# MAGILL'S
# LITERARY ANNUAL
## 2005

# MAGILL'S LITERARY ANNUAL 2005

*Essay-Reviews of 200 Outstanding Books
Published in the United States During 2004*

*With an Annotated List of Titles*

Volume Two
L-Z

*Edited by*
JOHN D. WILSON
STEVEN G. KELLMAN

**SALEM PRESS**
Pasadena, California     Hackensack, New Jersey

LIBRARY OF CONGRESS CATALOG CARD NO. 77-99209
ISBN 1-58765-217-X

FIRST PRINTING

PRINTED IN THE UNITED STATES OF AMERICA

# CONTENTS

## CONTENTS

# COMPLETE ANNOTATED LIST OF TITLES

## VOLUME 1

# COMPLETE ANNOTATED LIST OF TITLES

*From the European founding of American colonies to the twenty-first century,
mainstream attitudes toward American Indian spirituality have progressed from fear
and contempt, born of the Puritan conviction that Indian religion was little more than
devil worship, to reverent respect and admiration*

*In these essays, Sedaris uses his mocking tone to create affectionately humorous
portraits of life with his family during his youth and adult life with his partner in
France*

*Lycett draws a fresh and illuminating portrait of one of the major British poets of
the twentieth century, a powerful writer whose self-destructive life ended before he
was forty*

*Ricks brings his considerable critical skills to bear in an analysis of the lyrics of
songwriter Bob Dylan, with remarkable results*

*On the high plains of northeastern Colorado, four families find their lives inextri-
cably linked as they struggle to confront an uncertain future*

*Greene's book tackles two of the hardest questions in physics—"What is space?"
and "What is time?"—and shows how modern theorists seek to fashion one unified
theory about how space and time were created and work together*

*This novel's sweeping narrative records an unpredictable family history and
blends personal matters with the public account of the Love Canal ecological disaster*

*At College Sunrise, a small school for teenagers of wealthy families, a precocious
student is writing a novel that arouses the envy of the headmaster, who is himself trying to write a novel*

COMPLETE ANNOTATED LIST OF TITLES

COMPLETE ANNOTATED LIST OF TITLES

# VOLUME 2

COMPLETE ANNOTATED LIST OF TITLES

COMPLETE ANNOTATED LIST OF TITLES

COMPLETE ANNOTATED LIST OF TITLES

# COMPLETE ANNOTATED LIST OF TITLES

# MAGILL'S
# LITERARY ANNUAL
## 2005

# THE LINE OF BEAUTY

*Author:* Alan Hollinghurst (1954-    )
*Publisher:* Bloomsbury (New York). 438 pp. $25.00
*Type of work:* Novel
*Time:* 1983-1987
*Locale:* London

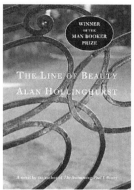

*Set against the background of the middle years of the Margaret Thatcher government,* The Line of Beauty *examines a young man's coming of age, from his ambiguous rise to his elegiac fall*

*Principal characters:*
> NICK GUEST, a doctoral candidate newly
>    arrived in London
> TOBY FEDDEN, Nick's host in the city and
>    the object of his crush
> CATHERINE FEDDEN, Toby's sister
> GERALD FEDDEN, Toby and Catherine's father
> WANI OURADI, Nick's lover

With its title drawn from William Hogarth's famous treatise *The Analysis of Beauty* (1753), Alan Hollinghurst's novel *The Line of Beauty* is a meditative set of variations on style: literary, personal, political, sexual, cultural, artistic, architectural. Although it may or may not be the author's best novel, *The Line of Beauty* is certainly his most ambitious and something of a capstone. It completes the loosely connected quartet of novels—with *The Swimming-Pool Library* (1988), *The Folding Star* (1994), and *The Spell* (1998)—that examine gay identity in the "ghastly" decade of the 1980's. It is easy now to forget the impact that *The Swimming-Pool Library* had and how influential its handling of gay life has been. As Hollinghurst has explained,

> From the start I've tried to write books which began from a presumption of the gayness of the narrative position. To write about gay life from a gay perspective unapologetically and as naturally as most novels are written from a heterosexual position. When I started writing, that seemed a rather urgent and interesting thing to do. It hadn't really been done.

Now it has, and yet, the more some things change, the more they remain the same. No sooner did Hollinghurst win the Booker Prize than the British tabloids began describing *The Line of Beauty* as a gay novel, even a gay sex novel (perhaps even part of a gay conspiracy, as the chairperson of the judges, Chris Smith, former minister of media, culture, and sport, was also Britain's first openly gay cabinet member). Hollinghurst does not object to being thought of as a gay novelist:

I only chafe at the "gay writer" tag if it's thought to be what is most or only interesting about what I'm writing. I want it to be part of the foundation of the books, which are actually about all sorts of other things as well—history, class, culture. There's all sorts of stuff going on. It's not just, as you would think if you read the headlines in the newspapers, about gay sex.

Divided into three parts and framed by two British elections (1983 and 1987), *The Line of Beauty* tells a more or less straightforward story of its protagonist's rise and fall against the backdrop of the middle years of Margaret Thatcher's government. It is a telling that artfully combines *Bildungsroman*, love story, comedy of manners, satire, lyricism, and elegy and that manages to be at once accessible and finely written, scathingly funny and emotionally affecting, at times almost unbearably so. It follows the sinuous double curve, "the line of beauty," the ogee, that Hogarth saw in a chair leg (among other places) and the novel's central character finds more sensuously in a lover's hip.

The novel also follows the author's own life to a degree: "I was a gay, middle-class only child from the provinces, fairly innocent of real life, with a precocious knowledge of music, literature and architecture," like his aptly, allegorically named protagonist, Nick Guest, fresh from Oxford, a bit snobbish, arriving in London in the early 1980's, in awe of "the romance of London, the sense of expectation and possibility." The novel's epigraph, from *Alice's Adventures in Wonderland* (1865), suggests Hollinghurst's playfully skeptical as well as self-critical approach to Nick's adventures in the wonderland of Thatcher's London. The novel is loaded with literary (and other cultural) allusions, as befits its well-read (and at times culturally snobbish) protagonist. Henry James's *The Spoils of Poynton* (1897) looms large, as does the 1985 Merchant-Ivory film adaptation of E. M. Forster's *A Room with a View* (1908); Evelyn Waugh's *Brideshead Revisited* (1945); Oscar Wilde's plays, *Lady Windemere's Fan* (1892) in particular, with more than a touch of *The Picture of Dorian Gray* (1891); Hogarth's *A Harlot's Progress* (1732) and *A Rake's Progress* (1735); and, least directly but most evocatively, F. Scott Fitzgerald's *The Great Gatsby* (1925), about another Nick, Nick Carraway.

"What would Henry James have made of us?" a minor character asks. James would have made something similar to what Hollinghurst has, but not quite the same thing, and not just because it is impossible to imagine James being so direct in his treatment of sex (not that *The Line of Beauty* is nearly as sexually graphic as some reviewers have claimed) or of using juxtaposition quite the way Hollinghurst does: "[Nick] was reading Henry James's memoir of his childhood, *A Small Boy and Others*, and feeling crazily horny, after three days without as much as a peck from Wani. It was a hopeless combination."

By making Nick the novel's focal character but not its narrator, Hollinghurst allows the reader to know Nick intimately yet ironically. He arrives in London to begin doctoral studies, writing a dissertation on the styles of Joseph Conrad, George Meredith, and Henry James. More important, he arrives as a guest, a country mouse, in the family home of his city cousin, or more specifically his college roommate, Toby Fedden, the discrete object of Nick's obscure, closeted desire the previous three years. As the novel opens, Nick is alone in the house in recently gentrified Notting Hill with Toby's sister Catherine, whose latest psychological crisis prevents Nick from keeping a first date with Leo Charles, a black clerk, whom he met through a personal ad. (Tending to Catherine also keeps him from having his first real, as opposed to fantasized, sex).

Thus, in the first pages, the reader is introduced not just to Nick and the house but also to the novel's overall rhythm of expectation and delay. The reader is also introduced to Nick's di-

*∾*

*Alan Hollinghurst was educated at Oxford University. After moving to London, he became deputy editor of* The Times Literary Supplement *and began writing his well-received first novel,* The Swimming-Pool Library *(1988). In 1993 he was selected by* Granta *magazine as one of the "Best of the Young British Novelists."*

*∾*

vided nature: his innocence and ignorance on one hand, his desires on the other; his willingness to take risks coupled with a fearful hesitancy and "provincial squeamishness" (as the other Nick says of himself in Fitzgerald's novel). The reader is also introduced, a few pages later, to his two kinds of "arse licking," as Leo says after they finally do meet and have sex, in the private gardens shared by the Feddens and their neighbors.

Nick's cultural and social pretensions invite the reader's scorn—or would, were it not for Nick's genuine concern for Catherine and equally genuine appreciation for art, literature, and music. Similarly, his sexual fumblings would make him seem somewhat comical were it not for the internalized doubts that act, for a time, as a brake on his desire. It is this in-betweenness that gives Nick, and Hollinghurst's comedy of manners, a depth of insight and feeling as Nick struggles to be what he is and to prove himself in various ways, socially and sexually above all.

The conflict is especially evident later in the novel, when Nick, long after Leo has dumped him, wants to show off his rich Lebanese lover, Wani Ouradi, and wants to show off for him. Nick may be, as Leo says, a preppy twit, but he is not just a preppy twit. The novel mirrors this ambivalence in its structure and texture, mixing satire and lyricism, the empty dialogue of its mainly well-heeled characters (caricatures hoist on their own petards) and passages of introspection and sudden feeling.

What attracts Nick to Wani is his wealth, and Hollinghurst is (as one of his characters says of Anthony Trollope) "very good on money." That is, he is very good at depicting how unworthy the Feddens and others are of the fine things they so conspicuously consume. Toby and Catherine's father, Gerald Fedden, is one of the one hundred and one new Tory members of Parliament elected in 1983. Gerald has plenty of money and power and, of course, wants much more of both, while possessing no appreciation for his things or for anyone around him, including his psychologically fragile daughter. Specifically he wants a cabinet post. He lusts politically, if not sexually, for Thatcher (who, never named in the novel, is always "the PM") Gerald's triumph comes when she plays the role of honored, or at least coveted, guest at Gerald and Rachel's twenty-fifth anniversary party. Just as he lusts after the power Thatcher can provide, he loathes Barwick, the provincial town he represents in Parliament.

Nick, too, loathes Barwick, because it is where he grew up, the only child of the discretely homophobic Don and Dot Guest. Nick feels no nostalgia for his hometown or, for that matter, for his home, which was never quite a haven in a heartless world and was always subject, in its small-time way, to Thatcher's economic policies, *avant la lettre:* Don, an antiques dealer, invariably sold the furnishings whenever he found a buyer. Nick returns home driving the little Mazda that Wani paid for, the sign of his success as well of his status as Wani's "pretty boy." Nick's willingness to sell himself in this more or less discreet way is a bit like Wani's obsession with pornography: less a personal failing than a sign of the grossly commercial, pornographic times ruled by the arch dominatrix, the PM.

While neither Gerald (nicknamed the Banger) nor the PM have any redeeming features, coke-snorting Wani does: not his bedding Nick, not his giving Nick a job or allowing Nick to name both the film company and the magazine *Ogee*, not the car, and certainly not the five thousand pound check, which effectively puts Nick on notice and in his place. What redeems the dying Wani is his willingness to care for Nick by giving him a commercial building, the income from which should be enough for Nick to live on the rest of his life.

Like almost everything else in *The Line of Beauty*, this act of generous affection turns out to be as much curse as blessing. Once the old buildings on this Clerkenwell corner had been razed,

> Baalbek House, named by Wani as if he had written a poem, started to go up. Nick cast about but really he'd never seen a more meretricious design than that of Baalbek House. His own ideas were discounted with the grunting chuckle of someone wedded to another vision of success and defiantly following cheaper advice. And now this monster Lego house, with its mirror windows and maroon marble cladding, was to be Nick's for life.

Baalbek House goes up, much of everything else comes down, and the novel ends in a flurry of deaths (especially AIDS deaths) and precipitous declines (including the financial markets' and, not long after, Thatcher's). After narrowly winning reelection, Gerald finds himself embroiled in three scandals: one financial and the other two sexual, one with his assistant and the other involving Nick and Wani: "Gay Sex Link to Minister's House: Peer's Playboy Son Has AIDS." The first issue of *Ogee*, with his name on the masthead amid the glossy ads "for Bulgari, Dior, BMW, astounding godparents to Nick and Wani's coke-child," offer fleeting confirmation of Nick's place in the world, but the first issue is also the last.

The end comes just pages later, when Nick reluctantly departs the Feddens' home, where he was never quite the guest, or the family member, he believed himself to be—always instead something of an interloper or renter or paid retainer. However, it is not bitterness Nick feels and not even regret but Gatsby-like wonder, "as he looked in bewilderment at number 24, the final house with its regalia of stucco swags and bows. It wasn't just this street corner but the fact of a street corner at all that seemed, in the light of the moment, so beautiful." It is a pity that there is no one but the reader to pay Nick Guest the compliment that Nick Carraway pays Jay Gatsby: "You're worth the whole damn bunch put together."

*Robert A. Morace*

## Review Sources

*Booklist* 101, no. 4 (October 15, 2004): 389.
*The Christian Science Monitor*, October 26, 2004, p. 14.
*Entertainment Weekly*, October 22, 2004, p. 98.
*Kirkus Reviews* 72, no. 16 (August 15, 2004): 765.
*London Review of Books* 26, no. 9 (May 6, 2004): 25.
*The New Republic* 231, no. 24 (December 13, 2004): 47.
*The New York Times*, November 23, 2004, p. E1.
*The New York Times Book Review* 154 (October 31, 2004): 19.
*Publishers Weekly* 251 (September 20, 2004): 46.
*San Francisco Chronicle*, October 23, 2004, p. E1.

# LINKS

*Author:* Nuruddin Farah (1945-    )
*Publisher:* Riverhead Books (New York). 336 pp. $25.00
*Type of work:* Novel
*Time:* The early twenty-first century
*Locale:* Mogadishu, Somalia

*The novel provides a vivid picture of life in Somalia's ravaged capital, Mogadishu, and traces the adventures of a Somali exile who returns to the city for a visit*

*Principal characters:*
JEEBLEH, a native of Somalia who visits his
disordered homeland for the first time in
twenty years
BILE, Jeebleh's childhood friend who operates a refugee center in
Mogadishu called The Refuge
CALOOSHA, Bile's corrupt brother and a longtime enemy of Jeebleh
SEAMUS, Jeebleh and Bile's Irish friend who works in The Refuge
RAASTA, a young girl called a "miracle child" because of her special
qualities
SHANTA, Raasta's mother and Bile's sister
FAAHIYE, Raasta's father
AF-LAAWE, a questionable operative who shadows Jeebleh's movements

Nuruddin Farah's eight novels record the turbulent history of Somalia after it gained independence in 1960. Farah, however, has not lived in his native land since 1976—the year that his second novel, *A Naked Needle*, appeared in Europe. Traveling abroad at the time of the book's publication, Farah intended to return to his native country to resume his teaching duties at the university in Mogadishu. He called his brothers to give them details of his flight arrival, but they warned him not to return. At that time, the Marxist dictator Siad Barre ruled the country with an iron hand and suppressed all dissent. Because *A Naked Needle* was considered subversive in its depiction of the country's condition, Farah faced arrest and imprisonment.

Living in Europe, other parts of Africa, and the United States since then, Farah continued to record in fiction the plight of his fellow Somalians who endured Barre's tyrannical authority. His next three novels, *Sweet and Sour Milk* (1979), *Sardines* (1981), and *Close Sesame* (1983) form a trilogy called "Variations on the Theme of an African Dictatorship." The second trilogy, "Blood in the Sun"—*Maps* (1986), *Gifts* (1992), and *Secrets* (1998)—traces Somalia's headlong plunge into anarchy before and after Barre's fall in 1991.

*Links* continues Farah's extended narrative of the East African nation he calls "the country of my imagination." Like most of his earlier work, this novel focuses on a single character who faces personal conflicts that fuse with the political discord surrounding him. The protagonist, Jeebleh, returns to a devastated Somalia, which stands in sharp contrast to his comfortable environment in New York City. Shortly after his arrival at the airport, he discovers how deeply the country has sunk into violence when he witnesses a senseless killing carried out for fun by well-armed youths. The unease heightens as he is driven into the once-beautiful city of Mogadishu, which now lies in ruins. Both in this fictional account and in reality, Somalia remains a country in suspension. It has no recognized authority, no sanctioned leader, no national currency, no working municipality, nor any other feature associated with an established national system. There is a provisional government, whose officials, it is said, do little except embezzle foreign aid funds.

*Born in Baidoa, Somalia, Nuruddin Farah has lived in exile most of his adult life. He has taught at universities in various countries and now resides in Cape Town, South Africa. Farah has published eight novels and numerous essays that chronicle Somalia's postcolonial struggles. In 1998, he received the prestigious Neustadt International Prize for Literature.*

This state of political crisis dominates the narrative as Jeebleh settles into Mogadishu, renews old friendships, and sets out to fulfill the missions that have brought him to Somalia for a short time. A student of Dante when he attended university in Italy, Jeebleh draws parallels between the unending horrors he observes and the *Inferno* from Dante's *La divina commedia* (c. 1320; *The Divine Comedy*, 1802). At the beginning of part 2 of the novel, Farah quotes from canto 24 of the *Inferno* that conjures up "so many, such malignant, pestilences." The multiple forms of these pestilences assume substance, as Jeebleh experiences life in a city where the tamed vultures feast on the bodies that litter the streets. Ruled by competing warlords and their militias who are drugged from chewing a narcotic called *qaat*, the city lies divided by loyalties to such an extent that no one is safe: "In these unsettling times, everyone's fate, actions, dreams, hates, and aspirations were seen, understood, and interpreted in stark political contexts; distrust was the order of the day, and everyone was suspicious of everybody else." The way Jeebleh reacts to these frenzied conditions, mixes with the city's inhabitants, and observes the vain attempt to seek normality provides an unsettled background as the narrative progresses.

As well as reproducing Somalia's current plight in grim detail, the novel tracks the country's history in the late nineteenth and twentieth centuries. Jeebleh recalls at one point how many times the land had been invaded, conquered, and colonized. He notes that the aggressors always come by sea, for the long and narrow country, which is about the size of Texas, is bordered on the east by the Indian Ocean and on the north by the Gulf of Aden. Long ago, the Muslim invaders arrived, exploited the land, and converted the people to Islam, which remains the dominant religion. Once the Suez Canal opened, the Europeans found Somalia attractive, and the Italians, the French, and the British came, eventually squabbling over territory and dividing the country. Then Russia stepped in, followed by the United States. Although never directly stated in the novel, Somalia's tangled history stands as a metaphor for all of Africa and its tragic encounter with the colonial project.

Yet *Links* emerges as far more than an account of Somalia's present dismal state and its past upheavals. Typical of Farah's fiction, the political situation and the personal circumstances merge flawlessly. Jeebleh's adventures unfold like a classic mystery, full of intrigue and suspense. Farah is a skilled storyteller. Jeebleh has made the trip to Somalia for specific purposes and as he goes about his missions the tension mounts. Mysterious strangers follow him through the city's ravaged streets and into deserted buildings. His ignorant clansmen demand money to outfit their militia with weapons, and when he refuses they threaten him. The man called Af-Laawe, who obviously serves one of the warlords, pretends to befriend Jeebleh but more accurately intends to deceive him. He confronts his old enemy, Caloosha, whom Jeebleh believes was responsible for his imprisonment during the dictator's rule. Soon he receives indirect threats from Caloosha, who now serves a powerful warlord. The risks and dangers multiply as Jeebleh sets out to help rescue his friend Bile's niece Raasta, who has been abducted, and to honor his dead mother belatedly. It is interesting to note that in a country without a phone system, Somalis now rely exclusively on cell phones, which are administered by neighboring nations. This real-life phenomenon plays an important role in *Links*.

The portrayal of the child Raasta provides an excellent example of the way Farah combines traditional African ways and beliefs with European sensibility. Without explanation or apology, Farah establishes the nine- or ten-year-old girl as "a miracle child." From the time of her birth, she was recognized for her spiritual qualities. Soon her father's prediction that "peace of mind will descend, halo-like, on whoever holds the girl in his or her embrace" proved to be true. When she was a few days old, people fleeing from the war turned up at the compound where Raasta lived, having heard that she was "protected," and so would those who lived near her. Not only did she serve as a conduit for peace among the refugees around her, but she also gained everyone's trust where trust was uncommon. She also displayed remarkable intelligence. At age three, she could speak, read, and write three languages. By the time she was five, she had mastered more languages. Raasta, whose birth name, Rajo, means "hope," evolves into a symbol of hope in a place that is otherwise so full of despair. Although she was abducted and held prisoner for a long period along with her companion Makka—a little girl with Down syndrome—both are eventually restored to the compound that houses The Refuge, where Raasta continues her peacemaking.

As Jeebleh prepares to return to the United States, he "held a childlike trust that things would work better for more people now that Raasta and Makka were back at The Refuge and Caloosha was out of the way." Jeebleh had, through unnamed contacts and scheming, arranged for the death of his old enemy Caloosha. In a typical mixing of the two cultures that have formed him, Jeebleh justifies this act of violence by recalling Thomas Jefferson's statement that the blood of patriots and tyrants refreshes the tree of liberty from time to time.

The two major elements of the complex narrative—the resolution of Raasta's disappearance and Caloosha's assassination—intersect with Jeebleh's search for his mother's grave. Given the atmosphere in Mogadishu, even that noble motive meets with untold difficulties. Eventually, though, he manages to honor this faithful woman in death as he had not been able to do during her life. After he fled the country, he attempted to contact her and to assist her financially, but even matters so simple proved impossible because of the civil strife. After being duped and cheated, Jeebleh finally finds the place where his mother is buried. He orders an appropriate monument to be built, arranges for Muslim rites to be administered, and stages a traditional party in her memory. Jeebleh's elevation of his mother is significant, considering that Farah has long condemned the oppression of women in Africa. Throughout his fiction, he embraces the idea that the unparalleled strength and wisdom of Somali women will someday rescue the tormented country from the discord that men have created. That belief in the liberating power of women Farah indirectly extends to all of Africa.

Farah's sophisticated style, rich with metaphors and similes, uncovers both the horror and the beauty of the territory that he has made his own. His fiction freely integrates African customs, beliefs, and mythology with the European tradition. At various points in the narrative he relates African folk tales, quotes from the Bible, alludes to a German drama, and draws on Dante's *Inferno* to illuminate the inhabitants of the wasted city. Farah's dialogue always rings true and captures with exactness the characters' pain or joy. That English is Farah's second or third language lends his prose a rare resonance that a native writer in English could never accomplish.

Farah has been called Africa's most important modern novelist in his exploration of yet another facet of colonialism. His work is rooted in the period shaped by the Cold War led by the United States and Russia. The earlier novels reveal how one small, remote nation is affected by the international dispute far from its shores. *Links* shows the consequences of this intervention.

*Robert L. Ross*


## Review Sources

*Black Issues Book Review* 6, no. 4 (July/August, 2004): 20.
*Booklist* 100, no. 14 (March 15, 2004): 1264.
*Entertainment Weekly*, March 26, 2004, p. 77.
*Library Journal* 129, no. 6 (April 1, 2004): 120.
*The New York Times Book Review* 153 (April 11, 2004): 7.
*Newsweek* 143, no. 16 (April 19, 2004): 65.
*Publishers Weekly* 251, no. 9 (March 1, 2004): 48.

# LITTLE BLACK BOOK OF STORIES

*Author:* A. S. Byatt (1936-    )
*Publisher:* Alfred A. Knopf (New York). 240 pp. $21.00
*Type of work:* Short fiction
*Time:* The late twentieth century
*Locale:* England and Iceland

*In her fifth collection of stories, Byatt's ordinary people find themselves in extraordinary circumstances as their lives take on aspects of folklore, fantasy, and the bizarre*

The books of English author A. S. Byatt are an acquired taste, like fine wine or caviar, but well worth the effort. Readers are probably most familiar with her novel *Babel Tower* (1996) or the award-winning *Possession: A Romance* (1990), although her stories and novellas are held in equally high regard. She loves words and color, and her writing is precise, textured, with a bright palette and a preponderance of lists: "the endless shifts in the colour of the sky, trout-dappled, mackerel-shot, turquoise, sapphire, peridot, hot transparent red."

Byatt's childhood reading, and her later research for an unfinished dissertation on medieval religious allegory, reinforced her interest in the myths and folklore that appear in much of her work. She is a cerebral writer and yet a fabulist, examining always a collision of worlds: past with present, history with legend, art with science, appearance with reality.

Her collection *Little Black Book of Stories* adds five more tales to her oeuvre. Her American publisher should be applauded for resisting the temptation to translate the occasional Briticism: for example, "humbugs," which are actually small candies, or "blue john," a regional name for fluorite. This volume, its faded black jacket reminiscent of a dusty tome on a forgotten shelf, is indeed small enough to hold comfortably in one hand. Its most disturbing fictions, "The Thing in the Forest" and "A Stone Woman," were published in *The New Yorker* and may well become classics in themselves.

"The Thing in the Forest" takes place in England in the 1940's and again forty years later, and like some of Byatt's earlier work evokes memories of World War II, which always serves as an important formative experience for her characters. In the midst of the Blitz (the real world), two little girls are evacuated from an endangered city to the relative safety of the countryside, even as Byatt herself once was. Pale, thin Penny and plump, blond Primrose meet and become friends on the grimy evacuation train that carries them past wartime stations that have carefully blacked out their identification. The children are temporarily billeted in an impressive country house until foster families can arrange to take them.

After a lonely night, the city girls feel an urge to explore the nearby forest, a phenomenon they have never before encountered. A very small child named Alys begs to go with them, but they avoid her by running away. Once in the wood, they hear "a crunching, a crackling, a crushing, a heavy thumping, combined with threshing and thrashing," and inhale "a liquid smell of putrefaction, the smell of maggoty things" (the world of legend). Terrified, they hide from a ghastly Thing that slowly drags itself past them—a monstrous Worm, its body composed of "rank meat, and

~

*A. S. Byatt is the author of numerous short stories, novellas, novels, and nonfiction books. Her novel* Possession: A Romance *(1990) won Britain's illustrious Booker Prize. She is a dame of the British Empire.*

~

decaying vegetation" and a face of "pure misery." Later, when Alys fails to return to the great house, they realize that she must have followed them into the forest, but they say nothing.

Penny and Primrose are separated and sent to live in different foster homes until the war is over. They silently bear the guilt of another child's fate and their own inability to come to terms with what they have seen (and done). In adult life neither marries, yet both dedicate themselves to helping children—Penny as a psychologist and Primrose as an entertainer and storyteller. Four decades elapse before they meet, by chance, at the country house that is now a museum, where they find in an old book an illustration of the legendary Loathly Worm that once inhabited the area. Still, neither woman is certain that she ever really saw it. Penny admits, "I think there are things that are real—more real than we are—but mostly we don't cross their paths. . . . Maybe at very bad times we get into their world, or notice what they are doing in ours."

Each woman returns alone to the wood. Primrose, largely a creature of emotion, fashions a story out of her walk in the forest to calm herself; she "understood something, and did not know what she had understood." Penny, however, finds herself there at dusk and watches herself as in a dream (although she suspects that the Worm was no dream), but the creature does not show itself. The next day the women silently meet again at the train station, but this time they are mute. Penny, ordinarily a sensible woman, will go once more into the wood to face her fear, even though it may destroy her. Safe in the city, Primrose will tell her young audiences her story of the Worm, for that story enables her to make sense of horror.

"The Thing in the Forest" demonstrates Byatt's fascination with folklore. The Loathly Worm of English legend derived its name in part from the Old English *Wyrm*, which also meant a serpent or dragon; both symbolized evil. Here the creature may also represent the war itself, or even death (it smells of all kinds of rot) and misery (its sad face). In addition, the tale embodies a theme that is one of Byatt's favorites: the necessity of stories. People organize their experience through narrative, she believes and, like Primrose, they need stories to survive.

A quite different treatment of this idea occurs in "Raw Material," the most realistic yet perhaps the weakest of the *Little Black Book of Stories*. Novelist Jack Smollett, a one-book wonder who has been unable to repeat his success, finds himself teaching a creative writing class in Derbyshire. Jack is a familiar type: a charming, irresponsible seducer with a minimum of talent. Even when he advises his students to write about what they know, they thrive on invented melodrama and in-class rivalry. One quiet, elderly woman is able to write—exquisitely—of daily life in the past, of black-leaded stoves and old-fashioned wash days, but her envious classmates argue that her subjects are boring. The woman's genteel facade masks an appalling, bizarre existence, reminding the reader that stories that make reality bearable do not always reveal the truth.

"A Stone Woman" is almost Kafkaesque, as ordinary people and landscapes merge with the world of legend to reveal the transformation of Ines, a dictionary researcher who shares a flat with her mother. After the mother's death, Ines ages rapidly, developing an intestinal blockage that nearly kills her. Saved by surgery, she longs for an end to physical and emotional pain, but when her scar grows hard and begins to spread across her abdomen, she undergoes a chilling metamorphosis: "One day she found a cluster of greenish-white crystals sprouting in her armpit." Gradually she is turning to stone—not ordinary rock but minerals, semiprecious stones and volcanic glass, all of which Byatt lists in an explosion of textures and color. As Ines watches her body petrify, her blood is converted to molten lava.

Drawn to an English cemetery crowded with headstones, Ines meets and is befriended by a stonemason-sculptor, who offers to make a tombstone for her. She tells him, "I do not need a monument. I have grown into one." He, in turn, proposes to take her with him to his native Iceland, where legends claim that the stones are alive: "We are matter-of-fact about strange things. We know we live in a world of invisible beings that exists in and around our own. . . . Our tales are full of striding stone women." Once there, Ines finds herself thinking "human thoughts and stone thoughts" and can perceive nonhuman figures within the landscape. When they begin to move, to dance, she follows them, entering their world joyfully. The woman who once loved words becomes a woman who loves stones, able to behold the faces, bodies, and mythic life within them.

While the most dramatic metamorphosis belongs to the stone woman, in each of these stories at least one character undergoes some sort of transformation. "Body Art" focuses on gynecologist and abstract art lover Damian Becket and, to a lesser degree, on art student Daisy Whimple. Damian is a man of science, gifted in his field but awkward with emotion and intimacy. As a university student, his vision of a crucifix led him to a new credo ("A man is his body"), causing him to switch from reading literature to studying medicine. Science has enabled him to become detached, although he still nurtures a passion for modern abstract art. When spike-haired, tattooed Daisy, who has volunteered to decorate the gynecology ward, falls off a hospital ladder and into his arms, a strange relationship begins.

Damien and Daisy's story is complicated by a bequest left the hospital by its founder: a collection of medical instruments and curiosities that has never been cataloged. These curiosities include preserved human body parts that the avant-garde artist Daisy borrows for a student exhibit, during which her installation of the goddess Kali generates considerable attention. Soon a life-changing event intervenes, and Damian, who once renounced literature for science, is transformed from a dispassionate analyst to a man who is overwhelmed by emotion.

Finally, in "The Pink Ribbon," an aging classicist, James Ennis, has become the caretaker for his once brilliant wife. Reduced to furious incoherence, "Maddy Mad Mado" now suffers from Alzheimer's disease, while James is enmeshed in a terrible ambivalence toward the woman who has not recognized him in five years. His intense love has turned to resentment, but he represses his anger by little rebellions: tying his wife's hair with a pink ribbon, a color she always hated, and sticking pins in the Teletubby doll he bought for her.

When a young woman at his door cries out that she is being followed, James invites her in. Dressed in clinging red silk, she calls herself Dido, like the "passionate queen" of Carthage who died for love. James thinks, "She was the quick, and he was the dead," but apparently it is the other way around. Dido's appearance triggers early memories of his wife during World War II, when they were wildly in love. Later Dido reveals that she is the "Fetch," but she is apparently the alter ego or "etheric body" to Mado's clay. She reminds James that he is no longer thinking of his wife's real need, only of what she has unwillingly become. The characters here seem to suggest British author John Bayley and his wife, writer Iris Murdoch. (Byatt, a friend who was strongly influenced by Murdoch's work, has produced two critical studies of her novels.)

An intellectual writer, A. S. Byatt approaches her audience on the level of ideas as well as through the brilliance of sensory perception. She requires that her reader think. If she has a weakness, it may lie in the aesthetic distance that she maintains. Her characters become difficult to identify with because their experiences and emotions are so frequently objectified. Still, Byatt's world is delightfully complex—ancient, mythic, yet very modern.

*Joanne McCarthy*

## Review Sources

*America* 191 (October 4, 2004): 17.
*Booklist* 100, no. 16 (April 15, 2004): 1404.
*Kirkus Reviews* 72, no. 6 (March 15, 2004): 237.
*Library Journal* 129, no. 8 (May 1, 2004): 143.
*The Nation* 278, no. 23 (June 14, 2004): 24.
*The New York Times Book Review* 153 (May 9, 2004): 8.
*Publishers Weekly* 251, no. 18 (May 3, 2004): 171.

# LITTLE CHILDREN

*Author:* Tom Perrotta (1961-    )
*Publisher:* St. Martin's Press (New York). 355 pp.
    $25.00
*Type of work:* Novel
*Time:* 2004
*Locale:* The fictional suburb of Bellington, near Boston

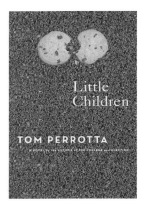

*Perrotta's satirical take on suburban America and family life is told through a battery of characters, all trapped in mundane lives of their own making*

*Principal characters:*
> SARAH, a former doctoral candidate and lapsed feminist, a housewife and mother to Lucy
> TODD, a former fraternity boy and football player who stays at home with his son Aaron while studying for the bar exam
> RONALD MCKORVEY, a man convicted for exposing himself to girl scouts, now released and living at home with his mother
> MAY, his mother
> RICHARD, Sarah's husband, a man secretly infatuated with an Internet sex club
> KATHY, Todd's wife, a documentary filmmaker
> LARRY MOON, a football teammate of Todd, a fallen police officer who is obsessed with McKorvey
> MARY ANN, a neighborhood mother who believes that she has complete control of her children through discipline and a rigorous schedule

As the author of *Election* (1998) and *Joe College* (2000), Tom Perrotta has distinguished himself as a literary satirist, offering savage examinations of American life. In *Election*, his focus was on high school overachievers and adolescent duplicity; in *Joe College*, he skewered the typical young-man-coming-of-age tale. In *Little Children*, Perrotta focuses his sights on suburban American home life.

*Little Children* particularly examines the lives of young parents who are finally and irreversibly entrenched in the day-to-day tedium of middle-class family life. Perrotta does not so much shed a light on the American Dream, such as it is, as he places under the microscope the expectations middle-class Americans either have foisted on them or impose upon themselves. Americans, Perrotta argues in *Little Children*, are not happy with health and respectable standards of living. Additionally, they all have to live out perfect dreams of realized ambitions, self-fulfillment, family togetherness, and community status.

Initially the reader is introduced to Sarah. Despite a passionate love affair with another woman during her undergraduate years, a major in women's studies, and a good deal of time in graduate school working on a Ph.D., she now finds herself a more or less typical American housewife with an older, self-absorbed husband, Richard, and a three-year-old toddler, Lucy. Sarah believes that "most people just fell in line like obedient little children, doing exactly what society expected of them at any given moment, all the while pretending that they'd actually made some sort of choice." Sarah spends most of her mornings at the playground with a group of banal young mothers whom she more or less loathes. The

*A native of New Jersey, Tom Perrotta graduated from Yale University and earned an M.A. in creative writing from Syracuse University. His first book was* Bad Haircut, *a collection of stories published in 1994. His other novels include* The Wishbones *(1997),* Election *(1998), and* Joe College *(2000).*

group is led by the aggressive and domineering Mary Ann, who not only keeps her children on a strict schedule for naps and snacks but even has her sex life scripted out in advance, penciling the act in for one night a week.

The dichotomies in Sarah's life are reflected by the reading material she packs in her diaper bag: Margaret Atwood's feminist dystopia *The Handmaid's Tale* (1985) rests next to the children's book *The Berenstain Bears Visit the Dentist*. She feels reduced to reminding herself, over and over, "I am a painfully ordinary person . . . destined to live a painfully ordinary life."

The novel's narrative abruptly changes focus, moving from Sarah to the good-looking househusband Todd, whom the playground mothers call "the prom king." A former athlete and graduate of law school, Todd is following his wife's plan to the letter. He will keep his three-year-old, Aaron, at home while his wife, Kathy, makes documentary films and Todd studies for the bar exam. When he passes the bar, their roles will change, and he will become a well-paid attorney, while she stays home with their son. The only problem is that Todd has already failed the bar twice and cannot work up the energy to throw himself into his studies for his third attempt.

Like Sarah, Todd and Kathy are shackled in their attempts either to hold onto their visions of who they perceive themselves to be or blindly to pursue the ambitious plans carefully laid in place before having a family. Each night when Todd finally makes his way to the library to study after his wife returns home, he first pauses to watch a group of teenage boys attempting skateboard stunts. The boys' willingness to defy the laws of gravity and risk life and limb above unforgiving concrete merely to show off, all caution tossed to the wind, appeals to Todd. A former football star in school, as well as a fraternity boy, Todd's life has lost all its recklessness and has been carefully plotted out by his resentful wife. Two things soon occur that will shock Todd out of his suburban doldrums, however. A neighbor, Larry Moon, invites him to play tackle football in an unofficial league, and one day at the playground, Sarah is dared to go speak to Todd. She takes the dare a step further, and they kiss. Before long, an affair between the two has begun in earnest.

One of Perrotta's points in this novel is that all people have their own dreams, disappointments, expectations, ambitions, and fears; in effect, everyone has his or her own stories. The novel's structure reflects this theme as well. Each large section is made up of smaller subchapters. Often, a scene is introduced through one character's perspective, and then the third-person point of view shifts to a different focus in the next section or subchapter, until the reader realizes that he or she is seeing divergent versions and perspectives of the same sequences of events. This shifting point of view and examination of various scenarios from multiple angles allow one not only a more objective take on the two protagonists, Sarah and Todd, but also help display the characters who would seem to be, in small ways, the antagonists of the novel.

For example, the entire suburban world of Bellington has been turned upside-down by the release from prison of Ronald McKorvey, a sex offender convicted for exposing himself to a Girl Scout selling cookies. Perhaps realizing that even the most tolerant reader would have difficulty identifying with a pedophile exhibitionist, Perrotta instead focuses more on Ronald's mother, May. Through her sorrow at her son's bitterness and loneliness, the reader also comes to feel pity for Ronald.

Similarly, Todd's teammate Larry is a police officer fallen from grace for accidentally shooting a young African American man who was carrying a toy pistol in a shopping mall. Larry is obsessed with Ronald McKorvey. He spray paints warnings such as "EVIL" on McKorvey's driveway, forms a one-man "Committee of Concerned Parents," places flyers about McKorvey's presence in the neighborhood on every telephone pole, and even sets a bag of dog feces on fire on the McKorveys' porch. Yet, just as the reader is prepared to find Larry utterly unsympathetic, Perrotta focuses the third-person narrative through Larry's perspective. One finds out how Larry lost his father to cancer and shot the young man by accident within one year. One learns that the accidental shooting resulted in his early retirement from the police force, and one sees how, without his job as a police officer, Larry's life seems meaningless and without purpose, and his wife wants a divorce. One realizes finally that Larry's obsession with McKorvey is his last-ditch effort to be a protective and supportive father to his sons.

Like Larry Moon and Ronald McKorvey, Sarah's older, middle-aged husband, Richard, is initially not a particularly sympathetic character. He is infatuated with a minor Internet porn star named Slutty Kay and even goes so far as to order panties through the mail that she has presumably worn. As unattractive as Richard is, however, Perrotta still manages to humanize him and to show that Richard is the same victim of disappointments, missed opportunities, and minor defeats as are Sarah and Todd. Perrotta affords even Mary Ann some sympathy, as the reader sees when granted a view of her disintegrating marriage late in the novel.

Each of the characters portrayed has what would seem to be modest desires, but that does not make their needs and wishes any more attainable. Todd wishes that his life were still full of the opportunity and promise that defined him as a younger man, and so he retreats to his younger years through watching skateboarders and becoming the quarterback on a team of disgruntled cops. Sarah seeks to unmake the past several years through winning her heart's desire—Todd—for the first time in her life. Larry wishes to prove that he is still a vital part of his children's lives and a capable father and so obsesses over McKorvey. Kathy is determined to hold onto her perfect plan of being a nurturing, stay-at-home mother and a successful documentary filmmaker at the same time, and so she pushes Todd further and resents him more. Married once before Sarah, with older children, Richard wishes that he could know the life of the (perhaps mythological) swinging bachelor, and so becomes infatuated with the swingers' lifestyle touted by Slutty Kay on her Web site. May McKorvey wishes for her son to somehow find an entry into normal life and to know some happiness and urges him to place personal ads in the paper and to go on dates. Only Ronald McKorvey's desires are enigmatic, torn as he is by his wish to abide by the rules of human conduct and his own destructive and indecent needs.

One is forced to realize that some desires are never granted and that some needs are unobtainable. This is first subtly spelled out when Sarah joins a book group that takes as its next subject Gustave Flaubert's *Madame Bovary* (1857). Forced by her nemesis Mary Ann to defend the novel, Sarah suddenly realizes that for the first time she identifies with Emma Bovary and her indiscretions. She no longer sees Emma's affairs as callow acts of selfish love but as acts of rebellion against the straitjacket a patriarchal society has placed on Madame Bovary. Perrotta is subtly teasing the reader here, however. Emma Bovary's taking of lovers may well constitute subversive behavior, but at the same time she is deceiving herself, and she eventually destroys herself. Similarly, Sarah is deluding herself when she thinks that somehow Todd and she can extricate themselves painlessly from their marriages, get married, and live together happily ever after.

In the end, *Little Children* suggests that the dreams and ambitions one creates for oneself are merely disappointments in waiting. By holding on to unrealistic, early expectations and aspirations, one is asking for heartbreak and disillusionment. The choice, instead, is to understand the lifelong commitment needed by children, who will need their parents beside them forever to help them weather the vagaries and disappointments—as well as the triumphs and victories—that make up life. In essence, the only choice is to become an adult.

*Scott Yarbrough*

## Review Sources

*Booklist* 100, no. 9/10 (January 1-15, 2004): 826.
*Kirkus Reviews* 71, no. 23 (December 1, 2003): 1378.
*National Review* 56, no. 11 (June 14, 2004): 50.
*The New York Times*, March 8, 2004, p. E7.
*The New York Times Book Review* 153 (March 14, 2004): 6.
*People* 61, no. 10 (March 15, 2004): 45.
*Publishers Weekly* 250, no. 49 (December 8, 2003): 43.
*The Washington Post*, March 9, 2004, p. C03.

# LITTLE SCARLET

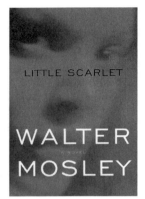

*Author:* Walter Mosley (1952-    )
*Publisher:* Little, Brown (New York). 320 pp. $25.00
*Type of work:* Novel
*Time:* 1965
*Locale:* Los Angeles

*In another of his mysteries featuring "Easy" Rawlins, Mosley shows the detective investigating a murder that took place during the Watts riots*

Principal characters:
> EZEKIEL ("EASY") RAWLINS, an African American school custodian and unlicensed detective
> RAYMOND ("MOUSE") ALEXANDER, a friend of Easy and a much-feared criminal
> MELVIN SUGGS, a white detective assigned to solve the Watts murder
> GERALD L. JORDAN, deputy commissioner of the Los Angeles Police Department, the powerful, ruthless official who has to ask for Easy's help
> GENEVA LANDRY, the dead woman's elderly aunt
> JACKSON BLUE, another friend of Easy, an ex-convict with a gift for technology

With the publication of *Devil in a Blue Dress* in 1990, Walter Mosley began his rapid ascent to his status as one of the United States' major mystery writers. Mosley soon developed a large and enthusiastic reading public, including, among others, President Bill Clinton, whose endorsement of Mosley in 1992 sent his sales skyrocketing. Reviewers praise Mosley's suspenseful plots, his vivid re-creation of time and place, and his skillful use of language. However, they agree that the author's greatest gift is characterization, which Mosley himself has said is his primary focus. Whether they appear in bit parts or in ongoing major roles, Mosley's characters are always believable and never stereotypical or predictable. Moreover, those who recur in several novels are shown changing as the times and their circumstances change and as they themselves grow older and more mature.

One can see this kind of development in Mosley's best-known detective, Ezekiel ("Easy") Rawlins. Easy first appears in *Devil in a Blue Dress*, which is set in 1948, when many returning veterans of World War II found themselves out of jobs and worried about paying their bills. As a twenty-eight-year-old African American man in a world dominated by whites, Easy has few prospects. Therefore, when a white man offers him cash to find a missing mistress, Easy takes the case. However, he soon discovers that things are not as simple as they seem and, moreover, that he has been thrust into a world of moral ambiguity, where, even with his best efforts, all he can achieve is an approximation of justice. Thus Mosley establishes the pattern

that will be followed in all the Easy Rawlins
books.

However, as America changes, the issues Easy
must deal with also change. *A Red Death* (1991),
is set at the time of the McCarthy witch-hunts in
the early 1950's. *Black Betty* (1994) takes place
in 1961, when the Civil Rights movement is under way. In *Bad Boy Brawly Brown* (2002), the
year is 1964, and Easy finds himself dealing with
activists, impatient at the slow rate of change,
who are forming an urban guerrilla movement
that will use violence to force a racial revolution.

~

*In 1990, Walter Mosley won the
Shamus Award of the Private Eye
Writers of America for his first Easy
Rawlins novel,* Devil in a Blue
Dress. *Mosley also was given the
Anisfield-Wolf Book Award for*
Always Outnumbered, Always
Outgunned *(1997), a collection of
stories featuring Socrates Fortlow.*

~

Over the years, Easy, too, has changed. In *Little Scarlet*, the year is 1965, and Easy
is forty-five years old. He has acquired some property, though he is careful to conceal
that fact from his long-time friends, most of whom are still living as they did a decade
before, and from his clients, many of whom come to him from the poverty-stricken
streets of South Central Los Angeles. He now owns a home, where he lives with
Bonnie Shay, a stewardess, whom he may well marry. He also has two adopted children, a son, Jesus, now a teenager, and a young daughter, Feather, whom he took in
when she was just a baby.

As Mosley has pointed out, during the 1960's African Americans began to enter
the professions in considerable numbers; therefore it is at this time that Easy begins to
think of himself not just as a casual, case-by-case investigator but as a professional
detective. Although he does not yet have a license, Easy does have an office and, as
his friend Jackson Blue points out, he even has an answering machine.

Given his own success, Easy is shocked and troubled by the Watts riots. On one
hand, he can understand why the blacks of Los Angeles are so angry. Many of them
are unemployed, and those who have found work are routinely underpaid. Even the
most respectable black citizens are subject to being stopped and harassed by white policemen, and none of them can count on being treated by whites as any more than inferior beings.

On the other hand, Easy knows that it is the African Americans themselves who
will suffer most when the white shopkeepers, who have, in many cases, been scrupulously fair to their black customers, decide not to rebuild their burned-out stores but
instead to flee the area, taking with them the jobs and services they provided for the
community. Moreover, though Easy understands that the widespread looting is as
much a by-product of cumulative anger as a demonstration of greed, he soon sees at
first hand that the fencing of stolen goods has become one of the most profitable busi-
nesses in the area.

Wisely, Easy decides to hole up in his office, emerging only to give aid or protection to the storekeepers in his immediate neighborhood. He is amazed when a white
detective, Melvin Suggs, seeks him out, offers to shake his hand, and asks his help in
solving a crime that remains unreported: the murder of Nola Payne, or "Little Scarlet." With Watts still smoldering, Easy knows that white policemen do not dare to

venture out alone to investigate. However, the case must be solved, for Nola was seen rescuing a white man from a mob and taking him into her apartment. The very rumor that a black woman might have been murdered by a white man, let alone one she had aided, would be enough to set Watts afire again, and the Los Angeles Police Department (LAPD) knows it. That is why Easy has been approached, and that is why the police have placed the dead woman's elderly aunt, Geneva Landry, in a mental institution, where she can be kept in a straitjacket, drugged and isolated, for fear she might tell someone what she knows.

After Suggs takes him to see Miss Geneva, Easy meets with Deputy Commissioner Gerald Jordan of the LAPD, a man hated by African Americans, who know only too well that his only religion is the raw exercise of power. Because he knows how badly Jordan needs him, Easy tries to see just how far he can go with him. Although it is evident that Jordan loathes having to treat a black man with respect, the fact that the LAPD official never loses his self-control convinces Easy that, as he suspected, the top echelons of the police force regard Nola Payne's murder as a ticking time bomb. It must be solved, and soon. Although Jordan is willing to negotiate a fee for Easy's services, the detective refuses. He will work on this case, he says, for the benefit of his own people. However, he does ask Jordan for a letter of authorization. That decision may well have saved his life, for the white police are seeking revenge for their humiliation during the riots, and they welcome any excuse to beat up an African American, any African American, guilty or innocent.

However, with his usual thoughtful evenhandedness, Mosley makes it clear that African Americans have as much to fear from their own race as from bigoted whites. Now that they have finished burning and looting, knots of men are standing on the street corners, looking for some other way to prove their manhood. All it takes is a look that can be interpreted as disrespectful or a wandering glance from a girlfriend, and the fight is on. Again, Easy has a trump card; he merely mentions the fact that he is a friend of Raymond Alexander, or "Mouse," a known killer who is feared throughout South Central Los Angeles. If the challenger does not take the hint, his friends usually hold him back, at least until Easy can make himself scarce.

The fact that Easy, a man of integrity, and the totally amoral Mouse are so loyal to each other illustrates one of Mosley's major themes: that people confronting a common enemy, in this case the white power structure, must finally depend for survival on their loyalty to each other. Although Easy tries to apply the test of right and wrong to his own actions, he does not expect his friends to live by the same code, and if they need his help, he will put his loyalty to them above the law.

At one point in the story, Mouse and his white business partner are giving Easy a ride in their truck, which is full of stolen merchandise, when they are stopped by the police. Easy does not hesitate; he pulls out his letter from Jordan and quickly concocts a lie, effectively preventing the police from examining the contents of the truck. On another occasion, Jackson Blue, who is just out of prison and has no fixed place of residence, asks Easy to let him give prospective employers the number of the answering machine Easy has in his office so that they will be able to contact him. Easy not only agrees to the request; disguising his voice, he calls in glowing recommendations. As he puts it, that is his way of getting a technical genius like Jackson into the white world, where he can make a future for himself.

Nonetheless, though Mosley shows the power structure as being in the hands of white men like Gerald Jordan, whose contempt for African Americans extends thoughout the LAPD, not all the whites in *Little Scarlet* are villainous. One of the tragic results of the Watts riots is that whites like Theodore Steinman, who Easy knows had never been unkind to an African American, has had his shop burned and his whole life virtually destroyed by the rioters. Steinman's essential goodness is demonstrated when, standing in the rubble, he can still say that it is his job and every-one else's to make sure that African Americans are treated fairly.

Deplorable as the riots were, Easy can see that they caused some whites to reexam-ine their attitudes and change their behavior. He suspects, for example, that a few days before, Detective Suggs would not have offered to shake hands with him or brought him coffee and doughnuts, as if they were colleagues and equals. Easy also notes that the riots have caused him to change, to demand respect. For the first time, he feels free to speak out on the subject of demeaning language, to point out that African American men do not like to be addressed as "son" and that African American women do not consider themselves "girls."

In Easy's encounter with Marianne Plump, the white receptionist at the mental in-stitution, he also recognizes his own ambivalence about the South. On one hand, Afri-can Americans who fled the South can remember its long history of racism. On the other hand, when Marianne apologizes to Easy for her behavior toward him, explain-ing that she is from Memphis, not only does he understand, but both of them also real-ize that the old days are gone forever, and now southerners of both races can base new friendships on their common roots.

Although he does sees such signs of hope for a better relationship between the races, Easy finds that the riots have left much unchanged. As long as whites are not put in danger, the authorities are still just as indifferent as before to a black woman's murder. Therefore as soon as the white suspect in Nola Payne's death is cleared and a black man is exposed as the killer, Suggs has to tell Easy that the authorities intend to take no action. The story ends with the innocent spared and a kind of justice ren-dered—but not by the LAPD.

Thus Mosley remains true to his goal: to tell the truth, in all its complexity, through the eyes of a highly principled man living in a largely unprincipled world. Like the best of its genre, *Little Scarlet* is not just a riddle with a solution; it is a thoughtful story of the eternal battle beween good and evil.

*Rosemary M. Canfield Reisman*

## Review Sources

*Black Issues Book Review* 6, no. 4 (July/August, 2004): 17.

*Booklist* 100, no. 17 (May 1, 2004): 1516.

*Kirkus Reviews* 72, no. 11 (June 1, 2004): 521.

*Library Journal* 129, no. 10 (June 1, 2004): 108.

*The New York Times*, July 5, 2004, p. E1.

*The New York Times Book Review* 153 (July 25, 2004): 19.

*Publishers Weekly* 251, no. 21 (May 24, 2004): 47.

# THE LOST LAND OF LEMURIA
## Fabulous Geographies, Catastrophic Histories

*Author:* Sumathi Ramaswamy
*Publisher:* University of California Press (Berkeley).
 334 pp. $60.00
*Type of work:* Anthropology, history, and history of
 science
*Time:* About 1840-2000
*Locale:* The Indian and Pacific Oceans

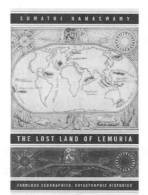

*Ramaswamy explores the genesis of the "lost conti-
nent" of Lemuria, explaining the appeal that such a scientific and cultural theory holds for diverse groups of people*

> *Principal personages:*
> PHILIP LUTLEY SCLATER, English zoologist
> ERNST HAECKEL, German biologist
> HELENA P. BLAVATSKY, Ukrainian-born occultist
> JAMES CHURCHWARD, Anglo-American inventor and writer
> WISHAR S. CERVÉ (HARVEY SPENCER LEWIS), American inventor,
>   writer, and occultist
> CHARLES D. MACLEAN, British civil servant in India

Lemuria made its first recorded appearance in an 1864 article titled "The Mammals of Madagascar" in *The Quarterly Journal of Science*. Its author, Philip Lutley
Sclater, was puzzled by the distribution of the lemur, the only primate inhabiting the
large island of Madagascar, off the southeastern coast of Africa. Sclater observed that
thirty species of lemur were to be found in Madagascar, while only a dozen or so lived
on the African mainland and only three in the region of India. Suggesting that Madagascar and India must have been connected at some remote time, Sclater went on to
wonder whether the supposed connection might have reached as far as the continents
of North and South America, as lemurs bear more resemblance to New World mon-
keys than to their Old World cousins. Sclater called this supposed land bridge or continent "Lemuria."

Speculation about such a landmass actually goes back to at least the 1840's, when
French natural historian Etienne Geoffrey Saint-Hilaire suggested that Madagascar
might be the remnant of a continent lying in what is now the Indian Ocean. The idea
was subsequently espoused by such prominent British scientists as Alfred R. Wallace.
Yet, as history professor Sumathi Ramaswamy points out in *The Lost Land of
Lemuria*, by naming the continent, Sclater gave it not just life but—paradoxically
enough for a place that never existed—a kind of immortality.

Lemuria was quickly taken up by those involved in biogeography (the study of the
distribution of plants and animals) and paleogeography (the study of earlier stages of
the earth's geography). During Sclater's life, these disciplines were burgeoning with

∽

*Sumathi Ramaswamy, an associate
professor of history at the Ann Arbor
campus of the University of
Michigan, is the author of* Passions
of the Tongue: Language Devotion
in Tamil India, 1891-1970 *(1997)
and editor of* Beyond Appearances:
Visual Practices and Ideologies in
Modern India *(2003).*

∽

the knowledge and data then being collected around the world, and the concept of Lemuria fit comfortably into the worldviews of the scientists collecting such data. Some even plotted the position of Lemuria and other "lost continents" on maps, lending the phantom bodies an even greater reality.

In 1870 German biologist Ernst Haeckel took up Sclater's creation with a passion, calling Lemuria the "probable cradle of the human race"—a theme that would resonate for years to come. Haeckel's work, translated into English in 1876 as *The History of Creation*, moved Lemuria far forward in time, although with little evidence. Haeckel was a confirmed evolutionist, inspired like so many of his colleagues by Charles Darwin's *On the Origin of Species by Means of Natural Selection* (1859). In seeking to trace the biological descent of humankind, the German scientist identified the lemur as a probable intermediate stage, and in a kind of compromise between those who favored either an African or an Asian origin, suggested Lemuria as the geographical site of human evolution. The land's disappearance beneath the waves also conveniently accounted for the lack of any hard evidence for Haeckel's hypothesis.

When Dutch anatomist Eugene Dubois discovered fossils of early hominids toward the end of the nineteenth century in what is now Indonesia, he dubbed his finds *Pithecanthropus erectus*. Although *Pithecanthropus* was the name that Haeckel had applied to one of his hypothetical stages of human evolution on Lemuria, Dubois was hesitant to endorse Sclater and Haeckel's ideas regarding the lost continent. Subsequently, however, amateur ethnologist Augustus H. Keane declared *P. erectus* to be an ancestor of the present-day inhabitants of Africa, Australia, and the Andaman Islands of the Indian Ocean—further proof that Lemuria or some similar body had once connected Africa with the lands to the north and east.

Yet throughout the final decades of the nineteenth century the idea of Lemuria was actually losing validity in most quarters. Sclater himself had done little to popularize or expand upon his brainchild. By 1875, in fact, the year before Haeckel's work was translated, he had backed away from the idea of an actual continent. Wallace, too, had second thoughts, deciding that the idea of subsiding continents was unacceptable and hypothesizing that a much wider occurrence of lemurs in the distant past might account for their present distribution.

A further blow was delivered to Lemuria in 1885 when Austrian scientist Eduard Suess proposed the former existence of a giant continent, Gondwanaland, that had slowly split into the continents known today. Somewhat similar to Suess's theory was another proposed in the early decades of the twentieth century by Alfred L. Wegener. The German meteorologist theorized a huge proto-continent he called Pangaea, which began to split apart approximately two hundred million years ago. In Wegener's hypothesis, India once lay close to Madagascar but has since drifted to its current position, creating the great Himalaya Mountains in the process.

Despite such setbacks, Lemuria had taken on a life of its own. It was adopted by Indian and Anglo-Indian anthropologists and ethnologists eager to make sense of the subcontinent's complex racial mix. Thus Lemuria was invoked by racial propagandists to account, in somewhat tortuous fashion, for the perceived gap in sophistication between India's northern and southern ethnic groups. According to one such scenario, a dominant lineage of humankind had long flourished in northern India, while the subcontinent's southern, that is "savage," inhabitants were later migrants from Lemuria. Again, the continent's presumed submergence was held to account for the paucity of physical evidence.

Even as Lemuria lost credence in the scientific community, it established a lasting foothold in the world of the occult as a kind of lost spiritual domain. In *Isis Unveiled* (1877) Ukrainian-born occult leader and cofounder of the Theosophical Society Helena P. Blavatsky identified Lemuria, which she more or less conflated with Atlantis, as the home of what she called the Fourth Root-Race, the ancestors of the world's more enlightened peoples. Three years later Madame Blavatsky (as she was known) argued that Lemuria was the home of a great and learned race whose subsequent dispersal accounts for the cultural similarities between widely separated cultures. Blavatsky would later relocate Lemuria to the Pacific Ocean with disarming ease, while subsequent Theosophists would assert that at one remote era Lemuria's inhabitants attained a degree of civilization under the guidance of the Venusians.

The Pacific region would prove to be a fertile breeding ground for other dreamers. In 1894 California teenager Frederick Spencer Oliver published *A Dweller on Two Planets*, a book recounting the life and teachings of one "Phylos the Tibetan," late of Lemuria and Atlantis but now inhabiting California's Mount Shasta. In 1908 Adelia Taffinder wrote that California itself had been the center of a Lemurian civilization antedating that of Atlantis. In 1924 Anglo-American inventor James Churchward began lecturing and writing about a lost continent he called Mu.

In discussing this latest incarnation of Lemuria, Ramaswamy reveals the depth of her research in what are admittedly murky realms, tracing the concept of Mu back to nineteenth century French archaeologists Brasseur de Bourbourg and Augustus LePlongeon, who had identified it as the Mayan name for Atlantis. Churchward himself claimed to have based his research on tablets written in an ancient language called Naacal and translated for him by a priest in India. Churchward later incorporated his ideas into several books, explaining that Mu had stretched some six thousand miles across the Pacific before its destruction twelve thousand years earlier.

The self-styled "Colonel" Churchward would, in turn, inspire another inventor, Wishar S. Cervé (born, more prosaically, as Harvey Spencer Lewis), to publish *Lemuria: The Lost Continent of the Pacific* (1931). The founder of the Ancient and Mystical Order of the Rosae Crucis (AMORC), Cervé placed the Garden of Eden in North America and dated Lemuria's (or Mu's) destruction to a far remoter age than Churchward. Cervé also claimed that the American Indians were descendants of the Lemurians and that the Mayans were the product of Lemurian and Atlantean intermarriage. Like Oliver before him, Cervé wrote that certain Lemurians survived within Mount Shasta, from which abode they emerged from time to time to trade gold nuggets.

Lemuria was taken up by fiction writers as early as 1898 with the publication of *The Last Lemurian* by G. Firth Scott, while A. Merritt worked the lost continent into his noted science-fiction novel *The Moon Pool* (1918-1919). Among the odder products of pulp publishing were the stories of Richard Shaver, whose purportedly factual accounts of a Lemurian world lying below the earth's surface enlivened the pages of the magazine *Amazing Stories* in the 1940's. More recently, Lin Carter has produced a series of heroic adventure novels about Thongor Valkarth of Lemuria.

In ironic contrast to earlier racist theories, Senegalese president Leopold Senghor invoked Lemuria as recently as 1974 to argue that the great civilizations of the Near East owed their origin to the people of color who had once inhabited the lost southern continent. Yet Lemuria's most fascinating modern manifestation may be found in the beliefs of the Tamils of southern India. Ramaswamy has written about the marginalized Tamils before, and in her new work she explores in great detail the role that Lemuria plays in their cultural and linguistic universe.

Colonial administrator Charles D. Maclean had incorporated Haeckel's speculations about Lemuria into *The Manual of the Administration of the Madras Presidency* (1885), suggesting that the subcontinent's southern inhabitants were its original settlers and that they may have migrated from a now-drowned homeland. Subsequently Tamil writers and public figures seized upon such speculation, identifying the lost, paradisiacal continent variously known as Lemuria or Kumari Nadu. Here Ramaswamy finds a living illustration of her book's central theme: the manner in which marginalized ideas and systems of thought retain their appeal for marginalized groups and individuals.

There have been a number of "lost" continents, beginning with the Atlantis of Greek philosopher Plato and including Archhelenis, which was thought to have linked Africa and Brazil. Yet aside from Atlantis and Lemuria, these have made no impact on the popular mind. Atlantis has, of course, been the subject of innumerable books, articles, films, and so on, but *The Lost Land of Lemuria* is the first work to treat its subject in such detail and from within such a variety of disciplines. Academic readers and researchers will appreciate the book's scholarly apparatus, and although general readers may be put off by Ramaswamy's occasional use of academic jargon and the density of her discussion of Tamil culture, they are bound to enjoy the fascinating byways she explores.

*Grove Koger*

# THE MADONNA OF EXCELSIOR

*Author:* Zakes Mda (1948-    )
*First published:* 2002, in South Africa
*Publisher:* Farrar, Straus and Giroux (New York).
    258 pp. $23.00
*Type of work:* Novel
*Time:* Approximately 1950-2003
*Locale:* Excelsior, South Africa's free state

*Using an event that occurred in 1971 involving out-lawed relations between the black and white races in South Africa, Mda demonstrates how apartheid laws affected the lives of people of both races and offers some hope for ra-cial reconciliation*

*Principal characters:*
    NIKI, black "Madonna"
    PULE, her husband
    POPI, her daughter
    VILIKI, son of Pule and Niki
    SEKATLE, the sometime friend of Viliki, a political opportunist
    FATHER FRANS CLAERHOUT, man, priest, and artist (referred to as the
        trinity) who paints the black Madonnas
    JOHANNES SMIT, a farmer who lusts after Niki
    STEPHANUS CRONJE, Niki's Afrikaner lover, father of Popi
    TJAART CRONJE, his son
    GROOT-JAN LOMBARD, the head of the police
    FRANÇOIS BORNMAN, the head cleric of the area
    ADAM DE VRIES, an Afrikaner lawyer

In his novel *The Madonna of Excelsior*, based on an event that occurred in Excelsior in South Africa in 1971, Zakes Mda begins in the middle of the plot, then returns to the past to explain how the significant event occurred, and then charts the results of that event. He devotes his first short chapter to a meeting between Niki, with her blue-eyed child, Popi, and Father Frans Claerhout, a priest who paints native women amid the South African landscape. Mda often begins chapters with descriptions of the paintings of Claerhout, a kind of Flemish expressionist whom Mda had actually met. The chapter ends with Popi thinking of Claerhout's canvases and the comparison of his work to "God's own canvas."

In the following chapter Mda presents Niki and Popi at a garden party that includes the "very cream of Excelsior society," especially, and ironically, the men who were accused of having had sexual relations with the black women of the town. At the party, Popi and Niki see Tjaart Cronje, who is Popi's half brother. By the end of the novel Popi and Tjaart, who are separated by race and economic status, are somewhat

∾

*Zakes Mda, novelist and playwright, has won every major South African prize for his work.* Ways of Dying *(1995) received the Olive Schreiner Prize, and* The Heart of Redness *(2000) was awarded the Commonwealth Writer Prize for the African region. After serving as writer-in-residence at the Market Theatre in Johannesburg, he was appointed as a professor of creative writing at Ohio University.*

∾

reconciled, just as the children of the black Madonnas painted by Claerhout will represent the new South Africa.

Following this prelude, in which readers learn of the Immorality Act prohibiting sexual relations between the races, Mda returns his readers to Niki's past. By beginning that past when Niki is a teenager capable of sexual relations, Mda implies that Niki's life begins when she is treated as sexual property by the Afrikaner men. Her first sexual experience occurs when Johannes Smit, known to Niki's friends as "Hairy Buttocks" and "Limp Stick," finally succeeds in raping her. Smit will continue to lust after Niki.

Niki marries Pule, who works in the distant South African coal mines, and has his son, Viliki. Pule sends her money, but his prolonged absences leave her alone and vulnerable. She feels that she is being raped by the eyes of the Afrikaners and is subjected to a strip search when she is suspected of stealing goods from her employer. At a cherry festival Smit makes a pass at Niki, but Stephanus Cronje helps her escape from Smit and then has sex with her. The relationship, which seems consensual, actually is not, given their unequal status, and it is hardly unique, as four other mixed-race couples join them at a barn where there is a sexual orgy (perhaps to his credit, Cronje does not share Niki with the other men). Ultimately, twelve pregnant black women and their Afrikaner partners are charged with breaking the Immorality Act.

To illustrate how miscegenation pervaded the Afrikaner power structure, Mda focuses not only on rich farmers like Cronje and Smit but also on Groot-Jan Lombard, head of the police, and on the Reverend François Bornman. In effect, government and religion implicitly sanction interracial sexual relations. Mda also focuses on the unequal treatment given to the Afrikaner men and the black women (the "Excelsior Nineteen"). While Adam de Vries successfully arranges bail for his Afrikaner clients, the black women are committed to jail until their trials. During their confinement, many of them, including Niki, give birth to mixed-race children.

Reactions to the charges also vary. Overcome with shame, Cronje commits suicide; and the Reverend Bornman, who attributes his actions to the seductive work of black women collaborating with the devil, botches his own suicide attempt, losing an eye but gaining the sympathy of his parishioners. Apparently the other Afrikaner men have no guilt or shame. Niki, fearful of Pule's reaction, attempts to make Popi into a black child by shaving her blond hair and by trying to "brown" her skin by holding her over a fire. When another series of miscegenation cases is brought to light, the charges against all the "guilty" black women are dropped. Mda suggests that when enough Afrikaner men are embarrassed, the laws are no longer enforced.

While Niki is the focus of the first half of the novel, it is Popi who is the main character of the second half, though Niki does remain the moral center of the story. For his painting of the "Blue Madonna," which Mda describes in great detail, Father Claer-hout uses Niki and Popi as models, suggesting that the savior of South Africa will be a woman. From this point, Popi and her brother, Viliki, become increasingly important in the narrative. With the end of apartheid, black South Africans come into power, al-beit in a limited way. The oppression by the Afrikaners is now succeeded by another kind of exploitation, and the black South Africans are again the victims. This time black South African politicians are the oppressors.

Prior to the official end of apartheid, Viliki and Popi become radicalized. Popi joins the Young Women's Union of the Methodist Church, which will eventually sup-ply her with a power base, and Viliki fights in the clandestine guerrilla revolutionary movement. Their model is Robert Mugabe, the revolutionary leader in what is now Zimbawe. The opposition is headed by lawyer Adam de Vries, the Reverend Born-man, Klein-Jan Lombard (who "inherits" the police from his father), and Tjaart Cronje, Stephanus's son and Popi's half brother. They are assisted by paid black in-formers. Because Viliki's friend Sekatle, an opportunist who aims to profit regardless of the outcome, accompanies Lombard when he comes to arrest Viliki, it is probable that Sekatle was the informer. While he is incarcerated for six months, Viliki is tor-tured (electric prods and pliers are applied to his genitals), but he manages to acquire a political following that battles the Afrikaners. In that brutal confrontation Popi, who as a bystander had not been political, is injured and then joins the black resistance.

After white rule ends, the battles continue, though now on the political front. De Vries, who had believed that the Afrikaners could retain their power, is marginalized, though he tries to become affiliated with the blacks, who now form the majority of the town council. The council deliberations act as a kind of microcosm for what is occur-ring throughout South Africa. Viliki, who has been elected mayor, is determined to make improvements in the town, but he is sidetracked by political and nationalistic questions, such as which language should be used for the minutes of the meeting. He is supported by Popi, also elected to the council. Tjaart Cronje is in the opposition. Sekatle, seeing an opportunity, wants to serve on the council and gains power by promising squatters property that is slated for decent housing. (Mugabe came to power in Zimbabwe using the same tactics.)

To her credit, Popi, who is slated to have one of the new housing units, refuses to use her political power for personal gain, and so her dwelling is not finished. Because Vikili will not pander to squatters, who want everything immediately, he is ousted as mayor; the corrupt Sekatle becomes mayor of Excelsior. As in Zimbawe, the "revolu-tionaries," once installed, become greedy.

Vikili and the "Seller of Songs," his significant other, become itinerant musicians. Popi, who did not run for reelection to the council, returns to a life of menial labor. Niki becomes the so-called Bee Woman.

Although the situation is hardly promising, Mda ends his novel on a positive note. In an interesting exchange with Popi, Smit explains that the red and yellow cherries are mixed in order to promote their cross pollination by bees. This discussion sets up the reconciliation between Tjaart and Popi. Tjaart, who has steadfastly refused to ac-cept the new Africa and who has been Popi's adversary on the council, becomes sick and sends for her. He acknowledges her as his half sister and offers her a jar of hair removal ointment to make her look better from an Afrikaner perspective. Though she resents his lack of insight, she accepts the gift, which he offers with the declaration that she is beautiful. His comment makes Popi aware of her beauty, and she tells her mother that she is now free of anger and shame, a statement that also frees Niki of her own shame.

At the end of the novel Mda resorts to Magical Realism as he describes the bees as the means of filling the gaping hole in Popi's heart and completing "the healing work that had begun with the creations of the trinity [the paintings of Claerhout]." Popi, Niki, and the bees then vanish from the canvas.

Although the story seems to be told by an omniscient narrator, there are several references to "I" and "we," suggesting that the narrator is a member of the Excelsior community—probably not an Afrikaner, because the only thoughts that are revealed to readers are those of Niki and Popi. Yet is it unlikely that even an articulate black South African would be privy to the thoughts of the two women. What is even more remarkable is that the narrator dispassionately records events without editorializing. Pule's death is the result of working in the coal mines, but there is no condemnation of the plight of the miners whose lungs are destroyed by the coal dust. While absentee husbands work in the mines, causing domestic problems for their wives, the situation seems to be presented as a given, and for the most part black South African men seem emasculated and marginalized in the novel.

Niki and Popi are, on the other hand, fully developed, but the narrator does not judge them. Niki seems imperfect, angry and scheming, but those are conclusions readers must draw. Perhaps the narrator as artist is similar to the "trinity," the painter: "His work was to paint the subjects, and not to poke his nose into their lives beyond the canvas." The similarity between the two painters is reinforced by the frequent juxtaposition of descriptions of the paintings and the actions of the novel. Both paintings and plot suggest that the two South African races are interdependent and that the new South Africa will be the "child" of both.

*Thomas L. Erskine*

## Review Sources

*Black Issues Book Review* 6, no. 4 (July/August, 2004): 20.
*Booklist* 100, no. 9/10 (January 1-15, 2004): 825.
*The Economist* 370 (February 28, 2004): 81-82.
*International Journal of African Historical Studies* 37, no. 2 (2004): 389.
*Kirkus Reviews* 72, no. 1 (January 1, 2004): 10.
*Library Journal* 129, no. 2 (February 1, 2004): 125.
*The New York Times Book Review* 153 (March 28, 2004): 8.
*Publishers Weekly* 251, no. 11 (March 15, 2004): 56.

# MAGIC SEEDS

*Author:* V. S. Naipaul (1932-    )
*Publisher:* Alfred A. Knopf (New York). 280 pp. $25.00
*Type of work:* Novel
*Time:* The 1980's and the 1990's
*Locale:* Berlin, India, and London

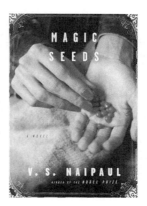

*This sequel to* Half a Life *(2001) takes its protagonist from Berlin to a rebel group in India and then to London as he struggles to adapt to his surroundings and discover some essential purpose and identity*

Principal characters:
WILLIE CHANDRAN, an English-educated
  East Indian
SAROJINI, his sister
BHOJ NARAYAN,
RAMACHANDRA, and
EINSTEIN, guerrilla squad leaders
ROJA, a rebel recruit
ROGER and PERDITA, old London friends of Willie
MARIAN, Roger's mistress
MARCUS, another old friend, now a retired ambassador

At the conclusion to *Magic Seeds*, Indian-born, English-educated Willie Chandran tells himself, "It is wrong to have an ideal view of the world. That's where the mischief starts." Coming from another writer, or at the end of any other novel, this judgment might be dismissed as a stagy literary sigh, a weary refusal to deal with ideas. During his long career, however, Nobel laureate V. S. Naipaul has witnessed and written about both ideals and mischief in India, Pakistan, South America, the Caribbean region, the United States, Indonesia, Africa, and Iran. Willie's remark comes from deep, prolonged observation, and if Naipaul seems obdurately jaundiced, he nevertheless speaks for people who have been cast loose from the protective mooring of nationality and culture.

Willie Chandran is such a drifter, and not by preference. *Magic Seeds* is the sequel to *Half a Life*. In the first novel, Willie leaves his family ashram in India to be a scholarship university student in England following World War II. It is a tremendous break for him, a door out of what he views as a confining, stifling Indian traditional life, opening onto a wide intellectual world. He founders, however, unable to grasp English ways, and although he publishes a book of short stories, he readily abandons his ambition to become a writer in order to marry and live the insulated life of a colonist in Africa. When a revolution ends that life, he abandons his wife and flees to Berlin to live with his sister, Sarojini, who has also left the family ashram to become a documentary filmmaker in Germany.

*V. S. Naipaul was born in Trinidad in 1932 and left to study at Oxford University at age eighteen. He became a freelance journalist for the British Broadcasting Corporation (BBC) and later a novelist and social commentator. His books earned him a knighthood, honorary degrees from American and British universities, and many literary prizes, including England's Booker Prize in 1971 and the Nobel Prize in Literature in 2001.*

*Magic Seeds* opens after Willie has spent six months with his sister in a pleasantly otiose, dreamlike existence. He has exasperated Sarojini with his indolence. She is an idealist in the sense that evidence of injustice angers her, and she makes documentaries for German television about revolutionaries who want to correct social inequities. She is impressed by an Indian thinker who proposes recasting his country without the class warfare that turned other revolutions into bloodbaths, and she pushes her brother to join the philosopher's rebel army, which has succeeded in taking over a rural region.

Willie acquiesces, thinking such a commitment to revolution might bring purpose to his life. After much hardship, he is taken to a rebel training camp, and in a sense the remainder of the novel is a tale about his new self that Willie wants to tell to his sister, the idealist. Long sections are in the form of letters to her.

Repelled at first by the brutal life of a guerrilla, he finds to his surprise that he is good at it. When his superiors make him a courier, because of his experience surviving an African revolution, he has a startling perception: Never having felt at home anywhere, he is yet able to look at home anywhere. The ability serves him well in evading police scrutiny, and he becomes trusted. He develops bonds with a series of squad leaders, recognizing that each of them has become a rebel out of some private need to leave society and strike out against it and not out of idealism; they are "action men," which is to say that they do not hesitate to kill.

The first, Bhoj Narayan, would appear to be an Indian success story, a man who came from a low-caste family to join the middle class, but in fact shame still dogs him. Hatred of Indian landlords, remnants of a feudal system, moves him to join the rebel army. He becomes Willie's mentor. For a while, Willie is content in his role. A poor recruit, Roja, is their downfall. Although likeable, Roja is unreliable and eventually betrays Willie to the police; however, Bhoj Narayan is accidentally captured in Willie's place. The episode teaches Willie two things: that an old veteran rebel can suddenly fail and that Willie himself can kill, for he executes Roja.

After that, two experienced leaders, Ramachandra and Einstein, both violently angry men, take Willie into their confidence. The first is killed in an ambush because he simply lacks basic combat skills, and the second, after woefully botching a kidnapping, surrenders to police and persuades Willie to do so, too. Willie realizes that the guerrillas are led by incompetent field commanders who have little idealism, while the leaders of the movement in general, the philosophers and strategists, do not understand the practicalities of the guerrilla warfare that they promote.

Willie enters an Indian prison, along with many of his former comrades. Their endless, repetitive, and vapid political discussions soon drive him to the verge of madness.
Through a bribe he gets himself transferred to the prison hospital, where he sinks into
inanition. He can only admit to himself that returning to India has been a mistake; he
can find no pattern or thread of meaning and views his experiences as no more a product of his will than his childhood development had been in the family ashram.

Luckily, however, Willie continues writing to Sarojini, and she comes to his rescue. She enlists the help of Roger, an old friend of Willie in London. On the strength
of Willie's single book of stories, Roger portrays Willie to prison authorities as a pioneer of postcolonial Indian literature. Willie thereby appears to have intellectual status in England, and because of it, he soon finds himself free and on his way to London
under Roger's sponsorship. The irony in this brilliant bit of plotting would be hilarious if it were not so damning. Though a murderer and a terrorist, Willie is set free because of a manufactured English testimonial about a book that no Indian has read. England is Willie's trump card, and in India it takes all tricks.

Yet it is only an abstraction of England that rescues Willie. Throughout his adult
life, he lived as though his mind was always catching up with his body. As a student in
England, he was bewildered, as his Indian childhood had not prepared him for that
life; as a planter's husband in Africa, he was buffered from Africans by his English
education; as a rebel, he counted upon the vague political idealism given him by his
sister to sustain him. In each case he fled before the consequences of his social separateness ruined him. Now in England, as a political refugee apparently not permitted
to leave, he has come to rest in a culture with which he is vaguely familiar, but his
prospects for finding a place for himself in the world look even grimmer.

Willie's friends Roger and Perdita appear to be a shining example of England's
new middle class. Roger is a successful lawyer; Perdita is a cultivated, elegant wife.
While Willie has been living precariously in former English colonies, they have
climbed in the world, grown moderately wealthy, and bought a large house in a fashionable district of London. Straightforward ambition and success, however, are often
the ruin of Naipaul's characters. Their glamorous life is in the process of undoing
them as Willie watches. Perdita has taken a lover, a former business colleague of
Roger, and soon she takes Willie as a lover, too. For his part, Roger faces serious legal
trouble because of his unwitting part in a shady real estate deal, and to bring some vitality into his life, he takes a working-class woman, Marian, as his mistress. The affair
fails. Eventually, Marian takes up with another of Roger's friends.

In the last two chapters of the novel, "Suckers" and "Magic Seeds," Roger reveals
how his own English attitudes have duped him. Despite a pretense of disdain for the
aristocracy, he has fawned on a wealthy lord, who becomes the source of his legal
trouble. Despite his wariness about the lower classes, he aligns himself with Marian,
who exposes him to her grasping, brassy, violent friends and family. Moreover, he
learns that for Marian sexuality is a kind of sport and a means of bettering one's lot,
nothing personal. These setbacks embitter him, and his reaction is to blame the very
culture that allowed his earlier success, or at least a chauvinistic ideal of that culture.

He laments to Willie that the "nicer sides" of Western civilization, such as the rule of law and compassion, are out of date in a changing world, that in fact they are being used as weapons against that civilization. Behind his remark is the old elitism embedded in the phrase "white man's burden."

In contrast to Roger's plight is the story of Marcus, which unfolds in the last scene of the novel. When Willie and Roger were young, Marcus, a young black diplomat from an African nation, was their friend. During the intervening years he held onto his job through one brutal dictatorship after another in his home country and became the ambassador to Great Britain. During it all, he pursued one simple ambition: to have sex with only white women so that eventually he would have a white granddaughter; he wanted to take walks with her in London and have the pleasure of hearing her call him grandfather in public. The final scene describes the marriage of Marcus's son to an aristocratic Englishwoman, a couple who have already had a boy and a girl. Marcus's happiness is complete.

In the meantime, Willie has made a discovery about himself. He has gotten a job as a fact checker for an architectural magazine in London, and his work there requires him to attend classes on architecture. He finds that the subject suits him and, for the first time, gives him an appreciation of the physical details and cultural continuity of London. Even though he is now past fifty, he decides to pursue architecture as a career, a calling. He feels that at last, on his own, he has found something good to tell Sarojini. Poignantly, when he tries, he cannot write her a letter about it because it entails a rejection of her ideal view of the world. At novel's end he is his own man for the first time.

*Magic Seeds* tells a wrenching tale despite Willie's rescue, for his story is consonant with the twenty-first century's postcolonial turmoil and international terrorism. How many Willie Chandrans are there in the world now, and how many will be suborned by idealists and zealots? The prospect is chilling. In his character, Naipaul portrays a vulnerable, patchwork mentality, such as multicultural crosscurrents can produce, and he does it with the graceful economy of style and spare plotting that gives his fiction unsettling power.

*Roger Smith*

## Review Sources

*Kirkus Reviews* 72, no. 20 (October 15, 2004): 980.
*London Review of Books* 26, no. 21 (November 4, 2004): 39.
*New Statesman* 133 (September 6, 2004): 50.
*The New York Times*, November 30, 2004, p. E1.
*The New York Times Book Review* 154 (November 28, 2004): 14.
*The Spectator* 296 (September 4, 2004): 37.
*The Times Literary Supplement*, September 3, 2004, p. 10.

# THE MAN IN MY BASEMENT

*Author:* Walter Mosley (1952-    )
*Publisher:* Little, Brown (Boston). 249 pp. $23.00
*Type of work:* Novel
*Time:* 2004
*Locale:* Sag Harbor, Long Island, and vicinity

*When wealthy Anniston Bennet rents Charles Blakey's empty basement, Blakey does not realize how the next few months will change both his identity and his understanding of the world*

> *Principal characters:*
> CHARLES BLAKEY, an unemployed black man with a mortgage on his
>     family home, no job, few friends, and fewer prospects
> ANNISTON BENNET, a rich white man who rents Blakey's cellar
> BIG CLARANCE MAYHEW, a friend of Blakey
> RICKY, Big Clarance's cousin and another friend
> MISS IRENE LITTLENECK, Blakey's eighty-year-old neighbor across the
>     street
> NARCISS GULLY, an antiques dealer and black historian
> BETHANY, a black woman who becomes another of Blakey's lovers
> EXTINE, a white woman whom Blakey befriends

Regular fans of Walter Mosley's fiction—and they are legion—may at initial contact be shocked by *The Man in My Basement.* The novel has none of the characters Mosley has created before (like Easy Rawlins or Fearless Jones), is not set in Los Angeles (as are most of his earlier works, such as the popular 1990 novel *Devil in a Blue Dress*), and is not a mystery—at least not in the ordinary sense of that genre. The novel does, however, have several of Mosley's trademark features: It is gripping and extremely well written, and it asks readers to think about its subjects. Mosley has always had this philosophical bent (note the name of his protagonist Socrates Fortlow in several earlier story collections, like the 1999 book *Walkin' the Dog*), and *The Man in My Basement* mines that serious vein, raising questions of power, justice, and morality that will not be answered soon in readers' minds.

Charles Blakey is not a promising fictional hero. At thirty three, he has no job, no chance for a job, no money, a mortgage on his house, and numerous other bills. As his sometime friend Big Clarance describes him, in an occasional burst of street language, "Unemployed, drunk loudmouth is what you is." Blakey lives alone in his roomy childhood home in what he tells readers is a secluded colored neighborhood of Sag Harbor, Long Island, and his life has become increasingly lonely and isolated since he lost his job as a bank teller nine months before and his last girlfriend soon after that. When he asks his friend Lainie, an officer at the bank, she tells him that he has been blacklisted from other jobs because of the petty thefts he committed while he worked at the bank. As usual, Blakey lies and denies the crimes. This antihero with

∼

*Walter Mosley has written fifteen
novels and short-story collections,
including* Bad Boy Brawly Brown
*(2002),* Six Easy Pieces: Easy
Rawlins Stories *(2003), and* Fear
Itself *(2003). He was born in Los
Angeles and now lives in New York.
He is the recipient of a Grammy
Award, the Anisfield-Wolf Book
Award, and other honors.*

∼

few redeeming qualities appears to have hit bottom, headed apparently for his own end.

His life changes radically when Anniston
Bennet shows up at his door and asks to rent
Blakey's empty cellar. The rich white man
knows everything about Blakey, including the
crucial fact that he needs money, and offers
him $50,000 to stay in his basement for sixty-
five days. Blakey initially refuses but then accepts the offer, and his life begins to change
almost at once. What Bennet wants, it turns out,
is to be caged in a nine-foot steel cell which
Blakey assembles and secures, after Bennet en-
ters it, with an ancient lock used on slaving ships that the prisoner provides. Blakey
brings him his meals but otherwise leaves the eccentric white man alone to read and
write and think. "This is my prison," he tells Blakey. "And you are my warden and my
guard." Bennet describes himself to Blakey vaguely as a criminal paying for his
crimes against humanity, but his actions are going to impact his jailer as profoundly as
himself.

Meanwhile, Blakey's life has already changed in significant ways. In cleaning out
his house in preparation for the arrival of his "guest," he unloads boxes of family heir-
looms on Narciss Gully, an antiques dealer who is interested in black history and particularly in some of the items that Blakey wants to sell. Blakey can trace his family
back generations to the first indentured servants (not slaves) who earned their freedom soon after their arrival in this area of New York in the eighteenth century. His
house has been in the family for generations and contains what to Narciss are treasures—like the three ivory "passport masks" which she reports were used for identification and go all the way back to tribal Africa. So Blakey is rediscovering his own essential black history, its roots growing back into the time of slavery—at the same time
that he is holding a rich white man in a cage in his basement. Bennet has made his
money in financial "reclamations," he tells Blakey, but it sounds more like "repara-
tions" are at work here, or better, perhaps, that it will be Blakey who is finally being
'reclaimed.'

What happens is that Blakey turns into a true jailer. In trying to uncover the concrete reasons for Bennet's self-incarceration, and frustrated by his vague and unsatis-
factory answers, Blakey imposes harsh restrictions on his prisoner, in effect torturing
him, and forcing him into a kind of solitary confinement. As in any number of actual
psychological experiments using lay subjects as both prisoners and warders, the roles
of jailer and detainee soon come to define their players, and the two main characters
here take on the behavior appropriate to their positions.

Although they seem at the beginning of the novel and on the surface worlds apart,
through their interaction Blakey and Bennet actually switch roles and become more
and more alike. It turns out that Bennet has killed people in the course of his powerful
international career, as he describes in graphic detail to his guard. At the same time,

Blakey realizes that he is not without guilt himself, in fact had a hand in the death of his hated Uncle Brent in this very house some years before. Further, Bennet is hardly the powerful figure he appears to be in the beginning of their interaction but reveals that his birth name was Tamal Knosos and that his father could have been Arab or African. It is Blakey, Bennet confesses, who is the true aristocrat, who can trace his genealogical lines back for centuries.

In learning the truth about Bennet, of course, Blakey is also uncovering truths about himself. He realizes how artificial his life has been, and what little intimacy he has had with others. Slowly his isolation melts, and he begins sexual relationships with both Narciss and Bethany, a black woman he meets through his friend Ricky, at the same time maintaining his secret life as Bennet's jailer. "My domination of him came from a personal conflict we were having. I didn't want to be another one of his slaves. I was foolish enough to believe that I could take his money and keep my freedom." Toward the end of the imprisonment, when he sees his prisoner growing weaker, Blakey relents in his treatment and begins to feed Bennet nourishing food but also to secretly tape-record his confessions.

Bennet has his own plan, however, and commits suicide by swallowing a poison he has carried into the cell. Blakey buries him and destroys the evidence that Bennet ever lived in his house. In a brief conclusion, Blakey tells readers that he has since opened up a museum of black history with Narciss (although they are no longer lovers) and is secure and relatively happy, although he does not think, because of what he's learned from his interaction with Bennet, that he will ever marry. So he ends his story less isolated than when he started it and with a great deal of knowledge of himself, his roots, and black history.

*The Man in My Basement* hardly ties together all the issues it raises. Rather, the story is like a mirror that is at the same time one-way and two-way: It lets the two characters observe, reflect, and learn from each other and finally reverse roles. The complex symbolism in the novel works toward those ends. Bennet is caged in Blakey's cellar, but it is Blakey who is truly isolated and "caged" in his own life, readers realize. Bennet, ironically, has the "key" to Blakey's freedom.

The passport masks Blakey finds in his piles of family history not only carry him back into the eighteenth century and his black lineage but represent the multiple personas both he and Bennet carry in the twentieth. Likewise, while African American literature has often played with the notion of underground characters—notably in Richard Wright's *The Man Who Lived Underground* (1971) and Ralph Ellison's *Invisible Man* (1952)—*The Man in My Basement* is a white man who perhaps has resided in the black collective unconscious from the beginnings of American history. Easy labels do not exist here; the novel raises issues of justice, morality, power, and manipulation but hardly concludes any of them. Racial stereotypes are again and again destroyed. Blakey feels as much guilt and fear as Bennet in the end, and it is Bennet who turns out to be the more violent, this small, bald man with a "huge" penis. The novel is dedicated to Harry Belafonte, "the man of the world," and few entertainers have done more in furthering racial understanding. Walter Mosley's novel is clearly an attempt to continue that tradition.

Mosley has always been one of the best writers of modern mysteries (certainly to be ranked with Michael Connelly and James Lee Burke), but with *The Man in My Basement* he shows himself to have moved permanently beyond whatever genre label he has carried in the past, for he has written a novel of profound and occasionally disturbing themes. If Mosley has literary ancestors here, they would be not popular modern authors, but Herman Melville, Franz Kafka, and other essentially philosophical writers. As in Melville's stories "Bartleby the Scrivener" and "Benito Cereno," for example, the narrator of *The Man in My Basement* is telling readers less about the title character than about Bennet's impact on his life. Like the works of Kafka, author of *Der Prozess* (1925; *The Trial*, 1937) and *Das Schloss* (1926; *The Castle*, 1930), the novel plays with notions of truth and justice, while it portrays a character caught in a maze he can only free himself from with difficulty. Walter Mosley's strange, taut tale is a novel of ideas that reveals a good deal about race and race relations in the United States in the twenty-first century.

*David Peck*

## Review Sources

*Booklist* 100, no. 4 (October 15, 2003): 358.
*The Boston Globe*, February 3, 2004, p. F2.
*Kirkus Reviews* 71, no. 21 (November 1, 2003): 1291.
*Los Angeles Times*, January 18, 2004, p. 88.
*The New Yorker* 79, no. 43 (January 19, 2004): 88.
*Publishers Weekly* 250, no. 50 (December 15, 2003): 54.
*The Washington Post Book World*, January 4, 2004, p. T09.

# MAPS OF TIME
## An Introduction to Big History

*Author:* David Christian (1946-    )
Foreword by William H. McNeill
*Publisher:* University of California Press (Berkeley).
   642 pp. $35.00
*Type of work:* History
*Time:* From the beginning of the universe to 2004
*Locale:* The universe, with emphasis on the Milky Way
   and Earth

*A cofounder of the Big History movement offers a "modern creation myth" that incorporates contemporary scientific findings and integrates human history with that of the cosmos*

The Big History movement was founded in the late 1980's, largely in response to two long-established intellectual trends: the diminishing significance of humanity in cosmological systems and increasing specialization in science and the humanities.

Over many centuries, Earth and the human race have been moved steadily away from the center of cosmology. In the Ptolemaic worldview, dominant through the European Middle Ages, Earth was innermost among concentric transparent spheres. In the sixteenth century, Nicolaus Copernicus argued that Earth revolves around the sun. A century later, Giordano Bruno suggested that other stars could be separate suns, perhaps with planets of their own. The notion of infinite time and space, dwarfing humanity, was common by the eighteenth century. By the twentieth century, cosmology made Earth and the human species seem so insignificant that Albert Camus could write of "the benign indifference of the universe." An important Big History goal is to put humanity back into the cosmological equation, without necessarily returning it to the core.

Meanwhile—in what some see as an inevitable trend—a given field of study in science or the humanities that has yielded new knowledge has tended to divide into subspecialties. As these proliferated, they have grown apart, sometimes ceasing to communicate. Ultimately, according to David Christian, a cofounder of the Big History movement, specialization presents obstacles to a supremely important intellectual achievement—a "creation story," a cosmology that would afford human beings a sense of their place in the universe. "It is one of the many odd features of modern society," he says, "that despite having access to more hard information than any earlier society, those in modern educational systems do not normally teach such a story. Instead, . . . we teach about origins in disconnected fragments. We seem incapable of offering a unified account of how things came to be the way they are."

Such a unified account is the objective in *Maps of Time: An Introduction to Big History*, addressed to lay readers and professional scholars alike. The book grew out

*David Christian, a cofounder of the Big History movement, is a professor in the Department of History at San Diego State University. In addition to* Maps of Time, *his published books include* Living Water: Vodka and Russian Society on the Eve of Emancipation *(1990),* Imperial and Soviet Russia: Power, Privilege, and the Challenge of Modernity *(1997), and* A History of Russia, Central Asia, and Mongolia—Volume 1: Inner Eurasia from Prehistory to the Mongol Empire *(1998).*

of Christian's Big History lectures, first at Macquarie University in Sydney, Australia, and later at San Diego State University in California. *Maps of Time* "unites natural history and human history in a single, grand, and intelligible narrative," asserts world historian William H. McNeill in the foreword. McNeill equates this achievement with those of Sir Isaac Newton, who "united the heavens and the earth under uniform laws of motion," and of Charles Darwin, who united "the human species and other forms of life within a single evolutionary process."

Big History has been but one of the forces seeking a unified modern cosmology. Actually, despite the specializing trend, much of the unifying impetus has come from scientists. For example, Stephen Hawking in *A Brief History of Time* (1988) took on the challenge of integrating theories from vastly differing spatial scales: the general theory of relativity and the theory of quantum mechanics. Preston Cloud's *Cosmos, Earth, and Man* (1978) aimed at integrating the largest timescales—from the creation of the universe to the creation of Earth—with the more modest scale of human history.

Christian takes an approach similar to these In *Maps of Time*; but, as one would expect from a historian, he focuses much more closely on human societies than Hawking the cosmologist or Cloud the biogeologist. Christian explains that Big History tries to put "human history in context, by seeing it as part of an even larger story that includes the past of the earth and the Universe as a whole. It therefore provides a natural bridge between the history discipline and the historical sciences of Biology, Geology and Astronomy."

Thus, the "modern creation myth" aims at reestablishing a place for humans in cosmology, while also reflecting "a growing sense among scholars in many fields that we may be close to a grand unification of knowledge." The word "myth" does not refer to the exploits of gods and heroes but conveys that the earliest chapters of the story, while plausible, cannot be scientifically verified. This creation myth, however, does incorporate the most recent findings of many scientific specialties; indeed, science relates more of the story than does history.

Christian's chronology begins with the big bang, "now the central idea of modern cosmology." (McNeill, in the foreword, recounts how, "in the course of a discussion about what sort of introduction to history the department at Macquarie ought to provide for its students, David Christian blurted out something like 'Why not start at the beginning?' and promptly found himself invited to show his colleagues what that might mean.") Christian is "looking at the past on all timescales," but detailing the human era, the way a computer file-management system displays expanded or collapsed file lists. The largest timescales—those immediately following the big bang that launched the universe—occupy relatively brief portions of the book. Part 1, "The Inanimate Universe," comprises three chapters covering the period from the big bang (about 13.5 billion years ago) to the creation of the Earth, some 4.5 billion years ago. Parts 2 and 3, totaling four chapters, cover the period from the origins of life to the beginnings of human history. Parts 4 and 5 provide a (relative) close-up on human history from the origins of agriculture through "the great acceleration of the twentieth century."

The book includes many reader-friendly features. Mindful of his general audience, the author defines technical terms on first use. Each chapter ends with a summary, and most chapters include timelines for the periods they cover. Two appendices present technical subjects—radiometric dating techniques and the second law of thermodynamics—simply and straightforwardly. The ending also features a "Chronology for the Whole of Time." Thus the book literally provides "maps of time," which can be helpful to the nonspecialist reader and to scientific specialists wishing to know how their disciplines are perceived to have contributed to the big picture.

Christian relates how the formation of life—intricate chemical combinations—was a consequence of a universal evolution from simplicity toward complexity. According to modern cosmology, the early universe contained little beyond vast hydrogen and helium clouds. Then, stars began to form from concentrations of hydrogen under the pull of gravity. As they coalesced, their extreme internal heat fused hydrogen into helium. Fusion produced energy that kept the interior from collapsing further, creating stable cores fueled by burning hydrogen. The larger stars exert even greater internal pressure, leading to the creation of more complex elements.

This tale of progressing complexity sets the stage for a major theme of the book: that certain patterns of transformation are repeated on all levels and all timescales, including human history. Christian notes, for example, that

> [i]n the early universe, gravity took hold of clouds of atoms, and sculpted them into stars and galaxies. . . . [B]y a sort of social gravity, cities and states were sculpted from scattered communities of farmers. . . . [I]n a striking parallel with star formation, new structures suddenly appeared, together with a new level of complexity.

The theme of transformational patterns is one means by which Big History seeks to reestablish humanity's place in the cosmological picture—but not at the center, for evolving complexity implies no inevitable culmination in humankind. In Christian's view, and that of modern biology, it was Darwinian natural selection that shaped the first organic chemicals, both in space and on the earth, and, about one billion years after the earth's formation, the organisms that became "the ancestors of all modern lifeforms." It was not Darwin but Herbert Spencer who popularized the term "evolution"; Spencer saw biological change "as a movement from 'lower' to 'higher' life-forms, as a form of progress." Darwin himself believed merely that certain life-forms had the traits most conducive to survival in their environment; hence, while others passed away without reproducing, these life-forms passed their genes and traits to succeeding generations.

Opposed to the concept of increasing complexity is another of the book's major themes: the tension between complexity and entropy, or as Christian describes it, the "endless waltz of chaos and complexity." Stars, galaxies, and living organisms were made possible by the unequal distribution of energy (gravitational force) throughout the universe, enabling the work necessary to develop and stabilize complex entities. According to the second law of thermodynamics, the amount of free energy available to do such work must decrease over large timescales until none is left in the universe, and complex entities are no longer possible. The "waltz of chaos and complexity" is not truly endless.

Paradoxically, complex entities may actually hasten the entropic process by dissipating huge amounts of free energy. Christian quantifies the energy used by entities at various levels of complexity, showing the ability of the most complex entities—animals, including humans; the human brain; and human societies—to handle large amounts of it without breaking down. But "they in fact generate entropy more effectively than do simpler structures."

Christian asserts that, in the near future at least, humanity can prolong its existence by limiting the expenditure of free energy, slowing down the inexorable march toward total entropy in an unimaginably distant future. He theorizes that in the medium term the race could direct its own evolution, through positive influence upon the environment resulting from language and "collective learning." He sees collective learning as another transformational pattern at work, the counterpart of the first "multi-celled" organisms formed through the "cooperation" of billions of single-celled organisms. Through collective learning, humans can rapidly teach one another new survival techniques, whereas genetic transmission of naturally selected traits is a far slower and chancier process.

*Maps of Time* may be evaluated in several ways: on its effectiveness in addressing its intended audiences; on its accuracy in presenting contemporary knowledge from many fields; and, of course, as a modern creation story. Telling the story of creation from its very beginning is a supremely ambitious undertaking, but Christian shows rare skill in communicating with two dissimilar audiences—general reader and specialist—through what are actually several retellings of the story in narrative, summary graphic, and tabular form. The book also succeeds as a rather ingenious synthesis of modern scientific and humanistic knowledge, integrating different scales of time and space and showing similar "patterns of transformation" between the human scale and other, vastly larger scales of time and space. The discovery that humankind partakes of these patterns restores the race to a significant role in the modern creation story.

Does *Maps of Time* succeed as a creation myth? Christian defines a creation myth as a story that provides "universal coordinates within which people can imagine their own existence and find a role in the larger scheme of things." He adds that creation myths "are often integrated into religious thinking at the deepest levels." In one sense, however, Christian seems to contradict that thinking, for he explicitly avoids and discourages the view that humankind was the goal of creation and evolution. He suggests that, "Instead, . . . we are one of the more exotic creations of a universe in the most youthful, exuberant, and productive phase of a very long life. Though we no longer see ourselves as the center of the universe or the ultimate reason for its existence, this may still be grandeur enough for many of us."

One reviewer comments, "For some this may perhaps suffice; for most, I think not." Still, Christian declares that by sharing in, and being an outcome of, the forces working on all scales of time and space, humanity is "remarkable, unusual, and profoundly important."

One's own answer may depend on whether one accepts the nonanthropocentric version of the creation story. Eastern religion believes in a universe in which humans are not the center, in which they lead only an ephemeral existence but in which they can rejoice. The best emblem of the author's view may be the book's epigraph from the Diamond Sutra (c. fourth century C.E.):

> Thus shall ye think of all this fleeting world:,
> A star at dawn, a bubble in a stream,
> A flash of lightning in a summer cloud,
> A flickering lamp, a phantom, and a dream.

*Thomas Rankin*

## Review Sources

*American Scientist* 92, no. 4 (July/August, 2004): 379.
*History: Review of New Books* 32, no. 4 (Summer, 2004): 131.
*Library Journal* 129, no 1 (January 15, 2004): 150.
*New Scientist* 181, no. 2430 (January 17, 2004): 46.
*Science News* 165, no. 11 (March 13, 2004): 175.

# MARTIN LUTHER

*Author:* Martin Marty (1928-     )
*Publisher:* Viking/Penguin Group (New York). 199 pp.
    $20.00
*Type of work:* Biography
*Time:* 1483-1546
*Locale:* Germany

*This biography of Luther, the most prominent leader of the Protestant Reformation in the early sixteenth century, describes his personal theological struggles as well as the social environment of his time*

Principal characters:
> MARTIN LUTHER, founder of the Protestant
>     movement that eventually broke with the
>     Catholic Church
> JOHANN VON STAUPITZ, Luther's superior and mentor at the monastery
>     in Erfurt, Germany
> JOHANNES TETZEL, a Dominican priest who sold indulgences
> LEO X, the pope, elected in 1513, who completed the building of
>     St. Peter's basilica in Rome and excommunicated Luther in 1521
> ALBRECHT, ARCHBISHOP OF MAINZ, the highest Catholic authority in
>     central Germany
> FREDERICK THE WISE, the ruling prince in Wittenberg who provided pro-
>     tection for Luther from Catholic persecution
> CHARLES V, elected Holy Roman Emperor in 1519, a powerful antago-
>     nist of Luther
> PHILIP MELANCHTHON, fellow professor at Wittenberg, a friend and
>     supporter of Luther
> KATHERINE VON BORA, a former nun, Luther's wife and mother of their
>     six children

This relatively brief biography of Martin Luther is intended for the general reader. The challenge of such an undertaking is to make Luther's verbal clashes with his Catholic opponents, as well as with his evangelical colleagues, comprehensible for the modern reader. The author, Professor Martin Marty, focuses on critical events in Luther's journey of faith. He provides informative background about Luther's antagonists and supporters. He also gives a historical context showing how Luther eventually came to characterize the pope as the Antichrist and to make a complete break with the Catholic Church.

Luther was born in 1483 in the town of Eisleben, Germany, about one hundred miles southeast of Berlin. He attended schools in Magdeburg and in Eisenach (which became famous later as the birthplace of composer Johann Sebastian Bach). Luther enrolled as a university student at Erfurt, where he graduated in 1505 at the age of twenty-two. His father wanted him to continue his education in law school. However, Luther shocked his parents and friends by announcing that he had decided to become a monk. This sudden decision was provoked by a stroke of lightning that hit very near him while he was out on a walk, frightening him into thinking that he might soon die and have to face the judgment of a wrathful God.

In the summer of 1505, Luther applied to join the Augustinian order of monks, founded by Saint Augustine in the fifth century. Luther was accepted into the monastery at Erfurt, where he lived in an unheated chamber and had to follow strict rules regarding prayer, fasting, and confession. He was obsessed with feelings of sinfulness and struggled to find his personal faith. It is hard for the modem mind to understand the extreme depth of his anxiety, which led him to make confessions to his superior that sometimes lasted for several hours. In 1507 he was ordained as a priest, which authorized him to perform the holy sacrament of Communion. His father attended his first Mass, a very special celebration. Unfortunately, the father chose this occasion to confront Luther regarding his disobedience to the Fourth Commandment (to honor father and mother) when he had decided to become a monk instead of study law. A strained relationship between father and son persisted for many years.

*Martin Marty is professor emeritus at the University of Chicago, where he taught for thirty-five years and published numerous articles and books on religious history. Bill Moyer, the television interviewer, described him as "the most influential interpreter of American religion." Marty was awarded the prestigious National Humanities Medal in 1997.*

In 1508, Luther was appointed by his Augustinian superior, Johann von Staupitz, to fill in temporarily as a professor at Wittenberg, where a new university was struggling to become established. This position provided Luther with his first experience in lecturing to students and participating in public discussions of theological issues. In late 1510 or 1511, Staupitz assigned Luther to make a journey to Rome, where he spent about four weeks. He was shocked by the filth of the city and the lack of piety among priests. One of his memorable experiences was climbing the Scala Santa, or sacred steps, brought to Rome from Jerusalem, which Jesus was believed to have climbed at the court of Pontius Pilate. Luther made the climb on his knees and said a prayer on each step, hoping thereby to shorten the time that his parents would have to spend in purgatory, according to the teachings of the Church. When he reached the top step, however, Luther later recalled that doubt entered his mind: "Who knows whether this is really true?" It was at that moment that he started to question the authenticity of Church doctrine.

In 1512, Luther was accepted as a regular faculty member at Wittenberg, where he remained for most of his life. He lectured on the letters of Saint Paul in the New Testament and continued to struggle with his personal faith. When doubts dominated Luther's thinking, Marty describes his mental state as being "in an abyss of despair." However, he later claimed a positive outcome from such experiences: "Such despair offered sinners opportunities to grow in faith. The assaults [of doubt] robbed them of all certainty, until they found no place to go except to the God of mercy and grace." Luther identified himself with the story of Jacob in the book of Genesis, who wrestled with God through the night until he finally obtained God's blessing.

In the early sixteenth century, many people, both inside and outside the Church, had become highly critical of the Church for using people's fear of purgatory as a ploy to raise money. At the cathedral in Wittenberg, Prince Frederick the Wise collected thousands of relics from biblical times, which supposedly included " . . . thorns from Jesus' crown, hay stalks from Christ's manger, some milk of the Virgin Mary, and body parts of . . . innocent infant victims massacred by King Herod's soldiers." People who paid to view such relics were assured that their time in purgatory would be reduced. Also in this region of Germany, a priest named Johannes Tetzel was notorious for selling indulgences, which were documents that promised purchasers a reduction of their time in purgatory.

Such scandalous, corrupt practices caused Luther in 1518 to write a long letter to the archbishop, which became the famous Ninety-five Theses that Luther purportedly nailed to the door of the Castle Church at Wittenberg. In the academic world, a thesis is not an established conclusion but an assertion intended by the writer to provoke discussion. Some of Luther's theses were quite radical: that popes and priests did not have the power to shorten one's time in purgatory, that selling indulgences was exploitation, and that penance was a churchly invention. Marty states that the Ninety-five Theses probably would have been merely a local squabble except that Wittenberg and other cities had acquired the recently invented printing press. They were able to publicize Luther's message which, much to his surprise, found a wide audience of interested and supportive readers.

Events moved rapidly from 1519 to 1521 and included a public debate on the authority of the pope; Luther's publication of three essays further attacking Church practices; his excommunication from the Catholic Church and his refusal to recant when given an opportunity to do so; Luther's faked kidnapping and confinement for his own safety; and the Edict of Worms, which banned Lutheran teachings in the Holy Roman Empire.

Luther was secluded at Wartburg for about ten months. During that time he undertook to translate the New Testament of the Bible from Greek and Latin sources into colloquial German. He wanted common people to have direct access to the Bible, as it was to become their infallible guide to salvation, replacing the pope. Marty writes that "'Scripture alone' became a banner of the whole movement."

In March of 1522, Luther secretly traveled from Erfurt to Wittenberg, where he was warmly welcomed. One Roman Catholic priest complained that 90 percent of the people in Saxony (central Germany) apparently had become supporters of Lutheranism, making it impossible to enforce the Edict of Worms. Luther gave eight sermons in as many days and had them published to reach congregations elsewhere. He encouraged priests and nuns to free themselves from their vows, which many did. Priests were not permitted to marry according to Catholic tradition, but some were openly living with mistresses and illegitimate children. In such cases, Luther said they should get married.

In 1522, Luther helped to free a group of nuns from their convent near Wittenberg. One of them, Katherine von Bora, became his wife in 1524, when Luther was forty-two years old. Over the next ten years they had six children, four of whom survived. Luther wrote that raising children was a vocation with a special calling like the priesthood, and that sexual expression was a valued part of married love. The family lived in the cloister at Erfurt, which had been converted from the monastery where Luther earlier had become a priest. Some glimpses of family life are preserved in a book of notes kept by visitors to the Luther household, titled *Table Talk*.

Luther's boldness in breaking free from the authoritarian teachings of Roman Catholicism had great popular appeal. However, the release from traditional patterns of church life generated strong disagreements within the Protestant movement. One particularly troublesome group were the Anabaptists, who promoted the idea of adult baptism. They argued that infant baptism, as done by the Catholic Church, was not valid. They rebaptized adult believers who were mature enough to make a faithful commitment. Luther strongly opposed this practice, arguing that baptism was a pure gift initiated by God. In 1528, the Holy Roman Empire banned adult baptism and declared its practitioners subject to the death penalty. Eventually, even Luther came to view Anabaptists as guilty of blasphemy, which justified death or exile. It is difficult to understand how this policy could be harmonized with Luther's view that faith should not be obtained by coercion.

Luther was a prolific writer. He translated both the Old and the New Testament into colloquial German. He wrote commentaries on most of the books of the Bible. He composed a Small Catechism for instructing young people and a Large Catechism addressed primarily to pastors. Many of his sermons, such as *The Eight Wittenberg Sermons*, were published. He wrote numerous pamphlets and tracts, defining his theology, defending himself from criticism, and attacking his opponents. He wrote many hymns, his most famous one being "A Mighty Fortress Is Our God." He wrote letters, which often were preserved by the recipients because Luther was a celebrity during his lifetime. Marty refers to the writings of Luther collected into no less than fifty-five volumes.

In summing up Luther's contributions to theology, Marty makes a list of some apparent contradictions. He freed his contemporaries to make choices based on conscience but stressed obedience to authority. He was a hero to common people but sided with the ruling princes to put down even a legitimate revolt. He personally gave free-spirited interpretations of the Bible, but his advocacy of "Scripture alone" led others to a rigid literalism. He commended Jews for their devotion to biblical study but supported their persecution when they refused to convert to Christianity.

The picture of Luther that emerges from this biography is a person with a mixture of self-doubt and self-confidence in his lifelong mission to bring the church back to a genuine faith in God.

*Hans G. Graetzer*

## Review Sources

*America* 191, no. 6 (September 13, 2004): 27.
*Booklist* 100, no. 11 (February 1, 2004): 936.
*Christianity Today* 48, no. 5 (May, 2004): 68.
*Commonweal* 131, no. 6 (March 26, 2004): 22.
*Kirkus Reviews* 71, no. 23 (December 1, 2003): 1394.
*Library Journal* 129, no. 2 (February 1, 2004): 100.
*Publishers Weekly* 251, no. 3 (January 19, 2004): 73.

# THE MASTER

*Author:* Colm Tóibín (1955-    )
*Publisher:* Charles Scribner's Sons (New York). 338 pp.
 $25.00
*Type of work:* Novel
*Time:* 1895-1899
*Locale:* Venice, Florence, London, and Rye, England

*Feeling creatively exhausted, Henry James sought a new career in 1895 as a playwright, and after his play* Guy Domville *failed, he turned inward and embarked on the most fecund period of his writing career*

*Principal characters:*
> HENRY JAMES, American novelist now relocated in England
> CONSTANCE FENIMORE WOOLSON, novelist, grandniece of James Fenimore Cooper, and close friend of James's who committed suicide in 1894
> MINNY TEMPLE, James's cousin and inspiration for a number of his heroines
> ALICE JAMES, Henry's younger sister and the sibling with whom he felt the greatest kinship
> WILLIAM JAMES, Henry's older brother with whom he had a competitive and uneasy relationship

*The Master* begins with perhaps the greatest professional disappointment of Henry James's illustrious career, the opening performance of *Guy Domville* in London in January, 1895. James's novels were no longer selling, and he felt blocked as a writer; drama, he believed, would bring a steadier income and reach a wider audience. James left the theater during the performance, and when he returned for a curtain call, he was hustled onto the stage and forced to endure the catcalls and insults of a disappointed audience.

Retreating to his London apartment, James began burying himself in the production of a series of new and increasingly more experimental, daring novels. Colm Tóibín burrows into James's consciousness as he licks his wounds and reviews his life. Thus the novel shuttles back and forth between the late 1890's and events throughout the writer's life, continually examining his friendships and his reticent involvement in others' lives and affections. Tóibín's James is a consummate observer, carefully watching the lives of others and his own, as if they were objects worthy of clinical examination.

Given Tóibín's consideration of the novelist in his study of gay life, *Love in a Dark Time: Gay Lives from Wilde to Almodovar* (2002), it should not be surprising that one of the novel's central concerns is James's ambiguous sexuality. Various biographies and memoirs have attempted to account for his sexual identity, with Leon Edel, the most comprehensive of James's biographers, regarding the novelist as essentially a

*Colm Tóibín was born in Ireland. His works* The Blackwater Lightship *(2001) and* The Master *were short-listed for the prestigious Booker Prize, and his first novel,* The South *(1990), won an* Irish Times *Literature Award. His nonfiction includes* Walking Along the Border *(1987),* The Sign of the Cross: Travel in Catholic Europe *(1994), and* Lady Gregory's Toothbrush *(2002). He lives in Dublin and Spain.*

celibate who may have had homosexual inclinations. Tóibín sides with those who see James as unquestionably gay but a man so profoundly repressed he could not admit his desires to others, much less himself. The chapter in which playwright Oscar Wilde is destroyed during a court trial because of his homosexuality is magnificent for revealing James's curious fascination with Wilde, whom he regarded as a moral degenerate, yet about whom he was thrilled and terrified to hear the latest gossip of the playwright's degradation.

Tóibín considers four episodes that reveal the novelist's tortured sexual attraction to other men. The first occurs in James's youth when he shares a bed with college friend Oliver Wendell Holmes during a vacation and cannot sleep because of agonizing longing. A second comes as a result of an attraction to Paul Jarowsky, an artist in Paris, who did not reciprocate James's feelings. A young James spends a night planted on a rainy street, staring mournfully at the artist's window, a perfect symbol illustrating Tóibín's image of a man living at a distance from life.

A third encounter, one of Tóibín's creation, occurs during a vacation in Dublin with an army corporal named Hammond who is assigned as James's manservant. Althought the two barely speak, James increasingly yearns for the man's ministrations. The final relationship is with Hendrik Andersen, a Norwegian American sculptor James met in Rome and later invited to stay with him at his new house in Rye, England. Although in letters to Andersen James's attraction seems palpable, the relationship in *The Master* is one of indirection and understatement. The young sculptor teases the older man with attention yet tries to manipulate him, to no avail, to advance his dubious career. The sexual tension in James's novels, which is extraordinarily elliptical, finds its analogue in the writer's life; indeed, Tóibín suggests, James wrote as he lived.

In his friendships and relationships with family members, James fares no better. He is the boon companion of his sister, Alice, during their youth, yet as they mature, he grows more distant. He disapproved of her close relationship with Katherine Loring, Alice's nursemaid and companion. Tóibín hints that relationship may have been more intimate than simple friendship. James fails to invite his sister to Europe late in her short life and then after her death worries that he may have injured her. Similarly his relationship with his cousin Minny Temple is another exercise in attraction and rejection, and once again a woman sends James letters hinting at a visit that is never forthcoming.

The most disturbing of these friendships is that with Constance Fenimore Woolson, a novelist with whom James shared an animated correspondence. After she commits suicide by throwing herself from a balcony in Venice, James relives their relationship, searching for the reasons for her despair. He exonerates himself from guilt, and Tóibín is careful not to contradict the writer's self-justification but shows the likelihood that James's inattention may have contributed to his friend's ultimate despair. James refuses to attend Woolson's funeral. He visits her apartment later and puts himself in charge of her papers, another self-serving action which allows him to destroy much of their correspondence. When asked to dispose of her clothes, he is at a loss, and decides to ferry them out into the Venetian lagoon she loved to visit and dump them overboard.

> Before he reached for the first dress, Tito [the gondolier] blessed himself and then he laid the garment flat on the water as though the water were a bed, as though the dress's owner were preparing for an outing and would shortly come into the room. Both men watched as the color of the material darkened and then the dress began to sink. Tito placed a second and then a third, each time tenderly on the water, and then continued, working with a slow set of peaceful gestures shaking his head as they floated away each time, and moving his lips at intervals in prayer. Henry watched but did not move.

The gondolier responds with genuine emotion, while James, ever detached, remains immobile and simply observes. No sooner do Woolson and her effects seem finally gone than the garments return. "Some of the dresses had floated to the surface again like black balloons, evidence of the strange sea burial they had just enacted, their arms and bellies bloated with water." As Tito struggles to submerge the unsubmergible, James continues merely to watch, mentally recording the spectacle.

The scene is yet another of Tóibín's tantalizing symbols of James's curious relationships with friends and the world. He continually stands apart, largely taciturn, and forever observing, watching life as if it were a spectacle, something alluring but separate. The novel continually suggests that James was incapable of conflict; he would prefer to avoid, or simply drown, the disagreeable, and retreat to the kingdom of his thoughts. However, just as with Woolson's dresses, the world, friendships, and his troubled sexuality float back up and demand attention and action.

For James the action, of course, was vicarious. He solipsized his friends, his guilts, and his desires in his fictions. Tóibín does a masterful job of charting the many ways in which James transformed the raw material of life into the art of his life. After Temple's death, the narrator clarified that she did not haunt the writer so much as "he haunted her. . . . He could control her destiny now that she was dead, offer her the experiences she would have wanted, and provide drama for a life which had been so cruelly shortened."

The American Civil War forced James further into his solipsism, thus he may have feigned a back injury to avoid military service, which led him to live the war in his imagination and in his early fiction. As he writes, rather prophetically, in one of those stories, "My own taste has always been for unwritten history and my present business is with the reverse of the picture."

The fourth significant relationship is with James's older brother William, the famous, public man, a figure much more comfortable with other people and one who appeared to enjoy life as a popular professor and lecturer. However, William was a continual source of doubt and difficulty in Henry's life, and one reason for the author's long sojourn in Europe was simple physical removal from the irritant that was his brother. In 1899 William visited during a lecture tour of England, and for once the seemingly urbane, invincible older brother revealed himself to be physically frail and emotionally vulnerable. For Henry the visit, though difficult, is also liberating.

Tóibín's triumph is his ability to invade James's consciousness in a way no biographer could hope to achieve. He manages to weave various remarks from letters, journals, and public pronouncements into a portrait of an extraordinary man who lived an almost thoroughly unspectacular life. One of the novel's tantalizing treats, especially for avid readers of James, is the parade of allusions to various novels and stories and the curious origins of many of these works. One of Tóibín's central concerns is the revelation that such a private man put so much of his personal life into his public art, though most readers, like brother William, have felt that James wrote of little more than the brittle and hypocritical manners of Europe and America's privileged class.

While Tóibín does not fall into the trap of imitating James's baroque style, he does create a verbal texture that is reminiscent of James. Almost all the important scenes in the novel can be read in multiple ways, and ambiguity prevails. However, what remains unambiguous is James's lifelong embrace of solitude. When visiting injured soldiers at a field hospital during the Civil War, James has a long interview with one man and concludes, "He realized that his own separateness was complete, inviolate, just as the soldier could never know the comfort and privilege which came from being the son of Henry James Senior, who had been kept away from the war."

Ultimately, despite all his social graces and acquaintances, James valued "being left alone . . . the governing comfort of his life." In his essay "The Art of Fiction," James issued the famous dictum that a writer should "be one of the people on whom nothing is lost," and that lesson is hardly lost on Tóibín. *The Master*, an ironic title to describe such a detached figure, is an apt description of the Irish writer who has made compelling fiction of a less than compelling life.

*David W. Madden*

## Review Sources

*Booklist* 100, no. 15 (April 1, 2004): 1350.
*Kirkus Reviews* 72, no. 7 (April 1, 2004): 297.
*Lambda Book Report* 13, nos. 1/2 (August/September, 2004): 31.
*Library Journal* 129, no. 8 (May 1, 2004): 142.
*Los Angeles Times*, June 6, 2004, p. R6.
*New Statesman* 133 (March 8, 2004): 54.
*The New York Times*, May 31, 2004, p. E10.
*The New York Times Book Review* 153 (June 20, 2004): 10.
*Publishers Weekly* 251, no. 16 (April 19, 2004): 39.
*The Spectator* 294, no. 9162 (March 13, 2004): 39.

# THE MAZE

*Author:* Panos Karnezis (1967-    )
*Publisher:* Farrar, Straus and Giroux (New York). 364 pp. $24.00
*Type of work:* Novel
*Time:* 1922
*Locale:* Western Turkey

*A Greek brigade retreats from a disastrous military campaign in Turkey in 1922; loss of faith in their purpose among the officers, as well as decadence in a Greek-dominated village that the brigade briefly occupies, shows that an era in Western civilization has ended*

*Principal characters:*
BRIGADIER NESTOR, commander of a retreating Greek brigade
MAJOR PORFIRIO, brigade chief of staff and a secret communist
FATHER SIMEON, Eastern Orthodox priest, brigade chaplain
MEDIC, the brigade's only medical officer
MAYOR, chief administrator of a Greek town in western Anatolia
MR. OTHON, the town schoolmaster
MADAME VIOLETTA, French owner of the town brothel
ANNINA, Violetta's maid
YUSEF, an Arab gardener

Panos Karnezis' lovely novel *The Maze* is a story of despair, loss of faith, madness, addiction, and treachery that conveys the absurd heroism of a military disaster. The disaster comes three years after a Greek military force has attacked and occupied western Anatolia (Turkey) to protect the ethnic Greek population there, which first colonized the area in classical times. Nationalist Turkish forces mustered from the collapsed Ottoman Empire eventually stop and crush the attack. The focus of the novel is on a retreating Greek brigade of a thousand soldiers and later an unnamed, Greek-dominated town near the Aegean Sea coast. Despite hardship, crumbling discipline, and a haunting war memory, the brigade, accompanied by the Greek townsfolk, reach the sea and safety; by the time they do so, it is clear that the last vestige of Greek's colonial empire and ancient civilization is leaving with them. An epoch is ended. Karnezis does not leave things at that, however. He uses the love story of two naïfs and an idealistic medic to hint at what kinds of bonds will replace traditional Western culture.

Just as the original Greek colonization of Turkey occurred in the age of myth, so does Karnezis try to give his plot a mythlike aura. Aside from allusions to specific ancient myths, the techniques he uses are, for the most part, stylistic. He has a vividly imagistic style, and he focuses on objects and scenery that recall the distant Hellenic past, such as an ancient temple destroyed by the brigade to make a defensive fortification, or that underscore the long Greek presence in Turkey, such as architectural style and clothing. Karnezis' prose is also sonorous and slow-paced, which help sustain the grave, deliberative tone of the book.

*~*

*Born in Greece, Panos Karnezis moved to England in 1992, where he studied engineering and then earned a master's degree in creative writing from the University of East Anglia. His collection of short stories,* Little Infamies*, was published in 2003 to critical acclaim.*

*~*

The chief technique, however, comes in his handling of the characters. They never are given complete names. Either the name is formal and suitable to the person's station in life—such as Brigadier Nestor and Mr. Othon, for the professional class and simply first names for servants—or no name is given at all, only an occupation—mayor, medic, cook, war correspondent. This restrained particularity has two effects. Its sets the major characters in sharp contrast with the minor characters, a quality of heroic literature, and it makes the major characters sound as if they are equivalent to the legendary figures in ancient histories, such as those by Herodotus or Xenophon.

The impression is reinforced by Karnezis' fondness for leaving the reader guessing at the beginning of a chapter or section of a chapter about the character being discussed: He uses pronouns alone until the subject finally becomes obvious (or the reader is on the point of complete confusion). The suspension of naming injects the characterizations with a tantalizing bit of mystery. Moreover, only a few soldiers and civilians appear in the story, and the focus on them highlights character development rather than narrative action.

With all this emphasis upon characterization, the reader infers that the characters represent types, or ideas, rather than simply individuals, and that is the case. The principal character is Brigadier Nestor, commander of the retreating Greek column. Like his namesake in Homer's *Iliad* (c. 725 B.C.E.), he is an old man who represents tradition. He is among the leaders in the expeditionary force, which is intended to save Greek towns from mistreatment by Turkish nationalists. He is also something of an amateur scholar, and his passion is ancient myth. An able tactician, he has foreseen the futility of the campaign, and after the collapse of the Greek front, he leads his troops through the desert toward the sea and evacuation, seemingly against all hope.

Nestor is also a deeply flawed character, and each flaw hints at something troubling about the civilization he loves. He has lost his wife and is in despair because of it. This despair, coupled with the infirmities of age, drives him to use morphine to remain calm and sane; he is an addict, although he refuses to admit it. His fierce adherence to the past—the myths of Greek culture and his personal history—gives his heroic struggles an air of decay and obsolescence. During the course of the novel, a further cause of torment is revealed: The brigadier ordered a massacre of the people in the town that helped the enemy adjust artillery fire against his troops, a barbarity that belies Greek humanistic values.

Moreover, Nestor is tormented by two internal challenges to his authority. The graver of them is a series of clandestine broadsheets spread throughout his brigade that criticizes the war and espouses communist ideology. This is the challenge of the new and treasonous. A more traditional challenge comes from thefts. The thefts are minor, involving such luxury items as cigars and wine, but they strip the brigadier of accustomed pleasures and vex him. He spends much time fruitlessly seeking the culprits. Slowly and inevitably, he is worn down and retreats into deepening addiction.

The internal challenges come from the two officers whom Nestor least suspects, both of whom are defenders of a faith. Father Simeon is the brigade chaplain, an Eastern Orthodox priest. He is dogmatic, ineffectual, and ridden with guilt for not having tried to prevent the massacre; he embodies a Christian formalism that seems feckless in the desert. His faith weakens as he blames God for visiting undeserved hardships upon him, even while stealing from other officers, the brigadier included, to replace his dwindling supplies for church services, such as wine for Eucharist. Major Porfirio is the ideal military officer, brave, meticulous, austere, and dutiful; however, he is a secret communist, and with fanatical determination he prints and distributes antigovernment pamphlets with the help of his single convert, a cavalry corporal whom the major has cruelly manipulated.

After increasingly hopeless wandering through the maze of the Anatolian desert, the brigade comes upon a town. The relationships among townsfolk mirror that of the brigade officers. Just as the brigadier, major, and chaplain form a triangle of competing faiths, so do the corrupt mayor; pedantic schoolmaster, Mr. Othon; and brothel owner Madame Violetta form a decadent love triangle. By the time the brigade reaches the town, Violetta has spurned the schoolmaster for the mayor, who promises her a more lucrative future, but she quickly tires of him. She herself is a fugitive, having murdered a government minister in her native Paris. The rival suitors, once close friends, become enemies.

Both sets of character conflicts reach a climax after the brigade occupies the town. Major Porfirio's treason is exposed, and although the brigadier has long regarded him virtually as a son, he has the major executed. In a hapless attempt to save the major, the priest confesses his theft to the brigadier. In his case the brigadier is forgiving, but the leniency drives the priest into an insane, expiatory fantasy: He decides to remain in the town and become a missionary to the poor Muslims there. The execution and a bizarre, destructive storm soon afterward convince the brigade to leave, and the Greek residents of the town, fearing the Turkish nationalists that will soon take power, leave with the soldiers. Madame Violetta is among them, and she breaks her engagement to the mayor, who then resumes his friendship with Mr. Othon. The love affairs appear directionless and barren.

Father Simeon remains behind with his dreams of a heroic mission, but his would-be converts loot the town and leave a day after the Greeks. The column reaches the sea at last, where boats wait to carry the soldiers and townspeople to the homeland. It seems like a great success after great struggle—and the war correspondent accompanying the column promises to make the story famous as just that—but, in fact, the evacuation marks a departure of Greek (and Western) civilization. After his first glimpse of the Aegean, the brigadier collapses, defeated, in a morphine stupor, and none of the characters appears to have much of a future.

There are two exceptions, and in them Karnezis points to a cultural transformation after the damage done to traditional societal and intellectual structures by World War I, the fall of the Ottoman Empire, and the failed Greek expedition in Turkey. First is the brigade medical officer, the closest thing to a saint in the novel. His compassion in treating soldiers (Greek and Turkish) and his dedication to the scientific method contrast perfectly with the vindictive faiths of Father Simeon and Major Porfirio. The medic's own faith in the beneficial influence of science suffers a setback, but he yet represents a positive force for the future—the humane pursuit of knowledge.

The second exception is the love between Annina, Madame Violetta's maid, and Yusef, a gardener in the town. Both are castoffs from their societies: Annina was a homeless waif in Paris when Violetta found her, and Yusef became a wanderer from his native Egypt after disease left him a hunchback. During the evacuation, they decide to marry and travel back east, instead of west, to find a life for themselves. They represent a romantic mingling of culture. The medic and lovers shift the novel from a story of futile, anachronistic Western adventurism to a story of tentative, modest hope.

The maze of the title is psychological. Characters struggle to escape from a maze of their own guilt, obsessions, venality, and economic plight. That Karnezis succeeds in making the characters represent ideas, as well as personalities, makes the maze cultural, too. It is a brilliant conception, and Karnezis delivers it movingly, even though the novel can wear upon the reader's indulgence. The techniques used to create a tension between individuality and idea in the main characters sometimes falter, and then characters may seem like actors in a morality play, or museum statues.

Also, one may wonder whether Karnezis overplays the significance of the failed Greek military adventure altogether: Has traditional Western culture really contracted so dramatically? For readers who doubt it, Karnezis uses a clever ploy throughout the book. Every time there is an allusion to ancient Greek myth, he explains it in a footnote at the bottom of the page. At first readers might wonder why and be annoyed that he explains tales well known to the educated. That is just the point. Readers trained at universities in the liberal arts may well understand the allusions on their own, but such readers are a minority—an increasing minority. These footnotes are a tricky device, but Karnezis is right that in the retreat of classical education, the old legends and myths have become footnotes to modern life, not guides.

*The Maze* is Karnezis' first novel. Considering its stylistic dexterity and the intellectual depth of its story, he promises to be an author of unusual insight and cultural breadth.

*Roger Smith*

### Review Sources

*Booklist* 100, nos. 9/10 (January 1-15, 2004): 824.
*The Economist* 370 (February 14, 2004): 80.
*Kirkus Reviews* 71, no. 24 (December 15, 2003): 1416.
*The New York Times Book Review* 153 (March 21, 2004): 16.
*Newsweek* 143, no. 13 (March 29, 2004): 60.
*Publishers Weekly* 251, no. 2 (January 12, 2004): 35.
*The Times Literary Supplement*, January 30, 2004, p. 21.

# MOANIN' AT MIDNIGHT
## The Life and Times of Howlin' Wolf

*Authors:* James Segrest (1961-    ) and Mark Hoffman
(1952-    )
*Publisher:* Crown Pantheon Books (New York). 398 pp.
$27.00
*Type of work:* Biography
*Time:* 1910-1976
*Locale:* The United States

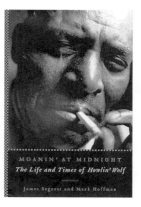

*A fascinating compilation of recollections about a leg-
endary musician whose experiences personified the blues*

*Principal personages:*
HOWLIN' WOLF (CHESTER A. BURNETT),
   charismatic blues musician
LILLIE BURNETT, his wife
LEONARD CHESS, his record producer
HUBERT SUMLIN, his longtime guitarist
MUDDY WATERS, his Chicago blues rival
EDDIE SHAW, his bandleader

*Moanin' at Midnight* includes these thoughts by singer and musician Bonnie Raitt:

> If I had to pick one person who does everything I loved about the blues, it would be Howlin' Wolf. It would be the size of his voice, or just the size of him. When you're a lit-tle pre-teenage girl and you imagine what a naked man in full arousal is like, it's Howlin' Wolf. When I was a kid, I saw a horse in a field with an erection, and I went, "Holy shit!" That's how I feel when I hear Howlin' Wolf—and when I met him it was the same thing. He was the scariest, most deliciously frightening bit of male testosterone I've ever experi-enced in my life.

Howlin' Wolf was indeed a unique force of nature, performing gutbucket blues as if possessed by supernatural powers. He left behind myriad memories, a legion of fans, and a treasure trove of classic recordings that blended the down-home Delta sound he honed as a youth with the electrified style that was a Chicago blues trademark.

    Embarking on a labor of love, blues aficionados James Segrest and Mark Hoffman faced two daunting tasks in writing this biography: how to assess the accuracy of sto-ries distorted or embellished over time, and how to capture in words the emotional power of Wolf's recordings and the riveting magnetism of his live performances. To judge from favorable reviews by blues historians, the authors fared well on both counts. Among *Moanin' at Midnight*'s many virtues are its descriptions of the Missis-sippi Delta of Wolf's youth, the Memphis and Chicago music scenes at mid-twentieth century, and Wolf's influence on 1960's groups in Great Britain and the United States.

*James Segrest, a teacher in
Notasulga, Alabama, wrote liner
notes for the Grammy-nominated
album* A Tribute to Howlin' Wolf
*(1998) and has written for* Blues
Access. *A resident of Bainbridge
Island near Seattle, Mark Hoffman
has written for numerous blues
publications, including* Living
Blues, Blues Access, *and* Blue
Suede News.

Born in 1910 and named for America's twenty-first president, Chester Arthur Burnett had a miserable youth. He claimed he got his lupine nickname from a grandfather who scared him with stories about wolves in the woods. Abandoned by his mentally unstable teenage mother, he moved in with a great-uncle who treated him like a beast of burden. Fleeing a bullwhip beating at age thirteen, he reunited with his father, a sharecropper. He sang ditties behind a plow pulled by mules and paid fifteen cents for his first harmonica.

In 1927 Chester's father brought in a good crop and bought his son a guitar. As was also the case with Delta legend Robert Johnson, bluesman Charlie Patton was Wolf's most important influence. Wolf claimed he would sit outside a juke joint on Dockery's Plantation and try to imitate his mentor until one day Patton invited him to join him. Compared to farming, the life of a traveling entertainer was exciting but dangerous. Patton once had his throat cut from ear to ear during a barrelhouse brawl. A chain smoker with a weak heart, he died in 1934 at age forty-two. In a recording studio some thirty-five years later, Wolf recalled Patton being "a hard-luck boy like me." Recalling his childhood in "Hard Luck," Wolf sang:

> Well, rocks is my pillow. Cold ground is my bed.
> Highway is my home and I'd just rather be dead.
> I'm walkin'. And Lord, I don't have nowhere to go.
> The road I'm travelin' on, the road is mud and cold.

In 1930 Funny Papa Smith released "Howling Wolf Blues." Around then Wolf set out on his own, performing in juke joints in Arkansas and Mississippi, sometimes for as little as a fish sandwich plus tips for requests. He also played on street corners for coins. Sonny Boy Williamson II (Alex "Rice" Miller) taught him to play harp, and the two sometimes appeared together. Wolf had such striking blue-gray eyes, feral magnetism, and ribald mannerisms that many thought he had sold his soul to the devil (including his mother, who rebuffed several efforts to establish contact). In addition to Wolf's trademark howl, he gyrated suggestively, crawled like a snake, played the guitar behind his head, and got down on all fours simulating fornication while singing, "Let Me Hump You, Baby."

Wolf enjoyed the pleasures of many women. Israel "Wink" Clark claims Wolf "had a wife near about everywhere he went." Frenzied females would jump on his back and ride him across the floor. One girlfriend plunged a butcher knife in his leg for flirting with a rival; Wolf allegedly kept on singing right out the door before rushing to a hospital. Once he made a hasty retreat ahead of his sexual partner's husband, jumped out a second-story window, and ran into barbed wire. In the darkness, he first believed he had been stabbed. Another cuckold severely beat a woman Wolf was seeing. Enraged, Wolf hit the man with a cotton hoe, slicing off part of his head and killing him instantly.

In Pace, Mississippi, after a white woman asked Wolf to play on her porch, her husband had him arrested. Released from jail a week later, Wolf fled, leaving behind a son and common-law wife. Having been pressured to join the Army during World War II, he reacted poorly to the regimentation and languished several months in a hospital before receiving an honorable discharge.

Widespread adoption in the South of mechanical cotton harvesters meant less money for juke-joint performers. In 1948, Wolf moved to West Memphis, Tennessee, took up the electric guitar, formed a band called the House Rockers, purchased a DeSoto touring car, and got a fifteen-minute radio spot on KWEM, which proved useful for publicizing gigs. In 1950 Sam Phillips, the future Sun Records mogul, heard Wolf on KWEM, lured him into a studio, and sent cuts of "Moanin' at Midnight" and "How Many More Years" to Leonard Chess in Chicago, who turned them into a double-sided rhythm and blues hit record. Two years later, Chess convinced Wolf to move North.

At the time, Muddy Waters was the Chess label's star. The two men were rivals for the following twenty years, although as time went by the competition was increasingly friendly. Muddy's style was laid back compared to Wolf's over-the-top showmanship. As Waters acknowledged: "When he's finished, man, he's sweatin'! Feel my shirt, it's soaked, ain't it? When Wolf finishes, his jacket's like my shirt!"

Chess once said he preferred sales of thirty thousand on everything he released to so-called hits. This philosophy helped Wolf, whose recordings did moderately well in numerous regional markets. A surprise rhythm and blues seller, "No Place to Go," led to a triumphant return to Memphis, where Wolf played the Hippodrome, along with Muddy and Little Walter. A year later he appeared on an Apollo Theater bill in Harlem with Bill Doggett, Bo Diddley, the Harptones, the Flamingos, and seventeen-year-old Etta James. The week before in Cleveland, aspiring rockers Little Richard and James Brown joined him on stage.

Wolf had a violent, authoritarian streak, perhaps because of his abused childhood, as well as a gentle, sentimental side to his personality. He once whacked a tardy band member on the back of the head with his guitar, knocking the man out. He fined those who got sloppy drunk or who did not dress properly but cared enough to pay musicians' social security taxes so they could collect unemployment and other benefits. He was like a stern father to guitarist Hubert Sumlin, who first met Wolf when he got up on a pile of empty coke cases to peer into a juke joint window, lost his balance, and fell onto his head. The surprised performer allowed the youngster to stay and even drove him home.

Wolf mellowed somewhat after meeting thirty-two-year-old Lillie Handley, who became the love of his life. She helped him with business affairs, and he doted on her daughters. Unlike Waters, whose yearly Cadillac came from future royalties, Wolf controlled his own finances and avoided the fate of comrades who died penniless (the authors defend the Chess brothers against charges that they exploited their stable of artists). Unschooled as a youth, Wolf took courses in reading and math as well as guitar lessons but retained his earthy down-home sound and ribald stage persona and continued to play out-of-the-way southern venues where people showed up riding mules.

In 1960 Wolf recorded "Wang Dang Doodle," which was based on "Bull Daggers Ball," a tune popular with lesbians and attributed to Willie Dixon (who claimed credit for many old standards). In Memphis Wolf used a cooking spoon as a phallic symbol despite kids being in the audience, and the concert promoters closed the curtain on him. He reprised the routine at the august First International Jazz Festival in Washington, D.C. Thanks to blues fan David Hervey, he also played for Delta Kappa Epsilon fraternity at the University of Mississippi a year before African American James Meredith's appearance to register for classes there caused a riot.

In 1964 Wolf made the first of several trips to Europe. "Smokestack Lightnin'" became a hit in Great Britain, and he played the Cavern Club, the Beatles' old Liverpool haunt. Quite agile despite weighing nearly three hundred pounds, he reminded one critic of a pacing gorilla. Another believed his clownish mannerisms—eyes rolling, for instance, as he simulated masturbation—resembled an old-fashioned carnival act. Yet he could emit a baleful stare that signaled (in the words of Peter Wolf), "Look out! Proceed with caution."

British groups idolized him, and he was gracious to young unknown musicians who backed him overseas. Before the Rolling Stones went on the television show *Shindig*, they insisted that Wolf or Waters be booked. Describing Wolf's network appearance, Segrest and Hoffman write: "Wolf made the most of it—stabbing his massive finger at the camera, shaking his rear end like an elephant suffering a seizure, and blasting blues harp into prime-time TV land." The Rolling Stones sent a limo to escort the Burnetts to their Chicago gig. The next evening, Stones members Ron Wood and Bill Wyman showed up for a soul food dinner Lillie had prepared and spent the night drinking and merrymaking.

Future Electric Flag bandmates Michael Bloomfield and Barry Goldberg went to Silvio's, and the black patrons froze when they walked in. Wolf recognized Bloomfield, who had been frequenting blues clubs since the age of fourteen, and invited them up to play piano and rhythm guitar on "Killing Floor." Goldberg recalled: "It was like playing baseball in Yankee stadium with the Yankees." On the other hand, once somebody approached Wolf's guitarist Hubert Sumlin about sitting in, and Wolf knocked him off the stage.

Some eighteen thousand people at the 1966 Newport Folk Festival witnessed Wolf's entrance in bib overalls, work shirt, and straw hat, carrying a broom. He pretended to sweep the stage before launching into the sexual lyrics of "Dust My Broom." Among the groups who recorded his songs were the Rolling Stones, the Animals, the Yardbirds, and the Doors. Led Zeppelin used parts of "Killing Floor" in their hit "The Lemon Song" and later settled a lawsuit brought by Chess Records. Wolf's label pressured him into doing a "psychedelic" concept album; predictably, it tanked. Opening for Alice Cooper, he doggedly finished his set despite chants of "Alice, Alice." A 1971 recording session with Eric Clapton, Ringo Starr, Mick Jagger, Charlie Watts, Bill Wyman, and other notables yielded a critically acclaimed album that reached number nineteen on the "Billboard 200."

Slowed by health problems, Wolf was still performing his down-and-dirty routine shortly before he died. An admirer noticed him grab his chest as he snaked along on the floor, pause to take a pill, and then continue. On the evening of his burial, the authors note, "a full moon rose over Chicago. At the Brookfield Zoo, three miles from Wolf's grave, the captive wolves howled long into the night." A successful lawsuit against ARC Music and Chess Records allowed his family to live in comfort. Lillie devoted her life to securing Wolf's proper legacy.

In addition to a lively text, Segrest and Hoffman provide plentiful notes and photographs as well as a valuable discography and sessionography. Like Robert Gordon's *Can't Be Satisfied: The Life and Times of Muddy Waters* (2002), their work provides a compelling guide to the Chicago blues scene. Other records of Wolf's life and work include "The Chess Box," a three-CD compilation that includes the performer talking about his life and craft, and *The Howlin' Wolf Story: The Secret History of Rock and Roll*, a prizewinning 2003 documentary. In the end, however, Wolf remains enigmatic. A survivor against great odds, he poured his frustrations and unleashed fury into unforgettable compositions.

*James B. Lane*

## Review Sources

*Blues To Do* 22 (June, 2004): 3.
*Booklist* 100, no. 17 (May 1, 2004): 1536.
*Library Journal* 129, no. 9 (May 15, 2004): 90.
*The New York Times*, July 21, 2004, p. E1.
*The New York Times Book Review* 153 (June 13, 2004): 13.
*Publishers Weekly* 251, no. 15 (April 12, 2004): 50.
*USA Today*, June 22, 2004, Life, p. 6.

# THE MOLD IN DR. FLOREY'S COAT
## The Story of the Penicillin Miracle

*Author:* Eric Lax (1944-    )
*Publisher:* Henry Holt (New York). 308 pp. $25.00
*Type of work:* History of science and medicine
*Time:* 1881-2004
*Locale:* Great Britain and the United States

*Through the lives and contributions of four scientists—Alexander Fleming, Howard Florey, Ernst Chain, and Norman Heatley—Lax debunks several myths as he tells the complex story of how penicillin was discovered, developed, and made into the antibiotic that saved numerous lives*

> *Principal personages:*
> ALEXANDER FLEMING (1881-1955), Scottish bacteriologist who first discovered penicillin
> HOWARD FLOREY (1888-1968), Australian pathologist who developed penicillin into an antibiotic for human use
> ERNST CHAIN (1906-1979), German biochemist who studied the chemical nature of penicillin and transformed it into a valuable clinical drug
> NORMAN HEATLEY (1911-2004), English chemist who developed techniques for making penicillin on which American drug companies capitalized

Throughout the ages, war and disease have been great killers of human beings, and the story of penicillin cannot be understood without first considering these destroyers of life. Many historians of medicine have argued that the discovery and development of penicillin before and during World War II was the most important medical event of the twentieth century. The four people that Eric Lax situates at the heart of the penicillin story—Alexander Fleming, Howard Florey, Ernst Chain, and Norman Heatley— were profoundly affected by the more than ten million deaths in World War I, many of them as a consequence of bacterial infections. They were also acutely aware of the more than twenty million people who perished during the influenza epidemic of 1918. By the twentieth century these and other scientists had learned much about the nature of various diseases, but they knew very little about how to cure them. Despite the disagreements, jealousies, and hatreds among the scientists most responsible for developing penicillin as a drug, these individuals managed to create an antibiotic that saved many lives during World War II and many more in the postwar period.

Lax became interested in such events after reading an obituary in *The New York Times* in 1999 of the first person whose life was saved by penicillin. In 1942 this thirty-three-year-old woman was dying from blood poisoning in a New Haven, Connecticut, hospital when she was given penicillin. Her complete recovery was followed by more than fifty years of fulfilling life, and her death at ninety stimulated Lax to wonder why it took so long between Fleming's recognition of penicillin's antibacte-

rial power in the late 1920's and its use to save human lives in the 1940's. While having dinner with
his British publisher, Lax mentioned his puzzle-
ment, and the publisher told him that solving this
puzzle might make an interesting book.

For the following five years Lax did research
at many libraries and archives in England and the
United States. Although most of the scientists in
the penicillin story had died by the time Lax
started his project, several of them had written
their versions of the events. Lax studied these and

*Eric Lax, a freelance writer, has
published articles in such
magazines as* Life, Vanity Fair,
*and* Esquire. The New York Times
*chose his* Life and Death on 10
West *(1984) and* Woody Allen: A
Biography *(1991) as notable books
for their respective years.*

also was able to interview Heatley over the course of several months. Furthermore,
Lax was given access to Heatley's personal diaries, and this material enlivens his narrative, besides bringing belated recognition to one of the unsung heroes of the penicillin story.

Lax, who is best known for his two books on the filmmaker Woody Allen, might at
first seem an unlikely person to write about penicillin. However, he also wrote *Life
and Death on 10 West* (1984), an insider's portrayal of life in a California medical research clinic told through profiles of certain doctors and patients. The books on Allen
and on the bone marrow transplantation ward combined biography with critical analyses of relevant issues. Similarly, *The Mold in Dr. Florey's Coat* combines biographies of Fleming, Florey, Chain, and Heatley with a critical analysis of their contributions. Because Lax is neither a trained medical researcher nor a professional historian
of science, he emphasizes the human elements in his quadribiographical account. As
an adept storyteller, he communicates to the reader not only pertinent events in the
lives of these scientists but also important chemical and medical information in its social, political, and historical contexts.

Like several scholars before him, Lax is highly critical of the mythologization of
Fleming as the pivotal person in the discovery and development of penicillin. Instead,
his goal is to bring out the significance of the achievements of Florey, Chain, and es-
pecially Heatley, without whose work Fleming never would have won a Nobel Prize.
In 1945 Florey and Chain shared the Nobel Prize with Fleming, but, in Lax's view,
Heatley was unjustly neglected.

Lax acknowledges that, in 1928, Fleming, while working in St. Mary's Hospital
Medical School in London, discovered penicillin and recognized its ability to kill certain bacteria. After the horrors that Fleming had witnessed in World War I, he dedicated himself to discovering ways of conquering infectious bacteria. His first important discovery was lysozyme, an antibacterial agent that was useless against virulent
strains. His next, more important discovery occurred serendipitously. During the
summer of 1928 he left London for his annual vacation in Scotland. Upon his return
he, by chance, noticed in an uncovered Petri dish a green mold in a colony of staphy-
lococcal bacteria. Surprisingly, a clear space existed around the edges of the mold, indicating that some substance from the mold had killed the bacteria. Fleming later
stated that the spore of the mold came through an open window, but scholars have dis-

covered that the likeliest route was from a mycological laboratory on the floor below, up a stairwell and through the open door of Fleming's laboratory.

Eventually the mold was identified as a variant of *Penicillium notatum*, and so Fleming named the secreted substance "penicillin." He found that penicillin was effective in killing the bacteria that caused pneumonia, gonorrhea, and diphtheria. He also tested penicillin's toxicity and discovered that it was no more poisonous than broth. However, his penicillin was extremely unstable, and its effectiveness against bacteria was short-lived. Fleming published his results in 1929 in a paper that, despite its flaws and omissions, became a milestone in the history of modern medicine, not because of Fleming's subsequent work but because, several years later, his paper stimulated others to do much better work on penicillin.

Howard Florey, who had come to Oxford University from Australia as a Rhodes scholar in 1929, became interested in his medical specialty in an unusual way. He suffered from a rare disease, achlorhydria, in which a deficiency in hydrochloric acid secretions in the stomach causes digestive disorders. Florey, a trained pathologist, consequently became interested in bodily secretions and the pathology of the digestive system. After he became head of the William Dunn School of Pathology at Oxford, he hired Ernst Chain, a Jewish refugee biochemist from Germany, to study the chemistry of antibiotics, because Florey believed that bacteriological progress depended on biochemical progress. He also hired, as Chain's assistant, Norman Heatley, an expert in applying microchemical methods to biological problems.

In later years Florey and Chain told different stories of how the Oxford group began their work on penicillin. Florey claimed that he was the first to recognize penicillin as an important subject of research, as it had implications for the theory of antibiotics. Chain, on the other hand, claimed that, after reading Fleming's 1929 paper in 1938, he informed Florey about penicillin's power as an antibiotic—with the potential to save soldiers' lives in the war that was looming. Neglected in these retrospective accounts of Florey and Chain was the crucial contribution of Heatley. While Chain concentrated on purifying penicillin and determining its chemical nature, Heatley worked on faster and more efficient techniques for making large amounts of penicillin.

Because of clashes between Chain and Heatley, Florey hired Heatley as his assistant, while allowing him to continue to work under Chain. Despite such personal clashes, the Oxford group produced sufficient penicillin to begin tests on laboratory animals. In 1940 two groups of mice were infected with streptococcal bacteria, but one group was also injected with penicillin. Within hours, all the untreated mice died, whereas the mice treated with penicillin remained healthy. These experiments were done while Nazi bombs were falling on England. Heatley, who feared that a Nazi invasion was imminent, suggested that the members of their research team rub spores of *Penicillium notatum* into their laboratory coats, so that they could continue their research if they had to flee to another country. This action is what led Lax to call his book *The Mold in Dr. Florey's Coat*.

Seven members of Florey's group jointly published a paper on their penicillin research in the summer of 1940, but because of the London blitz the article generated little interest. Nevertheless, the Oxford group forged on, beginning tests on humans in 1941. They were able to bring about a dramatic reversal in a horrifying infection of a police constable's face, eyes, and scalp, but their lack of sufficient penicillin for continued treatments resulted in his relapse and eventual death. Clearly, much more penicillin was needed.

Because of the war, little financial help was available from British sources, and Florey and Heatley traveled to the United States to generate interest and support for penicillin production. They were able to convince Alfred Newton Richards, chairman of the Committee on Medical Research and Development, of penicillin's importance. Richards persuaded governmental agencies and such drug companies as Merck, Squibb, and Pfizer that penicillin was not only a lifesaver but also a moneymaker. After the Japanese attack on Pearl Harbor, the U.S. War Department made the production of penicillin its second-highest priority (the first was the secret atomic bomb project). The infusion of American money and labor resulted in success. American researchers found a new *Penicillium* mold and developed a new medium for its growth from corn syrup. In a relatively short time twenty-six drug companies were manufacturing massive amounts of penicillin. In the last two years of the war these billions of units of penicillin saved thousands of lives.

The wonders of penicillin quickly became public knowledge, and journalists on both sides of the Atlantic Ocean crowned Fleming as king of his medical marvel. With his blue eyes, handsome face, and modest demeanor, Fleming proved to be the hero that people needed and wanted. On the other hand, the antagonisms among members of the Oxford group led to less than ideal relations with the media. It took time before scholars were able to excise the legendary elements in the popular accounts of penicillin's discovery and development, but enough was known in the postwar period that the Nobel Prize rewarding work on penicillin went to Fleming, Florey, and Chain.

However, at the Nobel ceremonies Florey refused to speak to Fleming, and the prize failed to mend the broken relationship between Florey and Chain. After he received the Nobel Prize, Fleming saw his popularity continue to increase, and he received more than fifty honorary doctorates and other awards. A smaller number of honors came to Florey and Chain. Both were knighted, and Florey became president of the Royal Society. Toward the end of his life, Heatley was finally celebrated for his contributions when Oxford University conferred on him the first honorary doctor of medicine degree in its eight-hundred-year history.

Scholars have often noted the stark differences between scientists' accounts of discoveries in formal publications and the messy and complex reality of how flawed human beings actually make their discoveries. Lax's account is excellent in detailing the human aspects of the penicillin story, but it is weaker in its analysis of the biological, chemical, and medical details. For example, American scientific and technological expertise was very important in making penicillin inexpensive and widely available, yet Lax says very little about this work. Indeed, the British, who first discovered and developed penicillin, ended up having to pay royalties to American drug companies for using their patents.

The story of penicillin continued through the rest of the twentieth century, but with the growth of antibiotic resistance the picture would become less rosy than it was in the postwar years. Furthermore, to bring new drugs to market began to cost millions of dollars, whereas penicillin's early development had cost only thousands. Nevertheless, because bacterial diseases continue to kill many humans, the search for relevant antibiotics will continue to be important in the twenty-first century, as will the need for medical researchers like Fleming, Florey, Chain, and Heatley to conquer these new threats to human health.

*Robert J. Paradowski*


## Review Sources

*Booklist* 100, no. 14 (March 15, 2004): 1251.
*JAMA: Journal of the American Medical Association* 292, no. 13 (October 6, 2004): 1620.
*Kirkus Reviews* 72, no. 4 (February 15, 2004): 166.
*Library Journal* 129, no. 5 (March 15, 2004): 98.
*Nature* 428 (April 22, 2004): 801.
*The New England Journal of Medicine* 151, no. 16 (October 14, 2004): 1697.
*Publishers Weekly* 251, no. 6 (February 9, 2004): 67.
*The Times Literary Supplement*, April 30, 2004, p. 29.

# MONTE CASSINO
## The Hardest-Fought Battle of World War II

*Author:* Matthew Parker
*Publisher:* Doubleday (New York). Illustrated. 414 pp.
  $27.50
*Type of work:* History
*Time:* 1943-1945
*Locale:* Monte Cassino, Italy

*A historian's epic chronicle of a battle whose casualties numbered a quarter of a million soldiers; Monte Cassino could be called a prelude to the invasion of Normandy and yet also be seen as a battle that should never have been fought*

*Principal personages:*
FRANKLIN D. ROOSEVELT, the U.S. president
WINSTON CHURCHILL, the British prime minister who, at Casablanca in January, 1944, reached agreement with Roosevelt on guidelines for the invasion of Italy
SIR HAROLD ALEXANDER, the Allied commander at Monte Cassino
MARK CLARK, the commander of the U.S. Fifth Army
SIR BERNARD FREYBERG, a leader of New Zealand units in the field and his country's top strategist in the Mediterranean region
WLADYSLAW ANDERS, a general of the Polish Corps
ALPHONSE JUIN, a general of the French forces
ALBERT KESSELRING, the leader of German forces defending Monte Cassino; replaced by General Fridolin Von Senger
FRED L. WALKER, a major general in the U.S. 36th (Texas) Division
ERNIE PYLE, an American combat correspondent
DON GREGORIO DIAMARE, the abbot of a monastery destroyed in the battle

By the time American victories in the Pacific region and in North Africa had downsized the debacle at Pearl Harbor, World War II was moving into its fourth year. The Allies in both theaters had reason to be confident. Hitting Japanese bastions, though costly in casualties, caused their fall much more quickly than had been expected. With attrition working against Japan and U.S. production ballooning on the homefront, Japan would last only as long as the Philippines. In the European theater, the Allies were poised to conquer a Third Reich that was being softened up by Soviet resistance on the eastern front. By mid-January, 1943, the noose had tightened around Stalingrad.

On January 14, 1943, U.S. president Franklin Roosevelt and British prime minister Winston Churchill met in the newly liberated city of Casablanca, Morocco, to plan the invasion of Italy. From this point, Matthew Parker launches *Monte Cassino*, his

∾

*Matthew Parker is the author of* The
Battle of Britain *(2000). Based in
London, he is a writer and editor
specializing in modern history.*

∾

study of what, justifiably, he calls in the book's
subtitle *The Hardest-Fought Battle of World
War II*. Behind Casablanca's outward shows of
Allied unity lurked serious disagreements about
strategy. The Americans, the young British military historian declares, wanted to proceed with
the invasion of Europe across the Channel from
Britain to Normandy, through France, and into Germany. Churchill believed the
Allies were not yet ready to take on the Germans. That he was right is proved for
Parker by the Normandy landings which, although battle-ready and precise in design,
proved to be no walkover.

At issue, however, was what to do with large numbers of idle soldiers until D day.
Winston Churchill proposed to lay siege to Italy, despite sensing the opposition of
Gen. Bernard Montgomery to a campaign "Monty" saw as lacking overall direction.
He was relieved of duties in Italy. Sir Harold Alexander, a hero of World War I, would
become Allied commander at Cassino. The British got their way. Preparations were
made for the invasion of Sicily, a prelude to the bloody battle of Cassino.

"Americans were unwilling participants in Churchill's 'Mediterranean adventure.'" writes Parker. It "fed the distrust and dislike between the two principal Allies,
which was to reach its grim conclusion at Monte Cassino." With most of the Italian
army surrendering, the Allies thought they could look forward to an easy walk to the
eternal city. The Germans, however, fought on under their formidable commander,
Field Marshal Albert Kesselring. At the center of one of Europe's strongest natural
defensive positions was Monte Cassino, the site of an ancient Benedictine monastery.

Founded by Saint Benedict himself around 529 C.E., the abbey loomed in its wartime guise less spiritually than imperiously: a fortress from which the Gustav Line defenders could train their guns relentlessly downward. New Zealand brigadier general
Howard Kippenberger stated the infantrymen's case best: "It was impossible to ask
troops to storm a hill surrounded by an intact building such as [the monastery], capable of sheltering several hundred infantry in perfect security from shellfire and ready
at the critical moment to emerge and counterattack."

U.S. Fifth Army commander Mark Clark opposed bombing the abbey longest, but
for Parker, who presents the American general as an inept publicity seeker, U.S. opposition shows that the British commanders were more in touch than the Americans
with the feelings of the frontline troops. Lancaster Fusiliers soldier Fred Majdalany,
one of uncounted survivors whose testimony enriches this book, describes how the
abbey spooked him and his buddies as they approached the ridge on which it stood:
"You began to have the feeling the monastery was watching you. When you have
been fighting a long time, you develop an instinct for enemy observation . . . it is like
being suddenly stripped of your clothes. We were being watched by eyes in the monastery."

By the start of 1944, when attacks on the Germans had failed, with staggering
losses, it was decided to bomb the monastery, despite pleas from the pope. Allied
Commander Alexander said that "bricks and mortar, no matter how venerable, cannot

be allowed to weigh against human lives." On February 15, 1944, bombers turned the monastery into rubble, providing the Germans with new positions when the Allies went on the offensive one month later. Fridolin Von Senger's crack troops held on until May. In June the Allies finally entered Rome, which would soon have fallen anyway. Invasion of Normandy, the jugular blow to Hitler, started a few days later.

If they take away the many Italian place-names and leave in only the actual battle descriptions, readers of books like Erich Maria Remarque's *Im Westen nichts Neues* (1929; *All Quiet on the Western Front*, 1969) and Robert Graves's *Goodbye to All That: An Autobiography* (1929) may be struck by a similar feel in *Monte Cassino* to the descriptions of trench warfare. As in the battles in Flanders, there was occasionally an unwarlike

> "lightening up" between German and Allied soldiers. In a fire-fight for a hill not far from Cassino an [Allied] stretcher bearer approached [the German position] under a white flag to ask for a cease-fire in order to pick up wounded. . . . For half an hour Germans, British and Indians worked side by side bearing away the injured. When the Germans ran out of stretchers, they were lent some blankets by the British to help carry away their wounded.

In minutes the truce was over, and men on the two sides resumed killing each other. While seeking to explain the strategic and tactical compromises and waffling that led to the battles, Parker's *Monte Cassino* is not a polemic. "This book focuses on the human experience of the men there at the time, rather than playing 'what if?' games or 'weighing' the performance of the generals." Whether the costly Italian drive pinned down German divisions that could have been used elsewhere in Europe or whether the Allies should have stopped at the "Gustav Line, content to have retained vital air bases in the south for attacking inner Germany and thereby forcing the Nazis to keep large troop concentrations in Italy anyway"—this and other unanswerable cruxes are brilliantly described, but not argued, in the story Parker tells magnificently through eyewitnesses in their own words.

*Richard Hauer Costa*

### Review Sources

*Booklist* 100, nos. 19/20 (June 1-15, 2004): 1691.
*The Economist* 368 (September 20, 2003): 80-81.
*Kirkus Reviews* 72, no. 7 (April 1, 2004): 316.
*Library Journal* 129, no. 8 (May 1, 2004): 127.
*Publishers Weekly* 251, no. 15 (April 12, 2004): 54.

# THE MOUNTAIN POEMS OF MENG HAO-JAN

*Author:* Meng Haoran (689-740)
Translated from the Chinese by David Hinton
*Publisher:* Archipelago Books (New York). 81 pp. Paperback $14.00
*Type of work:* Poetry
*Time:* Eighth century C.E.
*Locale:* China

*Meng Haoran is considered the first major poet of China's medieval Tang dynasty; he invigorated Zen poetry with his sharp focus on concrete images and his keen expression of Daoist philosophical ideas*

*Principal characters:*
>THE PERSONA, a poet who resides alone on a mountain and travels through eighth century China
>WANG WEI, a younger Tang poet and friend of the Persona
>CHANG CHIU-LING, high government official and friend of the Persona
>VARIOUS ZEN MONKS, visited and admired by the Persona
>WOMAN PICKING AN ORANGE, in whom the Persona sees a kindred spirit

With *The Mountain Poems of Meng Hao-jan*, accomplished translator and poet David Hinton has made available in English a significant selection of the poems of the classical Chinese poet Meng Haoran. More than twelve hundred years after Meng composed them, his mountain poems still inspire a modern reader. This is accomplished by the poems' clear vision of the cyclical character of all life. The seasons come and go in Meng's beautiful mountain landscape, and humans feel like guests participating in the endless cycle of birth, blossoming, ripening, death, and rebirth.

To introduce the reader to the thinking of Meng Haoran, David Hinton opens his selection of Meng's poems with his translation of "Autumn Begins." Here, the advent of fall is shown as a gradual process, like many changes in life. For the untrained or distracted observer, the event may nearly be missed. "Nights slowly lengthen" during this transitory time, and only "little by little" is "summer's blaze giving way." Yet to those who clear their minds, this process offers a revelation. As he turns his eyes down the stairs from his thatched mountain hut, the Persona suddenly sees how "lit dew shimmers" in the colder autumnal grass. Thus unexpected beauty is revealed in a harsh season.

As Hinton explains in his excellent introduction, which also includes a map of Meng's medieval China, Meng's poetry is celebrated for its fusion of concrete images and Daoist philosophy aided by Zen meditation. In this, Meng follows China's earliest poetic tradition. From its beginning in the late fourth century C.E., China's mountain and river (shan-shui) poetry sought to show how China's natural landscape could reveal the Daoist view of an empty cosmos suddenly filled with life. Yet life flour-

ishes only briefly, to disappear again. However, after a momentary pause, there starts
another cycle of birth, flowering, and death.
Hinton calls this momentary state a "pregnant emptiness" that applies both to the universe ready to bring forth life again and
Meng's mountain landscape when it is ready
to emerge from the cold lifelessness of winter. At the core of many of Meng's poems,
there is a desire to reveal exactly this transitory state of life and the shift from emptiness
to fullness.

*Meng Haoran became a famous recluse
poet who chose an independent lifestyle.
His Zen poems rejuvenated Chinese
poetry after centuries of stagnation. He
became wildly admired and inspired a
powerful next generation of celebrated
poets. Because he destroyed his own
work, only the 270 poems that he sent to
his friends survived.*

In "On Reaching the Ju River Dikes, Sent to My Friend Lu," Meng evokes nature's
capacity for renewal and reflects on the universe's power to create life out of apparent
nothingness. Sitting on his exhausted horse overlooking a river landscape in the evening, the Persona notices that the traces of winter have disappeared. The "Lo River . . .
free of snow" is lying before him. Beneath "empty skies" and over mountain peaks,
"twilight clouds" show their "lit/ colors surging elemental and swelling." They are
seen as primal creatures ready to burst with new life. Awestruck, the Persona writes
the poem for his friend, telling him how he observes this moment of imminent rebirth
and "how it just keeps unfurling, unfurling." The "pregnant emptiness" of winter (in
Hinton's words) is about to deliver the force of spring.

Even though Meng's fame is founded on his image as a recluse, and mountain ere-
mite, his poetry shows the reader that the mountain poet valued friendship and conversation with fellow humans. In "Lingering Out Farewell with Wang Wei," Meng
states that "nurturing isolate depths of quiet" is not everything his life is about. To the
contrary, he longs for the company of "kindred spirits" like his friend Wang Wei, and
others who are mentioned in his poems. Indeed, Meng's poems reveal that he lived an
active social life. Ironically, it is as a result of his social contacts that Meng's poetry
survived. Only the poems he sent to his friends such as Wang Wei still exist, as Meng
destroyed all his other works as failures. In turn, it was Wang who would write an
obituary poem for Meng and continue to work in his poetic tradition in the next generation of successful Tang poets.

With his friends, Meng also enjoyed drinking wine and playing the qin, a harplike
instrument similar to the Japanese koto or a Western zither. In "Listening to Cheng
Yin Play His *Ch'in*," the Persona is elated as there is "a fresh tune for each cup of
wine." In "Inscribed on a Wall at Li's Farm, for Ch'i-wu Ch'ien," the Persona joyfully describes as he is "Bringing out my *ch'in*, I came to sip wine . . . savoring idleness." As Hinton points out in his *Mountain Home: The Wilderness Poetry of Ancient
China* (2002), mountain poets like Meng Haoran and his followers loved to drink
wine to blur the distinction between themselves and the things they observed. In contrast, they drank tea to raise their awareness of this distinction. Hinton's *Mountain
Home* also contains his translation of a few of the poems presented in *The Mountain
Poems of Meng Hao-jan*, as well as those of earlier poets and those in part inspired by

Meng. Hinton's earlier book reveals the translator's long and deep concern with his subject, and his efforts in creating a definitive translation for these classical poems.

As revealed in *The Mountain Poems of Meng Hao-jan*, Meng did not limit his friendship to fellow poets and drinking companions. He also treasured the company of Chang Chiu-ling (Zhang Jiu Ling in Pinyin), a high Tang dynasty official. Chang gave Meng the only official government job he held in his lifetime, as a regional supervisor. Characteristically for his unconventional spirit, Meng was appointed in the fall of 737 and resigned in the spring of 738, two years before his death at age fifty-one. In "On Peak-Light Tower with Prime Minister Chang Chiu-ling," the Persona indicates his respect for this friend, a "man walking so alone" under the burden of high responsibility. The Persona rejoices that even though it is winter and he is homesick on his journeys through China, "finding you/ know me all" makes him forget home because another person understands him so well. This is high praise for the power of friendship that can overcome even the despair brought on by the cold, dormant season of a harsh Chinese winter.

Meng's friends include many Zen monks, who practice the form of meditation and spiritual life his poetry celebrates. Hinton's selection in *The Mountain Poems of Meng Hao-jan* presents quite a few of Meng's poems that deal with his relationship with Zen monks. In "Spending the Night at Abbot Yeh's Mountain Home, Dragon-Cascade Monastery, I Await Master Ting Who Never Arrives," the time of day is dusk, as so often in Meng's poems. Because they represent a moment of transition, dawn and dusk are favorite moments for Meng. Just as night changes to day, or day to night, the Daoist universe is in a constant flux of changing from nothing to fullness, and from fullness to emptiness again. In this poem, characteristic of Meng's concrete images, he describes how the "late sun crosses beyond western ridgelines,/ leaving canyons and valleys suddenly dark." As night falls, the human inhabitants of the landscape, indicated here by the conventional woodcutters of Chinese mountain poetry, "make their way back home" as "mist begin settling in." As if to remind the Persona of the unpredictability of human affairs, his friend who meant to be "coming tonight" fails to show up, and the Persona is left alone with his qin, to "wait out an overgrown path."

Comparing Hinton's translation of this poem to an earlier English translation, done almost a quarter century before Hinton's work, reveals much of the translator's approach to the classical Chinese of Meng's poetry in *The Mountain Poems of Meng Hao-jan*. In his well-researched biography *Meng Hao-jan* (1981), Paul W. Kroll renders the opening lines of the poem thus: "Evening's sunglow has crossed the west ridge;/ The serried straths suddenly, now, are dark-cast." As Hinton explains in his *Mountain Home*, classical Chinese poetry consists of ideograms, or characters, that refer to mostly uninflected verbs that register action. There are mainly descriptive rather than functional words, such as prepositions or conjunctions. In sum, Meng's original Chinese lines are "mostly a list of images" that posts a challenge for the English translator.

Hinton's translation seeks to re-create a sense of the stark sparseness of the concrete images of Meng's poetry. Hinton prefers "late sun" over Kroll's "evening's sunglow," the latter alluding more to the conventions of a Western elevated poetic style. While Kroll's alliterative "serried straths" seeks to capture the series of similar sounds of the original Chinese characters, Hinton's "canyons and valleys" are a much more concrete translation.

For the modern reader, Hinton's decision to translate Chinese names, places, and some key terms by using the older Wade Giles system of transliteration can be problematical. Since its official adoption by the People's Republic of China in 1979, the Pinyin system of transcribing Chinese characters into the Roman alphabet has become most widely accepted worldwide. Thus, beginning with the transliteration of the poet's first name (his last name, Meng, coming first in the Asian tradition), Hinton's rendition of Hao-jan is at some odds with the Pinyin transliteration as Haoran. While this may not concern a reader primarily interested in the power of Meng's mountain poetry, it may make a search for places like his hometown frustrating (for the town called Hsiang-yang by Hinton is commonly referred to as Xiang-yang in modern geography). A similar problem exists concerning the proper names of Meng's friends and associates.

Overall, Hinton's translation in *The Mountain Poems of Meng Hao-jan* offers the reader a powerful view of the work of this major and influential Tang dynasty poet. Hinton's selection of Meng's poetry also reveals the poet's appreciation of a kindred spirit in a person of the opposite gender. Even as a mountain recluse and often lone traveler, Meng appreciated feminine company as well. In "Courtyard Oranges," the Persona's gaze is fixed on fruits that "hang like pure gold" as a late frost recedes from the orchard. Suddenly, he notices a woman who picks the oranges. He observes how she is "touched at how they grow in pairs," and reveals that both he and she "feel this mind we share," a mind conscious of the universal desire for companionship. The Persona also appreciates the other as a woman, for he notices the "scents clinging to kingfisher hairpins" in her hair, mixing her perfume with the smell of the oranges. When "she brings a bowlful," both she and the Persona are taken by the oranges' "allure in groves of quiet mystery." Even in a garden, nature shows its fundamental mysteries.

It is perhaps Meng's deep appreciation of nature and wilderness that make his poetry so appealing to a modern reader. A reader more familiar with Western poetry may feel reminded of the poetry of American Gary Snyder or the work of the romantic English poet William Wordsworth or even Henry David Thoreau's *Walden* (1854), when reading Meng's poems. What distinguishes Meng's mountain poems is his Daoist belief that the universe is forever oscillating in a constant cycle of birth, death, and rebirth and that ultimately emptiness lies at the core of all existence. This emptiness should not be mistaken for mere barrenness. For Meng, it always holds the promise of a sudden reemergence of all life. An appreciative reader should feel elated that Hinton has made available so much of Meng's classical poetry. Hinton's well-crafted English successfully maintains the sparse, imaginist character of Meng's Chinese original.

*R. C. Lutz*

# MR. PARADISE

*Author:* Elmore Leonard (1925-    )
*Publisher:* William Morrow (New York). 291 pp. $26.00
*Type of work:* Novel
*Time:* 2004
*Locale:* Detroit

*A homicide detective investigating the murder of an octogenarian multimillionaire and his beautiful, paid mistress becomes involved with killers on a bloody rampage and con men trying to loot the old man's estate*

> *Principal characters:*
> FRANK DELSA, the acting lieutenant of Squad Seven, Homicide Section, Detroit Police Department
> KELLY BARR, a gorgeous blond model who becomes his lover
> CHLOE ROBINETTE, an equally gorgeous blond, $900-a-night prostitute working—and mostly vacationing—as Paradiso's mistress at $5,000 a week
> ANTHONY PARADISO, a retired personal injury attorney, nicknamed Mr. Paradise; a half-senile, nearly impotent but still lecherous multimillionaire
> MONTEZ TAYLOR, Paradiso's yes-man, procurer, and "number-one walking-around guy"
> LLOYD WILLIAMS, Paradiso's live-in houseman, who once served 108 months for armed robbery
> SERGEANT JACKIE MICHAELS, street-smart homicide cop
> JEROME JUWAN JACKSON (THREE-J), ambitious drug dealer who becomes a C.I. (confidential informant) for Delsa
> AVERN COHN, defense attorney who contracts murders of drug dealers and provides a legal shield for the hired killers
> CARL FONTANA, middle-aged contract killer responsible for at least nine recent murders
> ART KRUPA, Fontana's equally trigger-happy partner in crime

Elmore Leonard was born in Louisiana but grew up in Detroit and still lives in the Detroit area. He has set several of his novels in Florida, Cuba, California, and Mississippi, but in this book he returns to crime-ridden, ethnically diverse Detroit with gusto. Many of his characters are African American, and Leonard delights and excels in mimicking the unique, sometimes poetic brand of English spoken by his underprivileged but resourceful, defiant, and intrepid black characters. He might almost be called a modern-day Mark Twain.

Montez Taylor has been working for Mr. Paradise for ten years. He is forced to dress in conservative suits and ties to look like a private secretary. He keeps his true feelings, which are hostile and greedy, to himself, waiting for the old man to die and leave him the two-story mansion worth about two million dollars, as Mr. Paradise has often promised. Then Montez learns that his employer, who enjoys tormenting and tantalizing relatives and retainers alike, has changed his mind and is leaving the house to a granddaughter.

Montez decides to have his employer murdered while he still retains control of a safety box containing unknown documents, thought to be worth millions to Chloe Robinette, Mr. Paradise's mistress. Montez believes she will share the fortune with him in gratitude for preserving the documents and expediting the creepy, perverted old man's death. Otherwise, he can threaten her with the same fate that befell their employer.

*Elmore Leonard is regarded as the grand master of crime fiction. His genre novels are treated with unprecedented critical respect, largely because of his avant-garde narrative technique and his flawless ear for dialogue, rivaling Dashiell Hammett. Many of Leonard's novels, including* Get Shorty *(1990),* Out of Sight *(1996), and* Rum Punch *(1992) have been made into big-budget films.*

Leonard's plots are always complicated and hard to follow. They frequently depend on coincidence and happenstance. Montez has contracted with the crooked attorney Avern Cohn to have Carl Fontana and Art Krupa, two fearless and ruthless but moronic hit men, invade the Paradiso mansion at a specific date and time. They are supposed to break a window and steal a few items to make the entry look like a more-or-less random home invasion.

As usual in a Leonard novel, the characters have their own ideas. They are not stick figures like characters in many genre novels. Leonard has often stated that his creative method is to create a cast of interesting characters with conflicting motivations and let them work out their own destinies. The typical Leonard novel contains long periods of nothing much happening, followed by explosions of unexpected violence. Although the story contains many murders, most violence occurs off the page or in the past tense. Leonard's fans enjoy suspense rather than gore. They feel sure that something very bad is going to happen eventually, with all the greedy, unprincipled characters involved—but what, how, and when are the questions that keep them turning pages.

Chloe does not show up on the night she is supposed to act as a half-naked University of Michigan cheerleader while Mr. Paradise, reliving his past, watches an old Rose Bowl game on videotape. Instead, Chloe arrives the next night and brings along her roommate Kelly Barr to assist her. The two young blondes look very much alike in their blue-and-beige cheerleader outfits. Montez has been unable to contact Cohn or either of the hit men to postpone the hit. He is ordered to take Kelly upstairs, while Mr. Paradise tries his best to make love to Chloe in front of the television set.

The unhappy factotum has to stand helplessly by while Fontana and Krupa enter, shoot the old man dead, and then kill Chloe to eliminate a witness. When Montez runs downstairs to talk to the killers, Kelly comes out into the hallway overlooking the foyer and sees the hit men taking their leave. She is now in danger of being killed by Fontana and Krupa—or by Montez, who decides on the spur of the moment to have Kelly assume the identity of Chloe so that she can forge Chloe's name, cash in on the documents, which turn out to be stock certificates, and share the proceeds with him. After seeing what has happened to her girlfriend, Kelly agrees to go along with Montez's scheme. Montez himself is under tremendous pressure because he owes the killers $50,000 for their handiwork and really cannot expect to inherit anything from his employer.

It does not take detective Frank Delsa long to figure out that Kelly is Kelly, and she is relieved to be able to confess. He promises to protect her, not only because she is a valuable witness but also because he is already falling in love with her. The basic plot is that Kelly probably can identify the two killers. They, in turn, will rat out Montez in order to get a reduced sentence, and Montez will rat out Avern, who gave the contract to Fontana and Krupa. With so much at stake, Kelly's life is in danger. Delsa must protect her, but she must use her own sharp wits and feminine charms to protect herself as well. Delsa, being a homicide cop in one of the United States' most drug-ridden, murder-ridden cities, has other cases to pursue. He is chronically overworked and shorthanded, and he is at least temporarily in charge of the whole homicide department. Fortunately, it turns out that many of the murders on his current case load are traceable to the same few individuals, principally Fontana and Krupa.

Leonard writes every scene from the point of view of one of the participants. Much of his novel is told in dialogue. The effect is comparable to that of a modern motion picture in which scenes are shot from several different angles by multiple cameras and then spliced together in the cutting room. There is no intrusive narrator explaining what is happening. Descriptions of settings are minimal. Leonard makes the traditional third-person narrator—such as the omniscient narrator of Theodore Dreiser's *An American Tragedy* (1925)—as well as the first-person narrator—such as Raymond Chandler's Philip Marlowe and Mark Twain's Huckleberry Finn—seem tedious and old-fashioned. He eases back and forth in time with nonchalance because he can always use a viewpoint character's memories to relive the past. An example of Leonard's technical virtuosity, which is what has made him a favorite of discriminating readers and elevated his genre books to the rank of "serious literature" or "quality fiction," can be found in chapter 24. Here Acting Lieutenant Delsa is investigating another humdrum unnecessary shooting during an armed robbery at a McDonald's restaurant while munching French fries and simultaneously remembering the night before, when he and Kelly had sex for the first time.

> Delsa was conducting an interview but thinking of last night, looking through scenes in his head, stepping into the shower and Kelly turning to him, water streaming over her naked body, her perfect breasts, her navel, Kelly smiling at him and laughing out loud as he said, "Heil Hitler," and says to the McDonald's counter girl, "Do you know Big Baby's real name?"

Big Baby is the armed robber who shot the terrified, totally submissive McDonald's manager, just to see what it felt like to kill somebody. Delsa says "Heil Hitler" because Kelly models skimpy underwear for famous merchandisers like Victoria's Secret, and her Brazilian-style bikini wax leaves only a trace of hair resembling Hitler's famous mustache. It was this observation that enabled Delsa, when he saw her photographs in lingerie catalogs, to identify her as Kelly rather than the dead, unshorn Chloe.

When Montez finally gets his hands on the documents that Paradiso had already signed over to Chloe, he still tries to persuade Kelly to forge Chloe's signature and cash them in, even though he fully realizes she has confessed her true identity to the police. His method of persuasion is simple and direct: If she does not cooperate, he will have her killed by the same two men who killed Paradiso and Chloe. Kelly is not a hooker, but she is not compulsively ethical either. She is tempted to cooperate with Montez until she discovers that the power company stocks, which were worth $81.40 a share one year ago, have dropped to 53 cents a share, with the company headed for bankruptcy. The game is not worth the gamble.

Leonard always tries to orchestrate the casts of his novels. There are only three female principals in *Mr. Paradise*, and Chloe dies early on. Tough-talking, street-smart Sergeant Jackie Michaels seems to have been created mainly to add another woman to the cast. Jerome Juwan Jackson, whose street name is Three-J, seems to have been invented mainly to provide another point of view that can allow the narrator to remain invisible. This young delinquent attaches himself to Fontana and Krupa, who let him think they are a couple of plainclothes detectives. Much of their action and dialogue is seen and heard through the eyes and ears of the naïve but intelligent Three-J. Fontana and Krupa are too stupid and too similar to merit their own points of view.

When the two white killers find out they have been identified, they decide to revisit the Paradise mansion and use it as their hideout, taking Three-J with them. Along the way, they kidnap their attorney-agent Avern. Meanwhile Montez has kidnapped Kelly and brought her to the mansion, so all the principals are gathered together for the climax when Delsa arrives, looking for Kelly. Nobody trusts anybody else. A lot of guns are out on the breakfast table. Almost everybody has a reason for shooting somebody else, while everybody also has a reason for refraining from initiating the carnage. Fontana and Krupa, for example, would like to eliminate Montez as an informant, but Montez still owes them $50,000 for doing the job. Montez is one of several who would like to kill Kelly, but he is still hoping to get her to forge Chloe's name to the stock certificates and enable him to salvage at least a little compensation for his ten years of toadying to Mr. Paradise. Delsa would like to kill Montez, Fontana, and Krupa, because all of them have very good reasons to murder Kelly. Three-J, from whose point of view much of the denouement is described, is fascinated by what he regards as an exceptional out-of-school learning experience. This thoroughly satisfying, state-of-the-art page-turner ends with an explosion of violence, followed by a predictable love scene with Delsa and Kelly lying comfortably in her bed.

*Bill Delaney*

# Review Sources

*Kirkus Reviews* 71, no. 21 (November 1, 2003): 1290.
*Los Angeles Times*, February 15, 2004, p. R16.
*The New York Times Book Review* 153 (February 1, 2004): 6.
*Publishers Weekly* 250, no. 47 (November 24, 2003): 42.
*The Washington Post*, January 18, 2004, p. T15.
*The Washington Times*, February 1, 2004, p. B6.

# MY LIFE

*Author:* Bill Clinton (1946-    )
*Publisher:* Alfred A. Knopf (New York). Illustrated. 957 pp. $35.00
*Type of work:* Memoir
*Time:* 1946-2002
*Locale:* Hope, Hot Springs, Fayetteville, and Little Rock, Arkansas; New Haven, Connecticut; Washington, D.C.; New York; many of the world's major capitals

*The forty-second president of the United States presents a detailed and forthright account of his life from its beginnings through his two terms as chief executive*

Principal personages:
BILL CLINTON, forty-second president of the United States
HILLARY RODHAM CLINTON, his wife
CHELSEA VICTORIA CLINTON, their daughter and only child
VIRGINIA KELLEY, Bill Clinton's mother
MONICA LEWINSKY, the White House intern with whom Clinton had sexual contact
KEN STARR, the prosecutor in Clinton's impeachment trial

When Bill Clinton completed his term of office in January, 2001, he faced the immediate task of writing his memoirs, under contract to Alfred A. Knopf. It is rumored that Clinton actually hoped to fulfill his contractual obligation to Knopf by writing two books, one detailing the years leading up to his governorship in Arkansas and one detailing his political growth during four terms as governor of Arkansas, then as a major figure during his two terms as president of the United States.

Although his publisher allegedly urged him to write a single book, *My Life* is, in a way, two books. The first part is a perceptive analysis of what made Clinton the man he became. Had he not entered an extensive course of family counseling following the Monica Lewinsky scandal, it is doubtful that he would have possessed the insights to view his first thirty-odd years with the clarity that he brings to this analysis of his early life.

The second part of the book focuses on Clinton's political activities and of his rise from the lowest paid governor in the United States to president. Much of this portion of *My Life* is an extended catalog of the many functions and involvements in which Clinton was involved as president, but these details are far more than a mere recounting of his presidential activity. The book, written at breakneck speed, has a locomotive force that, despite its bulk of 957 pages plus forty-three additional pages of index and acknowledgments, quickly draws readers into its drama and dynamics, making it compelling reading.

Clinton repeatedly refers to the parallel lives he has lived. Of his father, William Jefferson Blythe, Jr., who died in an automobile crash three months before Clinton's birth on August 19, 1946, he writes, "My father left me with the feeling that I had to live for two people, and that if I did it well enough, somehow I could make up for his

*Bill Clinton, a Rhodes scholar and professor of law at the University of Arkansas, was elected governor of Arkansas in 1978, becoming the youngest governor in the United States. Defeated for a second term, he ran again in 1982 and was elected. He served as governor for a total of twelve years before being elected president of the United States in 1992 and again in 1996.*

life." The theme of parallel lives pervades the book, but Clinton takes this theme beyond the obvious dichotomy between the public and private figure and delves as well into the inner consciousness, the psychological substrata, of each.

Clinton's was not a typical childhood. Not only was his father dead when he was born, but his mother, Virginia, soon had to go to New Orleans for training as a nurse anesthetist, leaving her infant son in the care of her parents, who were thoroughly good, loving people. Upon his mother's return to Arkansas and her remarriage to Roger Clinton, young Bill adopted the surname of his stepfather, with whom he was generally on good terms.

Roger Clinton, however, became mean and violent when he drank, leading to frequent crises within the household. Finally, during one of Roger's drunken physical attacks upon Virginia, Bill, still in his teens, stood up to his stepfather and threatened him with a golf club as he was beating his mother. Recalling the incident, Clinton writes, "I suppose I was proud of myself for standing up for Mother, but afterwards I was sad about it, too. I just couldn't accept the fact that a basically good person would try to make his own pain go away by hurting someone else." The family tensions Clinton endured were lodged deep within him and not shared with anyone. From his earliest years, Bill became adept at keeping secrets and repressing emotions.

During the years that he lived in Roger Clinton's home, Clinton learned to distance himself psychologically from the tumult that often surrounded him there. Throughout his career, he relied on his ability to keep separate the diverse strands of his life, making it possible for him to rise above many of the attacks upon him during his years as a public official. During the impeachment woes that threatened to destroy his presidency, Clinton attended to affairs of state simply by closing from his mind the immediate threatening pressures upon him.

Shortly into his presidency, intimations of financial improprieties surrounding his involvement in Whitewater came to light. Clinton, convinced that he and his wife, Hillary, had nothing to hide, urged the appointment of a special counsel to investigate the matter. Ken Starr, a right-wing conservative obsessively opposed to Clinton and to all he stood for, became special counsel. Starr pitted himself against Clinton from the beginning, using every tactic he could employ to discredit the president. He ultimately succeeded in bringing the Clintons to the verge of bankruptcy before the president's two terms in office ended. The situation became muddied when Clinton's womanizing became an issue and when the president dealt with Paula Jones's accusations of sexual harassment by settling with her out of court to bring closure to a matter that threatened to become a prolonged distraction.

Although Starr never proved malfeasance on the part of either of the Clintons in regard to Whitewater, he brought to public attention the suggestions of so many scandals related to them that they were broadly discredited among conservatives and even among some moderates. The Starr assault reached its acme when the Monica Lewinsky scandal came to light. In this matter, the president openly and knowingly lied to the American public, denying a sexual relationship that DNA testing subsequently affirmed.

Starr pressed for the impeachment which became a blight upon Clinton's final years in office, even though the impeachment hearings ultimately failed to convict him. Throughout this extremely trying period, Clinton functioned productively as president, largely because of his ability to compartmentalize the various elements of his complex existence. For example, Clinton enumerates ten major national and international activities, many of them with global consequences, in which he engaged during the first week of May, 1994. He ends this enumeration with the simple statement that he was sued that week by Paula Jones, commenting wryly that it was just another week at the office. Clinton also admits that sometimes the pressures of the job left him totally exhausted. He claims that it was at such times that he was vulnerable to making the sorts of bad decisions that resulted in his inexcusable dalliance with Lewinsky.

The book is filled with interesting vignettes that reveal much of the activities that preceded history-making events. Clinton presents the details of a major logistical matter that had to be resolved before Palistinian president Yasser Arafat and Israeli prime minister Yitzhak Rabin could meet at the White House, following months of negotiating a Palestinian-Israeli peace accord, an initiative that Clinton had labored hard to bring about. This historic meeting was to be televised worldwide.

Arafat requested that he and Rabin shake hands. Rabin resisted strenuously at first, blaming Arafat's aggressions for the fact that hordes of young men and women lay buried in Israeli cemeteries. Finally, however, Clinton persuaded Rabin that this handshake was what the world expected, so the prime minister agreed, rationalizing that one does not make peace with one's friends. He drew the line, nevertheless, at kissing. In the Middle East, the conventional greeting is an embrace and a kiss on both cheeks. Rabin would have none of this. Finally, acknowledging how much rested on the public appearance of the two opponents and recognizing as well that the kiss in a situation like this was more or less a reflex among Arabs, Clinton had to devise a way that the two could shake hands publicly but that would not result in Rabin's being kissed by Arafat. Clinton's first thought was that he might shake hands with both men and that if Arafat did not kiss Clinton, he would be unlikely to kiss Rabin. This solution, however, was not sufficiently foolproof. He mentioned his dilemma to National Security Adviser Tony Lake, who said he knew of a way to prevent the kiss. Clinton describes reviewing strategy with Lake: "I played Arafat and [Tony] played me, showing me what to do. When I shook his hand and moved in for the kiss, he put his left hand on my right arm where it was bent at the elbow, and squeezed it; it stopped me cold." In this way, Clinton was able to control the essential, televised White House handshake between Arafat and Rabin.

Shortly after George W. Bush was elected president in 2000, Clinton met with him in the Oval Office to discuss security issues. Bush told Clinton that national missile defense and Iraq were his top security priorities. Clinton pointed out that his eight years in office had led him to different conclusions. He considered Osama bin Laden and al-Qaeda the greatest security risks to the United States, followed closely by unrest in the Middle East. As Clinton perceived it, tensions between India and Pakistan, both nuclear powers, also loomed large, as did Pakistan's links to the Taliban in Afghanistan and al-Qaeda. North Korea and its nuclear weapons program were next on Clinton's list of priorities, followed, finally, by Iraq. History demonstrates that Bush did not share Clinton's priorities.

Given what Hillary Clinton referred to as attacks on the Clinton administration by a right-wing conspiracy, one well may marvel that *My Life* is not a mean-spirited retaliation. Instead it is a fair, relatively objective account of its author's life and public service. The only signs of vindictiveness in it appear in Clinton's statements about Ken Starr. Even then, Clinton acknowledges that Starr was doing his job. Some of Newt Gingrich's duplicity is also revealed, but not in a mean-spirited nor personal way. In this book, Clinton emerges as the effective conciliator that he was throughout his presidency, ever attempting to understand both sides of controversial issues and seeking a middle ground from which bipartisan action could proceed.

*My Life* is both the most personal and the most detailed presidential memoir of any twentieth century president. As such, it is a quintessential historical document that will inform historians for decades to come.

*R. Baird Shuman*

## Review Sources

*Booklist* 100, no. 22 (August 1, 2004): 1866.
*The New York Review of Books* 54, no. 13 (August 12, 2004): 60-64.
*The New York Times*, June 20, 2004, p. A1.
*The New York Times Book Review* 153 (July 12, 2004): 1.
*Newsweek*, July 5, 2004, p. 13.
*Publishers Weekly* 251 (June 28, 2004): 5-7, 14.
*Time* 163 (June 28, 2004): 26-39.
*The Times Literary Supplement*, August 27, 2004, pp. 3-4.

# NATALIE WOOD
## A Life

*Author:* Gavin Lambert (1924-    )
*Publisher:* Alfred A. Knopf (New York). 370 pp. $26.00
*Type of work:* Biography
*Time:* 1938-1981
*Locale:* Hollywood, California

*A portrait of the legendary film star who drowned at the age of forty-three*

*Principal personages:*
NATALIE WOOD, a Hollywood film star
ROBERT WAGNER, her first and third husband
MARIA GURDIN, her ambitious, Russian-born mother
NICK GURDIN, her alcoholic, Russian-born father
RICHARD GREGSON, her second husband
NATASHA GREGSON WAGNER, her older daughter
COURTNEY WAGNER, her younger daughter

Surprisingly, *Natalie Wood: A Life* is only the third biography of the legendary actress to be published after her tragic death in 1981. Suzanne Finstad's *Natasha: The Biography of Natalie Wood* (2001) provided an engrossing account of the actress's life, replete with Hollywood gossip and juicy details, while Lana Wood's *Natalie: A Memoir by Her Sister* (1986) was as much about Lana as Natalie and does not really qualify as a legitimate biography. Lambert, who knew Wood both as a friend and as a colleague—he wrote the screenplay for *Inside Daisy Clover* and was sleeping with Wood's first love, bisexual director Nicholas Ray, at the same time she was—received full assistance and blessing in this effort from Wood's widower, Robert Wagner.

Natalie Wood was born Natalia Nikolaevna Zakharenko on July 20, 1938, in San Francisco, to Russian émigré parents Maria and Nick, who changed their surname to Gurdin upon becoming U.S. citizens. When a motion-picture company was filming in Santa Rosa, California, where the Gurdins were living at the time, three-year-old Natalie was cast as an extra. Maria's already strong ambitions for her beautiful little girl were intensified. Convinced that her child was destined for stardom, she moved the family to Hollywood, changed Natalie's last name, and three years later Maria's persistence and Natalie's talent earned the child a starring role in *Tomorrow Is Forever* (1946), with Orson Welles.

Hollywood took notice of Wood's quiet but intense presence in the film, and her career took off. Between 1947 and 1949, she appeared in six Fox productions, including the classic *Miracle on 34th Street* (1947). She worked almost nonstop, making

*Born and educated in England, Gavin Lambert is the author of four biographies*—On Cukor *(1972),* Norma Shearer *(1990),* Nazimova *(1997), and* Mainly About Lindsay Anderson *(2000). He has written seven novels and several screenplays. He is also a film critic and has edited the film journals* Sequence *and* Sight and Sound.

nine films between the ages of ten and fourteen. By 1953, roles for the now adolescent Natalie were offered less frequently, and she filled the void of her "awkward years" with a television situation comedy, *The Pride of the Family*, and work in several television dramas.

Finally, in 1955, *Rebel Without a Cause* presented Natalie Wood with the role that would break her out of the "child star" mold, earn her an Oscar nomination, and begin to establish her reputation as a serious actress. Influenced by her costar James Dean and director Nicholas Ray, she began to view acting as a serious pursuit, rather than just a way to please her parents. She was drawn to the new method school of acting, espoused by Dean, and began for the first time to break away from the powerful influence of both her mother and the studio and to think for herself.

After *Rebel Without a Cause*, Wood worked steadily in a series of mediocre films assigned her by Warner Bros. but did not have another opportunity to showcase her talent properly until her work in 1961's *Splendor in the Grass*, directed by Elia Kazan and also starring Warren Beatty. In order to win this role, she had to pretend not to want it, so that studio head Jack Warner, who intensely disliked her, would demand that she do it. This role, for which she received an Oscar nomination, marked the beginning of the peak years of her career.

Her next film, *West Side Story* (1961), was her most successful, although she did not reap its rewards, having opted for a $50,000 bonus rather than 5 percent of the profits (a mistake that she would not repeat with the 1969 hit *Bob and Carol and Ted and Alice*, for which she received 10 percent of the profits). Although her singing voice is dubbed in *West Side Story* (she was not informed until after filming that her voice would not be used) and she disliked director Robert Wise, it remains one of her signature roles. *Love with the Proper Stranger* (1963), *Inside Daisy Clover* (1965), and *Bob and Carol and Ted and Alice* marked the remaining high points in Wood's career. She received her third Oscar nomination for *Love with the Proper Stranger*.

Wood made very few films after 1969, although she appeared in some noteworthy television dramas, including *Cat on a Hot Tin Roof* (1976) with Robert Wagner and *From Here to Eternity* (1979). She was filming *Brainstorm* (1983) with Christopher Walken when she drowned in 1981 at the age of forty-three.

Lambert stresses the strong influence of Wood's family on her life, particularly that of her mother. Maria was told by a gypsy that she would give birth to an exceptional child, so when her second, dark-eyed, beautiful child was born, she was convinced the gypsy's prophecy had come to pass. From the time she pushed Natalie on the director in Santa Rosa, she was a full-blown "stage mom," reveling in her status as mother of the star. At the age of six, Natalie was not only expected to support her family, but she was also responsible for her mother's identity and self-esteem. Her family's life revolved around her career, to the extent that her mother was paid to answer her fan mail and her father was hired by the studio to work as a carpenter. Maria impressed upon Natalie that she was never to acknowledge her father on the set, because she was a star and he was the hired help.

This biography makes much of the fact that Nick Gurdin may not have been Natalie Wood's biological father. Maria had a lifelong affair with fellow émigré George Zepaloff, the "great love" of her life; according to Lambert, she hinted on occasion to Natalie that he, not Nick, was her real father. It remains unclear whether Wood ever caught her mother's implications, or took them seriously if she did, but after Wood's death enough information came to light to convince Wagner and Wood's two daughters that this was true. Although Lambert returns repeatedly to this line of inquiry, he fails to make the case that this fact changes Wood's life story in any way. Nick was an ineffectual alcoholic whose only influence on Wood's life was through his absence as an effective father figure, but it is clear that George would have been an even less effective parent.

Lambert also explores the dichotomy in Wood's character between her desire to be both a serious actor and a glamorous film star. One of the last products of the old studio system, she maintained a very professional attitude toward her work, appearing in the mediocre fare assigned to her by the studio, often in exchange for the freedom to then do something of her own choosing. However strongly she was attracted to the idea of acting as a serious art form, she nonetheless was meticulous about her appearance, often making "movie star" type demands for a particular costume designer (she was partial to Edith Head) or makeup artist in order to protect her glamorous image. She also cultivated the "old Hollywood" image when she went out as well, making sure her "star" face was on when she appeared in public.

Lambert does not fail to "dish the dirt," particularly when it comes to Wood's love life. The reader learns that she lost her virginity at the age of sixteen to forty-three-year-old Ray, the director of *Rebel Without a Cause*, while at the same time conducting an affair with her twenty-year-old costar Dennis Hopper. She had an on-and-off affair of many years with singer Frank Sinatra and attempted suicide after breaking up with Beatty. She also had brief flings with California attorney general (and future governor) Jerry Brown and with actor Steve McQueen. Her second marriage to Wagner appeared to be successful, although in the last year of her life, when her alcohol and drug use increased, she was carrying on a flirtation, if not an affair, with costar Walken, who was present the night of her death.

Unfortunately, Lambert's insider status does not shed much new light on what has become the most fascinating aspect of the Natalie Wood story: her mysterious death by drowning in 1981. He examines the details of that fateful Thanksgiving weekend thoroughly, using the police and autopsy reports and interviewing many of those involved, including Wagner, whose vague recollections of a very drunken weekend are not particularly revealing. Lambert was unable to get more information from the key witness, Walken, than he has given in the past, so this book is no more helpful in unraveling the occurrences on the Wagners' boat than any previous source.

While Lambert's knowledge of Wood's private life is extensive, his encyclopedic knowledge of the motion-picture business is even more impressive, although it sometimes gets in the way of the book's narrative flow. He offers such extensive background material on each film and filmmaker mentioned that the reader can feel bogged down in the kind of extraneous detail appreciated by only the most devoted students of film. This habit of presenting extensive background information on nearly every person introduced, however tangential to Wood's life, becomes distracting and, finally, annoying.

Although bursting with intriguing details only an insider can provide, this biography may finally suffer more than profit from the author's close association with Wagner. Because this work received his full cooperation and support, the reader cannot help but feel that the version of Natalie Wood presented here is perhaps too heavily filtered through Wagner's protective lens and that Wagner's own role in her life is somewhat whitewashed. The author is extremely censorious of Maria Gurdin and Natalie's sister Lana (perhaps deservedly so) and is totally uncritical of Wagner. Although Lambert's portrait of Wood, drawn from personal experience, is sensitive and insightful, he does tread lightly on her darker side. Nonetheless, his status as an insider and his extensive knowledge of the film industry make this biography a valuable addition to Hollywood history as well as a well-researched examination of one of its biggest stars.

*Mary Virginia Davis*

## Review Sources

*Booklist* 100, no. 8 (December 15, 2003): 718.
*Kirkus Reviews* 71, no. 22 (November 15, 2003): 1352.
*Library Journal* 129, no. 1 (January 15, 2004): 116.
*The New York Times Book Review* 153 (January 18, 2004): 8.
*People* 61, no. 2 (January 19, 2004): 46.
*Publishers Weekly* 250, no. 49 (December 8, 2003): 57.
*The Times Literary Supplement*, July 2, 2004, p. 16.
*Variety* 393, no. 12 (February 9, 2004): 95.

# NATASHA, AND OTHER STORIES

*Author:* David Bezmozgis (1973-    )
*Publisher:* Farrar, Straus and Giroux (New York). 147
  pp. $18.00
*Type of work:* Short fiction
*Time:* 1980-2004
*Locale:* Toronto

*Bezmozgis's first book is a collection of short stories about a family of Russian Jews from Latvia that immigrates to Toronto in 1980 and slowly assimilates into North American culture*

*Principal characters:*
> MARK BERMAN, the narrator, the son of Roman and Bella, who grows up
>   observing the divided world of immigrant Russian Jews in Canada
> ROMAN BERMAN, his father, a former weightlifting coach
> BELLA BERMAN, his mother, who suffers from depression
> JANA, his older cousin
> ZINA, a Russian Jew who marries Mark's uncle
> NATASHA, Zina's fourteen-year-old daughter
> SERGEI FEDERENKO, a Soviet weightlifting champion
> RUFUS, Mark's friend, a drug dealer
> RABBI GURVICH, the head of the Hebrew school that Mark attends as a
>   boy
> HERSCHEL, an elderly resident at an assisted living apartment building
>   for Jews

While one cannot judge a book by its cover, the themes of David Bezmozgis's first book, *Natasha, and Other Stories*, are nicely reflected by the Russian nesting dolls—or *matryoshka*—that replace the letter As in the title on the otherwise spartan cover of the book's first Farrar, Straus and Giroux edition. The use of the nesting dolls ostensibly conveys the Latvian-Russian cultural heritage at play in Bezmozgis's collection of stories. At the same time, however, the nesting dolls—those oval, hollow dolls made so that each doll in a succession can fit inside the next larger doll—serve as a primary metaphor for Bezmozgis's stories. Over and over again, Bezmozgis's characters are people who are not wholly one thing or another. Rather, they are always nesting inside a shell imposed upon them by themselves or by the various societies around them. In Soviet Latvia, the Berman family members were Jewish; in Canada, they are Russian immigrants trying to assimilate but at the same time trying not to become too assimilated. They are never completely freed of external scrutiny, never allowed to shed their shells until the final, smallest, most fragile figurine is all that remains.

As a collection of stories, *Natasha, and Other Stories* follows solidly in the tradition established by Sherwood Anderson with *Winesburg, Ohio* (1919) and carried on

~

*David Bezmozgis emigrated with his
family from Latvia in the waning
years of the Cold War and grew up
in Toronto. After majoring in
English at McGill University, he
attended film school at the
University of Southern California.
He directed the critically successful
short documentary* L.A. Mohel
*(1999) about Jewish circumcisions
in Los Angeles.* Natasha, and Other
Stories *is his first book.*

~

in books such as *Go Down Moses* (1942) by William Faulkner. Although the book is purportedly a collection of short stories, the tales in each of these books are united by either themes or characters or both. Through their unity and cohesion, the collection of stories form a kind of novel. *Natasha, and Other Stories* is particularly unified through both its use of characters and its consistent themes. It manages to present the best of both genres: the brief, concise, brilliant images that one associates with a collection of short stories, combined with the weight and impact of a novel.

The stories are all told by Mark Berman, who is six years old in the first story and an adult in the last two stories of the book. A family of Russian Jews who have immigrated to Toronto from Latvia, the Bermans immediately seek to learn the language and customs of their new home, although they are constantly reminded of the differences between themselves and their new neighbors. Initially, only Mark and his cousin Jana are successful in learning English and have to translate for their parents. Even within Toronto's Jewish community, other Jews see them as foreigners.

In the story "Roman Berman, Massage Therapist," Mark's father, Roman, a former weightlifting coach and massage therapist in Latvia, is struggling to open his own massage parlor, having quit his job as a laborer at the chocolate factory. He is told to seek out Kornblum, a rich Jewish man who sometimes helps immigrants. The Bermans attend a dinner party at the Kornblum residence in hopes of gaining Kornblum's aid. Over the course of the evening, however, they realize that Kornblum is more interested in learning how horrible things are in the old country for Jews. Tales of anti-Semitism allow him to wax on about his own life in Canada, and the Bermans realize that Kornblum's help of immigrants serves as an excuse for him to demonstrate his own successes and triumphs.

The early stories portray the difficulty the family has in becoming Canadian. At the same time, however, the Bermans are provided with a number of reminders about how much better off they are in Toronto than they were in the Soviet Union, despite their occasional feelings to the contrary.

In "The Second Strongest Man," Sergei Federenko, a weightlifting champion coached by Roman Berman in Latvia, is participating in an international contest in Toronto, and Roman is asked to be one of the judges. During this time, Roman is approached by the team's KGB supervisor, who wishes help finding a dentist. Although their meetings are innocent enough, they are shrouded with fear caused by the agent's power. "Don't ever forget," Mark's father tells him. "That is why we left. So you never have to know people like him." Later, Sergei is invited to the Bermans' apartment. He has just lost his first-place standing and knows that before long his privileges at home will begin eroding away. Sergei compliments Roman on his great success, and Roman protests, saying, "I'm not lying. Every day is a struggle." Sergei replies, "Look, I'm not blind. I see your car. I see your apartment. I see how you struggle. Believe me, your worst day is better than my best."

Similarly, in "Natasha," an older Mark realizes how much his troubles as a typical sixteen-year-old Canadian pale beside the life lived by the fourteen-year-old Natasha in Moscow. As the title of the story indicates, "Natasha" serves as the centerpiece of the collection. In "Natasha," Bezmozgis intertwines Mark Berman's coming of age—both sexually and emotionally—with the primal survivalism exhibited by Natasha and her mother, Zina. Zina marries Mark's aging bachelor uncle in an arranged marriage as a way of gaining entrance to Canada from Russia; she also brings her fourteen-year-old daughter, Natasha.

Thrown together by the adults, it is not long before Mark understands that Natasha has led a harsh life. As she initiates Mark sexually, Natasha not only informs him that her mother has more or less worked as a prostitute but that she herself has performed in pornographic films. Stuck in teenage doldrums, Mark has befriended drug dealers and is spending most of his time stoned. When events with Natasha finally reach their climax, however, and she runs away to move in with his drug dealer friend Rufus, Mark realizes that, unlike Natasha and Zina, he is free to choose his destiny. After leaving Rufus's house, Mark states, "By the time I got home I had already crafted a new identity. I would switch schools, change my wardrobe, move to another city." He is not shackled by the past.

While still a boy, however, Mark does struggle with the multiple identities thrust upon him. As related in "An Animal to the Memory," he finds it difficult to be Latvian, Jewish, and Canadian all at once and strives, through purposefully bad behavior, to have himself removed from Hebrew School. After an unruly encounter with an enemy on Holocaust Day, he is confronted by Rabbi Gurvich, the headmaster of the school. The rabbi asks him if he is indeed Jewish, given the lack of respect demonstrated by his altercation with the other schoolboy. Mark narrates, "I may have considered myself a tough little bastard, but when Gurvich gripped me I understood that mine was a boy's shoulder and that his was a man's hand. He put his face very close to mine and made me look at him. I could smell the musky staleness of his beard. For the first time, I felt I was going to cry." Gurvich grasps his shoulder harder and harder, forcing him to cry out "I'm a Jew!" over and over. When Mark is finally overwhelmed with fear and thoroughly intimidated by Gurvich, the headmaster releases him, telling him, "Now, Berman . . . now maybe you understand what it is to be a Jew."

As Mark grows older, however, he does become more interested in preserving his heritage. In "Choynski," he is an adult seeking to find everything he can about a Jewish boxer named Joe Choynski, a turn-of-the-twentieth-century contemporary of boxer Jack Johnson. Juxtaposed with Mark's interest in Choynski are his grandmother's fatal illness and the fatal stroke of the boxing expert he befriends, Charlie Davis. Davis's son has no interest in the boxing lore in which his father was so invested, and thus represents a severance with his heritage and past. Similarly, Mark's dying grandmother comes to represent his heritage as a Jew and a Latvian. Although he feels that her passing does not entirely affect him, the story ends with Mark looking for her dentures, which he hopes to place in her grave with her. He loses them in the deep, new fallen snow around the grave, but rather than leaving them there, he cannot stop searching for them; he is conscious that a vital link has gone out of his life and, for the first time, realizes that he cannot surrender his heritage so easily.

The final story in the collection, "Minyan," is a fitting capstone to a book chronicling the complexities of assimilation and Jewish identity. The term "minyan" refers to the requisite number of ten Jewish men who must be present for an orthodox Sabbath service to be held in a synagogue. When Mark's grandfather moves into an assisted living apartment house for elderly Jews, he meets two men who will be his neighbors, Herschel and Itzik, who are also immigrants to Canada. Mark eventually realizes that Herschel and Itzik are homosexual lovers and that the apartment building's residents disapprove of the two. When Itzik dies, the community wishes to drive Herschel out, so that others may have the coveted apartment he had shared with Itzik. Despite the pressures brought to bear, however, the Rabbi Zalman, who runs the building's synagogue, refuses to censure Herschel or influence the building's manager to have him removed; to Zalman, Herschel is a Jew first. His status as a Pole, a Canadian immigrant, and a homosexual all come second. Like Mark, Herschel is a man caught between many worlds at once; like Mark, he can never be quite sure which of his external shells most closely resembles his true internal self.

One of the differences between unified collections such as *Natasha, and Other Stories* and traditional novels is that the canvas is never completely painted. One is not sure how Mark cleaned up his act, attended school, or started a career, and the reader never finds out for sure what happens to his depressive mother or whether his father truly succeeds in his career. At the same time, the images, anecdotes, and portraits presented in these stories, scattered as they are in time and subject matter, present a truer picture of the overall diaspora of Jewish immigrants to North America from the former Soviet Union. It is a tribute to Bezmozgis's gifts that such brief renderings in a short book provide the reader with such an overwhelming effect.

*Scott Yarbrough*

## Review Sources

*Booklist* 100, no. 15 (April 1, 2004): 1345.
*Kirkus Reviews* 72, no. 7 (April 1, 2004): 284.
*Library Journal* 129, no. 5 (March 15, 2004): 109.
*London Review of Books* 26, no. 24 (December 16, 2004): 26.
*The Nation* 279, no. 12 (October 18, 2004): 38.
*The New York Review of Books* 51, no. 14 (September 23, 2004): 75.
*The New York Times*, June 8, 2004, p. E6.
*The New York Times Book Review* 153 (June 27, 2004): 6.
*Publishers Weekly* 251, no. 16 (April 19, 2004): 36.

# NEW AND SELECTED POEMS

*Author:* Michael Ryan (1946-    )
*Publisher:* Houghton Mifflin (Boston). 148 pp. $22.00
*Type of work:* Poetry

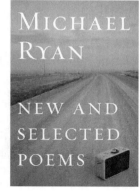

*A fine collection of new and old poems that captures a poet's need to grapple with such human issues as love, loss, death, reconciliation, and forgiveness*

*New and Selected Poems* is Michael Ryan's fourth poetry collection and his first in fifteen years. His debut collection, *Threats Instead of Trees*, was published in 1974 and won the Yale Series for Younger Poets Award. This was an auspicious start for Ryan. The collection also was a finalist for a National Book Award. His second collection, *In Winter*, appeared in 1981 and was a National Poetry Series Selection. Ryan's third collection, *God Hunger*, was published in 1989. The poem "My Dream by Henry James" appeared in this collection. Its opening—"In my dream by Henry James there is a sentence:/'Stay and comfort your sea companion/ for a while,' spoken by an aging man/ to a young one"— introduces characters and moves the story line forward. Ryan has stated that this beginning "made a window I would eventually see the rest of the poem through in language I found compelling." This poem is a fine example of how Ryan takes satisfaction in the melding of language and meaning. *God Hunger* won the 1990 Lenore Marshall Poetry Prize.

Ryan's *New and Selected Poems* includes eleven poems from his first collection, twelve poems from his second, thirty-four from his third, and thirty-one new poems. Most of the new poems previously appeared in such prestigious publications as the *American Poetry Review*, the *Kenyon Review*, *The New Yorker*, *Poetry*, *Slate*, and the *Threepenny Review*. For this volume, Ryan took the time to revise significantly some of the poems that first appeared in his previous collections, especially the poems from *Threats Instead of Trees*. A selected edition like this gives the poet the opportunity to alter the past, to improve what came before. It forces the serious reader to locate the earlier collections in order to do a line-by-line comparison. It is well within the poet's prerogative to change poems from the distant past, but to leave the older poetry alone would have served as a gauge of where the poet began and how he had since grown as a poet.

In such poems as "Speaking" and "Prothalamion," there is a dark tone that touches on the anguish found in loneliness. The poem "Speaking" opens with "I'm speaking again/ as the invalid in the dark room./ I want to say thank you/ out loud to no one." In "Prothalamion," Ryan expresses his uneasiness with a relationship in such lines as "The love we've defined for ourselves/ in privacy, in suffering,/ keeps both of us lonely as a fist. . . . " This theme is revisited in a poem from the collection *In Winter* titled "The Pure Loneliness." The poem opens with "Late at night, when you're so

∽

*Michael Ryan is an award-winning poet and author. He is also a highly acclaimed professor of English and creative writing at the University of California, Irvine.*

∽

lonely,/ your shoulders curl toward the center of your body,/ you call no one and you don't call out./ This is dignity. This is the pure loneliness/ that made Christ think he was God./ This is why lunatics smile at their thoughts." These striking poems fit in well with this new collection, but they may not be a totally accurate representation of the poet's first two poetry volumes. Ryan also has been acclaimed for his autobiography, *Secret Life* (1995), a volume of essays *A Difficult Grace: On Poets, Poetry, and Writing* (2000), and a memoir, *Baby B* (2004).

As Ryan has included so many poems from his third collection, *God Hunger*, a reader must conclude that the poet wishes to be judged more for the poems that he wrote at that stage in his development than any other. Out of the eighty-eight poems included in *New and Selected Poems*, only twenty-three come from his first two books. While craft and the concept of being poetic served Ryan well enough in his first two collections, for *God Hunger* he took his subject matter more directly from life experience. Ryan comes across as a poet attempting to be honest with himself and the reader. In some poems, there can be seen a hard-drinking writer who chases women. At times, there is the misunderstood poet who wonders how he will find his place in the world. The collection is full of life in all of its permutations. Common occurrences and odd events are laid bare before the reader for close examination. While the poems found in *Threats Instead of Trees* have been described as verging on the mannered and in love with ideas, the poems of *God Hunger* take on themes of love and death in a much more direct approach.

For the most part, Ryan has given up on the surreal language that was very evident in his first two collections. Mysteries exist in the everyday for all to discover, for all to unravel in their own way. As a witness to how these everyday events can make an impact on any life, Ryan employs his distinctive poetic voice in order to give a deeper meaning to the seemingly ordinary. In the poem "Not the End of the World," the poet relates the experience of a small bird that mistakenly flies down his chimney. The poem opens with "What flew down the chimney/ into the cold wood stove/ in my study? Wings/ alive inside cast iron/ gave the cold stove a soul/ wilder than fire, in trouble." The poet does his best to recognize what has happened and act accordingly. He wishes to help the "dull brown bird no bigger/ than my fist hopped modestly/ out, twisting its neck like a boxer/ trying to shake off a flush punch." With great care Ryan "scooped" the bird up and "sat it outside on the dirt." He waited to see if the bird would regain its balance and true calling to be a creature of flight. Ryan then attempted to go back to his own life, to the "work I had waiting," but it was impossible to do. In the last stanza of the poem, he confesses that he stayed away "for all of a minute," and in that minute everything changed, in that minute the bird vanished. For the poet, all that remained was "a space so desolate/ that for one moment I saw/ the dead planet." Ryan has filled *God Hunger* with revelations that emerge out of life. He contemplates the tragedy of a friend's suicide, the pain of his own childhood, the impact

of a Bernardo Bertolucci film, and more. He does this in various poetic forms, including free verse, a villanelle, and metrical quatrains.

Ryan continues to explore the human condition with wit and inner resolve in the
thirty-one new poems found in *New and Selected Poems*. He refuses to turn away
from a close examination of the unflattering elements from a person's past. As he sees
it, it is impossible for him to understand fully who he is without coming to terms with
the demons that inhabit his soul. In his 1995 autobiography, *Secret Life*, Ryan details
how he was molested as a child by a neighbor. The honesty with which he faced this
ugly episode has carried over to his poetry. It was necessary for him to shine a light on
the tragedy in order to move forward. For him to grow as a man and as a poet, he had
to face down the demons.

Of the thirty-one new poems, more than half of them are short, with rhyming quatrains. In the poem "Tutelary," the poet talks about how the relationship between father
and child can be a perverse one. The poem opens with "What a fuckup you are./ What
dumbshit you do./ Your father's voice/ still whispers in you,/ despite the joys/ that
sweeten each day." Loved ones can be the worst offenders, can do the most harm to
those closest to them. What some people must endure is poignantly expressed in the
poem "Chronic Severe Incurable." It begins with the lines "There's nothing more you
can learn from pain,/ but here it comes again—with its monotone,/ its idiot drone." The
poem ends with "Pain:/ *payment, penalty, punish, revenge*–/ all these miseries inhering
in the word:/ you must think no word for what you feel./ The being pain is being is you."

While the shorter poems tend to examine the darker sides of the human condition,
the longer poems are free-wheeling and sometimes terrifying. The poem "My Other
Self" has to be considered one of craziest, most hilarious, and scariest poems written
by an American poet. The poem delineates a road trip. A married couple is not traveling alone. They are taking a road trip with other selves, with alter egos, with doubles
who think they know everything. "My Other Self" opens with "He could have
smacked you/ for running out of gas, at midnight,/ in December, in a middle-of-
nowhere place . . . " and ends with "since the next one's got to be the starlet in the
Jaguar/ wrapped in a mink with nothing underneath." Ryan clearly believes in the
power of poetry to illuminate the human condition, to help in piecing together the human jigsaw puzzle. Since the publication of his first collection in 1974, he most certainly has matured as a poet and has grown into a more caring person.

*Jeffry Jensen*

## Review Sources

*Atlanta Journal and Constitution*, April 18, 2004, p. M4.
*Library Journal* 129, no. 5 (March 15, 2004): 82.
*Los Angeles Times Book Review*, April 11, 2004, p. 13.
*The New York Times Book Review* 153 (May 2, 2004): 22.
*Publishers Weekly* 251, no. 17 (April 26, 2004): 58.

# A NEW WORLD ORDER

*Author:* Anne-Marie Slaughter
*Publisher:* Princeton University Press (Princeton, N.J.).
   341 pp. $30.00
*Type of work:* Current affairs
*Time:* The late twentieth and early twenty-first centuries

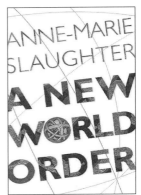

*A scholar of international relations (and international law) describes an ongoing, radical transformation in the way nation states relate to one another, a transformation which offers new global opportunities for more effective problem solving, lasting peace, and enhanced justice*

In *A New World Order*, Anne-Marie Slaughter gives a detailed account of global politics in transformation. Slaughter, who holds a law degree as well as a Ph.D in international relations, describes a world in which the predominance of unitary nation states is being complemented, and perhaps even partly supplanted, by a system of multiple networks in which disaggregated nation states (that is, agencies and branches within national governments, as opposed to heads of state) interact cooperatively with one another as well as with international organizations. Because news media and other observers remain geared to the highly visible and more easily interpreted actions of unitary governments, the great abundance and rich variety of international ventures at the disaggregated level falls below the radar for most of the public and even for some experts on global politics.

This is unfortunate, according to Slaughter, for a number of reasons. On the most basic level, it leads to a distorted view of how international relations really works and is likely to develop as the twenty-first century unfolds. It also keeps observers from seeing the most likely solution to what Slaughter calls "the globalization paradox," that is, the condition of "needing more [world] government and [at the same time] fearing it." At present, debate about the issue of world governance tends to pit national sovereignty versus world government. As such, it conceptualizes little or no middle ground between an anarchic, conflict-laden system of sovereign nation states battling each other for predominance, on the one hand, and the specter of an autocratic, hyperbureaucratic, and essentially undemocratic unitary world government, on the other. In the emergence of numerous cooperative international relationships at the disaggregated level, Slaughter sees the possibility of highly effective world governance without the dangers associated with a unitary world government. She also thinks that such a system can, ultimately, enhance world justice. As a result, Slaughter believes that the transformation she describes should not only be better understood but also actually encouraged for the sake of the entire global community.

After an introduction in which Slaughter gives a concise road map to her main arguments, three chapters give a detailed look at the types of international cooperation that are radically transforming the world system. Slaughter begins in chapter 1 by describing numerous efforts in the field of government regulation. In the fields of global trade and finance, the environment, and law enforcement, among others, the regulators of different nations are becoming more and more interdependent. This is true in terms of public policy making, in cases where national interests overlap; and also the sharing of information, in cases where nations face common problems. Slaughter describes such regulators as "the new diplomats" and reports that the volume of such interaction is already substantially large and continually growing.

In the second chapter, Slaughter describes the interactions of judges and lawyers from around the world in constructing a global legal system. This includes the making of provisions for orderly and authoritative transnational litigation as well as laying the basis for global standards (and enforcement) in the area of human rights, an area in which Slaughter herself is expert. In the third chapter, she describes the, as yet underdeveloped, interactions of national legislative bodies. She also suggests the route that greater cooperation between legislatures might take. In chapter 4, Slaughter discusses the totality of these developments as constituting a newly emergent "disaggregated world order," one which differs significantly from the system of unitary nation states that has previously been predominant. More specifically, she distinguishes between the "horizontal" and "vertical" dimensions of this new world order, horizontal referring to interaction between government officials of different nations, vertical referring to interactions between such officials and international organizations with some measure of coercive power.

While Slaughter sees the need for both the horizontal and vertical dimensions, she does point out that an excess of vertical interactions can threaten national sovereignty and also lead to counterproductive national competition for influence over international organizations. Slaughter then moves on in chapter 5 to the argument that this new world order is more effective (in terms of solving international problems) than the old, and that, if consciously cultivated, it can be made more effective still. Thus, the disaggregated world order is not only treated as an emergent reality but also as a desirable goal which will make for more successful efforts to deal with global problems as disparate as terrorism and environmental pollution. Implicit in this claim is the dream of an eventual lasting world peace. Presumably, as cooperation and interdependence between disaggregated nation states becomes more and more routine, it becomes less likely that nations will want, or even be in a position, to go to war with one another.

*Anne-Marie Slaughter is dean of the Woodrow Wilson School of Public and International Affairs at Princeton University and president of the American Society of International Law. She holds a Ph.D in International Relations from Oxford University and a law degree from Harvard University. Slaughter has worked on collaborative efforts to formulate procedures by which war criminals can be brought to justice before international courts. She is coeditor of* The European Courts and National Courts: Doctrine and Jurisprudence *(1997) and has written numerous scholarly articles and op-ed pieces on the global transformation described in* A New World Order *as well as on related topics.*

In chapter 6, Slaughter goes further, making what is, perhaps, her boldest claim. She argues that the newly emerging world order she describes may well not only be more effective but also more just. Interestingly, this normative (that is, morally prescriptive) chapter is also the book's most tentative, indicating that Slaughter is well aware of the complexities involved in defining (and actualizing) justice, on the domestic as well as on the international level. This includes dealing with the tricky relationships between global prescriptions, national sovereignty, and cultural diversity. Slaughter's own conception of justice in this book centers on procedural democracy and human rights. While she clearly recognizes the existence in the world of haves and have-nots, in terms both of wealth and political clout, these inequalities are not the focal point of "justice" as discussed in this book. A brief conclusion wraps the book up.

There are certain undeniable appeals to *A New World Order*. The book is supremely well organized, and Slaughter provides a rich account of the sort of changes that are taking place as well as those she would like to see take place in the future. The book is also sure to provoke discussion, which is one of the things a good book is supposed to do.

That is not to say that all of the discussion of this book will be positive. For one thing, the prose is somewhat typical of books treating thorny issues in social science, which is to say the style is turgid and, on occasion, a bit difficult for nonspecialists to penetrate. In terms of the book's substance, Slaughter has stepped on the toes of too many ideologues of one stripe or another to avoid criticism. True believers in the free market may well see Slaughter's presentation as overrating the ability of governments to act efficiently in pursuit of public goods, either on the domestic or international level. Avid critics of world government probably will not be assuaged by the fact that the massive international cooperation envisioned by Slaughter will be decentralized, instead seeing an equally daunting threat to national sovereignty. They may also see the complex web of activity described by Slaughter as a mere stepping stone to unitary world government. Avid opponents of globalization will note that Slaughter offers little, if any, antidote to the hegemonic powers of the stronger nation states or the economic might of multinational corporations. Globalization supporters, on the other hand, may well disagree with Slaughter's emphasis on the need for a complex web of government regulations, as opposed to a more spontaneous, business oriented perspective.

Read carefully, Slaughter's book provides sensible answers to the objections raised in the previous paragraph. There are, however, two difficulties that are less well addressed in her book. For one thing, Slaughter actually describes a hybrid system, with vestiges of the unitary nation state system clearly still predominant, for example, when nations engage in high diplomacy and when, diplomacy failing, they go to war. Slaughter is aware of the potential for conflict between the unitary and disaggregated systems, and, in particular, the danger that, instead of the disaggregated world order leading to lasting peace, warring states will disrupt the emerging network of international cooperation. She does not, however, offer a satisfying discussion of the problem.

A second nagging difficulty with *A New World Order* is that the chapter on global justice does not measure up to the rest of the book. Throughout most of the text, Slaughter does an impressive job of balancing her realistic description of what exists against her idealistic (and pleasingly optimistic) account of what could and should exist in the future. In the section on justice, however, Slaughter is decidedly unrealistic, basing her hopes for a more just world on voluntary national compliance with several principles related to the maintenance of democratic procedure and the preservation of human rights. This seems uncharacteristically naïve on Slaughter's part. She also, for some observers, will fall short on the idealistic side as well, because, as mentioned above, she does not substantially address issues of global (or, for that matter, domestic) equality. In connection with this, Slaughter's discussion of justice appears to be largely oblivious to the most acute suffering going on in the global community, with many millions of people struggling to survive the ordeals of starvation, disease, or political oppression. For many readers, this sort of misery is what comes immediately to mind when the issue of global justice arises. Slaughter's other writings make it clear that she, too, is concerned with these issues, and that, in all likelihood, she sees the disaggregated world order as a pragmatically possible beginning point in the quest for a world system in which all people can enjoy the fruits of global prosperity as well as social and political justice.

*A New World Order* would be an even better book than it is if the link between Slaughter's incremental procedural goals and those of substantive justice were made more explicitly. As it stands, Slaughter's discussion of justice is bloodless and unconvincing. Still, this is a highly worthwhile book, one which provides a wealth of information about the rapidly changing world as well as hope for a better future. As such, it deserves to be widely read and discussed.

*Ira Smolensky*

## Review Sources

*Foreign Affairs* 83, no. 3 (May/June, 2004): 136.
*Perspectives on Political Science* 33, no. 3 (Summer, 2004): 182.
*Publishers Weekly* 251, no. 6 (February 9, 2004): 72.

# NIGHTINGALES
## The Extraordinary Upbringing and Curious Life of
## Miss Florence Nightingale

*Author:* Gillian Gill (1942-   )
*Publisher:* Ballantine Books (New York). 535 pp. $28.00
*Type of work:* Biography
*Time:* The eighteenth and early nineteenth centuries
*Locale:* England and the Crimea

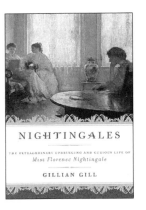

*The intimate story of the life of an influential and controversial public figure, explored through the complex relationships of her extended family and the Victorian era*

*Principal personages:*
> FLORENCE NIGHTINGALE, nurse, hospital reformer, and philanthropist
> WILLIAM SMITH, her maternal grandfather
> MARTHA FRANCES SMITH, her "Aunt Patty"
> WILLIAM EDWARD NIGHTINGALE (WEN), Florence's father, born W. E. Shore
> FRANCES SMITH NIGHTINGALE (FANNY), Florence's mother
> MAI SHORE SMITH, WEN's sister and Florence's favorite aunt
> PARTHENOPE NIGHTINGALE, Florence's older sister
> MARY CLARKE (CLARKEY), Florence's close friend in Paris
> SELINA (SIGMA) and CHARLES BRACEBRIDGE, friends of Florence
> SIDNEY HERBERT, secretary at war and Florence's friend

Biographies of Florence Nightingale have focused on her roles as the heroine of the Crimean War, the organizer of public health reforms, or the founder of modern nursing. What makes this biography different is its focus on Nightingale's multigenerational extended family and the intricate relationships within the Nightingale-Shore-Smith-Nicholson-Bonham Carter clan. Gillian Gill re-creates the Victorian era and the world in which Nightingale lived for modern readers and, in keeping with the subtitle of the book, *The Extraordinary Upbringing and Curious Life of Miss Florence Nightingale*, depicts Nightingale's life as an engaging drama of the Victorian era, rather like a Jane Austen novel.

Gill begins the introduction in storybook fashion in 1849, when Nightingale is twenty-nine, with her rejection of Richard Monckton Milne, her suitor for more than six years. She cared for Richard, who was popular and well connected, but "she dreamed of becoming a nurse, of developing nursing as a profession for educated, dedicated, capable young women like herself, of making Britain a healthier, safer, happier place for all its citizens, of reassessing and rebuilding the whole system of health care in public institutions."

Gill explores the serious financial and social consequences of Nightingale's decision. Her father, WEN, born William Edward Shore, had inherited the lands and estate of his great-uncle Peter Nightingale through an entail, thereafter taking the name of Nightingale. Florence's only sister, Parthenope, was a chronic invalid and unlikely to marry. With no prospect of a male heir in the family, the Nightingale assets (including two large estates—Lea Hurst in Derbyshire and Embley Park in Hampshire) could not be left to his wife or children because they were females. Upon WEN's death, the property would pass to his sister Mai, and after her death, to her son, leaving WEN's wife and two daughters without a home. The Nightingale entail and Florence's refusal to marry troubled the entire family.

*Gillian Gill is a Ph.D. in modern French literature from Cambridge University and has taught at Northeastern, Wellesley, Yale, and Harvard Universities. She is the author of* Agatha Christie: The Woman and Her Mysteries *(1990) and* Mary Baker Eddy *(1998).*

The chief protagonists—WEN, Nightingale's doting father; Fanny, her mother; and her sister, Parthenope—could not understand her desire to enter nursing. Given the inferior social position of women and the low status of nursing in nineteenth century England, it was a radical notion for an upper-class, educated young woman to want to nurse. Ironically, the Nightingale family history and their social connections with the English aristocracy contributed to Nightingale's decision and to her extraordinary place in history.

Nightingale's mother's family, the Smiths, were a fascinating family of dissenters and Unitarians who were opposed to the Church of England and suffered social and political discrimination. Florence's grandfather, William Smith, was a prominent member of the merchant class from the industrial Midlands. In addition to his country home in Essex, he owned a London townhouse, had a library of more than one thousand volumes and an extensive art collection that included three works by Rembrandt and paintings by Joshua Reynolds and Thomas Gainsborough. Smith helped found the National Gallery. Even though it was not in his own financial interests, he was opposed to slavery and became a member of the House of Commons, where he was known as a strong abolitionist and advocate for civil rights for religious minorities.

The Smiths had ten children—five girls and five boys—and, by all accounts, were a happy family. They loved strenuous hiking holidays and were accustomed to braving the rough roads and travel conditions of the day. The Smith women were strong nonconformists and well-educated by the standards of the day. Nightingale was strongly influenced by her "Aunt Patty" (Martha Frances), the oldest child, and "Aunt Ju" (Julia), the youngest, who were radical spirits, independent early feminists, and unorthodox volunteers and activists. Although Nightingale was a conventional Victorian with reservations about her aunts' fervent idealism, she too was a nonconformist and, like her Aunt Patty, was to become a confirmed spinster and hypochondriac. (Nightingale took to her bed after a debilitating illness in the Crimea and was a recluse for almost fifty years.)

Nightingale's Aunt Anne married a wealthy man, George Nicholson of Waverley. Another aunt, Joanna, married John Carter, who came into a large inheritance from his bachelor cousin John Bonham and became John Bonham Carter.

When William Smith suffered severe business losses and had to sell everything to meet his debts, his daughter Fanny was fortunate to marry William Edward Nightingale (WEN), a wealthy Unitarian. During an extended honeymoon in Italy, their daughter, Parthenope, was born in 1819, and Florence was born in the city of her name in 1820. WEN's sister, Mary Shore ("Aunt Mai"), married Fanny's brother, Samuel, and became Florence's devoted friend and protector. (William's sons Benjamin and Octavius became independently wealthy businessmen. Another son, William Adams, was something of a "black sheep" and never married, and the youngest son, Frederick, went to India when his father's business crashed.)

These families—the Nicholsons, the Bonham Carters, and the Smiths—were Nightingale's social support system, and she and her sister had frequent contact with twenty-five cousins while growing up. They corresponded, visited one another, traveled together, and cared for one another. Nightingale frequently "escaped" to their homes when the expectations of her mother and the demands of her emotionally dependent sister became oppressive. There were passionate friendships between Nightingale and some of her cousins—male and female—leading some biographers to suspect that Nightingale was a lesbian. Gill refutes this charge—passionate, but chaste, friendships were common in Victorian times.

WEN was a devoted father and educated his daughters himself from 1831 to 1839, Nightingale's happiest years. He gave her intellectual self-confidence. When she was seventeen, the Nightingale family made an extended tour of Europe and called on Mary Clarke ("Clarkey"), who organized an intellectual salon in Paris and would marry Julius Mohl, the leading Orientalist of his day. "Clarkey" and Florence became steadfast friends. During this year, Florence experienced a call to serve God, but it was not until 1844 that she realized hospital work was to be her calling. It would be several years before her family gave up their resistance to her ambitions.

After returning to England in May, 1839, the girls were presented at court. Fanny was a prominent hostess, and the Nightingales' circle of friends included the reformers Lord Palmerston, the future prime minister, and Lord Ashley, the future Lord Shaftesbury. From them Florence gained invaluable political connections and learned to network and form alliances to reach her goals. Lord Shaftesbury supplied Florence with reports about hospitals and public health that she meticulously analyzed, while managing the considerable housekeeping tasks of her family's estate helped her to develop the organizational skills she would later use in her hospital work.

Although brilliant and entertaining at social functions, Nightingale hated her superficial life. The constant conflicts within her family as she tried to resist traditional roles made everyone miserable. She secretly learned everything she could about health care, and whenever there was a birth or anyone in the family was sick or be-reaved, Nightingale was there to provide comfort and care. She loved her visits to Grandmother Mary Evans Shore and Great-Aunt Elizabeth Evans at Lea Hurst, the family home in the Midlands. There she became aware of the great gap between the rich and the poor, organized evening classes for mill women, gained experience in nursing the sick among them, and came to respect their strength and independence. (Later this work helped Nightingale to establish rapport with nonofficer patients in the Crimean War hospitals and contributed to her egalitarian nursing policies.)

In 1846, "Sigma" and Charles Holte Bracebridge became Nightingale's most in-fluential and supportive friends, and she was permitted to accompany them to Italy (1847-1848). There she became friends with Elizabeth and Sidney Herbert, the future secretary at war, and Mary Stanley (a friend who would infuriate her by challenging her role in the Crimea and bringing another group of nurses there.) She was again al-lowed to travel with the Bracebridges in 1949-1950 to Egypt and Greece and Ger-many. In Germany, she visited hospitals and spent two weeks at Kaiserswerth, a reli-gious institution that trained lay deaconesses to serve the poor.

Nightingale was euphoric, but her mother was enraged and demanded that she de-vote herself to her sister, an invalid. Only when she was called on to help Aunt Mai nurse her Great-Aunt Evans was she relieved of this duty. Finally, her loving care dur-ing her father's battle with blindness gained his active support, and in the summer of 1851, she was allowed to train at Kaiserswerth. In 1853 Clarkey and Julius Mohl ar-ranged for her to visit public medical facilities in Paris, but her work was cut short when she was needed to care for her Grandmother Shore. WEN was touched by all she had done for his mother, and in 1853, with his blessing, she became the superin-tendent of Harley Street Hospital for Gentlewomen, where she did a remarkable job of improving conditions.

In October, 1854, Herbert, the secretary at war, asked Nightingale to be "superin-tendent of the female nursing establishment in the English General Military Hospitals in Turkey" and take a group of nurses to the Crimea. Newspaper reports had made the mismanagement of the war and terrible suffering of the wounded known to the British public. Accompanied by her good friends the Bracebridges, Nightingale accepted the challenge. She was made into a national heroine by the press and "the Lady with the Lamp" was front-page news for twenty-one months.

Nightingale's attempts to improve the deplorable conditions in army hospitals, de-spite the resistance from the medical authorities, are legendary. The soldiers loved her, the public idolized her, and her criticisms inspired a government investigation of conditions in the military. Following her collapse from so-called Crimean fever and long recuperation in Scutari, she returned to England and enjoyed a popularity rival-ing that of Queen Victoria.

Nightingale became a recluse, but through correspondence and meetings with gov-ernment officials she worked unceasingly from her bed and used her enormous popu-larity to improve the status of nursing and bring about better sanitation and care in army hospitals. Her post-Crimea reforms and influence on nursing were probably her greatest contribution. To everyone's surprise, Parthenope married, and her husband,

Sir Harry Verney, promoted Florence Nightingale's health and sanitary measures in Parliament.

Gill's account is balanced. Nightingale was not an angel—she could be self-pitying, extremely critical, unforgiving, and ungrateful—but she was an extraordinary woman who had a significant impact on her time and future generations.

For all its romantic nuances and Victorian tone, reminiscent of Judith Martin's Miss Manners columns, this is a scholarly, well-researched biography. It includes a genealogy chart that makes the complex history of this big, affluent, close-knit family easier to follow, sixteen pages of photographs, and copious chapter notes. There are extensive quotations from diaries and numerous letters, including those from the uncataloged archives at Nightingale's sister Parthenope's home. More than ten thousand Florence Nightingale letters survive; she kept drafts of many of her own letters. They provide accounts of her travels, valuable information abut her thoughts and feelings, and details of painful events, which may have helped Nightingale cope with grief.

*Edna B. Quinn*

## Review Sources

*Booklist* 100, no. 21 (July 1, 2004): 1808.
*Entertainment Weekly*, September 3, 2004, p. 79.
*Kirkus Reviews* 72, no. 12 (June 15, 2004): 567.
*Library Journal* 129, no. 12 (July 15, 2004): 92.
*Ms.* 14, no. 3 (Fall, 2004): 90.
*The New York Times Book Review* 154 (October 24, 2004): 8.
*Publishers Weekly* 251, no. 24 (June 14, 2004): 52.

# THE 9/11 COMMISSION REPORT
## Final Report of the National Commission on Terrorist Attacks upon the United States

*Author:* National Commission on Terrorist Attacks upon the United States
*Publisher:* W. W. Norton (New York). 604 pp. $20.00
*Type of work:* Current affairs
*Time:* 1992-2001
*Locale:* New York City, Washington, D.C., and Pennsylvania

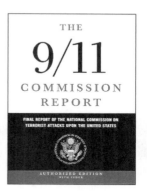

*The official U.S. government version of events surrounding the terrorist attacks of September 11, 2001*

Principal personages:
GEORGE W. BUSH, the forty-third president of the United States
RICHARD CLARKE, national counterterrorism coordinator from 1997 to 2001
CONDOLEEZZA RICE, Bush's national security adviser
BILL CLINTON, the forty-second president of the United States
MOHAMMED ATTA, the tactical leader of the terrorist attacks of September 11, 2001
OSAMA BIN LADEN, the head of al-Qaeda
KHALID SHEIKH MOHAMMED, the mastermind of the September 11 attacks

On the morning of September 11, 2001, the United States experienced the most devastating and deadly homeland attack in its history. Millions watched as two jet airliners slammed into the towers of the World Trade Center. Plane crashes also occurred at the Pentagon and in a rural Pennsylvania field. Americans at first were stunned and angry but soon became resolute in finding and punishing the individuals who masterminded these attacks. Many questions remained. How could this have happened, given the heightened level of security throughout the summer of 2001? How could armed hijackers gain access to commercial airliners so easily? Why did the Federal Bureau of Investigation (FBI) and the Central Intelligence Agency (CIA) overlook or ignore obvious warning signs of an impending attack?

At the urging of the loved ones of the victims of the attack, the independent, bipartisan National Commission on Terrorist Attacks upon the United States, better known as the 9/11 Commission, was created by Congress. Putting partisan politics aside and guided by the strong and steady leadership of chairman Thomas H. Kean, the ten commissioners succeeded in presenting a fair and comprehensive account. The official public report was released on July 22, 2004, and was made available through the Government Printing Office and bookstores.

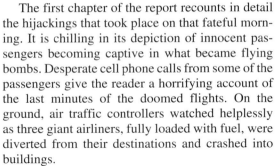

*The 9/11 Commission consisted of five Democrats and five Republicans chosen by Congress. Thomas H. Kean, former governor of New Jersey, chaired the committee. Lee H. Hamilton, former congressman from Indiana, was vice chairman.*

The first chapter of the report recounts in detail the hijackings that took place on that fateful morning. It is chilling in its depiction of innocent passengers becoming captive in what became flying bombs. Desperate cell phone calls from some of the passengers give the reader a horrifying account of the last minutes of the doomed flights. On the ground, air traffic controllers watched helplessly as three giant airliners, fully loaded with fuel, were diverted from their destinations and crashed into buildings.

Meanwhile, brave passengers on United Airlines Flight 93 struggled to subdue hijackers and gain control of the plane. There is no doubt that if they had not attempted to defeat their attackers, the White House or the Capitol building would have been hit. Although Air Force jet fighters could have scrambled to find Flight 93 in an effort to shoot it down, they would have arrived too late. As was later revealed, air traffic controllers did not know the exact location of the plane until after it had crashed in a field in rural Pennsylvania. The male and female passengers and crew of Flight 93 will forever be remembered as heroes.

To understand the motivation for these attacks, the commission chronicled the rise of the al-Qaeda movement and its shadowy leader, Osama bin Laden. As far back as 1992, Muslim extremists' hatred of the United States encouraged them to declare a jihad, or holy war, against the United States. Hiding out in the rugged mountains of Afghanistan, bin Laden set up training camps for terrorists and convinced many to join the cause. The U.S. government was well aware of bin Laden and the threat he posed to Americans, but most security analysts in Washington were more concerned about attacks against American interests overseas than those on American soil.

It was not until 1996 that the U.S. government realized that bin Laden was the inspiration and organizer of what the commission called the "new terrorism," meaning that such groups were not known before. When it became evident that bin Laden was not only the spiritual leader of the movement but also was actively seeking and training recruits, efforts were made by the CIA and other agencies to track his movements, freeze his assets, and eventually attempt to capture or kill him.

In August of 1998, however, bin Laden struck first, bombing U.S. embassies in Kenya and Tanzania. An all-out effort to find bin Laden and bring him to justice would prove frustrating and ultimately unsuccessful. As far back as December 4, 1998, President Bill Clinton was warned in an intelligence briefing that bin Laden was planning attacks on the United States, including the hijacking of airplanes. The lack of specific information made it extremely difficult to prepare or respond, but clearly America was in danger.

It is now known that the October 12, 2000, attack on the American Navy destroyer USS *Cole*, which killed seventeen crew members, was a full-fledged al-Qaeda operation, with the target having been selected by bin Laden himself. The question for the United States was how to respond. Several attempts to kill bin Laden either were deemed to be too risky or were called off at the last minute, to the frustration of many in the government. Several times it appeared that there was a reasonable chance of killing or capturing bin Laden, but such opportunities were lost.

The next chapters chronicle the movements of the hijackers as they begin to prepare, two years in advance, for the attacks. The 2003 capture and interrogation of Khalid Sheikh Mohammed, mastermind of the September 11 attacks, reveals that he was considering another attack on the World Trade Center (which had been bombed in 1993) as early as 1995. It was his idea to abandon the idea of hijacking and hostage taking in favor of suicide flight missions that would involve crashing into buildings. With the blessing of bin Laden, planning began in earnest in 1998.

The inclusion of biographies of the men who carried out the attacks provide insight into their motivations. Most came from poor families and led troubled lives when they were young. Collectively, they had little success in education or careers. Radical Islam fueled their hatred for Western values and for the United States in particular. All were eager for what they considered revenge.

So many warning signs, which appear obvious in hindsight, failed to capture the attention of authorities. Several of the hijackers took lessons at various American flight schools, telling their instructors they were not interested in learning how to take off and land jet aircraft, only in flying and navigating them. Many traveled in and out of the country with falsified passports, for which only one potential terrorist was apprehended. A plot to blow up Los Angeles International Airport on the eve of the new millennium was nearly successful and was averted only by a border agent's alertness. In the summer of 2001, U.S. security personnel were alerted by increased cell phone activity between known al-Qaeda operatives as well as a direct threat from bin Laden himself that an attack on the United States was imminent. Most within the government were convinced that if an attack came, it would most likely be overseas or possibly a domestic airplane hijacking followed by a hostage situation. All U.S. embassies, as well as overseas military installations, were placed on high alert.

Part of the problem was the change within the White House. The 2000 election was in dispute for more than a month, shortening the typical transition period for a new president. The organizing of the George W. Bush administration took away some of the momentum of the fight against terrorism; new staffers had to be briefed and trained and President Bush needed to form his own strategy for combating international terror.

The only person who recognized the imminent danger was Richard Clarke, the National Counterterrorism Coordinator, who served in both the Clinton and Bush administrations. A month before the attacks, Clarke made an impassioned plea to Bush's staff, warning them not to get bogged down in what he called bureaucratic inertia. "Decision makers should imagine themselves on a future day when the CSG [Counterterrorism Security Group] has not succeeded in stopping al Qida [sic] attacks and hundreds of Americans lay dead in several countries, including the US," Clark wrote in a memo to Condoleezza Rice, Bush's national security adviser. Unfortunately, Clarke was written off as being "obsessed" with bin Laden and was characterized as being an alarmist. Clarke's warnings would turn out to be frightfully accurate.

At the heart of the government's intelligence problem was a serious breakdown in communication. The lack of shared information between the FBI and the CIA allowed many obvious clues to go unnoticed until it was too late. In addition, airline security proved to be woefully inadequate.

In a chapter appropriately titled "Heroism and Horror," the commission chronicles the events at "Ground Zero"—the World Trade Center—on that awful day. The firefighters and police officers who responded to the distress calls had no idea of the incredible horror that faced them. In spite of the magnitude of the attack, they climbed stairways to rescue as many people as they could, unaware that both towers would soon collapse. Communication by radio contact made it difficult for rescuers to send and receive information. Orders given over the public address system to office workers, other employees, and visitors was contradictory, advising people either to evacuate or to stay in their offices; such instructions may have cost precious time and lives. Meanwhile, firefighters at the Pentagon battled flames and were informed (wrongly) that a possible second plane was headed their way, forcing an evacuation of the entire building.

The narrative is compelling, inspiring, horrifying, and sad. In attempting to explain the events of September 11, the commission did a thorough and commendable job. The background information relating to the history of terrorist groups in the Afghan region places the events in an important and informative context.

What was deemed most important, at the conclusion of this report, was to make specific recommendations. First and foremost among those was a recommendation to continue to disrupt terrorist networks. Cooperation with other countries, particularly Afghanistan, Pakistan, and Saudi Arabia, is crucial in this regard. In addition, the United States needs to provide a moral example to the world. Muslim countries should be encouraged to reject extremism and work with the United States to create a safer world. It is also extremely important that groups such as al-Qaeda not gain access to weapons of mass destruction, which they would most surely attempt to unleash on the United States. Security of U.S. borders, airports, and seaports must be upgraded. In order to unify the antiterrorism initiatives, the commission recommended a reorganization of government agencies to expedite the flow of information and "see the enemy as a whole." This would include rebuilding the CIA and the FBI.

This book stands as the official account of a day that changed America forever. As with many historical tragedies of this magnitude, the complete story of the causes and events may never be brought to light. What the report provides is an opportunity to understand, reflect, mourn, and plan for the future. To those who will never forget September 11, 2001, this book will stand as a stark reminder and a cautionary tale. For those too young to remember or those yet to be born, it can be read as a timeless account of a day, as the commissioners put it, of "unprecedented shock and suffering."

*Raymond Frey*

## Review Sources

*The Economist* 372 (August 7, 2004): 69.
*Foreign Affairs* 83, no. 6 (November/December, 2004): 149.
*The New York Review of Books* 51, no. 14 (September 23, 2004): 6.
*The New York Times*, October 24, 2004, p. 21.
*Progressive* 68, no. 9 (September, 2004): 45.
*Publishers Weekly* 251, no. 33 (August 16, 2004): 56.
*Time* 164, no. 5 (August 2, 2004): 60.

# NOTHING LOST

*Author:* John Gregory Dunne (1932-2003)
*Publisher:* Alfred A. Knopf (New York). 335 pp. $25.00
*Type of work:* Novel
*Time:* 2003
*Locale:* The Midwestern United States

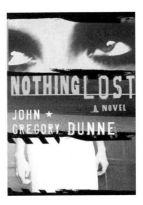

*The brutal torture and murder of a black man in the American Midwest provokes a national response that brings a collection of malignant types out of the cultural woodwork and exposes some long-kept secrets*

Principal characters:
> MAX CLINE, a former state district attorney, suddenly thrust into the legal spotlight once more
> TERESA KEAN, a former victim's rights advocate who defends a pair of indefensible killers and hires Cline to assist her
> J. J. MCCLURE, the assistant district attorney assigned to prosecute the murder case
> POPPY MCCLURE, the district attorney's neoconservative wife, who harbors aspirations to be governor
> EDGAR PARLANCE, the African American victim of an apparent hate crime

*Nothing Lost* opens with its end—"That is the end of the story. Or almost the end. I'm not sure I'm the one who should be telling it, but if I don't, nobody will, so what the hell"—and then orbits recent events in American history. The plot revolves around the mutilation and murder of an itinerant black man in a Great Plains state called South Midland.

The gruesomeness of the murder catapults those involved into the national spotlight, as one figure after another seeks to take advantage of the death. Max Cline, the narrator, is an outsider drawn into the vortex of swirling events. Once a deputy state district attorney, Cline is forced out of office for "lifestyle differences" (he is gay). Teresa Kean is hired as lead defense counsel by Carlyle, a teenage model who is the half sister of one of the defendants. Cline is then asked to join the defense team.

The narrative now veers off to tell a number of different stories—that of Kean's past; her romantic involvement with the prosecutor, J. J. McClure, during the trial, which results in her disbarment; Carlyle's machinations to use the trial to her professional advantage; and the secret history of victim Edgar Parlance, also known as Wonderman. The array of incidents is dizzying, as motives and identities veer off in all directions. Underscoring the often bewildering array of characters and events is the collagelike narrative method, emphasizing parallel stories as multiple narrators take whole sections of the novel.

Reading any of John Gregory Dunne's novels is a vertiginous experience, for his

works inevitably blend fiction with the historical record. His method, however, is something
more destabilizing than simple historical fiction.
With Dunne, fiction challenges—even competes
with—history until the familiar is rendered utterly unfamiliar. The quintessential example of
this method is *True Confessions* (1977), his first
novel, which swirls around the grisly 1947 Los
Angeles slaying known as the Black Dahlia murder. That novel is equal parts social commentary
on Irish American life and the novelist's attempt
to solve an insoluble mystery.

Similarly, *Nothing Lost* oscillates wildly between the fictional and late-twentieth century social history. The central event, the killing of a
black man in a small town in the middle of the
United States, is starkly reminiscent of the Texas

*John Gregory Dunne began his
career as a journalist for* Time
*magazine and became associated
with the New Journalism movement
of the 1960's. Besides screenplays
written with his wife, Joan Didion,
Dunne published nonfiction, the
most startling of which was* The
Studio *(1969), an exposé of the film
industry. His best-remembered
novel is* True Confessions *(1977),
which chronicled the lives of Irish
American brothers set on a collision
course with disaster. Dunne died
suddenly of a heart attack in 2003.*

murder in June, 1998, of James Byrd, Jr., by three white men, one a former convict.
Byrd's body was dragged three miles behind a truck. The character Edgar Parlance
has his tongue cut out and is skinned alive before his death.

Byrd's funeral, like that of Parlance in the story, drew glaring media attention,
with basketball star Dennis Rodman paying for a burial attended by the Reverends
Jesse Jackson and Al Sharpton. In the novel, a player named Jamal Jefferson pays for
Parlance's interment and inveigles the National Basketball Association (NBA) to establish a memorial award for racial tolerance. Both funerals are spectacles for publicity hounds and grasping politicians. In Dunne's hands, the glitter of celebrity of whatever stripe is always tinged with something darker and unfailingly mendacious.

Dunne began his writing career as a journalist, and his concerns with social issues,
racial injustice, and American current events have remained unabated through all of his
articles and books. In *Nothing Lost* he is particularly interested in the "culture wars,"
showing that they have far less to do with culture and the health and future of the United
States than with bare-knuckled combat. At the center of these debates in the novel is
Congresswoman (or as she prefers, "Congress*man*") Poppy McClure, who regularly
appears on news programs as a resident talking head and self-appointed social engineer. Her methods are aggressive and destructive, and her motives are predictably
self-serving and intensely focused: She lusts after the governorship of South Midland.

The novel's title—taken from a passage in Robert Penn Warren's *All the King's Men*
(1946)—can refer not only to the secrets the characters try to hide but also to the premise of
any social critic: Everything deserves consideration and should be uncovered. The
phrase is also reminiscent of Henry James's famous dictum that a novelist is someone on
whom nothing is lost. All interpretations apply to narrator Cline and novelist Dunne.

As critic and novelist, Dunne delights in peeking behind comforting social bro-
mides, and the satirist in him excoriates the United States' cannibal culture. This is a
social milieu that delights in human vulnerability and finds its sport intruding into

others' personal lives, which explains, in part, Cline's disinclination to reveal much about his relationship with Dr. Stanley Poindexter, his companion.

Most of the novel's characters are animated by purely venal aspirations of self-aggrandizement, and perhaps the most nakedly selfish and self-involved is seventeen-year-old model Carlyle, half sister of one of the accused killers. A multimillion dollar industry figure and a creature brimming with self-importance, she cannot imagine anything more compelling than her own ever-changing appetites and whims. As if she does not already have enough exposure and attention, she uses her half brother's arrest and trial as an opportunity to splash her name across front pages by underwriting his defense, appearing at the trial, and publishing a collection of local-color photographs with her face in the foreground.

The media, who turn all embarrassment and tragedy into a carnival, are like piranha in search of fresh blood. They are quick to elevate sadists to grim celebrities and to tear down the reputation of an attorney who spent her professional life working on behalf of those without resources or advantages. Dunne's treatment is hardly revelatory, but the relish he takes in exposing such unscrupulousness gives the novel much of its wild energy.

Basketball player Jefferson, who lunges into the spotlight and plays up his altruism, is another in the novel's cavalcade of frauds. Like so many professional athletes, Jefferson's lucrative promotion contract with a sporting goods firm, headed by an executive who is also a Hollywood investor, lands the athlete a potential starring role in a film about Parlance's life. With the possible exceptions of Cline and Kean, all the characters in the novel are on the take or out to advance themselves.

One of Dunne's major themes is the disjunction between appearance and essence. Nothing is as it appears, and the murder of Edgar Parlance is perfectly illustrative of this condition. At the beginning of the novel, the reader assumes that Parlance's killing is random, a hate crime, and that Parlance is inoffensive and unknown, "the kind of black man white people can most easily grasp unto themselves." This does not prove to be accurate.

Parlance's legal record, with which no one initially seems concerned, shows a conviction for auto theft. In jail in Colorado, however, he knew one of his accused killers and also ran a ring of jailhouse prostitutes and forced the defendant into whoring himself. Parlance was known then as Earnest Wonder, or Wonderman. The defendant went by the moniker Princess, thus the "P" carved in the dead man's chest was not short for his surname—it was a calling card from his killer.

One of the novel's central ironies is that, even though every person carefully constructs a false front, they are still incapable of seeing through the falsehoods surrounding them. The main exception is narrator Cline, a confirmed cynic who sees behind the dizzying array of facades to the core of corruption and venality. At one point, Kean believes there are two kinds of people, "the scrutinizers and the scrutinized." Indeed, Cline appears to be one of the few scrutinizers. The affair between prosecutor J. J. McClure and Kean, a violation of professional ethics, is actually a liaison between two desperately alienated people.

To capture such a confusing, two-faced world, Dunne employs a dramatically self-conscious style. The narrative stands as an assemblage of scattered sources from a variety of different points of view: newspaper clippings presented in direct, reportorial prose; Kean's private diary, unearthed from deep in her computer's hard drive; McClure's fevered recollection of his baby brother's drowning; surveillance logs of a woman's random activities caught on a casino's hidden camera; and most important, Cline's sardonic observations. Cline's voice is a heady mix of pugnacious assurance and flippant ambivalence:

> As fact, it might be suspect, but as truth it is as close as I can get. If you were the filter, your facts, or your memory of them, might be equally suspect, but the truth, presupposing your honesty or as close as you could get to it. But you weren't there, and . . . I think I got it right. Mostly. And if I didn't, it's the available version.

Max's singular style, often composed of sentence fragments and random associative juxtapositions, is reminiscent of the disaffected, nonchalant prose of Dunne's wife, Joan Didion. Often such narration is annoying and disingenuous, yet Dunne adjusts the style and reminds readers that he is also capable of remarkably incisive observations, for instance this brief obituary and narratorial comment: "'He is survived by his second wife, from whom he was recently divorced, and by a stepson from his first marriage.' Think of the moral and sexual misdemeanors woven into that simple sentence, the mosaic of small, mean betrayals."

The novel is top-heavy with a panoramic collection of characters, although most are sufficiently compelling in themselves, readers will need a scorecard to keep them straight. Ultimately, they amount to an embarrassment of riches and create narrative diffusion. One wonders whose story this is and how all these personalities fit together. Some of this overwriting may come from the fact that Dunne is extending the implications of his earlier novel, *Playland* (1994), in which Kean's biological parents' chaotic lives are elaborated.

Nevertheless, Dunne has written a personal swan song. He has always been a brash, no-holds-barred voice in American writing, and *Nothing Lost*, in spite of its faults, reveals a singular sensibility. Like the Irish brawler that he was, Dunne leads with his chin and takes no prisoners.

*David W. Madden*

## Review Sources

*Booklist* 100, no. 14 (March 15, 2004): 1243.
*Kirkus Reviews* 72, no. 6 (March 15, 2004): 240.
*Library Journal* 129, no. 8 (May 1, 2004): 139.
*Los Angeles Times*, May 9, 2004, p. R3.
*The New York Times*, April 27, 2004, p. E1.
*The New York Times Book Review* 153 (May 2, 2004): 9.
*Publishers Weekly* 251, no. 11 (March 15, 2004): 51.
*San Francisco Chronicle*, May 4, 2004, p. E1.
*The Washington Post*, May 9, 2004, p. T01.

# NUCLEAR TERRORISM
## The Ultimate Preventable Catastrophe

*Author:* Graham Allison (1940-    )
*Publisher:* Times Books/Henry Holt (New York). 263 pp.
  $24.00
*Type of work:* Current affairs

*A distinguished American political scientist sounds the alarm on the possibility of a nuclear attack in the United States, arguing that if present policies are continued, such an attack, possibly of Hiroshima magnitude, is inevitable but is preventable if the policies the author recommends are adopted*

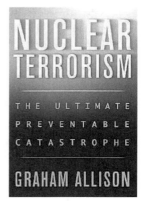

In October, 2001, just weeks after the September 11 terrorist attacks, a tense drama unfolded in New York City. Unknown to the public, a team of scientists was walking the city's streets with disguised equipment to detect the radioactivity of an atomic weapon. On October 11, George Tenet, head of the Central Intelligence Agency (CIA), informed President George W. Bush that the CIA had received word through an agent code-named Dragonfly that al-Qaeda had smuggled a 10-kiloton nuclear device into New York City. The team of scientists attempting to locate the weapon found themselves searching for something more difficult to find than a needle in a haystack. It was, they said, more like looking for a needle in a haystack of needles—practically impossible. Fortunately, the agent's message was a false alarm.

That a nuclear terrorist attack on the United States is a clear and present danger is a terrifying thought, but just this possibility is the focus of Professor Graham Allison's arresting jeremiad, *Nuclear Terrorism: The Ultimate Preventable Catastrophe*. It might be called, with little exaggeration, the most important book calling the American public to action since Thomas Paine published *Common Sense* in January, 1776. Allison, founding dean of Harvard University's Kennedy School of Government, lays out a painstaking and thoroughly convincing case that a nuclear attack on American soil is not only possible but, if present policies persist, inevitable. Such an attack would not emanate from a rogue state launching intercontinental ballistic missiles but from terrorists smuggling nuclear weapons from abroad or even constructing them within the United States.

How is it that such a nightmarish claim can be made by a figure of academic stature and credibility, a former Defense Department official? Why does the author declare nuclear attack to be inevitable if present U.S. policies remain unaltered, and what, if anything, can be done to avoid catastrophe? These questions occupy the substance of Allison's book.

First, who might be plotting such attacks? The obvious answer is al-Qaeda, especially in view of the many credible reports of its interest in using nuclear weapons against the United States. Al-Qaeda's second-highest-ranking official, Ahyman al-Zawahiri, has publicly boasted that the organization possesses nuclear weapons, though his boast may be empty. While empty one day, however, such boasts may be true the next.

Al-Qaeda is hardly the only terrorist organization interested in reducing American cities to radioactive rubble. Another is the Asian al-Qaeda affiliate Jemaah Islamiyah, which has perpetrated terrorist outrages in the Philippines, Indonesia, and Singapore. In October, 2002, this organization carried out the bombing of a Bali nightclub, killing 202 people, mostly Australian tourists. Such threats merely represent the tip of the iceberg. Chechen gangsters could also acquire nuclear weapons on the Russian black market. Their target of choice would be Moscow, but the Chechens might provide weapons to their Islamist brethren in al-Qaeda.

*Graham Allison, professor of government at Harvard University and dean of the Kennedy School of Government, is director of the Belfer Center for Science and International Affairs. He served as Assistant Secretary of Defense for Policy and Plans in the administration of President Bill Clinton and is author of* The Essence of Decision: Explaining the Cuban Missile Crisis *(1971).*

Next on the list of potential nuclear conspirators is what Allison calls "the A-team" of Islamic terrorists: Hezbollah, the powerful, supremely violent Middle Eastern Islamist terrorist organization centered in Lebanon. Hezbollah was responsible for the attack on the Marine barracks near Beirut in October, 1983, that killed 241 American personnel. Hezbollah's primary target is Israel, which it seeks to destroy. A secondary target is Israel's friend and protector, the United States.

Finally, there is a welter of doomsday cults around the world, some of which would relish the opportunity to bring about the "end of days" and which might target the United States. In the 1980's one such group, the Japanese cult Aum Shinryko, scoured Soviet Russia, loaded with cash, searching for a nuclear warhead to detonate in Japan. Allison believes there are a large number of such organizations, mostly under the radar of public knowledge but potentially extremely lethal. After all, for those seeking universal fame and supreme excitement, a nuclear attack meets all requirements.

Second, what weapons might be used? On this subject the news is especially grim. Since the days of the Hiroshima and Nagasaki bombs, nuclear weapons have been substantially miniaturized. Allison includes photographs of the diminutive American battlefield "Davy Crockett" tactical nuclear weapon, two thousand of which were once deployed in Europe. Each of these devices delivers the punch of 100,000 sticks of dynamite—a quarter-kiloton. The Soviet Union deployed some twenty-two thousand small battlefield weapons of various descriptions. Today, terrorists could choose among several hundred varieties of these small nuclear devices.

The destructive force of such weapons is difficult to imagine. The Hiroshima blast, which destroyed a large city, measured some 12 kilotons, equivalent to 12,000 tons of TNT. The bomb hunted in New York in October, 2001, was said to have been 10 kilotons. Other bombs rumored to exist and to be missing from Soviet arsenals are the so-called suitcase bombs, providing one kiloton of explosive power. Even these weapons would inflict awesome damage. An attack on a nuclear reactor could release into the atmosphere hundreds of times the radiation released by the two World War II bombs.

Do the rumored Soviet-era suitcase bombs exist, and if they do, might some be in terrorist hands? Despite much investigation, no one knows. What Allison believes, however, is that if they exist, such bombs can be set off by terrorists without secret codes or radio signals from Moscow. Further, hope that they will not explode because their shelf life has expired is unavailing. Even if such weapons failed to detonate properly, a partial explosion (known as a "fizzle") would be catastrophic. Such a "disappointing" explosion could kill 250,000 people within a week if detonated in Times Square, New York City, on a weekday. Besides suitcase weapons, there are other easily transportable "backpack" bombs, American versions of which weigh 50 to 65 pounds.

Third, from what sources might nuclear weapons be obtained? The principal source of illicit weapons is undoubtedly Russia, where thousands of weapons or forms of nuclear material are imperfectly stored, ill-guarded, and subject to theft. Of great concern is the fact that within post-Soviet Russian society there exists a wide range of mores. Terrorists may be scouting for black-market devices in a nation that has spawned far-flung organized crime syndicates that care nothing about the loss of human life. In a nation where bribery is ubiquitous and moral inhibition scarce, there can be little doubt that black-market procurement of nuclear weapons is a realistic possibility, given the nihilism of Russian organized crime.

Attempts to smuggle radioactive materials are hardly uncommon. Allison mentions, for example, that after the United States provided Russia monitoring equipment to staunch the exit of radioactive materials, some 275 cases of attempted transport of radioactive materials were detected. In Bulgaria, weapons-usable material was discovered and removed from the trunk of a car. Russia, however, is not the only source of nuclear weapons or the materials from which to construct them. Pakistan, North Korea, Iran, and elsewhere—even the United States itself—are possible sources.

Fourth, when could terrorists attack? The short answer is "any time." The world is awash in the makings of nuclear weapons that can be constructed with minimal equipment. Plans for such weapons are readily available, for example on the Internet. To drive this point home, Allison himself publishes a rough design for a nuclear weapon. In doing so, he gives nothing away. He relates, tellingly, that as an experiment, the heads of the U.S. National Laboratories attempted to build an "off the shelf" nuclear weapon from readily available materials. They had no difficulty succeeding—breaking no laws in the process. However, making one's own weapon is required only if buying or stealing a ready-made device is not feasible.

Fifth, how could terrorists deliver weapons to their targets? This is a question easily answered. U.S. borders are porous. Successive presidential administrations have pointedly refused to close off the southern border with Mexico. The George W. Bush administration is no exception. Trade agreements now allow thousands of trucks, few of which are inspected, to cross the border daily. Thousands of illegal immigrants, mostly Mexicans but also those from numerous nations, including those in the Middle East, cross each day as well. At one Indian reservation on the border, dozens of smugglers nightly carry backpacks containing up to 100 pounds of drugs. Other materials might easily be transported.

In addition, tens of thousands of ship-borne freight containers, only a small percentage of which are inspected, arrive daily at U.S. harbors. To illustrate this danger, in 2003 ABC News successfully smuggled nuclear material from Indonesia to downtown Los Angeles. American coasts and harbors, where many thousands of small craft arrive annually, are also imperfectly guarded. Moreover, terrorists would have no difficulty in bringing weapons smuggled into Canada across the U.S. northern border. They might ship such cargo via Federal Express.

Having terrified the reader with this litany of horrific possibilities, Allison sets about inquiring how nuclear catastrophe can be prevented. Nuclear catastrophe is inevitable (meaning a likely event in the next decade, he believes) only if government policy does not change. However, policy can and must be changed. One difficulty, the author argues, is that the war in Iraq has deflected American attention from the key task at hand, defeating Islamofascist nuclear terrorism—not "terrorism" in general. Instead, Allison calls upon the United States to focus on the prevention program he outlines in part 2 of *Nuclear Terrorism.*

Allison summarizes his program as the "three no's" and the "seven yeses." The "no's" are no loose nukes; no "new nascent" nukes; and no new nuclear powers. The first item of the program requires that all nuclear materials and bombs be secured in accordance with a new "gold standard" of secure lockdown. The "loose nukes" that especially need securing are the thousands scattered around Russia. The Russian situation requires a far more substantial, faster program than the one now in place. Nations such as Pakistan and North Korea are also possible sources, and they are not alone.

Second, there must be no more legally constructed nuclear facilities capable of producing the highly enriched uranium or plutonium required to build a bomb. Loopholes in the Nuclear Proliferation Treaty must be plugged and nations compensated for giving up the right to construct nuclear devices. The machinery to enrich uranium must be embargoed and international nuclear proliferation of all kinds criminalized. Here, Iran is the most dangerous player, and its weapons program must be stopped by a carrot-and-stick method—the stick being the threat of U.S. military action.

Third, there must be no new nuclear powers. Iran, again, is one of two nations in the spotlight, there being much evidence collected over the past two decades of its nuclear ambitions. The other nation is North Korea, believed to have one or more weapons as of 2004. Allison offers another carrot-and-stick approach in bilateral (not multilateral) talks.

Finally, Allison outlines a detailed plan of action for the federal government, incorporating the above strategy. He issues a strong warning that such a program (the "seven yeses") must become an "absolute national priority" for the president and his administration. He is also adamant that Congress, prodded by an aroused citizenry, become more actively involved.

*Nuclear Terrorism* reads like America's worst nightmare—but the author is not dreaming. Allison's offering is an exercise in sober, informed thinking on the subject and is ignored or marginalized at the United States' peril. It took the attacks of September 11, 2001, to awaken the United States to one kind of threat confronting it. Will it require an American Hiroshima—or simultaneous Hiroshimas—to awaken the nation to the reality of the nuclear threat?

*Charles F. Bahmueller*

## Review Sources

*Booklist* 100, no. 22 (August 1, 2004): 1878.
*Kirkus Reviews* 72, no. 12 (June 15, 2004): 563.
*Publishers Weekly* 251, no. 27 (July 5, 2004): 48.

# OBLIVION

*Author:* David Foster Wallace (1962-    )
*Publisher:* Little, Brown (New York). 329 pp. $26.00
*Type of work:* Short fiction
*Time:* 2004
*Locale:* The United States

*A collection of postmodern, surreal, and satirical short stories that displays the obsessions and cultural idiosyncrasies of the United States*

From the publication of his first books, *The Broom of the System* in 1987 and *Girl with Curious Hair* in 1989, David Foster Wallace has shown himself to be a keen observer of American popular culture. In fiction and essays, his challenging prose has skewered American preconceptions, trends, and obsessions, particularly in terms of hipster culture and corporate chic. His mammoth novel *Infinite Jest* (1996) runs to more than one thousand pages; its publication revealed that the perspicacity of Wallace's insight was matched by his wildly ambitious energies. His ability to turn his satirical microscope on various icons of modern culture is particularly on display in his book of essays *A Supposedly Fun Thing I'll Never Do Again* (1997), which takes on such cultural idiosyncrasies as cruise ships, state fairs, and competitive tennis.

Wallace's new collection of stories, *Oblivion*, provides free rein to his enormously creative muse. Perhaps because of their brevity and economy, short stories are a more forgiving genre for experimentation in fiction than are novels. It might prove difficult for an author to dedicate a whole book, for example, to a narrative written as if it were a report on a marketing focus group, or to sustain a lengthy narrative about a husband accused of snoring who turns out to be a dreaming wife, or to linger for hundreds of pages with the first-person, posthumous recounting of a suicide. In the short-fiction form, however, Wallace can actually create such stories successfully.

The label of postmodern has haunted Wallace since he began publishing. This often employed literary descriptor seems to mean something different each time it is used. Sometimes postmodern merely means countercultural; at other times, it means experimental, surreal, or metafictional. Each of these terms serves to describe various stories in *Oblivion*.

Wallace's fiction often does not follow the linear plot progressions of realistic texts. While the intellectualism of his prose and his need to challenge the reader on a number of levels clearly owes something to the deep modernism of James Joyce, Virginia Woolf, and William Faulkner, Wallace's work rarely indulges in the poetic impressionism of modernism. His satirical insights and focus on the cultural *Zeitgeist* reflect the fully grown flower sprung from seeds planted by such earlier postmodern writers as John Barthes and Don DeLillo.

∽

*A native of Ithaca, New York, David Foster Wallace earned an A.B. from Amherst College and an M.F.A. from the University of Arizona. Works such as* The Broom of the System *(1987),* Girl with Curious Hair *(1989), and* Infinite Jest *(1996) have cemented his place in the canon of postmodern fiction. He has been nominated for a Pulitzer Prize and is the recipient of a MacArthur Foundation "genius grant."*

∽

One of the strengths of Wallace's prose in *Oblivion* is his ability to adapt an organic unity in his affectations of style. That is, the style of a given story in some way or another reflects the purpose and theme of the story itself. For example, "Mister Squishy" is about an advertising focus group that is being asked to try a new form of Mister Squishy snack cakes. Thirty-four-year-old Terry Schmidt is the facilitator of the focus group. Unlike most members of the group, he is conscious that they are being covertly tested, manipulated, studied, and analyzed in a perplexing number of ways. The prose style of the narrative of "Mister Squishy" follows a similar approach as a focus group's narrative report. The narrator of the story, for instance, casually notes details that seemingly have nothing to do with the story's development, observing at one point that:

> There were four pairs of eyeglasses in the room, although one of these pairs were sunglasses and possibly not prescription, another with heavy black frames that gave their wearer's face an earnest aspect above his dark turtleneck sweater. There were two mustaches and one probable goatee. A stocky man in his late twenties had a sort of sparse, mossy beard; it was indeterminable whether this man was just starting to grow a beard or whether he was the sort of person whose beard simply looked this way.

This breakdown of eyeglass and facial hair trends bears little overall relation to the story, yet in its ridiculous attention to detail and its fixation on minutia, this approach mirrors the narrative style of a marketing focus group report, which must note and explore every mundane element in order to investigate what influence those various factors might have on consumer purchases. Wallace obviates the absurdist facets of corporate culture and anomalies like "targeted focus groups" further by introducing a surreal element: in this case, a wall-scaling, potential sniper or assassin. Tellingly, the story is never resolved, and the reader never discovers whether the climbing gunman carries out an attack on anyone.

"The Soul Is Not a Smithy" is one of the stronger stories in the collection and also reflects unity of style and theme. Like "Mister Squishy," "The Soul Is Not a Smithy" largely eschews paragraph breaks. The story is ostensibly about four fourth-grade students held hostage for a short while by a substitute teacher who suffers a psychotic episode and who is later shot in front of the four children. The story is narrated some years later by one of the students, who presumably has some form of attention deficit disorder. Seated by the window during the crisis, he ignores the panic of his classmates as well as the teacher writing "kill them" on the board. Instead, he uses the grid of panels on a mesh-covered window to imagine a long and poignant comic strip about a missing dog and a family's series of tragedies.

The narrator's anxieties over the substitute teacher do manifest themselves in his consciousness, however, through the appearance of increasing violence and trauma in the imaginary comic strip. Yet the story takes a strange turn and also paints a brief and sad portrait of the narrator's father. Even as the narrative displays the lack of communication between the external world and the narrator's internal world during a crisis, the narrator comes to understand how his father was cut off from life and isolated by loneliness.

As writers have known since the days of Jonathan Swift, the danger of satire is that the absurdity of a given scenario or the bitter humor of the tone may interfere with the reader's immersion in the text. Rather than being compelled by the plot of prose of a work, she or he may withdraw and feel that a work is overintellectualized. Postmodern and experimental writing also runs the risk of alienating the reader. For example, "Another Pioneer," like "Mister Squishy" and "The Soul Is Not a Smithy," is told in one long single paragraph. ("The Soul Is Not a Smithy," at least, is occasionally broken up by retrospective interludes written in all capital letters.)

"Another Pioneer" follows an oddly intricate narrative path. Presumably, one anthropological expert overhears another on an airplane describing the life of a Third World child from a remote rainforest village who seems supernaturally precocious. The child becomes a religious seer and the leader of his tribe until elders and shamans from rival tribes work to discredit him. Although the plot of the story is, in itself, somewhat interesting, one is not sure what is gained by the stylistic choice of narrative that follows the form of a lecture or discussion, without paragraphing or quotation marks or direct dialogue. Nor does the aesthetic or thematic benefit of the story's odd origins—an anthropological discussion overhead on an airplane voyage and recounted and discussed at length—become readily apparent.

Similarly, the titular story, "Oblivion," seems to be about a man who is going through a stressful period in his relationship with his wife. She accuses him of snoring too much, and he believes that she is imagining it. At the same time, her daughter (his stepdaughter) is leaving for college, and possibly the stress of empty-nest syndrome is affecting the couple. The text is ambiguous, and the reader is never sure what to think in "Oblivion." At first, it seems that the narrator is unreliable and is the problem; then it seems likely that his wife is unreasonable; and then it seems possible that he has been an abusive parent. At the end of the story, it turns out that the whole narrative— presumably told from the husband's point of view—has been dreamed by the wife. Although the twist is clever, it seems unworthy of the themes developed throughout the story.

At their best, however, Wallace's postmodern renderings do what they are supposed to do: They surprise readers and remove them from their comfort zones; they make them think, work, worry, and sweat with the stories. By way of example, "Good Old Neon," possibly the best story in the collection, uses metafictional twists late in the narrative to add a poignant dimension to the tale. As a literary term, "metafiction" generally means that a given text is calling attention to the fact that it is a text (rather than an unfolding story that a reader is somehow witnessing) and usually comments upon the text itself or its creation or its goals.

In "Good Old Neon," the subtle intrusion of metafiction near the end of the story makes it clear that the narrator, a man who considers himself a fake and a fraud, was a classmate of Wallace and that the present story, presumably (and absurdly) told from the vantage of a peaceful afterlife by a man who committed suicide, is the author's attempt to understand the narrator's suicide. As he dies, the narrator describes the actions of various people in his life and then states that "David Wallace blinks in the midst of idly scanning class photos from his 1980 Aurora West H.S. yearbook and seeing my photo and trying, through the tiny little keyhole of himself, to imagine what all must have happened to lead up to my death in the fiery single-car accident he'd read about in 1991." Later, the narrator points out how Wallace, back then, had imagined the narrator to be "as happy and unreflective and wholly unhaunted by voices telling him that there was something deeply wrong with him that wasn't wrong with anybody else."

Wallace's project as a writer is perhaps best spelled out by the final story in the collection, "The Suffering Channel." The story seems to be about a lot of things: a middle-aged reporter for a fashionable magazine who is trying desperately not to be outdated, the sadistic elements behind the American zeal for "reality" programming, and, finally, about a man who seemingly can create works of art with his own feces. The artist does not work on the feces after he has excreted them; rather, they emerge fully formed as works of art. Wallace seems to be saying that the world is full of mundane, trivial, at times alarming or disgusting detritus. The job of the artist, the writer, however, is not to sweep away the petty remains and offal of modern, everyday American life. Rather, the writer must examine these ruins of common existence at length for the truths they hold and to somehow shape those truths into an art that sustains one's intellect and curiosity.

*Scott Yarbrough*

## Review Sources

*Booklist* 100, no. 18 (May 15, 2004): 1600.
*Entertainment Weekly*, June 18, 2004, p. 89.
*Kirkus Reviews* 72, no. 9 (May 1, 2004): 422.
*The New Republic* 231, no. 6 (August 9, 2004): 26.
*The New York Times*, June 1, 2004, p. E8.
*The New York Times Book Review* 153 (June 27, 2004): 7.
*Publishers Weekly* 251, no. 21 (May 24, 2004): 42.
*Review of Contemporary Fiction* 24, no. 2 (Summer, 2004): 125.
*Time* 163, no. 23 (June 7, 2004): 123.

# OCCIDENTALISM
## The West in the Eyes of Its Enemies

*Authors:* Ian Buruma (1951-    ) and Avishai Margalit
(1939-    )
*Publisher:* Penguin Press (New York). 214 pp. $21.00
*Type of work:* History
*Time:* From the eighteenth century to 2004

*Demonstrates that the anti-Western hatred found in the Islamic world has its roots not in Islam but in revolutionary groups and ideas that have appeared in the West and elsewhere since the early nineteenth century*

Americans watching the nightly television news about terrorist threats to the United States from the Islamic world frequently ask the bewildered question: Why do they hate us so much? It is difficult for Americans, so convinced that their country stands for freedom and democracy, to imagine why such apparently worthy goals could arouse such fierce opposition. In *Occidentalism: The West in the Eyes of Its Enemies*, Ian Buruma and Avishai Margalit answer this question in an unusual way. They do not immediately cover the prevalent views of the West among those in the Islamic world. Instead, they examine extreme anti-Western views, which they call Occidentalism, that have emerged from within the West itself, from where such ideas have spread to the Islamic world. The authors identify several strands of Occidentalism that can be found wherever the phenomenon has occurred: hostility to city life; opposition to science and reason; contempt for the settled, mediocre bourgeois lifestyle; and hatred of the infidel, who must be destroyed.

Hostility to the sinful city, given to pleasure and commerce rather than to the worship of God, was dramatically revealed on September 11, 2001, when Islamic terrorists attacked the Twin Towers in New York, symbol of American power and commerce. Hatred of cities as perceived centers of corruption is not a new phenomenon. It can be traced as far back as Juvenal's satire of ancient Rome and the hatred of the early Christians for Babylon, which they referred to as the great whore—a metaphor that has endured because it expresses the idea that in a city, the highest goal is the pursuit of wealth, which means that everything is for sale. Everything has a price—but nothing has a soul.

The hatred of cities became focused on the West largely because of the growth of the great European urban centers of the nineteenth century. Trade and individual and political freedom went hand in hand, but this attracted censure from those who saw cities as centers of self-interest and greed. Friedrich Engels, for example, identified the selfishness and individualism of city life as unnatural, something that human nature rebelled against. The association of universal trade and capitalism, concentrated

∾

*Ian Buruma is currently Luce*
*Professor at Bard College. His*
*previous books include* God's Dust
*(1989),* Behind the Mask *(1984),*
The Missionary and the Libertine
*(2000),* Playing the Game *(1991),*
The Wages of Guilt *(1995),*
Anglomania *(2000), and* Bad
Elements *(2001).*

∾

*Avishai Margalit is Schulman*
*Professor of Philosophy at the*
*Hebrew University of Jerusalem.*
*His previous books include*
Idolatry *(1992),* The Decent
Society *(1996),* Views in Review:
Politics and Culture in the State of
the Jews *(1998), and* The Ethics of
Memory *(2002).*

∾

in cities, appeared to Occidentalists as a conspiracy to destroy everything that was authentic and spiritual. Capitalism was, in a sense, the victory of the city over the country, and it generated a backlash in those who idealized stable, rural cultures that had endured for centuries. During the 1920's and 1930's, many European intellectuals espoused disdain for the city life, perceived as shallow, rootless, and materialistic, and this aspect of Occidentalism spread to other continents, too. In the twentieth century, it manifested in Mao Zedong's war against the bourgeois and the intellectuals in the city, as well as in Cambodia, where the Khmer Rouge marched into the Westernized city of Phnom Penh and destroyed it.

In their next chapter, "Heroes and Merchants," the authors discuss the contrast between Western liberal democracies, perceived by their enemies as soft, decadent, and addicted to pleasure, and those who subscribe to a heroic ideal of revolutionary action and self-sacrifice, including death. They point to Germany after its victory over France in 1871 and its growing worship over the following seventy years of martial self-discipline and the "warrior state." For German nationalists, Germany was a nation of heroes willing to sacrifice themselves for a higher ideal, in contrast to the commercial values of Britain and France, interested only in material goods that brought physical comfort. Because commercialism needed security and peace in order to flourish—war was bad for business—nations dominated by commercialism adopted liberal democracy because it was the political system that suited them best. Conflicts of interest were resolved through negotiation and compromise.

The Occidentalists, however, saw no virtue in this. In their view, the West was unheroic, mediocre, superficial, and soft. The liberal ideals so cherished by the West, of civilization, freedom and peace, undermined the potential grandeur of a people, nation, or religion. War was needed for regeneration, or so the German nationalists thought. This aspect of Occidentalism spread to Japan, which was the most Westernized country in Asia in the 1930's, and culminated in the kamikaze pilots of the last years of World War II, who considered themselves intellectual rebels against the Western corruption of Japan. The most notorious Occidentalists today, Osama bin Laden and his al-Qaeda organization, as well as other Islamic fundamentalist groups, have borrowed from the Occidentalism of Nazi totalitarianism and the Japanese kamikaze spirit. This is basically the same point made by Paul Berman in his book *Terror and Liberalism* (2003), that the anti-Western beliefs of today's suicide terrorists have their roots in Western political and philosophical ideas and practices that began in the nineteenth century and culminated in the totalitarian movements of Soviet communism, Italian fascism, and German Nazism.

Buruma and Margalit then turn their attention to the Occidentalist assault on the mind of the West. The Western mind may be efficient, in a coldly practical sense, but it knows nothing of the higher values in life and therefore can really do nothing right, economic success notwithstanding: "Western man, in this view, is a hyperactive busybody, forever finding the right means to the wrong ends." Various antitheses to the Western mind have emerged at different times in different countries. Nineteenth century Russian thinkers extolled what they called the "Russian soul," and their thinking was a model for later intellectuals in India, China, and the Islamic countries.

The idea of the Russian soul was, in fact, rooted in German Romanticism, which was prompted by a reaction to the German fear of France, seen as the quintessential West. The German Romantics believed, as did their counterparts in England, that excessive rationalism had destroyed the West. Battling a sense of national inferiority, German Romantics contrasted "their own deep inner life of the spirit, the poetry of their national soul, the simplicity and nobility of their character, to the empty, heartless sophistication of the French."

In the case of Russia, the Westernizing policies of the eighteenth century rulers Peter the Great and Catherine the Great were followed in the nineteenth century by an ideological battle between the Westernizers and the Slavophiles, who idealized the almost mystical entity of the "Russian soul," believing that it had been betrayed by Russia's Westernizers. Using the work of the German Romantics, especially the philosopher Friedrich Wilhelm Joseph Schelling, philosophers such as Ivan Kireyevsky claimed that the West was built on rotten foundations—spiritually, politically, and socially. The mind of the West, in this view, was narrowly rationalistic, cut off from the wholeness of the world, whereas "the organic Russian mind . . . is guided by faith and able to grasp the totality of things." The problem with excessive rationalism was its insistence that science was the sole source of knowledge, which left no place for religion. This belief in the superiority of reason, according to the Russian nineteenth century Occidentalists, had made the West arrogant, insisting on its own superiority.

In the next chapter, "The Wrath of God," the authors make a distinction between secular and religious Occidentalism. The religious strain of Occidentalism was created in Manichaean terms, as a holy war fought against evil. The modern manifestation of this appears in certain strains of Islamicism which regard the West as a form of idolatrous barbarism. The term is *jahiliyya*, which is translated as ignorance or barbarism. The West, in this Manichaean view, is made up of barbarians who worship matter, the things of the earth, rather than the things of the spirit.

Like Berman in *Terror and Liberalism*, Buruma and Margalit highlight the work of an influential Islamic thinker and activist named Sayyid Qutb, who was a member of the Egyptian Muslim Brotherhood. Qutb spent two years, from 1948 to 1950, studying in the United States, where he was shocked by what he saw as the frivolous, pleasure-seeking American lifestyle. This helped to transform him into a fervent Occidentalist with a strong anti-Semitic cast. For Qutb, *jahiliyya* was, in the authors' summary, "the culture of animals . . . of supremely arrogant animals who try to play God." Qutb did not advocate violent attacks on the West. Instead, he reserved his fire for the Westernized rulers of Egypt and other nations. He paid the price for his views, being imprisoned and then hanged in 1966 by Egypt's military leader, Gamal Abdel Nasser.

After considering the origins of the Wahhabi sect in Saudi Arabia, which began in the eighteenth century and has since been exported everywhere in the Muslim world to become the main brand of Occidentalism today, the authors point out that what makes the terrorism practiced by such revolutionary groups so lethal is that it synthesizes religious zealotry and modern technology. The Occidentalists, while attacking the West, use the technology of the "barbarians" to do so. The authors repeat here one of Berman's main points in *Terror and Liberalism*, that many Islamic radicals, both today and in the past, live a cultural double life, having been educated in Europe and becoming as familiar with the culture of the "enemy" as with Islamic culture.

As for how to protect the West against its enemies, the authors warn against assuming that the West is at war with Islam, as most of the fiercest battles will be fought within the Muslim world; Muslims themselves must halt the radical Occidentalists. The authors also caution against taking refuge in the idea of colonial guilt or blaming the violence of Islamic revolutionary movements on American imperialism or global capitalism and the like, as every group should be held morally responsible for its actions. Nor should Westerners take the easy route of blaming religion, because organized religion can play a constructive role in offering community and spiritual meaning.

Finally, the authors argue that although the West must defend itself with force if necessary, it must be careful how it wages the battle. The ideas that have fueled the growth of Occidentalism could also contaminate the West "if we fall for the temptation to fight fire with fire, Islamism with our own form of intolerance." To do so would betray the very idea that the West is supposed to be defending.

*Occidentalism* is a valuable book because it gives some historical perspective to the Islamic terrorist campaign against the West. It is surely useful for any culture to try to understand how its enemies see it. However, some readers may regret that the authors spend so much time examining long-defunct enemies of the West, such as the nineteenth century Slavophiles or the Japanese in the 1930's and 1940's rather than probing more deeply and directly into the ideology that sustains today's Islamic terror groups.

*Bryan Aubrey*

## Review Sources

*Booklist* 100, no. 12 (February 15, 2004): 1008.
*Commentary* 117 (April, 2004): 21.
*The Economist* 370 (March 20, 2004 ): 90.
*Foreign Affairs* 83, no. 2 (March/April, 2004): 155.
*Kirkus Reviews* 72, no. 1 (January 1, 2004): 21.
*Library Journal* 129, no. 5 (March 15, 2004): 87.
*The New York Times*, March 27, 2004, p. B9.
*The New York Times Book Review* 153 (April 4, 2004): 11.

# ON LITERATURE

*Author:* Umberto Eco (1932-    )
Translated from the Italian by Martin McLaughlin
*Publisher:* Harcourt (Orlando, Fla.). 334 pp. $26.00
*Type of work:* Essays and literary criticism

*Essays and addresses on a variety of literary subjects*

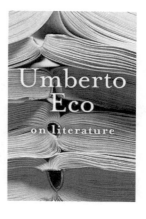

Collections of essays are, even at their best, mixed bags, even when written by someone like Umberto Eco, respected in the fields of semiotics, medieval studies, literary and cultural criticism, and fiction writing, to name a few. *On Literature* is an eclectic collection. Its "occasional writings" include five lectures, six conference papers, one closing address, two short newspaper articles, one preface, one afterword, one essay, and an indeterminate other, for which the explanatory endnote was omitted. All were delivered or published between 1980 and 2000 (and all but one after 1990), then revised. The publisher is inaccurate in claiming that the eighteen pieces cover "the course of his illustrious career," which began two decades before the publication of Eco's first novel, the improbable international best-seller *Il nome della rosa* (1980; *The Name of the Rose*, 1983). The publisher is also remiss in making it seem that the essays have not appeared in English before; some have, albeit in different form.

*On Literature* is clearly intended for American readers—or, more accurately, the American market. Although as a critic and semiotician, Eco has shown scant interest in literature's economic side—from which he has profited handsomely—the publication of this miscellany in 2004 cannot be separated from Harcourt's publication of the paperback edition of Eco's fourth novel, *Baudolino*, in 2003 and the impending publication of *The Mysterious Flame of Queen Loana*, the English translation of his fifth novel, *La Misteriosa fiamma della Regina Loana* (2004), in 2005.

In his theory of the "Model Reader," Eco puts crude economic matters aside, for the Model Reader is not the actual reader (least of all the one with $26) but that purely hypothetical being—or beings—created by the text itself. The semantic Model Reader only wants to know how the story turns out, and the semiotic or aesthetic Model Reader "asks himself what kind of reader that particular story was asking him to become, and wants to know how the Model Author who is instructing him step by step will proceed." Although he applies it only to narrative texts (especially novels), Eco's theory of model readers proves useful in trying to figure out exactly what kind of mixed bag *On Literature* is, as it takes on Dante's *La divina commedia* (c. 1320; *The Divine Comedy*, 1802), Karl Marx and Friedrich Engels's *Manifest der Kommunistischen Partei* (1848; *The Communist Manifesto*, 1850), Gerard de Nerval's "Sylvie" (1853; English translation, 1922), Miguel de Cervantes' *Don Quixote de la Mancha* (1605, 1615; English translation, 1612-1620), Aristotle's *De poetica*,

*Umberto Eco has made his mark both as an academic and as a writer of popular essays and especially novels that are at once erudite and highly popular. Professor of semiotics at the University of Bologna, Eco achieved popular success with his postmodern detective story* Il nome della rosa *(1980;* The Name of the Rose, *1983), an international best-seller set in a medieval monastery.*

(c. 334-323 B.C.E.; *Poetics*, 1705), Piero Camporesi's *Il sugo della vita* (1988; *Juice of Life*, 1995), and Oscar Wilde's aphorisms, as well as literature in general, paranoid symbolism, style, intertextuality, the representation of space in words, the power of falsehoods, and Eco's own fiction-writing habits in particular.

What the book's eighteen pieces have in common is Eco's having been invited to write or deliver them—for a book, a conference, an anniversary, a convocation, and the like. The Model Reader being constructed by the collection as a whole is quite different than the Model Reader being constructed by any one of its parts (an address at a conference of Italian semioticians, for example, or the readers of an Italian newspaper). However varied the actual audiences and the Model Readers of the individual essays undoubtedly were, and are, *On Literature*'s Model Reader is not someone who has an interest in one or more of these specific topics. Rather, he or she is someone who delights in the play of Eco's well-stocked mind in these eighteen walks in the narrative woods (to borrow the title of one of Eco's earlier books) and who delights equally in the sound of Eco's voice, as rendered on the page. Martin McLaughlin's translation is so wonderfully consistent and remarkably transparent that the reader cannot doubt that this is exactly how Eco sounds—in English.

Always the affable guide, Eco invites the reader to ramble with him, dotting the journey with bits of his distinctive brand of intelligent, gently mocking as well as self-deprecating humor: "I remember the shivers I experienced as a young man, feeling as marginalized as a young homosexual in Victorian society, when I discovered that the Anglo-Saxon tradition had continued to take Aristotle's poetics seriously, and without interruption."

Eco's sentences are often miniature versions of his overall method of labyrinthine twists and turns: "[Philosopher and historian Paul] Ricoeur (quoting [Jacques] Derrida on this topic, who says that in Aristotle the defined is implicated in the person who defines) observes that, in order to explain metaphor, Aristotle created a metaphor, borrowing it from the order of movement." It is a method Eco intuitively discovered early and which explains the affinity between his novels and his nonfiction, between his scholarly and fictional sleuthing:

> When I was examined for my graduating thesis on the problem of aesthetics in Thomas Aquinas, I was struck by one of the criticisms of the second examiner (Augusto Guzzo, who, however, later published my thesis as it was): he told me that what I had actually done was to rehearse the various phases of my research as if it were an inquiry,

noting the false leads and the hypotheses that I later rejected, whereas the mature scholar digests these experiences and then offers his readers (in the final version) only the conclusions. I recognized that this was true of my thesis, but I did not feel it to be a limitation. On the contrary, it was precisely then that I was convinced that all research must be "narrated" in this way. And I think I have done so in all my subsequent works of nonfiction.

As a result, I could refrain peacefully from writing stories because in fact I was satisfying my passion for narrative in another way; and when I would later write stories, they could not be anything other than the account of a piece of research (only in narrative this is called a Quest).

This narrative leaves the semantic Model Reader fully satisfied. The aesthetic Model Reader may feel differently, however, as if Eco were inviting further decoding. What appears at first glance straightforward may be something more duplicitous. Like Nathaniel Hawthorne in his "Custom House Introduction" to *The Scarlet Letter* (1850), Eco seems to keep his innermost self hidden behind a veil. Lured by Eco's dance of the seven semiotic veils, the aesthetic Model Reader discerns what the semantic Model Reader misses: that "How I Write" bears an uncanny resemblance to Edgar Allan Poe's "Philosophy of Composition," discussed elsewhere in *On Literature*. Revealing himself in this concealing, parodic way allows Eco to retain for himself what critic Mikhail Bakhtin called a loophole, an unspoken final word.

Thus the tenacity with which Eco pursues a subject is complemented by the pleasure he takes both in the pursuit itself and in the narrative of that pursuit: his tales of scholarly sleuthing, of tilting at intellectual windmills. At once Sherlock Holmes and Don Quixote, Eco sallies forth not, as in James Joyce's *Portrait of the Artist as a Young Man* (1916), to fashion the uncreated conscience of his race but instead on a series of seriocomic intellectual adventures in a collection that resembles nothing so much as an episodic novel in which the breadth of interests is offset, or linked, by a sameness, even saneness, of method.

There is the opening gambit, often followed by a discussion of a term's etymology, followed in turn by several speculative walks in the interpretive woods (the bulk of each essay), and ending with a conclusion that seems at once definitive and provisional or penultimate. Many of these speculative walks combine Eco's passion for narrative and his passion for endless classification, for splitting semiotic hairs: Eco the semiotician in the Peircean mold morphing into a character in one of Samuel Beckett's plays or novels—Molloy, perhaps, sucking his sucking stones, turn and turn about. "You must go on I can't go on I'll go on."

The result is often illuminating, occasionally maddening, nowhere more so than in "The Mists of the Valois," the longest work in the collection. It begins:

I discovered *Sylvie* when I was twenty, almost by chance, and I read it knowing very little about Nerval. I read the story in a state of total innocence, and I was bowled over. Later I discovered that it had made the same impression on [Marcel] Proust as it did on me. I do not remember how I articulated this impression in the vocabulary I had then, especially as now I can only express it in Proust's words from the few pages he devotes to Nerval in *Contre Sainte-Beuve* (*Against Sainte-Beuve*).

Eco translates the forty-five years he has spent, off and on, with "Sylvie" into the thirty-four-page reworking of a part of the afterword to his Italian translation of Nerval's story. Eco marshals charts, tables, and parallel columns in an exhaustive (and exhausting) attempt not merely to explain to the reader but also to understand for himself both Nerval's mazelike handling of time and space and his effect on Proust (who, Eco contends, devoted his life to the challenge of outdoing Nerval).

"The Mists of the Valois" makes a prime example of the role intertextuality plays in Eco's conception of literature in general and in his critical methodology: a *mise-en-abime* of texts within texts. Eco can understand Nerval by understanding Proust, who not only wrote after Nerval wrote but whom Eco read after reading Nerval.

In "How I Write," Eco explains that in order to create a novel he must create a world, and to create a world he must spend years on research in order to create a world out of texts. The intricacy of the worlds Eco creates in his fiction and his nonfiction, and the enormous pleasure that readers take in both, mask a wistfulness on Eco's part and perhaps on his reader's as well. This wistfulness is especially evident in "On Symbolism," in which Eco examines the fate of the symbolic in a wholly secular world, and in the far more playful "A Portrait of the Artist as a Bachelor."

In the latter, Eco plays the role of genial guide through a labyrinth of his own making. He begins not, as with his novels, with an image but with an invitation: to speak on the anniversary of the conferral of a bachelor's degree on Joyce. Invitation leads to word, "Bachelor," word leads to etymology, etymology to the courses that Joyce took and the papers that he wrote and lectures that he delivered on the way to earning his bachelor's degree, and from these to Dante's search for an Edenic, pre-Babel language, and from Dante's project for a perfect language through a twelfth century Irish grammatical treatise of which Joyce may have known, *Auraicept na n-Éces* (*Auraicept na n-Éces: The Scholars' Primer*, 1917), to one that he certainly knew or at least had seen, *The Book of Kells* (800 C.E.). Eco—playing the parts of Ariadne, Theseus, Daedalus, Stephen Dedalus, Don Quixote, Sancho Panza and perhaps his horse Rozinante, too—takes his readers to a conclusion as bold and sweeping as it is tenuous:

> Perhaps we are living inside a *Book of Kells*, whereas we think we are living inside Denis Diderot's *Encyclopédie*. Both *The Book of Kells* and [Joyce's] *Finnegans Wake* are the best image of the universe as contemporary science presents it to us. They are the model of a universe in expansion, perhaps finite and yet unlimited, the starting point for infinite questions. They are books that allow us to feel like men and women of our time, even though we are sailing in the same perilous sea that led Saint Brendan to seek out that Lost Island that every page of *The Book of Kells* speaks of, as it invites and inspires us to continue our search to finally express perfectly the imperfect world we live in.

Eco himself "invites and inspires," as well as delights. Like intertextuality (which he perversely calls "intertextual irony"), this reluctant postmodernist "provides revelations to those who have lost the sense of transcendence" and in this way unites author and reader "in the mystic body of worldly Scriptures."

*Robert A. Morace*

## Review Sources

*The Independent*, January 27, 2004, p. 35.
*Sunday Times*, January 9, 2005, p. 42.

# ON THE GROUND

*Author:* Fanny Howe (1940-    )
*Publisher:* Graywolf Press (St. Paul, Minn.). 64 pp. Paperback $14.00
*Type of work:* Poetry

*A challenging collection of innovative poems by Howe, winner of the 2001 Lenore Marshall Poetry Prize, that is both political and spiritual*

Fanny Howe is a postmodernist poet with a following that reaches beyond readers of this form. Interestingly, she has moved from more commercial publishers toward independent presses. Her first works, short stories, poems, and novels, were published with Houghton and Avon, but she has moved toward collectives and respected small presses as her work has become more experimental. It is certainly the reverse of many career trajectories to go from Houghton and Avon to Sun & Moon Press, but Howe has the courage of her convictions and is writing now for a small audience of enlightened readers. While her main themes of social injustice and the spiritual dimension of life remain constant throughout all of her literary output, her style has become more edgy and boundary-challenging as her work has progressed.

Howe's first work, *Forty Whacks* (1969), was a book of short stories about women in difficult situations, and it has a cool, *New Yorker*-style sophistication. After her marriage in 1968 to a fellow writer, Carl Senna, she began to open up her style to multiple possibilities and interpretations. Even her first book of poems, *Eggs* (1970), is a step in this direction, and she has proceeded in this direction since, some of her later works including a mingling of prose and poetry. Her novel *Saving History* (1992), for instance, intersperses the narrative with poetry. The 1970's brought her wholly into the realm of the experimental writer, where she has steadfastly remained.

In fact, Howe is often thought of as a member of the Language Poets of the 1970's, together with Charles Bernstein, Lyn Hejinian, Leslie Scalapino, and others. Howe is currently known for elliptical, open-ended poems and novels that defy the conventions of narrative. Her poetry is not experiment for experiment's sake, or mainly to explore the limitations of language. She has recurrent, insistent subjects to which she returns. Her subjects tend to be the marginalized and the oppressed, especially women in extreme situations, the danger and instability in the current world, and the need or quest to define a spiritual dimension in a world that seems bent on self-destruction.

Postmodern poetry is fluid. As Wallace Stevens said, though, "Thought tends to collect in pools," and so it does in this work, which returns again and again to the same quests, ironies, conflicts. Concerns of religion, especially Catholicism, surface—but always in a sidelong, quirky way. The saints, the Mass, the Catholic beliefs, large and small, thread through the poems as motifs. There is no doctrine here, only exploration; this version of Catholicism is one way to affirm the mystery but not to define it away. Exploration is always the center of these poems, which seem quest-poems, voyages past signposts but not to a destination. This collection, and indeed Howe's work generally, consists mostly of longer poems, some a couple of pages, some much longer. The poet takes the space required to explore in many directions, follow down byways, and come back.

Quoting samples of the poems is of little use in the discussion of this kind of poetry, because streams of thought combine and separate, and there are glimmers or glitters in the depths that cannot be separated from the streams that produced them. The poems shift and twist through rocks, and the reader follows them willingly, finding now and then a faintly legible guidepost that lets one know one is emotionally and intellectually with the poem still.

~

*Fanny Howe has been a professor at University of California, San Diego, and at Bard College, among other institutions. A novelist and children's writer as well as a poet, she has won numerous awards, including a National Endowment for the Arts fellowship grant, a National Poetry Foundation award, and the Lenore Marshall Poetry Prize.*

~

*On the Ground* is a collection of ten poems, or perhaps sequences, that explore experientially the nature of human existence—what it means to be on the ground, grounded, what it feels like to experience the trauma and trivia of daily life. The title is ironic because to be on the ground in this collection is to be a part of a metaphysical as well as a physical reality—to be, in other words, in the air. The book is examining political grounds and grounding too, as war, destruction, terrorism, and oppression loom in and out of the scene, like trucks coming over a hill. This, however, is not a negative book, filled only with the rot of current social ills. The idea of a postmodern metaphysic seems to be an oxymoron, as the postmodern movement is, in part, a denial of the "transcendental signifier" that was the foundation of earlier poetics. Howe's poems are soul-seeking, and they include the spiritual dimension even in a time of overwhelming social chaos. If the title *On the Ground* suggests matter and the material, these poems are not resting on the ground, and in fact seem to be grounded in motion.

The poems of *On the Ground* are difficult, and it is a characteristic of Howe to string together incongruities, returning again and again to an obsessive image. It is the obsession, sometimes obliquely identified, that holds the poem together. Her points of return and also of irritation are Christianity, social injustice, violence, and the family, and these concerns both conflict and overlap. There is never a resting place in the poem, allowing the reader to pull it all together or to follow the poet's reflections and collocations—there are only glimpses, half seen in the headlong rush. Even the book's end is no stopping place.

On the page, these poems are typical of postmodern work. No rhythmic patterns or eye stanzas appear; the lines are mostly short, and a lot of white space separates them. There is little in the way of direct metaphor or realistic imagery; these poems are layered but not in a modernist mode. The poems are open-ended and suggestive. The relationships between parts of the poem are deliberately blurred through quirky juxtaposition and pronoun slippage. Allusions are rare but difficult; a highly specific and cryptic image often precedes an abstraction. Yet there is a power and a sense of urgency in the poetry. These poems seem to ask for a special mode of reading. The poems seem to yield most when read quickly at first, to catch the obsessive motifs and the flow of the poem, and then reread slowly, stopping at certain lines and following connections, and then reread again quickly, to let the images and concepts fall into place again. The poems deliberately frustrate expectations at every turn—words and concepts slip from their moorings, and metaphorical equations are deconstructed. There is an "I," but it seems to be neither the poet nor a defined speaker but a disembodied I, an eye. The emotion in the poems, too, seems to be separated or detached from any person, and yet it is there, floating between subject and object, ready to attach itself to the reader. The poems burn with an almost abstract passion.

Action dominates this work, and the poems offer multiple means of transport: bus, taxi, walking, boats, planes, and so forth. The reading of them seems itself a vehicle, as they move very swiftly and without transition between familiar and unfamiliar terrain. They arrive in a foreign territory full of indistinct shapes and sudden sharp images, shapes which nevertheless communicate impressions, points of view, even political stances. There are layered parables and sudden shifts of perspective, and there are the motifs that recur throughout the book as brief stops on its route. There is no decoration. Michael Palmer said of her work, "Fanny Howe employs a fierce, always passionate, spareness in her lifelong parsing of the exchange between matter and spirit." The spareness contributes to the effect of rapid motion, of thought on a headlong linear trajectory.

The last poem (or poem sequence) is the longest and perhaps the most complicated. A long poem with multiple parts and excursions, "The Kneeling Bus" covers more than a third of the book. It begins with the image of the city bus which lowers a side ramp to accept wheelchair-bound passengers and is referred to as a "kneeling bus." The metaphor is taken literally—an interesting postmodern technique; instead of making metaphors, Howe will take metaphors apart, providing a hard, impenetrable surface rather than a symbolic narrative to be delved into for meanings. The "kneeling bus," then, becomes a church as well as a bus. From the perspective of the bus rider, on a trip located in time and place ("The M-11, / February, 2003.") The bus trip, through lots of misery and occasional exaltation, touches on the poor, the mad, terrorists, the September 11, 2001, terrorist attacks, time, and God, never slowing down, dissolving identity into plurality and reconstituting it again after the manner of poet Walt Whitman. The trip ends with the comparison of the kneeling bus/church with other of the speaker's places of worship, other ways of approaching, appealing to, or recognizing divinity. The last line, with its terminal word, "live," seems to suggest all the odd coincidences and the tenuous chains of events that constitute existence. It all adds up to a sense of the vital.

> My church is this machine rolling
> the people along and sometimes
>
> my church is a public latrine, sometimes
> I drop on my knees and fall

across a chair like a coat in an empty room.

. . . . . . . . . . . . . . . . . . . . . . . . . . . . . . . . .

Sometimes my church is a Franciscan chapel
near Penn Station. Beads rattle.

People sleep, mutter and curse.

When I leave this bus

a *thanks* to the driver is to cross and live

These poems of *On the Ground* are not going to be well received by all readers, or even all poetry readers; their elliptical breathlessness and their quirky juxtapositions are not characteristic of mainstream poetry and are not what readers who pick up occasional copies of the National Book Award-winning works have come to expect. The poems are enigmatic and darting in movement. They pay no attention to the readers and do not stop for them. The mixture of matter and spirit, poetics and politics, as well as the sudden gleams of insight that illuminate them, have strong appeal to those who are never willing to settle for easy solutions and who appreciate poetry on the edge.

*Janet McCann*

### Review Sources

*Ploughshares* 30 (Fall, 2004): 215.
*Publishers Weekly* 251, no. 25 (June 21, 2004): 58.

# ONE DAY THE ICE WILL REVEAL ALL ITS DEAD

*Author:* Clare Dudman
*First published: Wegener's Jigsaw*, 2003, in Great
  Britain
*Publisher:* Viking (New York). 405 pp. $26.00
*Type of work:* Novel
*Time:* 1883-1931
*Locale:* Berlin and Hamburg, Germany; Copenhagen;
  Graz, Austria; Iceland; and Greenland

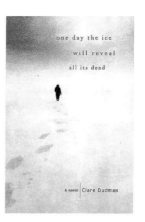

*A historical novel about the meteorologist whose revo-
lutionary ideas about continental drift led the way to the
theory of plate tectonics*

Principal characters:
> ALFRED WEGENER, a German meteorologist
>   and geophysicist
> KURT WEGENER, his older brother and closest friend during their youth
> JOHAN KOCH, a German cartographer, Alfred's friend
> ELSE KÖPPEN WEGENER, Alfred's young wife, a schoolteacher
> VLADIMIR KÖPPEN, her father, a professor of meteorology and Alfred's
>   loyal supporter
> LUDWIG MYLIUS-ERICHSEN, a Danish explorer, organizer of the first
>   Greenland expedition

During his lifetime, Alfred Wegener was ridiculed by his colleagues, and even today, though the theory of plate tectonics is familiar even to schoolchildren, the name
of the German meteorologist who first suggested that land masses are constantly in
motion is not widely known. In *One Day the Ice Will Reveal All Its Dead*, Clare
Dudman reminds the world how much it owes to a man who stood up to abuse by his
colleagues with the same courage that led him onto the glacial ice of Greenland and finally to an early death.

The author of the book was drawn to her subject by her fascination with the idea of
continental drift, first proposed by Wegener. By the time she was ready to begin her
university education, Dudman already knew enough about Wegener to describe him
to university interviewers as the famous scientist she would most like to meet. However, Dudman would complete her doctorate in chemistry, pursue a career in research
and teaching, and publish a children's novel before she was ready to embark on a
book about Wegener.

After eighteen months of research, including a trip to Greenland, Dudman had ample material for a scholarly biography. However, she chose to write Wegener's story
as a historical novel. By having Wegener tell his story in the first-person voice, often
in the present tense, Dudman is able to explore the inner conflicts she believes defined
Wegener's life, the struggle to hold to his own perception of truth in the face of almost

universal scorn and the even more difficult battle
with his conscience as he saw his family suffering
for his convictions.

*One Day the Ice Will Reveal All Its Dead* begins with a two-part preface, in which Dudman introduces the two symbolic constants in her work:
ice and death. The preface begins with what the
speaker describes as an explanation of ice. Although in the succeeding paragraphs this narrator,
who presumably is Wegener, does present a good
deal of factual material, his tone is not that of an
objective scientist but of a man with a passion for
his subject. Halfway through this poetic disquisi-

*Clare Dudman is a Ph.D. in
physical organic chemistry and
has worked as a research scientist
and a teacher. In 1995, she won
the Kathleen Fidler award for her
children's novel* Edge of Danger.
*In 2001, an excerpt from her first
adult novel,* Wegener's Jigsaw,
*won an Arts Council of England
Writers Award.*

tion, Wegener speculates that perhaps at some point in the future "the ice will reveal
all its dead," and dead bodies from throughout history will arise from their unmarked
graves in the Arctic. From this passage, in which ice and death are symbolically
united, the American version of Dudman's book derived its title. Wegener concludes
by pointing out that at present, the ice continues to conceal even the graves of those
who love it.

The question of what is meant by "the present" points to a flaw in what is otherwise
an impressive book. Neither in this preface nor in the rest of the novel is it made clear
just where in time Wegener, the narrator, is positioned. The preface seems to suggest
that Wegener is speaking from beyond the grave; however, most of the episodes he relates could well be simply his recollections in later years, as he assesses his past life,
or even in his final days, as he waits for death.

In any case, the author does not leave the reader uncertain as to Wegener's fate.
The last part of the preface is an italicized passage in which an unspecified, objective
observer describes a scene on the Greenland ice cap. An exact date is given: it is
May 12, 1931, or six months after Wegener vanished. Dogsleds appear, bringing people to dig at a site marked with skis. Suddenly someone announces finding some hair,
then an animal skin, then a fragment of clothing which is declared to be "his." As the
preface ends, the diggers are still at their grim task.

If the preface to *One Day the Ice Will Reveal All Its Dead* suggests that Wegener's
passion took him to a tragic death, the last two pages of the novel offer a very different
perspective. Here Dudman reprints an article from *The New York Times* in which the
famous artist and writer Rockwell Kent urges public support for the work of the German scientists in Greenland, and the scientist who is Wegener's successor offers to
work without pay in order to carry on the work of his leader and friend. Clearly the
preface and the final extract are meant to serve as a frame for the narrative itself. The
preface equates ice with death; the conclusion suggests that Wegener and his passion
not just for the poetic beauty he finds in the ice, but also for truth, will live on.

That this historical novel is actually a work about the pursuit of scientific truth is
evident in the titles of the four sections into which the book is divided: part 1, *Die
Einleitung* (The Introduction); part 2, *Die Hypotheses* (The Hypothesis); part 3, *Die*

*Methode* (The Method); and part 4, *Der Schluss* (The Conclusion). Thus Dudman suggests that Wegener's life can be equated with his progress in finding and proving one scientific idea. What made his story so poignant, she goes on to show, was that he was not just a scientist; he was also a human being, sensitive to criticism and only too conscious of his responsibilities to those he loved.

Wegener's first memory is of breaking loose from the clutches of an older sister and an older brother in order to catch the light in a patch of water. He ends up in a Berlin canal. Obviously, he is already too curious about the world around him to worry about his own survival. This same curiosity later leads young Alfred and his brother Kurt to watch their older brother Willy producing little explosions by mixing ingredients from the kitchen. After Willy's untimely death, Alfred and Kurt keep on experimenting. However, although late in his university career Alfred finally develops an enthusiasm for science and earns his doctorate, he does not like being cooped up in a laboratory. He would rather be adventuring with Kurt, climbing a mountain or establishing a record for the longest flight in a balloon. It is as much his thirst for adventure as his interest in science that accounts for Alfred's accepting the offer of the Danish explorer Ludwig Mylius-Erichsen to serve as a meteorologist on a scientific expedition to Greenland.

At the time, Wegener does not realize that he will find himself forced to decide between his affection for his family and his need to know more about the world. He can understand why his mother would worry, but he is surprised when his father protests, calling the expedition a foolhardy escapade. What really stuns Wegener, however, is his realization that Kurt feels betrayed because, for the first time, Alfred is venturing forth without him. However, even in the face of his family's disapproval, Alfred never wavers in his decision.

While he is in Greenland, Wegener discovers that according to his calculations, Greenland has been moving west. At the time, Wegener does not realize the importance of his discovery. He is too busy learning to survive all that the pursuit of scientific truth may entail: physical discomfort, exhaustion, hunger, loneliness, and ever-present danger. When the ice breaks under him, Wegener nearly drowns. He is saved by a man who becomes his close friend and companion, Johan Koch, a German cartographer. Mylius-Erichsen is not so lucky. For all his experience, he loses his life to the ice.

Two important events take place in the second section of the book. Wegener falls in love with Else Köppen, the daughter of Vladimir Köppen, a Hamburg professor who has befriended him, and he happens onto the idea that will dominate his life. While browsing in the library at the University of Marburg, where he is a tutor, Wegener sees an article pointing out similarities between fossils found on both sides of the Atlantic Ocean. Although the scientific community believes these likenesses prove that the continents were once connected by land bridges, Wegener remembers his observations about Greenland and considers other possibilities. Noticing how closely the coastlines of Africa and South America could fit together, he comes up with a different explanation: that the continents had once been joined but had slowly, inevitably drifted apart. Wegener now has his hypothesis; what he must do is prove it.

Though he finds happiness in his marriage to Else and in their growing family, Wegener now has new worries, for the appearance in 1915 of his book *Die Entstehung der Kontinente und Ozeane* (*Origin of Continents and Oceans*, 1922) has made him an object of scorn in the scientific community. His public lectures arouse nothing but hostility; his colleagues treat him with contempt. For nine years, he cannot obtain a position at any decent university, and even after he is hired by the University of Graz in Austria, thus obtaining the first economic security in his married life, he still finds his hypothesis first mocked and then, even worse, largely forgotten.

From the beginning, Else has been supportive of Wegener, waiting patiently for him to return from Greenland, enduring poverty when he could not find anyone to hire him, never diminishing in her love for him. However, in 1930, when Wegener, now fifty, is asked to make another expedition to Greenland, Else finally opposes him. She argues that he is too old and that he is needed at home. As if her pleas were not enough, Wegener's three daughters also beg their father not to leave. This may perhaps be the most difficult test of Wegener's resolve, for while he can stand up to hostile colleagues, he finds it difficult to see his wife and his children so unhappy. Again, his devotion to science wins out. Seeing how adamant he is, his daughters finally give in, and Else seems to believe his solemn promise that he will return to his family. He does not. In the brief fourth section of *One Day the Ice Will Reveal All Its Dead*, Wegener bids his farewells and goes on to Greenland, where he disappears a few months later.

Wegener was never to know that his detractors would be discredited or that his own hypothesis would become the basis of the theory of plate tectonics. He would not even know that, as *The New York Times* story indicates, his work in Greenland would go on. However, in his final moments, Dudman has her protagonist turn his head to look at the ice gleaming in the setting sun, a sight he finds so beautiful it hurts.

*One Day the Ice Will Reveal All Its Dead* is an impressive achievement. Not only is it is a fictional work that captures the essence of a real person, but it is also a book that convinces one how truly poetic a life can be that is devoted to the pursuit of scientific truth.

*Rosemary M. Canfield Reisman*

## Review Sources

*Booklist* 100, no. 12 (February 15, 2004): 1035.
*Kirkus Reviews* 71, no. 24 (December 15, 2003): 1411.
*Library Journal* 129, no. 3 (February 15, 2004): 160.
*The New York Times Book Review* 153 (April 4, 2004): 18.
*Publishers Weekly* 251, no. 6 (February 9, 2004): 58.

# OPENING MEXICO
## The Making of a Democracy

*Authors:* Julia Preston and Samuel Dillon
*Publisher:* Farrar, Straus and Giroux (New York). 594
   pp. $30.00
*Type of work:* Current affairs and history
*Time:* From the 1960's to 2004
*Locale:* Mexico

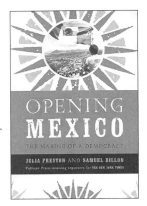

   *The authors, two reporters from* The New York Times,
*relate the background and the possible consequences of
Vicente Fox's victory in Mexico's 2000 presidential campaign*

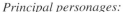

   *Principal personages:*
      VICENTE FOX, president of Mexico, candi-
         date of the National Action Party (PAN)
      MIGUEL DE LA MADRID, president of Mexico, 1982-1988, Institutional
         Revolutionary Party (PRI)
      CARLOS SALINAS, president of Mexico, 1988-1994, PRI
      ERNESTO ZEDILLO, president of Mexico, 1994-2000, PRI
      FRANCISCO LABASTIDA OCHOA, PRI candidate in 2000, who was
         defeated by Fox
      CUAUHTEMOC CARDENAS, 2000 presidential candidate and son of former
         president Lazaro Cardenas

   On July 2, 2000, Mexico changed, perhaps forever. On that date, Vicente Fox, the
candidate of the opposition National Action Party (PAN) was elected president of
Mexico. For the first time since the Mexican Revolution of 1911, an opposition candidate was chosen president in an open democratic election. In *Opening Mexico*, Julia
Preston and Samuel Dillon relate the story of Mexico's single-party rule and its 2000
transition to a successful multiparty democracy in, as one would expect from two
prizewinning newspaper correspondents, an involving journalistic style. *Opening
Mexico* combines the authors' personal experiences from 1995 to 2000, when they reported events in Mexico for *The New York Times*, as well as other visits to Mexico,
with a narrative of the events and personages that led up to the 2000 election.
   For most of the twentieth century, the party of government, and of much else in
Mexico, was the Institutional Revolutionary Party (PRI) or its predecessors. Through
the decades, political opposition to the PRI was either nonexistent or minimal and irrelevant. The PRI had many accomplishments to its credit. In comparison to most
Latin American nations, the PRI had provided Mexico with political stability. In the
first decade or so after the revolution of 1911, Mexico's political leaders often died violently, including two presidents who were assassinated in the 1920's. To end the cycle of violence, the official National Revolutionary Party (PNR) was established in

the early 1930's. Under Lazero Cardenas, in about 1940 the PNR was renamed the Party of the Mexican Revolution (PRM), which in turn became the Institutional Revolutionary Party (PRI) in 1946.

Thus from the early 1930's, a single political party dominated Mexican politics, and after its founding there were no military *coups d'état*, no man-on-horseback syndrome, and no caudillo phenomenon, unlike elsewhere in Latin America. Every six years political power was transferred peacefully from the president to his successor. However, the selection of the future president was not a democratic process. There were no primary elections in which the voters had any input, and there were no political conventions where delegates determined the candidate. The public's participation in what was a mock-drama was that every six years they got to vote, although in reality there was only one person for whom to vote. The incumbent president's was the only vote that truly counted because he, and only he, chose his successor, and with only one party, the chosen candidate always triumphed. The results were predestined by *el sistema* (the system). Under the guise of democracy, the system was a dictatorship.

*Samuel Dillon was Mexico City bureau chief for* The New York Times *and was awarded Pulitzer Prizes for his Iran-Contra scandal reporting and for his series on Mexican drug corruption.*

*Julia Preston, a* New York Times *correspondent in Mexico from 1995 to 2000, shared the 1998 Pulitzer Prize for international reporting and has received the Maria Moors Cabot Prize for coverage of Latin America.*

The PRI had accomplishments other than order and stability. One of the causes of the 1911 revolution was the demand for land reform. Too few Mexicans (and some foreigners) owned and controlled too much land. In the aftermath of the revolution, and particularly during the presidency of Cardenas in the 1930's, a significant (if not complete) restructuring of the landed resources of Mexico took place. Cardenas also nationalized the mineral resources of Mexico, particularly the oil reserves, a decision that caused considerable enmity between the Mexican government and foreign, mostly American, oil companies. Educational opportunities increased, as did the availability of medical care. The PRI and its supporters had much to be proud about, again particularly in comparison to many other Latin American nations, but pride can lead to hubris, and power tends to corrupt. Over the decades, abuse of power and various modes of corruption, political and economic, invaded and infiltrated the governing system.

The PRI leadership and its ordinary members equated the PRI to Mexico itself. To be against the PRI was to be against the state, to be unpatriotic. For many Mexicans, particularly workers and peasants, the PRI's appeal worked. They enthusiastically supported and voted for the PRI candidates on both the local and federal levels, even though through the years Mexico's majority did not improve, rather the reverse.

The PRI, however, went further than just wrapping itself in the Mexican flag. Elections were often uncontested—or if contested, the opposition candidates and parties had no chance of political victory. Nevertheless, the PRI took no chances. Ballot boxes were stolen or stuffed with votes by nonexistent voters. PRI buses transported voters from polling place to polling place so that multiple fraudulent ballots could be cast for PRI candidates. In rural villages, washing machines were distributed as bribes, and at factories, PRI-controlled unions ensured that the members would vote only for approved PRI candidates. Opposition candidates were excluded from the PRI-controlled media, particularly television, and the opposition press faced the possibility of not receiving sufficient newsprint on which even to publish.

As a last resort, PRI goons resorted to physical intimidation and violence against both the left and the right. The goal became the maintenance of political power and the perquisites that went with power, notably wealth. It was cynically said, even by PRI officials, that a politician who is poor is a poor politician. Traditionally, when a president completed his *sexenio* (six-year term), he had acquired numerous mansions and millions of pesos, often deposited in foreign banks.

Opposition to the PRI came from both the political left and the political right. Critics on the left claimed that the PRI had turned its back upon its revolutionary heritage. Peasants and workers did not benefit, only the politicians of the PRI. Communists and socialists were placed beyond the law, and even students faced the brutal force of the PRI, most infamously in 1968 just prior to the Mexico City Olympic Games, when, at Tlatelolco plaza, government security agents, acting with the knowledge of President Diaz Ordaz, murdered and injured hundreds of demonstrating students. In the aftermath, in what the authors call the first mass democratic movement in Mexican history, hundreds of thousands of demonstrators, many of them from the middle class, marched against the PRI regime. The Tlatelolco massacre was a turning point for many Mexicans, who concluded that the governing party had lost its political and moral legitimacy.

On the right, the National Action Party (PAN) was often the only opposition party during the decades of PRI domination. Founded in 1939 by a group of Catholic lawyers, PAN was ideologically more conservative than the PRI. It occasionally fielded candidates, particularly in local elections, but they rarely were elected, and if they were victorious the election would be stolen through ballot manipulation or legal maneuvering because the legal system was also controlled by the PRI. Perhaps the most infamous example of the PRI stealing an election occurred in 1986, when in the gubernatorial election in the state of Chihuahua, the PAN candidate, although leading three to one in some polls, was "defeated" by the PRI candidate. The blatant theft mobilized antigovernment sentiment across the ideological divide, gaining the conservative PAN liberal allies who were disgusted with the PRI's corrupt practices.

The 1990's was a culmination of democratic aspirations, and developments during that decade paved the way for Fox's victory in 2000. The democratic movement in Mexico evolved over time, sparked by such events as Tlatelolco and Chihuahua, and the participants were less concerned about advancing a particular ideology than the democratic process itself. The presidents of Mexico played major roles, mostly negative, in "opening Mexico" to democratic change, because they held so much power as heads of state but also as heads of the PRI. Among the increasingly numerous advocates of democracy, there was no single figure who personified the movement, as did Nelson Mandela in the antiapartheid campaign in South Africa.

Rather, it was many Mexicans in numerous organizations and demonstrations who were committed to ending *el sistema*. The authors brilliantly interweave the activities of ordinary Mexicans with the actions of the ruling elite. *Opening Mexico* tells the stories and experiences of dozens of ordinary Mexicans who played parts in the democratic drama, and on occasion, the authors step out of the third-person narrative of journalism and history and provide first-person vignettes about what they encountered.

The PRI president most responsible for assuring Fox's peaceful accession in 2000 was Ernesto Zedillo. His predecessor, Carlos Salinas, had been the choice of Miguel de la Madrid and was duly elected in 1988, but Salinas's victory was clouded by accusations that the election had been stolen from the PAN candidate. In 1994, at the end of his *sexinio*, Salinas chose Luis Donaldo Colosio as his successor, but Colosio was assassinated in Tijuana during a campaign appearance. (Six years later it was announced that the assassin was mentally deranged and had acted alone.) By default, Zedillo was chosen as Colosio's replacement. In the election that followed, Zedillo defeated two opposition candidates, in what was, given the PRI's history of corruption and intimidation, a relatively clean election. As president, Zedillo was something of a PRI outsider and not always comfortable to the traditional political culture of the PRI. He supported political reform in which the law would be supreme, not *el sistema*, and it was Zedillo's commitment to a more democratic process that ensured Fox's subsequent election.

Fox, at six feet, six inches tall and wearing his trademark cowboy boots, was a charismatic campaigner. A former executive at the Coca Cola Company, he got into politics in the late 1980's, joining PAN, which was becoming popular with Mexico's growing middle class. After serving as governor of the state of Guanajuato, he began his campaign for president in 1997, an unprecedented early start by Mexican standards. His PRI opponent in the 2000 election was Francisco Labastida Ochoa, who had loyally served the party for more than thirty years, and by PRI standards was relatively uncorrupt. Cuauhtemoc Cardenas, the son of the former PRI president Lazaro Cardenas, was a third candidate. The 2000 campaign was not without incidents of vote buying and intimidation, but Zedillo, much to the pain and anger of many PRI minions, guaranteed that Fox, if he legitimately had the votes, would become Mexico's next president.

Fox's victory in 2000 did not immediately bring change to Mexico. Crime and kidnapping continued unabated, drug smugglers persisted in their murderous forays along the border with the United States, the polluted air in Mexico City ranked it among the worst of the world's large cities, and the Zapatista Indian uprising in Chiapas remained unresolved. Nevertheless, 2000 was a watershed year in Mexican history. Whatever the challenges and problems in the future, *el sistema* had seemingly been vanquished, and a multiparty democracy had established permanent roots in the Mexican soil. In *Opening Mexico*, Preston and Dillon relate this important development with drama and with insight.

*Eugene Larson*

## Review Sources

*Booklist* 100, no. 11 (February 1, 2004): 946.
*Business Week*, March 29, 2004, p. 24.
*Foreign Affairs* 83, no. 2 (March/April, 2004): 167.
*Kirkus Reviews* 71, no. 24 (December 15, 2003): 1442.
*Library Journal* 129, no. 2 (February 1, 2004): 110.
*The Nation* 278, no. 15 (April 19, 2004): 25.
*The New York Times Book Review* 153 (March 28, 2004): 10.
*Publishers Weekly* 251, no. 4 (January 26, 2004): 244.

# ORDINARY WOLVES

*Author:* Seth Kantner (1965-    )
*Publisher:* Milkweed Editions (Minneapolis). 324 pp.
 $22.00
*Type of work:* Novel
*Time:* The 1970's and 1980's
*Locale:* Northernmost Alaska and the cities of Fairbanks
 and Anchorage

*Cutuk Hawcly, raised in the wilderness of Alaska, must balance the traditional Inuk ways he has been taught with the attraction of popular culture*

Principal characters:
> CUTUK HAWCLY, a boy raised in the wilds
>  of Alaska
> ABE, his father, an artist who left Chicago for Alaska
> IRIS, his sister
> JERRY, his brother
> ENUK WOLFGLOVE, a traditional hunter
> DAWNA WOLFGLOVE, Enuk's granddaughter
> CHERYL, Cutuk's friend in Anchorage

   Seth Kantner, in his first novel, *Ordinary Wolves*, writes about a world that he knows firsthand, having grown up in similar circumstances to his protagonist, Cutuk. The love and respect that he has for a disappearing lifestyle and exploited land are apparent, and he is able to transfer these feelings to his audience, who is made aware of the seriousness of the loss.

   *Ordinary Wolves* is the story of the boy Cutuk, but it is also the story of the land. Cutuk, five years old when the novel begins, grows up in the remote regions of Alaska, learning the traditional ways and dreaming of being a hunter like the Iñupiaq village elder and family friend Enuk Wolfglove. Cutuk lives with his eight-year-old sister, Iris, and his ten-year-old brother, Jerry, in a sod igloo built by their father, Abe, in an area so remote that Takunak, the nearest village, is two days away by dogsled. Abe, an artist with a temperament and a profession that is suited to such isolation, left Chicago for a life in harmony with the rhythms of nature. It is a position that Cutuk comes to understand. Cutuk's mother, of whom he has few memories, has returned, for reasons unexplained, to the lower United States.

   The family is close to being self-sufficient. They make clothing from caribou and beaver. Old sweaters are recycled into vests and mending yarn for socks. Buttons and zippers are salvaged from worn-out clothes. As the children learn quickly, nothing is wasted. They obtain food from hunting, fishing, and gathering. From a slain moose, all is used except the windpipe, lungs, and stomach contents. Meals might be dried meat and seal oil or pot-roasted lynx eaten with a salad of springtime shoots, such as fireweed

~

*Seth Kantner, who received a bachelor's degree in journalism from the University of Montana, is a wildlife photographer and writer. Ordinary Wolves, his first novel, won the Milkweed National Fiction Prize. Kantner, his wife, and their daughter live on the Bering Coast in Alaska and return in spring and fall to the sod house where he was raised.*

~

and bluebell. For the money that the family needs, Abe makes wood furniture and paints Alaskan scenes to sell in Anchorage. However, his best oil paintings, especially those of wolves, he burns.

Life in a sod igloo on the arctic tundra is challenging. Abe and the children change clothes only once a month because of the burden of doing laundry. They use a chamber pot in the winter to avoid breaking a trail to the outhouse. Such a life is potentially dangerous, as the climate is so unforgiving. Winter temperatures are often thirty degrees below zero, so cold that the kerosene for the lamps congeals, so cold that their sled dogs stand on three legs in order to thaw the fourth, and so cold that Cutuk will warm his hands in the pooling blood of a slain moose.

Because of their remoteness, the children are home-schooled, and visits from their rare guests are occasions for celebration. Two or three times a year, the family travels to Takunak, a town of 150 people. These trips, which must coincide with the freezing and "Breakup" of the Kuguruk River, are to get mail and to purchase necessities, such as flour, powdered milk, gun powder, and occasionally a bag of apples and vanilla for snow cones. Because his family are outsiders, these trips bring anguish to Cutuk, who, feeling the stigma of being white, prefers his Inuk name to his English one of Clayton, tries to flatten his nose, and is ashamed of his blond hair and blue eyes.

Cutuk is stared at because "no one had ever learned not to stare," ostracized, and bullied, even though he is more knowledgeable of the Inuk ways than the other children. One of the few who befriend him is Dawna, Enuk's granddaughter, and at twelve he is enamored with her: "I wanted her to be the first person I ever kissed—after I learned how."

Cutuk and his siblings are taught traditional ways by their father and Enuk. They sew caribou socks, mukluks (boots made from skins), and rawhide-and-birch snowshoes. They tan hides with sour dough, and skin foxes in order to sell the pelts. They know to ice the runners of the sleds with bear fur dipped in water and to bite off with their teeth the ice balls that form between the toes of the sled dogs.

Abe and Enuk teach Cutuk respect for the land and its game. Honoring a slain wolf, Enuk cuts its throat to release its spirit. Hunting moose with his father, Cutuk is reminded not to shoot wolves that are not needed by the family. After Abe has left their campsite to take some of the moose meat back to their home, ten-year-old Cutuk is left to guard the rest of the meat. During the night he hears the wolves howling and the sounds of one chasing a small animal. He aims at a wolf but does not shoot, recognizing the intrinsic value of the wolf: "That wolf—how many miles and years had he walked under this smoky green light [aurora borealis]? Walked cold, hungry in storms, wet under summer rain; walking on this land I'd always called *my* home. He knew every mountain, every trail along every knoll so much better than I ever would."

The traditional ways that Abe knows and teaches his children are not followed by the native inhabitants of the region. Cutuk's clothing—caribou parka, beaver hat, and wolverine mittens—is not that worn in the village, its teenagers wear nylon jackets and jeans, clothing from catalogs that does not stand up to the challenges of the environment. Even the diet of the villagers has changed: On a trip into town Cutuk is surprised to be served canned stew, not the usual caribou or bear. Electricity and satellite television are curtailing the outdoor lifestyle of the natives. The biggest change, and the most disastrous for the environment, is the snowmobile or, as it is locally termed, snowgo, which allows for incursions into the wild and promotes killing for sport, not just for food and clothing.

Cutuk and his siblings feel the pull of the outside world. Jerry finds work as a contractor in Fairbanks; Iris visits that city in preparation for college. As she talks to Cutuk, now sixteen, about her experience, he is amazed at her revelations about store-bought ice, roller skates, buses, pizzas, and dances. Suddenly what he does seems insignificant:

> A dance! While Iris was gone I'd mushed my dogs north, climbed a pass in the Dog Die Mountains. I tracked and shot a wolverine beyond treeline . . . I skinned it there . . . Days later on the way home . . . a brown bear charged out of alders . . . I shot from the sled. The bear fell, rose, and bounded into the thickets. Cautious and alone, I snowshoed after the wounded animal and took the bear's meat home . . . Now in the thud of one heartbeat it was nothing worth telling.

Cutuk realizes that he must experience contemporary city life before he can make a choice about his future. He questions whether he can ever fit in; he is not like Iris, who is comfortable in both worlds: "She could gut a caribou and talk to strangers." Cutuk spends the last year of high school in Takunak. Seduced by the idea of a snowgo, he buys one with his Alaska Permanent Fund check, a yearly dividend from Alaskan oil revenues.

Like the villagers, he uses the snowgo to hunt down a wolf: "In half a minute I was beside him. His mouth panting wide, his head pounding up and down with supreme effort." He shoots, "My stomach wrenched, recognizing this moment, this first slam of death, when an animal was suddenly writhing and wounded, already a creature with terror eyes and . . . no way back to perfection." He knows that he will never do that again. Later, though, he trades the wolf for rum in an effort to fit in with the local teenagers.

At twenty-two, Cutuk goes to Anchorage and works in a junkyard washing parts with solvent to make them look new. He lives with January Thompson, a friend of his father who once shot wolves from a plane for the bounty, and finds a girlfriend, Cheryl. All that most Americans take for granted, such as cars and running water, he experiences for the first time, and his confusion is palpable. Without knowledge of popular culture, he is again an outsider, this time among his own people who cruelly mock and ridicule him. He is afraid to answer a simple question about ice cream, "'You ever try Pralines 'n Cream?' . . . in case it was a common narcotic, or some kind of bent-over sex everyone else had had."

It is the constant noise that defines the city for Cutuk: "I realized finally that, more than in wind or cold or Breakup, the power and the absoluteness of wild earth resided in its huge uncompromising silence," something he does not find in the city.

After a year in Anchorage, Cutuk, still searching for his way, wonders what is important. His answer brings him back to the wilderness:

> The pastel of evening sky over snow. Caribou clicking past. Ravens on the wind. . . . The fire crackling in the morning. The smell along the riverbanks of grass and tundra and highbush cranberry. Fox tracks in fresh first fall snow. Ermine tracks by the *quaq* pile. Out on the river ice, otters nuzzling beside deadly open water. Wind moving the tops of spruce.

Not only does he miss the beauty, he also misses the directness and simplicity of that life where "water came from the river, heat from wood, meat from animals." So he returns to Takunak and visits his sister who, now a teacher, sees firsthand the problems faced by the Native Americans. Modern changes bring convenience but also boredom, alcoholism, and suicide.

Cutuk then visits his father, who has moved to a cabin downriver, owns solar panels and a short wave radio, and has a small boat but prefers the reliability of a dogsled. Even with the changes, Abe remains part of the natural world. After Cutuk helps his father put up caribou for the coming winter, he returns to live in the sod igloo of his childhood and catches fish, hunts caribou, and gathers berries for his own winter supply. He wonders about his future and about the possibility of Dawna sharing such a life.

The novel is an engrossing coming-of-age tale, but it is also an elegy for a lost way of living and for a landscape that is being irrevocably damaged. It is a criticism of the "Everything-Wanters," of the expensively dressed tourists and sport hunters who turn the land into a "playground wilderness," of the "native worshipers" and of the social anthropologists who promote schemes such as the Cultural Edification Project, with its plans to put all Iñupiaq knowledge on compact discs: "They're gonna have classes, teach how to be Eskimo, just learn on your computer." It is a criticism of the Alaska Natives who are forgetting their heritage. Most of all *Ordinary Wolves* is an honest portrayal of the Alaskan wilderness: Jack London, author of *Call of the Wild* (1903), sensationalized it; Kantner does not.

*Barbara Wiedemann*

## Review Sources

*Anchorage Daily News*, May 28, 2004, p. F1.
*Booklist* 100, no. 17 (May 1, 2004): 1545.
*E Magazine: The Environmental Magazine* 15, no. 4 (July/August, 2004): 60.
*Kirkus Reviews* 72, no. 8 (April 15, 2004): 350.
*Library Journal* 129, no. 5 (March 15, 2004): 106.
*The New York Times*, July 25, 2004, p. 16.
*Poets and Writers* 32 (July/August, 2004): 44.
*Publishers Weekly* 251, no. 18 (May 3, 2004): 170.

# OUR KIND
## A Novel in Stories

*Author:* Kate Walbert (1961-    )
*Publisher:* Charles Scribner's Sons (New York). 208 pp.
$23.00
*Type of work:* Novel
*Time:* The mid- to late twentieth century
*Locale:* Washington D.C., New York, and Connecticut

*Women who came of age in the postwar era look back on early marriages, lost careers, years of child rearing, and divorces to find that so many of life's disappointments were shared by their friends*

As young women, the characters in *Our Kind* disappoint their teachers and forsake their talents, dropping out of graduate studies to fulfill the roles society expects of women. Their innocence and lack of skill to please their mates bring out criticism and cruelty—even, in one case, on the wedding night. While their husbands are absent at work, these women live empty, lonely lives, raising children practically by themselves. Once divorced, with their children gone, it is the women who stay together as friends. In flashes of memories, they reminisce about their dreams of romance, most of which turned into traumatic and humiliating experiences. Comparing notes, only now do they find how similar their lives have been, filled with disappointment and hurt. Finally free, they understand one another and share what is left of their lives, doing what they choose although still living far removed from their once-innocent dreams of the lives they hoped to have.

*Our Kind* is Kate Walbert's third novel. It consists of ten stories, each of which could be published separately. The stories are presented in vibrant, beautiful flashes of memory from different stages in the lives of women who came of age in the 1950's. This is the generation of Walbert's mother, to whom this book is dedicated. In this, like in Walbert's previous books, a story was first published in *The Paris Review* and then used to develop a whole novel for and about women. Interesting and educational, the stories are not didactic or moralizing, because the prose is mannered and detached. It sparks flashbacks, explosions of memories and scenes from lives past. At the same time, Walbert's talent for storytelling keeps the story thread on at least two, constantly intertwined, levels, "then and now," offering depth and new perspectives.

The writing is loaded with effervescent life details that could easily be missed if the stories are not carefully read. The fluffy, informal language also makes the work an attractive and easy read. The narrative also leaves much to the imagination, with its unfinished sentences and things unsaid. It motivates one to read actively and alertly to capture all the nuances. The writing almost engages the reader and writer in a dialogue. By virtually becoming part of the group and entering the scene, the reader will

*The author of* Where She Went *(1998) and* The Gardens of Kyoto *(2002), Kate Walbert is the recipient of a grant from the Connecticut Commission on the Arts and fellowships from MacDowell and Yaddo. She teaches writing at Yale University and lives in New York City with her family.*

understand the double meanings, symbols, and foreshadowing. Walbert chooses to deliver her message indirectly, thus allowing her characters and readers to make their own decisions.

Walbert shows respect (although it is coated with mild humor) for strong women. For example, Grandmother Nettle dares to stand up to President Roosevelt, demanding that he act as a gentleman. With an O. Henry-esque touch, and almost en passant, Walbert depicts young women, who lack mothers and family tradition to fall back upon, teaching their babies to be strong like aviator Amelia Earhart and orderly like style guru Martha Stewart.

In the first story, "The Intervention," the whole group of women friends is gathered around Canoe's swimming pool to plan a joint action to save their idol, a man who is part of their pasts and who replaces their husbands and sons, for he has always been there for them. In the end, they find out, it is they who need to be saved. He has been taking care of himself—at their cost—all along.

In "Esther's Walter" a woman, once talented and attractive, has married a man without looks or money. After years of a childless marriage, she becomes a widow. This is the only story in which love is not ridiculed. Rather, it tells of a lifelong commitment. The family house, symbol of Esther and Walter's marriage, was once beautiful enough to attract Andrew Wyeth for some sketches. Now it is dilapidated and disintegrating. On the anniversary of Walter's death, Esther invites friends for a celebration. The atmosphere is ghostly—even the dogs are hungry and skinny as skeletons. Esther suggests a toast, then dramatically fixing her eyes on her husband's portrait, drinks in the name of love. The drink is, her friends learn later, some kind of arsenic usually used on vermin. The toast, however, makes them realize how long it has been since anyone touched them. None of them can claim love. They are only the onlookers in life.

In "Bambi Breaks for Freedom," a once-talented pianist, now in a wheelchair, makes midnight calls to a man whom she "adored from the first minute" when she was eighteen. The next story, "Screw Martha," portrays the group of women friends engaged in the protection of endangered species. The story is about life and death and the emptiness and loneliness in between.

"Come as You Were" is a flashback to the times of the characters' innocence, early marriages, disappointments never fully named or recognized, and romantic dreams starring only made-up lovers, for lack of any other kind. This is the story in which the memory of Grandma Nettle hovers as a role model of a strong woman standing up for women's rights even when the president acts like a man, not a gentleman.

"Sick Chicks" takes place in a hospice, now changed from the days of the women's youth, when they came there with their children for recreation. Now they gather in the Sunshine Room for a book-club activity, to discuss Virginia Woolf's *Mrs. Dalloway* (1925), about women of their age. Some of them are gradually dying, reminding the group of the inevitability of what "a certain age" holds. Never before did they like or understand *Mrs. Dalloway* as they do now. Each word brings to them their own memories, their own interpretations. Woolf's words "*First the warning, musical; then the hour, irrevocable!*" remind Betsy Kroninger of cancer and Viv of Big Ben and the death knell. That is when all of them laugh together, realizing, they decide, that they would "rather not" die. That story is a powerful collective voice of final victory of life, endurance, and friendship, in spite of everything.

"Warriors" recalls the days when the friends raised their babies, trusting best-selling pediatrician Dr. Spock's every word. A photographer who comes to take a picture of the naked babies ends up shooting a nude and pregnant Louise, who looks like an overripe watermelon and who goes into labor at the end of the story.

"Back When They Were Children," has the women remembering their own childhoods through those of their daughters'. They have their daughters wear self-made hats and then take their picture, wondering what the girls feel "on the inside." Those girls are already different from them, belonging as they do to a different time. They will, later, be involved in statutory rape, smoke marijuana, be caught naked at the cemetery, and spend time in the juvenile center.

"The Hounds, Again" recalls the German dogs, cruel and bloodthirsty. In this story, Christmas is approaching; the kids, busy in college, will not come home. Like Little Red Riding Hood, they do not recognize the hounds with their red, hungry tongues, already claiming them.

"The Beginning of the End" recalls the end of college and also of the women's innocence. Contemporary events include innuendo about artist Salvador Dali's sex life. Some of the girls have already said "yes" to their boyfriends. They wear small promise rings, not really knowing why they are making a decision to marry. Professors are disappointed: The best students are trading their talents for a small ring and "fuzzy thinking." Some already think fuzzily, while unconsciously, almost archetypally, falling into the traps society has prepared for them. Later they will be angry at life, like their mothers. Yet, like their mothers, they never will say anything to their daughters about "those things," so their daughters will have no choice, either. The mothers, however, are noticing their daughters are already different, not raised only by them but by society, the times, and new mores. The daughters have less innocence and more experience in experimenting. Will that make them happier, free to be in charge of their lives?

The new generation is making different decisions (not necessarily better ones). The times are changing so drastically that the experiences of the past are only partially relevant, leaving room for new discoveries, new errors, and new experiences necessary for evolution. This book is detached yet touching, and Walbert's narrative is fractured yet lyrical, as has been noted by critics. Like that of her characters, her language is alive, fluid, youthful, and challenging. With both *Where She Went* (1998) and *Our Kind*, the author shows that women can take freedom into their hands, to invent and reinvent themselves. Walbert reveals and dismantles taboos, educating without preaching. Hers is a book to be read and reread.

*Mira N. Mataric*

## Review Sources

*Booklist* 100, no. 12 (February 15, 2004): 1039.
*Kirkus Reviews* 72, no. 2 (January 15, 2004): 60.
*Library Journal* 129, no. 7 (April 15, 2004): 127.
*The New York Times Book Review* 153 (April 4, 2004): 7.
*Publishers Weekly* 250, no. 48 (December 1, 2003): 38.

# PABLO NERUDA
## A Passion for Life

*Author:* Adam Feinstein
*Publisher:* Bloomsbury (New York). Illustrated. 497 pp.
$32.50
*Type of work:* Literary biography
*Time:* 1904-1973
*Locale:* Chile

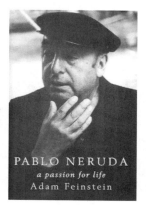

*The first comprehensive English-language biography of the Chilean Nobel Prize winner comprehensively illustrates the poet's work and life*

Principal personages:
PABLO NERUDA, a famous poet
JOSÉ DEL CARMEN REYES, his father
MARIA ANTONIETA HAGEMAAR
VOGELGANZ, his first wife
DELIA DEL CARRIL, his second wife
MATILDE URRUTIA, his third wife
SALVADOR ALLENDE, the president of Chile

The life of Pablo Neruda (1904-1973), winner of the 1971 Nobel Prize in Literature, was anything but peaceful. In a biography that appears on the centenary of the Chilean poet's birth, Adam Feinstein, a journalist and translator of Spanish and Latin American poetry, conveys the reader directly into Neruda's exciting, tantalizing life. Just a recounting of the famous people Neruda encountered—Pablo Picasso, Federico García Lorca, Diego Rivera, Leon Trotsky, Jorge Luis Borges, Jawaharlal Nehru, Arthur Miller—would be book enough without any of the other episodes that make up Neruda's resplendent life.

Like many (or perhaps most) great writers, Neruda, whose real name was Neftalí Reyes, suffered during a difficult childhood. In 1904, he was born into a poor family in Parral, Chile, which the poet described as a "grey dirty dump." His mother, Rosa Neftalí Basoalto Opazo, died from complications during his birth, and his never-happy father, José del Carmen Reyes, punished him constantly. The poet was sick as a child and spent a great deal of time in bed listening to the rain falling. This rainfall, he came to identify as the primary character in his childhood. His father sired an illegitimate girl and a boy with the same woman and for years failed to acknowledge them. Within all the tension and chaos, Neruda found peace in his lifelong fascination with nature, with the ocean in particular, and came to love his gentle, supportive stepmother, Trinidad Candida Marverde ("Mamadre") and his half sister Laura ("Laurita").

Oftentimes somber and melancholic, at age sixteen Neruda changed his name and left his hometown of Temuco for the big city, Santiago. At the university there, he

*Adam Feinstein is a journalist and translator who writes about Spanish and American literature. He is also a short-story writer and has translated poetry by Federico García Lorca and Mario Benedetti. Feinstein has worked as a correspondent for the British Broadcasting Corporation (BBC) and* El Mundo. *He lives in London.*

came to be greatly influenced by French Symbolist poetry, which inspired him cunningly and originally to combine elements of surrealism and impressionism in his first collection, *Veinte poemas de amor y una canción desesperada* (1924; *Twenty Love Poems and a Song of Despair*, 1969), which made him an instant sensation throughout the Spanish-speaking world. However, desperately angry about Chile's economic problems, the young poet soon began to long for greener meadows to nourish his capacious appetite for experience.

After his university years, Neruda served as a diplomat wandering between various Argentinean, French, Japanese, Chinese, Spanish, Mexican, and Indonesian outposts, where he experienced great loneliness and longing and gathered grist for his poetry mill. Wherever he went, he reached out to the downtrodden. For example, in Ceylon he was particularly struck by the arrogant British landowners and their Sinhalese laborers. "The path of poetry," Neruda wrote in 1953, "leads outwards, through streets and factories; it listens at the doors of all the exploited." During this lonely exile, he found himself "yearning for communion," and in love with two Chilean women simultaneously, Albertina Azocur and Laura Arrue, whom he wrote to constantly, pleading with each to marry him.

According to Feinstein, throughout Neruda's life the driving forces behind his work remained his passionate commitment to politics and his obsession with women. It was in Java, Indonesia, that he met his first wife, Maria Antonieta Hagemaar Vogelganz, a Javanese woman of Dutch origin who spoke only English and whom he called "Maruca." No doubt, the instability in his wandering life, coupled with extreme loneliness, prompted Neruda into this marriage. It was unhappy from the start. Although the couple had a daughter, she was unhealthy from birth and died early. During the 1930's, while a diplomat to Spain, Neruda fell in love with the much older artist, Delia del Carril, his second wife, who influenced him to become a communist. By then, the acclaim for his love poems made Neruda a household name.

In addition to loving multiple women, Neruda was also obsessed with left-leaning politics, especially after the Spanish Civil War. Heroically, he ferried Spanish refugees across the Atlantic Ocean in 1939. In the 1940's, he became a senator representing northern Chile, where copper miners lived in nearly complete deprivation. Neruda despised the incursions of American mining corporations into Chile. Filled with the desire to make a social difference, in his thirties and forties Neruda traveled around South America, gaining the stuff of his poetry out of the sufferings of the people. In 1948, as a member of Chile's Communist Party who saw in Joseph Stalin a personal hero, Neruda criticized the president of Chile and was forced, consequently, to flee on horseback over the Andes Mountains. In 1952 he returned to Chile and ran for president. A central figure among the cultural Left, his devotion to communism never wavered, although his continual support of Stalin and his great admiration for China under Mao Zedong caused him ongoing problems. Ironically, despite his love of politics and his passion for the betterment of the underprivileged, Neruda's poems that center on politics, most critics agree, remain his weakest.

The poems that concern Neruda's other obsession—women and love—are considered his best. His three marriages and numerous love affairs inspired him to compose what many see as the most brilliant love poetry ever written in the Spanish language. Critics propose that women adored Neruda, who was plump and not handsome, because oftentimes he would act like a child, desiring certain food and even throwing tantrums. Some critique that the sense of absence and longing that mark his poetry came about through Neruda's constant need to replace the mother he lost at birth. Matilde Urrutia became his third wife. Neruda possessed an insatiable thirst for women; at one point he had an affair with his third wife's niece.

Given Neruda's James Bond lifestyle, it would be easy for Feinstein to fall into the mere telling of the poet's life. However, the biographer stays on task and focuses instead on the work that grew out of Neruda's highly adventurous life. In all, politics and love inspired him to produce the work that many cite as the best poetry of the twentieth century. In such varied works as *Crepusculario* (1923; book of twilights), *Twenty Poems and a Song of Despair*, his more mature *Residencia en la tierra* (1933, 1935, 1947; *Residence on Earth, and Other Poems*, 1946, 1973) and his later *Memorial de Isla Negra* (1964; *Isla Negra, a Notebook*, 1981), the reader finds a touch of the surreal intermingled with epic and myth. For instance, his great poem "Canto general," a hymn to the Americas, came to him through the inspiration of the natives who built Machu Picchu. Neruda, whose work is at times complex and at other times shatteringly simple, longingly desired to associate himself with physical labor, calling himself later in life a poet-baker and a poet-carpenter. However, he sensibly came to understand he could do the most good, or perhaps bring about the most social change, by obeying the inner voice of his calling—writing poetry.

Although Neruda came to enjoy something of a friendship later on in life with Chilean socialist president Salvador Allende, the poet's life ended as it began, in deep, dark suffering. In 1973, during the dictator Augusto Pinochet Ugarte's United States-backed, right-wing coup, Neruda was dying of prostate cancer. As soldiers burst into his house at Isla Negra, the poet maintained a heroic stance, crying out: "the only thing of danger you'll find here is poetry." His house in Santiago was destroyed. His funeral cortege sadly paraded through the capital's streets, amid machine gun-toting soldiers. Indeed, Feinstein evokes tears in the final chapters of *Pablo Neruda: A Passion for Life*.

No doubt Feinstein loves Neruda's poetry with his whole soul. Without such deep affection, there is no way he could otherwise have written such a remarkable biography. He successfully attempts to untangle the contradictions that make up Neruda. However, although he uses the poet's memoirs as a primary source of information,

Feinstein rightfully does not trust Neruda's biased memory. In true journalistic style, the biographer painstakingly questions everyone and anyone associated with the poet. Also, although he makes clear that Neruda, like many brilliant poets before and after, was deeply flawed, Feinstein skillfully avoids judging his subject. He succeeds in this effort by focusing intently on the author's work—the pristine poetry. The book contains beautiful photographs.

*M. Casey Diana*

## Review Sources

*Library Journal* 129, no. 17 (October 15, 2004): 63.
*New Statesman* 133 (August 9, 2004): 38.
*Publishers Weekly* 251, no. 31 (August 2, 2004): 64.
*The Spectator* 295 (August 14, 2004): 33.
*The Times Literary Supplement*, November 5, 2004, p. 8.

# THE PARADOX OF CHOICE
## Why More Is Less

*Author:* Barry Schwartz (1946-    )
*Publisher:* Ecco Press (New York). 288 pp. $24.00
*Type of work:* Psychology

*An investigation into why increasing prosperity and the growing number of choices available to Americans in all areas of their lives tend to be accompanied by decreasing personal happiness and satisfaction*

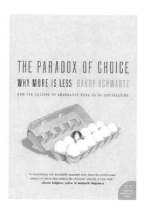

The Paradox of Choice by Barry Schwartz, a social scientist at Swarthmore College, is itself a paradox. It presents detailed research in choice and decision-making conducted by psychologists, economists, market researchers, and decision scientists. It has a humorous, upbeat approach that will be absorbing to the general reader. The book provides "aha" experiences, a sense of new knowledge unfolding that is, at times, counterintuitive. It also offers justification for some underlying suspicions that readers may have held all along. Perhaps that is part of the power of this book. In addition to explaining how and why people make the choices that they do, the author's argument gives credence to the noted sense that something is wrong in a society when the proliferation of available options leaves individuals feeling more and more dissatisfied with the choices they make and less happy with their lives in general.

Schwartz opens with a personal example involving the purchase of a pair of blue jeans. He tends to wear his jeans, Schwartz says, for a long time, so when he found it necessary to buy a new pair at The Gap a few years back, he was unprepared for the options he would find. Schwartz asked the young saleswoman for size 32 waist and 28 inseam, the size he had always worn. He expected to be out of the store with his purchase in just a few minutes. However, she started to ask questions: Did he want slim fit, easy fit, relaxed fit, baggy, or extra baggy? Did he want stonewashed, acid-washed, or distressed? Did he want button-fly or zipper-fly? Did he want faded or regular? Schwartz confesses to being stunned, then sputtering out that he just wanted a pair of regular jeans, the kind that used to be the only ones available.

Not knowing what that kind might be, the saleswoman spoke with an older colleague and was able, eventually, to point Schwartz in the right direction. By that time, however, he was starting to second-guess himself. Did he really want the old-fashioned kind? Perhaps one of the other options would be better. He did not know what the differences among the designs were, and the diagrams in the store were no help. Nonetheless, he became convinced that one of them would certainly be preferable. He decided to sample them all. Although Schwartz says he tried on all kinds of jeans that day, he still could not figure out which were the best.

Schwartz ended up with the "easy fit," and he says they worked out fine. He came

~

*Barry Schwartz is the Dorwin Cartwright Professor of Social Theory and Social Action at Swarthmore College. His articles have appeared in leading social science journals. He is the author of five previous books, including* The Battle for Human Nature: Science, Morality, and Modern Life *(1986) and* The Costs of Living: How Market Freedom Erodes the Best Things in Life *(1995).*

~

away thinking, though, that buying a pair of pants should not be such an ordeal. Given that people have different preferences and body types, having some options is good. However, it does not necessarily follow that more choices are better. As Schwartz explains, "Before these options were available, a buyer like myself had to settle for an imperfect fit, but at least purchasing jeans was a five-minute affair. Now it was a complex decision in which I was forced to invest time, energy, and no small amount of self-doubt, anxiety, and dread." From his experience, Schwartz had ventured into what he calls the darker side of freedom, where a plethora of choices can not only be irritating but also debilitating, and—he suggests—even tyrannizing.

Schwartz then extends his investigation of consumer options to the supermarket. He reports that at his local market he found—among other things—85 kinds of crackers, 285 varieties of cookies (21 options among chocolate chip cookies alone), 175 salad dressings, and 230 kinds of soups. In the electronics store, there were 45 different car stereo systems, 42 different computers, and 27 kinds of computer printers. He also studied the 20 mail-order catalogs that came to his home each week and the cable television offerings, compiling staggering examples.

Schwartz explains that the standard thinking among social scientists is that added options can only make things better for the consumer. People feel happy and empowered when they have more from which to choose, and one who does not want to sift through the options can simply ignore them. However, Schwartz shows the opposite to be true, citing evidence from studies such as a series titled "Why Choice Is Demotivating," published in *Journal of Personality and Social Psychology* in 2000. Throughout the book, he examines why unchosen options detract from the satisfaction that results from the choices people make. "Having too many choices produces psychological stress," Schwartz states, "especially when combined with regret, concern about status, adaptation, social comparison, and perhaps most important, the desire to have the best of everything."

Connecting one's emotional state to the abundance of options is disturbing enough on the level of simple shopping, where irritation is a common result. Schwartz goes further, however, drawing examples from areas such as education, religion, friendship, romance, work, health care, and so on. He asserts that, "as a culture, we are enamored of freedom, self-determination, and variety, and we are reluctant to give up any of our options. But clinging tenaciously to all the choices available to us contributes to bad decisions, to anxiety, stress, and dissatisfaction—even to clinical depression." Consider the large numbers of adults, he says, who find it increasingly difficult to decide what career to pursue or to choose their life partner. People find it difficult to decide what city to live in (or what state or country) or even—with the proliferation of cosmetic surgeries—to know how they want their bodies to look. These are areas, Schwartz says, where an overabundance of options is doing serious damage.

Schwartz connects the proliferation of choices with statistics that show that the American "happiness quotient" has been falling for more than a generation. Studies indicate that individual happiness is related to human interaction, and Schwartz believes that the social fabric of society is no longer a birthright. Relationships have to be consciously chosen, he says, and Americans are finding this harder and harder to do. Instead of being seduced by an overload of options, Schwartz suggests that people should embrace voluntary limits on freedom of choice and accept what is "good enough" rather than try to have the best of everything.

Schwartz also suggests that people lower expectations about the results of the choices they make and start thinking of decisions as irreversible. In addition, Schwartz advises his readers to care less about what other people are doing. He speaks strongly and directly, stating that until the American public realizes that having too many choices is a problem, people will not be able to ignore the seemingly endless alternatives that are proliferating and make more satisfying decisions. This book is Schwartz's attempt to bring such knowledge to light.

An important issue underlying the material that Schwartz presents involves the question of whether one is a maximizer or a satisficer. He offers a short quiz to his readers (courtesy of the American Psychological Association), who can in this way learn where they stand on the maximizer/satisficer scale. So-called maximizers are people who demand the very best and believe that every purchase or decision must be at that level. Satisficers, on the other hand, are able to settle for something that is good enough, without worrying that there might be a better alternative somewhere. Of course, no one is all maximizer or all satisficer in every situation. The tendencies, though, are real and thought-provoking. Schwartz explains that "to a maximizer, satisficers appear to be willing to settle for mediocrity, but that is not the case. A satisficer may be just as discriminating as a maximizer. The difference between the two types is that the satisficer is content with merely excellent as opposed to the absolute best." Schwartz continues, "I believe that the goal of maximizing is a source of great dissatisfaction, that it can make people miserable—especially in a world that insists on providing an overwhelming number of choices, both trivial and not so trivial."

*The Paradox of Choice* has been well received, though subject matter that features the words "freedom" and "choice" is likely to touch nerves in the public arena. Some criticism has centered around the concept of self-help. Some people would like more of a "cookbook" approach to action than Schwartz provides; others have said that the nine steps to happier living Schwartz offers in his short, final chapter detract from the real strength of the work, which involves the unresolved, not-so-tidy questions the book raises. Such controversy is perhaps unavoidable, and criticism from neither side seems particularly damning.

Some of the suggestions Schwartz offers may sound like platitudes, such as number six, "Practice an 'Attitude of Gratitude'" and number seven, "Regret Less." Others are rich and ripe for rumination. For example, Schwartz explains in step one,

"Choose When to Choose," that people should consciously decide "which choices in our lives really matter and focus our time and energy there, letting many other opportunities pass us by." This is easier said than done, but Schwartz argues convincingly that is it worth pursuing. He does not infantalize the task by cheering his readers on. In fact, Schwartz warns that taking these steps will be hard and may even require a new way of thinking. *The Paradox of Choice* provides solid reasoning to enable its readers to do so.

This book succeeds in bringing option overload into the reader's consciousness and sparking discussion. Those who have already considered the subject may find that *The Paradox of Choice* supports some of their ideas and undermines others. Readers who have not given the subject much consideration are likely to be enticed to do so. Schwartz has blended personal anecdotes and other commonplace examples with academic research studies, basic psychology concepts, and—every once in a while—a great *New Yorker* cartoon.

References to researchers, academic studies, and results are included in such a way that they enhance, rather than disturb, the wholeness of Schwartz's argument. Detailed explanations and citations are provided in endnotes for readers who want more. *The Paradox of Choice* is a provocative book in which readers will recognize themselves and their society, complete with quirks and quandaries. It is likely to make people look at their own decision-making in a new light. Some may be surprised, at least initially, by the objective research that Schwartz presents and its reflection in everyday American experience. Readers will probably come away from this book with more questions than answers and with a renewed sense of the possibility for—and the necessity of—change.

*Jean C. Fulton*

## Review Sources

*Booklist* 100, no. 6 (November 15, 2003): 550.
*Business Week*, April 26, 2004, p. 25.
*The Christian Science Monitor*, January 6, 2004, p. 18.
*Library Journal* 128, no. 20 (December 15, 2003): 148.
*New Statesman* 133 (June 7, 2004): 49.
*The New Yorker* 80, no. 2 (March 1, 2004): 91.
*Psychology Today* 37 (March/April, 2004): 79.
*USA Today*, January 20, 2004, p. 4D.

# PLAN OF ATTACK

*Author:* Bob Woodward (1943-    )
*Publisher:* Simon & Schuster (New York). 467 pp.
$28.00
*Type of work:* Current affairs
*Time:* 2000-2004
*Locale:* Washington, D.C., Iraq, and Kuwait

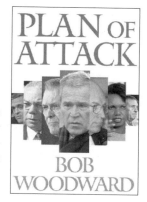

*Based on interviews with President George W. Bush and seventy-five high-ranking government officials, this book reveals how the Bush administration justified attacking Iraq preemptively in order to topple dictator Saddam Hussein*

Principal personages:
> GEORGE W. BUSH, forty-third president of
> the United States
> RICHARD CHENEY, vice president
> CONDOLEEZZA RICE, national security adviser
> KARL ROVE, one of Bush's major political strategy advisers
> COLIN POWELL, secretary of state
> DONALD RUMSFELD, secretary of defense
> JOHN ASHCROFT, attorney general
> GEORGE H. W. BUSH, forty-first president of the United States and
> George W. Bush's father
> BRENT SCOWCROFT, George H. W. Bush's national security adviser
> BOB WOODWARD, investigative reporter for *The Washington Post*

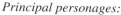

The stated purpose of *Plan of Attack* is to provide a detailed account of why U.S. president George W. Bush, spurred on by his supporters and his advisers, engaged the United States in an unprecedented preemptive war against a sovereign country, Iraq, to bring down its dictator, Saddam Hussein. Hussein was undeniably a cruel and power-crazed despot who ruled by brutalizing Iraqis who opposed him in any way. Famed journalist Bob Woodward's major question, nevertheless, is whether the United States could successfully justify conducting an offensive against Iraq, thereby violating the sovereignty of an independent nation.

In his earlier book *Bush at War* (2002), Woodward delved into the president's motivations for considering a preemptive attack on Iraq. In preparing to write *Plan of Attack*, Woodward had Bush's full cooperation. The heart of the book is based on three-and-a-half hours of interviews Woodward conducted in the White House with the president on December 10-11, 2003. Woodward interviewed defense secretary Donald Rumsfeld as well, for more than three hours during the autumn of 2003.

Bush directed other government officials to cooperate with Woodward, who subsequently interviewed more than seventy-five people crucially involved in events that resulted in the war against Iraq. These included White House staff members, key fig-

∾

*A Pulitzer Prize-winning
investigative reporter for* The
Washington Post, *Bob Woodward
is coauthor (with Carl Bernstein)
of* All the President's Men *(1974),
a Watergate exposé, and the
author of* Bush at War *(2002).*

∾

ures in the Departments of State and Defense, officials of the Central Intelligence Agency (CIA), and members of Bush's war cabinet. It was agreed that these interviews would be conducted for background information, which meant that Woodward was free to use information gained through them but was not free to identify his sources directly or individually.

According to *Plan of Attack*, the Bush White House, from its inception, was supportive of more hawks (war-backers) than doves (negotiators or compromisers). Bush's top-level team members referred to themselves as "the Vulcans." They were Richard Cheney and Donald Rumsfeld, both former secretaries of defense; Colin Powell, former chairman of the Joint Chiefs of Staff; Paul Wolfowitz, former undersecretary of defense; Richard Armitage, former assistant secretary of defense; and national security adviser Condoleezza Rice. The only moderate among these six was Powell, who clearly favored diplomacy over war.

The administration's justification for launching a war against Iraq was that Hussein had weapons of mass destruction (WMDs) that placed the free world in imminent danger of attack and destruction. The events of September 11, 2001—when commercial airliners loaded with fuel were flown into the World Trade Center and the Pentagon, with a fourth plane aimed at Washington, D.C., presumably to destroy either the White House or the Capitol—heightened international awareness that terrorism was indeed a palpable threat, against which drastic measures seemed justified.

Shortly before Thanksgiving of 2001, although Hussein had not been convincingly linked to the catastrophic events of September 11, Bush took Rumsfeld aside and asked him to begin, in concert with Tommy Franks, the combatant commander of the area around Iraq, to devise a plan to protect the United States, one that would topple Hussein's regime. After a cabinet meeting, Bush again met privately with Rumsfeld and told him to devise a war plan against Iraq. When Bush emphasized that Rumsfeld was to discuss this plan with no one, Rumsfeld pointed out the need for input from George Tenet, director of the CIA, who would, it was hoped, provide the documentary justification for such a plan.

Bush met with Tenet in Rice's office and was provided with information about Hussein's alleged WMDs. Bush was somewhat suspicious of the information Tenet proffered and asked him if what he had given him was the best he could provide. Tenet twice told Bush that there was no need to worry, that this was, in his words, a slam-dunk case.

Bush was scheduled to speak in Cincinnati, Ohio, on October 7, 2002. He intended to use this address as the occasion to make his case against Hussein and in favor of the United States' taking preemptive action against the Iraqi dictator. A draft of the speech mentioned that Hussein had purchased from Niger uranium oxide, a necessary ingredient for constructing nuclear weapons. Draft 6 of this speech was altered considerably, and the portion about an Iraq-Niger connection was omitted.

Word of this connection did not surface again until January 28, 2003, when Bush included sixteen words in his state of the union address that referred to an Iraq-Niger connection which, indeed, had never existed. Accounts of it were based on forged documents that were later discredited wholly. Nevertheless, the word was out, and this development was useful to Bush as he attempted to establish his bases for attacking Iraq and destroying Hussein's regime.

The CIA in February, 2002, dispatched retired diplomat Joseph Wilson to Niger to see if he could find evidence that Niger had sold uranium to Hussein. After a comprehensive investigation, Wilson concluded that there was no evidence of the alleged sale. He filed his report with the CIA. When Wilson heard, almost a year later, that Bush had referred to the discredited information in one of the most important speeches of his career, he realized that Bush had ignored totally information readily available to him which declared the Iraq-Niger connection nonexistent.

Woodward writes, "There was no acknowledgment that they lacked 'smoking gun' evidence. Bush instead suggested only a larger risk, one that Rice had publicly raised a month earlier: 'Facing clear evidence of peril . . . we cannot wait for the final proof, the smoking gun, that could come in the form of a mushroom cloud.'" Using these scare tactics, the administration hoped to justify acting as it did in the face of faulty information. Wilson's account of the Bush administration's retaliation against him for writing an op-ed piece in *The New York Times* titled "What I Didn't Find in Africa" is presented in detail in Wilson's book *The Politics of Truth* (2004).

Woodward examines the dynamics of the Bush administration in other ways. He records Powell's discomfort with many of the decisions made regarding going to war. For example, Powell tried to steer Cheney toward a philosophical middle ground as preparations for the war moved forward, but, Woodward writes, the "vice president was beyond hell-bent for action against Hussein. It was as if nothing else existed. Powell attempted to summarize the consequences of unilateral action," but Cheney simply said that Hussein was the issue, rather than the international reaction to a unilateral action on the part of the United States.

The relationship depicted between George H. W. Bush and his son is particularly interesting. The elder Bush has consciously stayed out of his son's way in matters of decision making. When George W. Bush was asked whether he had conferred with his father about going to war against Iraq, Bush the younger replied that his counsel came from a higher father.

Nevertheless, some people speculate that the elder Bush tried obliquely to reach his son through his close friend and associate, Brent Scowcroft, who served as national security adviser during the first Bush presidency and who has remained close to George H. W. Bush through the intervening years. In an op-ed piece published in the August 15, 2002, edition of *The Wall Street Journal* titled "Don't Attack Hussein," Scowcroft voiced his fear that the real Middle Eastern threat to the United States came not from Hussein but from al-Qaeda, an organization with which Hussein has never been convincingly connected. Scowcroft labeled Hussein an anticlerical socialist and, while stating that Hussein harbored a vision of dominating the Middle East, he could not reasonably be linked to terrorist organizations and certainly not to the September 11 tragedies. Scowcroft warned that there was little international sentiment in favor of going to war against Iraq and that doing so would be a go-it-alone operation which would be extremely costly in both lives and dollars.

Scowcroft's sentiments were thought to reflect significantly those of the elder Bush, and they clearly challenged the president's judgment. Following the appearance of the op-ed piece, Powell called Scowcroft to thank him for giving him some running room. Powell had clearly been opposed to entering the war but, as a good and loyal soldier, had not expressed to the president his reservations, feeling that it was not his place to do so unless he was specifically asked—which he never was.

Scowcroft also received a telephone call from Rice about his *Wall Street Journal* piece. She rebuked him sharply, implying that the editorial had not set well with the administration. Scowcroft responded that he did not want to do anything to create a rift with the administration but that he had expressed similar sentiments on television ten days earlier, with no repercussions. Little was heard from Scowcroft after that, probably because the elder Bush did not wish to do anything to lessen his son's confidence at such a crucial time in his administration.

As the nation moved toward the war which was finally begun in March, 2003, Bush appeared to have a single-minded dedication to pursuing the conflict. Karl Rove, one of Bush's major political advisers, had tentatively organized between twelve and sixteen fund-raisers for February, March, and April. The president was to appear at each of these fund-raisers, which were to benefit his campaign budget by as much as two hundred million dollars. Bush, however, made short shrift of these plans, telling Rove, "We've got a war coming . . . and you're just going to have to wait." Rove reminded him that his father had lost the election of 1992 in part because his campaign had started too late, but the president was not swayed by this argument. By Woodward's account, Bush was determined to wage war against Iraq, even though he had no clear exit plan, and he would allow nothing to stand in the way.

*R. Baird Shuman*

## Review Sources

*Business Week*, May 17, 2004, p. 26.
*Entertainment Weekly* 764 (May 7, 2004): 9.
*The New York Times Book Review* 153 (May 9, 2004): 7.
*The New Yorker* 80, no. 11 (May 10, 2004): 98-102.
*People Weekly* 61 (May 3, 2004): 81.
*Publishers Weekly* 251 (May 3, 2004): 18.
*Time* 163 (May 3, 2004): 23.
*U.S. News and World Report* 136 (May 3, 2004): 13.

# THE PLOT AGAINST AMERICA

*Author:* Philip Roth (1933-        )
*Publisher:* Houghton Mifflin (Boston). 361 pp. $26.00
*Type of work:* Novel
*Time:* 1940-1942
*Locale:* Newark, New Jersey, and Washington, D.C.

*In an alternative history that reflects current preoccupations with national identity and political repression, Roth imagines the catastrophic consequences, especially to American Jews, of Charles Lindbergh's election to the U.S. presidency*

> *Principal characters:*
> PHILIP ROTH, the narrator, recalling his life when he was seven to nine years old
> SANDY ROTH, his older brother, talented at drawing
> HERMAN ROTH, his father, an employee of a large insurance company
> BESS ROTH, his mother
> ALVIN ROTH, his orphaned older cousin who comes to live with them
> WALTER WINCHELL, a crass, popular radio commentator
> SELDON WISHNOW, a bright, lonely young neighbor
> AUNT EVELYN, Bess's sister, wife of Rabbi Lionel Bengelsdorf
> LIONEL BENGELSDORF, a Conservative rabbi, chief Jewish apologist for the Lindbergh administration

In a sense, every novel is alternative history, an attempt to imagine how things might have been. A specific genre of popular fiction proceeds from the premise that a familiar public event occurred differently—for example, the South won the Civil War, Napoleon never met his Waterloo, the Spanish Armada conquered England—and extrapolates from there to depict the likely consequences of one dramatic change. In more than twenty books of fiction published since his first collection of short stories, *Goodbye, Columbus,* in 1959, Philip Roth has been more interested in examining the inner lives of fictional figures than in speculating about large historical contingencies. In *The Counterlife* (1986), Roth offers contradictory histories not of the Normandy Invasion but of his recurring character Nathan Zuckerman. When, in *The Ghost Writer* (1979), Zuckerman encounters an Anne Frank who managed to survive the Holocaust, Roth is more intent on examining Zuckerman's personality than in pondering how different the world would have been if the Nazi genocide had been less thorough. *Operation Shylock* (1993) imagines alternative personal identities, two antagonistic characters each named Philip Roth.

However, though the plot of *The Plot Against America* is refracted through the eyes of a boy named Philip Roth, this novel has its sights on broad historical developments. It asks the reader to accept the premise that Charles A. Lindbergh, the aviator who became a national hero by flying solo across the Atlantic Ocean in 1927, defeats Franklin D. Roosevelt in the 1940 presidential election. Lindbergh is an isolationist and a Nazi sympathizer, and once he moves into the White House, the United States

*Recipient of the Pulitzer Prize, the National Book Award, the National Book Critics Circle Award, and the PEN Faulkner Award, Philip Roth emerged as an important force in American Jewish literature with the publication of his first book,* Goodbye, Columbus, *in 1959. Set before and during World War II,* The Plot Against America *follows a sequence of three works—*American Pastoral *(1997),* I Married a Communist *(1998), and* The Human Stain *(2000)—that examine postwar American culture.*

pursues cordial relations with Germany and does not enter World War II. American Jews, including Roth and his family, find themselves in an increasingly precarious position.

A postscript to the novel reprints a speech that Lindbergh actually gave on September 11, 1941. Addressing a rally of the America First Committee in Des Moines, Iowa, Lindbergh—who had visited Adolf Hitler and expressed admiration for him—noted that Jews wielded inordinate influence over the media and the government of the United States. He criticized them for pursuing parochial self-interest and pushing the country into war with Germany. By including Lindbergh's speech, along with verifiable information about public figures, including Lindbergh, Roosevelt, Walter Winchell, and Henry Ford, Roth encourages the reader to examine how he fictionalized history and to ponder the plausibility of his inventions. That it could indeed happen here is the implication of Roth's mingling of fabrication with verifiable facts.

*The Plot Against America* is Philip Roth's fictional memoir of a man named Philip Roth who recalls a crucial, fearful time in his childhood and in the history of his country. He evokes a generally happy household comprising his parents, his older brother, Sandy, and his orphaned cousin, Alvin, in Weequahic, a Jewish neighborhood of Newark, New Jersey. When Metropolitan Life, the company that employs his father, Herman, offers to make him manager of a branch office in nearby Union, he declines rather than move the family to an area in which Jews are vastly outnumbered and profoundly disliked. During an outing to Washington, D.C., the Roths encounter blatant bigotry. Revulsion at the horrors of the Holocaust would, a decade later, drive most anti-Jewish sentiment in the United States underground, but within the context of a society in which anti-Semitism is already widespread and widely accepted, the young Philip experiences persecution and pogroms as consequences of official policy.

At seven, Philip is more concerned about his stamp collection than national politics. He becomes aware of Lindbergh's isolationist campaign and his electoral victory over the incumbent Roosevelt chiefly while listening with his family to the radio and while overhearing anxious conversations among adults. For an American Jew growing up in a largely secular household, the growing threat of ethnic intolerance is brought home by members of his own family. Disgusted with the Lindbergh administration's entente with Germany and intent on fighting Nazism, Philip's cousin Alvin slips off to Canada to enlist in the war against Hitler. After losing a leg during combat in France, he returns to New Jersey to share a bedroom and his bitterness with Phil.

In contrast, Philip's brother, Sandy, cannot understand the opposition to Lindbergh, which he attributes to ignorance and parochialism. Convinced that Jews must cease to set themselves apart from other Americans, Phil's brother participates in "Just Folks," a federal program to provide Jewish children with experience in the Christian heartland. After spending a summer on a tobacco farm in Kentucky, Sandy is a convert to the cause of assimilation and an ardent spokesman for "Just Folks." As prospects for the Jews of New Jersey grow increasingly grim, the Roth apartment echoes with arguments between Phil's mother and father over whether they should flee to Canada or stay where they are and try to defend their way of life.

"Just Folks" is the invention of Lionel Bengelsdorf, a Conservative rabbi from Newark who becomes the principal Jewish apologist for Lindbergh and Lindbergh's director of the Office of American Absorption, a federal agency designed to erase ethnic distinctions. At first, Herman Roth and most other Jews despise Bengelsdorf as a sanctimonious quisling, an opportunist who betrays his own people in order to advance his career. "Koshering Lindbergh for the goyim" is Alvin's verdict on what Bengelsdorf is doing. When Phil's Aunt Evelyn marries Bengelsdorf, more than thirty years her senior, Herman cannot contain his hostility. When Evelyn and Lionel Bengelsdorf attend a state dinner at the White House in honor of the German foreign minister, Joachim von Ribbentrop, Alvin refuses to have anything more to do with them.

Lindbergh keeps his promise to keep the United States out of war, and, amid general prosperity, most Jews begin to wonder whether Bengelsdorf might not have been right all along about the good intentions of the handsome aviator-president. Perhaps stubborn contrarians such as Herman Roth and his nephew Alvin are merely unhinged, rendered paranoid by their willful isolation from mainstream America.

At least until later in the novel, when a Jewish challenger to Lindbergh is assassinated and anti-Jewish riots erupt throughout the United States, Roth the author maintains a delicate balance between Alvin and Sandy, between partisan contempt for Nazi collaborators and a willingness to integrate into the larger culture, to set Americanness ahead of Jewishness. Even at the end, when, amid general havoc, Lindbergh disappears, his motives remain ambiguous. One could even believe, as Bengelsdorf does, that the plan to relocate Jews away from coastal cities and into the sparsely populated interior is good for the Jews rather than a prelude to genocide.

Phil's childhood coincides with dire public developments, but a neighbor's suicide affects him more deeply than any of the oratory at the 1940 Republican National Convention that, echoing off radios throughout Weequahic on a warm June night, puts the boy to sleep. Yet he is burdened by uneasy dreams. Though helpless to avert the carnage that is enveloping the planet, Phil is nevertheless troubled by a sense of responsibility. He feels compelled to assist Alvin with his prosthetic leg, and he is bound by ineradicable guilt to a pesky young neighbor named Seldon Wishnow for having indirectly caused the death of that precocious but lonely boy's mother.

*The Plot Against America* reimagines a world in which the mass media of radio, newsreels, and newspapers create celebrities, and celebrities—commentators as well as aviators—amass power. Through his radio broadcasts, Winchell, a dauntless Jewish demagogue, galvanizes opposition to the Lindbergh presidency. He is shot dead while campaigning to replace the object of his antipathy and become the first Jew to occupy the White House. Broadcast weekly, Winchell's fulminations are crude and hyperbolic, a stark contrast to the finely nuanced prose of Roth's novel.

A brief allusion to the future assassination of Senator Robert F. Kennedy suggests that, despite diverging from the public record by positing a Lindbergh administration in the 1940's, the author has restored the familiar lines of history by 1968. Not even Philip Roth could have imagined a liberal Democrat making a serious run for the White House in 1968 if the trajectory set in motion by a victory for America First in 1940 had continued. Ultimately, according to the novel, the Lindbergh presidency turns out to be a twenty-two-month interlude followed immediately by a landslide victory by Franklin Roosevelt for a third presidential term, a Japanese attack on Pearl Harbor, and the American entry into World War II.

All of that leads to the present and to the realization that current concerns mirror those of the 1940's. Despite a note to the reader that insists *"The Plot Against America* is a work of fiction," this historical novel is rooted in modern America. Released in the midst of an acrimonious battle for the presidency between George W. Bush and John F. Kerry, Roth's book examines the issues of patriotism, faith, and security that divided the United States in 2004.

"Fear presides over these memories, a perpetual fear" is the way the narrator begins his account, and that fear has not been dispelled by the time he tells his story in the aftermath of the September 11, 2001, attacks on the World Trade Center and the Pentagon. Terrorist alerts were being issued by the newly created Department of Homeland Security while Roth was conjuring up a childhood dominated by dread. Prominent national figures were proclaiming the United States "a Christian nation" while he was imagining a scheme to marginalize Jews by relocating them in remote rural areas. Roth's previous novel *The Human Stain* (2000) offered an oblique critique of prigs and hypocrites who hounded Bill Clinton during his two terms as chief executive. *The Plot Against America* is a secular American Jew's nightmare about the ascendancy of fervent Christians who define American identity in terms that exclude the Roths of Weequahic.

*Steven G. Kellman*

## Review Sources

*The Atlantic Monthly* 294 (November, 2004): 143.
*Los Angeles Times*, September 22, 2004, p. E1.
*The Nation* 279, no. 17 (November 22, 2004): 23.
*New Criterion* 23, no. 3 (November, 2004): 54.

*The New York Review of Books* 51, no. 18 (November 18, 2004): 4.
*The New York Times*, September 21, 2004, p. E1.
*The New York Times Book Review* 154 (October 3, 2004): 1.
*The New Yorker* 80 (September 20, 2004): 96.
*Newsweek* 144, no. 12 (September 20, 2004): 56.
*Publishers Weekly* 251, no. 28 (July 12, 2004): 44.
*Time* 164, no. 13 (September 27, 2004): 67.
*The Times Literary Supplement*, October 8, 2004, p. 21.

# POLITICS
## Observations and Arguments, 1966-2004

*Author:* Hendrik Hertzberg (1943-    )
*Publisher:* Penguin Books (New York). 683 pp. $30.00
*Type of work:* Essays and current affairs
*Time:* 1966-2004
*Locale:* The United States

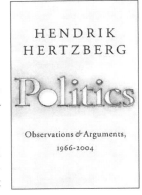

*A book of the author's essays on politics and culture that illuminates the development of national affairs over four decades*

Hendrik Hertzberg has been one of the most influential and thoughtful essayists about American politics and culture over the past four decades. From his editorial posts at *The New Republic* and *The New Yorker* he has written with wit and style about the evolution of public life during the last quarter of the twentieth century. He was a speechwriter for President Jimmy Carter during the 1970's, so he has the perspective of a one-time insider and the insight of a careful critic of the foibles of politicians and their antics. *Politics* is one of those rare volumes of collected prose that will provide pleasure and stimulation even though much of what Hertzberg writes about seems now to be part of a very different past in the United States.

This book brings together Hertzberg's journalism over four decades. It thus provides the interested reader with a panoramic view of American life from the age of Lyndon Johnson to the presidency of George W. Bush. For such now-distant episodes as the election of 1988, which pitted Michael Dukakis as the Democratic nominee against the winner, President George H. W. Bush, Hertzberg recaptures the spirit of that empty campaign. He is equally thoughtful about those controversies which once seemed so important but now have faded from memory. He has some wise things to say, for example, about the failure of John Tower's nomination to be secretary of defense in 1989, the intellectual limits of Newt Gingrich as a political thinker, and the continuing controversy over the fairness and wisdom of the death penalty.

Hertzberg approaches politics from the perspective of a detached, skeptical liberal, but he is as hard on the foibles of the Democrats as the Republicans. He has a soft spot for the predicament of Bob Dole in the Republican primaries of 1988, when the sardonic senator from Kansas proved no match for the hardball tactics of the elder George H. W. Bush. While he is scathing about Vice President Dan Quayle's efforts as a young man to avoid the risks of service in Vietnam, he also provides an understanding analysis of Quayle's intellectual limits as a candidate and a person.

One of the strengths of Hertzberg's writing is his willingness to take a searching look at his own motives. In dealing with how young men such as Quayle responded to the choices that the Vietnam War posed, Hertzberg candidly outlines his own course as a draft-age male in the mid-1960's. No better brief explanation exists of the dilemmas that confronted men who opposed the war and faced the draft in that troubled period than Hertzberg provides.

*A prolific commentator on American politics and culture, Hendrik Hertzberg was a speechwriter for President Jimmy Carter and an editor of* The New Republic. *He is currently a staff writer and editor at* The New Yorker.

At bottom, Hertzberg's best essays turn on his ability to get beyond the surface aspects of "personality" on which so much of modern print and television now depends. During the decades of Hertzberg's career, journalism and punditry have moved away from an engagement with serious policy issues and evolved instead into a concentration on the interplay of individual characteristics of prominent individuals. Many of the author's reporter colleagues believe they have said something meaningful when they opine that George W. Bush seemed like someone to have a beer with or that John Kerry seems "French." This style of reportage enables scribes who have little interest, or perhaps even less competence with complex policy questions, to escape into high school-style gossip and innuendo, which are less demanding on their intellectual resources.

Hertzberg rejects such inane commentary in favor of probing into what public figures actually mean in their public statements and how their substantive choices will have consequences for the American public. In short, he treats his readers as adults rather than children with short attention spans. Thus, speaking about the differences between George W. Bush and Al Gore in the 2000 election, he notes the emphasis on their contrasting personalities: "Personality apparently excludes, if not intelligence itself, then such manifestations of it as intellectual curiosity, analytic ability, and a capacity for original thought, all of which Gore has in abundance and Bush not only lacks but scorns."

This, then, is not a book for those with short attention spans and a disdain for nuance. Like H. L. Mencken and Murray Kempton, two of Hertzberg's distinguished ancestors in this format of essay journalism, Hertzberg expects the reader to have some knowledge of the context of daily events and an awareness of American culture beyond the scope of Fox News and the animated series *The Simpsons*. These demands of literacy and social awareness may shrink the book's audience, especially among television journalists, but those who come to *Politics* with an open mind and appreciation of lively prose will find many delights and rewards.

One of the most interesting aspects of the book is the author's interest in the way democracy does and does not work in modern times. Two incisive essays look at the ways that the filibuster distorts the legislative process in the U.S. Senate. Having to muster sixty votes to shut off debate in the upper house puts lawmakers at the mercy of forty-one senators with enough resolve to oppose whatever bills are being considered. The filibuster has long been an antidemocratic feature of political life, and Hertzberg identifies its adverse effects on public policy in a thoughtful and persuasive manner. Almost as great a problem, Hertzberg argues, is the inability of the American people to change the membership of the House of Representatives, so gerrymandered has that body become. To deal with this dilemma, he advocates a system of proportional representation, to make votes actually count for something. That is not likely to occur any time soon, but credit goes to Hertzberg for being willing to advance the idea as a way out of the rigidities of the current political box.

Hertzberg's interests cover many features of the current scene, from pop culture to the mass media. In the latter connection, there is a superb feature on the rise and spread of tabloid journalism from the 1920's to 2004. The *New York Daily News* and the *New York Post*, the modern incarnations of these earlier newspapers, are part of a tradition of popular, often vulgar, journalism that goes back to the period just after World War I. "Tabloids," Hertzberg writes, "have become one of those subsided cultural treasures that we New Yorkers get to enjoy simply because we live in New York." He understands that these newspapers speak to something enduring in the American character that seeks to know what is happening today in all aspects of life from the trivial to the consequential. Cable television, for all of its tawdriness, is an electronic extension of what the tabloids first set out to accomplish. Here again, Hertzberg provides, in a brief space, permanent insights into how society functions right now.

In his four decades as a writer and sometime participant in politics, Hertzberg has rubbed elbows with many of the great and near-great in public life. He treats these figures with respect but without undue reverence. His examination of Ronald Reagan's memoirs, for example, makes clear how that empty, tedious volume came into being and why it reflected so little of the former president's personality and style. Ronald Reagan's "perfect obliviousness to the feelings and thoughts of others protected him from emotional turmoil," the author concludes. That observation tracks the revelations of Reagan's intimates who often commented on his inability to connect with even his most faithful aides as real individuals.

As stated, Hertzberg worked as a speechwriter for Jimmy Carter, and he looks back on his experience in the White House with a mixture of regret and pride for what he and his boss accomplished between 1977 and 1981. Hertzberg is too realistic a thinker to argue that Carter was a success in the Oval Office. He does show why Carter was so much more effective as a former chief executive, in situations where his moral values could be put to use outside the corridors of power. His judgment that Carter was "a saint" may be a little over the top. Nonetheless, Hertzberg makes as good a case as possible for Carter's worth as a human being and does so in a thoughtful way that will carry the reader a long way toward agreement.

The final section of *Politics* looks at the presidential election of 2000, its troubled aftermath, and the response of the George W. Bush administration to the events of September 11, 2001. Hertzberg is not a great admirer of G. W. Bush, either as a candidate or an executive. If the Bush presidency runs into the troubles that often afflict administrations during a second term, Hertzberg's analysis will provide a wise guide to some of the danger signals that emerged during the first Bush campaign and the early days of the presidency. He respects the president's skill as a campaigner and his ability to frame issues in a manner that voters applaud. Some of his observations have come to seem telling in the perspective of the passage of time since September 11, 2001. "The world will be policed collectively or it will not be policed at all,"

Hertzberg announced in *The New Yorker* on September 24, 2001. Time will tell whether that judgment is accurate, as Americans grapple with a war in Iraq and the continuing difficulties of uprooting international terrorism.

Hertzberg also explores the contradiction that has emerged since September, 2001, between the need to mobilize the United States for a protracted war with a terrorist enemy and the evident desire of the Bush administration for a small, unobtrusive national government. In such areas as raising armies to fight abroad, educating young people for the global struggle, and ensuring a healthy, motivated population, the White House is faced with hard choices. As Hertzberg puts it, "whatever one may think of the global democratic-imperial ambitions of the [Bush] administration, they cannot long coexist with the combination of narrow greed and public neglect it thinks sufficient for what it is pleased to call the homeland."

Hertzberg's *Politics* is thus an illuminating tour through many of the paradoxes of American life at the start of the twenty-first century. The author is such a good writer that his prose is rewarding even when the reader comes to disagree with his conclusions. Witty, civilized, and discerning, Hertzberg's essays re-create the immediate past with a sense of energy and power that makes these receding events live again in the mind. Weekly journalism often disappears very quickly as the pace of history overtakes what a columnist has said. Hertzberg's work will continue to be read by historians seeking to recapture what the mood of the country was like in such troubled decades. That elusive target, the general reader, will find the author a superb guide to things that happened, in the phrase of Frederick Lewis Allen, "only yesterday" and which still shape the lives and future of Americans.

*Lewis L. Gould*

## Review Sources

*The American Spectator* 37, no. 8 (October, 2004): 55.
*Booklist* 100, nos. 19/20 (June 1-15, 2004): 1689.
*The Economist* 372 (October 9, 2004): 80.
*Kirkus Reviews* 72, no. 9 (May 1, 2004): 430.
*Library Journal* 129, no. 12 (July 15, 2004): 103.
*The New York Times Book Review* 153 (July 4, 2004): 7.
*Publishers Weekly* 251, no. 22 (May 31, 2004): 62.

# THE POLITICS OF TRUTH
## Inside the Lies That Led to War
## and Betrayed My Wife's CIA Identity

*Author:* Joseph Wilson (1949-    )
*Publisher:* Carroll & Graf (New York). 513 pp. $26.00
*Type of work:* Current affairs and memoir
*Time:* From the 1990's to 2004
*Locale:* Washington, D.C.; Gabon; Iraq; Kuwait; numerous other African and Middle Eastern countries; and Bosnia

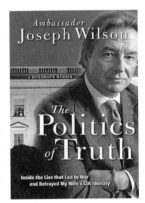

*A knowledgeable investigator's examination of the claim that Iraqi dictator Saddam Hussein bought uranium from Niger showed that the allegation was false; Wilson's politically unpopular conclusion led to unpleasant personal consequences for him and his family*

Principal personages:
> JOSEPH WILSON, a retired diplomat
> VALERIE PLAME, his wife, an undercover agent for the Central Intelligence Agency (CIA)
> ROBERT NOVAK, a columnist for *The Washington Post*
> GEORGE W. BUSH, the forty-third president of the United States
> RICHARD CHENEY, vice president
> KARL ROVE, one of Bush's major advisers
> LEWIS "SCOOTER" LIBBY, Cheney's chief of staff
> ELLIOTT ABRAMS, a neoconservative member of the Bush administration

History, from the times of the ancient Egyptians, Greeks, and Romans through subsequent centuries, is rife with kill-the-messenger tales. Bearers of bad news and purveyors of unpopular conclusions have always revealed their information at considerable risk. Such is the case with Joseph Wilson, a highly regarded retired diplomat who served in the administrations of Gerald Ford, Jimmy Carter, Ronald Reagan, George H. W. Bush, and Bill Clinton. Wilson served in various diplomatic posts in Africa and, before his retirement in 1998, was ambassador to Gabon. He was also knowledgeable about Middle Eastern politics and served as acting ambassador to Baghdad when the Iraqis invaded Kuwait in 1990. As such, he was the last U.S. ambassador in Iraq prior to the collapse of Saddam Hussein's regime.

In good standing with the George W. Bush administration at its inception, Wilson was asked by the CIA to go in February, 2002, to Niger, a country with which he had great familiarity and in which he had many dependable, high-level contacts. He was charged with investigating allegations from an Italian source that Niger was selling Hussein uranium, an element vital in the production of nuclear weapons.

Wilson agreed to accept this mission on a pro bono basis, billing the U.S. government only for his transportation and per diem costs. He approached his assignment with an open mind and with the heartfelt conviction that the Bush administration was genuinely interested in knowing the true facts about the rumored Niger-Iraq uranium sales.

Upon his return from Niger in March, 2002, Wilson briefed the CIA and filed his report, in which he expressed strong doubts that the uranium transactions had ever taken place. After a thorough investigation, he uncovered nothing to suggest that Hussein had purchased from Niger any uranium from which the Iraqis could make weapons of mass destruction. Nevertheless, in September of the same year, a British white paper, later discredited, charged that there was a uranium connection between Niger and Iraq.

*Joseph Wilson was a career diplomat from 1976 until 1998, occupying various diplomatic posts in Africa before becoming United States Ambassador to Gabon. He was acting ambassador to Iraq when the Gulf War erupted in 1990. In 2002, he investigated for the Central Intelligence Agency allegations that Iraq had tried to buy uranium from Niger.*

Little more was said about the matter until Bush's State of the Union address on January 28, 2003. In this speech, the president included sixteen crucial words that unleashed the furor about which Wilson is writing: "The British government has learned that Saddam Hussein recently sought significant quantities of uranium from Africa."

Some six weeks later, on March 7, 2003, the International Atomic Energy Agency publicly discredited the British white paper as having been based on obvious forgeries. The following day, a spokesperson for the Department of State admitted that the Bush administration had been deceived. On the same day, Wilson revealed on the Cable News Network (CNN) that the government had considerably more information about the matter than it had admitted, citing his own report that was apparently ignored by an administration seeking any means possible to justify waging a preemptive war against Hussein.

Shortly after Wilson's CNN interview, a rattled administration met in Vice President Richard Cheney's office to discuss damage control. Those present presumably included Cheney, Lewis "Scooter" Libby, Newt Gingrich, and other Republican officials. The focus of the meeting was on producing a workup on Joseph Wilson, aimed at revealing information with which to discredit him.

Three months later, on *Meet the Press*, Condoleezza Rice, Bush's national security adviser, denied that any of the senior administration knew how unreliable the claims of a Niger-Iraq uranium connection were, although she admitted that some lower-ranking members of the administration might have had such knowledge. Little more was said of the matter until July 6, 2003, when Wilson's op-ed piece "What I Didn't Find in Africa" appeared in *The New York Times*. On the same day, Wilson, a guest on *Meet the Press*, gave detailed information about his trip to Niger and explained why he was convinced that Niger had sold no uranium to Hussein.

Two days later, a friend of Wilson, someone thought to work in the White House, encountered Robert Novak, a columnist for *The Washington Post*, on Pennsylvania

Avenue not far from Wilson's office. As the two walked along together, Novak off-handedly told his companion that Valerie Plame, Wilson's wife, was a CIA operative. Obviously, this represented a significant breach of confidentiality because it is important that the cover of no CIA operative be compromised. The nature of the agency's work requires that its operatives maintain low profiles. Novak also made some unflattering comments about Wilson and speculated that his wife had arranged for his invitation from the CIA to make the investigative trip to Niger, which some members of the administration later characterized as a boondoggle. After finishing his walk with Novak, Wilson's friend went immediately to Wilson's office to report this troubling conversation to him.

When Wilson, almost immediately afterward, confronted Novak with an account of what he had been told, Novak apologized, and the matter appeared settled. Nevertheless, six days later, on July 14, Novak publicly outed Plame in his *Washington Post* column, writing: "Wilson never worked for the CIA, but his wife, Valerie Plame, is an agency operative on weapons of mass destruction. Two senior administration officials told me Wilson's wife suggested sending him to Niger to investigate the Italian report."

On July 20, Andrea Mitchell, NBC's Washington bureau chief, called Wilson to inform him that senior White House officials were out to discredit him in any way they could. The following day, *Hardball* host Chris Matthews told Wilson that he had just talked with Karl Rove on the telephone and that Rove said of Plame that she was fair game in the White House's effort to cast Wilson in a bad light. The Intelligence Identities Protection Act had apparently been violated, which constitutes a felony, conviction of which can carry a ten-year prison sentence.

On September 28, it was announced that the Justice Department, headed by Attorney General John Ashcroft, was launching a full-scale investigation into the leak that had resulted in outing Plame. The following day, *The Washington Post* reported that before the publication of Novak's column, two high-level White House officials had called at least six journalists, disclosing to them the fact that Plame worked for the CIA. Early in October, Bush gave his assurance that the Justice Department would find out how the leak occurred and who was responsible for it.

Ashcroft recused himself from the leak investigation on December 30, 2003. By January 21, 2004, a grand jury had begun hearing evidence. On February 5, it was announced that federal law enforcement officials had obtained reliable evidence that two officials attached to Cheney's office had apparently leaked information, but it made no accusations at that point against Rove or the vice president. It was inferred that indictments for criminal misconduct would be forthcoming against the two and possibly against other White House officials.

Wilson names names in his book. He speculates that, although Rove may not have been involved directly in the leak that outed Plame, two employees attached to his office, Libby and Elliott Abrams, possibly acting with Rove's knowledge, were the culprits.

Libby is Cheney's chief of staff and, according to Wilson, had both the motive and the opportunity to find out that Wilson's wife was a CIA operative. Once Rove had set in motion the investigation designed to discredit Wilson, it was relatively simple for any senior official in Cheney's office to gain access to much of the classified information that was not readily available to anyone who was not a high-ranking administrator.

Abrams, who had served in the administration of George H. W. Bush, was convicted in 1991 on two charges that he committed perjury in denying to Congress that the government had illegally supported the contra rebels of Nicaragua. A staunch neoconservative, Abrams was granted a pardon by George H. W. Bush in 1992 and later became involved in the administration of George W. Bush as an employee of the vice president.

The last official action of the grand jury before Wilson's book went to press was to subpoena the telephone logs of the presidential plane Air Force One from July 7-12, 2003, and records of the White House Iraq Group from July 6-30. The investigation remained open and had the support, at least nominally, of the Bush administration.

Wilson's is an intriguing story. It could have been told more succinctly, but his writing style is so polished and clear that readers are more likely to rejoice in the excess verbiage than to complain about it. The cloak-and-dagger elements of the Bush administration's effort to bring dishonor upon Wilson make for a compelling and disturbing tale.

The implications of Wilson's account are indeed far-reaching. If they are accurate, they support the belief, widely held by some, that George W. Bush, from the earliest days of his presidency, was determined to wage war against Iraq and was merely seeking some justification for making his preemptive strike. The destruction of the World Trade Center with its massive casualties as well as two other air assaults on the same day clearly demonstrated that terrorism is a real threat, but responsibility for these destructive acts could not legitimately be laid on Hussein's doorstep.

The contention that Bush made up his mind to attack Iraq before he had the kind of justification that would support such an action is echoed in Bob Woodward's *Plan of Attack* (2004), based on three-and-a-half hours of interviews with Bush and buttressed by revealing interviews with seventy-five other high-level officials. Wilson's findings on his investigation in Niger in no way suggested that Hussein was buying from Africa the materials to make weapons of mass destruction.

*The Politics of Truth* is filled with small nuggets of wisdom, the mining of which will richly reward perceptive readers. One of the more memorable statements of this sort occurs in a passage in which Wilson comments on Bush's contention that Hussein was a madman who had to be brought down, using this argument to defend his preemptive strike against Iraq. Wilson comments, "Indeed, Saddam was dangerous, and perhaps mad; but was he an urgent or unique threat to our national security that could be managed only by war? We structure our armed forces to defend our country against foreign threats, not to fight madmen."

*R. Baird Shuman*

## Review Sources

*The New York Times*, May 5, 2004, p. E7.
*The New York Times Book Review* 153 (May 23, 2004): 9.
*Publishers Weekly* 251, no. 18 (May 3, 2004): 185.
*The Quill* 92 (May, 2004): 31.

# POWER, TERROR, PEACE, AND WAR
## America's Grand Strategy in a World at Risk

*Author:* Walter Russell Mead (1952-    )
*Publisher:* Alfred A. Knopf (New York). 226 pp. $20.00
*Type of work:* Current affairs
*Time:* From the 1990's to 2004

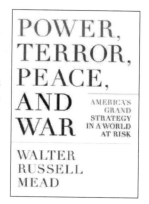

*The author discusses the challenges facing American foreign policy in the aftermath of September 11, 2001, including the subsequent war in Iraq*

*Principal personages:*
GEORGE W. BUSH, president of the United
    States, 2001-
BILL CLINTON, president of the United
    States, 1993-2001

Walter Russell Mead has written widely on United States foreign policy, and his *Special Providence*, published in 2002, received the Lionel Gelber Award as the year's best study of international relations. In *Power, Terror, Peace, and War*, Mead continues his discussion and analysis of American policy in the light of the Iraq war, initially waged against the regime of Saddam Hussein. Unlike some writers on foreign affairs, Mead approaches U.S. foreign relations from a historical perspective, believing that ignoring the historical dimension of current affairs can lead to wrong-headed policies and serious misadventures.

Like most commentators, Mead agrees that September 11, 2001, was a watershed date in American history but says that, in retrospect, the terrorist attacks of that day were not entirely unexpected. He claims that the years from the fall of the Berlin Wall in 1989 to September 11, 2001, were lost years for American foreign policy, and during the post-Cold War years, events abroad were creating challenges to American security and world primacy that culminated with the attacks on the Pentagon and New York City's World Trade Center.

At the core of Mead's analysis is what he calls the "American project," which he defines as the quest to assure American security domestically while establishing a world order made up of democratic states tied together by common values and economic prosperity. The American project is not a recent development. The United States has had global concerns stretching back to the founding of the republic. However, the nineteenth century was Britain's century, and it was only after the sun set on Britain's empire that the United States was forced to become the "gyroscope" of world stability, a position enhanced as the result of the collapse of the Soviet Union. In the post-Cold War world, the United States, according to Mead, must play the role on a global scale that Rome and China had historically played on a regional basis.

The use of power is central to the American project, according to the author, and to ignore the realities of power will lead to failure on a global basis. One type of power is

*Walter Russell Mead is the Henry A. Kissinger Senior Fellow in United States Foreign Policy, Council on Foreign Relations. Mead graduated from Yale University, and his* Special Providence *received the Lionel Gelber Award in 2002 for the best book in English on international relations.*

"hard power," or military power. In the early twenty-first century the United States dominates the world with its military capacity, even though, as evidenced in Iraq, there are limits to even America's resources. To prevent the Middle East, with its oil resources, from becoming a "theocratic terror camp," Mead strongly supports the George W. Bush administration's use of military force against Afghanistan's Taliban and al-Qaeda's Osama bin Laden.

There is also so-called sticky power, or economic power. Mead argues that sticky power can potentially prevent the use of military power. The current economic relationships between the United States and China, he believes, will militate against the use of military force over such contentious issues as the future of Taiwan. China, the emerging superpower, is less likely to rely upon military force if it is entangled in the sticky power of economic interrelationships. In addition to hard power—military and economic—there is what Mead calls sweet power, which is the attractiveness of American culture and values in much of the rest of the world. The example of pop culture, with its movies and music, is an obvious example, but so is the United States' stated commitment to human rights.

As the sole superpower at the beginning of the twenty-first century, the United States is the world's hegemonic power, and hard, sticky, and sweet power together account for America's paramount position and will likely do so in the future. Mead argues that the United States has an obligation to use its several powers, not least in the Middle East. In his opinion, American involvement, past and present, does not so much seek to gain access to oil to fuel American cars but rather to temper the impact of Middle Eastern oil resources on the world as a whole.

Mead also compares and contrasts what he calls the "Fordist" economic and social system that dominated much of the twentieth century with the "millennial capitalism" of the early twenty-first century. Fordism was a reaction to laissez-faire capitalism of the nineteenth century and was a result of the Progressive and New Deal movements. A relationship of bureaucracies of business and labor administered by powerful government agencies as honest brokers and with numerous social welfare programs, Fordism proved its worth, not least in the Cold War. However, Mead argues, capitalism is an economic system that rewards—demands—innovation. The kinder, gentler Fordism was a suitable system for one era, but the times have changed, and Fordism is no longer the most efficient method by which to organize capitalist economies. The new, less bureaucratic millennial capitalism, which he admits is currently more popular within the United States than elsewhere, is not a retreat to nineteenth century laissez-faire policies, but government regulation will be more flexible and adaptable to the changing economies of the present.

Leading the American project are what Mead calls American Revivalists, advocates of the new millennial capitalism, which, they believe, will result in the spread of

American power and values throughout the world. The Revivalists, the author argues, can be called Hamiltonians, because, like Alexander Hamilton, first secretary of the Treasury, they believe in the necessity of having a strong government to support the economy. In the early twenty-first century, government will advance the millennial economy rather than rely on the New Deal Fordist model.

Some of the Revivalists, the neoconservatives, have also accepted a new Wilsonianism, or the spread of American ideals and values universally. The current Wilsonians differ from their namesake Woodrow Wilson by being unwilling to believe that international institutions are a necessary centerpiece in the propagation of American ideals and values, and they are more influenced by evangelical Christians.

Still another element of American Revivalism is what Mead refers to as the "Jacksonians," who are against big business, big government, and big labor as well as distrustful of "experts" and the traditional elites. This, Mead argues, coincides with millennial capitalism, and he suggests that the future will see a further reduction in middle management and tenured positions in American society, as the outsourcing of certain services continues. The author claims that the millennial economy and the American Revivalists, with the support of the Jacksonians and evangelical Christians, have, under the Bush administration, largely supplanted the traditional foreign policy elites and the latter's focus upon Europe and commitment to international institutions. This movement away from the traditional Eurocentric policy began earlier, and Mead faults the Clinton administration for failing to make clear to the European governments the new redirection of American policy after the end of the Cold War.

Mead is suspicious of the efficacy of international institutions such as the United Nations, which he associates with two factions, the "Party of Heaven" and the "Party of Hell." The first, represented by Canada and Germany, claim that if the United States subjected its power to the United Nations, peace would inevitably result. The second, represented by Russia and France, envision a world of multipolarities, as in the past, and an ending to America's present hegemony. The author argues that to place American power in either the naïvely idealistic or the self-interested hands of other nations is patently unrealistic.

American Revivalism and the American project are not and will not become the monopoly of one political party, Mead predicts, and the permanent ascendancy of the Republican Party is not assured, but, writing early in 2004, Mead is largely favorable toward the Bush administration's foreign policy. He argues that the focus upon maintaining American hegemony in the face of hostile opponents and ensuring continued development of the world's economy have been the essentials of American foreign policy for many decades. However, there were fundamental changes that occurred in the aftermath of the September 11, 2001, attacks, including Bush's declaration of a "war on terror." Mead finds that phrase useful but misleading in that the war on terror is not directed against all terrorists but mainly against al-Qaeda and its associates because they threaten the global economy and security upon which rests the American project. Even the Bush doctrine of preemptive war, disturbing to many, was not without precedent, and Mead cites President John F. Kennedy's threats during the Cuban

Missile Crisis as an example. He also says that strong language can be justified as a deterrent.

The Bush administration's decision to remove Saddam from power was correct, Mead argues. He does fault the administration for relying almost exclusively on the existence of weapons of mass destruction as the only justification for invasion. The administration was also grossly wrong and irresponsible in implying that the war would not require significant sacrifices. In addition, although Mead does not believe that the use of American power should be vetoed by the United Nations or other international organizations, he argues that the Bush administration was too arrogant and brusque in its diplomatic dealings. In addition, if the removal of Saddam was justified, the administration has thus far failed in its postwar strategy in creating a democratic Iraq.

In the future, the Middle East and the Far East will be the focus of American policy rather than Europe, and Mead argues that the administration's East Asia policy has been largely successful, particularly in its relations with China. The Bush administration, however, has "been too choppy and uncertain, its ability to formulate and express its strategic direction too crude and unconvincing, and it has not yet found a way to articulate a positive agenda for the United States and the world that can win sympathy beyond our frontiers." In other words, it is not the package but the packaging that is at fault; the strategy was correct, but the tactics were inept, not least in its public diplomacy.

The author envisions that American foreign policy will continue to be challenged by "grand terror," which was largely ignored by both the Clinton and Bush administrations prior to September 11, 2001. Mead suggests that a policy of what he calls "forward containment" is a possible approach, differing from the containment policy of the Cold War by being more proactive in its use of military and other kinds of power rather than merely reactive. An international consensus in the battle against what the author calls "Arabian Fascism" is desirable, but ultimately American power and the willingness to use it will be decisive. Islam is not the enemy, and Mead, perhaps too optimistically, sees the possibility of a common cause of spirituality and morality shared by evangelical Christian America and the majority of Muslims.

*Power, Terror, Peace, and War* is a timely book. In his general approval of the Bush administration's policies and its response to the events of September 11, 2001, Mead will undoubtedly alienate many liberals as well as some conservative isolationists. In his criticism of the tactics of the Bush administration, he will likely anger administration supporters and admirers. In spite of perhaps an excessive reliance on jargon—American project, Arabian Fascism, American Revivalism, hard and sticky power—the author presents valuable insights about U.S. foreign policy, past and present and perhaps the future.

*Eugene Larson*

## Review Sources

*Booklist* 100, no, 18 (May 15, 2004): 1583.
*Esquire* 141 (June, 2004): 42.
*Foreign Affairs* 83, no. 6 (November/December, 2004): 151.
*Kirkus Reviews* 72, no. 5 (March 1, 2004): 212.
*National Review* 56, no. 10 (May 31, 2004): 45.
*The New York Times Book Review* 153 (June 13, 2004): 27.
*Publishers Weekly* 251, no. 14 (April 5, 2004): 57.

# PREACHING EUGENICS
## Religious Leaders and the American Eugenics Movement

*Author:* Christine Rosen

*Publisher:* Oxford University Press (New York). 286 pp. $35.00

*Type of work:* Ethics, history of science, medicine, and religion

*Time:* 1883-1938

*A timely exploration of the way in which religious leaders collaborated with scientists and social reformers in an audacious, unprecedented, and controversial movement designed to narrow the hereditary characteristics of the human race*

*Principal personages:*

> KENNETH MACARTHUR, Protestant minister whose family won the American Eugenics Society's Fitter Family Context
>
> ALBERT EDWARD WIGGAM, flamboyant eugenics speaker who devised a new ten commandments for the eugenically minded
>
> PHILLIPS ENDECOTT OSGOOD, rector of Saint Mark's church in Minneapolis and winner of the 1926 American Eugenics Society's Eugenics Sermon Contest
>
> WALTER TAYLOR SUMNER, dean of the Cathedral of Saint Peter and Paul in Chicago, who required all couples he married to have health certificates from a reputable physician
>
> HARRY EMERSON FOSDICK, a leading liberal Protestant minister and member of the American Eugenics Society
>
> JOHN A. RYAN, one of the liberal Catholic clergy members to become involved in the eugenics movement
>
> STEPHEN WISE, one of the principal Jewish rabbis to express support for eugenics

In 1883, Francis Galton, a British scientist and cousin to Charles Darwin, invented the term "eugenics," which he derived from a Greek word meaning "good in birth." Galton sought to employ the powers of modern science to harness the unruly creativity of nature. "What nature does blindly, slowly, ruthlessly, man may do providentially, quickly, and kindly," Galton confidently argued.

To the devoutly religious, Galton's program for human improvement should have seemed blasphemous. His words suggested that human beings could usurp God's role. Especially disturbing to religious thinkers was the growth of eugenics organizations that advocated mass sterilization of the "feebleminded" and birth control programs that would prevent the weaker members of the human species from reproducing.

Certainly the Catholic Church regarded the eugenicists with suspicion, if not outright condemnation. (That came in 1930, in Pope Pius XI's encyclical about family planning.) Catholic teaching affirmed natural law and the dignity of the individual as defined by Saint Thomas Aquinas (c. 1225-1274). To presume to interfere with the divine order of nature, to decide which human beings could reproduce and which could not, defied Church doctrine.

*Christine Rosen, who earned her Ph.D. at Emory University, is a fellow at the Ethics and Public Policy Center in Washington, D.C., and a senior editor of* The New Atlantis: A Journal of Technology and Society. *This is her first book.*

Similarly, most other conservative Christians—especially evangelicals and fundamentalists—reacted with horror at the idea of scientists—or any secular body of human beings—interfering with family life in such drastic and dangerous ways. Indeed, eugenicist organizations aspired to a power over family planning that the Church saw as its province. On the face of it, then, eugenics and virtually all forms of religious belief would seem poles apart.

Yet, as Christine Rosen demonstrates in *Preaching Eugenics: Religious Leaders and the American Eugenics Movement*, during the first two decades of the twentieth century, eugenics commanded the attention and sometimes the enthusiastic support of religious leaders. Most of them—Protestants, Jews, and even a few Catholics—were progressives or liberal reformers. They responded to eugenics as simply a movement aimed at human betterment. In most cases, these clergyman had little grasp of the fundamentals of science, and so their sermons emphasized the positive outcome eugenics promised rather than the means that would achieve that laudable goal.

Otherwise well-educated ministers also saw eugenics as a way to assert their modernity and show that their churches were relevant to contemporary society. This was a period when writers such as Bruce Barton wrote books about Jesus (*The Man Nobody Knows*, 1925), which suggested that if Jesus were alive in the twentieth century, he would be a businessman and a eugenicist. Eugenicists such as Albert Edward Wiggam traveled the United States with a missionary zeal—lecturing with a charismatic power that rivaled the style of evangelists such as Billy Sunday.

Moreover, the eugenicists were keen to make common cause with those ministers who seemed susceptible to persuading their flocks to adopt the new "scientific" view of human improvement. The word "scientific" has to be put in quotation marks here, because the eugenicists' claims that they would be able to improve the hereditary characteristics of the human race were false. By the 1920's, geneticists had demolished the eugenicist argument, although it took a full decade more for the bogus and dangerous aspects of eugenics to become apparent to certain clergyman and others.

In retrospect, Rosen points out, eugenics obviously seems like a terrible idea. Laws passed in the 1920's that permitted the sterilization of the so-called feeble-minded engendered crimes for which state governors are still apologizing. The very idea that heredity could be controlled through sterilization or birth control seems unscientific, to say the least, as well as immoral.

However, at the advent of the twentieth century, progressive thinkers like Theodore Roosevelt worried about "race suicide." Intermarriage between persons of different races and religious faiths seemed to be a growing problem and was feared to lead to social, political, and religious strife—not to mention unhappiness for the individuals involved. Novels and plays confronted what was deemed the chaotic rush of immigrants to America. By the 1920's, nearly a third of New Yorkers were Jewish, and one eugenics study suggested that 60 percent of them might be "feebleminded."

Indeed, the obsession with the feebleminded seems, in retrospect, an extraordinary fantasy. Sermons, newspaper articles, and books, however, treated this phenomenon as fact. Society—the world, really—was degenerating, the eugenicist-minded announced. Eugenicists made studies of families and communities that were found to be so debased that only sterilization or segregation of the enfeebled could save society from their polluting presence. One eugenics study suggested that the Pine Barrens sections of New Jersey ought to be separated from the rest of the state. That region's inhabitants were a menace to their fellow citizens, the state's governor concluded.

Toward the end of her book, Rosen suggests that the liberal religious thinkers who made common cause with the eugenicists lost their bearings; that is, the ministers, driven by the demands of a social gospel that focused on the good of society, not the salvation of individuals, abandoned their traditional role. Their attempt to be more meaningful to secular society ultimately diluted their religious principles, and by the late 1930's—when eugenicists began to acknowledge the importance of environment, not just heredity—most of the clergy had already drifted away from the movement.

Any lingering attachments to eugenics was annihilated during World War II, when the Nazi experiments on human beings, the death camps that included among their prisoners the so-called enfeebled, and mass sterilization programs demonstrated the horrifying consequences of looking at the world eugenically.

It seems logical to ask what happened to all those feebleminded American people the eugenicists kept identifying in alarming numbers. Rosen does not quite address the issue, except to suggest that, driven by an obsession, the eugenicists were always able to find what they were looking for. A good many of the putative feebleminded were probably suffering from vitamin deficiencies and other health problems. Others were simply poorly educated. In a period when Jews and Slavs, for example, were deemed inassimilable into American life, is it any wonder that eugenicists—who decried the declining birthrate among Mayflower descendants, the original settlers of America—should believe the country was headed for a steep, chaotic decline? To some extent, as Rosen might have made clearer, political interventions such as the New Deal in the 1930's focused efforts on improving the environmental factors that produced the putative feebleminded. When nutrition, labor conditions, and public benefits were improved, concerns about the feebleminded diminished rapidly. Readers unaware of these developments may find it puzzling that Rosen never quite explains what happened to the masses of defective people who were supposedly dragging the United States down to its doom.

In her conclusion, Rosen implies that the idea of eugenics is not quite dead in an age that is testing the limits of genetic engineering. After all, polls seem to indicate that Americans see nothing wrong with tampering with the genetic code of their offspring for both medical and cosmetic reasons. Rosen does not believe that genetic engineering is the same as eugenics, but her language implies a level of disapproval that she is not quite willing to make explicit: "Thus, parents meddling with the genetic composition of their unborn children does not suggest to most people the same assault on free will and individual rights that forcible eugenic sterilization does." To use the term "meddling" suggests a degree of distress that the author does not develop.

There is one puzzling aspect of Rosen's conclusions that requires further thought:

> The liberal tenor of religious participation in the eugenics movement also serves as a reminder that eugenics was never exclusively a conservative movement. Eugenic ideas rested comfortably within the mainstream of progressive American reform in the early decades of the twentieth century. It was a movement that the liberals of its day wholeheartedly embraced as an effective form of social engineering and one that political leaders viewed as providing justification for a range of state interventions, including immigration restriction and compulsory sterilization.

How, one wonders, can Rosen write about eugenics as "never exclusively a conservative movement"? In what sense was it conservative at all? If by the word "conservative," she means a political position, then her book supplies no evidence of conservative support for eugenics. If she is applying the word "conservative" to parts of the religious establishment, then, again, where is the evidence? Only the most liberal Catholics tended to have any sympathy with eugenics, and even those were wary. Most other Protestant and Jewish eugenics supporters were liberal. The conclusion to be drawn from Rosen's book seems quite the opposite: Only the religious conservatives saw early on the sinister implications of eugenics. What political conservatives made of the movement will remain a mystery to readers of this otherwise well-researched and well-argued study.

Quite aside from the intellectual and religious arguments that Rosen canvases, her book offers a panoply of colorful personalities (many of them appear in portrait photographs) that help to show how eugenics was sold to the public. The minibiographies of the eugenics stars, so to speak, help to make this an entertaining as well as an instructive work of scholarship. While it is useful to have these photographs included at those places where the subjects are mentioned in Rosen's argument, it would have been helpful, for reference purposes, if she had also included a list of illustrations. Her detailed notes and comprehensive bibliography make this an essential resource.

*Carl Rollyson*

## Review Sources

*Books & Culture*, July/August, 2004, p. 7.
*Commentary* 118, no. 1 (July/August, 2004): 49.
*Commonweal* 131, no. 9 (May 7, 2004): 32.
*History: Review of New Books* 33, no. 2 (Winter, 2005): 59.
*The Wall Street Journal* 243, no. 79 (April 22, 2004): D10.
*The Wilson Quarterly* 28, no. 3 (Summer, 2004): 126.

# QUEEN OF SCOTS
## The True Life of Mary Stuart

*Author:* John Guy (1949-    )
*Publisher:* Houghton Mifflin (Boston). Illustrated.
   581 pp. $28.00
*Type of work:* Biography
*Time:* 1542-1587
*Locale:* Scotland, France, and England

*Drawing largely on original documents, Guy presents the life of Mary Stuart, queen of Scots, in the political and religious context of sixteenth century Europe*

*Principal personages:*
   MARY STUART, queen of Scotland and
      France, claimant to the English throne
   MARY OF GUISE, her mother
   ELIZABETH I, the queen of England
   FRANCIS II, the king of France, Mary Stuart's first husband
   HENRY, LORD DARNLEY, Mary Stuart's second husband
   JAMES HEPBURN, the earl of Bothwell, Mary Stuart's third husband
   JAMES STUART, the earl of Moray, Mary Stuart's half brother
   CATHERINE DE MEDICI, Mary Stuart's mother-in-law; mother of
      Francis II
   WILLIAM CECIL, LORD BURGHLEY, the chief minister to Queen Elizabeth

Being queen of Scotland in the sixteenth century was not a position; it was a predicament. The difficulties began with Scotland itself, which was still feudal. In *Queen of Scots*, John Guy observes that "violence was endemic in [the country]. Politics were tribal, based on organized revenge and the blood feud." Adding to the factionalism were religious differences arising from the Reformation. While Scotland's official religion was Protestantism, many, if not most, of its subjects were Catholic.

Compounding tribal and theological differences were foreign allegiances and hostilities. Ever since the 1290's, England had been trying to annex Scotland, which maintained an uneasy independence despite repeated military defeats. To balance England's greater military resources, Scotland allied itself with France; but some within Scotland favored an Anglo-Scottish accord. Even a French alliance did not always help England's northern neighbor. James IV of Scotland had been killed at the battle of Flodden Field in 1513, and in late 1542 James V's forces suffered a humiliating defeat when a border raid went badly wrong. Already ill from syphilis and other maladies, James V died on December 14, 1542, six days after the birth of his daughter Mary, his only legitimate child.

Mary Stuart thus became an infant queen, as her father had been an infant king. In both cases a regency was established, exacerbating power struggles, factionalism,

and political instability. Mary Stuart would be
a pawn. England's Henry VIII wanted to annex Scotland by force or marriage, and when
Mary was only a few months old he sent Sir
Ralph Sadler to Edinburgh to negotiate her
marriage with his five-year-old son, Edward.
Mary's mother, a member of a leading French
family, wanted no part of such a union, favoring closer ties with France.

*Born in Australia, John Guy received his Ph.D. from Cambridge University in 1973. His books include the popular* textbook Tudor England *(1988),* The Reign of Elizabeth I *(1995), and* Thomas More *(2000). He is a fellow in history at Clare College, Cambridge University.*

Thwarted politically, Henry turned to military action in what was known as the "Rough
Wooings," which would persist even after Henry's death. While the English never
conquered Scotland, they did inflict severe casualties. These repeated invasions
prompted the new French king, Henry II, to promise to help Scotland and to engage
his heir, Francis, to Mary Stuart, who sailed for France in 1548.

This union put Mary, already queen of Scotland, in line to become queen of
France. As great-granddaughter of Henry VII of England, she also had a claim to the
English throne. Catholics never recognized the marriage of Henry VIII and Anne
Boleyn, so in their eyes Henry and Anne's daughter, Elizabeth, was illegitimate. In
1536 the English Parliament, at Henry's urging, had declared her so, and that statement had never been revoked. In his 1544 Third Act of Succession, Henry VIII had
restored Elizabeth's claim to the throne and excluded the Stuarts, but Catholics did
not accept this law. They regarded Mary Stuart as third in line to succeed Henry, after Edward VI (Henry's son) and Mary Tudor (Henry's elder daughter, herself a
Catholic).

In France, Mary Stuart was well educated. Though she was not the scholar that her
cousin Elizabeth Tudor was, she did learn Latin, Italian, and some Greek. She studied
French poetry under Pierre de Ronsard, France's leading writer of the day, and became his patron. A decade after arriving in France, Mary wed Francis. He was fourteen, she fifteen. The marriage occurred in April, 1558.

In November, Mary Tudor, the queen of England, died. Elizabeth became queen,
but France refused to recognize her as such. Instead, the French court added the heral-
dic arms of England to those of Scotland and France on the plates and furniture
of Mary and Francis. Mary's uncle Charles Valois, cardinal of Lorraine, lobbied
Pope Paul IV to declare Mary queen of England instead of the Protestant Elizabeth.
Philip II of Spain, however, hoped to marry Elizabeth, and the papacy needed Spanish
support. The pope therefore rejected Mary's claim. Even Henry II feared the ambitions of Mary's French relatives.

Again, death soon intervened to influence Mary's fortunes. On July 10, 1559,
Henry II died after being wounded in a joust. At the age of sixteen, Mary was queen of
France. Her Guise relatives were free to pursue their dynastic ambitions. The new
royal seal of Scotland called Francis and Mary "by grace of God, king and queen of
France, Scotland, England and Ireland." The Guises also sought to impose Catholi-
cism on Scotland, thus provoking a revolt led by James Stuart, Mary's illegitimate

half brother. Mary of Guise was deposed as regent and replaced by a council of twenty-four nobles. When French forces restored Mary of Guise, Elizabeth sent troops to Scotland to aid the rebels.

In 1560 England and France concluded the Treaty of Edinburgh, which recognized Elizabeth as England's queen and allowed the council of twenty-four to rule Scotland as long as Mary Stuart remained out of the country. Francis and Mary had not been consulted about the treaty, and Mary refused to ratify it. On December 5, 1560, Francis II died. His ten-year-old brother, Charles IX, succeeded him. Catherine de Medici, the Queen Mother, became regent and rejected a marriage between Charles and Mary. With no power in France, Mary returned to Scotland to reign.

Domestically, Mary tried to balance the various religious and political factions. Internationally, she wanted Elizabeth to recognize her claim to the succession as queen of England, while at the same time she tried not to antagonize her cousin. For Guy, Mary's nemesis as she pursued her policies was William Cecil, an ardent Protestant who feared Mary's religious and dynastic ambitions. He would use his considerable influence with Elizabeth and, with various Scots, to thwart Mary and eventually have her killed.

When Mary officially entered Edinburgh as Scotland's queen on September 2, 1561, Calvinists staged anti-Catholic pageants. One showed a priest burned at the altar as he elevated the Host. In another, a dragon, representing the pope as antichrist, was set on fire. Mary agreed not to meddle with religion but insisted on toleration for Catholics.

In 1562, religious wars erupted in France. Elizabeth aided the Protestants, hoping to secure a channel port in France. Mary kept Scotland neutral, but she was also maneuvering for a husband to gain support for her claim to succeed Elizabeth. In July, 1565, she married the Catholic Henry, Lord Darnley, who had blood ties to English royalty. Elizabeth was not pleased, and some Protestant Scottish lords, led by James Stuart rebelled. Defeated, they fled to England.

Mary and her new husband quickly quarreled, and she resolved to deny him the crown matrimonial, thus retaining power herself. Darnley now allied himself with the rebel lords, promising to let them keep their lands if they supported his bid to become king. The rebels secured their pardons, but Darnley did not get the crown. To excuse his recent policies, Darnley blamed Mary's private secretary, David Rizzio, who was assassinated while at dinner with her.

Mary was furious, and soon various lords were also angered by Darnley's policies, including his desire to impose Catholicism on Scotland and to invade England. On February 10, 1567, James Douglas, earl of Morton, and James Hepburn, earl of Bothwell, assassinated Darnley. Mary was unaware of the plot and suspected that her half brother James was responsible. She feared she might be the next victim, and so she turned to James's chief opponent, Bothwell, whom she married on May 15, 1567. Bothwell's increased power led his former allies to fear him.

In June, the confederate lords seized power. Bothwell was allowed to flee, but Mary was imprisoned and forced to abdicate in favor of her son, then one year old. Bothwell fled to Norway, where he was arrested; he died in captivity in Sweden in

1578. In May, 1568, Mary escaped and organized an army, but her forces were defeated outside Glasgow on May 13, 1568. Mary fled to England to seek her cousin's support in regaining her throne.

The confederate lords claimed that Mary had been deposed because she had conspired in the death of Darnley and had committed adultery with Bothwell. To support these charges they sent Elizabeth eight "Casket Letters" that Mary had written, so called because they were supposedly found in a casket. The originals have disappeared. Guy has examined French and English transcripts and has concluded that while the letters were indeed by Mary, the confederate lords added incriminating dates and occasional lines, thereby distorting their meaning. For example, the first Casket Letter, while indeed by Mary (according to Guy), was not sent to Bothwell and was not written just before Darnley's assassination, as the confederate lords claimed.

Ultimately, nothing came of the Casket Letters. Mary was not tried on the charges leveled by the confederate lords, but neither would Elizabeth free Mary or help her regain her throne. Nor would Elizabeth declare Mary her successor. For the next eighteen years Mary was kept in captivity, sometimes more restrictive, sometimes less, while Elizabeth wrestled with the problem her guest posed.

In 1586, Mary committed herself to the Babington Plot, organized by the Catholic Antony Babington and the former Spanish ambassador to England, Bernardino de Mendoza, to assassinate Elizabeth and make Mary queen of England. Elizabeth's secret service read every letter the conspirators wrote. On the outside of the letter in which Mary agreed to the plan, the chief decoder, Thomas Phelippes, drew a picture of a gallows.

Even after Mary was convicted of conspiracy to kill Elizabeth, Elizabeth hesitated to sign Mary's death warrant. She wanted Mary dead, but she felt that sentencing a monarch would set a dangerous precedent. Elizabeth wrote to Sir Amyas Paulet, Mary's captor, asking him to kill Mary. Paulet refused. She considered hiring Robert Wingfield, a paid assassin. At length, she signed the warrant, and Mary was beheaded at Fotheringay Castle on February 8, 1587.

Elizabeth would outlive her Scottish cousin by sixteen years, but when she died in 1603, Mary's son succeeded to the English throne; Mary's dynastic claim was recognized at last. All of England's rulers since James I are direct descendants of Mary, not Elizabeth. In 1612, James erected monuments to Elizabeth and Mary in Westminster Abbey and had his mother reburied there. (She had been buried at Peterborough Castle in 1587.) Elizabeth's monument cost 765 pounds; Mary's monument cost 2,000 pounds. As Guy concludes, "If Elizabeth had triumphed in life, Mary would triumph in death."

Guy tells his story well and provides rich details to show how life was lived in the sixteenth century, whether luxuriously with painted ceilings and finely carved woodwork at Linlithgrow Palace, where Mary Stuart was born, or in the damp Tutbury Castle, one of the places where Mary was imprisoned. Guy defends Mary, as have most modern historians, and rejects the view that she allowed her passions to sway her decisions, whereas her cousin Elizabeth used her head. *Queen of Scots* shows how powerless Mary finally was, and how her actions were rational, even if unsuccessful. This is a worthy companion to Antonia Fraser's 1969 biography of Scotland's ill-starred queen.

*Joseph Rosenblum*

## Review Sources

*Booklist* 100, no. 13 (March 1, 2004): 1129.
*The Guardian*, January 24, 2004, p. 12.
*History: Review of New Books* 33, no. 1 (Fall, 2004): 23.
*History Today* 54, no. 5 (May, 2004): 68.
*Library Journal* 129, no. 7 (April 15, 2004): 95.
*The New York Times Book Review* 153 (April 11, 2004): 11.
*The Times*, January 3, 2004, Weekend review, p. 10.
*Times Higher Education Supplement*, April 16, 2004, p. 23.

# A QUESTION OF BLOOD

*Author:* Ian Rankin (1960-      )
*First published:* 2003, in Great Britain
*Publisher:* Little, Brown (Boston). 406 pp. $23.00
*Type of work:* Novel
*Time:* 2004
*Locale:* Scotland

*Edinburgh's popular fictional policeman is again on the case and in trouble in this installment in the best-selling John Rebus series*

> *Principal characters:*
> JOHN REBUS, a detective inspector with a past and an attitude
> SIOBHAN CLARKE, a detective sergeant
> ALLAN RENSHAW, Rebus's relative by marriage and father of a murder victim
> JACK BELL, an opportunistic member of the Scottish Parliament
> LEE HERDMAN, a suicide and alleged murderer
> TERI COTTER, "Miss Teri," a teenage Goth
> PEACOCK JOHNSON, a dealer in "replica" guns
> MARTIN FAIRSTONE, a lowlife and murder victim
> DOUGLAS BRIMSON, the owner of a local aviation service

Ian Rankin's *A Question of Blood* is the fourteenth novel featuring Edinburgh detective inspector John Rebus. Begun in 1987, the series, which also includes a novella and two collections of short stories, has a new Rebus book appearing just about every year. Rankin also published six other novels in the 1980's, early in his career, including three under the name Jack Harvey. He began supplanting Irvine Welsh on the Scottish and British best-seller lists in the late 1990's, about the same time he won the coveted Golden Dagger award for *Black and Blue* (1997) and started attracting a large American following. Although he did not invent the so-called tartan noir, Rankin certainly increased its visibility and advanced the art, while adding to the international allure of modern Scottish writing.

*A Question of Blood* begins the day after a seemingly senseless shooting at a private school in South Queensferry, ten miles from the city center, has left two students dead and another wounded. Dead too, by his own hand, is Lee Herdman, a former member of the Special Air Service (SAS), an elite commando unit with a history of its members "losing it." Knowing of Rebus's brief stint in the SAS, the officer in charge of the investigation, Bobby Hogan, asks for his help.

However, the problems associated with Rebus's involvement are many. First, he is in hospital with two badly burned hands, scalded, he says, when he drunkenly fell into his bath. Second, the same night Rebus injured his hands, a nefarious character named Martin Fairstone, who had been harassing Rebus's closest colleague, Detective Sergeant Siobhan Clarke, died in a fire, just hours after Rebus had been seen drinking

∼

*Since the publication of Ian
Rankin's* Knots and Crosses *(1987),
the Rebus books have been
translated into twenty-two
languages, and three of them have
been televised. The winner of many
literary prizes, Rankin was awarded
the Order of the British Empire in
2002 and is Great Britain's best-
selling crime writer.*

∼

with him at a pub and entering his apartment. (Rebus will be suspended from his duties, pending an investigation.) Third, Rebus turns out to be related to one of the dead students; thus one of the meanings of the novel's title and a situation which calls for Rebus to make the relationship known (which he does not) so that he can be disqualified from the investigation (which he is not). Before the cases are solved, there will be two more deaths, several subplots, and plenty of red herrings.

The novel's structure is as simple as the plot is intricate. The story unfolds in seven parts, or "Days" (workdays), further divided into twenty-seven chapters plus a short epilogue. As the novel and the investigations proceed, the pace picks up. Chapters in Days One and Two average twenty pages each; in Days Six and Seven, just twelve and eight, respectively. Questions arise, complicating the obvious, with the first big break coming a little more than a quarter of the way through the novel, when forensic pathologist Dr. Curt unofficially tries to help Rebus by explaining exactly how Fairstone died.

Rebus pokes the first hole in the SAS/Dunblane explanation of the school shooting. (Dunblane was the site of a March, 1996, school shooting that left sixteen students and one teacher dead.) Why, Paul asks, did the supposedly deranged Herdman walk past a schoolyard full of kids before shooting anyone? Why did he shoot these three students? Why, if the explanation is so straightforward, has SAS sent two of its own to investigate for a full week? The nascent forensic science and straightforward causality of Sherlock Holmes's day has given way to the Butterfly Theory that Rebus has distantly heard of but intuitively understands. Rebus does eventually put the pieces together—a photograph, Webcam, diamond, and Land Rover here, a military helicopter crash years before, a blood-spray pattern there. One of the novel's epigraphs is *Ita res lumina rebus* (thus one thing throws light upon others). Putting the pieces together, however, does not mean that justice will prevail and order be restored, and so the novel's other epigraph reads: "We find . . . no prospect of an end."

With his badly scalded hands, Rebus is in hot water in more than one sense and forced to battle with his hands tied, or at least bandaged. He is at once the badly tarnished knight errant who eschews the rules and a man haunted by his own past: separated from his former wife and his daughter, drifting away from his most recent girlfriend, retreating more into his work, his apartment, and his drinking. He is a good deal more like the alleged shooter than he would like to admit. In fact, it is his SAS file that is marked, not Herdman's, signifying the high probability that someday he will "lose it." (Rebus's time in the SAS is explained in the 1987 book *Knots and Crosses*.)

Rebus is fiercely loyal to his job, or rather, to solving cases, punishing wrongdoers, finger-in-the-dyke fashion. He is also fiercely loyal to a chosen few. He never knew the murdered boy who was his blood relative, even though he lived a few minutes' drive away, but Rebus is deeply concerned about Andy Callis, a uniformed cop on sick leave, severely depressed following the death of his wife and an incident in which he shot at a teenager armed only with a replica gun. The trade in replica guns will become an important element in Rebus's investigation into Fairstone's death and the school shootings. A second meeting with the teen will leave Andy dead, though whether the result of accident, murder, or suicide neither Rebus, who has a death wish of his own, nor the reader will ever know.

The person to whom Rebus is closest is Clarke, whose importance to Rebus and to the Rebus novels has grown steadily the past few years. Alternately Rebus's colleague, mother, sister, and daughter substitute, but never girlfriend, Clarke is mainly a younger, female Rebus: an outsider by virtue of her sex and English accent, estranged from family, having no real friends, prone to panic attacks rather than drinking, and loyal—to Rebus, anyway.

Clarke's future looks bright to Mullen, the internal affairs officer looking into Rebus's role in Fairstone's death: "'Inspector within five years, maybe chief inspector before you're forty . . . that gives you a whole ten years to catch up on DCS Templer.' He paused for effect. 'All of that waiting for you, if you manage to steer clear of trouble.'" Clarke's friend Rebus may embody trouble, but Clarke puts loyalty and trust over personal advancement, despite her own doubts about Rebus's innocence.

Rebus and Clarke are the central characters, but much the of the pleasure of reading this and other Rebus novels derives from the large supporting cast that is enormously vared and deftly drawn. Besides Hogan, Callis, and Mullen, brief appearances are made by Rebus's immediate superior (and former lover) DCS Gill Templer and by Claverhouse and Ormiston from the Drugs and Major Crime division (as well as from Rankin's 2001 book *Resurrection Men*). There is less interest in internal affairs than in some of the previous books, and the role of bad cop is assigned to the two SAS investigators, Whitehead and Simms. Rankin's latest girlfriend, Jean Burchill, curator at the Royal Museum of Scotland, is barely mentioned, their relationship all but over. The other characters cover a great deal of ground, geographically, professionally, socioeconomically, and generationally. Represented are the dead and the living, the old and the young, the well-off judge, the member of Scottish parliament, the struggling middle-class single parent, preppies, Goths, and schemies (who live on the city's impoverished housing estates), the vulnerable female college student and the sleazy tabloid journalist, hard men and soft touches, long-time criminals and those just starting out. There are also the psychologically wounded: Allan Renshaw and Callis and ex-SAS, too, including Rebus. Interestingly enough, Rebus's frequent nemesis, the kingpin of the Edinburgh underworld, Big Ger Cafferty, plays no part here.

Much of *A Question of Blood* is devoted to dialogue—half distinctive, half generic, and always sharp—but it is in the brief sketches (of characters, places, groups, and the like) that are especially effective. More than just efficient ways of introducing characters, places, or groups, these sketches put readers in Rebus's mind, enabling them to see not just what he sees but how he sees, with the same quick eye for detail and possible significance.

No less integral to Rankin's art is the city he has helped make Britain's "crime capital"—in fiction, not in fact: The number of homicides in Edinburgh and throughout Britain is actually quite small. Edinburgh is more than a setting that adds local color to Rankin's grim cases. It is certainly not a place where, as an American reviewer mistakenly claimed, "universal themes transcend geography." Rankin depicts his adopted city not only in all its specificity and topographical as well as socioeconomic extremes, but as having (along with Scotland more generally) a very specific and largely deleterious effect on its inhabitants: breeding violence and poverty as well as boundless opportunities for greed at all levels. Rankin's Edinburgh is at once realized, historicized, and mythologized. It is a city both changeless, because it is haunted by its own dark past, and changing, especially since the referendum on devolution (1997) and the opening of the first Scottish Parliament in three hundred years (1999).

Rebus has changed, too. He is no longer the detective sergeant of *Knots and Crosses* who "really needed their pats on the back, their congratulations on a job well done, their acceptance" and who "needed someone to assure him that it was going to be all right. That he would be all right." He is not so much more self-assured as more withdrawn. He is also older. Forty when the series began and a year older with each novel, Rebus is fifty-five now, just five years away from mandatory retirement age. Rebus's crime investigation division headquarters has already been retired, a casualty of the new Scottish Parliament, its demise inscribed in the novel's dedication: "In memoriam, St Leonard's CID." Fortunately, Rankin has been preparing for that inevitability by making Clarke more prominent. That is good news for readers, who are as addicted to Rankin novels as the Edinburgh junkies are to heroin in Welsh's *Trainspotting* (1993). It is good news for publishing in Britain, where the Rebus books account for fully 10 percent of all crime fiction sales.

*Robert A. Morace*

## Review Sources

*Booklist* 100, no. 7 (December 1, 2003): 627.
*The Guardian*, August 30, 2003, p. 23.
*Kirkus Reviews* 71, no. 24 (December 15, 2003): 1428.
*Library Journal* 129, no. 1 (January 15, 2004): 166.
*New Statesman* 132 (October 6, 2003): 53.
*The New York Times*, February 9, 2004, p. E8.
*The New York Times Book Review* 153 (February 22, 2004): 7.
*Publishers Weekly* 251, no. 1 (January 5, 2004): 43.
*The Spectator* 293 (September 6, 2003): 44.
*The Times Literary Supplement*, September 5, 2003, p. 8.

# RAMBLIN' MAN
## The Life and Times of Woody Guthrie

*Author:* Ed Cray (1933-    )
*Publisher:* W. W. Norton (New York). 488 pp. $30.00
*Type of work:* Biography
*Time:* 1912-1967
*Locale:* The United States

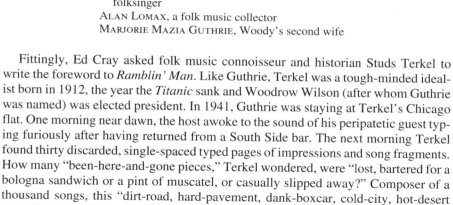

*An intimate yet critical account of America's most famous Depression-era balladeer, a restless spirit and author of the autobiographical 1943 novel* Bound for Glory

*Principal personages:*
> WOODROW WILSON GUTHRIE, a folksinger
> PETE SEEGER, a folksinger
> HUDDIE "LEADBELLY" LEDBETTER, a folksinger
> ALAN LOMAX, a folk music collector
> MARJORIE MAZIA GUTHRIE, Woody's second wife

Fittingly, Ed Cray asked folk music connoisseur and historian Studs Terkel to write the foreword to *Ramblin' Man*. Like Guthrie, Terkel was a tough-minded idealist born in 1912, the year the *Titanic* sank and Woodrow Wilson (after whom Guthrie was named) was elected president. In 1941, Guthrie was staying at Terkel's Chicago flat. One morning near dawn, the host awoke to the sound of his peripatetic guest typing furiously after having returned from a South Side bar. The next morning Terkel found thirty discarded, single-spaced typed pages of impressions and song fragments. How many "been-here-and-gone pieces," Terkel wondered, were "lost, bartered for a bologna sandwich or a pint of muscatel, or casually slipped away?" Composer of a thousand songs, this "dirt-road, hard-pavement, dank-boxcar, cold-city, hot-desert gamin" man (Terkel's words) was also a soda jerk, sign painter, mariner, radio entertainer, writer, spinner of yarns, labor organizer, and left-wing propagandist.

Oklahoma's Okfuskee County, Guthrie's birthplace, was a bastion of white racism. In 1911, a mob lynched thirty-four-year-old Laura Nelson and her fourteen-year-old son Lawrence in retaliation for the death of a policeman. Guthrie's go-getter father had a budding realty business in the oil-boom town of Okemah before suffering financial ruin during the post-World War I depression. Misfortune dogged him. One home lost its roof to a tornado; another burned down.

Guthrie's mother, Nora, sang Scots-Irish and parlor ballads to her children but was mentally unstable and never recovered from an incident that occurred when Guthrie was six. Grounded unfairly, Guthrie's sister Clara set her clothes on fire to scare her mother and died from the burns. A few years later, Nora doused her husband with kerosene and set him on fire. It took eighteen months for him to recover. Nora was institutionalized with Huntington's chorea, a disease Guthrie inherited.

*A journalism professor at USC's Annenberg School for Communication, Ed Cray is the author of solid biographies of General George C. Marshall and Chief Justice Earl Warren as well as anthologies of ribald verse, including* The Erotic Muse: American Bawdy Songs *(1968).*

Free to roam, Guthrie became fascinated with the harmonica playing of a "shoe shine boy" named George. He saved up enough money for his own harmonica and learned blues songs. For coins, Guthrie sang, jig-danced, and played the bones, sometimes in blackface. Forgoing his last two years of high school, he moved to the Texas Panhandle oil town of Pampa in 1929 to help his father manage a flophouse. He also worked in a drugstore whose owner sold "jake," an alcoholic concoction that sometimes caused paralysis.

Guthrie's Uncle Jeff taught him guitar chords, and on a nearby farm they would spend hours "woodshedding" with accomplished musicians. An acquaintance described Guthrie's infectious good spirits: "He would ride the freight train within two miles of our house and come down the lane singing and playing his guitar." Guthrie's first combo, the Corncob Trio, played hoedowns, minstrel tunes, and square-dance numbers.

In 1933 Guthrie married the teenage Mary Jennings. Two years later, drought and wind turned the Panhandle into a dustbowl. On Palm Sunday, the sky became black as night. The young couple "hunkered down in their shotgun shack," struggling, Cray writes, to "catch a good breath as the fine dust filtered through cracks until the naked electric light hanging on a cord from the ceiling glowed no brighter than a lighted cigarette." The following day, humorist Will Rogers died in a plane crash. From then on, Guthrie emulated the droll, cracker-barrel aura of Oklahoma's favorite son, although Guthrie was more impish and antiestablishment.

An indifferent husband, though affectionate toward children, Guthrie left his pregnant wife and daughter to go west. As Cray puts it, he "stuffed his paint brushes in a hip pocket, slung his guitar over his shoulder, and put up his thumb. Out there, at the end of Route 66, lay California and opportunity." Before reaching Los Angeles, the brushes had been stolen and the guitar swapped for food. His confidence intact, he teamed up with his cousin Jack Guthrie, who "could sell ice cubes to Eskimos," as a mutual friend put it.

Crooners Ken Maynard and Gene Autry had made cowboy music popular, and Jack landed the Guthries a show on radio station KFVD. They received no salary but hoped to parlay the exposure into guest appearances on other shows. When Jack tired of the gig, Woody found a woman partner. The act received thousands of fan letters from "Okie" migrants exploited by big growers. In 1938 Guthrie became a self-styled roving "hobo correspondent" for a fledgling weekly, the *Light*, which was promoting the gubernatorial candidacy of progressive Democrat Culbert Olson. Guthrie drifted from Hoovervilles to skid rows, witnessing the desperate conditions thrust upon proud "workhunters" despite five years of Franklin D. Roosevelt's New Deal. Guthrie determined to be the voice of "people living hungrier than rats and dirtier than dogs in a land of the sun and a valley of night breezes."

Back at KFVD, Guthrie befriended Communist Ed Robbin, who hosted a program of news commentary. After Olson, now governor, pardoned political prisoner Tom Mooney, Guthrie penned and performed "Mister Tom Mooney" ("Done got a pardon from the old jail house warden/ Mr. Culbert L. Olson's decree") at a victory rally. He started a folksy, left-leaning column called "Woody Sez" for *People's World*. His family arrived, but he was frequently gone and was a notorious womanizer.

After the Nonaggression Pact signed by Adolf Hitler and Joseph Stalin left California Communists in disarray, KFVD terminated Robbin and Guthrie. The Guthries returned to Pampa in a 1929 Chevrolet with a cracked engine block, breathing exhaust fumes all the way. Guthrie soon set out for New York, on actor Will Geer's suggestion. Hitchhiking through Pennsylvania, he nearly froze to death in a snowstorm. Staying with the Geers, he scrounged up enough money in Bowery bars to land in a grimy hotel near the New York Public Library. There he wrote "This Land Is Your Land," a retort to Irving Berlin's "God Bless America." The tune he borrowed from the Carter Family's "Little Darling, Pal of Mine."

The darling of the Left, though too undisciplined to be anything more than a fellow traveler, Guthrie resumed "Woody Sez" in the *Daily Worker*. At a fund-raiser, folklorist Alan Lomax heard him perform "Pretty Boy Floyd."

> Yes, he took to the river bottom along the river shore,
> And Pretty Boy found a welcome at every farmer's door.
> The papers said that Pretty Boy had robbed a bank each day,
> While he was setting in some farmhouse 300 miles away.

Impressed, Lomax got Guthrie to come to the Library of Congress, where he recorded his songs and stories and met twenty-one-year-old banjo player Pete Seeger. In a 1939 Plymouth purchased on credit, Guthrie took the straight-laced Seeger on a cross-country trip. Encountering stark poverty and racism, it was (Seeger later said) his "coming out into the world."

Guthrie landed a show on CBS radio called *Pipe Smoking Time* (the sponsor was Model Tobacco Company). His theme song was "So Long, It's Been Good to Know You." The producers wanted hillbilly songs, not social commentary, and after just seven shows Guthrie quit and was off to California, encouraged by Lomax to write his autobiography. He grew despondent until an offer suddenly came to write songs for a documentary celebrating public power and the building of Bonneville Dam. ("Roll On, Columbia, Roll On," later became Washington State's official folk song). When Seeger invited Guthrie to join the Almanac Singers, Mary refused to go with him, saying her wandering days were over. Cray writes: "There was no argument, not even tears as they parted."

The war years were Guthrie's most creative. He played union halls on tour with the Almanac Singers in Duluth, Detroit, and other heartland venues and wrote songs based on current events. Though often slovenly, he was capable of bursts of self-discipline. He found time to finish his autobiography, *Bound for Glory*. He fell in love with a married woman, Marjorie Mazia, and shipped out three times as a mess man on Liberty ships. Jim Longhi's *Woody, Cisco, and Me: Seamen Three in the Merchant Marine* (1997) contains fascinating anecdotes showing Guthrie's bravery and outrage at the segregated arrangements on board.

By this time the Federal Bureau of Investigation was following him, among other leftists. The Office of War Information cancelled a radio appearance of the Almanac Singers, and a naval intelligence official purloined Guthrie's seaman's papers. He was drafted and served on a base near East St. Louis, Illinois. Seeger, returning from the Pacific, started a political music project called People's Songs. Guthrie moved in and out of the group. The light of his life was daughter Cathy, whom he called "Sackabones." One day while Marjorie, now Guthrie's wife, was across the street buying milk and oranges, a short circuit in a radio cord sparked a fire that, with unbelievable suddenness, took Cathy's life. Crushed, Guthrie succumbed to alcoholism, which probably hastened the onset of Huntington's chorea.

In 1947, the Broadway hit *Finian's Rainbow* featured a character named Woody Mahoney, based on Guthrie, who expressed regret that the romantic lead had abandoned his wanderings to settle down. The following year Guthrie appeared at Progressive Party rallies for presidential candidate Henry Wallace. Guthrie's marriage disintegrating, he went to California and married a twenty-one-year-old woman after he and Marjorie divorced.

In a Florida hovel without electricity, Guthrie splashed kerosene on his sleeve one morning while preparing a fire and burned his arm from the shoulder to the fingers. Flames had taken his sister and daughter and maimed his father; now him. He would never play guitar again. Morose, his behavior veered toward the violent and lecherous. His final ramble landed him in several jails. On September 16, 1954, he checked himself into Brooklyn State Hospital.

In 1956, a benefit took place in New York's Pythian Hall for the Guthrie Children's Trust Fund. In the audience, the forty-three-year-old honoree was so ill his voice was nearly silenced, and his elbow was too twisted to hold a guitar. Led by Pete Seeger, friends sang thirty "hard hitting songs for hard-hit people" (the phrase became the title of a 1967 anthology by Lomax, Guthrie, and Seeger). The audience sang the final chorus of what many considered to be their national anthem: "This land is your land, this land is my land,/ From California to the New York Island./ From the redwood forest to the Gulf Stream waters,/ This land was made for you and me."

Summing up his subject's legacy, Cray does not resort to hyperbole. According to him, Seeger did more to keep American folk music alive, but Guthrie was "the most important writer-performer of songs that expressed a personal political view"—at least until Bob Dylan came along. One of scores of Guthrie's disciples, the Minnesota native affected jerky, mumbling mannerisms that seemed to mimic Guthrie in the early stages of Huntington's.

Had Guthrie not been such a narcissist, his life story could have been more heroic. Okemah first resisted efforts to memorialize its famous citizen, but in 1996 the town hosted the first annual Woody Guthrie Festival and unveiled a bronze bust in his likeness. In making good use of newly unsealed material from the Woody Guthrie Archives, Cray has produced a worthy update to Joe Klein's admirable *Woody Guthrie: A Life* (1980).

Cray achieves the main objectives of a biographer by capturing what Guthrie loved and conveying his importance. As Guthrie put it: "About all a human being is, anyway, is just a hoping machine." Cray provides lengthy introductions to people who were important musical influences, such as Huddie "Leadbelly" Ledbetter, and furnishes cogent background information on the Red Scare. *Booklist* reviewer Joanne Wilkinson wrote: "A man of contradictions, the songwriter emerges as an intellectual who took pains to hide his intellect and as a crusader for social justice who neglected his own family. His second wife, Marjorie, takes on near-heroic stature as the caregiver who, though they were long divorced, looked after him during the last decade of his debilitating illness."

*James B. Lane*

## Review Sources

*Booklist* 100, no. 12 (February 15, 2004): 1017.
*Entertainment Weekly*, February 13, 2004, p. 77.
*Kirkus Reviews* 71, no. 23 (December 1, 2003): 1388.
*Library Journal* 129, no. 1 (January 15, 2004): 113.
*Los Angeles Times*, February 15, 2004, p. R3.
*The New York Times Book Review* 153 (April 11, 2004): 21.
*Rolling Stone*, April 1, 2004, p. 101.

# RATS
## Observations on the History and Habitat of the City's Most Unwanted Inhabitants

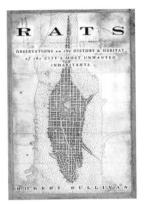

*Author:* Robert Sullivan (1963-    )
*Publisher:* Bloomsbury (New York). 242 pp. $24.00
*Type of work:* Nature and history
*Time:* 2001-2002
*Locale:* New York City

*For a year, Sullivan spent his nights watching rats in an alley and here provides his observations and a natural history of rats, their behavior, and their relationship with humankind*

On the first page of this fascinating study, New York writer Robert Sullivan tackles the question many readers may wonder: Why did he choose to write a book about rats? His explanation illustrates his dispassionate, yet conversational and often humorous tone: "One answer is proximity. Rats live in the world precisely where man lives, which is, needless to say, where I live." Acknowledging that many people find rats frightening and disgusting, Sullivan asserts, and goes on to demonstrate, that the history of rats is bound up with that of humankind, whose garbage they eat. Sullivan's research into New York City brings to life many historical figures, from American naturalist John James Audubon, whose painting of rats inspired this book, to the Civil Rights movement agitator Jesse Gray, who challenged authorities to eradicate rodent infestation in Harlem tenements, to Isaac Sears, who mobilized a mob of American colonialists against British soldiers just before the Revolutionary War began.

With a scientist's accuracy and with pleasing informality, Sullivan reports his methods: "All I did was stand in an alley—a filth-slicked little alley that is about as old as the city and secret the way alleys are secret and yet just a block or two from Wall Street, from Broadway, and from what used to be the World Trade Center." He describes his observations of the nightlife, mentioning passersby, local loiterers without obvious residences or occupations, and taverngoers who step outside the taverns for cigarettes and are sometimes surprised to see a man standing in the dark alley with night-vision gear. "To know the rat is to know its habitat, and to know the habitat of the rat is to know the city." After describing this part of the city, he describes the rats, occasionally with aversion but always with interest and delightful characterization: "Rats command a perverse celebrity status—nature's mobsters, flora and fauna's serial killers."

Sullivan devotes his second chapter to describing the rat that lives in Manhattan, *Rattus norvegicus*, also called the Norway or brown rat. The animal is a marvel of evolution, with its excellent sense of smell and taste, its incisors which grow five inches per year, its steel-strong teeth, its ability to mate as often as twenty times a day, and its phenomenal birthrate: "A single mating pair can produce up to 15,000 offspring a year." (This number seems sensationalistic, unless he means to include the offspring of offspring.)

*Robert Sullivan is the author of* The Meadowlands *(1998) and* A Whale Hunt *(2000), both New York Times Notable Books of the Year. He has received a National Endowment for the Arts creative writing fellowship. Sullivan is a contributing editor to* Vogue *and a frequent contributor to* The New Yorker.

Sullivan chronicles how rats made their way to America from Asia and how they can invade buildings, basements, and subway stations with their powers of gnawing and digging. He also evokes sympathy for these mammals by detailing the many ways in which they can be killed, from automobiles and hawks to determined exterminators armed with traps and poisons. Sullivan employs the word "thigmophilic," meaning "touch-loving," to explain that rats like to touch walls and corners as they travel, which is perhaps why white rats are used so often in laboratory tests of maze-traversing and memory. Finally, in this chapter Sullivan brings up the folklore of the Rat King. He will return to each of these topics at expanded length throughout the rest of his book.

After hunting for a suitable observation point, Sullivan selected Edens Alley, and the history he provides, as well as his vivid, smell-resplendent descriptions, conjure this alley to life. Employees at nearby restaurants toss bags of garbage into the alley, so that its cobblestones are greasy and dirty, creating a veritable rat heaven. The rats gnaw open the bags and feast, then carry bits of food down their holes to other, nesting rats. Quotes from Sullivan's journal detailing his observations on a winter evening illustrate his gift for the well-placed literary allusion and his sense of humor:

> More garbage comes up out of the bottom of the Irish bar. One bag lands on a rodent bait station that is ancient and nearly destroyed. The garbage tide is rising. I am reminded of [poet John] Milton, in "Lycidas": "tomorrow to fresh woods and pastures new." Though when I am reminded of it the words *woods* and *pastures* are replaced by *trash*.

A little further down this page, Sullivan shows his patience and philosophical temperament: "What exactly am I waiting here for? Nature, even rat nature, does not answer mortals, even rat-interested mortals. If the alley speaks, it is obscure: *Claude os et audit!*" (Close your mouth and listen!)

Sullivan relates his research into Edens Alley, which once was a street in a neighborhood of craftspeople and bakers and designers of gold jewelry and which, before that, was a grassy hill above a swamp. This alley, connecting Fulton and Gold Streets in the Fulton Fish Market neighborhood of lower Manhattan, is antique. It was named for a friend of Aaron Burr. Sullivan discovers that the first "battle" (or, at any rate, fighting in the streets) of the American Revolution occurred at the top of Edens Alley in 1770, and he narrates the colorful biography of Isaac Sears, charismatic chieftain of New York and leader of that fight against the English soldiers. Ever entwining the history of humans with rats, he describes how *Rattus norvegicus* arrived in America in 1776 on the ships of England's navy as the British sailed over to put down the revolutionaries.

Using anecdotes and interviews with exterminators (or "pest control technicians"), Sullivan makes clear that rats are everywhere, even if people do not see them. He quotes an epidemiologist in the New York health department: "The general consensus is that if you see one, then there are ten, and if you see them during the day, then you don't know what you've got" in the way of numbers, because rats are normally nocturnal, and sightings during the day are symptoms of hungry rat overpopulation.

Sullivan documents how the terrorist attacks on the World Trade Center on September 11, 2001, interrupted his visits to Edens Alley, which was blocked off for some months. He grimly interconnects terrorism with contagious disease, with which rats are so closely linked in the minds of so many people.

Sullivan's reading of newspapers from 1900 and 1901 exposes a horrifying chapter in American history—the appearance of bubonic plague in San Francisco's Chinatown and its subsequent coverup by newspaper editors and businessmen who were afraid of losing tourist dollars. By mid-1901, states around the union had threatened a national quarantine against California, and the outcry succeeded in producing a cure, though the plague infestation did not end until 1904. The ongoing threat of bubonic plague in North America—mostly in rural areas—is illuminated in the case of a married couple from New Mexico who were hospitalized in New York in 2002 and diagnosed with the plague.

In the chapter called "Catching," Sullivan recalls being allowed to accompany New York health department agents on outings to trap live rats and test their blood, as part of a project to discover how the city's rat populations would react in case of an outbreak, whether accidental or engineered by terrorists. The author intersperses accounts of their adventures with information about bubonic plague. The use of plague as a biological weapon is under study by the Centers for Disease Control, and Sullivan documents Japanese plague-bombing of China during World War II, as well as experimentation with bioweaponry in the United States in the 1950's and 1960's, unleashed upon an unwitting populace. (Sullivan does not moralize, but the message is clear: Rats are accidental vectors of disease and innocent victims of plague-carrying fleas, but humans spread death on purpose.) Sullivan and his health agent friends are impressed by the strong constitutions of the rats they capture, rats who take repeated doses of anesthesia before falling asleep, and he explains that rats are difficult to catch because they are so cautious about anything new in their environment, including traps.

Sullivan is excellent as both historian and natural historian, and his respect and liking for pest control technicians convinces his audience. He quotes conversations with exterminators at length, cherishing rat-encounter anecdotes and explaining the many different ways in which rats are exterminated. His history of sanitation in New York City is filled with frightened residents and the efforts—or promises—of politicians, both sincere and corrupt. Sullivan tells the (usually unfortunate) results of rats who swim into toilets and elaborates on the alarming tale of a 1979 attack on a woman in Ann Street by a large pack of rats.

Animal lovers will enjoy the passages about rat behavior, which Sullivan describes, if not with loving detail, then at least with sympathy and amazement. Chapter 8, titled "Food," is entirely entertaining, as Sullivan recounts a summer evening in Edens Alley in which he undertakes to examine his rat population's dietary habits. As lyrically as the subject of rats scrabbling in garbage bags will allow, he describes his alley as a wildlife refuge and the happiness of rats with a lot of food available to them. The list (reprinted from a 1953 article) of foods in garbage heaps that rats will eat, from most-liked to least-liked, will provoke laughter: high on the list are scrambled eggs, macaroni and cheese, and potatoes, and at the bottom are fresh fruits and vegetables—though Sullivan describes jogging after a rat that was determined to keep an apple core it had found. Sullivan notes that the rats in his own alley were particularly fond of cheesy Italian dishes, which might also provoke some gratitude in the reader that oversized, unfinished portions in restaurants are not going to waste after they are carried from the table.

Rat dietary habits become, in Sullivan's capable hands, a brilliant metaphor for a city as an organism that consumes and expels in a vast, never-ending system. The book is at times a natural history of New York as a living creature, and in describing it thus Sullivan provides a new way to look at this old city that will enlighten both its residents and those who know it only from cinema, literature, and anecdote. His book cannot be said to romanticize Manhattan—except, perhaps, for some moments in its history; nor does he romanticize the rat (he admittedly hesitates to describe the romantic life of the rat). He never sentimentalizes the animal. However, Sullivan succeeds in drawing an appreciative and open-minded portrait of rats, a summation devoutly to be wished in view of the fact that these creatures share the world closely with humans and, as scavengers, lessen the size of human garbage dumps. The book is guaranteed to join the canon of natural history studies.

*Fiona Kelleghan*

## Review Sources

*Booklist* 100, no. 15 (April 1, 2004): 1338.
*The Boston Globe*, April 28, 2004, p. F2.
*Discover* 25, no. 5 (May, 2004): 74.
*Kirkus Reviews* 72, no. 2 (January 15, 2004): 77.
*Natural History* 113, no. 4 (May, 2004): 58.
*The New York Times*, April 6, 2004, p. E8.
*The New York Times Book Review* 153 (April 4, 2004): 8.
*Newsday*, April 11, 2004, p. C37.
*Publishers Weekly* 251, no. 5 (February 2, 2004): 65.
*The Washington Post Book World*, May 5, 2004, p. C04.

# RE-ENCHANTMENT
## Tibetan Buddhism Comes to the West

*Author:* Jeffery Paine (1944-    )
*Publisher:* W. W. Norton (New York). 278 pp. $25.00
*Type of work:* Religion and history
*Time:* 1923-2004
*Locale:* The United States and Tibet

*An overview of the unlikely resurgence of Tibetan Buddhism after its attempted destruction by Communist China in the 1950's, told largely through personal vignettes of some of the religion's most prominent adherents, past and present*

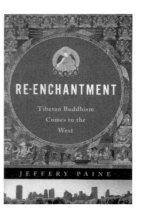

Principal personages:
   ALEXANDRA DAVID-NEEL, American
      explorer and author
   THOMAS MERTON, Catholic monk and author
   HAROLD TALBOTT, JR., American student of the Dalai Lama
   THE FOURTEENTH DALAI LAMA (TENZIN GYATSO), exiled leader of
      Tibetan Buddhism
   LAMA YESHE, Tibetan exile and Buddhist teacher
   CHOGYAM TRUNGPA, Tibetan exile and Buddhist teacher
   ROBERT THURMAN, American scholar and former monk
   JETSUNMA AHKON LHAMO (ALICE LOUISE ZEOLI), American teacher
      and Buddhist *tulku*, or reincarnation
   TENZIN PALMO (DIANE PERRY), British teacher and Buddhist nun

Throughout history, an untold number of once-thriving religions have ceased to exist. Some of them disappeared passively, as their popularity faded and their adherents gradually died out with no younger generation to carry on the flame. Other religions were violently conquered or assimilated into competing, more materially powerful faiths.

By all odds, Tibetan Buddhism should today be numbered among the latter type of casualty, after its bloody attempted extermination by Communist China in the mid-twentieth century. The unlikely sequence of events that has allowed the religion not only to survive but also to grow and thrive today across various continents is the story that Jeffery Paine undertakes to tell in *Re-enchantment*.

Though the book's somewhat staid subtitle, *Tibetan Buddhism Comes to the West*, hints at a measured, academic-style account of the people and cultural forces involved, Paine's book is anything but that—his narrative is fast-paced, funny, and thoroughly modern in tone and approach, seemingly crafted to appeal to Western readers with zero vested interest in the subject of Buddhist teachers or their teachings (a premise not without its drawbacks, as will be discussed). Fortunately, the author also weaves in a substantial enough primer on the basics of Buddhist thought to give readers who come to this volume out of simple curiosity a good idea of the reasons for Buddhism's wide-ranging appeal.

The Tibetans who managed to escape into exile during the Chinese purges of the 1950's were, by most standards, woefully unprepared for life in the larger world. Their home country, with a land area roughly equal to the state of Texas but with icy mountain peaks, was for thousands of years both geographically remote and culturally insular. Tibetans were taught that Americans, although skilled at technology, were so morally and intellectually adrift as to border on insanity. Likewise, the Chinese government portrayed Tibetan Buddhism to the rest of the world as a childishly outdated amalgam of magic and superstition.

The first person successfully to break through that mutual wall of fear and suspicion was Madame Alexandra David-Neel (1868-1969), a rich

*Jeffery Paine is a contributing editor at* The Wilson Quarterly *and has written for many newspapers and various literary periodicals. He has taught at Princeton University, the New School for Social Research, and the Volksuniversiteit Amsterdam. Paine is the author of* Father India *(1998) and the editor of the anthology* The Poetry of Our World *(2000).*

and adventurous Frenchwoman so obsessed by the little she knew of otherworldly Tibetan culture that she taught herself the language and, in 1923, adopted a series of disguises in order to cross undetected into the holy city of Llasa, which was off-limits to foreigners. To say that the odds were against her is an understatement, as Paine relates here:

> An endangered culture may, at the last moment, attract an alien witness who records its unique way of life before it perishes. . . . But to preserve Tibet's story, Alexandra David-Neel was, obviously, the wrong person entirely. First of all, she was exactly that, *she*, a woman, who undertook excursions and perils in which men perished like swatted flies. A trained athlete in prime condition could hardly have endured the ordeals she encountered, yet when she began her mad march to Llasa she was fifty-five, then considered the threshold of old age. Well-provisioned expeditions had perished on those treacherous wintry routes, but Alexandra embarked on them with a single companion and with no provisions at all. Her subsequent account, *My Journey to Llasa*, describes a Parisienne on an insouciant lark, but her jaunty attitude played down the actual facts—starvation; threats from brigands; danger from wild beasts; uncharted icy wastes—that made every day a game of Russian roulette. Later journalists and feature writers, puzzled how she survived at all, invariably resorted to some variation of (to quote one account) "It was the most remarkable journey a white woman has ever made."

Once David-Neel settled in, her written accounts were far from the breathless, touristy gossip one might expect. Instead she became, to the extent she was able, a Tibetan—befriending the thirteenth Dalai Lama, going on months-long solitary spiritual retreats, and eventually living what she described as a fairy-tale existence in the palace of the prince of Sikkim (a dashing figure more than twenty years her junior), wearing gold brocade robes, and helping the prince administer his kingdom's monasteries. Though she had no background in anthropology, she nonetheless wrote about Tibet and Buddhism with a degree of scientific rigor that would, by the time of her death at the age of one hundred, help dispel many of the world's misconceptions about the storied land.

The next prominent Westerner to have his life's course changed by Tibet was a monk named Thomas Merton (1915-1968), America's premier Catholic intellectual and author of such classic spiritual works as *The Seven Storey Mountain* (1948). Although he had an affinity for Taoism and Zen, he had largely dismissed Tibetan Buddhism as primitive. In 1968, however, Merton was on an Asian tour when he met the Dalai Lama and other Tibetan monks and made a dramatic intellectual turnaround. Merton wrote in his journal:

> The Tibetan Buddhists are the only ones at present who have a really large number of people who have attained to extraordinary heights in meditation and contemplation. . . . We need the religious genius of Asia to inject a dimension of depth into our aimless threshing about. May I not come back [to the United States] without having settled the great affair.

He however, eagerly made plans to begin a year-long study of Buddhist practice in India, the Dalai Lama's home in exile. Then, on a side trip to a religious conference in Thailand, Merton died in a freak accident—he slipped in a bathroom shower and was electrocuted by a faulty floor fan. His change of mind and heart, though, had already made its impact.

In fact, the spiritual odysseys of Merton and David-Neel could not have come at a more propitious point in history. As China's violent crackdown on religion in Tibet continued, more and more Tibetan monks began finding their way to the United States—by chance coinciding with the large cultural revolution in the United States in the 1960's. As Paine describes that era:

> A generation of young "rebels" . . . launched a protest against the perceived despiritualization of contemporary life. Hippies and other middle-class youth joined the protest against what they considered the unenlightened policies of their society (e.g., racial discrimination, war in Vietnam), often by turning to the East to pursue a different kind of enlightenment. Probably at no other time, before or since, could Tibetan Buddhism have thus landed on American shores and enjoyed such a welcoming reception.

The central section of *Re-enchantment* is an account, told through personal vignettes, of the ups and downs of two prominent Buddhist teachers and two of the movement's most prominent Western disciples. In both pairs of cases, the individuals profiled could not be more opposite. Lama Yeshe, though highly unconventional in his methods, was an able founder of new Buddhist centers and, after his untimely death from a heart ailment, was almost universally revered by his students as a holy man. Chogyam Trungpa, by contrast, was both a charismatic leader and an eccentric known for his heavy drinking and sexual exploits; his reputation largely imploded in scandal, and he died of alcohol abuse at the age of forty-seven.

It was likewise for the two students-turned-teachers. Diane Perry, later named Tenzin Palmo, was a student of the erratic Chogyam Trungpa and yet became a sedate and respected Buddhist nun who spent twelve years in solitary retreat in a Himalayan cave. Whereas Jetsunma Ahkon Lhamo (born Alice Louise Zeoli, in Brooklyn, New York) took instruction from an august Tibetan rinpoche, or reincarnated lama, but became an erratic and flamboyant leader whose popular retreat center came apart in a financial scandal.

The author's explanation of how such paradoxes make sense when examined from a Buddhist perspective is one of the most articulate and enlightening portions of his book and goes a long way toward remedying what is otherwise the most significant weakness of his narrative approach. Focusing on the most outrageous examples of any phenomenon is great for entertainment value but bad for balance, and Paine's choice of material runs the risk of giving a lurid, tabloidesque glow to a system of thought that is apparently, for the vast majority of its new followers, a largely rational and understated—albeit life-changing—experience.

Paine himself best describes the root effect of Buddhism on current religious thought with this striking image: "Picture a large cathedral symbolically dominating the landscape; then picture a modest American home or urban apartment with a little sunlight streaming through the window. Buddhism was, peculiarly enough, one of the forces that helped rehouse religion from the first sort of dwelling to the latter."

In a nutshell, Tibetan Buddhism as explicated in *Re-enchantment* is best expressed by a quote attributed to the current Dalai Lama: "I like to joke that religion is a luxury item. Kindness is not." Unlike many other faiths, Buddhism tends to value pragmatism and human compassion above dogma and theology. Indeed, some make the case that Buddhism is less a conventional religion than it is an ethical system, a philosophy, a science, or all three combined. Buddhist monks have variously described their vocation as "a science of mind," and "an alternate method of comprehending the universe." In contrast to more mainstream religions that vigorously pit their biblical truths against the findings of science, as in the current controversy over teaching creationism alongside evolution in schools, the Dalai Lama has famously said, "If the words of the Buddha and the discoveries of modern science conflict, the former have to go."

Ironic as it seems, a religion once derided as primitive and superstitious has conceivably become the most modern and cutting-edge of them all. The Dalai Lama is known as an avid student of science, medicine, and physics and convenes gatherings of experts who discuss with him in detail the latest knowledge in a wide range of fields. Some of those exchanges are featured in the 2004 book *The New Physics and Cosmology: Dialogues with the Dalai Lama*, by Arthur Zajonc, of which reviewer Doug Brown writes: "Buddhism has several core tenets which are shared by science. According to Buddhism, two causes of suffering are making assumptions about the world and ignorance. Discussions within Buddhism, as in science, work to expose statements that are unsupported by data and peel them away." As a result, the notion of accepting an idea "on faith" from some religious authority is foreign to Buddhism, which urges its followers to question the teachings of even the Buddha.

The remainder of *Re-enchantment* examines Hollywood's recent fascination with Buddhism and Tibet—such major films as *Kundun* (1997), *Seven Years in Tibet* (1997), *Little Buddha* (1993), and others in the works—and in the harrowing chapter, "To Hell and to Jail," profiles Jarvis Jay Masters, a prisoner on death row who converted to Buddhism while in San Quentin. Masters's dark story has a parallel in Buddhist history: Milarepa, a poet and one of Tibet's best-loved yogis, was a murderer before he repented and atoned for his crimes. Paine's concluding chapter, a reflection upon Buddhism's future in the West, is cogent and thought-provoking.

In an afterword, the author argues persuasively—but not convincingly—for his decision not to include a bibliography with his text, basically saying that *Re-enchantment* is not a scholarly book but is intended for the "common reader." Considering the dazzling array of topics the book covers, even some common readers will likely miss having a bibliography to guide their further reading. Still, *Re-enchantment* is a vibrant and compelling introduction to a system of thought that is of growing influence in American culture.

*Carroll Dale Short*

## Review Sources

*Booklist* 100, nos. 9-10 (January 15, 2004): 794.
*Library Journal* 129, no. 1 (January 15, 2004): 121.
*Publishers Weekly* 250, no. 45 (November 10, 2003): 57.

# THE REFORMATION
## A History

*Author:* Diarmaid MacCulloch (1951-      )
*Publisher:* Viking Press (New York). 792 pp. $35.00
*Type of work:* History and religion
*Time:* 1490-1700
*Locale:* Europe, England, and Scotland

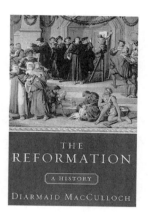

*MacCulloch traces in detail the events of both the Protestant Reformation and the Catholic, or Counter-Reformation*

*Principal personages:*
MARTIN LUTHER, father of Lutheranism
JOHN CALVIN, father of Reformed Protestantism
HERASMUS GERRITSZOON (DESIDERIUS ERASMUS), noted humanist
CHARLES V, Holy Roman emperor (1519-1556)
ELIZABETH I, queen of England (1558-1603)
FERDINAND I, Holy Roman emperor (1558-1564)
HENRY III, king of France (1574-1589)
HENRY VIII, king of England (1509-1547)
JAMES I, king of England (1603-1625); also known as JAMES VI, king of Scotland (1567-1625)
MARY STUART, queen of Scotland (1542-1587)
MARY I, queen of England, known as Bloody Mary (1553-1558)
PHILIPP MELANCHTHON, follower of Luther
PHILIP II, king of Spain (1556-1598)
FRANCISCO XIMÉNES DE CISNEROS, central figure in the Spanish Inquisition
HULDRYCH ZWINGLI, reformed innovator of the presbytery system

In *The Reformation*, Diarmaid MacCulloch's opening chapter "The Old Church, 1490-1517" identifies its two pillars as the Mass, with its close relation to the belief in Purgatory, and papal primacy. The chantry evolved as a place where Masses could be sung to buy time off in Purgatory, a practice open to abuse in the selling of indulgences. Martin Luther ranted about indulgences as "clerical confidence tricks" and contradictions of his teachings about salvation through faith.

Such voluntary organizations as guilds and confraternities, with clergy paid by the laity, accommodated the laypeople's hunger for prayer. Pilgrimages to holy sites and the growth of a cult of Mary signified a need for devotion of another sort. Questions about the Mass led to Thomas Aquinas's explanation, derived from Aristotle, that the Communion bread and wine underwent a process of transubstantiation in which the accidents, or outward sensory properties, stayed the same, while the substance (that

~

*Diarmaid MacCulloch is a fellow of St. Cross College, Oxford University, and professor of the history of the Church at Oxford. Among his books are* Suffolk and the Tudors *(1986), winner of the Royal Historical Society's Whitfield Prize, and* Thomas Cranmer: A Life *(1997), winner of the Whitbread Biography Prize, the James Tait Black Prize, and the Duff Cooper Prize.*

~

which stands under, unavailable to the senses) became the body and blood of Christ. Those in the "Roman obedience" generally accepted this account, "but in sixteenth-century Europe, thousands of Protestants were burned at the stake for denying an idea of Aristotle, who had never heard of Jesus Christ."

The second pillar, papal primacy, withstood a challenge from John Wyclif (1328-1384) and his Bible-believing Lollard supporters in England, but after Jan Hus was burned at the stake in 1415, a Czech rebellion established an independent Hussite Church in Bohemia. The Hussites used Czech instead of Latin and insisted that worshipers receive wine as well as bread at the Eucharist (Communion). Many Church leaders held that the Church was better run by a collective authority than solely by the bishop of Rome, but this argument for "conciliarism," or governance by a council of bishops, was defeated by Pope Alexander VI and Pope Julius II.

In the fifteenth century, noble families took over many Church properties, selecting powerful laymen known as commendators to run the abbeys, often with "genuine idealism." During the rise of secular governments, or commonwealths, in the sixteenth century the Valois monarchy in France kept its distance from the pope, and England's Henry VII started a struggle for independence that his son Henry VIII later won.

The fall of Constantinople to the Turks in 1453 threatened Europe until the end of the seventeenth century, with modern estimates of around one million Christian Europeans enslaved between 1530 and 1640. The Muslims were repulsed only in the Iberian kingdoms, where the Castilian Francisco Ximénes de Cisneros achieved administrative reforms for the Castilian Church but brutalized Jews during the Inquisition. At the same time, Spanish and Portuguese penetration of the New World advanced the Church across the Atlantic Ocean.

Giovanni Pico della Mirandola celebrated free will, but the "bleak picture of human worthlessness" that Saint Augustine inferred from Saint Paul's epistle to the Romans smothered the genial humanist vision of Desiderius Erasmus and dominated the thought of Martin Luther and John Calvin. Their grim teachings about predestination, original sin, irresistible grace, and the elect obviously contradicted any hopes for human effort and led to desperate sophistries to dodge accusations of antinomianism. Luther argued that the body and blood of Christ were physically present in the Eucharist, but he rejected it as a good work, made the Bible central for Christians, accepted sacred art, and insisted on infant baptism. Philipp Melanchthon of Wittenberg became Luther's ardent disciple, but a group of Zurich reformers, led by Huldrych Zwingli, took an independent stand on several of these points. Zwingli organized assemblies to synods, or presbyteries, on matters of worship that antedated the English parliamentary system. After Zwingli's death, his follower Heinrich Bullinger taught Zwingli's interpretation of the Mass as symbolic and presented baptism and the Eucharist as "seals" of God's covenant with his people.

The period from 1524 to 1540 witnessed increased tensions between civil and ecclesiastical powers. It began with the Peasants' War and was marked by the travails of the Anabaptists in Moravia, led in a separated Church by Jakob Hutter. Luther and Melanchthon met with other theologians in 1529 at Marburg, where all agreed on fourteen articles that evolved into the Augsburg Confession, the cornerstone of various Protestant faiths, especially Lutheranism. Millenarian fervor moved the Anabaptists to seize Münster in 1534, but the bishop's forces starved out the rebels and executed Anabaptist leaders in "exercises in exemplary sadism."

Protestants and Catholics made no progress toward reconciliation in the sixteenth century, but inspired leaders emerged on both sides. Ignatius Loyola founded the Society of Jesus, whose members soon assumed crucial positions in missionary work, and John Calvin reorganized the Genevan Church and preached on predestination and the elect. Calvin rejected Luther's stand on the physical presence of the body and blood in the Eucharist, and he was skeptical about images of the sacred and honoring Mary.

The Peace of Augsburg in 1555 accepted the religious division of the Empire but did not reconcile the Lutherans and the Reformed on the Mass. The Catholic faith revived briefly under Queen Mary in England from 1553 to 1558, but Queen Elizabeth's accession in 1558 quickly produced the Religious Settlement that has been the foundation of the Church of England—and thus worldwide Anglicanism—ever since.

During the same decade, Scottish Protestants created a new church, the Kirk. The Habsburg archduke Ferdinand supported Catholicism with a determination that eventually fueled the Thirty Years' War (1618-1648). The last session of the Council of Trent, from 1561 to 1563, despite its unresolved debate over whether final authority should rest with the pope or with the bishops, influenced papal policies for the future. The council did nothing, however, to prevent the brutal wars of the period between Protestants and Catholics in France.

By 1570 the Protestants dominated northern Europe but were split into Lutheran (or "evangelical") and Reformed branches, divided on such doctrinal issues as the Eucharist, the proper use of images and ceremony, and predestination. The Catholic Church, eager after the Council of Trent to reassert its primacy, enjoyed widespread advances in Poland and Lithuania largely through the excellent schooling opportunities offered by the Jesuits. The partition of the Low Countries created today's Roman Catholic Belgium and the Protestant Netherlands.

Jacobus Arminius modified the Calvinist doctrine of irresistible grace, preaching that some reject God's grace and suffer damnation through their own willfulness, a damnation that God foresees but does not decree. Subscribers to this "Arminianism," known as Remonstrants, were soon locked in a struggle with the Calvinist powers that was resolved when the Synod of Dordt "formulated conclusions under five headings that would remain the reference points of developed Calvinism: the unconditional decree by God of election, the limiting of Christ's atoning death for humanity to those elected to salvation, the total corruption of humankind, the irresistibility of God's grace, and the unchallengeable perseverance in saving grace of God's elect."

In Scotland, King James VI submitted to the flourishing of presbyteries, thereby strengthening the Kirk's role alongside the Scottish Parliament. England's Queen Elizabeth faced two antagonists: the Puritans, who favored presbyterianism over episcopacy, and the Catholics, whose hopes were dampened by the execution in 1587 of Mary, Queen of Scots. Richard Hooker criticized Reformed theology in his *Laws of Ecclesiastical Polity*, but William Perkins developed a sophisticated theory of covenants that afforded an escape from charges of antinomianism, the claim that free grace nullified moral law. The bloodshed went on, with England "judicially murdering more Roman Catholics than any other country." Whereas the Tudor government's respect for Welsh culture helped bring the Welsh into English Protestantism, different circumstances and English mistakes ensured the success of the Counter-Reformation in Ireland.

Catholicism continued strong in southern Europe, especially in Italy, where vernacular Bibles were ceremonially burned and evangelicalism was eradicated by the Roman Inquisition. Venice successfully resisted the centralization of authority promoted by the Council of Trent, but Milan under Archbishop Carlo Borromeo maintained strict control while developing an impressive educational system. King Philip II of Spain promulgated Tridentine decrees and used the printing press to spread the faith, while Jesuit intellectuals invented a historic past and the clergy promoted a large increase in funeral Masses. The interaction over centuries of Judaism, Christianity, and Islam fostered "currents of mystical spirituality" that bore Teresa of Avila and John of the Cross. The Church in southern Europe assumed responsibility for spreading its religion worldwide, and Spanish evangelism succeeded widely in Central and South America. It had meager results in Asia, except in Japan, where it bloomed until the Tokugawa family's cruel suppression of Christians in the early seventeenth century.

In central Europe, the Austrian branch of the Habsburg family joined a succession of Wittelsbach dukes in forming a Counter-Reformation notable for the Jesuits' persistent championing of a cult of Mary. An independent Protestant Church evolved in Transylvania, Reformed but not Calvinist, only to wither in the late seventeenth century when the ruling Rákóczi family converted to Catholicism.

The machinations of Spain's King Philip II and Catholic extremists drove France's King Henry III to have the duke of Guise assassinated in 1588, prompting an uproar that led to Henry's murder in 1589 and his succession by the king of Navarre as Henri IV, whose weary remark—not at all substantiated—that "Paris is worth a Mass" suggests everybody's exhaustion with years of bitter polemic. In 1598 Henry made peace with Spain and crafted the Edict of Nantes, guaranteeing religious freedom. The edict's revocation in 1685 produced the contempt for the established Catholic Church that wracked France a century later. "It is striking how the areas in the south that after 1572 formed the Protestant heartlands continued to form the backbone of anticlerical, antimonarchical voters for successive Republics, and even in the late twentieth century they were still delivering a reliable vote for French Socialism."

The Thirty Years' War (1618-1648) proved to be one of Christianity's bloodiest chapters, marked by the imperial army's devastation of the Free City of Magdeburg in 1631 and the end of Catholicism's hope "to become a coherent, bureaucratic, and centralized state." In England at this time James I, a Reformed Protestant, was working for a universal peace. Upon his succession in 1625, Charles I, with William Laud, bishop of London, attempted a "Counter-Reformation without the Jesuits." Charles's subsequent campaign against the Protestant establishment came apart in 1642 when Parliament split into "Presbyterian" followers of Scottish church structure and "Independents" who urged a minimum of central organization in English religious life. The Independents won a *coup d'état* leading to Charles's execution, and the profusion of Protestant denominations that then sprang up led to the separatist movement that plagued Charles II after his restoration in 1660.

MacCulloch's last section surveys "how it felt to live during Europe's Reformations and Counter-Reformations." His chapter "Changing Times" summarizes the witchcraft scare, and the chapters on love and sex are fluent, witty, and informative, especially in his account of the background to attitudes toward homosexuality. *The Reformation* presents a long and tangled drama with an extended cast of saints and villains, and it is hard to imagine anyone else covering the whole narrative with more gracefulness.

*Frank Day*

## Review Sources

*America* 191, no. 11 (October 18, 2004): 24.
*The Economist* 369 (December 13, 2003): 82.
*History: Review of New Books* 33, no. 2 (Winter, 2005): 76.
*Kirkus Reviews* 72, no. 4 (February 15, 2004): 167.
*Library Journal* 129, no. 6 (April 1, 2004): 107.
*London Review of Books* 26, no. 14 (July 22, 2004): 22.
*Publishers Weekly* 251, no. 13 (March 29, 2004): 58.

# THE REST OF LOVE

*Author:* Carl Phillips (1959-    )
*Publisher:* Farrar, Straus and Giroux (New York). 70 pp.
$20.00
*Type of work:* Poetry

*In his seventh collection of poems, Phillips explores physical and spiritual love and questions the possibility and even the nature of belief in his characteristically spare, austere style*

*The Rest of Love* is not easy poetry, but it is work that repays the effort spent rereading and thinking about it. From the beginning of his poetic career, Carl Phillips has clothed his challenging themes and concepts in richly allusive, lyrical garb. His poems deal with the flesh and the body, but they are not body-poems; rather, their specificity is merged with myth, so that their smallest images seem weighted. His subjects include the gay world, the natural world, and the possibility of a world beyond. Of another book, *Cortège* (1995), critic Kay Murphy commented, "The encoded diction of the gay subculture can slight the uninitiated; the disregard for narrative that forces an alternate means to meaning can challenge even the most active reader. These poetics shape Phillips's originality, courage, and sheer vitality within a tradition." Other critics have commented on the open-endedness of the poems, their susceptibility to multiple interpretations, and their use of complex and layered images. In fact, while browsing through Phillips's books the reader may conclude that over the years the work has become even more dense, spare, and allusive. The enigmatic nature of Phillips's poetry contributes to its attraction.

Phillips studied classicism—in fact, he has translated Sophocles' *Philoktētēs* (409 B.C.E.)—and the tales of the classics are a major part of his image bank, but the familiar (and sometimes unfamiliar) figures are deconstructed and reinterpreted to make part of a new mythology. Classical allusions abound in *The Rest of Love*, which melds body and spirit in poems that explore the nature of desire on all levels and seems to seek a point at which all desires meet as one. The mythical characters become real, and real people and places develop layers of mythology. Unexpected sidelights are discovered in the classical tales, possibilities of meaning so far unexplored.

These are spare, terse poems; perhaps half Phillips's lines do not stretch half the way across the page in this slim book. He writes in free verse and does not nod to the contemporary practice of including a few sonnets or villanelles in a group. The poetry is highly condensed, and there is not a hint of cliché here, in image, form, or diction. There are motifs, and the images and ideas group and regroup, teasing the mind into following them. The collection is divided into three sections: "The Sanctum," "The Way as Promised," and "The Rest of Love." Often the free verse is organized into flexible tercets, and sound-echoes and rising and falling rhythms provide the poems' music. The scenes in the poems are of nature and myth. They question what one derives from nature, from the observation of natural phenomena and the meditation on what presents itself. The question of whether anything rests behind nature, whether the surface glitter is its only light, is examined from multiple perspectives, and the answer derived may depend more on the reader than on the poem.

Even the titles are teasing in this way, as the names of these sections seem to point toward a central metaphysics that may or may not be there: the sanctum inside, the promised way, the rest of love—the invisible part of love, or the end of it, or its relaxation or release. If the work is read as a theological inquiry of sorts, the natural images are somewhat like those of Amy Clampett, whose quizzical theological investigations also provided open-ended answers. The combination of ambiguity and precision in *The Rest of Love* evokes emotional responses in the reader which may be directed as the reader chooses, as the poems are so open to multiple in-

*A professor of English and African American studies at Washington University in St. Louis, Carl Phillips has won major awards for his poetry, including the Samuel French Morse Poetry Prize for* In the Blood *(2002) and the Kingsley Tufts Poetry Award in 2002 for* The Tether *(2001). His work appears in* The Best American Poetry *(1994, 1995, 1996, 2000) and* The Best of the Best American Poetry.

terpretation—toward a tentative definition of spiritual or of physical love, or possibly of both. The physical world glitters with meaning—but is this illusion, or not? Part of the theme of the poems is that one desires it not to be.

For those who are not always willing to engage with difficult, multilayered poetry, what often makes the difference is the imagery, which has to have enough power to it to hook the reader into the challenge of the poem. Cleverness and rich allusiveness are not enough for readers not already on the same wavelength. These poems have the powerful images which make readers interrogate the poem and their readings of it. The power of the images and their elusiveness is underscored by the punning, teasing titles and the inconclusive endings, the use of the familiar strangely, the use of the strange familiarly. The poet strikes a note of seriousness, of authority, and the reader is willing to accept it and follow into the freighted lines of convolutions and mysterious devotions. Describing Phillips's style, David Orr in *The New York Times* comments, "He likes to play complex syntax against free-verse line breaks, allowing the ostentatious control of the former to challenge the inherent arbitrariness of the latter much the way that waves build and disperse across a beach." In fact, Phillips's style seems often to be a matter of placing one concept or image on the grid of another, dissimilar one; his juxtapositions throw each other into relief.

Stylistically, the poems are illusively easy to follow, and their scenes intersperse brief, memorable images with speculation and meditation. Their recurrent images of music, especially the bell, and birds, and other animals seem to suggest the physical-spiritual debate, sometimes sacramentalizing the physical, sometimes giving body to the spiritual world. Poems of birds and music have to be, in some sense, enlightening, and so these are; the birds and bells of the poems suggest ascent of the body and spirit. These poems have some of the suggestions of medieval metaphysical poetry which makes of physical love a metaphor for spiritual, sometimes dissolving the boundaries between these two forms of love.

Tortured syntax brings the reader back and forth between forms of love, sometimes without clear signals as to which is the dominant mode. "Conduct" is an example. Its title is not only semantically but also syntactically double. The shirt, handed to the speaker by his lover "after," is the conductor of electricity, not to mention intimacy. "*Here—/ your shirt*, he said,/ after. Lifting it. Bringing it/ to me as if it were/ not a shirt/ but a thing immaculate,/ or in flames. . . ." The shirt is compared also with a "sacred heart" transfixed, and other things, metaphors retreating into mirrors—until finally the poem arrives at how the issue of a brutal truth both attracts and keeps away the perceiver by its capacity to burn: "How turn away? How/ not rush forward,/ and fold it—in flames, immaculate—/ in your arms?" It is a flaming shirt, its mythic meanings of sexual betrayal and treachery muted, present under erasure but still present, the truth of burning shirts. The electricity it conducts is a dazzle of mixed lights— transcendence, purification, destruction, and the sexual burning. The intimacy of the lovers, marked by the transfer of the ordinary and daily garment, the shirt, melds with the desire for intimacy with the quintessential, the truth at the center of things.

Some of the poems seem to demand comparison with well-known poems that have a similar premise or image. "The Grackle," for instance, brings to mind Sylvia Plath's "Black Rook in Rainy Weather" so immediately by its images and thoughts that the reader wonders if the Plath poem is its genesis and if Phillips's poem is in part a reflection on Plath's conclusion, that is, that the momentary perception of beauty in nature is enough to clarify for a moment the dulled vision, delight the alienated soul. Plath's poem wonders about the "trick of radiance" as if indeed, radiance must be a trick. The speaker remains totally separate from the scene, an observer. In "The Grackle," the viewer and the grackle merge, instinct and knowledge, physical and metaphysical become one desire. The validity of the vision is not in question. In the flight of the poem, the descent of the grackle becomes the heart's trajectory. The melding of bird and perceiver is done deftly enough not to confuse or distract the reader. The grackle's descent is "yet another variation/ . . . on/ how it must be,/ to be distractible/ only by what is/ immediate to—/ and knowable by—/ the senses," but the mind intrudes with its preoccupations, and the questioning mind and the bird in flight become one image of desire. Unlike the watcher in "Black Rook," this observer becomes participant. This poem is followed by "Pleasure," a poem which seems to analyze the components of pleasure and to measure the distance between pleasure and joy, to attempt to ascertain the point at which pleasure transcends itself.

The poems are followed by a few notes, reverences to Ivan Turgenev, Sophocles, Anton Chekhov, Heinrich Heine, John Donne, the Psalms, and other sources. Like most good notes to poetry, they tell the reader little. The notes remind the reader of other thinkers on similar themes whose meditations feed into Phillips's, but they do not unlock the secrets of the poetry. Rather, they point to works which might enrich the reading of Phillips's poetry, or they simply locate a source for those who might be curious.

*The Rest of Love* is not for everyone. It is for those who enjoy both the modernists and the postmodernists, for Phillips uses devices of both. It is for lovers of the open query and unanswered questions, poetry readers, and writers who like layered imagery and a sense of illumination that can never be pinpointed. "Piqued, stimulated, challenged, [the reader] feels grateful for what is overheard as this disciplined mind wanders, grateful for the lyric gift that outstrips all diversionary maneuvers," Carol Moldaw said in *The Antioch Review* of Phillips's previous book, *The Tether* (2001). Indeed, attempts at explication tend to self-destruct; every reading seems to overlook something or to incorporate shades of meaning which may not be there. Nevertheless the poems remain satisfying emotionally. Where the light comes from in *The Rest of Love* remains partly a mystery, but it is there.

*Janet McCann*

## Review Sources

*Booklist* 100, no. 12 (February 15, 2004): 1025.
*Library Journal* 128, no. 18 (November 1, 2003): 87.
*The New York Times Book Review* 153 (April 18, 2004): 20.
*Ploughshares* 30, no. 1 (Spring, 2004): 182.
*Poetry* 184, no. 5 (September, 2004): 387.

# THE RETURN OF THE DANCING MASTER

*Author:* Henning Mankell (1948- )
*First published: Danslararens aterkomst,* 1999, in Sweden
Translated from the Swedish by Laurie Thompson
*Publisher:* The New Press (New York). 291 pp. $25.00
*Type of work:* Novel
*Time:* 1999-2000
*Locale:* Germany, Sweden, Scotland, and Argentina

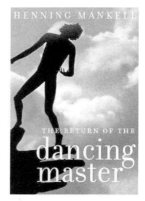

*Inspector Stefan Lindman, recently diagnosed with cancer of the tongue, sets out to learn the truth about the murder of a former associate and discovers not only the identity of the killer but also an international neo-Nazi conspiracy*

*Principal characters:*
> STEFAN LINDMAN, a young Swedish police detective
> ELENA, his lover
> GIUSEPPE LARSSON, a middle-aged police detective
> HERBERT MOLIN (formerly AUGUST MATTSON-HERZEN), murder victim, retired police detective
> VERONICA MOLIN, Herbert's daughter
> ARON SILBERSTEIN (alias FERNANDO HEREIRA), a German Jew seeking vengeance for the death of his father

Post-World War II Sweden has long been heralded by the *cognoscenti* as a model of democratic progress. In the left-leaning 1960's and 1970's its quasi-socialist, equalitarian reforms were celebrated in countless press reports conferring upon Sweden near utopian status for its minuscule crime rates (in comparison to other Western democracies); its cradle-to-the-grave health care and welfare system; its tolerant sexual mores (on American television, at any rate, where beautiful, muscular Swedish girls seemed to view uninhibited sex as a sort of hygienic exercise); and its progressive views on capital punishment, gun control, and other issues. That image has been sullied a bit in recent years. The bureaucratic nanny-state does not seem quite so glamorous anymore, and Sweden's crime rates (not to mention its suicide rates) have begun to rise. Enter Henning Mankell, whose enormous international popularity as a writer of crime fiction may have something to do with his unflinching diagnoses of the Swedish reality as opposed to the mythical image.

Inaugurated in the early 1990's, Mankell's Kurt Wallander series established its author as one of the finest living Swedish writers and its protagonist as among the most memorable in modern crime fiction. Now in his mid-fifties, Mankell has introduced a protagonist who may return in future installments of a new series. Stefan Lindman, in *The Return of the Dancing Master*, is in many ways a younger version of Wallander. Both are small-town Swedish cops: Wallander in Ystad, at the southern tip of the country; Lindman, in Boras, along the southwest coast. Wallander is divorced and desperately lonely, has a guilty relationship with an aging father who disapproves of his career, and has a troubled rapport with a daughter who lives in Stockholm. Lindman, at thirty-six, has lost both his parents and maintains a tenuous relationship with his older lover, Elena.

~

*Internationally acclaimed Swedish mystery writer Henning Mankell has produced dozens of plays and more than thirty books.*

~

Both detectives suffer health problems: Wallander drinks too much and suffers from diabetes; Lindman, in the opening pages of the new book, learns that he has a cancerous lump on his tongue. Both men brood incessantly about the lurking possibility of death, though neither is particularly religious. Finally, while neither Wallander nor Lindman can be described as highly intelligent—no startlingly Holmesian deductions here—they are both intensely dedicated and painstaking policemen. It is their frailties, conjoined with their honesty and perseverance, that make them such emotionally attractive characters.

Mankell's writing is praiseworthy on a number of levels. His terse, almost minimalistic prose (though it can, at moments, seems merely plodding) is often charged with a repressed, threatening energy. Like the snow-swept Swedish landscape, the writing is stark but quietly captivating. His characters, even the minor ones, are memorable, often marked by some subtle eccentricity of speech or manner suggestive of hidden psychic wounds or trauma.

Perhaps most compelling are Mankell's crime scenes. Among current writers of crime fiction, few can equal Mankell's eye for the bizarre but psychologically grounded murder. Such scenes are constructed not simply to shock but also to provide a multilayered and symbolic view of the mind of the killer. Rarely in the history of the murder mystery have crime scenes "spoken" with such mute eloquence.

In Mankell's sixth Wallander novel, *Femte kvinnan* (2000; *The Fifth Woman*, 2000), for example, a serial killer constructs each of her killings as a cryptic, artfully contrived testimony to the sexual abuse that has maimed her, the first involving the murder of an elderly and seemingly harmless birdwatcher, who is impaled in a ditch on a bed of bamboo staves.

Equally unforgettable is the crime scene in *The Return of the Dancing Master*. Here, another elderly recluse, Herbert Molin, is assaulted at dawn in his remote forest home near Sveg, in north-central Sweden. His unseen attacker lobs teargas through his windows, driving the terrified Molin out of the house, whereupon he is run down in the woods and beaten slowly to death. When the police arrive on the scene, what they find is at once gruesome and mockingly inscrutable. Molin's corpse "wasn't really a man at all, just a bloody bundle. The face had been scraped away, the feet were no more than blood-soaked lumps, and his back had been beaten so badly that the bones were exposed." Entering the house, they find among other things a strange pattern of bloody footprints and, in the bedroom, a life-size, fully inflated female doll. Puzzling over the footprints, Giuseppe Larsson, the lead detective from nearby Ostersund, realizes that their pattern is familiar—they are tango steps. Larsson thinks at first that the doll "was some kind of sex toy used by the lonely Molin, but the doll had no orifices. The loops on its feet suggested that it was used as a dancing partner." Other than these cryptic indicators, the police are left utterly perplexed about the identity of the killer or the motive.

The reader, on the other hand, is aware of the killer's identity well before the police. In a series of chapters running parallel to the main story line, one learns that Molin's murderer, Aron Silberstein, is a German Jew whose father, the eponymous dancing master, was murdered by Molin in Berlin at the end of the war. Silberstein was a child at the time and later left Berlin for Argentina to make a new life for himself. For over half a century he has been nursing dreams of revenge but has only recently—and by happenstance—discovered the identity and whereabouts of his father's killer. Mankell, of course, risks a good deal by revealing the identity of the murderer so early in the novel—it is, after all, the job of the murder mystery to generate suspense through the withholding of the murderer's identity. Mankell manages to overcome this liability, partly by revealing Silberstein's motive only gradually over the course of the narrative, so that the reader's full possession of the truth coincides with Lindman's at the end of the novel, where the two narratives converge. This is deftly handled, on the whole, but seems at times a bit contrived.

Lindman reads in the national papers of the murder and wonders if the victim was the same Herbert Molin under whom he had served years earlier, while still a fledgling detective. Lindman has just been told of his life-threatening cancer and, out of work on medical leave, must wait for three weeks before his therapy is scheduled to commence. Learning that the victim is indeed the same Molin, Lindman ignores his doctor's advice that he take a seaside vacation and travels north to Ostersund, knowing full well that his presence as an "outsider" will be resented by the local police. Nonetheless, he remembers Molin as a mentor, if not a close friend, and needs desperately to find some distraction from his thoughts of the cancer "cells multiplying out of control . . . like a pack of wild dogs careering around inside [him]." While Larsson and his associates do greet Lindman's arrival with some hostility, Larsson recognizes that Lindman's past knowledge of the victim may be of some help and offers him a peripheral role in the investigation.

An uneasy friendship grows between Lindman and Larsson as they work to piece together Molin's mysterious past, a past which the victim himself has deliberately attempted to erase. Lindman quickly begins to see that the man "he thought he'd known" was in fact "a complete stranger." When he had worked under the older detective, Lindman had learned to respect him for his expertise, but Molin had rarely communicated any personal history. Lindman also recalls that Molin was always a bit paranoid, as though he feared the possibility of attack by an unseen enemy. A search of public records reveals that Molin had, in fact, changed his name in 1951. His birth name had been August Mattson-Herzen, his parents seemingly solid Swedish patriots. Moreover, several years preceding Molin's becoming a policeman are unaccounted for. When Molin's daughter, Veronica, turns up in Ostersund, she seems unwilling to talk about her father's past, and Lindman has the impression that the beautiful but distant Veronica is doing most of the interrogating.

A breakthrough in the case occurs when Lindman interviews an elderly friend of the victim, Elsa Berggren, a retired dance teacher who had for some years been Molin's ballroom partner. Lindman and Larsson are able to establish that the inflatable female doll found in Molin's home was, in fact, a practice "partner." The significance of the pattern of footprints remains elusive. However, Lindman suspects that Berggren is withholding something and returns to search her house. In one of the closets he finds a man's Waffen SS uniform. Questioning Berggren about it later, he learns that the uniform belonged to her deceased father, who fought for the Nazis during the war. Further interrogation reveals that Molin himself fought on the side of the Nazis. To the dismay of the somewhat self-righteous Larsson, Berggren is far from penitent about her father's Nazi past. She reveals, in addition, that Molin, too, had always remained proud of his service to the National Socialist cause.

Lindman is now convinced that he has the key to Molin's mysterious past, which, he believes, will somehow explain the particular ferocity with which he was attacked and killed. That the murder was motivated by revenge he and Larsson are all but certain. This conviction is reinforced after Lindman revisits the crime scene to make another search.

In a storage shed behind Molin's home, Lindman notices something that does not "fit into the pattern" of the victim's attention "to symmetry and order." The tools are all "neatly arranged," the firewood perfectly stacked, but some of the tiles in the floor are "not orderly in the same way as the rest." Finding that the tiles are loose, Lindman removes them and uncovers a package containing a diary and a bundle of letters. These provide abundant evidence of Molin's Nazi history, of his recruitment by the SS, his near death on the Russian front, and, most important, of his presence in Berlin in the chaotic months after Adolf Hitler's death (though Lindman does not realize yet the full significance of this fact).

Clearly, the tiles which do not quite fit the pattern of Molin's life are also an ironic metaphor for the investigation itself. Lindman's intuitive perception of an anomaly in the pattern of appearances leads to a deeper insight into the hidden pattern of events that led to Molin's death. It is one of the virtues of Mankell's writing that he introduces metaphors of this kind with such matter-of-fact subtlety.

However, Mankell's skill as a stylist notwithstanding, there is much in the final part of *The Return of the Dancing Master* that chafes against the limits of plausibility. For example, Molin's diary reveals the name of a Swedish portrait painter, Emil Wetterstedt, who, Lindman believes, may provide further information about Molin's death. However, the chapter devoted to his visit with Wetterstedt hardly rises above caricature. The painter proves to be an old man who, during the National Socialist era, was favored by the Nazi high command with a number of portrait commissions and who keeps behind a curtain in a special room—a shrine of sorts—paintings of Hitler, Hermann Göring, and his deceased wife. "This is where I keep my gods," Wetterstedt says. As if this were not sufficiently melodramatic, Mankell provides Wetterstedt with a youthful Aryan assistant, whose shrill, fanatical stammerings call to mind the young Nazi lieutenant who betrays the von Trapp family in the film *The Sound of Music* (1965).

Sweden had its share of Nazi sympathizers during the 1930's and 1940's, and so it is not unlikely that a few of them—like Berggren and Wetterstedt—have lived on to wax nostalgic about the good old days when Hitler knew how to deal with the Jews and immigrants and other such stock. As the plot of *The Return of the Dancing Master* unfolds, the reader is required to believe in the existence of a worldwide Nazi conspiracy, one directed by Internet-savvy businesswomen like Veronica Molin, and to believe that such conspiracies are worthy of serious attention. Fortunately, these are merely the ghosts that haunt the liberal imagination in a postliberal age.

*Jack Trotter*

## Review Sources

*Booklist* 100, no. 13 (March 1, 2004): 1142.
*Kirkus Reviews* 72, no. 2 (January 15, 2004): 64.
*London Review of Books* 25, no. 22 (November 20, 2003): 24.
*The New York Times Book Review* 153 (March 28, 2004): 12.
*Publishers Weekly* 251, no. 9 (March 1, 2004): 52.
*Time* 163, no. 23 (June 7, 2004): 121.

# THE ROMANS
## From Village to Empire

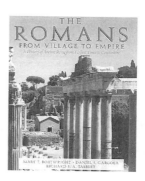

*Authors:* Mary T. Boatwright (1952-    ), Daniel J.
  Gargola (1947-    ), and Richard J. A. Talbert
  (1947-    )
*Publisher:* Oxford University Press (New York). 544 pp.
  $35.00
*Type of work:* History
*Time:* c. 4000 B.C.E.-337 C.E.

*A comprehensive survey of the history of the Roman
people, their culture, and the Roman Empire from prehis-
toric times until the reign of the emperor Constantine the
Great*

Histories of Rome have traditionally focused on the city's political, military, and
institutional history. As the evolution of the city is traced from a village on the River
Tiber to the capital of a great empire, historians have inevitably dealt with the transition from monarchy to republic to imperial autocracy and with the deeds of great Romans like Romulus, Scipio Africanus, the Gracchi brothers, Cicero, Julius Caesar,
and a succession of emperors, both good and bad. *The Romans* puts this traditional
history in a broader context by juxtaposing political and military events with social,
cultural, and economic developments. The result is a full historical picture of the Romans and their world.

*The Romans*—intended as a companion to *Ancient Greece: A Political, Social,
and Cultural History* (1999) by Sarah B. Pomeroy, Stanley M. Burstein, Walter
Donlan, and Jennifer Tolbert Roberts—was written not for scholars but for general readers. Discussion of archaeological research and scholarship is integrated
into broad, yet academically sound, overviews of the period. In sidebars scattered
throughout the volume are excerpts from primary materials representing a variety of
ancient sources, including histories, inscriptions, and so on. The result is a wide context for historical events.

The eleven chapters of *The Romans* are arranged chronologically, beginning with
the prehistorical evidence and ending with the reign of the emperor Constantine. Each
chapter includes a discussion of the types of evidence available. The early chapters
rely most heavily on the archaeological record. For later chapters, written evidence is
increasingly used. Accompanying the text are approximately ninety black-and-white
illustrations and photographs. References to these images of Roman art, coins, archaeological site plans, tombstones, and buildings are, for the most part, integrated
into the fiber of the narrative, so that text and image create a coherent picture of the
Roman world. Each chapter concludes with a short bibliography of suggested readings. Occasionally these bibliographic citations are accompanied by useful descriptive citations.

〜

*Mary T. Boatwright is professor of ancient history and chairwoman of the Department of Classical Studies at Duke University in North Carolina. She is also the author of* Hadrian and the Cities of the Roman Empire *(2000).*

〜

*Daniel J. Gargola is associate professor of history and director of graduate studies at the University of Kentucky in Lexington. He is also the author of* Lands, Laws, and Gods: Magistrates and Ceremony in the Regulation of Public Lands in Republican Rome *(1995).*

〜

*Richard J. A. Talbert is William Rand Kenan, Jr., Professor of History at the University of North Carolina at Chapel Hill. He has served as director of the American Philological Association's Classical Atlas Project and is the editor of the* Barrington Atlas of the Greek and Roman World *(2000).*

〜

Thirty-five black-and-white maps of Rome, Italy, and the Mediterranean region at various stages in the history of Rome and its Empire accompany the text. These handsome maps were designed specifically for this volume with technology developed at the Ancient World Mapping Center at the University of North Carolina at Chapel Hill and are available in digital form free of charge at the center's Web site (http://www.unc.edu/awmc/downloads). By consulting these maps, readers of *The Romans* are better able to follow the events described in this book. Individual maps are devoted to such events as Roman expansion into the Iberian peninsula during the Punic Wars, veteran settlements in Italy by Sulla, Julius Caesar, and Augustus in the first century B.C.E., and the military campaigns of Julius Caesar, Marcus Aurelius, and other great generals. Such maps trace the social and political changes in the Roman world and put historical events in a broader context.

Several other features of use to the general reader are provided in the end matter of *The Romans*. In a time line divided into four columns, the authors outline significant events in the West, Rome and Italy, and the East, as well as important cultural landmarks. For example, the time line shows that writing appeared in Italy about the same time that the first Italian city-states were formed, in the eighth century B.C.E. Rome issued its first coinage about the time the city fought the war against King Pyrrhus of Epirus (c. 280 B.C.E.). Glassblowing technology developed in Italy about the time that Julius Caesar was writing his *Commentaries* about his campaigns in Gaul (58-51 B.C.E.). Mount Vesuvius erupted in southern Italy (79 C.E.) about the same time that a major fire devastated the city of Rome (80 C.E.)

The Romans also contains a glossary in which many Roman terms are defined. Often the general meaning of the word is accompanied by the literal meaning. For instance, the Latin word *ambitio* originally meant "going around" but came to mean "legal canvassing" of votes by Roman politicians. The term *vigiles* (watchmen) referred to the corps of fire patrols instituted by Augustus for the city of Rome. In a separate list the authors also provide basic information about the principal ancient authors and texts mentioned in the book.

In the first five chapters of *The Romans*, Gargola describes early Italy and the first centuries of Rome's history. Important topics include the rise of cities in Italy, the role of Greeks and Etruscans in the development of the culture of the Italian peninsula, and the emergence of Rome as an independent city. Socioeconomic conflicts between the classes known as patricians and plebeians highlight the internal affairs of the city in the fourth century B.C.E. Also important in this period is the relationship between Rome and its neighboring cities in Latium and in the rest of Italy. Gargola further traces the city's epic military conflict with Carthage in the Punic Wars (264-146 B.C.E.), the beginnings of Empire in Sicily, Spain, and Greece, and continued social and political strife marked by the careers of Tiberius and Gaius Gracchus in the late second century B.C.E.

Gargola uses archaeological evidence from the elaborately decorated sixth century palace at Murlo, near modern Siena, to illustrate the kind of monumental architecture found in early Italy. He also refers to the archaeological record in the Roman Forum to describe the rise of the city in its first centuries. Excavations at the third century Cosa show how early Roman colonies were built. The complex second century "House of the Faun" at Pompeii indicates how the growing wealth of Romans affected their domestic architecture.

In order to provide some ancient witness for important events of the period, Gargola includes excerpts from ancient historians in text boxes. A passage about Romulus's founding of Rome comes from Plutarch's *Bioi paralleloi* (c. 105-155 C.E.; *Parallel Lives*, 1579), and a description of a religious procession at the *ludi romani* (Roman Games) comes from Dionysus of Halicarnassus's *Roman Antiquities*. Gargola also provides the historian Appian's account of the triumph of Scipio Africanus at the end of the Second Punic War in 201 and the historian Strabo's report concerning the slave trade on the Greek island of Delos.

In chapters 6 through 9, Talbert picks up the narrative in the late second century. At this time the Empire was endangered by a war with King Jurgurtha of Numidia. Italy was threatened by external invasion by the Gauls and by the internal dissension of the Social War between Rome and the Italians. Talbert devotes some attention to changes in the Roman army, administration of the provinces during this period, and the lives of Roman women. However, most of his chapters, of necessity, deal with the traumatic political events of the first century B.C.E. These include Sulla's proscriptions, the Catilinarian conspiracy of 63 B.C.E., and civil wars, first between Julius Caesar and Pompey the Great and then between Caesar's heir, Octavian, and Marc Anthony.

The defeat of Marc Anthony and Cleopatra VII at the naval battle of Actium in 31 B.C.E. established Octavian as *princeps* (leading figure, or prince), meaning sole ruler, of the Empire under the imperial name of Augustus (revered). Talbert's description of Augustus's political settlement includes sections on the problems of imperial succession, the role of the Senate and *equites* (knights), and Augustus's building programs in the city of Rome. Here Talbert also surveys Latin literature in the first century B.C.E., especially the poetry of Catullus, Vergil, Horace, and Ovid.

Like Gargola, Talbert supplements his narrative of political events with important archaeological information. His account of the role of Praeneste (modern Palestrina) in the conflict between Marius and Sulla is accompanied by a description of the ancient site. Sulla's settlement of military veterans in the colony of Pompeii is associated with information about the city's innovative amphitheater. Excavations of a large villa near Cosa and of an artificial fishpond near Circeii (modern Circeo) provide evidence for the private lives of wealthy Romans in the late Republic. Talbert also uses a plan of the Roman Forum in the late first century B.C.E. to illustrate ways that Julius Caesar and his successor, Augustus, used building projects to enhance their own political reputations. Various images of Cleopatra VII and of Augustus provide a context for discussing the political importance of these two prominent figures of the late first century B.C.E.

Talbert enhances his narrative with text boxes containing Sallust's account of Marius's political ambition, excerpts from Cicero's successful speech in defense of Sextus Roscius, and an oath of loyalty to Augustus sworn by officials in southern Spain. The connection between the historical narrative and the text box containing the entire *Laudatio Turiae* (eulogy for Turia), a funerary inscription erected by a wealthy husband to his deceased wife, is less obvious. Perceptive readers, however, will note references in this *laudatio* to the political proscriptions which were so prominent a feature of the period.

In the last four chapters Boatwright traces the history of the Roman Empire from the death of Augustus in 14 C.E. to the death of Constantine in 337 C.E. The reigns of the Julio-Claudian emperors (14-69 C.E.) are followed by the institutionalization of the principate under the Flavian emperors (69-96). The prosperity under the five "good emperors" of the second century (Nerva, Trajan, Hadrian, Antoninus Pius, and Marcus Aurelius) leads to the civil and military transformation of the Empire in the late second and third centuries and to significant political changes under Diocletian (r. 284/285-305) and Constantine (r. 324-337). In many ways, the increasingly Eastern and Christian orientation of the Empire under Constantine, who moved his capital from Rome to Constantinople and gave legal status to Christianity, marks the beginning of the Byzantine Roman Empire and provides a natural end point for *The Romans*.

Boatwright includes in text boxes several noteworthy primary sources which bring the period to life. The oratorical style of individual emperors is evident in Claudius's speech regarding the admission of the Gauls to the Roman Senate (48) and in Hadrian's address to his troops in North Africa in 128. The realities of life in the Roman Empire appear in the sophist Aelius Aristides' description of a plague in 165, Pliny's famous letter to the emperor Trajan about the Christians (c. 112), and Dio Cassius's account of the deification of the emperor Pertinax in 193.

Boatwright uses a variety of archaeological artifacts to describe private life in imperial Rome, including a first century funerary monument from Mogantiacum (modern Mainz, Germany), the early first century statue of the wealthy matron Eumachia from Pompeii, and a bilingual (Latin and Greek) funerary inscription from Odessus (modern Varna, Bulgaria) of the second half of the second century. The public life of the period is illustrated by discussion of features of the triumphal arch of Titus, the Column of Trajan, and the Arch of Constantine, all in Rome.

The authors of *The Romans* have brought to life the chronicle of Rome's development from a small Latin village on the Tiber River to the ruler of the entire Mediterranean basin. Their thoughtful combination of historical narrative, archaeological materials, artwork, photographs, and excerpts from primary sources creates a vivid picture of the Romans and the world in which they lived.

*Thomas J. Sienkewicz*

## Review Sources

*Booklist* 100, no. 12 (February 15, 2004): 1020.
*Library Journal* 129, no. 2 (February 1, 2004): 104.
*Publishers Weekly* 251, no. 2 (January 12, 2004): 43.

# THE RULE OF FOUR

*Authors:* Ian Caldwell (1976-      ) and Dustin Thomason (1976-      )
*Publisher:* Dial Press (New York). Illustrated. 372 pp. $24.00
*Type of work:* Novel
*Time:* Easter weekend, 1999
*Locale:* Princeton, New Jersey

*Over Easter weekend of their senior year at Princeton University, four suitemates risk their lives to solve the mysteries encoded in a five-hundred-year-old book*

*Principal characters:*
> THOMAS CORELLI SULLIVAN, a senior, the book's narrator
> CHARLIE FREEMAN, a pre-med senior
> GIL, a senior business major and president of Ivy, Princeton's most prestigious eating club
> PAUL HARRIS, a senior history major
> BILL STEIN, a graduate student in history
> KATIE, Thomas Sullivan's girlfriend, a sophomore
> VINCENT TAFT, a fellow of the Institute for Advanced Study at Princeton
> RICHARD CURRY, the owner of a large New York auction house and a trustee of Princeton's art museum

In 1499, the Venetian humanist scholar-editor Aldus Manutius published a curious book titled *Hypnerotomachia Poliphili*, which translates as "Poliphilo's battle of love in a dream." Rarer than the Gutenberg Bible (1455), it is regarded by book lovers as the supreme achievement of the printing press in the fifteenth century because of what Helen Barolini, in *Aldus and His Dream Book* (1992), calls "the harmony of illustration and text." The work contains more than two hundred woodcuts by an unknown artist (who signed only one illustration, and that with an enigmatic "b"). These include eleven full-page pictures and thirty-nine floral capitals.

The text itself is something of a mystery, written in a mixture of Italian, Venetian dialect, Latin, Greek, Hebrew, Chaldean, and Arabic. The woodcuts include various hieroglyphic and pseudo-hieroglyphic signs. Ostensibly, the *Hypnerotomachia Poliphili* tells the story of the love of Poliphilo for Polia. As the book begins, Poliphilo awakens on May Day from a dream of Polia. In the longer part 1, he undertakes a journey in quest of her, but the text often strays into discussions of architecture and antiquity. The shorter part 2 is more of a love story, in which Polia initially resists Poliphilo's entreaties. Finally she yields to him, but then she vanishes and Poliphilo awakens.

Questions about the work begin with its authorship. The book is signed only with an acrostic and a pun. The initial letters of the chapters spell out *Poliam Frater Franciscus Colonna peramavit*, "Friar Francesco Colonna deeply loved Polia." In part 2, Polia tells Poliphilo, "You are the solid column and culmination of my life." In Italian "column" is "colonna." Francesco Colonna was a friar living in the monastery of Saints Giovanni and Paolo in Venice. Polia may have been the niece of Colonna's bishop, but in Greek *polia* means old age or antiquity. Is Poliphilo's quest in fact not for a woman but for classical learning?

The book's subtitle states that in the *Hypnerotomachia Poliphili* all human endeavor is shown as a dream. The dedication, written by Leonardo Crasso, who commissioned and paid for the printing of the work, states that the text contains matter not to be revealed to the common reader. Perhaps, then, this curious encyclopedia of antiquity contains secrets concealed in codes of various sorts. Fifteenth century humanists were fascinated with cryptography. Already in 1600 François Béroalde de Verville's adaptation included an essay on the alchemical lore in the work. The pictures, too, are enigmatic. For example, one series (reproduced in the novel) shows a naked winged boy in a cart being drawn through a forest by two naked women, while another woman, clothed, looks on from behind some trees. The boy is holding a whip. In the second picture the boy is cutting up the women with a sword, and in the final image the boy is flying away, while a lion, a wolf, an eagle, and a mythical beast devour the women's limbs. The illustrations appear to be an allegory of something, but of what?

*Ian Caldwell and Dustin Thomason grew up in Fairfax County, Virginia, where they began collaborating on writing projects in third grade. Like Thomas in* The Rule of Four, *Caldwell attended Princeton University, from which he graduated Phi Beta Kappa in 1998, and then went to work for a time at a dot-com company before quitting and moving to Blacksburg, Virginia, to write. Thomason graduated from Harvard University in 1998 and then attended Columbia University for medical school while continuing to work on* The Rule of Four.

In *The Rule of Four*, that is part of the mystery that Thomas Sullivan, Sr., Vincent Taft, and Richard Curry had set out to solve in the 1960's, when they met as young men. Curry found a contemporary diary by a Genoese harbormaster, who recorded that an aristocratic Roman named Francesco Colonna was expecting a secret shipment, and when two people tried to discover the nature of this cargo, they quickly died. When Colonna's goods finally arrived, they were easily transported, even by an old woman. The implication is that these were books and pictures. Curry and Sullivan believe that the diary holds a key to the meaning of the *Hypnerotomachia Poliphili*. Taft dissents. The men quarrel, and one evening someone breaks into Curry's apartment and steals the diary. The men separate. Sullivan goes to Ohio State University, where he writes a book about his theories, drawing on a letter recording the death of two men who were working for Colonna. Taft, who has moved to Princeton's Institute for Advanced Study, savagely reviews the work. Curry pursues a career in art and becomes the owner of a well-known New York gallery.

In the 1990's Sullivan's son, Thomas Jr., arrives at Princeton University, his father's alma mater, where he rooms with Paul Harris. Paul is drawn to Thomas because of Thomas's father's work, but Thomas does not completely share Paul's enthusiasm. Yet when Paul decides to write his senior thesis on the *Hypnerotomachia Poliphili*, Thomas becomes ensnared in the project. It begins to consume him, as it had his father (who died in a car crash), to the extent that he ignores his devoted girlfriend, Katie. Curry provides money to send Paul to Italy to research his thesis, directed by Taft, and aided by Bill Stein, a graduate student who shares Paul's interest.

In many ways *The Rule of Four* imitates Colonna's book. Thomas's quest for Katie resembles Poliphilo's for Polia. Colonna's digressions into architecture are mirrored in discourses about the underground tunnels and eating clubs of Princeton. The fifteenth century book's discussions about classical antiquity are replaced with accounts of Florence in the 1490's. According to Paul's interpretation of Colonna's book, the *Hypnerotomachia Poliphili* involves a pact among four friends, the possibility of death, and the quest for learning that is threatened by malevolent forces. A summary of *The Rule of Four* would be rather similar, as Paul, Thomas, and two other students, Gil and Charlie, work together to recover the missing harbormaster's diary, try to solve two murders, and risk death themselves. Even the 1497 bonfire of the vanities in Florence that supposedly impels the composition of Colonna's work is repeated when Ivy, a Princeton eating club, goes up in flames near the end of the book.

Among the influences on Colonna's book is Dante's *La divina commedia* (c. 1320; *The Divine Comedy*, 1802). Both, for example, begin in a wood, and both recount the quest for reunion with a dead woman. *The Rule of Four* similarly draws on Dante's work. Most obviously, the novel unfolds, like the *Inferno*, over Easter weekend. Authors Ian Caldwell and Dustin Thomason so wanted to use this particular weekend that they moved the first snowstorm of the season (needed for the Nude Olympics, a now-abolished Princeton tradition in which the sophomore class runs naked on the quad to mark the first snowfall of the season) to Easter. The holiday signifies redemption and a return to life, themes that inform the novel. For Dante, betrayal of friends and benefactors is the worst of sins. In *The Rule of Four* the characters repeatedly must choose whether to help or desert those closest to them.

Like the *Hypnerotomachia Poliphili*, then, *The Rule of Four* works on many levels. It offers a love story in which Thomas and Katie are the protagonists. While Katie is Polia as woman, the deciphering of Colonna's secrets is Polia as antiquity, and that is the Polia of Paul's quest, for which he is willing to risk his life. While *The Rule of Four* does not appear to contain any acrostics or hidden messages, it certainly is a murder mystery, though admittedly with a limited number of suspects. On another level, the novel is a coming-of-age story, especially for Thomas, as he begins to understand his dead father and himself.

*The Rule of Four* is a remarkable achievement for two men still in their twenties. For one thing, the book discloses the authors' familiarity with a wide range of Renaissance literature and art that is unusual for recent graduates of even the Ivy League schools the authors attended. For another, *The Rule of Four* seems wise beyond the years of its writers. The libraries, museums, and faculty of Princeton and Harvard could inform Caldwell and Thomason about Aldus and Leon Battista Alberti, Pomponia Letto and Lorenzo Valla, but these young men also understand the siren song of scholarship. They create characters who are willing to die, and kill, for knowledge. Thomas, Sr., devoted his life to one book, and his son, though warned by his father's example, chooses to help Paul solve one of Colonna's riddles rather than spend even an hour with Katie on her birthday. Both Paul and Thomas become like the Francesco Colonna that Paul believes is revealed in the *Hypnerotomachia Poliphili*. Such devotion on one level is shown to be madness, but it is a kind of divine madness. In both the 1490's and 1990's it leads to death, but it also results in the preservation and advancement of learning. Without taking sides, *The Rule of Four* shows well the conflict between art and life.

*Joseph Rosenblum*

## Review Sources

*Booklist* 100, no. 15 (April 1, 2004): 1350.
*Kirkus Reviews* 72, no. 6 (March 15, 2004): 237.
*The New Republic* 231, nos. 7/8 (August 16, 2004): 21-26.
*The New York Review of Books* 51, no. 14 (September 23, 2004): 66-69.
*The New York Times*, May 6, 2004, p. E11.
*People* 61, no. 18 (May 10, 2004): 55.
*Publishers Weekly* 251, no. 11 (March 15, 2004): 51.
*The Times Literary Supplement*, June 4, 2004, p. 22.

# THE RULES OF ENGAGEMENT

*Author:* Anita Brookner (1928-     )
*Publisher:* Random House (New York). 273 pp. $24.00
*Type of work:* Novel
*Time:* From the 1950's to 2004
*Locale:* London

*Solitary widow Elizabeth Wetherall looks back on her life, reviewing especially her troubled relationship with her closest childhood friend and the damaging affair they each had with the same married man*

*Principal characters:*
> ELIZABETH WETHERALL, a lonely woman whose life is filled with regrets
> BETSY NEWTON, Elizabeth's vulnerable, romantic childhood friend
> DIGBY WETHERALL, Elizabeth's dull husband
> EDMUND FAIRLIE, the married lover of both Elizabeth and Betsy
> CONSTANCE, Edmund's inscrutable wife
> DANIEL DE SAINT-JORRE, Betsy's unbalanced French lover
> NIGEL WARD, Elizabeth's second, uninspired lover

*The Rules of Engagement* is narrated by Elizabeth Wetherall, a lonely woman whose life has mysteriously taken a wrong turn. This circumstance she shares with a lifelong friend, Betsy Newton. They also share the same first name and the same birthday, and Elizabeth comes to realize that Betsy was the one constant in her life, acting as a mirror, an alter ego, or a variation on her own baffling situation.

Elizabeth's empathic but ruthlessly honest consciousness envelops this story from the beginning to the end, providing illumination and insights which are the consequence of living a closely examined life. As she tells the reader a surprisingly suspenseful story of the complicated love triangle that secretly developed among herself, Betsy, and a charming philanderer, Elizabeth is capable of devastating insights, not only into her oldest friend but also into her own nature. Having been encouraged to develop a smiling, uncomplaining persona even in the face of her parents' unhappy marriage and her own disappointing love life, Elizabeth has, as a result, become so self-contained and so used to concealment that she lives a life of almost total emotional isolation. Raised in a prosperous environment, Elizabeth satisfies her parents' expectations by marrying a dull but successful older man, Digby Wetherall. Almost immediately afterward, she finds herself bored and lonely and establishes a pattern of long, aimless walks around London which she will follow for the rest of her life.

In desperation, Elizabeth takes as a lover her husband's stockbroker, the worldly Edmund Fairlie, who seems to feel no guilt at keeping a flat expressly for the purpose of sexual liaisons. The fairly long relationship he and Elizabeth sustain is not only without empathy or curiosity on his part but seems also to demonstrate a moral disengagement that Elizabeth finds increasingly disturbing. Realizing there has actually been no love in her life, despite having had a husband and a lover, Elizabeth ends her relationship with Edmund when her husband dies suddenly, as if each man were somehow a function of the other. She attempts to put her life back together by taking another lover, the recessive, lonely Nigel Ward.

*Anita Brookner was born in London and, apart from several years spent in Paris, has lived there ever since. She trained as an art historian and taught at the Courtauld Institute of Art until 1988.* The Rules of Engagement *is her twenty-second novel.*

With indications that Nigel may prove to be a second Digby, Elizabeth's waning interest in him is compounded by her realization that she has not recovered from her affair with Edmund, which left her with a legacy of regret and guilt and with a conviction that she is destined to wait for a true love that will never materialize. In addition to this disillusionment, she is haunted by the fear that her affair did real spiritual harm to herself and genuine damage to her marriage. These regrets and scruples, Elizabeth believes, make her a marginal figure in a society she sees as devoted to self-interest and self-satisfaction, to the exclusion of a morality now dismissed as having belonged to a previous generation. She begins to feel that her pangs of conscience are dismissed by the larger world as tiresome, unattractive, and irrelevant— and she begins to wonder if the world is not right and she is missing her chances at life.

This theme has preoccupied author Anita Brookner quite often in her work—on one hand, she suggests, modern society is constituted of beautiful and selfish neo-pagans who pursue pleasure without regard to scruples or conscience. On the other hand are the saints and martyrs who perform good works for others or practice virtues increasingly deemed old-fashioned and ripe for exploitation.

The period in which Brookner claims this type of modernity came to fruition is exactly the time in which the major action of this novel is set: the 1980's. This decade exerts a subtle presence in the novel, so although *The Rules of Engagement* is essentially a psychological study, Brookner opens it up to a social context in which the prevailing view is that one should be free of all constraints and prohibitions. This libertarian spirit—associated in England with the rise of Prime Minister Margaret Thatcher—is that one Brookner suggests took over the whole of human behavior at this time. It is within this societal ambience that Edmund and his sophisticated wife, Constance, began to conduct themselves as if they were the favorites of the gods, immune from traditional moral precepts or obligations.

This sense of an entire society fragmenting into small units of personal self-interest meant, Elizabeth suggests, that women with more traditional values and expectations were increasingly demoralized. For instance, Edmund fails to see how his expectation that Elizabeth see herself as a free agent, without romantic yearnings, leaves her feeling not liberated and empowered but lonely and frightened. Although she has experimented with living life as do Edmund and Constance Fairlie, Elizabeth continues to wonder if freedom and virtue are reconcilable, and she worries if punishment indeed still awaits those who behave badly.

While Elizabeth's marriage and love life are coming apart, her more free-spirited and impecunious friend Betsy has moved to Paris and become involved with an unstable young Frenchman, Daniel de Saint-Jorre. Although the two are in love with each other, Daniel is perhaps too much like Betsy—both are lost souls and have difficulty facing cold reality. Unlike Elizabeth, who was brought up by two parents in an intact, albeit unhappy, household, Betsy is an orphan whose years in the custody of a pallid aunt left her both emotionally needy and with a tendency to idealize men as potential knights in shining armor. With no other childhood models, Betsy has premised her love life on the romantic Hollywood films of her childhood and on the heightened emotional scenarios of all-consuming love rendered by the seventeenth century French playwright Jean Racine.

A trusting, romantic soul, Betsy has none of the dark knowledge that Elizabeth has assimilated into her consciousness. It is this fact that concerns Elizabeth when, after Daniel dies in a quasi-suicidal accident, Betsy settles in London and is seduced by Elizabeth's former lover, Edmund. Even though she feels compelled to warn Betsy that the Fairlies are a shameless, demoniac couple, the habitually secretive Elizabeth does not tell Betsy of her own previous relationship with Edmund— a crucial decision in the life of both friends. The sweetly innocent Betsy goes on to devote herself not only to Edmund but also to Constance, who is apparently aware of the love affair and prepared to use it to her own advantage. Betsy's guilt, her yearning for family life, and her intense need to please lead her to live in almost unending, uncompensated obligation to the Fairlies, who exploit and humiliate her without compunction. Betsy's passionate attachment to Edmund and her selfless devotion to his wife and children leaves her with no time to look after herself, and as a result she is hospitalized with cancer, which has been diagnosed too late for effective treatment.

Once Betsy becomes ill, the Fairlies literally disappear, selling their home and decamping to parts unknown. It is up to Elizabeth to be Betsy's sole consolation and companion. After Betsy dies, Elizabeth spends much time alone, searching for answers to the inexplicable feelings of failure and despair that have darkened her life and that of her friend. She realizes, however, that she took pains to keep Betsy's trusting soul as safe as possible, knowing that Betsy could never bear the knowledge that the more realistic Elizabeth had of the dark side of the Fairlies and, indeed, of life itself. Elizabeth understands that she is stronger than Betsy and is able to face the truth about her life in a way that was impossible for her more vulnerable friend. She wonders if her protecting Betsy's innocence was the right thing to do—whether it was a good thing to have preserved Betsy's idealistic and romantic illusions, or whether it was a form of destructive false hope. It is a question that Brookner leaves open, inviting the reader to consider the issue thoughtfully, as Elizabeth has.

In considering the question of Betsy's romantic nature and its value, Elizabeth is led to face the fact that she also has remained a young romantic at heart, even though her life, like Betsy's, has been spoiled by a damaging love affair. The notion of damage looms increasingly large in Elizabeth's consciousness, along with a feeling that her love life and Betsy's both required the denial of their essential natures. Elizabeth understands that Betsy was fundamentally a simple, loving person who had been denied the parental care that would have allowed her to thrive and whose yearning for affection doomed her to masochistic suffering in her adult life. Elizabeth can admit to herself that her own romantic relationships have cheated her as well and, furthermore, that her affair with Edmund may have put her in danger of being converted to his way of thinking, which would have corrupted her hopelessly.

It may come as a surprise to the reader that the seeming stasis of Elizabeth's life is quietly resolved in the wake of Betsy's death. Almost without the reader's realizing it, Elizabeth has turned a figurative page. Avoiding romantic entanglements, she pursues volunteer work in the hospital where Betsy died, makes new woman friends, and starts finding that time now passes quickly. She remains solitary and still enjoys her long, reflective walks, but her sleep is no longer troubled by disturbing dreams. One senses that her life is a good one. Elizabeth ends her story not with the nightmares that have plagued her in the past but with a waking dream in which she is young, joyful, and safe at home with the parents who loved her. This final image demonstrates how much she has lost since her childhood, but it is also a kind of blessing. Despite the loss that the dream suggests, the return in her dreams of her youthful, beloved self shows that Elizabeth has been rewarded in the end for her care of Betsy and that the accidental death of Edmund's beloved son during this same period can be read as form of punishment for her former lover's bad behavior.

The very subtle suggestion of a fairy-tale ending, in which good is rewarded, is of a piece with Brookner's delicate transformation of a bleak narrative into one in which Elizabeth achieves a deeper understanding of herself and others. In this regard, Elizabeth's tremendous isolation becomes a valuable resource, her solitude a necessary stage in an important awakening. Elizabeth's soul-searching has the happy result of dismantling her false, compliant self, with her enlarged vision and deepened feeling leading to reform and release. Additionally, it is important to realize that what appears to be a spare narrative of constricted lives is, in fact, a study of love in the spirit of Racine, the playwright who was Betsy's tutelary spirit. Like Racine, Brookner has made the process of consciousness evolving a subject of great dramatic intensity, bringing powers of psychological analysis, exquisite sensitivity, and spiritual strength to her fascinating study of love and loss. While Brookner may share a kinship of temperament and talent with the classic French playwright, in this novel she further consolidates her reputation as a major modern English novelist.

*Margaret Boe Birns*

## Review Sources

*The Atlantic Monthly* 293, no. 2 (March, 2004): 107.
*Booklist* 100, no. 5 (November 1, 2003): 458.
*The Boston Globe*, February 1, 2004, p. H7.
*Entertainment Weekly*, January 9, 2004, p. 87.
*Library Journal* 129, no. 1 (January 15, 2004): 151.
*Los Angeles Times*, January 4, 2004, p. R9.
*The New Republic* 230, no. 4 (February 9, 2004): 32.
*The New York Times Book Review* 153 (December 28, 2003): 5.
*Publishers Weekly* 250 (December 22, 2003): 38.

# RUNAWAY

*Author:* Alice Munro (1931-      )
*Publisher:* Alfred A. Knopf (New York). 335 pp. $25.00
*Type of work:* Short fiction
*Time:* The late twentieth century
*Locale:* Western Canada

*Munro collects eight stories about a theme that has permeated her writing: the desire to run away—whether from family, situation, or location, and the consequences of flight*

Principal characters:
>     CARLA, an abused wife in "Runaway"
>     SYLVIA, her well-intentioned neighbor
>     CLARK, her abusive husband
>     JULIET, the protagonist of "Chance," "Soon," and "Silence"
>     ERIC PORTEOUS, her husband, a prawn fisherman
>     CHRISTA, Eric's lover and Juliet's friend
>     GRACE, the protagonist of "Passion"
>     MAURY TRAVERS, her would-be fiancé
>     NEIL, Maury's alcoholic half brother
>     LAUREN, the teenage protagonist of "Trespasses"
>     DELPHINE, a waitress who believes that Lauren is her daughter
>     ROBIN, the protagonist of "Tricks"
>     NANCY, the protagonist of "Powers"
>     TESSA, a woman with clairvoyant powers
>     OLLIE, a journalist who marries Tessa

"Runaway," the first story in Alice Munro's collection of the same title, concerns two runaways: Carla, whose abusive husband, Clark, inspires her to run away, and Sylvia, her neighbor who encourages Carla's runaway attempt. Sylvia's husband has passed away, and she comes to rely on Carla for help around her house and develops an obsessive concern for her abused friend. Sylvia's friends describe her affection for Carla as a crush. While Carla resents Clark's abuse, it seems apparent that without Sylvia's planning and urging she would not have taken a bus out of town, only to get off the bus and call Clark to come and get her. Significantly, Carla, who is wearing some of Sylvia's clothes, decides that the clothes do not "fit" her.

Sylvia, who later moves to an apartment in town, also may be considered a runaway. Besides the two women, there is another runaway: Flora, Carla's pet goat, who mysteriously vanishes and returns in supernatural fashion when Clark threatens Sylvia physically. The goat's sudden appearance saves Sylvia, and then Flora again vanishes. After Carla returns to Clark, she finds Flora's bones in the woods. She speculates about how Flora died and then absolves Clark of any guilt—something she has

*Canadian Alice Munro has received many awards and prizes during her distinguished writing career. Three of her books have won the Governor General's Award, Canada's highest literary prize:* Dance of the Happy Shades *(1968),* Who Do You Think You Are? *(1978), and* The Progress of Love *(1986).* The Love of a Good Woman *(1998) and* Runaway *both won the Giller Prize.*

to do if she is to go on living with him. In effect, she runs away from the truth; Flora's fate could become hers.

As in *The Moons of Jupiter* (1982), *Runaway* contains three stories featuring the same protagonist, in this case, Juliet. Like many of Munro's characters, Juliet is an intellectual who does not "fit" into society. A classical scholar, she is out of place in a traditionally male field, and she has been encouraged to get out of academia and into the "real world." When she receives a letter from Eric Porteous, a man she once met on a train, she leaves the school where she teaches and goes to Whale Bay, where Eric lives. Upon arrival, she finds that Eric's wife has died and that her funeral had occurred that day. Eric spends the night with Christa, with whom he has been having an affair. He then returns home to find Juliet and "claim" her. They eventually marry.

If chance provides a happy ending (Christa even becomes Juliet's friend and confidante), time will alter Juliet's happiness. In "Soon," she returns to her hometown with her daughter, Penelope, named after Homer's character in the *Odyssey* (c. 725 B.C.E.), to see her parents. The unsuccessful return to the past to resolve relationships is another of Munro's themes. Juliet discovers that her parents' marriage has deteriorated as her father's independent streak and her mother's onset of senility have increased the gap between them and left them complaining about each other to Juliet. Juliet's obsession with a painting titled "I and the Village" also indicates that she is aware of her own lack of belonging in the community; to the villagers, she is "the girl who speaks Latin."

She decides to write to Eric that *"I don't know what I'm doing here. I can't wait to go home."* At the end of the story she reconsiders and thinks that her home is with her parents and that her duty is to "protect, as best you can . . . what happens at home." Unfortunately, when her mother reaches out to her, she cannot or will not reply. Instead, she turns her attention to cleaning up the kitchen. The last line, "She had put everything away," applies not only to dishes but also to her parents. She has, in effect, run away again, this time from relationships.

In "Silence" Juliet reaps the results of not having responded to her mother; Penelope runs away from her. Since the events in "Soon," Eric has drowned and, in classical Norse fashion, his body has been set out to sea on a burning boat. Juliet has become a television personality who specializes in interviews. This is ironic, as Juliet does not communicate well with her own daughter. As "Silence" begins, Juliet travels to the Spiritual Balance Centre, where she is informed that Penelope has experienced loneliness and unhappiness.

Juliet dismisses the comments about Penelope, but the "silence" continues, broken only by an occasional birthday card from her daughter, some not even signed. When Juliet visits her friend Christa (whom she resents because Penelope has spoken openly with her), Juliet cannot resist bringing up the past, which includes Eric and Christa's affair. That affair, which Juliet could never forget, had essentially destroyed Eric and Juliet's marriage.

Once again, Juliet had run away. Eventually the cards stop coming, but Juliet learns that Penelope has married, has children, and is living in Alaska. Juliet, who has a few affairs, returns to her doctoral work, only to give it up and focus on Heliodorus of Emesa's *Aethiopica* (c. 320 C.E.; *Heliodorus His Æthiopian History*, 1622). This romance deals with an Ethiopian queen who searches for her lost daughter and then saves her from death. Juliet's life does not echo fiction, however, and at the end of the short story she has to accept the fact that "Penelope does not have a use for me."

Another story, "Passion," involves a return to the past, this time from the perspective of Grace, who goes to the Traverses' summer house in the Ottawa Valley, where many of Munro's stories are set. Although she is "summer help" and consequently not on equal footing with her employers, her intelligence and appealing manner win over Mrs. Travers and Maury, her son. Maury's plans to marry Grace are ruined when, at a party, she cuts her foot and is taken to the hospital by Neil, Maury's half brother, an alcoholic physician. Neil and Grace then go for a long drive. After they park and Neil passes out with a bottle, Grace drives his car to her dormitory, leaving him to drive back to his family's summer home. The next morning she finds out that Neil has died in a car crash.

When Maury sends her a note asking her to say she did not want to go with Neil, her reply—that she did want to go—ends their relationship. When Mr. Travers tries to buy her off with a check for one thousand dollars, Grace thinks about tearing it up but does not. The check gave her "enough money to insure her a start in life." Munro is ambiguous about the result of Grace's return to the area, forty years later: Does a feeling "of relief pass over you, of old confusions or obligations wiped away"?

"Trespasses," is told from the perspective of Lauren, a teenager enrolled in a new high school. Her parents, who frequently drink and fight, have moved to the small town where Harry, her father, spent his summers as a child. Lauren has trouble fitting in but befriends Delphine, an older waitress at a café. Their relationship quickly deepens, and Delphine seems to know a lot about Lauren's family. Lauren is upset about finding a box of her sister's ashes and, when told that her sister died as a baby, suspects that she herself may have been adopted. Delphine then tells Lauren a story about her friend Joyce (obviously Delphine), who gave up her baby for adoption and then goes looking for it.

When her parents find Lauren sick at home and learn of Delphine's relationship with her, they travel to the woods with Lauren and Delphine, tell Delphine that her baby, whom they had adopted, died, and they disposed of the ashes. The impact on Lauren is illustrated by the burrs that stick to her clothes; she cannot get them off.

Even though her mother may take them off when they get home, other "burrs" will remain for Lauren. A return to the past, a mother searching for a daughter, and attempted flights from the truth—all are recurrent Munro themes.

Unlike the "trespasses," the sins of commission by the adults in the last story, the problem in "Tricks" is an act of omission, a missed opportunity for Robin, a young woman who yearly attends a performance of a William Shakespeare play in order to escape from her dull life. After she attends a play one year, she discovers that she has lost her purse. A stranger, an immigrant from Montenegro, helps her and before she returns home promises to meet her next year after a performance of *As You Like It* (pr. c. 1599-1600). For a year Robin thinks of the stranger constantly, but when she arrives early at his place after the play, he shuts the door in her face. She runs away in shame.

Years later, Robin finds a man with a similar name in a hospital psychiatric ward and learns that he is the twin brother of the man who helped her. The wrong twin had shut the door. Robin was the victim of mistaken identity, just like the characters in *As You Like It*, but the ending is not comic. Although a mature Robin concludes that the relationship would not have worked out, she is tormented by the missed chance.

The last story in the collection is a curious mix of diary and third-person narration (limited and omniscient by turns), with the focus on Nancy, an impertinent, egocentric young woman who never seems to understand what is occurring. She marries Wilf but is also attracted to Ollie, Wilf's journalist brother. She introduces Ollie to Tessa, a clairvoyant. After Ollie writes a feature story about Tessa, Nancy, with mixed motives, rebukes him for invading Tessa's privacy and then warns Tessa about the exploitive Ollie. To Nancy's amazement and dismay, Ollie and Tessa marry.

Years pass, and the curious Nancy visits Tessa, who is in a mental asylum. Nancy promises to write to Tessa, but she does not. Nancy later meets Ollie, but he knows a relationship between them, which might have been possible years ago, would not work now. At the end of the story she is removed from them and alone, like many of Munro's women characters. Though Munro's characters are interesting, few of them are likable. The men characters are almost tangential to Munro's stories.

*Thomas L. Erskine*

## Review Sources

*Booklist* 101, no. 2 (September 15, 2004): 180.
*Kirkus Reviews* 72, no. 18 (September 15, 2004): 887.
*Maclean's* 117, no. 40 (October 4, 2004): 48.
*Ms.* 14, no. 4 (Winter, 2004/2005): 90.
*New York* 37, no. 38 (November 1, 2004): 79.
*The New York Times*, December 7, 2004, p. E1.
*The New York Times Book Review* 154 (November 14, 2004): 1.
*People* 62, no. 20 (November 15, 2004): 47.
*Publishers Weekly* 251, no. 41 (October 11, 2004): 53.

# ST. PATRICK OF IRELAND
## A Biography

*Author:* Philip Freeman (1961-    )
*Publisher:* Simon & Schuster (New York). 216 pp.
  $23.00
*Type of work:* Biography
*Time:* About 390-460
*Locale:* Britain and Ireland

*This biography of Saint Patrick is based on his two autobiographical letters and on writings by Roman historians who commented on ancient Britain and Ireland*

Principal personages:
  SAINT PATRICK, the patron saint of Ireland
  CALPORNIUS, his father
  POTITUS, Patrick's grandfather
  PALLADIUS, the first bishop of Ireland and Saint Patrick's immediate predecessor as the bishop of Ireland
  COROTICUS, a British king who kidnapped and killed Christian converts in Ireland

Although Saint Patrick is revered by the Irish and those of Irish descent around the world, most people attribute to him mythical accomplishments, such as driving the snakes out of Ireland or using the shamrock to teach the mystery of the Trinity. In this excellent biography, Philip Freeman shows that the actual life of Saint Patrick is much more complex and interesting than such legends of medieval origin associated with the patron saint of Ireland. Freeman, who specializes in both classical and ancient Celtic studies, is extremely well qualified to describe the actual conditions of daily life in ancient Britain and Ireland because he has published extensively on archaeological discoveries in ancient Britain and Ireland and can also read both Latin and ancient Irish, the two languages in which the extant documents related to Saint Patrick and the Ireland of his lifetime were written.

Sometime near the end of his life, Saint Patrick wrote in Latin two letters that contain almost all the factual information that exists about his life. Freeman includes an excellent English translation of these two letters and gives bibliographical references to Latin editions of these letters so that readers can read the originals in Latin. In his "Letter to the Soldiers of Coroticus," Saint Patrick excommunicates a British king named Coroticus who had killed Christian converts in Ireland and had taken other Christians from Ireland into slavery in England. Without consulting British bishops, Saint Patrick called upon all people in England to shun the criminal named Coroticus who had so egregiously sinned against God. In his second letter, traditionally called his confession because he calls it in its last line a confession, Saint Patrick describes his life as a youth, his six years as a slave in Ireland, his escape

~

*Philip Freeman is a professor of*
*classics at Washington University*
*in St. Louis. He earned his Ph.D.*
*in classical languages and Celtic*
*studies at Harvard University.*
*This is his third book on ancient*
*Ireland.*

~

from slavery, his return to his parents' house in Britain, and his years of service as a missionary in Ireland.

Unlike his eminent contemporary and fellow bishop Saint Augustine of Hippo, Saint Patrick did not write a formal autobiography in his confession. His is, rather, a description of his spiritual development, from indifference to religion to a very strong commitment to Christianity. Although some critics have compared these two confessions by leading fifth century bishops, there is no proof that Saint Patrick ever read Saint Augustine's more famous autobiography.

Saint Patrick's two letters contain numerous surprises for those who know little about ancient Britain and Ireland. Saint Patrick, whom Irish people have admired as the very model of an Irishman, was born in Britain and may have died in Britain as well. Near the end of his confession, Saint Patrick expresses the wish that God allow him to die among his beloved Irish, but no one knows where Saint Patrick actually died. In his confession, Saint Patrick reports that he was born in the British village of Bannaventa Berniae. Freeman indicates that no other ancient source refers to this British village. He argues persuasively that Bannaventa Berniae had to be located near the western cost of Britain, but there is no way to determine whether Bannaventa Berniae was located in the current country of Wales, Scotland, or England. Saint Patrick may thus have been Welsh, Scottish, or English, but he was certainly not Irish.

In his confession, Saint Patrick describes his extraordinary transformation from a spoiled youth into a committed Christian. Although his father, Calpornius, was a deacon and his grandfather Potitus was a priest, the young Patrick was indifferent to religion. Freeman points out that the Catholic Church then permitted priests to marry. Patrick's family was relatively wealthy, and his family belonged to the ruling class in Roman Britain when he was born, perhaps around 390.

When Patrick was just fifteen years old, Irish pirates invaded his British village and dragged Patrick and others from his village in chains into slavery in Ireland. Although Patrick does not describe in great detail the horrors of his six years of slavery somewhere in Ireland, Freeman does an admirable job in explaining how terribly slaves were treated in the Roman Empire, in which approximately one quarter of all people endured slavery and were subjected to physical and psychological torture from their masters.

In a story that may well remind his readers of many later slave narratives, Saint Patrick indicates that he maintained his dignity and grew spiritually. While he was a slave, he learned ancient Irish and came to understand ordinary Irish people, especially women and slaves, whom cruel husbands and masters exploited unmercifully. Although his masters beat him and treated him abominably, he kept his optimism. After six years of slavery, Saint Patrick twice heard the voice of God telling him to cross Ireland on foot and to take a boat back to England. Like so many later slaves, Saint Patrick refused to accept the permanence of his lack of freedom. He fled from his master, and, despite the very real danger of recapture and death, he succeeded in persuading a ship's captain to take him to England, where his parents received him with joy and disbelief.

Most escaped slaves would have been delighted to have regained their freedom, but this was not sufficient for the heroic Saint Patrick. After his return to Bannaventa Berniae, Saint Patrick heard the voice of God and also saw God in the person of God the Holy Spirit.

The Holy Spirit explained clearly to Saint Patrick that he had been chosen by God the Father, God the Son, and God the Holy Spirit to convert the Irish to Christianity. Saint Patrick was certainly not going to disregard all three members of the Trinity. Although his formal education ended at the age of fifteen, he persuaded the bishop in his region of Britain to accept him as a candidate for the priesthood. After his ordination, Saint Patrick returned to Ireland. Palladius, the first bishop of Ireland, met the spiritual needs only of those who were already Christians. Saint Patrick undertook to convert all the Irish to Christianity despite the overt opposition of Irish kings, druids, and pirates.

It is not known when Saint Patrick arrived in Ireland or for how many years he worked there as a missionary. In his "Letter to the Soldiers of Coroticus," he indicates that he had worked as a priest in Ireland for a long time. If he was born around 390 and returned to Britain at the age of twenty-one, it is safe to assume that he began his missionary work around 420. Freeman believes that Saint Patrick probably died around 460. Saint Patrick's service as a missionary may well have lasted almost four decades. Legend has it that Palladius served only from 430 to 431 as the bishop of Ireland and that Patrick immediately succeeded him.

In his confession, Saint Patrick states that there had been very few Christians in Ireland before his arrival. He described Ireland as being located at the edge of the known world, and this is largely true. Previous missionaries had labored within the Roman Empire, but Saint Patrick felt that to become truly universal, as the word "catholic" means, the Catholic Church needed to reach out to all people. Saint Patrick's contemporaries believed that Ireland was literally at the western edge of the world. In their minds, there was no country west of Ireland. Saint Patrick believed that he was teaching Christianity at the edge of the world, and Freeman points out that it is not difficult for those who look at the Atlantic Ocean from the western coast of Ireland to imagine there is no land to the west.

Like all effective missionaries, Saint Patrick adapted to the culture of those whom he was serving, without modifying at all the religious message that he was presenting. In ancient Ireland during his lifetime, slavery was omnipresent; women had no real rights, and more than one hundred regional kings controlled their areas of Ireland.

In his confession, Saint Patrick tells English bishops that he paid Irish kings money so that they would allow him to try to convert men, women, and slaves under their control. Other bishops might object to such a use of church money, but Saint Patrick states that no contributions were used for his own benefit but only for the salvation of souls. Paying tribute to pagan kings might appear unseemly to bishops who live in more "civilized" countries, but Saint Patrick had to resort to unconventional methods in order to do God's work in Ireland. Saint Patrick points out to his fellow bishops that he returned to new converts all the gifts that they gave him because he did not want any person to believe that he was acting for his personal benefit. He needed to protect the reputation of all Christian missionaries so that no one could question his motives.

Saint Patrick was skillful in limiting the influence of druids, as the pagan priests in Ireland were then called, because he persuaded Irish kings that the Christian God and Christian priests were more trustworthy and predictable than druids and pagan deities. Saint Patrick successfully appealed to the self-interest of local Irish kings and even converted many of their sons and daughters.

As a former slave who had endured six years of horrendous mistreatment, Saint Patrick was especially proud of the very real comfort that he had brought to slaves and women who were so badly treated in ancient Ireland. Saint Patrick's profound concern for those whom society had exploited resounded positively with generations of Irish people who believed that Christianity, as he had presented it to their ancestors, enabled them to overcome extreme suffering.

Freeman explains well that Saint Patrick, who had intended only to share the Christian faith with the Irish, was especially important because he convinced them that each man and woman possessed dignity and an immortal soul. This is an excellent biography of a revered saint whose actual life was not generally well known until the publication of this book.

*Edmund J. Campion*

## Review Sources

*Booklist* 100, no. 13 (March 1, 2004): 1123.
*Kirkus Reviews* 71, no. 24 (December 15, 2003): 1436.
*Library Journal* 129, no. 3 (February 15, 2004): 132.
*The New York Times Book Review* 153 (March 14, 2004): 20.
*Publishers Weekly* 251, no. 3 (January 19, 2004): 72.
*School Library Journal* 50, no. 6 (June, 2004): 180.

# SCOTLAND'S EMPIRE AND THE SHAPING OF THE AMERICAS, 1600-1815

*Author:* T. M. Devine (1945-    )
*Publisher:* Smithsonian Books (Washington, D.C.).
   474 pp. $32.50
*Type of work:* History
*Time:* 1600-1815
*Locale:* Scottish and British colonies in North America
   and the Caribbean region

*An overview of the early years of England's empire building and of Scotland, the nation that played a key role in the formation of the British Empire*

When most people are asked to give their impressions of Scotland, they rarely advance beyond the famed Highland views or the cool, damp climate. Then there are the persistent clichés that seem to dog the Scots at every step: bagpipe playing, kilted and tartan-clad inhabitants, countless sheep, single-malt whiskey, and golf. Aside from these images, there seems to be little distinction in the popular imagination between England and its chilled neighbor to the north. T. M. Devine's splendid book *Scotland's Empire and the Shaping of the Americas, 1600-1815* informs the reader that there is much more to this nation than the stereotypes often associated with it.

While modern Scotland is part of Britain, Devine reminds the reader that this was not always the case. Scotland and England, it is important to note, have been steadfast foes throughout much of their joint history. From about the late thirteenth century, patriots such as William Wallace sought to keep Scotland free and independent from its larger and more powerful neighbor to the south. In practical terms, this meant that the two countries were economically, as well as ethnically, distinct well into the seventeenth century. It is true that—at least on paper—England, Scotland, and Ireland achieved a synthesis of sorts upon the death of Queen Elizabeth I in 1603. At that time, James VI of Scotland became the monarch of all three countries as King James I, the so-called Regal Union.

It was from this time that Britain came to encompass these discrete cultural and linguistic entities. It was less a marriage than an uneasy courtship. As Britain slowly assembled its growing empire in the seventeenth century, Scotland had relatively little to do with such ventures as the American colonies. As Devine makes clear, the Scots were the consummate wanderers from the seventeenth through the nineteenth centuries. This was less a matter of choice than of necessity. Due to its unpredictable climate and poor, rock-strewn soil, Scotland was never very well off and nearly always one step away from starvation. As a result, the most mobile members of each generation—unmarried young men—were compelled to travel abroad, both to feed their families and earn their keep. Although the subject of Devine's book is Scotland's role

~

*One of Scotland's best-known
historians, T. M. Devine has
authored numerous books about
his native land, including the
international best-seller* The
Scottish Nation *(1999). His
historical research has garnered
him several academic awards,
among them the prestigious
Royal Gold Medal in 2001.*

~

in empire building, he wisely precedes that discussion with an examination of how the groundwork was laid in the seventeenth century.

The Regal Union failed to unite the three disparate nations, partly because of prejudice but also as a result of substantive legal barriers: England's trade restrictions against Scotland were not lifted, and both nations had their own independent parliaments. Scotland began its role in empire building by first helping other European nations build theirs. In the early seventeenth century, for example, it is astonishing to learn that a significant portion of Scotland's emigration was directed toward Poland. Granted, much of this consisted of peddlers seeking a ready market for their goods, but a few Scots worked their way into the Polish government.

Devine is to be commended for unearthing these little-known facts, which prove that the famous Scottish wanderlust extended far beyond the British Empire. It was the reputation of its soldiers, however, that really made Scotland's presence felt by the various European nations. This was due in part to the culture of Scotland's Highlands, where the idea of a warrior society flourished before 1600. Again, the same climatic and economic forces that made peddlers ply their trade in Poland also compelled Scotland's young men to sell their services abroad as professional soldiers. In Scandinavia, Devine notes, Scottish officers managed to work their way into key government positions; in Russia, one Thomas Dalyell was named a general in that nation's army. Of greater importance, though, was the Thirty Years War (1618-1648), where the vast scale of the conflict demanded a steady supply of new recruits. For the Scots, homeland famine compelled young men to feed the European war machine.

Scotland's contribution to British imperialism effectively began with emigration to Northern Ireland. The British government actively encouraged Scottish settlement of confiscated Irish lands as a means of firmly planting Protestantism in that manifestly Catholic nation. Once again, this was a case of the Scots following the path of least resistance. Chronic penury and geographic proximity motivated this relatively easy move, but there were salient differences between this and the earlier emigrations in terms of both quality and duration. Whereas previous movements had consisted of brief excursions by independent merchants and soldiers of fortune, the shift to Ireland consisted of families—closely related groups of people who came to establish a permanent presence and till the soil. This was the beginning of what came to be known as the Scots Irish or Ulster Scots (after the province of the same name).

Aside from easing population pressures at home, the expanded market for Scottish goods created by the move marked the first significant shift in Scottish trade from continental Europe toward the West. This is not to say that Scotland had severed the continental connection entirely. One of the most significant factors in the movement of the Scots abroad—from at least the seventeenth century onward—was the fact that Scotland's desperately poor people were comparatively well-educated. It is well known that the founding fathers of the American republic were deeply influenced by the intellectual ideas of the Scottish Enlightenment. What Devine clarifies is the fact that this intellectual heritage came to a large degree from Scotland's ties to the Netherlands. Indeed, many members of Scotland's legal and medical professions continued to be educated at Leiden long after the westward shift. So close was this relationship with the Dutch that some felt a union with the Netherlands was actually preferable to one with Britain.

By the early eighteenth century, it was apparent to many that the Regal Union had failed to bring its member states into a close working relationship. A new arrangement was necessary, both for economic reasons and for blatant political necessity. Those political reasons were linked, in part, to the need for a more united kingdom during the process of empire building. A more pressing reason for greater unity was the fact that the Stuart line of kings had ended forcibly in 1688, and a closer relationship between Scotland and England would help to quell the Stuart supporters, the Jacobites.

From a modern perspective, it seems obvious that neither England nor its northern neighbor had much choice. This is the best portion of Devine's book, for he demonstrates that the outcome was far from certain, and he leaves no doubt that this change was critical to England's future as an imperial power. Despite Scotland's small size, it consisted of several competing factions whose interests were antithetical to one another. There were the Highland Scots or Gaels, whose clan associations perpetuated Scotland's reputation as a land of fierce warriors and who favored independence; the Lowland Scots, a more urbanized population that was desirous of union; and the Presbyterian Church, which wanted its own assurances of independence from the Anglican Church.

In the end, the Scottish church hierarchy received that pledge, but it was England's guarantee that all trade barriers against Scotland would cease that finalized the agreement. This was the concession that the Scots had long sought, the change that would enable them to participate fully in the burgeoning Atlantic trade. More than any other factor, this was the incentive that prompted the Scottish Parliament to vote itself out of existence and thus make the Union of 1707 a reality. Although few people realized it at the time, this new arrangement—which was rather shaky in its early years—made Britain's empire possible. With the collapse of trade barriers between the two countries, Scottish emigration dramatically shifted to the New World. At last, Scotland found an effective safety valve for its growing population and a source of virtually unlimited arable soil. This was an emigration that affected all of Scotland, and the fact that this was a well-educated nation of artisans and farmers meant a greater likelihood of achieving success in the new land.

The Scots have long had a considerable reputation for their business acumen, and the skills that they had honed on the European continent were soon directed westward after the Union of 1707. New World commodities such as chocolate and coffee began to attract the attention of Europe, and where there is a need for the importation of goods there is also a demand for those who would grow and transport them. For Scotland, it was tobacco that put England's northern neighbor on the international commercial map. Although the modern world has become increasingly aware of the health risks of tobacco, eighteenth century Europe was intoxicated with this strange plant and what was perceived to be its medicinal value. One of the impressive qualities of Devine's book is his skillful use of statistical evidence. Thus, when he discusses the profound effect of the tobacco trade upon the Scottish economy, he notes that in 1761 its merchants imported forty-seven million pounds of the plant from Virginia and Maryland.

Aside from the profits generated by the sale of tobacco at home and abroad, the plantation owners who grew this crop created a market for finished goods from the Old World. It is daunting to consider the fact that, in just a few decades, one of the poorest nations in Europe became one of the biggest players in international trade, with Glasgow being its center. Devine effectively pinpoints the long-lasting consequences of the increased commerce, some of which pertained to Scotland and others which affected the burgeoning colonies. For Scotland, the Atlantic trade proved the old adage that one needs money to make money. With the increased cash flow, the business community was able to invest heavily in Scotland's nascent moves toward industrialization.

No one can dispute the profound effect of the Scots upon American history, but Devine's book is praiseworthy for the thorough manner in which he teases out the distinct strands of Scottish ethnicity in the New World. It was the Scots Irish who constituted the bulk of Scottish immigrants to eighteenth century America. These were the small-scale farmers who formed close communities, settled on the frontier, and were responsible for many of the bloody encounters with American Indians during the French and Indian War (1754-1763). They also constituted the basis of American Protestant evangelism and largely supported the rebel cause in the American Revolution. Native Scots, on the other hand, came much later in the century, tended to be better educated, and were for the most part loyal to the Crown during the rebellion.

With the separation of the mother country from its colonies, the emigration of native Scots shifted to Canada, and highlanders cemented their reputation as fierce warriors in the service of Britain's empire in India and the West Indies. *Scotland's Empire and the Shaping of the Americas, 1600-1815*, is a fine study of a remarkable nation and its role in shaping British colonialism.

*Cliff Prewencki*

## Review Sources

*Contemporary Review* 284 (May, 2004): 316.
*Publishers Weekly* 251, no. 23 (June 7, 2004): 41.
*The Times Literary Supplement*, October 23, 2003, p. 4.

# SEARCH PARTY
## Collected Poems of William Matthews

*Author:* William Matthews (1942-1997)
Edited by Sebastian Matthews and Stanley Plumly
Introduction by Plumly
*Publisher:* Houghton Mifflin (Boston). 314 pp. $26.00
*Type of work:* Poetry

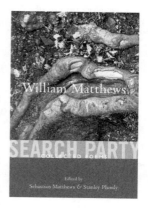

*This collection confirms Williams's status as one of the wittiest and most elliptical poets of the latter half of the twentieth century*

William Matthews died abruptly from a heart attack on the day after his fifty-fifth birthday in 1997. As a poet accustomed to producing a new book approximately every three years, he was both prolific and critically well regarded: His book *Time and Money* (1995) won the National Books Critics Circle Award, and in 1997 he received the Modern Poetry Association's Ruth Lilly Award. All told, for close to thirty years Matthews's enigmatic but increasingly accessible and entertaining poems earned him a substantial reputation. In the course of his career he received Guggenheim and National Endowment for the Arts fellowships, and he taught creative writing at Cornell University, the University of Washington, Columbia University, and the City College of New York.

Raised in Cincinnati, Ohio, Matthews graduated from Yale University and the University of North Carolina at Chapel Hill. His early poetry collections such as *Ruining the New Road* (1970) and *Sleek for the Long Flight* (1972) reflect the political and aesthetic ferment of the 1960's and the early 1970's, but all of his work displays a connoisseur's bent for the good things in life. He appreciated classic blues, jazz, gourmet food, and wine, and these topics often serve as poetic tropes in his works. His poetic themes include postmodern self-reflection on the nature of poetry, the landscape as a kind of text, and the nature of identity in relation to love, death, and loss. His philosophical and witty poems tease the reader with hints of personal crises that he was reluctant to expose. As editor Stanley Plumly writes in his introduction to *Search Party:* "[Matthews's] brilliance and volubility are inseparable from his reserve—the tension between them is the core dynamic of his kinetic mind and demanding language."

*Search Party*'s organization is unusual for a volume of collected poems because its two editors exclude so many of Matthews's previously published work, both in books and in periodicals. While the poems are arranged in chronological order with two samples of uncollected poems, the contents do not comprise a complete collection. For instance, the title sequence of poems included in *Flood* (1982) are not included. In his introduction, Plumly explains that he and Sebastian Matthews (William's son), tried to edit the collection in accordance with Matthews's strict selective process in

~

*Ohio-born William Matthews was
the author of eleven books of
poetry. His tenth book,* Time and
Money *(1995), won the National
Book Critics Circle Award. His
other notable books included*
Blues If You Want *(1992),* A
Happy Childhood *(1984),* Rising
and Falling *(1979), and the
posthumously published collection*
After All: Last Poems *(1998).*

~

which "either a poem played in concert with the concept of the whole manuscript or it didn't." In effect, the editors' selection of poems streamlines and unites Matthews's corpus. In his introduction, Plumly charts how the poems move from the "imagistic, aphoristic seventies to the more directly autobiographical eighties to the more meditative, introspective nineties," but what comes through the most is their consistency. While the resulting collection is admirably cohesive, the quality of Matthews's poetry leaves one wishing for more.

In earlier works such as *Sleek for the Long Flight* and *Sticks and Stones* (1975), Matthews's poems tended toward the surreal with their dreamlike associations. They are often shorter, more imagistic, and thus harder to follow than the later work, with many of these poems reflecting on the aesthetic choices that underlie them. The prefatory poem to his first book, *Ruining the New Road*, "The Search Party," establishes how Matthews anticipates his readers' interpretations. As soon as his narrator tells the story of participating in an anxious search party for a lost child, he turns on the reader: "by now you must be sure/ you know just where we are,/ deep in symbolic woods./ Irony, self-accusation,/ someone else's suffering./ The search is that of art." He denies this interpretation, however; it is a "real" search party, and the searchers eventually find the child alive. With its ironic shifts, "The Search Party" questions the set of assumptions the reader tends to bring to a poem. By calling attention to his poetic strategies, Matthews wants to have it both ways.

Matthews's poetry often reflects on the functions of art, the role of the poet (as he writes in "The Search Party," "I'm in these poems/ because I'm in my life"), and the relationship between art and life. Matthews liked to view landscape as a kind of poetic text. For instance, in another early poem, "Faith of Our Fathers," the narrator notes the portents of the dead in "graves in rows like a tray full of type," while the "pages of the hymnal" become "beach grass swaying in the wind . . . riffling, turning/ at last by themselves." As in the case of Philip Larkin's "Churchgoing," with the loss of faith, only the landscape remains, with the grass turning in the wind like the pages of a book without a reader.

Again and again, Matthews finds an *ars poetica* in unlikely places depending on the moods of his personae. For instance, in "Jilted," when the narrator finds that his lover will not arrive, his world becomes ominous with anxiety: "How quickly the landscape fills/ with figures, with code, with the palpable unspoken." Even the poet's penis in "Pissing Off the Back of the Boat into the Nivernais Canal" leaks "a whole sentence in Latin" in his pants. Matthews's poetry continually tries to interpret for the reader the various codes of experience, finding signs and symbols for itself everywhere.

Matthews's appreciation for jazz and blues musicians also allows him other ways to consider the foundations of art. In poems that concern John Coltrane, Charles

Mingus, Buddy Bolden, and others, Matthews divides his interests between that of the appreciative audience and that of the practicing poet who can learn from these musicians' technique. In "Smoke Gets in Your Eyes," he writes: "I love the smoky libidinal murmur/ of a jazz crowd . . . I like to slouch back/ with that I'll-be-here-awhile tilt/ and sip a little Scotch and listen."

Partaking in a tradition that stretches back to T. S. Eliot's experimentation with jazz rhythms in his poetry, Matthews is alert to the example of these masters as an artist. In "Coleman Hawkins (d. 1969), RIP," Matthews notes how "When [Hawkins] blew ballads/ you knew one use of force:/ withholding it," a line that explains Matthews's characteristic reticence. In *Foreseeable Futures* (1987), "The Accompanist" extends this meditation on aesthetics to the level of subduing oneself for one's art: "Don't play too much, don't play/ too loud, don't play the melody" so that "pain and joy eat off each other's/ plates," providing a kind of union of understated opposites.

While the blues influence seeks to commute pain and despair into joyful art, the jazz form also offers the poet an aesthetic of improvisation. In addition, Matthews never has any problem making allusions to the work of and paying tribute to other poets as well, especially W. H. Auden, Robert Frost, Wallace Stevens, and Eliot. Matthews makes allusions to Eliot's image of smoke moving like a cat along the ceiling in "The Love Song of J. Alfred Prufrock" repeatedly in various poems, in effect riffing and improvising on a strain of music that he enjoys.

Like Auden, Matthews experiments with a wide range of formal techniques, but in his reticent way he likes to disguise the formal structures of his work, creating a deceptive naturalness that hides the work he put into every line. He very rarely uses end-stopped rhymes, and when he does, he hides them with devices such as enjambment. As in Wallace Stevens's work, Matthews's poems suggest a meter without strictly adhering to it. When he describes the "latch" in his knee "not catching" in the poem "Strange Knees," the line breaks, as if to make the body of the entire poem fragment in sympathy.

Matthews was drawn to the ways an oral sound can correspond to a poem's topic. For instance, in "Promiscuous," his description of those who sleep around alliterates the letter s to a logically promiscuous, comic extreme: "all who slurred/ slavered, slobbered,/ slumped, slept or lapsed, slink of relapsed, slackened/ (loose lips sink ships) or slubbed, or slovened." Much of the time, Matthews disguises his formal choices, so as to not distract the reader with overt signs of artistry.

The humor of Matthews's poetry shows his increasing concern with audience. While some poets get more abstract and difficult with time, Matthews's poetry becomes more accessible and entertaining. To judge from Sebastian Matthews's memoir of his father, titled *In My Father's Footsteps* (2004), the elder Matthews was especially good at reading his work for an audience, and his characteristic display of wit would breathe air into the academic world surrounding him. For instance, in "Note Left for Gerald Stern in an Office I Borrowed, and He Would Next, at a Summer's Writers' Conference," he describes academia as a "methadone program for the depressed." In "Sticks & Stones" he describes how a poet's "marriage poems/ are really about his writing students—/ may his divorce poems/ be better."

Matthews even finds a kind of graveyard humor in his father's funeral, his wife's bout with cancer, and his grandmother's refusal to satisfy her family's desire for her to live to be one hundred in "Grandmother, Dead at 99 Years and 10 Months." Matthews's jokes about pigs tie in neatly to his characteristic themes. "Truffle Pigs" explores how in searching for truffles, "They know what to ignore;/ those pigs are innocent of metaphor," a thought which effectively links their search to the poet's search for beauty. In "Photo of the Author with a Favorite Pig," Matthews has the author's verbosity diminished next to the pig's frank "squint," which once again gains profundity from its reserve: "The copious pig/ has every appearance of knowing,/ from his pert, coiled tail to the wispy tips/ of his edible ears, but the pig isn't telling."

Throughout his oeuvre, Matthews's poetry celebrates moments of artistic mastery and grace in the midst of death and the body's decline. For instance, in "Slow Work," Matthews writes of how "the body of work" becomes "suppler and more vivid" while the "work of the body is to chafe and stiffen." Be it through the appreciation of a meal, a blues riff, or an erotic encounter, his poetry finds ways to affirm—but in a way that neatly balances that affirmation with the transience and the destructive elements of existence. With its concision, wit, philosophical depth, and human feeling, Matthews's poetry exemplifies the restorative power of art. Even a well-cooked meal can redeem, as the reader finds in one of his last poems, "Misgivings":

> Listen
> my wary one, it's far too late
> to unlove each other. Instead let's cook
> something elaborate and not
> invite anyone to share it but eat it
> all up very very slowly.

*Roy C. Flannagan*

### Review Sources

*Booklist* 100, no. 8 (December 15, 2003): 721.
*Library Journal* 129, no. 1 (January 15, 2004): 118.
*The New York Times Book Review* 153 (January 18, 2004): 11.
*Poetry* 183, no. 6 (March, 2004): 352.
*Publishers Weekly* 250, no. 46 (November 17, 2003): 59.

# SECOND SPACE
## New Poems

*Author:* Czesław Miłosz (1911-2004)
Translated from the Polish by Robert Hass, Renata
  Gorczynski, and Miłosz
*Publisher:* Ecco Press (New York). 102 pp. $24.00
*Type of work:* Poetry

*In this posthumously published collection, the Nobel
Prize-winning Polish poet focused his attention on ultimate questions about life and death, Nature and God,
doubt and faith, the body and the soul*

The death of Czesław Miłosz in Krakow, Poland, on
August 14, 2004, at the age of ninety-three marked the end
of one of the most important poetic careers of the twentieth
century. Described by his fellow émigré Nobel Prize-winner Joseph Brodsky as "one
of the greatest poets of our time, perhaps the greatest," Miłosz also has the distinction
of being one of the longest-lived. His first poems were published in 1931; *Second
Space* appeared seventy-three years later.

Miłosz was unique in many ways—in his rural Lithuanian boyhood and the youth
he spent in Nazi-occupied Warsaw; in the lifelong connection he maintained with his
Polish audience, even during the decades when his work was officially banned, and in
his sense of his vocation as a bard of his people and witness to his time; in his religious
faith and his resistance to the secularism that characterizes much of modern art in the
West; in writing all of his poems in Polish through thirty-nine years of exile from his
native land, spent first in Paris and then in Berkeley, California. He was also something very rare: a writer who continued to work at the highest level of his art into his
tenth decade and, in the process, provided his readers with a perspective that is seldom found in literature.

Miłosz was not a late bloomer, but wide recognition of his poetic achievement certainly came late in his life. Since his work was prohibited in Eastern Europe, for most of
his career it was all first published by obscure Polish émigré journals and publishing
houses and had to be passed hand-to-hand in his native land. Most readers in the United
States do not pay much attention to modern poetry, and there was even less interest in
Polish poetry in translation during the Cold War years. Miłosz was known in Western
Europe and the United States, but until the end of the 1970's his reputation was primarily based on his prose and scholarship: on his study of intellectuals under communism,
published in English as *The Captive Mind* (1955) and his *History of Polish Literature*
(1969), on his anthology *Postwar Polish Poetry* (1965), and his early novel *The Seizure
of Power* (1955). He was sixty-eight and still largely unknown as a poet when he was
awarded the prestigious Neustadt International Prize for Literature in 1978 and seventy when he received the Nobel Prize in Literature in 1980 and first gained real fame.

*Czesław Miłosz defected from
Poland to France in 1951. In 1960,
he became a professor of Slavic
languages and literature at the
University of California at
Berkeley. He wrote the standard*
History of Polish Literature *(1969)
and edited and translated the
anthology* Postwar Polish Poetry
*(1965). His own work has been
published in twenty-five books of
poetry and prose translated into
English. Miłosz was awarded the
Nobel Prize in Literature in 1980.*

At a time when most people retire, he then began one of the most productive periods of his long artistic life. In fact, more than half of the work gathered in his 747-page *New and Collected Poems, 1931-2001* (2001) was written after he received the Nobel Prize. Like the poems written in his seventies and eighties—published in English as *Provinces* (1991), *Facing the River* (1995), *Road-Side Dog* (1998), and *This* (2001)—the poems written in his nineties and collected in *Second Space* display the art of a master who lost few of his artistic powers and none of his ambition.

This collection is not just Miłosz's last book, it is also a book focused on last things—on meditations from the vantage of the final years of a long life about the body and the soul, time and eternity, youth and age, memory and desire, appearance and reality, pride and guilt, faith and doubt, past, present and future, earth, Heaven and Hell, the nature of Nature and of God. The book begins with thoughts of the "heavenly halls" and the desire to go beyond the physical world of earth to recapture "that other space" of Heaven and Hell; it ends with Orpheus, the poet returned from Hell, unable to raise the dead yet warmed by the earth. In between, the book's five sections never lose sight of either this world or the next.

The first section consists of a series of short lyrics of self-assessment, memory, longing, and observation. The second, "Father Severinus," is a sequence of eleven meditations by a priest who struggles with religious doubt. In the twenty-three poems of the third part, "Treatise on Theology," Miłosz recalls his youth, his own early struggles with religious doubt, and the influence of the ideas of the great Polish poet Adam Mickiewicz and the philosopher Jakob Boehme on his quest for understanding. In part 4, "Apprentice," Miłosz returns, as he has in so many of his works, to the story of his cousin, the poet and philosopher O. V Miłosz, and the influence that he and Emanuel Swedenborg had on the younger Miłosz's beliefs about humanity and God. Finally, in part 5 Miłosz retells the story of Orpheus and Eurydice.

Each of the five parts of *Second Space* is powerful in its own way, although the extensive historical, biographical, and autobiographical notes attached to it are, perhaps, the most interesting part of "Apprentice." The first and last sections of the collection will suggest both its themes and tone. Some of the lyrics in the first part confront the losses of old age, with wit and without self-pity. "High notions of oneself are annihilated/ by a glance in the mirror,/ by the impotence of old age,/ breath held in the hope that some pain/ won't return," Miłosz writes in "Degradation." "My body doesn't want to take my orders," he notes in "New Age." "My most honorable eyes, you are not in the best of shape," he says in "Eyes," though "you saw many things."

If there are losses, there are also consolations. "Without eyes, my gaze is fixed on one bright point,/ That grows large and takes me in," he says at the conclusion of "Eyes." "Not soon, as late as the approach of my ninetieth year,/ I felt a door opening in me and I entered/ the clarity of early morning." In this "Late Ripeness," his former lives depart, "together with their sorrow," and "the countries, cities, gardens, the bays of seas/ assigned to my brush came closer,/ ready now to be described better than they were before." In old age, he writes in "I Should Now," "Memory composes a story of shames and amazements./ The shames I closed inside myself, but the amazements,/ at a sun-streak on a wall, at the trill of an oriole, a face,/ an iris, a volume of poems, a person, endure and return in/ brightness."

Another sequence of lyrics turns back to Poland and Lithuania, re-creating moments and people from long ago. "A Stay" describes his time in "that city" (San Francisco) as a dream that lasted for years, while he only cared about hearing "a voice dictating verses." "I am and will be lame," he concludes, turning the cane he needed in his last years into a metaphor for the sense of difference and inadequacy that came with his vocation. "I pretended to work like others from morning to evening," he says in "Nonadaptation," "but I was absent, dedicated to invisible cities." These "invisible cities" are both the cities of his past, invisible to the people around him, and the "other spaces" that he believes in but cannot see.

Recalling one of the major Polish poets of his youth, Jaroslaw Iwaszkiewicz, in "A Master of My Craft," Miłosz chides the older poet for falling in love with death. "The passing away of people and things is not the only secret of time," he insists. "Which calls us to overcome the temptation of our serfdom./ And to put on the very edge of the abyss a table,/ And on the table, a glass, a pitcher, and two apples,/ So that they magnify the unattainable Now."

That same embrace of the "Now" in spite of the reality and inevitability of death reappears in another form in "Orpheus and Eurydice"—a small masterpiece that would be a deeply touching and fitting coda to Miłosz's life's work even if it were not the last poem in his last book. In it, his poetry ends by recounting the myth that is an appropriate metaphor for his entire oeuvre.

Like Orpheus, Miłosz was a poet who tried to use his verses about the world of the living to rescue the dead, a poet obsessed with remembering the lost even though sixty years of trying had taught him that his quest to bring them back to life through his art could never quite succeed. Like Orpheus, his thoughts and art looked back—to memories of the past, looked beyond—to the prospect of Heaven and Hell, and always, ultimately, looked around—drawing him back to the beauty of this world.

Like his self-laceratingly honest and intensely moving diary of 1987—the year his wife of more than fifty years died—called *A Year of the Hunter* (1994), the opening of his version of the Orpheus tale seems a tribute to her and an indictment of his own failings. "He remembered her words: 'You are a good man,'" Miłosz writes of his Orpheus. "He did not quite believe it. Lyric poets/ Usually have—as he knew—cold hearts." As "Only her love warmed him, humanized him./ When he was with her, he thought differently about himself. He could not fail her now, when she was dead."

Later, as he begins the ascent from Hell with Eurydice—"Her face no longer hers, utterly gray"—walking behind him, he weeps as he realizes that he has lost "the human hope for the resurrection of the dead. . . . He knew he must have faith and he could not have faith." When he violates Persephone's conditions and turns back to look for Eurydice just as he approaches the mouth of the exit to the world above, he loses her again and forever. When he emerges into the light, "everything cried to him: Eurydice!/ How will I live without you, my consoling one!" But also "there was the fragrant scent of herbs, the low humming of bees,/ And he fell asleep with his cheek on the sun-warmed earth."

It is hard to imagine a more subtle or evocative description of the mysterious process by which the absolute despair and sense of desperation that comes with the irretrievable loss of a loved one is somehow diminished and ultimately overcome by the power of the world to seduce us back to life—or a more fitting conclusion to both *Second Space* and Czesław Miłosz's life and work.

*Bernard F. Rodgers, Jr.*

## Review Sources

*America* 191, no. 10 (October 11, 2004): 35.
*Booklist* 101, no. 3 (October 1, 2004): 299.
*Library Journal* 129, no. 15 (September 15, 2004): 61.
*Los Angeles Times*, October 10, 2004, p. R3.
*The New York Times*, August 15, 2004, p. 41.
*The New York Times Book Review* 154 (November 21, 2004): 22.
*Publishers Weekly* 251, no. 42 (October 18, 2004): 60.
*The Washington Post*, October 10, 2004, p. T15.

# SECRETS OF THE SOUL
## A Social and Cultural History of Psychoanalysis

*Author:* Eli Zaretsky (1940-      )
*Publisher:* Alfred A. Knopf (New York). Illustrated.
    429 pp. $30.00
*Type of work:* Psychology and sociology
*Time:* About 1856-2004

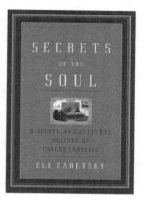

*A history of psychoanalysis, beginning with the work of Sigmund Freud, that attempts to place it in its social and economic context*

> *Principal personages:*
> SIGMUND FREUD (1856-1939), Viennese
>     physician and founder of psychoanalysis
> ANNA FREUD (1895-1982), daughter of
>     Sigmund Freud and prominent figure in
>     the psychoanalytic movement
> ALFRED ADLER (1870-1937), early disciple and ally of Sigmund Freud,
>     who split from Freud and introduced his own psychoanalytic ideas
> CARL JUNG (1875-1961), follower of Sigmund Freud, first seen as
>     Freud's heir; later became a bitter rival and founded the approach of
>     analytic psychology
> MELANIE KLEIN (1882-1960), influential figure in British psychoanaly-
>     sis and rival of Anna Freud

Psychoanalysis has been one of the most influential intellectual movements of modern times. From its beginnings in the late nineteenth century, it has also been one of the most controversial. Many academic psychologists today reject psychoanalysis as a pseudoscience, and today practicing psychiatrists generally rely more on other therapeutic approaches. At the same time, though, scholars and intellectuals in a wide variety of fields maintain that psychoanalytic ideas offer useful insights into human behavior and literature. In *Secrets of the Soul*, Eli Zaretsky avoids passing judgment on his subject. Instead, he tries to understand the history of psychoanalysis by placing the movement in a larger cultural and economic setting.

Zaretsky argues that the origins of psychoanalytic thinking and its changes can be traced to a society being shaped by economic developments. He divides the book into three parts, intended to reflect the forms of the economy and their resulting social styles. The first part, "Charismatic Origins: The Crumbling of the Victorian Family System," considers Sigmund Freud's founding of psychoanalysis during the years from 1890 to 1914. Zaretksy argues that these were also the early years of "the second industrial revolution." During the first Industrial Revolution, beginning a little more than a century earlier, Western economies had moved from a basis in agriculture to a basis in factory production. The second industrial revolution involved the develop-

∼
*Eli Zaretsky is professor of history*
*in the graduate faculty at the New*
*School University in New York City.*
*He specializes in cultural history,*
*the history of the family, and the*
*history of psychoanalysis. Zaretsky*
*is also the author of* Capitalism, the
Family, and Personal Life *(1976).*
∼

ment of mass-produced goods and, later, a consumer culture.

The early years of the second industrial revolution saw the freeing of individuals from the controls of family-centered life, according to the author. Zaretsky describes late nineteenth and early twentieth century Vienna as a new center of cultural life focused on the private self. The idea of the personal unconscious and a new fascination with individual sexuality emerged in response to such concern with the private self. Freud's theories expressed these concerns, and Freud became the charismatic founder of a new movement. It was unknown whether, as a new movement, psychoanalysis would become absorbed into the mainstream of medical practice or remain on the margins of intellectual life as a sect following Freud. By 1910, with Freud's split from Carl Jung and Alfred Adler, psychoanalysis was largely excluded from official acceptance and became a mostly Jewish sect.

The second part, "Fordism, Freudianism, and the Threefold Promise of Modernity," considers psychoanalysis from the years of World War I to World War II. Cases of shell shock (post-traumatic stress disorder among soldiers) and battlefield neuroses of World War I further inspired the attempts to understand psychological problems. Such cases also moved Freud to adapt his theories by developing his ideas on the death drive or death instinct in human behavior. The spread of Freudian approaches accompanied a new era in industrial history.

The term "Fordism" refers to Henry Ford, whose factories mass-produced automobiles, transforming these machines from luxury items for the wealthy to widely marketed goods for general consumers. Ford-type mass production had two contradictory aspects. On one hand, it required standardization; people had to show up at jobs and function as efficient workers. On the other hand, the consumer economy encouraged individualism. Freudian analysis promised to meet both requirements, as it seemed to be a means of curing inconvenient forms of nonconformity through therapy, and it also catered to the self-examination of individual patients.

While Freudian psychoanalysis responded to the market economy, it also flirted with the major industrial competitor of the market system. Several of Freud's associates were socialists, and for a time the psychoanalytic movement had loose ties to the Bolsheviks in Russia. Leon Trotsky, one of the major figures of the Russian Revolution who was forced into exile by Joseph Stalin in the late 1920's, was interested in psychoanalytic theory. Apparently, Freudian ideas appealed to Trotsky for the same reason they appealed to his capitalist rivals: Psychoanalysis seemed a promising means of social control. In 1918, during the brief period of Communist control in Hungary, the psychoanalysts held a congress in Budapest at the invitation of Hungarian leader Bela Kun.

During the years following World War I, psychoanalysis also became tied to another movement for social change, the women's movement. By 1930, women had joined the ranks of the most dominant figures in psychoanalysis, originally an almost exclusively male occupation. Anna Freud, the daughter of Sigmund, became a leading light and her father's most obvious successor. Karen Horney, a psychoanalyst who became a feminist critic of Freud, developed ideas about women's sexuality and the psychological development of women. Melanie Klein, who was to become Anna Freud's great rival, emphasized the role of the mother in the lives of children, a sharp contrast to Sigmund Freud's emphasis on the influence of the father.

This rise of women in the psychoanalytic movement, in Zaretsky's view, was another consequence of the evolving economy of the second industrial revolution. During and after World War I, women began to participate more actively in employment outside the household and in public life. The family became a place where goods were consumed, rather than produced, and women were central figures in the new, consumption-oriented family. The turn toward the mother in psychoanalysis, then, mirrored events in the surrounding culture.

World War II marked the end of Zaretsky's second period. With the rise of Nazism and Fascism, psychoanalysis was driven out of its Central European birthplace. In united Germany and Austria, a distorted "non-Jewish" version of psychoanalysis rose under the leadership of Matthias Göring, a cousin of Nazi leader Hermann Göring. The exile of Freud and his disciples encouraged the spread of psychoanalysis throughout the world, and the movement put down important roots in England and the United States. While Sigmund Freud tried to keep his theories separate from politics, many of the exiled psychoanalysts, opponents of Nazism, drew closer to left-wing politics. These included the Austrian Wilhelm Reich and members of the Institute for Social Research in Frankfurt, Germany, such as Erich Fromm, Max Horkheimer, and Theodor Adorno.

Zaretsky identifies the period after World War II as the third development in the history of psychoanalysis. This era, particularly from the late 1940's through the 1970's, was the time of the welfare state in Britain, the United States, and Western Europe. The role of the mother became even greater in this postwar welfare psychoanalysis. In the United States, psychoanalysis became institutionalized as a technique for social control, but some theorists also began to discover radical possibilities in psychoanalytic teachings. The tumultuous 1960's had charismatic, radical Freudians such as Norman O. Brown and Herbert Marcuse as prominent figures for the utopian New Left. The society of mass consumption also encouraged the proliferation of therapies, and psychoanalysis began to break down into many approaches to therapy and to merge with other theories and philosophies. In France, Jacques Lacan became something of a cult figure by linking psychoanalysis to structuralism and fashionable ideas about the nature of language.

While psychoanalytic theories addressed many of the concerns of the second half of the twentieth century, the psychoanalysts themselves had begun to become outdated. The culture of the 1960's seemed narcissistic and overly concerned with the self, and the new therapies that had arisen out of psychoanalysis began to replace it. In the 1960's, fewer individuals applied for membership in the American Psychoanalytic Association, and the average age of members rose rapidly.

By the 1970's, psychoanalysis had broken down into two main projects that had little in common with each other. Psychoanalysis was a medical technique that aimed at providing therapy for mental and emotional disorders. It was also a humanistic theory for the study of culture. Both of these projects faced challenges as the twentieth century ended. Neuroscience and psychopharmacology began to replace psychoanalysis as medical approaches. Many mainstream psychology departments in universities ignored Freudian ideas completely. Humanistic psychoanalysis came under assault from cultural studies, feminist theory, and other new trends in academic interpretation. There were indications of renewed interest in psychoanalysis, but there were also many who proclaimed that the movement had been an intellectual dead end.

This book is an important look back at psychoanalysis, and the ambitious effort to look at the movement as a reflection of its historical setting offers a fascinating perspective. Some questions about Zaretsky's argument may occur to many readers, though. It is not clear exactly what connection Zaretsky believes has existed between psychoanalysis and a culture resulting from modern mass production. It may be that there is a personal unconscious and that sexuality does play the role in human psychology that Freud described. If so, the second industrial revolution may have simply created the conditions for discovering these vital truths about human nature. Another possibility, however, is that human nature is so flexible that it changes in response to economic and social influences. In that case, the Freudian description of the personality in the early twentieth century may have been true for people in Vienna in 1910 but no longer true for twenty-first century Americans and Europeans. One more possibility is that psychoanalysis has been simply a series of illusions produced by modern consumer culture.

Some readers may also raise against Zaretsky the same criticism that philosopher Karl Popper raised against Freud. Popper objected to psychoanalysis as a scientific theory because he claimed that there was no way to prove whether it was true or false. Similarly, it may be interesting to think about psychoanalytic theory and practice as somehow reflecting cultural and economic trends, but even if one knew exactly what connection Zaretsky believes has existed between psychoanalysis and the second industrial revolution, such a connection might be very difficult to prove or disprove.

Although the author lapses into an academic style on occasions, in general the book is well written, and readers who are not familiar with psychoanalytic jargon can understand and enjoy it. Whether or not readers accept Zaretsky's claims about the influence of economic setting on psychoanalysis, most will agree that the division into three periods provides a helpful way of thinking about the history of these concepts. The book gives clear accounts of the basic views of Sigmund Freud and his followers and of how those views changed over time. Anyone who is interested in a general history of psychoanalysis and in its major figures and divisions will find this an extremely useful work.

*Carl L. Bankston III*

## Review Sources

*Booklist* 100, no. 17 (May 1, 2004): 1526-1527.
*Library Journal* 129, no. 10 (June 1, 2004): 162.
*The New York Times Book Review* 153 (September 5, 2004): 9-10.
*Publishers Weekly* 251, no. 21 (May 24, 2004): 52.
*The Wilson Quarterly* 28, no. 3 (Summer, 2004): 125.

# THE SEDUCTION OF UNREASON
## The Intellectual Romance with Fascism from Nietzsche to Postmodernism

*Author:* Richard Wolin (1952-    )
*Publisher:* Princeton University Press (Princeton, N.J.).
  375 pp. $20.00
*Type of work:* History and philosophy

*Wolin presents a powerful analysis of the intimate con-*
*nection between extremist politics of the Right and the*
*postmodern philosophy that attained widespread influence*
*in American universities in the late twentieth century*

Richard Wolin is a professor of history and comparative
literature at the City University of New York. In *The Se-*
*duction of Unreason: The Intellectual Romance with Fas-*
*cism from Nietzsche to Postmodernism*, he explores the
paradoxically intimate relationship between ideas fashionable in leftist circles today
and the insights of extremist right-wing philosophers of the early twentieth century.
What unites these wildly disparate bodies of thinkers is a vehement rejection of the intellectual legacy of the eighteenth century Enlightenment, expressing itself in a radical distrust of reason and a scornful dismissal of universal humanist rights and values.

This sinister synergy of ideas, the proverbial meeting of the far Left and Right, is
what animates Wolin's analysis. This is an angry book. Though solidly buttressed by
an impeccable scholarly apparatus, it is also a very political book. Wolin makes no secret that he is a committed man of the Left. He is dismayed, however, by the attraction
of many on the Left to postmodern ideas that he regards as morally suspect and politically self-defeating. By exploring the intellectual genealogy of postmodernism, and
redeeming the philosophical legacy of the eighteenth century, Wolin self-consciously
hopes to point the way to a more rational and enlightened future.

Wolin has long believed that postmodernism is an intellectual movement with feet
of clay. He is the author of volumes exploring the long and often intimate association
between the hugely influential German philosopher Martin Heidegger and National
Socialism. At the same time that Heidegger's Nazi affinities became a *cause célèbre*,
it was learned that Paul de Man, popularly known as the ambassador of postmodernism to the United States, and before his death a professor of philosophy at Yale
University, also had Nazi skeletons in his closet. The research that resulted in *The Se-*
*duction of Unreason* flowed naturally from these revelations.

In an irony that exasperates Wolin, ideas tainted by these dubious connections
took American universities by storm in the last two decades of the twentieth century.
Philosophers such as Michel Foucault, Jacques Derrida, and Jean Baudrillard became
intellectual icons, exerting enormous influence. These thinkers pursued a variety of
philosophical agendas. They were united in their intellectual debt to Friedrich Nietz-

sche and Heidegger, whose powerful critiques
of modernity inspired and framed the boundaries of postmodern philosophy. Nietzsche and
Heidegger launched a massive assault on society as they found it. They deplored the effects
that democracy and capitalism had on the human spirit. They attacked the philosophical tradition that underpinned these developments.
To borrow a postmodernist term, they deconstructed modern life, finding it shallow and obsessed with ephemera, with the people lost in it
alienated and adrift.

~

*Richard Wolin holds a Distinguished
Professorship of History and
Comparative Literature at the
Graduate Center, City University of
New York. He is the author or editor
of eight books, including* The Politics
of Being: The Political Thought of
Martin Heidegger *(1990) and*
Heidegger's Children *(2001).*

~

Nietzsche and Heidegger provided a philosophic rationale for the post-World
War I world T. S. Eliot described in his poetry as a wasteland inhabited by hollow
men. In doing this, Nietzsche and Heidegger laid the foundations for twentieth century existentialism. They also upended traditional conceptions of reason and truth,
casting both loose from any mooring in a metaphysical absolute. Dissociated from
any absolute, as Nietzsche famously put it, in a world where God was dead, truth and
value became relative. Nietzsche and Heidegger thus gave a powerful intellectual impulse to cultural relativism.

In the hands of their postmodern progeny, the profound insights of Nietzsche and
Heidegger, suitably elaborated, have launched a thousand academic ships. Their de-
throning of reason and truth has led to the textual acrobatics of literary decon-
structionism. Their relativism has spawned modern multiculturalism. Thus, in an
irony Nietzsche certainly would have appreciated, the universities that many Americans regard as temples of reason are often strongholds of philosophical ideals reso-
lutely hostile to the purposes for which these institutions were founded.

Although Wolin would probably not appreciate the comparison, his analysis bears
striking similarities to that of the conservative scholar Allan Bloom in his best-selling
*The Closing of the American Mind* (1987). Bloom was concerned about the coruscat-
ing effects of cultural relativism on American education and, by extension, on the
American character. Both Nietzsche and Heidegger figured prominently in his book
as sources of relativism. Bloom described in detail how their ideas migrated to the
United States with Central European refugees from the National Socialists in the
1930's and 1940's.

From an initial vantage point in the universities, the relativistic vision spread
across the country, getting an added impetus from the social disruptions of the 1960's.
The ready acceptance of these ideas was surprising because the political institutions
and ethos of the United States are firmly rooted in the Enlightenment. The Declaration of Independence and the Constitution, with their invocation of natural rights en-
dowed by a creator, belong to a moral universe antithetical to that of Nietzsche and
Heidegger. For Bloom, the paradox was resolved by the way that European relativism
was Americanized. In the secure confines of the United States, morally fraught ideas
seemed much less consequential. To a remarkable degree, Americans simply ignored

718  *Magill's Literary Annual 2005*

the implications of the ideas that they were embracing. The result was, as Bloom famously put it, nihilism with a happy face.

Wolin does not possess Bloom's gift for the rhetorical flourish, but he does paint a similar picture. Postmodernism took hold in American universities in the last two decades of the twentieth century, at a time when the terrible moral and political challenges posed by totalitarianism were beginning to recede. It offered a generation of American academics soured by the experience of the Vietnam War and Watergate a philosophic rationale for rejecting authority. It also provided its jaded audience a refined form of intellectual titillation, with its grandiose claims and derision of tradition. Wolin sees postmodernism as a species of philosophic fraud, its promise all artifice and affectation.

Foucault promulgated a discourse of power devoid of value. Such was Foucault's nihilism that he ended his days as a cheerleader for the tyrannical revolution of the mullahs in Iran. Derrida, the father of literary deconstruction, decried "logocentrism" and the "tyranny of reason." Yet his eccentric explications of texts took his readers down endlessly recursive halls of mirrors leading nowhere.

Wolin notes that outside their initial vogue in France and Germany, and then the United States, the ideas of the postmoderns did not travel well. In regions of the globe where intellectuals were struggling to free themselves from the domination of slowly expiring dictatorships, postmodern quips about reason as oppression did not resonate. Vapid posturings were of little use to men and women confronted by the realities of modern police states. As the Soviet Union and its empire collapsed, Eastern European intellectuals eagerly embraced the liberal political principles of the Enlightenment. They saw these as invaluable resources in the effort to re-create decent and humane states out of the ashes of communist totalitarianism.

Even in France postmodernism lost its cachet. During the 1980's, a new generation of French thinkers rebelled against the postmoderns' fashionable nihilism. The European eclipse of the postmoderns was accelerated by the rise of far-right political parties in the 1990's. Several of the leaders of these parties self-consciously borrowed from the intellectual repertoire of postmodernism to denounce the Enlightenment legacy of respect for human rights. Most of these parties drew their energy from popular antipathy to immigration from North Africa and the Middle East. Politicians demagoging this sensitive issue appropriated the postmodern language of multiculturalism to mount a defense of what they termed European culture. For Wolin, this use of postmodernist ideas reflects an affinity for extremist politics that can be traced back to its intellectual origins.

Most of Wolin's book is devoted to an extended historical dissection of the often intimate links between postmodern thinkers and fascism. He begins with the philosophers of Counter-Enlightenment, figures such as Joseph de Maistre, who during the period of the French Revolution argued vehemently against Enlightened assumptions about natural rights and the primacy of reason.

Nietzsche and Heidegger drank deeply at the Counter-Enlightenment well in framing their critique of modernity. Wolin takes pains to develop Nietzsche's apocalyptic political vision. This side of Nietzsche has been forgotten during the last half-century in the English-speaking world. One reason for this is the frightening nature of Nietzsche's writings on politics. He aestheticized violence and called for a radicalized form of power politics. He prophesied wars so intense and far-reaching that not even the destruction of the World Wars could compare.

The recent trend in philosophy has been to distance Nietzsche from fascism. Wolin argues that earlier estimates and the Nazis' own protestations of intellectual indebtedness are closer to the mark. He then proceeds to examine the lives and work of Carl Jung, Hans-George Gadamer, Georges Bataille, and Maurice Blanchot. What these thinkers all have in common is importance to the development of postmodern thought and a willingness to accommodate fascism, whether in Nazi Germany or the collaborationist regime of Vichy France.

Only in the 1960's did the ideas of these men become associated with the Left. The postmodern generation of Foucault, Derrida, and Baudrillard squared this circle. They looked to Nietzsche, Heidegger, and the rest for intellectual inspiration, all the while professing to be men of the Left. In doing so, they assimilated tendencies of reactionary extremism into the Left that made it vulnerable to the cynical aggrandizement of political demagogues in the 1990's.

Wolin also argues that, to the extent that the Left accepted postmodern ideas, it absorbed reflexes fundamentally totalitarian and cut itself off from the Enlightenment tradition that nurtures humane societies in the modern world; hence for Wolin, the supreme irony of the success of postmodernism in the United States, an irony that mirrors the paradox for Bloom of the prevalence of value relativism in the United States. Postmodernism is a complex of ideas deeply implicated in the history of European fascism. In Europe that history is now widely acknowledged, and postmodernism has ceased to be a vital influence. The United States alone can embrace postmodernism because America does not share the troubled history that gave it birth.

Adding to the irony is the rampant anti-Americanism of the postmodernists. Since the days of the Counter-Enlightenment thinkers, the United States has been uniquely associated with Enlightenment values. It was a detested symbol of modernity for the generations of reactionary intellectuals who paved the way for the postmodernists. For Heidegger, the United States represented capitalism, democracy, individualism, and reason, all of which he feared and despised. For many fascists, these hated qualities were interchangeably associated with Jewishness, adding anti-Semitism to the heady mix inherited by the postmoderns. These thinkers, in turn, carried on this tradition of criticism, tamping down its most politically incorrect aspects.

For the postmoderns, America was the land of modern consumerist alienation par excellence, a soulless expanse of unchecked greed and materialism. The postmodern theorist Baudrillard regards the United States as a land of appearances, media-driven and otherwise, and nothing else. For him, America has no history, no culture; it is all surface and no substance. This glib view of American life informed his notorious response to the terrorist attacks of September 11, 2001. Baudrillard wrote that the terrorist attacks were justified by the baleful cultural role that America plays in the world. He argued that the Islamo-fascist terrorists acted not only for themselves but for all the people of the world as they struck symbols of American economic and military might.

This nihilistic response to genuine tragedy represents for Wolin the moral nadir of postmodernism. Implicated with political extremism, morally frivolous, postmodernism has nothing to offer the future. In Wolin's view, the Left in the post-September 11 world must reconnect with its humanistic roots in the Enlightenment in order to meet the moral challenges to come. In this impressive book Wolin does for the Left what Bloom did years ago for the Right; he makes a powerful case for a return to moral seriousness.

*Daniel P. Murphy*

## Review Sources

*Library Journal* 129, no. 5 (March 15, 2004): 79.
*The Nation* 278, no. 23 (June 14, 2004): 53.
*National Review* 56, no. 15 (August 9, 2004): 46.
*New Statesman* 133 (May 31, 2004): 48.

# SKINNY DIP

*Author:* Carl Hiaasen (1953-    )
*Publisher:* Alfred A. Knopf (New York). 355 pp. $25.00
*Type of work:* Novel
*Time:* 2002
*Locale:* Florida

*A satiric novel driven by anger over the fate of the Florida Everglades and by sheer wonder at the depths of human folly*

*Principal characters:*
> JOEY PERRONE, a woman whose husband believes he has murdered her
> CHARLES REGIS (CHAZ) PERRONE, Joey's husband, a crooked biologist
> RICCA SPILLMAN, a hairdresser, Chaz's mistress
> MICK STRANAHAN, a prematurely retired investigator for the state attorney's office
> SAMUEL JOHNSON (RED) HAMMERNUT, a rich, corrupt farmer and despoiler of the Everglades
> EARL EDWARD O'TOOLE (TOOL), Red Hammernut's hired gun
> KARL ROLVAAG, a police detective

In part perhaps because it is necessarily topical, in part because it is funny (and funny writing is treated as generically inferior), satire is often undervalued as writing. Discussions of American fiction are far more likely to include third-rate "literary" novelists than first-rate satirists such as Richard Dooling, Christopher Buckley, or Carl Hiaasen. Perhaps it is not a coincidence that Dooling, Buckley, and Hiaasen, different as they are from one another, are all three intimately familiar with public life and commerce and the levers of power, with the flow of money and all that it brings in its wake. Hiaasen's journalistic career has included work as a reporter and then for many years as a columnist at the *Miami Herald*.

In his work for the *Herald*, Hiaasen has kept an unblinking eye on his native Florida, particularly on its rapacious development. He has put his years of close study to good use in his fiction. Like all the best satirists, Hiaasen combines genuine outrage at human folly with palpable delight in recounting it. Also like all the best satirists, he runs the risk of nihilism. How does a writer who sees through everything manage to affirm the good that gives his satire moral force?

*Skinny Dip* is Hiaasen's tenth novel, not counting three early books cowritten with Bill Montalbano and a young adult novel, *Hoot*, which appeared just a few months before *Skinny Dip*. His previous novel, *Basket Case*, published in 2002 (featuring a song written for the book by Hiaasen and Warren Zevon and later recorded by Zevon), was his best to date, and there was no falling off with *Skinny Dip*, which enjoyed

∼

*Carl Hiaasen joined the staff of the*
*Miami* Herald *in 1976 as a reporter*
*and later became a columnist. After*
*three early novels cowritten with*
*journalist Bill Montalbano, Hiaasen*
*published his first solo novel,*
Tourist Season, *in 1986. His novel*
Skinny Dip *has been optioned for*
*filming by director Mike Nichols.*

∼

excellent reviews as well as a run on best-seller lists.

The novel begins with an attempted murder: A woman in her early thirties, Joey Perrone, is thrown overboard from the deck of a cruise ship by her husband, Chaz. Murder is a serious subject, but from the opening paragraphs there is something ridiculous about this particular crime, and when Joey avoids seemingly certain death by clinging to a floating, burlap-wrapped bale of marijuana that dropped from a smuggler's boat, the whiff of absurdity is unmistakable.

This is Hiaasen's trademark manner. His novels are loaded with unseemly, incongruous, bizarre happenings. (He might well say in reply that the archives of the *Herald* contain incidents stranger than any fiction.) He aggressively violates routine notions of propriety and verisimilitude. Unlike many absurdist writers, however, who offer simulations of chaos, Hiaasen has created a fictional world in which the good are rewarded and the wicked are punished. His understanding of how to distinguish the sheep from the goats differs from traditional criteria, but Hiaasen is a moralist through and through.

One way to distinguish Hiaasen's good guys (and good women) from his villains is by their attitude toward the natural world. When the first sentence of Hiaasen's 1999 novel *Sick Puppy* reports that "On the morning of April 24, an hour past dawn, a man named Palmer Stoat shot a rare African black rhinoceros," the reader knows that a moral monster has been introduced. On the other hand, the "ecoterrorist" who will torment Stoat, young Twilly Spree—who is driven to purposeful fury by the sight of a litterbug in action—clearly has Hiaasen's sympathies.

Chaz Perrone of *Skinny Dip* is a biologist for the state of Florida. If he is a biologist, he must be a good guy, right? No. Apart from being incompetent—typically a sign of moral weakness in Hiaasen—Chaz is crooked. His job requires him to monitor the presence of pollutants in a section of the Everglades subject to runoff from the property of a rich farmer, Red Hammernut. Chaz systematically misreports the results, making it appear that Hammernut is complying with environmental regulations when, in fact, his farms continue to pour pollutants into the ecosystem. For this service Chaz is well compensated—though he would enjoy a perfectly comfortable lifestyle in any case. He is not, however, simply dishonest and selfish. He loathes the natural world—an attitude that marks him, in Hiaasen's work, as an irredeemably flawed human being.

This is the sort of man who is capable of planning the cold-blooded murder of his wife, Joey, because he fears (wrongly) that she has figured out his arrangement with Hammernut. She has become an inconvenience, and Chaz's first thought—as if there were no alternative—is that he must get rid of her. He meticulously plans the attempted murder—which takes place on an anniversary cruise—and congratulates himself afterward on its flawless execution, unaware that Joey has survived.

In contrast, there is Mick Stranahan, the protagonist of Hiaasen's 1989 novel *Skin Tight*, in which the most conspicuous prevailing folly is plastic surgery. In *Skin Tight*, the thirty-nine-year-old Stranahan has just "retired" on disability from his job as an investigator for the Florida State Attorney's Office. In fact he is not disabled at all, but, having killed a corrupt judge in self-defense, he has become something of an embarrassment—hence the fiction that removes him from the public eye.

Stranahan is quite happy to be so removed. By the time of *Skinny Dip* he has been enjoying retirement for almost fifteen years, lately ensconced on an "island" that is really just a big lump of coral. When he needs to get provisions, he hops in his boat and makes a quick run to Miami. Most of the time he is blissfully alone, fishing and reading and lounging about, though at intervals he falls in love with a waitress here or there on the mainland, marries her, and soon falls out of love again. This has happened six times during his "retirement" (though the sixth short-lived marriage broke the pattern when he fell for a television producer).

While Chaz, the murderous incompetent, is almost pathologically uncomfortable in any place where nature is not entirely tamed, Stranahan is a natural man to a fault, even given to skinny-dipping. It is he who finds Joey naked and unconscious, still clinging to the bale. Once she has recovered and told him her strange tale, he agrees to help her exact revenge upon Chaz—another recurring scenario in Hiaasen's novels, where the good guys pay heed to their version of the natural law and ignore the law books and the courts and all of society's clumsy mechanisms, preferring to dispense rough justice as they see fit.

Clearly, according to the canons of Hiaasenland, Joey and Stranahan are made for each other. They are splendid physical specimens; they are resourceful and trustworthy; they follow their instincts. Unsurprisingly, they soon find themselves in bed together. Given their track records, the long-term prospects are not good, but for the span of this book at least they are in harmony, somewhat in the manner of movie couples in the fast-talking romantic comedies of the 1930's, where all the spats and misunderstandings are created only to be resolved.

If the novel were divided between such paragons (however unconventional their virtue) and the likes of Chaz, it would lack sufficient variety and ordinariness. Even readers not averse to a dose of wish-fulfillment may find Stranahan a bit much. (Imagine Ian Fleming's James Bond character as a beach bum, never at a loss, whether preparing a fresh-caught dinner or dealing with a violent thug. Stranahan's closest fictional ancestor, however, is John D. MacDonald's Travis McGee, to whom Hiaasen tips his hat.) Thus there are additional figures such as the police detective Karl Rolvaag, who is about to leave Florida for good and return to the Midwest. Rolvaag is an ordinary guy for the most part, an effective foil to the larger-than-life types, decent and competent, but he does own two large snakes: a quirk that signals his virtue, just as Chaz's satisfaction in running over a snake signals his depravity.

There is also the hulking Earl Edward O'Toole, known as "Tool." He is also a recurring figure in Hiaasen's fiction: the grotesque villain, perhaps most memorably imagined in *Skin Tight* in the character of Blondell Wayne Tatum, known as "Chemo," who after losing a hand (to a barracuda, during a failed attempt to kill

Stranahan) replaces it with a Weed Whacker, powered by a battery pack that he attaches under his arm. Like Chemo, Tool is a simple soul who begins by simply doing as he is told (and paid) to do but who comes (in the course of the book) to question whether he should continue to do so. In Tool's case the transformation is more dramatic; more than any of the other principal characters, he changes in the course of the book, toward what counts as enlightenment in Hiaasenland. If he is Hammernut's hired gun at the start of the book, by the end he is Hammernut's executioner, a tool of justice, for the corrupt farmer is not only a world-class polluter but also a deep-dyed racist, a sin which Hiaasen never leaves unpunished.

It is a tribute to Hiaasen's art that the moral transformation of such a grotesque can be moving; characters in a good satire have a way of taking on life like this, even as they remain firmly within the schematic requirements of the genre. So, too, with the fate of Chaz. He is a butt of satire from the outset, thoroughly unsympathetic. Having (as he supposes) killed his wife, he comes to believe that he must kill his mistress, Ricca, as well. This second bungled murder attempt is not only more wildly out-of-kilter than the first but also more disturbing, so that tangled up with black comedy there is genuine horror at the progressive evil. Chaz, too, will meet his avenging angel, that virtuous madman of the Everglades known as Skink or "captain," who appears in many of Hiaasen's novels.

One of the virtually unchallenged maxims of fiction-writing, laid down everywhere from junior high classrooms to the trendiest M.F.A. programs, is that good fiction is never didactic. This is simply not true, and there is no shortage of counter-examples, including the fiction of Hiaasen. For all its humor, dark and light, a book such as *Skinny Dip* is as overtly moralistic as one of those nineteenth century novels inspired by the temperance movement. Whether its moral vision, its scale of values, is ultimately persuasive is a question for another day.

*John Wilson*

*Booklist* 100, no. 17 (May 1, 2004): 1514.
*Kirkus Reviews* 72, no. 10 (May 15, 2004): 460.
*Library Journal* 129, no. 10 (June 1, 2004): 122.
*The New York Times*, July 12, 2004, p. E1.
*The New York Times Book Review* 153 (July 11, 2004): 17.
*People* 62, no. 5 (August 2, 2004): 47.
*Publishers Weekly* 251, no. 19 (May 10, 2004): 34.

# SNOW

*Author:* Orhan Pamuk (1952-     )
*First published: Kar,* 2002, in Turkey
Translated from the Turkish by Maureen Freely
*Publisher:* Alfred A. Knopf (New York). 436 pp. $26.00
*Type of work:* Novel
*Time:* The early 1990's
*Locale:* Kars, Turkey, and Frankfurt, Germany

*In a social setting as rigid as a snowflake's structure,*
*Ka's failed efforts to escape with the woman he loves are*
*mirrored by the "author's" attempts to capture events*

*Principal characters:*

"ORHAN," the "author" who investigates the
  death of Ka, only to fall in love with Ýpek
KA (KERIM ALAKUÞOÐLU), a Westernized Turk lost between civiliza-
  tions
ÝPEK HANIM, the woman whom Ka has loved for years
KADIFE HANIM, Ýpek's jealous sister and Blue's lover
TURGUT BEY, their father, an old-time political radical
BLUE, a modern Islamic revolutionary
MUHTAR, Ýpek's former husband, a political activist
NECIP, a young Islamic radical infatuated with Ka
SUNAY ZAIM, the head of an acting troupe and a counterrevolutionary
FUNDA ESER, his wife
SERDAR BEY, the publisher of *Border City News,* always written a day
  ahead
FAZIL, Necip's friend who marries Kadife after Blue's death
Z DEMIRKOL, a Turkish paramilitary agent

*Snow* is set in the small Turkish town of Kars, isolated from the rest of the world
for three days by a snowstorm. The plot of the novel is as intricate and symmetrical as
the pattern of a snowflake. At the beginning, the center of this rigid form is occupied
by the poet Ka, short for Kerim Alakuþoðlu, who arrives in Kars seeking Ýpek, a
woman on whom he had a crush many years before. Unfortunately, he finds himself
not only cut off from the outside world by the snowstorm but also by a military coup
(and increasingly by his own self-destructiveness). In the isolated town, much as with
a snowflake, the structure is rigid, with every person and group balanced and even
paralyzed by their opposites. At the center of all this stand Ka and later "Orhan," the
narrator, who plays an increasingly larger role, eventually taking the place of the murdered Ka so far as to fall in love with Ýpek.

At the start of the novel, Ka, who had returned to Turkey to attend his mother's funeral, travels to the remote town of Kars. Though seeking to court Ýpek, a love from

*Turkish writer Orhan Pamuk is the author of many books. Translated into more than twenty languages, his novels have received major Turkish and international literary awards, including the IMPAC Dublin Literary Award for* Benim adım kırmızı *(1998;* My Name Is Red*, 2001).*

his youth, he claims to be investigating a series of suicides among girls who refused the secular government's order to remove their religious head scarves in school.

No two characters agree about the motivation of the girls or even the truth of the reports. Some see faith as the motive, others the oppressed condition of women. Still others believe that the stories of these suicides are lies circulated by enemies of Islam. One girl still wearing a head scarf in protest says, "[A] suicide wish is a wish for innocence," even though suicide goes against the teachings of the Qur'ān. In this, as in so much else in the novel, people believe what they need to believe, while not affording the same liberty to others. Similarly, the citizens of the town have developed such a mistrust of government pronouncements that they do not even believe weather reports. In so rigid a society, those who seek the freedom to act as they wish, to wear the head scarf or not, for instance, allow no one else free choices.

At first, Ka feels taken back to his own childhood and its purity, but this innocence is as quickly muddied as fresh snow. Though claiming to having discovered faith, Ka enters a life of duplicity to win Ýpek's love and convince her to leave with him. Moreover, he is unable to prevent the betrayal that will cost him his own happiness and, after his return to Europe, his life. Willing to say anything to get what he wants, Ka is a pathetic hero, becoming more infantile over the course of the novel. Ever more dependent on Ýpek, he demands her total love the way a child would from his mother. Refused, he falls apart, as a child would, becoming rageful and finally murderous.

Most of the novel's characters find themselves in similar predicaments. Wanting something certain and pure, they have already been disappointed and are far from innocent themselves. Social pressures exacerbate the situation, undermining not just individual freedoms but also the ties binding couples together. The bonds at the heart of lasting relationships lie not between husbands and wives but among family members. Ka wants a dead mother's love, while Ýpek cares most for her father. Likewise, what attracts her to Blue, as the reader later learns, is not just Blue himself but a rivalry with her sister Kadife.

Ka attempts to circumvent all this through writing. Tormented by his unfulfilled passion and pressured by the events unfolding around him, Ka writes twenty poems that delineate the structure of a snowflake at the same time that the structure inspires the poems (and the novel). However, only nineteen poems are actually written down, and these are later stolen by Ka's assassin in Germany. The twentieth poem Ka extemporizes onstage during the town's first televised variety show just before it erupts into violence connected to a military coup. He needs this last poem to feel whole, but he can never return to Kars because of his guilt.

One true innocent, however, is Necip, struggling with the doubt that possesses him whenever he tries to articulate his faith or form bonds of love and friendship. "If you can't put your trust in people, you'll never get anywhere in life," he says. He fails to see that in the world of this novel, where no one ever questions their own beliefs, lack of communication between people makes trust and true friendship impossible. Trying to escape this predicament, Necip identifies himself as a science fiction writer, though he wishes only to tell his own story, set far removed in time and place to avoid the dilemmas of the present.

Necip emerges as an ardent follower of Ka, in a literal sense, turning up in many of the same places. He wants Ka to understand him and to explain him to himself. He puts his trust in Ka, and his shock during Ka's extemporaneous recitation of the missing poem onstage during the raucous variety show, a poem Necip "knows" is his, drives him to his feet. Whether he stands in surprise or protest cannot be known because he is immediately shot down by soldiers onstage, whose first volley strikes the audience more as theater than reality. After this point, with innocence simply impossible, Ka becomes more and more involved with the events of the coup, bringing about the destruction of all of his hopes.

Ka is asked to persuade Ýpek's sister Kadife to take off her head scarf in a production of an old play (mirroring the earlier stage show) written to support the secular basis of modern Turkey. Here again, with Sunay Zaim directing both the play and the coup, the book posits the parallel between theater and history, ruling out any objective truth. In return for Kadife's cooperation, Sunay will allow Blue, Kadife's lover, to escape. Just when Ka has convinced everyone to go along with this plan that promises his escape with Ýpek, Z Demirkol, a shadowy character who pops up throughout the novel, throws it all off by showing Ka that both Ýpek and Kadife have long competed for Blue's love and have been Blue's lovers at different times.

"Orhan," who has come to investigate his friend's murder and find the twentieth poem, refuses to believe that Ka bears responsibility for Blue's death, considering it just another paranoid rumor circulating around the town. Searching for the truth, however, he participates more and more in the life of Kars, like Ka had and, like Ka, is soon drinking more and more, losing his own bearings in the world. Ultimately, he even declares his love for Ýpek, the night before leaving town without her—or the completed poem—just as had Ka.

During "Orhan's" visit, Necip's friend Fazil, who has married Kadife, refuses to be reduced to fiction and be misunderstood by any Western reader. When he confronts "Orhan" about this, the writer protests, but Fazil dismisses all reassurance, insisting that "Orhan" cannot help but render him as a caricature, demanding that "you let me speak directly to your readers." "Orhan" complies by depicting their exchange and recording that request, so at the end, instead of reality passing as fiction, fiction passes as reality.

However, it is impossible to capture reality. While the coup is taking place, and tanks are rumbling through the streets, people are watching a rerun of the stage show, for instance, instead of looking out their windows. They are trapped inside the accounts of things. Without truth, the attempt to explain anything takes characters around and around in endless circles, with everything inexplicable but predetermined. A newspaper is printed the day before, and not just because it is so heavily censored.

The future, like Sunay's assassination, can be predicted because the plot's symmetry makes the events unavoidable, with each event balanced by its opposites. In the end, Sunay, leading both the acting troupe and the coup, must die, just as Blue does—the first shot down on stage by Kadife, the second betrayed by Ka. Indeed, it is "Orhan's" ultimate recognition of this fatal balance, more than any concrete evidence, that convinces him of Ka's guilt.

In keeping with the symmetrical structure of a snowflake, the social life of Kars forms a frozen network of opposites—faith and apostasy, love and betrayal, individualism and conformism, East and West. For instance, American pornographic films featuring Melinda mirror the Mexican soap opera *Mariana*, fantasies of two different kinds of loves that people watch instead of finding love in their own lives. The plot of the novel is driven forward not so much by the interaction of all these forces as by the frantic activity of Ka rushing back and forth between the pairs like a spider on its web. It is impossible to establish a position that is not counterbalanced by another, so the characters cannot resolve the conflicts between opposites, whom they actually empower. On the other hand, the attempt to discuss and compromise immediately opens the door to doubt. With both relativism and rigidity impossible stances to maintain, the characters and readers remain suspended uncomfortably in between.

Though slow reading at times, *Snow* has considerable appeal as a satire of a paralyzed society in which political and social groups are either too weak or too fanatical. Locked in perpetual conflict, none of them can establish a nuanced stance or interact, except violently. Consequently, over the course of the novel, the dilemma of each character becomes bleaker, each caught between the violence of Islamic radicalism and government crackdowns. Some Western readers, often seeing themselves as the victims, may gain a more nuanced grasp of the conflict and the almost impossible situation in which the people of the Middle East find themselves.

*Philip McDermott*

## Review Sources

*Booklist* 100, nos. 19/20 (June 1, 2004): 1704.
*Kirkus Reviews* 72, no. 11 (June 1, 2004): 512.
*Library Journal* 129, no. 12 (July 15, 2004): 73.
*London Review of Books* 26, no. 15 (August 5, 2004): 30-32.
*New Statesman* 133 (May 10, 2004): 53-54.
*The New York Times*, August 10, 2004, p. E6.
*The New York Times Book Review* 153 (August 15, 2004): 1.
*The New Yorker* 80, no. 24 (August 30, 2004): 98-99.
*Newsweek* 144, no. 10 (September 6, 2004): 69.
*People* 62, no. 11 (September 13, 2004): 55.
*Publishers Weekly* 251, no. 29 (July 19, 2004): 144-145.

# SOMERSET MAUGHAM
## A Life

*Author:* Jeffrey Meyers (1939-    )
*Publisher:* Alfred A. Knopf (New York). Illustrated.
   411 pp. $30.00
*Type of work:* Literary biography
*Time:* 1874-1965
*Locale:* England, Germany, Spain, Malaya, Samoa, Ta-
   hiti, Russia, Cap Ferrat, New York, and South Carolina

*Meyers retells the story of the long, unhappy life of
writer W. Somerset Maugham*

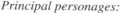

   *Principal personages:*
   WILLIAM SOMERSET MAUGHAM, English
      novelist, short-story writer, dramatist,
      essayist, most highly paid author of his time
   SYRIE BARNARDO WELLCOME, his wife, mother of his only child
   LIZA MAUGHAM, their daughter
   FREDERIC HERBERT MAUGHAM, Maugham's hostile brother, who rose to
      be lord chancellor
   ROBIN MAUGHAM, a nephew of Maugham
   GERALD HAXTON, Maugham's socially gifted but dissolute American
      companion for thirty years, the love of his life
   ALAN SEARLE, Haxton's successor, whom Maugham left a wealthy
      man

   Twenty-five years after Ted Morgan's definitive 1980 biography, and in three
hundred fewer pages, literary biographer Jeffrey Meyers has retold the story of
W. Somerset Maugham's life. Meyers, whose *Somerset Maugham: A Life* is his forty-
third book, told *Publishers Weekly* in 1995 that, "Speed is a big thing for me because
it lets me keep up a tremendous interest. I never get tired of what I do. I try to communicate this excitement to the reader. I write every day. I keep the pace up and never let
it drop." What one can anticipate in Meyers's work is exhaustive research, a readable style, and sound critical scholarship. Legions of readers have helped keep
Maugham's best books in print in the decades since his death; some, however, may be
displeased at how Meyers handles his subject in this work.
   "Maugham's homosexuality was well known but excited little comment in the tolerant literary world of London." So wrote Drew Middleton, veteran *New York Times*
writer, in a prominent sidebar to the paper's obituary of Maugham. So well did
Maugham guard the details of his sex life that an American academic, Richard
Cordell, who wrote the first book on Maugham in 1937 after the two had become well
enough acquainted to swap transatlantic visits, admitted he had known nothing of his
subject's sexual orientation.

~

*Jeffrey Meyers grew up in New York City, graduated from the University of Michigan, and received his doctorate from the University of California at Berkeley. He is the recipient of a Fulbright scholarship and a grant from the Guggenheim Foundation. He is the author of forty-three books, among them biographies of Joseph Conrad, F. Scott Fitzgerald, and Edmund Wilson.*

~

Once the word was out, Sanche de Gramont, an esteemed French journalist who changed his nationality to British and his name to Ted Morgan, became fascinated by the famous writer who had been born in Paris of English parents and spoke French as his first language until he was twelve. Morgan began unremitting research for the first full-scale biography with access to vital materials withheld on Maugham's orders by his literary executor. Morgan's 711-page volume was published in 1980 to acclaim that was, in part, prurient.

It is impossible to write of Meyers's book without referencing Morgan's. Meyers mentions his predecessor by name only once, although he lists fifty citations in endnotes. In three hundred fewer pages, Meyers follows Morgan's leads but, understandably, can add nothing significant. Although his admiration is as fervent, Meyers comes nowhere near as close to Maugham, the man whom novelist-biographer Victoria Glendinning, in her admiring review of Morgan's work, calls the Great Untouchable.

Morgan introduces his theme straightforwardly in his second chapter, while discussing Maugham's trials in school. "[Maugham's] homosexual inclinations had begun to show themselves at the King's School when his avoidance of participation in competitive games isolated him from his peer group. . . . He formed strong passions for boys who had the qualities he lacked."

Meyers concludes his opening chapter by trying to link Willie Maugham's schoolboy intimations of bisexuality with the overriding themes of duality, the problems of identity and selfhood. Scant evidence becomes no evidence when, in chapter 2, describing Maugham's medical training in London, Meyers egregiously comments that the young trainee "took every opportunity to practice giving enemas to his fellow students."

So dominant is homosexuality as his book's cohering theme that Meyers deploys it to summarize five of his first eight chapters. Chapter 2 dutifully records not only the five years at St. Thomas Hospital but also two earlier years of study in Germany, where at age seventeen Maugham came under the influence of his first lover, John Ellington Brooks, a brilliant dilettante ten years his senior. Meyers concludes with overconfident concision:

"[Maugham's] medical training destroyed his religious belief; but it . . . taught him to . . . adopt a cool, objective and clinical point of view. His emergent homosexuality . . . forced him to become reticent and secretive." However, Meyers earlier, and in similar buzzwords, cites Maugham's stammer as the force that "intensified his introspection, turned him away from people and toward his artistic vocation."

As is the case with many so afflicted, the stammer disappeared when Maugham was at ease. As for Maugham's homosexuality, there was apparently no rest. In chapter 4,

Meyers ushers the reader into the new century, seeing the "struggling author" at thirty as one whose "willed ambition" to succeed as a writer of plays about socio-sexual matters requires him to be "more careful than ever to conceal his own sexual life."

At the end of chapter 7, leading into a ten-page account of Maugham's work as a liaison agent in World War I counterespionage in Russia and elsewhere, Meyers contends that "[Maugham's] homosexuality, like that of the traitors Guy Burgess and Anthony Blunt, had taught him to be an undercover agent in both his life and his work." Such hemstitching of homosexuality into every aspect of his subject's life leads to overkill.

Writing in *The New Yorker* of the homosexuality of W. H. Auden and Stephen Spender, V. S . Naipaul declares that any mandate to formulate man as a sexual being "is breathtakingly reductive. . . . The ratio of one's sexual activity to other pursuits— say, earning a living, driving a car—is dismal even in one's prime."

Nothing is more pressing for a literary biographer who chooses to give primacy to his subject's homosexuality than to demonstrate how the "deviate" novelist—the term E. M. Forster favored—expresses that persuasion in his works. "Over the years," Meyers announces, "Maugham had found oblique ways to write about homosexual themes and characters." In the sense of "oblique" as signifying something deviously achieved, Meyers far surpasses Maugham.

"The Kite" (1947) is one of Maugham's most poignant stories because it is built on recent experience rather than culled from old notes. The story's narrator, Ned Preston (a stand-in for Alan Searle, Maugham's caretaker-companion), describes the character of young Herbert Sunbury, who marries a woman who interferes with his kite-flying. He returns to his parents, and she destroys his best kite. Meyers views "The Kite" as revealing a hidden theme—Herbert's latent homosexuality—which, according to Meyers, Maugham reveals in sexual language: "[He] sometimes panted . . . [and] couldn't get it up. . . . He doted on [the kite]. . . . It was grand to see that little black thing soaring so sweetly, but even as he watched it, he thought of the great big one. . . . In some queer way . . . " Meyers insists that "the soaring kite stands for the unfettered pursuit [by Maugham] of his own sexual destiny." He tries to reinforce his far-fetched theory by joining all the suggestive quotes with ellipses to make them appear consecutive. In the text, however, they are widely separated. The charming story soars on its own, beyond contrivance.

Meyers taught literature at the University of Colorado and at the University of California at Berkeley before devoting himself wholly to writing in the early 1990's. In *Homosexuality and Literature* (1977), a pioneering book on the subject, he demonstrates that authors such as Oscar Wilde, André Gide, Thomas Mann, Marcel Proust, Joseph Conrad, and Forster had to turn to the language of reticence and evasion to convey taboo themes, notably homosexuality. What worked for Meyers in the earlier book is doomed to failure in the present volume, for two reasons. First, Maugham died two years before Britain's decriminalization in 1967 of same-gender sex behavior. He remained covert in his life and in his writings. Second, Maugham was what Northrop Frye labels a "low mimetic" writer, meaning one whose style rarely lends itself to ambiguity.

If Maugham's homosexuality is to be inferred from Mildred's androgyny in *Of Human Bondage* (1915)—her boyish flat-chestedness—as one British critic averred in 1992—or ratified in *The Narrow Corner* (1932) from his rapturous description of the androgynous Chinese servant Ah Kay, as Meyers believes, what are readers to infer about William Faulkner from his lush descriptions of Eula Varner in the Snopes trilogy? Essayist Joseph Epstein quotes one of his students in a seminar on Henry James as suggesting there ought to be a statute of limitations on discovery of homosexuality in literature. Such a statute could be applied to biographers.

There are many fine things in Meyers's book. He is superb in finding literary and biographical kinships, respectively, between Maugham and Conrad and George Orwell. Meyers is the first to give full credit to the experience-based spy stories in *Ashenden: Or, The British Agent* (1928) for their acknowledged influence on Graham Greene and John le Carré. His segments on Maugham's Villa Mauresque and its "little Louvre" riches, the intrigue of his portrait-sittings, and the ferreting out from fictional characters their life models are all well handled.

Meyers has retraced Maugham's life story responsibly but without ardor, from Maugham's loss, at age eight, of his mother through the Paris years and the wandering years to his opulent dotage at the Villa Mauresque. The biographer sounds the long roll of peer admirers, from Theodore Dreiser to Orwell, and also of Wilson's cruel dismissal, in which Meyers favors Maugham. However, the biographer is too involved with the cult of personality to convey what he must know well; namely, Maugham's falling afoul of the prevailing mode in both prose and poetry during his most productive years: the elevation of text over temper, complexity over humanity, the artful over the life-affirming.

Meyers writes powerfully of his subject's devotion to the dissolute, American-born Gerald Haxton, the male love of his life, and of actress Sue Jones, who turned Maugham down but became the model for the unforgettable Rosie of *Cakes and Ale* (1930). He chronicles the disastrous marriage and the daughter Maugham tried to disown at the end of his life in a shaming attempt to adopt and enrich Searle, his always-faithful, always-maligned caretaker.

Reproached by Wilson and others for lacking a personal style (such that when one reads a page one knows at once who the author is), Maugham offered a riposte: Having "mannerisms" is just what he tries to avoid. After writing his last book at eighty-four and claiming he was glad to step down, Maugham repeated an old refrain: The critic for whom he was waiting was the one who would "inquire into what qualities my work must have to interest such vast numbers of people in so many countries." That critic has not emerged. What remains steadfast are the novels and stories.

*Richard Hauer Costa*

## Review Sources

*Booklist* 100, no. 12 (February 15, 2004): 1019.
*The Economist* 370 (March 6, 2004): 75.
*Kirkus Reviews* 71, no. 24 (December 15, 2003): 1440.
*Library Journal* 129, no. 3 (February 15, 2004): 126.
*The New York Review of Books* 51, no. 20 (December 16, 2004): 72.
*The New York Times Book Review* 153 (March 14, 2004): 9.
*Publishers Weekly* 251, no. 2 (January 12, 2004): 48.
*The Times Literary Supplement*, June 18, 2004, p. 28.

# SOMETHING ROTTEN

*Author:* Jasper Fforde (1961-    )
*Publisher:* Viking Press (New York). 310 pp. $25.00
*Type of work:* Novel
*Time:* The 1980's
*Locale:* Swindon, England

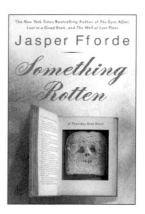

*In his fourth installment of the exploits of literary detective Thursday Next, Fforde returns Thursday from BookWorld to Swindon, where she once more attempts to restore her husband to reality, save the world from ultimate destruction by winning a croquet match, and find child care for her son, Friday*

> *Principal characters:*
> THURSDAY NEXT, a literary detective working in SpecOps, a special enforcement division responsible for solving literary crimes
> FRIDAY NEXT, her infant son
> LANDEN PARKE-LAINE, her husband, who was eradicated by the Goliath Corporation in an earlier book
> GRANNY NEXT, an elderly woman who cannot die until she has read the ten most boring books
> JOFFY NEXT, Thursday's brother and a pastor in the Global Standard Deity religion
> MYCROFT and POLLY NEXT, Thursday's uncle and aunt
> WEDNESDAY NEXT, Thursday's mother
> COLONEL NEXT, Thursday's father and member of the ChronoGuard, an elite police agency responsible for maintaining temporal stability
> PICKWICK, Thursday's pet dodo bird
> HAMLET, prince of Denmark, masquerading as Thursday's cousin Eddie
> YORRICK KAINE, a fictional character who has leaped into the real world and is attempting to become dictator of England
> BARTHOLOMEW STIGGINS, a reengineered Neanderthal and SpecOps agent
> BOWDEN CABLE, Thursday's partner at the Swindon Literary Detectives
> SPIKE STOKER, SpecOps operative, responsible for vampires and werewolves
> CINDY STOKER, Spike's wife, and an assassin known as "The Windowmaker"
> ST. ZVLKX, a thirteenth century saint whose prophecies often come true

In Jasper Fforde's fourth installment of the Thursday Next series, the literary detective returns to the real world, known as the Outland, from her stint as the BookWorld Bellman, the person in charge of the policing agency inside books whose task it is to maintain story lines within fiction, known as Jurisfiction. As a single mother (her husband having been eradicated in the second book of the series), Thursday has her hands full. Not only does she have her son, Friday, to care for, she also has her pet dodo bird, Pickwick, and Hamlet, the prince of Denmark, in tow.

Like the earlier books in the series, *Something Rotten* is set in Swindon, England, in the 1980's; however, this is a very different England from the one with which readers may be familiar and a very different 1980's from those that readers may remember. In this alternate reality, Wales is a socialist republic; croquet has the cachet of world-league soccer; fictional characters leap out of books, and real characters leap into them; dirigibles ply the sky rather than airplanes; extinct species such as dodos and Neanderthals have been genetically reengineered; and members of the ChronoGuard slip in and out of the time stream.

∿

*Jasper Fforde is the author of the Thursday Next series, comprising* The Eyre Affair *(2001),* Lost in a Good Book *(2002),* The Well of Lost Plots *(2003), and* Something Rotten. *Before writing his first book, he worked as a focus puller in the film industry. Fforde lives in Wales.*

∿

The wildly imaginative alternative reality and plot structures can be very confusing for the uninitiated reader, and the fourth book of the series is probably not the place to start an exploration into Thursday's world. Rather, a first-time reader ought to look up *The Eyre Affair* (2001) and read the other books sequentially to follow the complicated construction of a strange, yet oddly cohesive, alternate world.

For readers who have already met Thursday and her gang, however, *Something Rotten* offers another foray into a familiar, albeit wacky, landscape. The book picks up where *The Well of Lost Plots* (2003) closes. As *Something Rotten* opens, Thursday is still the Bellman and is still in BookWorld, tracking the escaped Minotaur by following a series of custard-pie-throwing incidents occurring unexpectedly in a number of Westerns. When Emperor Zhark comes to the rescue of Thursday and Colonel Bradshaw, destroying most of the book they are in, Thursday decides that she has had enough of the BookWorld and wants to return to Swindon, her home, and begin anew her search for her eradicated husband, Landen Parke-Laine.

The Council of Genres, however, refuses to accept Thursday's resignation and gives her a leave of absence instead, instructing her to deal with escaped fictional character Yorrick Kaine, who is trying to become dictator of England in the Outland. In addition, Thursday finds herself saddled with Hamlet, prince of Denmark, who is concerned that he is not being interpreted properly in the Outland. To complicate matters further, Thursday must find ways to provide child care for her son, including importing Mrs. Bradshaw (a dress-wearing gorilla married to the colonel) from the BookWorld.

The plot then branches in several directions. In one subplot, Thursday works toward reactualizing her husband by approaching the Goliath Corporation, which has now become a "faith-based corporate-management system" complete with "Apologaria," places where people who have been wronged by Goliath can go to receive apologies. In one such visit, Thursday encounters her former nemesis, Jack Schitt, and ultimately recovers her husband, although Landen flickers in and out of the time line for several chapters.

In a second subplot, Thursday tries to avoid being assassinated by the notorious hit woman known as the Windowmaker. In reality, the assassin is Cindy Stoker, mother of an infant child and wife of Thursday's friend Spike. Spike and Cindy's roles in the novel turn out to be crucial to the climactic ending.

Another branch of the plot occurs because of Hamlet's sojourn to the Outland. While Hamlet has been gone from BookWorld, his lover Ophelia has taken control of the play *Hamlet, Prince of Denmark* (pr. c. 1600-1601), turning it into a conglomeration of *The Merry Wives of Windsor* (pr. 1597) and the Polonius family called "The Merry Wives of Elsinore." Thursday must scramble to find a William Shakespeare clone in the Outland to rescue the play from Ophelia's crazed rewriting. In a further twist to this plot, Stiggins, the Neanderthal, helps Thursday find the place where both Shakespeares and Neanderthals were cloned. For Stiggins, this discovery may mean that the Neanderthals will be able to reproduce.

Meanwhile, Yorrick Kaine fans anti-Danish sentiment across the country, leading to the burning of books and persecution of all things Danish. As a result, Hamlet must pose as Thursday's cousin Eddie to avoid problems. Later, Thursday identifies the source of Kaine's frantic anti-Danish pogrom: Kaine is a fictional character from Danish writer Daphne Farquitt's romance novel "At Long Last Lust." By burning Danish books, Kaine hopes to eradicate all copies of the book where he belongs and thus prevent anyone from sending him back into fiction.

The return of St. Zvlkx, Swindon's patron saint, causes additional plot trauma for Thursday. St. Zvlkx speaks only Old English, and Fforde assigns him a different font from the rest of the text to mark this. The thirteenth century monk is known for his prophecies, which usually come true. One such prophecy is that the terrible Swindon croquet team, the Mallets, will win the SuperHoop competition. Although there is virtually no chance of this happening, Thursday's father, a member of the ChronoGuard, appears to Thursday and informs her that if the Mallets do not win the SuperHoop, the entire world will be destroyed in a thermonuclear explosion. Thursday, a former croquet player herself, becomes the manager of the Mallets and recruits a band of Neanderthals to play for Swindon. Yorrick Kaine and Goliath Corporation, however, try to sabotage the game for the Mallets by threatening their players. In order to have any chance at all, Thursday must take the field herself. The results of the game fulfill prophecy and place Thursday in mortal danger.

Fforde adds a final twist to the book with a scene between Thursday and Granny Next. A neat little surprise, the meeting between the young woman and the old is both touching and complicated as streams of time intersect and diverge from each other.

In addition to his signature plot gyrations, Fforde loads the book with puns, double entendres, literary inside jokes, and cameo appearances from some of literature's most famous characters. "The Cat formerly known as Cheshire" and Mrs. Tiggywinkle make frequent appearances, as does the historical character Admiral Horatio Lord Nelson in the midst of the Battle of Trafalgar. In a nod to both the television series *Buffy the Vampire Slayer* and Bram Stoker, the original author of *Dracula*, Fforde names Thursday's friend who heads the SpecOps division concerned with vampires Spike Stoker. Fforde also references George Eliot in the naming of Thursday's stalker, Millon de Floss. In a less literary example of Fforde's punning. the commander of the Swindon SpecOps Network is called Braxton Hicks.

Further, Hamlet provides some of the book's funnier moments. Angry with psychiatrist Sigmund Freud for suggesting anything improper in his relationship with his mother, Hamlet fills his days in the Outland watching film versions of his play and offers this critique before returning to BookWorld: "I liked [Mel] Gibson's because it has the least amount of dithering, Orson [Welles] because he did it with the best voice, [John] Gielgud for the ease in which he placed himself within the role and [Derek] Jacobi for his passion. By the way, have you heard of this [Kenneth] Branagh fellow? . . . I've got a feeling his Hamlet will be stupendous."

At its best moments, *Something Rotten* provides tongue-in-cheek social commentary, postmodern literary humor, and, at times, comments on literary theory. For example, Thursday explains to Hamlet why there are so many interpretations of any piece of literature, suggesting "the reader does most of the work." In a clearly stated summary of reader response theory, Thursday says, "Because every reader's experiences are different, each book is unique for each reader. . . . In fact, I'd argue that every time a book is read by the same person it is different again—because the reader's experiences have changed, or he is in a different frame of mind."

In its weaker moments, however, the book drags; there is a limit, after all, to the number of puns per page even the most patient reader can endure or the number of wild plot turns a reader will follow. Nevertheless, even at its lowest points, the book remains enjoyable. That this is so is largely because of Fforde's heroine, Thursday. In spite of the silliness, in spite of the crazy twisting plot, Thursday is utterly believable in a fully unbelievable universe. She is strong without being overbearing, smart without being smug, and true to her husband without being sentimental. She is a young woman who, quite simply and most endearingly, loves her family and her friends. Her understanding of and love for the Neanderthals, for example, demonstrate both tolerance and compassion; her steadfast devotion to her husband and son suggest both loyalty and strength. Most of all, Thursday is unflinchingly willing to take on tasks, no matter how dangerous or unpleasant, because they just need to be done for the welfare of the world. In the BookWorld or in the Outland, such a character is a treasure.

*Diane Andrews Henningfeld*

## Review Sources

*Booklist* 100, no. 21 (July 1, 2004): 1797.
*Entertainment Weekly*, August 6, 2004, p. 85.
*The New York Times*, August 5, 2004, p. E9.
*People* 62, no. 8 (August 23, 3004): 49.
*Publishers Weekly* 251, no. 33 (August 16, 2004): 44.
*School Library Journal* 50, no. 11 (November, 2004): 176.
*Time* 164, no. 5 (August 2, 2004): 80.
*The Washington Post*, August 15, 2004, p. T07.

# SONATA FOR JUKEBOX
## Pop Music, Memory, and the Imagined Life

*Author:* Geoffrey O'Brien (1948-    )
*Publisher:* Counterpoint Press (New York). 328 pp.
  $27.50
*Type of work:* Memoir

*The author, a poet and critic with a strong musical heritage and background, here traces the evolution and impact of recorded music in the twentieth century, drawing frequently upon his own recollections and reactions*

"This is a book written in the presence of music," observes Geoffrey O'Brien in the opening sentence of *Sonata for Jukebox*, an arresting, occasionally frustrating, and perhaps overlong rumination on the relationship between recorded music and the listener. Before long, it becomes clear that O'Brien's has been a life lived in the presence of music, almost from the moment of birth. By that time, in 1948, his father, Joe O'Brien, had risen from the status of journeyman radio announcer to that of minor celebrity as the early-morning disc jockey on New York's WMCA, heard by commuters throughout the tri-state area. Geoffrey's mother, Maggie, a stage actress and amateur pianist, was the daughter of a former small-time bandleader in eastern Pennsylvania. That gentleman, Bob Owens, known to his grandsons as Pop, figures prominently in O'Brien's early recollections, both for his presence and for his fleeting role in musical history.

During the early years of the Depression, Owens toured towns and colleges throughout the region with his optimistically billed Rainbow Club Orchestra, receiving ample publicity through live radio broadcasts. As O'Brien explains, there was no Rainbow Club, and the ten band members were, like Owens, blue-collar moonlighters. Money was always tight, and despite the radio exposure, no recordings were ever made of the Rainbow Club music. After a few years, O'Brien observes with an early hint of his sometimes overblown style, "They disappeared into that limbo where unrecorded dance bands play without interruption for the ghosts of the unremembered." By the time of his grandson's earliest memories, Pop was well into his sixties but always formally dressed, giving occasional piano lessons and mainly amusing himself at the keyboard. His story, told in the third chapter of *Sonata for Jukebox*, will reverberate throughout the volume, serving as a kind of cautionary tale for what is to follow. O'Brien is careful to note that Owens was born within two years after Thomas Edison's invention of the phonograph in 1887, underscoring the irony of the fact that his music, diffused by the later technological marvel of radio, was not to profit from the earlier invention of records.

Indeed, it is the twentieth century phenomenon of recorded music (the earliest recordings cited by O'Brien date from 1898) that informs both the theme and the title of

*Sonata for Jukebox*. Music, of course, has no doubt existed longer than history, but until Edison's invention began to take root, it was primarily a collective phenomenon, performed either by a group or by a soloist before an audience. Only after 1900 did the concept of the solitary listener become a possibility, and later a reality. Throughout the essays merged into *Sonata for Jukebox*, O'Brien explores the interactive potential of "canned" music, the possibility and extent of listener participation. In an early chapter, he recalls his earliest awakenings to sound and noise, some of which turned out to be music, either broadcast on the radio or played by

*Geoffrey O'Brien is a poet and prose writer whose other books include* The Phantom Empire *(1993),* The Browser's Ecstasy *(2000), and* Dream Time: Chapters from the Sixties *(1988). He has been honored with a Whiting Award and contributes regularly to* The New York Review of Books, Artforum, Film Comment, *and other journals. He is editor-in-chief of* The Library of America.

his two older brothers. The setting was a large house on the north shore of Long Island, a house strewn with musical instruments, records, and sheet music. In a prose style that swings between the poetic and the "purple," at times lapsing into obscurity, O'Brien muses upon what might be called the "aesthetics of reception" with regard to music, frequently citing his own experience and recollections. The result is a thought-provoking inquiry into the role of music in modern society and its possible effects, whether intended or not, upon individual lives.

Although addressed to the general reader, *Sonata for Jukebox* frequently assumes a level of musical "literacy" beyond the range of the average listener, and at times O'Brien risks losing the attention of readers too young to share his memories of certain songs in their temporal setting. His basic premise, however, is that the phenomenon of recorded music has somehow managed to "freeze time" into an eternal present. In certain cases, the performers cited are still alive but have retired or moved on to other projects; what remains, however, is the voice frozen in time, accessible as memory to the solitary listener.

It is significant that O'Brien tends to treat recorded songs as an organic whole, melody and lyrics taken together: In the opening chapter, an extended essay on the music and musical fortunes of composer Burt Bacharach, O'Brien opens the question of how Bacharach's music might have evolved without the urbane lyrics of Hal David or the interpretive skills of Dionne Warwick. His keenest observations and insights, however, deal with those who write and perform their own music, such as James Taylor, the Beatles, and the Beach Boys, whose works have become an integral part of his own memory.

In keeping with the book's title, *Sonata for Jukebox* is divided into three parts, "Exposition," "Development," and "Recapitulation," each consisting of five chapters. "Exposition" begins with the essay on Bacharach, moving forward through the author's childhood and his accounts of his grandfather's dance band and his father's career in radio, ending with an extended essay on Harry Smith's *Anthology of American Folk Music* (1952), an album of songs originally recorded "outside the mainstream" some twenty or thirty years earlier. Some of the performers, such as Uncle

Dave Macon, Dock Boggs, and the Carter Family, were then still alive and would benefit from Smith's "rediscovery." More significant, however, was the diversity of the recordings, a diversity that would, in time, reshape the "mainstream" itself.

"Development" begins in the early 1960's with the author's adolescence and the "top 40" songs played over the air by his father and other disc jockeys, moving on to O'Brien's personal experience of Beatlemania which, he says, began with a screening of *A Hard Day's Night* (1964). Subsequent chapters deal with the O'Brien family's move from Long Island back into Manhattan, specifically to a spacious apartment on Central Park West, coincidentally the title of a 1960 instrumental "ballad" recorded by John Coltrane. It was there that the O'Briens literally played out their musical destiny: Eldest brother Bob had married and moved on to a career in music publishing, and middle brother Joel would move in and out of the apartment as he tried out for a place in one or another rock band. Father Joe, meanwhile, increasingly felt the pressure of the expanding music business on his own career in radio. Music was still very much in the air as young Geoffrey developed a crush on a beautiful, troubled young classmate identified only as Susie, a girl who reminded him of songs which, in turn, reminded him of her.

As the narrative progresses, the reader learns of other songs, and other boys, attached to Susie, whose enigmatic presence seemed to inspire the writing of songs about her. During the same time span, brother Joel formed a band called the Kingbees, which disbanded after their first recording failed to reach the charts. Several of its members would form a new band around a young songwriter named James, newly arrived in New York, a friend of the guitarist. Susie would, between bouts of depression, followed by parental intervention and psychotherapy, form a strong bond with the songwriter, in whom she found a kind of soul mate. With the skill and cunning of an accomplished writer of mysteries, O'Brien interweaves his narrative of the music and the girl, building toward the climax of the girl's long-threatened suicide followed by "the song that did, finally, inevitably, get written about her." Although no surname is given, it is clear that James is none other than James Taylor and that Susie is the Susanne of "Fire and Rain." What O'Brien has done in this instance is to invite the reader's participation much as, in his view, popular music invites the participation of the listener.

O'Brien's third grouping, "Recapitulation," begins with a letter to a possibly imaginary, but probably real, former girlfriend appropriately named Rhonda, with whom he shared his experience of the Beach Boys and their unexpectedly groundbreaking music. What follows is a detailed, incisive analysis of Brian Wilson's evolution and accomplishments as singer and songwriter, together with an appreciation of music as an experience shared between lovers. A subsequent chapter, titled "The Rabbi's Playlist," explores the concept of the solitary listener, even when there is another person in the room. The "rabbi" was O'Brien's secret name for a friend whom he first met in college, and whose "Talmudic" approach to scholarship in casual conversation earned him that sobriquet. In the early 1970's, the heyday of Dave Loggins, Maria Muldaur, and the Eagles, O'Brien and the rabbi found themselves living in bachelor quarters a few blocks apart in New York City.

Displeased by the trends then current in popular music, the two friends would trade recordings and grievances, deliberately seeking the arcane or even the accidental, such as unseemly crowd noise on a live concert album. "Even between close friends," O'Brien recalls, "a darkness surrounded the act of listening." In time, the rabbi would retreat further and deeper into that darkness until he, like the doomed Susanne, would take his own life. O'Brien closes the chapter with a note to his friend, beyond the grave, informing him of what has happened on Earth—in politics, movies and, of course, music—since his untimely departure. The next chapter, "The Year of Overthrowal," takes the reader to 1979, with political upheaval taking place around the world against a background of protest music. The shah of Iran had been deposed, as had Idi Amin, Jean-Bédel Bokassa, Anastasio Somoza Garcia, and several other dictators. O'Brien's final chapters follow the development, diversity, and dispersal of music worldwide up to the end of the twentieth century, with the observation that "Hell is an oldies station that cannot be tuned out." In a brief coda, however, O'Brien recalls the final hours of his mother's life, playing off sound against silence. As Maggie's life draws to a close, the retired actress notes that no music can be heard in a house normally filled with it and asks that a record be played. Several hours later, family and friends gather around a table in a house atop a mountain to meditate upon life and death, and before long the people all start singing, show tunes, dance tunes, whatever comes to mind. Music, remembered from recordings, again comes alive as a counterpoise to silence and death—but only when shared by live voices.

Faulted by several reviewers for its idiosyncratic structure and occasionally overblown style, *Sonata for Jukebox* nonetheless amply repays close reading for its thoughtful examination of the phenomenon of recorded music and its keen insights into the potential of listener response. For those interested primarily in the facts, or in the history of popular music, there is no shortage of available sources, most of which are listed in O'Brien's exhaustive bibliography.

*David B. Parsell*

## Review Sources

*Kirkus Reviews* 72, no. 2 (January 15, 2004): 73.
*Los Angeles Times*, April 25, 2004, p. R8.
*The Nation* 278, no. 19 (May 17, 2004): 29.
*The New Yorker* 80, no. 17 (June 28, 2004): 105.
*Newsday*, March 14, 2004, p. C36.
*Publishers Weekly* 251, no. 6 (February 9, 2004): 73.

# SONTAG AND KAEL
## Opposites Attract Me

*Author:* Craig Seligman
*Publisher:* Counterpoint Press (New York). 251 pp.
 $23.00
*Type of work:* Literary criticism
*Time:* From the 1960's to the 1990's
*Locale:* New York City

*Seligman compares the styles and concerns of Susan Sontag, an eminent essayist, and Pauline Kael, an influential film critic, showing how these very different writers deal with art and society in the popular and high culture*

As Craig Seligman's subtitle suggests, his counterpointing of Susan Sontag and Pauline Kael is a personal choice. There is no particular reason that these two writers demand this kind of treatment in a book, except that they have profoundly influenced this critic, who chooses to write about them. Kael became a friend of Seligman, and his prose is liveliest when he portrays his memories of her. Seligman makes a point of emphasizing that he never met Sontag (who died in late 2004) and did not invite such an encounter, although it could have been easily arranged. Sontag stands in Seligman's consciousness as an aloof figure whose remoteness enhances her power and authority as a writer but also blinds her to the personal implications of some of her arguments.

Seligman not only realizes that Sontag and Kael are very different kinds of writers, but his book also implies that a proper critical consciousness ought to encompass— even if it cannot reconcile—their quite different approaches to art. Kael is at her best discussing individual films, allowing her critical criteria to arise out of the individual works on which she comments. Sontag, on the other hand, rarely focused on individual works of art in any significant detail. She tended to take a much broader view of art in its cultural context. Indeed, she shied away from the term "critic," as she did not see it as her task to judge works of art but rather to evoke their resonance. Her famous essay "Against Interpretation" exhorts critics to probe the sensuous properties of art and the forms that artists create rather than dissecting art for its content or message. Kael, however, derived great energy from praising and condemning films. Where these two writers are alike, perhaps, and where Seligman sees a convergence, is in the very enthusiasm for art that each writer, in her different way, is able to convey.

Perhaps because Seligman had not met Sontag, his view of her seems reverential. Whereas Kael appears in delightful anecdotes that capture her everyday affect as a person, Sontag remains distant and pristine. Indeed, any view that might shatter his iconic image of Sontag is treated with disdain. She is not beyond literary criticism— indeed Seligman surveys her faults—but any inspection of her motivations alarms him: "The charge that Sontag has used her beauty to further her career is drivel; the essays collected in *Against Interpretation* would have made a warthog famous. But she *has* used her beauty, and in the right way: to make herself interesting photographically."

Later on, Seligman reveals that in making such statements, he has in mind a certain "hostile, inept biography," *Susan Sontag: The Making of an Icon* (2001), by Carl Rollyson and Lisa Paddock, the title of which he fails to mention in order to make the point that its "single selling point was its documentation of her love affairs." The singular weakness of Seligman's book is that it does not take into account the considerable body of critical commentary that shows how she merged her iconic status with her role as cultural commentator. Some of this commentary is indeed hostile to Sontag, but much of it admires the way in which she fused her person and her work while maintaining the high quality of her perceptions and her prose.

∽

*Craig Seligman was educated at Stanford and Oxford Universities. He has been an editor at* The New Yorker, Food and Wine, *and* Salon *and has written criticism for a wide variety of publications, including the* San Francisco Examiner *(where he was a staff film and book critic in the 1980's),* The New Yorker, Salon, The New Republic, The Threepenny Review, The Village Voice, Artforum, Bookforum, *and* The New York Times Book Review.

∽

Seligman's treatment of Kael is more down-to-earth. Perhaps because of his friendship with Kael, he does not seem to be troubled—indeed he does not seem to notice—that like Sontag, Kael had to negotiate her way through the demands of art and commerce, writing, most of the time, for weekly deadlines set by *The New Yorker*.

The idea that Sontag is, in part, the creation of commerce enrages Seligman, who wants to view her in purely literary terms. Biographies that actually show writers engaged in career-making—Marion Meade's *Bobbed Hair and Bathtub Gin* (2004) is an excellent analysis of the business of writing—are apt to be dismissed as vulgar because writers are shown to have mixed motivations. They want to write well and be famous. Somehow such a formula, Seligman supposes, detracts from treating Sontag as a serious writer.

Seligman writes as though Sontag made a contribution to the history of photography by allowing herself to be photographed in provocative poses producing shots often resembling film stills. He also thinks there is something peculiarly honest about Sontag's self-advertising. She shows her age proudly, he asserts. Yet he does not mention those windblown, misty photographs of Sontag in which Annie Leibovitz specializes. How can Seligman ignore the way Sontag turned herself into a cult figure?

Seligman introduces Kael as the anti-Sontag. She is a good antidote to doses of a lofty writer who is a proselytizer for high art. Like many critics, Seligman seems uncomfortable with the Sontag who repudiates her essays of the 1960's, turning instead to historical fiction, a very conventional—indeed conservative form of art—and openly questioning her earlier appetite for what she came to regard as avant garde silliness.

Seligman seems embarrassed by Sontag's politics, especially as her harsh condemnations of her native country and her touting of so many communist regimes were so at odds with her sophisticated literary judgments. So he tries to have it both ways—first criticizing her and then seeking to soften the blow:

> To take a hard line about it: to the extent that she supported these absolutist societies, she participated in some of the conduct she most abhors, the persecution of dissident artists and intellectuals. To put it more generously, she recapitulated the progress of many earlier American Stalinists, from blindness to disillusion—or, more generously still, to enlightenment.

Why, though, did Sontag have this craving to recapitulate the blunders of an earlier generation of leftists? Seligman does not ask, let alone answer, such a question.

Even while trying to favor Sontag as a better writer than Kael, Seligman admits that readers of an early draft of his book asked why he hated her so much. His ambivalent fixation on Sontag is reminiscent of William Faulkner's Quentin Compson, who obsessively repeats in *Absalom, Absalom!* (1936) that he does not hate the South. The best Seligman can do to explain Sontag's many reversals of opinion, her evasive uses of the passive voice that allow her to slip free of responsibility for the statements she makes, is to call her a contrarian and an intellectual worrier who is always of two minds about any topic—for example, lauding Leni Riefenstahl, director of the Nazi epic *Triumph des Willens* (1935; *Triumph of the Will*), in one decade and denouncing her in the next.

Seligman turns away from such tortured reasoning—which is familiar to anyone versed in the literature about Sontag's work—to the ebullient and amusing Kael (like so many Sontag admirers, he has to admit his icon has no sense of humor). Here is a critic who worked hard every week and did not make a show of agonizing over sentences. Here is a critic who took on all comers, relishing films good and bad because she was so enraptured with the medium itself.

Kael, Seligman recognizes, is an Aristotelian whose views of art evolved from her concrete responses as a reviewer meeting a deadline. Over many decades she created a body of work that has the richness of a novel, he claims, with a cast of characters and a sense of drama that will, Seligman predicts, become a part of the literary canon. It seems much too early to make such judgments, especially when he makes extravagant claims for Sontag while denouncing most of her critics as "pygmies."

Seligman announces that he is gay and expresses sadness that Sontag did not come out of the closet until very late in her career. He fails to mention that she began to discuss her sexuality only after *Susan Sontag: The Making of an Icon* brought up the topic. The irony that he could not be having his say about Sontag's sexuality and its relationship to her work without the services of biography seems to escape Seligman. Indeed, the only biographical source that he takes seriously is Sontag herself.

Curiously, Kael herself provided Seligman with an attitude toward Sontag that he steadfastly refuses to address. When Sontag praised Jack Smith's film *Flaming Creatures* (1963) for "a sensibility based on indiscriminateness, without ideas, beyond negation," Kael "snorted"—to use Seligman's word—"I think in treating indiscriminateness as a *value*, she has become a real swinger." As Seligman reports, Kael believed Sontag was betraying the "standards the critic is supposed to be laboring to uphold." Indeed, if Sontag went on in this fashion, Kael concluded, "it's the end of criticism—at the very least." Yet Seligman immediately changes the topic and begins dealing with Sontag's moral earnestness—a non sequitur that suggests Seligman cannot or will not grasp Kael's point. He seems to think that she is being ironic.

Kael found Sontag unreadable, Seligman has to admit. "It took me many dutiful bursts of effort over a two-week period to get through Susan Sontag's essay on pornography, and when I finally thought I'd grasped it, it evaporated," Kael told Seligman. Yet all he has to say about her comment is that it was a "lapse of taste." He does not even seem curious as to why Kael reacted so negatively.

It is unfortunate that Seligman did not treat Sontag to the same searching and perceptive comments that distinguish his discussion of Kael's film criticism—but then, he does not want to know Susan Sontag in that intimate way. As a result, Sontag tends to dominate this book—in large part because Seligman shies away from exploring so many of her paradoxes and flip-flops.

*Lisa Paddock*

## Review Sources

*The Atlantic Monthly*, July/August 2004, p. 159.
*Booklist* 100, no. 13 (March 1, 2004): 1130.
*Harper's Magazine*, May, 2004, pp. 85-86.
*Kirkus Reviews* 72, no. 5 (March 1, 2004): 214.
*Library Journal* 129, no. 8 (May 1, 2004): 108.
*The New York Times Book Review* 153 (May 30, 2004): 7.
*San Francisco Chronicle*, June 1, 2004, p. E1.

# SOUL MADE FLESH
## The Discovery of the Brain—and How It Changed the World

*Author:* Carl Zimmer (1966-      )
*Publisher:* The Free Press (New York). Illustrated.
   367 pp. $26.00
*Type of work:* History, medicine, and science
*Time:* 1543-1675
*Locale:* England

   *The life and groundbreaking discoveries of English scientist and physician Thomas Willis, today considered the founder of modern neurology, set against a turbulent backdrop of plague, civil war, and the Great Fire of London*

The Discovery of the Brain—
and How It Changed the World

CARL   ZIMMER
Author of Evolution: The Triumph of an Idea

   *Principal personages:*
   THOMAS WILLIS, anatomist and physician
   ROBERT BOYLE, Irish-born natural philosopher and chemist
   WILLIAM HARVEY, physician
   ROBERT HOOKE, physicist and author
   RICHARD LOWER, physiologist, junior partner of Willis
   JOHN WALLIS, mathematician
   CHRISTOPHER WREN, architect and medical illustrator

   Throughout most of recorded history, the relative status of the human heart and the human brain was clear and mostly unquestioned. An observer at an ancient Egyptian embalming ceremony, for instance, would have seen the priests use a hooklike tool to perfunctorily scrape out the cadaver's brain through the nose and then pack the resulting empty skull with clean cloth before burial. The heart, by contrast, was carefully preserved in the body. As the seat of the soul and all intelligence, the heart was considered crucial for entering the afterlife, where it was weighed by the gods to determine whether the dead merited paradise or destruction.

   Even if one fast-forwards thirty-six hundred years to the world of science and medicine in Europe, the brain is still considered a mostly incidental organ. Philosopher Thomas Hobbes, who consorted with such great thinkers as Galileo, summed up the accepted view when he wrote: "For what is the heart but a spring; and the nerves but so many strings; and the joints but so many wheels, giving motion to the whole body, such as was intended by the artificer?" Hobbes considered the heart "the fountain of all senses," and taught that the rate of the heart's blood flow determined whether a person felt pleasure or pain, anger or fear.

   A contemporary of Hobbes, a young physician named Thomas Willis, was about to forever overturn that established hierarchy of anatomy—from considering the brain as, in philosopher Henry More's view, "something like a bowl of curds" to enthroning it as the seat of the modern soul. As contemporary psychologist and author Oliver Sacks (whose medical writings were the basis of the popular 1990 film *Awak-*

*enings*) has written, "Willis was the first man to come to grips with the human brain, to see how different parts of it had different functions, and how the human soul could be embodied in it."

The historical setting for Willis's research was as dramatic and contradictory as the discoveries themselves. Though historians would later refer to the period as England's "century of genius," it was also an era of revolution and persecution in which most people's lives were, in Hobbes's best-known phrase, "nasty, brutish, and short."

Willis and his close-knit group of colleagues, who came to be called the Oxford Circle, were viewed as dangerous heretics by the religious establishment of the day. By persevering in their experiments they risked being officially branded as atheists, which at the time could place both their careers and their survival in jeopardy.

*Carl Zimmer is the author of* Evolution: The Triumph of an Idea *(2001),* Parasite Rex: Inside the Bizarre World of Nature's Most Dangerous Creatures *(2000), and* At the Water's Edge: Fish with Fingers, Whales with Legs, and How Life Came Ashore but Then Went Back to Sea *(1998). He writes frequently for magazines including* The New York Times Magazine, National Geographic, Science, *and* Natural History.

This sprawling and multilayered story finds an able and eloquent teller in young science writer Carl Zimmer, winner of numerous journalism awards and author of a monthly essay in *Natural History* magazine, a prestigious forum he inherited from the late Stephen Jay Gould. Zimmer has a natural gift for putting complex topics into accessible language and for bringing a scene to life in short order. These gifts are put to the test many times over in *Soul Made Flesh*, as its narrative ricochets along wildly branching pathways: from the medical practices of ancient Greece to astronomy to modern brain-scan machines and antipsychotic pharmaceuticals. It is to Zimmer's great credit as a storyteller that the numerous digressions only occasionally leave the reader impatient to return to the main tale.

Thomas Willis thrived amid the vigorous stir of ideas and discussion made possible by the polymath collection of talents represented in the Oxford Circle. At the age of thirty-nine, he was a well-respected physician and author during the watershed events of 1660, when King Charles assumed the throne of England after years of bloody uprisings and revolution. Willis, now with friends in high places, had more freedom than usual to explore—at least in his lectures—new scientific theories that did not necessarily jibe with the accepted wisdom of such legendary authorities as Galen, the Greek physician whose ideas still dominated European medicine some fifteen hundred years after his death.

Ironically, that freedom and intellectual stimulation led Willis at first to doubt, and then to become severely disillusioned with, his formidable earlier achievements. It was of this time period that Willis would later recall:

I seemed to myself like a painter that had delineated the head of a man, not after the form of a master, but at the will of a bold fancy and pencil. . . . [I] had not followed that which was most true, but what was most convenient, and what was desired rather than what was known. Thinking on these things seriously with myself, I awaked at length sad, as one out of a pleasant dream. . . . I determined with myself seriously to enter presently upon a new course, and to rely on this one thing, not to pin my faith on the received opinions of others, nor on the suspicions and guesses of my own mind, but for the future to believe nature and ocular demonstrations.

His new project had the ambitious goal "to unlock the secret places of man's mind." And in the service of "believing nature" Willis determined to concentrate for a period of years on performing autopsies of the brain—or, as he inelegantly phrased it, "I addicted myself to the opening of heads."

With the help of his assistant Richard Lower, a skilled surgeon, and friend Christopher Wren, architect and artist with his sketch pad at the ready, Willis tried to approach his new study of the brain as if from scratch. (Wren's now-classic neurological drawings, featured alongside the chapter headings of *Soul Made Flesh*, are at once straightforward and yet almost mystical in their clarity.) As Zimmer notes, "Willis and Lower dissected the brain in a different way, coming at it from the underside and extracting the brain whole and intact. Willis would then hold it for his audience to see. Looking at the brain this way forced Willis and his friends to think about it in a new light: not as a nondescript mass of flesh glued to the inside of the skull but as an independent organ."

Along the way, the pioneering Willis discovered what he already suspected: that the revered Galen had gotten much of it wrong. Rather than being a homogenous mass, for example, the brain was actually a cluster of three distinct parts—so distinct, in fact, that Willis could cut each section free with a scalpel and study it individually. In his search he benefited greatly from new scientific techniques, many of which had been introduced by his Oxford colleagues. These included an early version of the preservative formaldehyde, which helped the brain tissue retain its consistency for days rather than hours; an arterial dye made of ink and saffron; and most significant, improved versions of a microscope designed by Wren and physicist Robert Hooke.

With these new aids, Willis was able to track the vast network of fibers known today as the nervous system, and to chart the ways they changed as they spread from the brain throughout the entire body. Up until then, the fact that the body's organs worked in cooperation with one another, despite being seemingly unconnected, was explained by Flemish biochemistry pioneer Joan Baptista van Helmont as the result of "mystical influences," which were somehow related to complex chemical processes he called "ferments."

Willis's observations proved that nerve fibers, not mystical forces, were responsible for coordinating the body's movements. Although he had no way of making the next intuitive leap—that the nerves' method of transmission was electrical in nature—he was remarkably close. As Zimmer describes it, "Descartes had envisioned the spirits of the body driven ultimately by the beating heart, which pushed them throughout the brain and into the muscles. Willis reorganized the body, making the brain the origin and the nervous system an explosive fountain. Just as the brain sent out spirits to the heart and other organs, the nerves picked up signals from the outside world and sent animal spirits flashing back into the brain."

In an intense three-year period of study, through voluminous autopsies and a number of grisly animal experiments, Willis and his colleagues compiled the material that would become his landmark book, *Cerebri anatomoe: cui accessit nervorum descripio et usus* (1664; *The Anatomy of the Brain and Nerves*, 1681). The volume would go through twenty-three editions, become required medical-school reading for at least the next 150 years, and bring into existence an entirely new field of medicine that its author christened "neurologie." There were, however, other, nonmedical, hurdles to overcome.

Despite Willis's professional prominence, his radical new version of anatomy was sufficiently at odds with religious authorities' interpretations of the Bible that he had to walk a political tightrope in order to avoid being condemned by the Church as an atheist. This fancy linguistic footwork involved, in part, a flattering dedication to the archbishop in which Willis professed that his only aim for the anatomical textbook was "to look into the living and breathing chapel of the Deity."

Somehow, his finesse worked to stave off any controversy. The book, complete with Wren's drawings, became a publishing sensation. By 1665, Willis was one of the richest men in England, and was lauded by a nobleman as "one of the most famed physicians in the world." Willis used part of his wealth to buy a High Street inn and convert it to a combination spa and hospital. Profits from the enterprise helped him provide medical care to the poor without charge, even as he occasionally ventured out of Oxford to treat a select number of patients among the nobility.

With the career of Willis at its zenith, his country was once again about to descend into suffering and chaos. A new plague began to spread through London, and soon thousands of its victims were dying each week as panicked city-dwellers fled into the countryside. When the plague tapered off in the summer of the following year after some 100,000 deaths, that September brought the infamous Great Fire of London, consuming thirteen thousand buildings over three days and producing a cloud of smoke that darkened skies sixty miles away.

As London recuperated, Willis continued to build his medical practice, politely declined a knighthood he was offered, and spent his spare time speculating on such topics as the role of sleep, dreams, and imagination in the new understanding of the brain he had brought about. After his wife died of tuberculosis, he fought grief by turning his attention to writing a book titled *De anima brutorum quæ hominis vitalis ac sesitiva est, excertitantiones duæ* (1672; *Two Discourses Concerning the Soul of Brutes*, 1683), his attempt at an anatomy of the soul, which some historians regard as his greatest work. It drew the ire of critics and played into a growing national debate about ghosts and witchcraft. In time he remarried and began writing a handbook of drugs that would be called *Pharmaceutice rationalis* (1674-1675; English translation, 1683). It was his final work. He died of pneumonia in 1675, at the age of fifty-four, and was buried with great ceremony in Westminster Abbey.

Zimmer is at his best in re-creating what the daily flow of experience might have been like for Willis and his cohorts during those years of vibrant discovery. With hindsight, a modern reader marvels at how the pioneers had time to achieve anything of importance, much less their world-changing breakthroughs, while negotiating both the crush of current events and the minefields of political and religious controversy. The parallels with the third millennium's cultural war between science and religion are striking and disturbing.

The final chapter of *Soul Made Flesh*, which attempts to synthesize Willis's legacy with an overview of modern brain studies, from dopamine to magnetic resonance imaging, is more intriguing than satisfying. There are far greater sins for an author, however, than to leave his audience wanting more. In a perfect world, the compressed nature of Zimmer's ending might signal a future sequel that would delve more deeply into this changed world.

*Carroll Dale Short*

## Review Sources

*Booklist* 100, no. 7 (December 1, 2003): 642.
*Library Journal* 128, no. 20 (December, 2003): 158.
*Natural History* 113, no. 5 (June, 2004): 52.
*Nature* 427 (February 12, 2004): 585.
*The New England Journal of Medicine* 351, no. 1 (July 1, 2004): 107.
*The New York Times Book Review* 153 (April 4, 2004): 16.
*Psychology Today* 37, no. 1 (January/February, 2004): 80.
*Publishers Weekly* 250, no. 47 (November 24, 2003): 52.
*Science News* 165, no. 20 (May 15, 2004): 319.

# THE SOUND ON THE PAGE
## Style and Voice in Writing

*Author:* Ben Yagoda (1954-    )
*Publisher:* HarperCollins (New York). 304 pp. $24.00
*Type of work:* Language

*Challenging the notion that the only proper style in writing is one of plainness, simplicity, and transparency, Yagoda argues that successful writers entertain and inspire their readers not necessarily by what they say but by how they say it*

"Style matters," observes author and writing teacher Ben Yagoda in his introduction to *The Sound on the Page*. When talking about writing, however, a solid definition of style is difficult to pin down. What does one mean by "style"? Is it merely an elegant turn of phrase? Does it follow a "convention with respect to spelling, punctuation, capitalization, and typographic arrangement" as the *Merriam-Webster's Dictionary* states? Is style the same as voice? How is style a reflection of a writer's personality and individuality? In what ways is style related to content, and how does it affect the way one reads? Yagoda addresses these questions in his erudite, informative look at the ways authors express their ideas—and ultimately their true selves—through their own unique and recognizable writing styles.

Interwoven with Yagoda's insights are excerpts from interviews he conducted with more than forty well-known authors, including Nicholson Baker, Dave Barry, Joan Didion, Harold Bloom, David Thompson, Cynthia Ozick, John Updike, Clive James, Elizabeth McCracken, Elmore Leonard, and Tobias Wolff. The result is a lively, engaging discussion about a subject that has perplexed readers and writers alike for centuries.

Tracing the historical development of the concept of style in literature, Yagoda begins with the ancient Greeks, who sparked the debate about style more than two thousand years ago. On one side of the issue, the sophist Gorgias argued that the "eloquence and persuasiveness" of words should be valued as ends in themselves. His opponent, the philosopher Plato, contended that words were merely a "necessary evil" and often obscured the truth. The conflict continues today. Taking Gorgias's side are writers such as Natalie Goldberg, who believes that style "means becoming more and more present, settling deeper inside the layers of ourselves and then speaking, knowing what we write echoes all of us." Other authorities, such as William Strunk and E. B. White, agree with Plato that style should be a "vehicle for content" instead of primarily a means of personal expression. Yagoda leans toward Goldberg and Gorgias, taking issue with Strunk and White's ideas on style, which reflect Plato's influence.

*Ben Yagoda is the author of* About Town: The New Yorker and the World It Made *(2000) and* Will Rogers: A Biography *(1993) and has written for* The New York Times Magazine, The American Scholar, *and* Esquire. *He is the director of the journalism department at the University of Delaware, where he teaches nonfiction writing.*

Something of an icon in the writing world, Strunk and White's *The Elements of Style* (first published in 1918) is widely viewed by publishing houses, newspapers, magazines, academics, and students as the ultimate word on style. Yagoda, however, criticizes Strunk and White (as the book is popularly called) for its advice to writers to "avoid fancy words" and strive for "transparent" prose by placing themselves in the background. Although he agrees with White that the issue of style is a "high mystery," Yagoda nonetheless views White's twenty-one suggestions for stylistic excellence as limiting and impeding creativity and self-expression.

*The Sound on the Page* is Yagoda's cogent response to Strunk and White's advocacy for a minimalist approach to writing style. In contrast to White's idea that writers should endeavor to keep their personalities in the background, Yagoda asserts that allowing one's individual style to shine is one of the hallmarks of great literature, as well as a window into the writer's "essence." "The style is the man himself," Yagoda quotes French naturalist George de Buffon as saying in 1753. Yagoda agrees, arguing that personal style goes beyond a writer's technique to reveal something fundamental about the mind that gives birth to the unique arrangement of the words on the page.

Is style really a reflection of the essence of the writer? In a chapter subtitled "Style and Personality," Yagoda acknowledges that often there is a difference between the public personality of writers and their writing personas. This discrepancy often comes as a surprise to readers who frequently believe they can deduce their favorite writers' personal characteristics from their style. According to Yagoda—and to several of his interviewees—such is not always the case.

For example, Yagoda notes that when he spoke with Thompson, he found him to be a quiet and subdued man, in contrast to his writing style, which is boldly assertive. Barry commented to Yagoda in an interview that "you are no more seeing the real me in my columns than you're seeing the real Jerry Seinfeld when you watch *Seinfeld*. Everything you see in the columns came from me, but there is much more to me." Ozick, who Yagoda notes comes across in print as "assured," admits, "I write in terrible fear. When I'm writing fiction, it is really terror . . . What do I do about it? I hide it. You can't write with fear showing, and you can't write with depression showing. You need to construct a mask."

In spite of what these writers say about themselves, Yagoda notes that, more often than not, personality and persona are integrated. He cites Russell Baker, Jamaica

Kincaid, Calvin Trillin, and Updike as examples of writers who, when talking with them in person, "you can almost see the words on the page."

If style reveals the essence of the man, Yogoda suggests that it does the same for the woman. At the beginning of "Engendering Style," one of five "Interludes" between the nine chapters included in the book, Yagoda cites quotes from various male and female authors who comment on the different ways men and women approach writing.

Then Yagoda asks a loaded question: "Do men and women have substantially different writing styles?" In his all-too-short assessment of the impact gender has on style, Yagoda answers his question with a qualified "yes." He cites three linguistic studies in which pieces of writing by both men and women were analyzed by a computer. In each case, the results showed identifiable differences between male and female authors concerning word choice, punctuation, and sentence structure. Yagoda also mentions the results of a Myers-Briggs Type Indicator personality test that showed "60 percent of men characteristically employ a 'thinking' style rather than a 'feeling' style, whereas 60 percent of women are 'feelers.'" He concludes that the results of various personality tests seem to indicate that "men display, women reveal." This apparent reinforcement of cultural stereotypes raises more questions than it answers and deserves a more in-depth treatment than Yagoda gives the issue here.

How have accomplished writers developed their own unique styles? Many say: by reading—and, to a certain extent, imitating other authors. One of the more intriguing chapters, titled "Finding a Voice, Finding a Style," deals with the influence of writers on writers. Again, Yagoda draws on interviews, letting the writers speak for themselves regarding the authors who have had the most impact on their work. He quotes Judith Thurman: "When I'm stuck I'll read Didion—she calms me down." Meghan Daum agrees: "Certainly there's no young writer in the country who hasn't been influenced by Didion." As Griel Marcus comments, "Pauline Kael, Leslie Fiedler, D. H. Lawrence's *Studies in Classic American Literature*. They dove into their subjects, wrestled with them, brought them to life." Abraham Verghese recalls that "[George] Orwell was a tremendous influence."

While many authors spoke admiringly of their mentors, some writers sounded a discordant note. Ernest Hemingway, who is generally thought to have had the greatest influence on twentieth century literature, drew mixed reviews from Yagoda's interviewees. Wolff, for example, is ambivalent: "Hemingway was my dominant influence. I didn't like it pointed out to me, but in my heart I knew it was true." Ozick, on the other hand, denounces Hemingway in no uncertain terms: "I hate Hemingway. I absolutely despise Hemingway. I can't tell you passionately enough how much I hate Hemingway. This naked prose . . . it seems so brutal. . . . There's no richness—no *mind*—to it. . . . What has [Hemingway] done to American writing? He's simply despoiled it." Instead, Ozick credits Henry James and E. M. Forster's evocative prose as her main inspiration in the early years of her career. Wolff's and Ozick's disparate views highlight Yagoda's point that writers' personalities, not an accepted convention, are often the driving force behind the decisions they make, whether it be in choosing reading material or developing writing styles.

Yagoda also explores the impact of technology on composition and style, a subject not often addressed in a book on writing, even though personal computers and word processors have been around since the late 1970's. Although some writers, including Thompson, Ozick, James Wolcott, and Camille Paglia, write their manuscripts in longhand, others such as Marcus and Andrei Codrescu have adapted to writing on the computer.

Codrescu, comparing the computer to the typewriter, makes an important point about composing on a computer: "The problem with the computer is that you lose the bottom of the page . . . There is also the problem of mistakes. In the typewriter you have to take them out with White-Out, so in a sense you have a record of your mistakes. On a computer you eliminate them immediately, so you're not conscious of them. I mean, they're gone without a trace." Losing a record of changes in a manuscript is not only a problem for writers, it is also a drawback for future students and admirers who study emendations in manuscripts order to gain greater insight into the creative processes of their favorite writers.

Although Yagoda claims that *The Sound on the Page* is not a how-to manual, in the last chapter of the book he offers strategies to help writers develop their own distinctive styles. Much of his advice, however, falls into the category of principles that are usually taught in beginning writing classes: Read widely; experiment with different styles through imitation; become a discerning reader of your own work, especially by reading it aloud; avoid clichés; and revise, revise, revise. While these principles are time-tested, they very nearly fall into the category of cliché themselves. After an engaging and innovative discussion on style, such suggestions seem pedestrian and out of place. If, however, experienced as well as novice writers often need to be reminded of the basics, this chapter accomplishes that purpose.

Trying to unseat entrenched ideas such at those found in *The Elements of Style* is never easy, yet Yagoda and his coterie of fellow writers attempt to do so with grace, wit, and candor. Although they never reach a consensus of what constitutes style, their conversation certainly upholds Yagoda's contention that style matters. Writers of all stripes would do well to read, mark, and inwardly digest the thought-provoking insights found here—and to keep this volume in a prominent place on their bookshelves.

*Pegge Bochynski*

### Review Sources

*Booklist* 100, nos. 19/20 (June 1-15, 2004): 1687.
*Library Journal* 129, no. 10 (June 1, 2004): 150.
*The New York Times*, July 23, 2004, p. B35.
*The Wall Street Journal* 243, no. 119 (June 18, 2004): W10.

# STALIN
## The Court of the Red Tsar

*Author:* Simon Sebag Montefiore (1965-    )
*First published:* 2003, in Great Britain
*Publisher:* Alfred A. Knopf (New York). Illustrated.
   785 pp. $30.00
*Type of work:* Biography
*Time:* 1878-1953
*Locale:* Russia and the Soviet Union

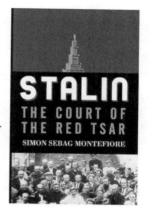

   *A very readable account of the life and devious rule of the Soviet Union's Georgian-born despot, with the "magnates" who served him developed in full*

    *Principal personages:*
      JOSEPH STALIN (JOSEPH VISSARIONOVICH
        DJUGASHVILI), secretary of Bolshevik
        Party (1922-1953) and premier of the Soviet Union (1941-1953)
      NADYA ALLILUYEVA, his second wife
      LAVRENTI BERIA, Politburo member in charge of nuclear bomb
      NIKOLAI BULGANIN, mayor of Moscow, Politburo member, defense
        minister
      LAZAR KAGANOVICH, Jewish Old Bolshevik, Stalin's deputy early
        1930's, railways chief, Politburo member
      NIKITA KHRUSHCHEV, Ukrainian First Secretary, Politburo member
      GEORGI MALENKOV, Central Committee secretary, ally of Beria
      ANASTAS MIKOYAN, Armenian Old Bolshevik, Politburo member, trade
        and supply minister
      VYACHESLAV MOLOTOV, Politburo member, premier, foreign minister
      ALEXANDER POSKREBYSHEV, Stalin's *chef de cabinet*
      ANDREI VYSHINSKY, ruthless prosecutor in the show trials
      NIKOLAI YEZHOV, "Blackberry," former NKVD head and brutal torturer
      ANDREI ZHDANOV, Politburo member, Leningrad boss, Central Commit-
        tee secretary, naval chief, Stalin's friend and heir apparent

    Joseph Stalin was born in the small Georgian town of Gori on December 6, 1878. His father, Vissarion, or "Beso," was a drunken cobbler who beat his wife, Ekaterina, or "Keke," who in turn beat the son, whom they called "Soso." In 1888 Soso entered the Gori Church School, and in 1894 he won a scholarship to the Tiflis Seminary, where he became an atheist and a Marxist before being expelled in 1899. He then joined the Russian Social Democratic Workers' Party, assuming the professional revolutionary name of Koba.

    Exiled to Siberia in 1902, Koba escaped and returned to Tiflis in 1904, where he married Ekaterina ("Kato") Svanidze, with whom he had a son, Yakov, before Kato died of tuberculosis in 1907. Mostly an absentee husband and father, Koba traveled

*Simon Sebag Montefiore studied history at Cambridge University before traveling widely in the former Soviet empire, reporting for journals and newspapers. His* Prince of Princes: The Life of Potemkin *(2000) was short-listed for several awards, and he has written two novels and several television documentaries.*

the Caucasus raising Party funds by brigandage. Sent back to Siberia in 1910, Koba fathered a son, Konstantin Kuzakov, by a young widow, Maria Kuzakova.

Escaping again, Koba went to Petersburg in 1912, sharing rooms with the twenty-two-year-old Vyacheslav Scriabin, who called himself Molotov, "the hammer," and taking his own industrial alias, Stalin, "steel." Exiled a final time in 1913, Stalin was back in Petersburg by 1917 under the Provisional Government and became, along with Leon Trotsky, one of five members of the Politburo (Political Bureau) formed by Vladimir Ilich Lenin as an organ of the Bolshevik Revolution begun in October, 1917. Stalin married the seventeen-year-old Nadya Alliluyeva, with whom he had a son, Vasily, and a daughter, Svetlana, before Nadya committed suicide in 1932.

Appointed general secretary of the party's Central Committee (CC) in 1922, with Lenin's death in 1924 Stalin was able to shove aside Trotsky and brutalize the Soviet Union for three decades. His ruthlessness emerged in his starvation of the kulaks, those peasants who resisted the collectivization judged vital to producing the food for the growing industrial machine. Author Simon Sebag Montefiore observes, "The resulting rural nightmare was like a war without battles but with death on a monumental scale." Stalin and his "magnates" lived sumptuously as one big Kremlin family, while the famine in the countryside was claiming perhaps more than five million lives and creating an uneasiness in the Politburo that inflamed Stalin's paranoia. Of the 1,966 delegates to the Seventeenth Party Congress in 1932, 1,108 would eventually be arrested, with few surviving.

The death of Sergei Kirov remains a mystery. He was one of Stalin's closest friends and a Politburo member, but as Leningrad chief he had annoyed Stalin by resisting his plan to end bread rationing. Kirov was assassinated in his office building on December 1, 1934, perhaps by a naïve tool of the NKVD (People's Commissariat of Internal Affairs). The evidence remains equivocal, but "Whether or not he killed Kirov, Stalin certainly exploited the murder to destroy not only his opponents but the less radical among his own allies." Declaring Kirov's murder a terrorist act, Stalin launched a series of executions, including those of two prominent old Leninists, Grigory Zinoviev and Lev Kamenev. In December alone, 6,501 people were shot in a crackdown followed by the show trials and designed to beat the party into submission.

Two months after Kirov's death, Stalin appointed Lazar Kaganovich railways chief and Nikita Khrushchev Moscow boss. Kirov was replaced as CC secretary by Nikolai Yezhov, a brutal "bisexual dwarf" nicknamed "Blackberry" by Stalin, and in the bloodbath that followed in 1937, Yezhov was the tireless instrument of the "democide, the class struggle spinning into cannibalism." The latest figures suggest 700,000 were shot in the Terror. Yezhov's dissoluteness and ill health, however, led

Stalin to replace him with a new favorite, the sadist Lavrenti Beria, who between February 24 and March 16, 1939, executed 417 important prisoners. Yezhov himself was shot in 1940.

With the internal threats suppressed, Stalin turned to dividing up Europe with Adolf Hitler, whose foreign minister, Joachim von Ribbentrop, arrived in Moscow on August 23, 1939, to sign a nonaggression pact, beginning what Molotov called "The Great Game." A week later Germany invaded Poland, and on September 17 Russian troops crossed into Poland from the other side. By November, 1940, Khrushchev had deported 1.17 million Poles, 30 percent of whom were dead by 1941.

Stalin then moved through Beria against certain officials' wives who were feared to be disloyal. President Mikhail Kalinin's wife, Ekaterina, was heard complaining on a bugged telephone and exiled. Dr. Bronka Poskrebysheva, wife of Stalin's *chef de cabinet*, Alexander Poskrebyshev, requested the release of her imprisoned brother and was never seen again. Sophia Kavtaradze, wife of Stalin's old Bolshevik friend Sergo Kavtaradze, was put in Lubianka prison and tortured. A list of 346 death sentences signed by Stalin on January 16, 1940, also included the distinguished writer Isaac Babel and Stalin's brother-in-law Stanislas Redens.

Despite advance intelligence from the spy Richard Sorge in Tokyo, as well as from the British government and from Mao Zedong, Stalin was still astonished by Hitler's wide-ranging attack on June 22, 1941. Only Marshal Georgi Zhukov on the southwestern front was able to muster any resistance, and even he suffered insults from Stalin, whose incompetence in military matters was glaringly exposed and whose murder of all of his enemies was the only thing that saved his position. Though Stalin collapsed into depression, Montefiore believes that much of his breakdown was a strategic withdrawal to strengthen his position.

By August, Leningrad was nearly cut off from the rest of the country, with Andrei Zhdanov, the city's helpless boss, replaced by Zhukov, who mustered such stiff resistance that Hitler abandoned the assault in the hope of starving the population into submission. With German troops within one hundred kilometers from the chaotic Kremlin in October, Stalin ordered Zhukov back to Moscow. Beria, Kaganovich, and the CC secretary, Georgi Malenkov, urged an evacuation to Kuibyshev, but Stalin had learned from Sorge that Japan was not planning to invade Russia, and he recalled 400,000 men from his Far Eastern Army along with a thousand tanks and a thousand planes to defend the capital. Zhukov lost 155,000 men in twenty days but stopped the German assault on Moscow on December 5, two days before Japan attacked Pearl Harbor.

Stalin's own incompetence as a military leader was compounded by the stupidity of the leaders he appointed. Lev Mekhlis, the Red Army political chief, launched an ill-considered attack in the Crimea that cost 176,000 men, four hundred planes, and 347 tanks. Khrushchev and Marshal Semyon Timoshenko blundered into a trap in the Caucasus that lost a quarter of a million men and twelve hundred tanks. Then, on August 13, 1942, with British prime minister Winston Churchill visiting the Kremlin, the German Sixth Army crushed Stalin's Fourth Tank Army to open the way to Stalingrad.

Fearing the loss of the oil supply from the Caucasus, Stalin sent his NKVD boss, Beria, to Georgia with orders to stop the Germans at any cost and to eliminate dissidents. The crisis at Stalingrad then forced Stalin to turn command of his military forces over to the professionals, Zhukov and Marshal Alexander Vasilevsky, whose Operation Uranus pitted a million men, 13,541 guns, 1,400 tanks, and 1,150 planes against Hitler's armies on November 19, 1942. On January 31 the Nazis' Field Marshal Paulus surrendered ninety-two thousand starving, exhausted troops in a crucial Russian triumph that "seemed to refresh Stalin."

On March 3 Field Marshal Erich von Manstein recaptured Kharkov and soon had a large Russian force almost cut off at Kursk. Stalin sent Zhukov and Vasilensky to the front, where they waited with more than a million men and six thousand tanks for Hitler to begin Operation Citadel with 900,000 men and 2,700 tanks. The carnage began on July 5 in a "colossal battle of machines in which fleets of metallic giants clashed, helm to helm, barrel to barrel." The Russians' success in this historic battle, Montefiore says, destroyed Hitler's last chance to win the war.

With the outcome of the war in sight, Stalin met with Churchill and American president Franklin D. Roosevelt in Teheran in November, 1943. Stalin got along well with Roosevelt, and they outflanked Churchill, who wanted a Mediterranean campaign before undertaking Operation Overlord, the cross-Channel invasion. Montefiore judges, "Roosevelt's deference to Stalin and shabbiness to Churchill were both unseemly and counterproductive." Roosevelt did, however, for political reasons refuse to discuss Poland, thereby encouraging Stalin's plans for a "tame Poland." Despite the badinage Stalin enjoyed with Roosevelt, he later admitted that he admired Churchill more and called him "the strongest personality in the capitalist world."

As the Russians drove the Germans back, Stalin swaggered and bullied his subordinates. His armies raped two million German women, prompting Milovan Djilas, the Yugoslav politburo member, to complain to the indifferent Stalin. In February, 1945, Stalin met again with Churchill and Roosevelt, this time in Yalta, where Stalin finally got his way with Poland and added Sakhalin and the Kurile Islands. Roosevelt and Churchill are commonly charged with selling out Eastern Europe to Stalin, but as Montefiore opines, if any sellout occurred, it probably came at the Moscow Foreign Ministers Conference in October, 1943. When President Harry Truman, whom Stalin loathed, informed Stalin at Potsdam in July, 1945, of the successful testing of a nuclear bomb in New Mexico, an event already reported to the Kremlin by its spies, Stalin chose Beria, whom he had come to despise but who was a proven administrator, to run the Soviet atomic project.

These happy postwar years were filled with nights of eating, boozing, and watching movies, regular rituals dreaded by most of the high-ranking lackeys, but they contributed to a serious heart attack Stalin suffered in October, 1945. Recuperating at Gagra on the Black Sea, Stalin acted quickly through Beria, Mikoyan, and Malenkov to keep Molotov in his place. Three years later, Stalin's favorite as his heir, Andrei Zhdanov, died of heart disease, leaving the succession open. After the establishment of the State of Israel, Stalin initiated an anti-Semitic purge, with Malenkov and the secret police chief, Victor Abakumov, in charge of a terror that sent even Polina

Molotov to Siberia. Two prominent Leningrad Politburo members, Alexei Kuznetsov and Nikolai Voznesensky, Stalin's heirs apparent as secretary and premier, respectively, fell into disfavor in 1949 and were disposed of by Beria in the so-called Leningrad Affair.

After one final deadly outburst against imaginary enemies, in this case, Jewish doctors, in January, 1953, Stalin collapsed with a severe stroke on March 1 and died four days later. The happiest of his critics was Beria, "a bulging but effervescent grey toad, glistening with ill-concealed relish." Beria's hopes were for naught. His proposal to free East Germany scared the other magnates, and under Khrushchev's direction he was arrested and executed with a bullet to his forehead. Beria's death was not the last chapter in the long story of Bolshevik crimes, but not many would dispute the appropriateness of its manner.

*Frank Day*

## Review Sources

*Booklist* 100, no. 15 (April 1, 2004): 1343.
*History Today* 54, no. 2 (February, 2004): 57.
*Kirkus Reviews* 72, no. 5 (March 1, 2004): 212.
*Library Journal* 129, no. 8 (May 1, 2004): 122.
*The New York Review of Books* 51, no. 8 (May 13, 2004): 2.
*The New York Times*, April 16, 2004, p. E31.
*The New York Times Book Review* 153 (April 18, 2004): 10.
*The New Yorker* 80, no. 14 (May 31, 2004): 81.
*Publishers Weekly* 251, no. 12 (March 22, 2004): 78.
*Time* 163, no. 15 (April 12, 2004): 69.

# THE STATE OF ISRAEL VS. ADOLF EICHMANN

*Author:* Hanna Yablonka
*First published: Medinat Yisrael Neged Adolf Eichmann,*
2001, in Israel
Translated from the Hebrew by Ora Cummings with
David Herman
*Publisher:* Schocken Books (New York). 319 pp. $26.00
*Type of work:* History
*Locale:* Israel

*Analyzing the process that led to the conviction and exe-
cution of Adolf Eichmann, a key perpetrator of the Holocaust, Yablonka shows how Eichmann's 1961 trial has
shaped Israel's national identity*

*Principal personages:*
ADOLF EICHMANN, Nazi war criminal, tried and executed in Israel
DAVID BEN-GURION, the first prime minister of Israel
GIDEON HAUSNER, Israel's attorney general

On May 23, 1960, Prime Minister David Ben-Gurion made an announcement to
the Knesset, the Israeli parliament: Agents of Mossad, Israel's secret service, had captured the Holocaust perpetrator Adolf Eichmann in Argentina and brought him to an
Israeli prison. As author Hanna Yablonka demonstrates, that arrest began a process
that transformed Israeli society and Jewish consciousness.

Born in 1906, Eichmann grew up in Austria and joined the Nazi Party in 1932. As a
member of the SS and the Security Service (SD), he developed expertise on Jewish affairs. Although Eichmann did not control the Third Reich's anti-Jewish policies, his
ties to Reinhard Heydrich, his SS superior, made him part of the inner circle that plotted and carried out the destruction of the European Jews. Eichmann played decisive
parts in implementing Nazi policy as it went from forcing Jews to emigrate from the
Third Reich in the late 1930's to deporting them to killing centers such as Auschwitz-
Birkenau, where millions were gassed from 1942 until the end of 1944.

In particular, Eichmann presided over the forced emigration of Austrian Jews in
1938. He participated in the Wannsee Conference, the infamous meeting held on January 20, 1942, at which Heydrich and other Nazi leaders coordinated plans for the so-
called final solution. Eichmann also supervised the deportation of Hungarian Jews in
the spring and summer of 1944, when approximately 435,000 Jews were sent to
Auschwitz within a few weeks. Such activities required his initiative and reflected his
ambition. Contrary to the impression that he was a banal bureaucrat or an indistinct
cog in the Nazi machine, Eichmann was never a merely obedient underling who followed orders, a characterization that was central but unsuccessful in his trial defense.

After World War II, Eichmann fled to Argentina, where he and his family lived
under the name of Klement. As early as September, 1957, German sources tipped Is-

raeli officials as to his probable whereabouts. Yablonka's narrative indicates that the Israelis responded cautiously, hoping that the Germans would extradite and try him. In 1960, when it became clear that the Germans would not act, Haim Cohen, Israel's attorney general at the time, authorized the capture and abduction. The Mossad snared Eichmann on May 11, 1960, and he arrived in Israel on May 22. At least for a time, those actions made Israel vulnerable to international criticism for violating Argentina's sovereignty.

After lengthy interrogation of Eichmann, which was carried out by Bureau 06, a police unit led by Avraham Zellinger and Avner Less, the trial started on April 11, 1961. Defended in the Jerusalem district court by the German lawyer Robert Servatius, Eichmann faced a fifteen-count indictment, which accused him of war crimes, crimes against humanity and, significantly, crimes against the Jewish people, a category that had not previously been used in postwar tribunals. Gideon Hausner, Israel's attorney general, was the chief prosecutor. The case was heard by three Israeli judges: Binyamin Halevi and Yitzchak Raveh from the district court, with Supreme Court justice Moshe Landau presiding. The testimony concluded on August 14. Four months later, on December 12, the judges found Eichmann guilty as charged and sentenced him to death. His execution by hanging took place at 1:00 A.M. on June 1, 1962. Eichmann's body was cremated. The ashes were scattered over the Mediterranean Sea, beyond Israel's territorial waters but not beyond Israeli identity and Jewish consciousness.

Although *The State of Israel vs. Adolf Eichmann* necessarily provides the background outlined above, Yablonka's book is neither a history of the Holocaust, a biographical study of Eichmann, a thorough account of the clandestine operation that led to his abduction, nor even a detailed, day-by-day account of the trial itself. Instead, she concentrates on the context, meaning, and significance of the eight-month judicial proceeding.

Yablonka examines the Eichmann trial from three perspectives. First, there are questions about what she calls its "public-legal dimensions," which include, for example, issues about where the trial would be held, how the judges were appointed, and which witnesses were chosen. Second, she assesses the trial's impact, a difficult task because Israeli society is multifaceted and complex. Surmounting the difficulties, some of Yablonka's best work is done in the chapters devoted to this part of her project, especially when she shows how Holocaust survivors were crucial in the trial's development, deeply affected by it, and—for the first time—warmly embraced by Israeli society during and after the proceedings. Third, Yablonka assesses what she calls the "historic-legal discourse" about the Eichmann trial. Was it merely a "show trial?" What contributions did the trial make to study and memory of the

*Born in Tel Aviv and residing in Givatayim, Israel, Hanna Yablonka is a professor of Jewish history at Ben-Gurion University of the Negev. She is the author of* Ahim zarim: Nitsole ha-Shoʾah bi-Medinat Yiśraʾel, 1948-1952 *(1994;* Survivors of the Holocaust, *1999). The Hebrew edition of* The State of Israel vs. Adolf Eichmann *won the 2001 Buchman Memorial Prize from Yad Vashem, Israel's national memorial to the Holocaust.*

Holocaust? Overall, her work not only presents the main Israeli figures in the proceeding—investigators, prosecutors, witnesses, and judges—but also explains how the trial promoted a deepened Israeli awareness of the Holocaust's significance.

The trial opened with a dramatic speech by prosecutor Hausner, who told the judges that he was not alone in bringing the case against Eichmann. "I am joined," he emphasized, "by six million prosecutors." Referring to the Holocaust's victims, Hausner told the court that "their blood cries out, but their voices are unheard." Hausner's insistence that he would speak on their behalf signaled that the trial's scope would not focus narrowly on specific actions taken by Eichmann but would broadly document the Holocaust and Eichmann's role in it.

At the time of the trial, Israel's population numbered about two million. Yablonka notes that one-quarter of them were Holocaust survivors. Although relatively few had any direct contact with Eichmann, his actions affected many of them immensely. Consequently, the trial put the Israeli survivors in the spotlight as never before. Previously many of them had been active in commemoration activities, including the 1959 campaign that produced the law establishing a national Holocaust Remembrance Day, but overall the survivors' place in Israeli life was both less visible and less appreciated than it came to be during and after the Eichmann trial.

In the 1950's, the survivors worked to re-create their lives, to raise children, and to build the State of Israel. Those concerns could not erase the Holocaust's trauma, but its expression was repressed. At the same time, an Israeli majority tended to have ambivalent attitudes toward the survivors. Those attitudes ranged from scarcely noticing the survivors to seeing them as "immigrants on whom fortune had smiled" or, especially with regard to those who were not identified with partisan resistance or ghetto uprisings, viewing them as people whose survival raised the accusing question, later understood to be misinformed and out of place, "Why didn't you resist?" Furthermore, the place of Holocaust survivors in Israeli society had been complicated by legal actions preceding the Eichmann case.

Enacted in 1950, the Nazi and Nazi Collaborators (Punishment) Law provided the foundation for the Eichmann trial, but in the 1950's the law reflected the fact that some survivors were accused of Holocaust complicity, if not collaboration, with the Germans. In the 1950's, Yablonka observes, "several dozen Jewish survivors were prosecuted in Israel" under this statute, "but not a single German. Until, that is, Adolf Eichmann was captured and tried." The most dramatic case, known as the Kastner trial, was a 1954-1955 proceeding in which it was decided that Dr. Rudolf Kastner, who headed the Hungarian Jews' rescue committee in 1944, had engaged in dealings with the Germans, Eichmann among them, to save a few privileged Hungarian Jews at the expense of the larger population. In January, 1958, that finding was overturned, but too late for Kastner, who had been assassinated at his home in Tel Aviv the previous March. Eichmann's name surfaced prominently in the Kastner trial, but he was far from its focal point, which concentrated instead on allegations about Jews that increased the ambivalence about Israeli survivors prior to Eichmann's trial.

The decision to focus broadly on the Holocaust during the Eichmann trial meant that documentary evidence would be augmented by survivor testimony. For the first time in Israel or elsewhere, survivor testimony about the Holocaust was widely shared in public and in depth. Of the 101 persons who were chosen as witnesses, all but nine were Holocaust survivors. Nearly all the survivors came from Israel, and most were carefully selected so that their testimony, which needed to be articulate and moving, described extensively the Holocaust's ghettos, camps, massacres, death marches, and resistance activities as well as its vast geographical scope. Although the 750 seats in Jerusalem's Bet Ha'am (House of the People) hall went not to the general public but mostly to journalists and diplomats, and despite the fact that the absence of television in Israel in 1961 meant that the first-ever filming of an Israeli trial was not accessible to most Israelis, the press and radio gave the trial wide coverage in the State of Israel. For the Israeli people, says Yablonka, and to some extent for Jews world-wide, the testimony of survivors such as Rivka Yoselewska, Moshe Beisky, the writer Yehiel Dinur, and the artist Yehuda Bakon "came to represent the Holocaust itself."

In Yablonka's judgment, the survivors' testimony built "a living bridge between 'there' and here." As Israeli empathy for the survivors' suffering grew, the survivors helped Israelis and Jews in the Diaspora to understand that the Holocaust was not cat-astrophic in some general way but that what had happened in Europe is profoundly a part of Israel's history and the legacy of every living Jew, for Eichmann and his peers intended the utter destruction of the Jewish people and their traditions. The Eichmann trial intensified Jewish solidarity, the view that Israel was an essential haven against anti-Semitism and future threats to the Jewish people, and a commitment to Holo-caust education, which had not been a high priority in Israel. The trial's most signifi-cant results also included the perception that the nations of the world had not inter-vened directly on behalf of Jews during the Nazi period. That conviction meant that the State of Israel could never entrust its security to another country. The Eichmann trial was a cathartic moment, a time when "attitudes of alienation and shame toward the Holocaust faded away" and when the Holocaust became increasingly powerful in Israeli consciousness, particularly among the nation's youth. As the Israeli poet Haim Guri put the point on September 10, 1961, a few weeks after the survivors' testimony had concluded, it was as though "the Holocaust has happened now."

Eichmann's conviction and execution did not bring closure. The trial left Israelis asking themselves whether Jews in the Yishuv, the pre-statehood Jewish community in Palestine, had done their best to help Europe's Jews during the Holocaust. Regret-ting the important information that was lost, Yablonka wonders why, even after Eichmann's conviction, historians were denied access to him. Moreover, what about the trial itself? What kind of proceeding was it? Yablonka emphatically rejects the criticism that it was a "show trial," but she also contends that the proceedings cannot simply be called a "criminal trial." Hausner had made clear early on that the trial would not only seek to carry out justice, which Yablonka understands to be the object of a criminal trial, but also it would have the educational, ethical, and political goal of bringing "people in Israel and the world closer to the enormity of the calamity."

Nevertheless, the proceedings were far from a show trial. The trial was not staged, and Yablonka credits especially the integrity of the Israeli judges, including those on the Supreme Court who heard Eichmann's appeal after the district court pronounced its verdict and sentence. Significantly, she suggests that written documentation weighed more heavily with the judges than the survivors' testimony, which the judges heard with great respect but not without criticism. Furthermore, in show trials the defendants are usually innocent. As research continues, Eichmann's role as a Holocaust perpetrator becomes increasingly evident.

Yablonka concludes that the Eichmann trial is best called a "historic trial," a term coined by the Israeli press while the proceedings were under way. It remains historic because the trial enabled the Holocaust to "become an integral part of Israel's national identity." Related to that outcome, a gnawing question persists about the Holocaust itself. "How," asks Yablonka, "could it have taken place in broad daylight?" *The State of Israel vs. Adolf Eichmann* does not answer that question, but this book stimulates thoughtful reflection about it.

*John K. Roth*

## Review Sources

*Booklist* 100, no. 12 (February 15, 2004): 1024.
*Library Journal* 129, no. 6 (April 1, 2004): 108.
*The Times Literary Supplement*, May 28, 2004, p. 8.

# STRANGERS
## Homosexual Love in the Nineteenth Century

*Author:* Graham Robb (1958-    )
*Publisher:* W. W. Norton (New York). 342 pp. $27.00
*Type of work:* History
*Time:* 1800-1918
*Locale:* England, Europe, and the United States

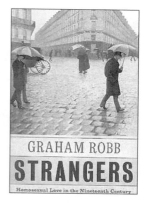

*A historical account of homosexuality in the nineteenth century that argues for the existence of a recognizable gay culture which, in spite of oppressive legal and medical discourse and practices, was produced by a vibrant international community of increasingly aware individuals*

*Principal personages:*
KARL HEINRICH ULRICHS (1825-1895),
German jurist and journalist; the author
of seminal tracts on the civic rights of "Uranians" and the first nineteenth century public figure to come out publicly
MAGNUS HIRSCHFELD (1868-1935), writer, editor, organizer of the Scientific and Humanitarian Committee, and tireless fighter for the rights of "the third sex"
OSCAR WILDE (1854-1900), famous Irish dramatist, wit, and aesthete; tried and sentenced for indecency in 1895 and subsequently elevated as a gay martyr
EDWARD CARPENTER (1844-1929), influential socialist writer, author of *The Intermediate Sex* (1908), and persuasive advocate for "homogenic love"
RICHARD VON KRAFFT-EBING (1840-1902), physician and academic whose *Psychopathia Sexualis* (1886) was a collection of case studies of homosexuals that focused more on their difference than their perversity

It was while doing the research for his biographies of the great nineteenth century French writers Honoré de Balzac, Victor Hugo, and Arthur Rimbaud that Graham Robb was struck by the intriguing material he kept turning up about homosexuality during that period. Not only was there a staggering amount of it, but it also seemed to contradict traditional notions of what life was like for Victorian gay men and women. The more Robb looked, the more his excavations revealed "curious fragments of what seemed a vanished civilization." It is this lost and largely unexplored gay culture that he has attempted to reconstruct in *Strangers*. By examining "homosexual love, the obstacles it faced and the societies it created," his hope was to "provide some credible reason to take a more cheerful view of the past."

Robb lays out his three-part plan with an equally crisp clarity: He will first show how homosexuals were treated by the legal and medical professions and by society at

*Graham Robb has published widely
on French literature and culture. His
critically acclaimed biographies
include* Balzac *(1994), the Whitbread
Biography Award-winning* Victor
Hugo *(1997), and* Rimbaud *(2001).*

large; he will then look at the beginnings of gay solidarity (how gay and lesbian people found their way to one another) and the early movement for gay rights; and he will finally address the various ways this vital gay presence made itself felt. It should be said that *Strangers* only fitfully follows this neat linear scheme, making instead excursions into rich literary, social, or statistical minutiae that regularly threaten to derail the main line of the argument. In the end, however, it is precisely the massing of all these concrete particulars that makes the book so valuable. What could have been an arid historical exercise becomes a colorful and moving mosaic of letters and journals, novels and poems, police and doctors' reports: a choir of nineteenth century voices which largely substantiate Robb's thesis of a thriving gay culture existing at a moment in history when some dispute not only the idea of such a culture but of such an identity category.

In making this claim, Robb consciously challenges the hegemony of Michel Foucault's theory about the history of sexuality. Foucault's social constructionist view holds that as identity is shaped by discourse and social practices (particularly the capitalist instruments of technological and bureaucratic control), there could not possibly be a real sense of homosexual identity until the discursive practices of the medical profession "invented" homosexuals as a new species (the word "homosexual" was coined only in 1868 by the Hungarian writer Karl Maria Kertbeny). Before such a distinct homosexual personality existed, there could be only a repertoire of sexual behaviors, acts judged sinful and criminal or noble and visionary, depending on the culture and the time. Arguing against innate sexuality, this theory finds problematic the existence of a transhistorical, cross-cultural homosexuality.

Robb's evidence suggests that, contrary to the Foucauldian view, there have always been people who were primarily or exclusively attracted to people of their own sex and who were able to identify themselves as such, often from a very early age. These people were perceived to be different by others as well and were treated by them with various degrees of tolerance. Whether able to call themselves homosexuals or not, these "mollies," "poufs," "pederasts," "chestnut gatherers," "lavender aunts," these women said to "eat garlic" or men said to "be musical" understood that they constituted an identity category different from most of their neighbors. Some were destroyed by this knowledge; others were persecuted when it was revealed. Still others, Robb suggests, were able to live reasonably happy, productive lives and to make connections with other gays and lesbians within an evolving international gay culture.

The first move Robb makes in *Strangers*, however, seems to subvert rather than advance this claim. He brings in a dense documentary record (an apparatus of charts and graphs and interpretive glosses showing the connection between antisodomy laws and prosecutions) which makes clear the criminal cast to Victorian homosexuality. This would appear to support the traditional view of the nineteenth century as a fiercely inhospitable epoch for sexual minorities, one in which they were bound by a set of inhumane laws and hounded from society by its enforcement. Robb, however, quickly dismantles this impressive statistical history, arguing that in most important ways such legal statistics are misrepresentative, focusing as they do on prohibited acts instead of on how desire played out in individual lives—something much harder to document.

It is true that in England sodomy was a crime punishable by death from 1533 until 1861, and indeed between 1810 and 1835, forty-six individuals were executed. Robb insists that within the law, gay people were not treated with "unusual severity." Punishment was not systematic and never a determining part of gay culture. If anything, there was a slight decrease in criminal prosecutions from the 1840's to the end of the century. If any period emerges as the most egregious for enforcing antisodomy laws, statistics show it is easily the mid-twentieth century, when prosecutions of homosexuals leapt off the charts, the effect of more stringently enforced legislation in France, Germany, the United States, and even Holland. Robb concludes that "nineteenth century homosexuals lived under a cloud, but it seldom rained." A history that presents them solely as victims has, he asserts, given too much weight to criminal evidence which looms disproportionately large only because so little other information is available.

As the nineteenth century unfolded, there was an explosion of medical and psychiatric interest in homosexuality, a shift in emphasis from prosecution to treatment: identifying symptoms, establishing causes, proposing cures. It is difficult to read these pages without feeling a mix of hilarity and pathos, so comically outrageous is most of the "scientific" thinking, so tragically devastating the implications of applying it to real people's lives. What is one to do with the information that "sexual inversion" can be caused by masturbation, or that gay men cannot urinate in a straight line, or that if thrown an object they will automatically close their legs, whereas a lesbian will open hers? People were told that this "contrary sexual feeling," in Carl Westphal's famous phrase from 1870, can be cured by visiting a brothel, or by "cold baths with outdoor exercise and the study of mathematics."

Even many of the medical figures behind such absurd prescriptions were forced to admit that there often was not much to "cure," that the homosexuals they saw were specimens neither of pathology nor physiological defect. The case studies they published in increasing numbers during the latter part of the nineteenth century had the curious effect of letting other gay people know they were not alone, not aberrant; works like Richard von Krafft-Ebing's *Psychopathia Sexualis* (1886) inadvertently became texts in which homosexuals could read their own lives in the medical studies of these other "cases" and could see themselves not as isolated deviants but as normal beings in a different community.

Members of this community, Robb writes, could find their way to one another fairly easily by the mid-nineteenth century. There was even a kind of Gay Grand Tour encompassing Europe to North Africa, and within most large cities there were places where gay men and women knew they could be sympathetically received. London, Barcelona, Naples, St. Petersburg, Capri—all had their gay terrains, like the plush interiors of Nathalie Barney's Paris salon or the winding paths of New York's Central

Park. There was also a coded system of communication—not only a means of survival but of secret enjoyment—specific allusions, colors, gestures, even floral arrangements that signaled identity. There were clubs, bars, baths, balls, societies, the sheer variety of which makes it difficult to identify a coherent gay community but which argues for a large and diverse gay presence.

In spite of Robb's desire to focus as much on the experience of gay women as of gay men during this century, his book is seriously weighted in the direction of men of higher economic classes. The reason for this is presumably that men occupied positions of privilege and had easier access to a wider world of relationships that were more likely to be documented. As well, the lack of antilesbian legislation meant that homosexual women had nothing specific to organize against—nothing, of course, except a more diffuse but maddeningly pervasive set of gender prejudices. Nevertheless, Robb brings in women when he can, highlighting the famous Ladies of Llangollen, Eleanor Butler and Sarah Ponsonby, as well as introducing lesser-known figures such as Anne Lister, a gentlewoman from Halifax who in the 1820's found women sexual partners from Yorkshire farms to Paris pensions.

Another goal Robb does not quite meet is his intention that *Strangers* not be a mere annotated list of famous nineteenth century gay people. Certainly it is more than that, and yet to an extent it cannot help being a colorful biographical survey of the leading gay personalities as well. There are telling sections on Pyotr Ilich Tchaikovsky, Johann Joachim Winckelmann, Hans Christian Andersen, Walt Whitman, Marcel Proust, and Emily Dickinson.

Perhaps the most satisfying profiles are of the century's real gay groundbreakers, the brave activists who forced the cultural understanding of homosexuality into new channels, in particular Karl Heinrich Ulrichs and Magnus Hirschfeld. Ulrichs was the first—the only—public figure to come out as a gay man, which he did before an audience of German jurists in Munich, 1867, giving a public defense of homosexuality as innate and of "Uranians" as citizens entitled to specific legal rights. With Hirschfeld the modern story of gay rights really commences. His organizing and research efforts had the effect of confirming and legitimizing homosexuality by articulating the view of this "third sex" as just another naturally occurring differentiation of human sexuality along a continuum. His annually published lists of "sexual intermediates" made visible what was once mostly hidden and, again, allowed homosexuals to view themselves as having a history, as standing within a tradition.

The last section of *Strangers* is a potpourri of cultural items, in which Robb aims to show how there was a distinct gay presence in religion, literature, and most interesting, at the heart of the new genre of detective fiction. He points to gay readings of the Scripture, particularly of Christ and the Apostles, and notes a general homoeroticism that was increasingly regarded as compatible with religious fervor. He even finds evidence that "some priests and vicars were prepared to perform marriages for homosexual men or lesbians." Turning to literature, he looks at the early portraits of homosexuals in the fiction of Balzac and Théophile Gautier, where they are not reduced to cheap "types," and at the more clinical presentations in fiction after 1880.

It is in the newly minted detective fiction that Robb locates his real nineteenth century hero and with which he concludes this sprawling history. Beginning with Edgar Allan Poe's eccentrically nocturnal aesthete Dupin and reaching its full flowering with Arthur Conan Doyle's equally eccentric Sherlock Holmes, this new modern hero—with his dual nature, his sexual ambiguity, his predilection for night life, his powers of deciphering secrets and reading clues—is the apotheosis of the urban gay male. Robb interprets the success of the homosexual detective as a positive sign, a way of bringing the scapegoat back into society as a personality to be admired and imitated. Perhaps it is so. In any event, this makes for a suitably heroic finale to a history that aims to present nineteenth century gay men and women less as victims than as striving, self-aware human beings.

*Thomas J. Campbell*

### Review Sources

*The Economist* 370 (January 10, 2004): 74.
*Harper's Magazine* 308, no. 1844 (January, 2004): 76.
*Kirkus Reviews* 71, no. 21 (November 1, 2003): 1303.
*Library Journal* 128, no. 20 (December 15, 2003): 147.
*New Statesman* 132 (December 8, 2003): 51.
*The New York Times Book Review* 153 (March 7, 2004): 10.
*Publishers Weekly* 250, no. 44 (November 3, 2003): 69.
*The Times Literary Supplement*, January 9, 2004, p. 9.

# THE SUNDAY PHILOSOPHY CLUB

*Author:* Alexander McCall Smith (1948-    )
*Publisher:* Pantheon (New York). 247 pp. $20.00
*Type of work:* Novel
*Time:* The early twenty-first century
*Locale:* Edinburgh

*After seeing a young man fall to his death from a concert hall balcony, Isabel Dalhousie attempts to discover why he died*

> *Principal characters:*
> ISABEL DALHOUSIE, a middle-aged Edinburgh woman who edits *The Review of Applied Ethics* and has a reluctant curiosity about other people
> CAT, her niece and closest friend, owner of a delicatessen
> TOBY, Cat's romantic interest
> JAMIE, a former boyfriend of Cat and still a close friend of Isabel
> GRACE, Isabel's housekeeper and confidante
> MARK FRASER, a young fund manager who meets a tragic death at a concert hall
> PAUL HOGG, the fund manager who supervised Fraser's department at work
> NEIL MACFARLANE, a lawyer in training
> HENRIETTA DUFFUS, known as Hen, who shared an apartment with Mark and Neil
> JOHN LIAMOR, Isabel's college lover, long gone but not forgotten

Although he has written more than fifty books over a long career, Alexander McCall Smith is best known for the No. 1 Ladies' Detective series novels featuring Precious Ramotswe, a woman of traditional build who solves mysteries in Gaborone, Botswana. The first five volumes of that series, beginning with *The No. 1 Ladies' Detective Agency* (1998), sold more than five million copies and were translated into more than thirty languages. Readers were charmed by Mma Ramotswe and her gentleness, her optimism, and her affirming insights into human nature. With *The Sunday Philosophy Club*, McCall Smith begins a new series, also featuring a woman detective with a sense that people are basically good.

Isabel Dalhousie, the main character, is an independently wealthy, middle-aged woman living in Edinburgh. Her mind is of a philosophical bent, and she is editor of a scholarly journal, "The Review of Applied Ethics," as well as head of an informal group that calls itself the Sunday Philosophy Club. She listens to classical music, collects valuable paintings, and begins her mornings with a cup of coffee and the crossword puzzle. She sips tea while working on manuscripts in the afternoon and sips good wine while chatting with friends in the evening. Like her spiritual cousin Precious Ramotswe, she is motivated by a genuine desire to live a good life, rather than by greed or jealousy.

As in the books of the No. 1 Ladies' Detective series, there is no violence and no blood in *The Sunday Philosophy Club*. Isabel is attending a thoroughly civilized concert by the Reykjavik Symphony at Usher Hall when she happens to see, in the novel's first sentence, a young man fall to his death from "the gods," or the hall's highest balcony. Although the death is horrible and sad, even when describing the body, the narrator's gaze remains firmly on the intimate details of the young man's humanity, "his legs twisted over the arms of the neighboring seats, one foot . . . without a shoe, but stockinged." Although it kills him, the fall from up high leaves the victim with a "halo of tousled dark hair and the fine features, undamaged."

*Alexander McCall Smith is the author of the No. 1 Ladies' Detective Agency series, which has brought him international acclaim since the publication of the first volume in 1998. Previously, he had published some forty books, including legal textbooks and books for children. Born in what is now Zimbabwe, he lives in Edinburgh, where he has retired from the university there as a professor of medical law.*

While the authorities examine the body and then take it away, Isabel climbs to the upper balcony to look for clues. She has none of the swagger or feisty impertinence of other amateur detectives like Lord Peter Wimsey or Miss Marple; in fact, when a man below sees her looking down from the balcony, Isabel is embarrassed: "What must he have thought of her?"

Isabel's decision to investigate the death is a reluctant one, and slow in coming. The morning after the young man falls, she tries to tell her housekeeper, Grace, about it, but her mind wanders, first to a memory of two Scottish poets and then to a long-ago news story about a man falling to his death on his honeymoon in South America. Trying to settle in with the crossword puzzle, Isabel reflects on the man who died, wondering, "Would she have felt differently if he had been somebody older? Would there have been the same poignancy had the lolling head been grey, the face lined with age rather than youthful?" She does not find the answer, but for whatever reason, the death nags at her.

It turns out that Isabel's niece, Cat, owner of a coffeehouse and delicatessen, slightly knew the dead man, Mark Fraser, because he lived in her neighborhood and was an occasional customer. Isabel's conversation with Cat, intended as an airing of Isabel's thoughts about the death, becomes instead a discussion of Cat's new boyfriend, Toby. Isabel invites them to dinner and develops an instant (and astute) dislike for the pretentious Toby, who wears corduroy trousers the color of crushed strawberries.

Listening to Cat and Toby, Isabel begins to reflect on the wonderful qualities of her own college lover, John Liamor. Brilliant, handsome and condescending, he was as arrogant and thoughtless as Isabel was reasonable and kind. Eventually they were married, in a way, but he soon proved unfaithful and eventually went to California with another woman. While Cat and Toby continue their dinner conversation, Isabel wonders "why we needed to be in love at all. The reductionist answer was that it was simply a matter of biology, and that love provided the motivational force that encouraged people to stay together to raise children." As easily distracted by philosophical digressions as she is, it is perhaps no wonder that weeks go by before Isabel begins to investigate Fraser's death in earnest.

As she interviews Fraser's roommates and acquaintances, Isabel begins to get a sense of the victim and his world. He was a fund manager, and Isabel has to learn a bit about the stock market and insider trading to understand her conversations with Fraser's supervisor, the pleasant Paul Hogg, who makes her acquaintance at an art exhibition. She visits Fraser's roommates unannounced, surprising them in bed together, but learns nothing other than their impression that Mark was a good man, happy and reliable. Before the end, there are several young, ambitious, beautiful people to consider, all bright and talented, each with something to hide. Each contact raises interesting philosophical questions in Isabel's mind, which she ponders for a few moments or discusses briefly with a friend before moving on. By the time the questions about Fraser's death are finally resolved, Isabel's curiosity about the case has fizzled out, replaced by broader questions about youth and ambition, and the story fades quietly away.

What Isabel is really interested in is love and how it shapes a life. She devotes a great deal of thought to looking for a way to bring Cat and Cat's old boyfriend Jamie together. She loves them both, but although Jamie pines for Cat, Cat simply does not return his love. Isabel feels tender sympathy for Jamie, in no small part because she has waited two decades for John Liamor "to walk through the door and say . . . : I'm sorry. All these years that we've wasted. I'm sorry." It seems safe to assume that McCall Smith will continue to weave the thread of Isabel's old love story through the rest of the series, as he will the themes of love and forgiveness.

McCall Smith has lived in Edinburgh since he was eighteen years old and offers *The Sunday Philosophy Club*, in part, as an introductory course in his beloved city and country. Through the novel, many readers who have not visited Scotland will pay their first visits to Usher Hall, where the unfortunate Fraser falls to his death, and to the Georgian New Town and various suburban neighborhoods. They will encounter the painter Elizabeth Blackadder, the poets Ruthven Todd and Hugh MacDiarmid ("the best poet and the wordiest poet in Scotland," respectively), the Scottish composer Hamish McCunn, Edinburgh's "lower" tabloid newspapers and the "morally serious papers," and the Scottish children's characters Oor Wullie, Soapy Soutar, and Fat Boab. Isabel even pauses in her ruminations about her new friend Paul Hogg to comment slyly on the former lord chancellor Quinton Hogg. McCall Smith surely realizes that many of these references will be lost on his international audience but nevertheless sprinkles them through the novel as homage.

Delightfully, some of the small details in the lives of Isabel and her friends come straight out of McCall Smith's life. Like her creator, Isabel lives in the neighborhood of Merchiston, near the Union Canal. Also like McCall Smith, Isabel's friend Jamie plays the bassoon, and another friend Peter is associated with the Really Terrible Orchestra, the orchestra in which McCall Smith and his wife, a flutist, play. One senses also that only someone who knows Edinburgh well could so successfully capture its chilly, foggy atmosphere, which here seems entirely realistic, not cartoonlike.

In spite of all the cheerful coincidences and energetic young characters, however, *The Sunday Philosophy Club* is ultimately unsatisfying. It skims the surface, hoping to enchant readers with local color and intelligent thought, but it never looks very deeply into the hearts of its characters, good or evil. Ethical issues are raised but not explored. Trivial and fascinating facts and opinions (a digression on how Anglo-Normans blew their noses, a comparison between a forgotten German emperor and a potato) are tossed in casually but without apparent cause or effect. The plot, not a strength of the author even in his most popular novels, limps along for almost a hundred pages before Isabel begins to investigate the mystery. Hints about intentional avalanches and insider trading are left unresolved. A tabloid reporter investigates the death the day after it occurs, reveals that he knows about Isabel's clue-hunting trip to the upper balcony, implies that he knows more about the death, and is never heard from again. The Sunday Philosophy Club itself never even holds a meeting.

An argument can certainly be made that it is inappropriate to expect an author to achieve—or even to attempt—the same kind of work in every book, and comparing Isabel Dalhousie to Precious Ramotswe may be unfair to both of them. Many of Mc-Call Smith's current fans have come to him through a real affection for Mma Ramotswe, whose ruminations never get in the way of true feeling. Isabel seems colder, more rational, and readers meeting her hoping only for a wealthier, more urbane version of Mma Ramotswe will be disappointed. McCall Smith has promised at least three volumes in this series, and the readers who stick with him will be those who are able to embrace Isabel on her own terms.

*Cynthia A. Bily*

## Review Sources

*Booklist* 100, no. 22 (August 1, 2004): 1872.
*Entertainment Weekly*, October 1, 2004, p. 76.
*International Herald Tribune*, October 4, 2004, p. 16.
*Kirkus Reviews* 72, no. 15 (August 1, 2004): 717.
*New Statesman*, September 6, 2004, pp. 52-54.
*The New York Times Book Review* 154 (October 3, 2004): 30.
*Newsweek*, October 4, 2004, p. 61.
*Publishers Weekly* 251, no. 31 (August 2, 2004): 51.
*USA Today*, October 14, 2004, p. 5D.

# SWEET LAND STORIES

*Author:* E. L. Doctorow (1931-    )
*Publisher:* Random House (New York). 147 pp. $25.00
*Type of work:* Short fiction

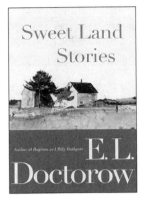

*Five long stories about attempts to fulfill personal dreams and ideals in America's "sweet land of liberty"*

E. L. Doctorow, author of *Ragtime* (1975), *Loon Lake* (1980), and *Billy Bathgate* (1989), is much better known as a novelist than as a short-story writer. Acknowledging that the novel has always been his typical rhythm, Doctorow said in an interview after the publication of *Sweet Land Stories* that while editing *Best American Stories: 2000*, he discovered that many authors were not writing the tight, epiphanic Chekhovian story but rather were going back to the more leisurely, plot-based story typical of the nineteenth century. The result of this realization are these five long stories, most of which originally appeared in *The New Yorker*.

The stories are primarily plot-based, recounted in a seemingly artless, casual tone—three told in first-person voice by deluded male narrators and two narrated in third-person voice by ironic storytellers. What is arguably "sweet" about these stories is the naïveté and innocence, thus ultimately the self-delusion, of the central characters as they seek to achieve the American Dream, find transcendence in a savior, or uphold their ideals in the face of political chicanery.

"A House on the Plains" is a comic horror, a con artist story told by the slow-witted son of a "merry widow" mother. After the father, whom Mama says was pretty smart "for a man," mysteriously dies, the widow thinks it best that she and her son leave Chicago for a small town where no one will jump to conclusions. Once settled, she takes in three orphans from a New York social organization and ominously declares soon after that if they do not come up with some money before winter, the only resources they will have is the insurance she took out on the three children.

Mama, a bigger-than-life, pragmatic believer in the American Dream, advertises for immigrant men, particularly Swedes and Norwegians, to join her in a partnership in a bountiful farm in the Midwest. One by one, the men who visit her disappear and her bank account increases from their insurance policies. The brother of one of the missing men arrives and begins to ask questions. Mama, nonplussed, formulates an escape plan that is treated as blithely as the rest of the horrors in this comic tall tale. Quite simply, she cuts off the heads of the nosey brother and her housekeeper to make it look as if she and her son have died in a fire. She frames her handyman for the arson.

The story ends with the handyman in jail, Mama in California, and the narrator son reunited with his sexual partner from Chicago. The fact that three orphans, several innocent men, and the housekeeper are all dead is just part of the comic tone of this tale that makes one admire Mama for achieving the American Dream of financial independence.

Doctorow has said that "Baby Wilson," chosen for inclusion in *Best American Short Stories 2003*, was inspired by his seeing a young woman in a long paisley dress walking along the Pacific Coast Highway in Southern California. Although Doctorow says he is not sure why he made this woman into Karen Robileaux, the kidnapper of a newborn baby, he thinks he must have decided as a premise for the story that while a man would kidnap a child for ransom, a woman would want the child for herself.

The story is told by Lester Romanowski, Karen's shiftless boyfriend. When she brings the stolen baby home, she declares it is her own newborn child that she is giving to Lester to be his son. Lester decides he is going to reform himself into a person who makes executive decisions. He wins some money at gambling, procures six fake credit cards, and goes to sleep thinking what a "great country this [is]."

*E. L. Doctorow has won the National Book Critics Circle Award three times, as well as the National Book Award and the PEN/ Faulkner Award. He has also received the William Dean Howells Medal of the American Academy of Arts and Letters and the National Humanities Medal.*

In a family van he buys with an American Express Gold Card, Lester and his "imitation wife and child" head west, to California. With the sun lighting their way like a "gold road," he has a revelation of a new life, in which he will become a dependable father with a full-time job. However, his dreams are dashed when he hears on the radio that the family of the kidnapped child has received a ransom note. "Can you believe the evil in this world?" he asks Karen, who articulates the theme of the story by saying that she has faith that people can be redeemed. To make a much-too-long story short, Lester and Karen drop off the baby at a church and head to Alaska, another place where people live in relative privacy, where nobody asks too many questions. When Karen gets pregnant, Lester declares himself alert and "ready for inspiration."

The heroine of "Jolene: A Life" also has her dreams, even though she is disadvantaged in several ways. She marries Mickey Holler when she is fifteen, to get out of a foster home where the father molests her and the mother beats her. This is a move from the frying pan into the fire, for Mickey and Jolene have to live with his Uncle Phil and Aunt Kay, and Uncle Phil has an eye for Jolene. In the comic fashion typical of these stories, Uncle Phil finally has his way with Jolene by coming up behind her one day while she is scrubbing the floor, picking her up with the scrub brush still in her hand, and carrying her into his bed. When Mickey finds out, he beats up Uncle Phil in a slapstick battle and then jumps off a bridge and kills himself.

Jolene is placed in a juvenile institution, but in a silly bit of good fortune, a woman in the place smashes a mirror and cuts her wrists with a sliver. When all the mirrors Have been removed and nobody there can see herself, Jolene begins a business of drawing portraits of the girls so they will know what they look like. She then makes friends with an admiring female attendant, but when the woman arranges Jolene's release from the facility, Jolene promptly leaves her and takes to the road, finally ending up, at age seventeen, in Phoenix.

Like other protagonists of these American Dream stories, Jolene appreciates the fact that in the West nobody cares much what one does. She meets a tattoo artist named Coco Leger, moves in with him, and starts working at his Institute of Body Art. One day, Coco's first wife shows up with a baby on her hip. Jolene finds Coco's cocaine, calls the police, and tells them about it. She then takes off after selling her wedding band for fifteen dollars.

Arriving in Las Vegas, Jolene, still young and shapely, gets a job dancing topless, and meets Sal, a distinguished, gray-haired man, who puts a diamond choker on her neck and asks her to move in with him. When Sal is killed by mobsters, Jolene takes off again, this time to Tulsa, Oklahoma, where she meets and marries Brad G. Benton and becomes a young matron of the upper class. After she has a baby and Brad starts to beat her, she gets a divorce, but Brad and his family get custody of the child. Finally, Jolene goes to Hollywood, the land of dreams and opportunity. The story ends in Doctorow's usual comic pathos, with Jolene thinking that maybe she will act in movies, so that one day she can go back to Tulsa in a Rolls-Royce, and her son will answer the door to meet his movie-star mother.

"Walter John Harmon" is also a story about self-delusion. The narrator is a former lawyer who has joined a religious group led by an uneducated garage mechanic named Walter John Harmon. The lawyer insists that he and his wife are not cult victims and allows his wife to take part in a "purification" sex ceremony with the cult leader. The community of believers survives because many of the followers are lawyers, accountants, public relations experts, and computer specialists, who know how to keep the outside world at a distance. The story focuses on the means by which Harmon maintains his charismatic hold on the community and how the members protect themselves from the outside world.

The followers' need to believe is so strong that even after Harmon deserts them with the narrator's wife, the elders, using the vague language and zany logic of philosophic sophistry and Messianic Christianity, argue that this immersion in sin and disgrace is a beautiful paradox of a prophecy fulfilling itself by means of its negation. The narrator basks in the glory of his unfaithful wife, who has been chosen to join Harmon.

Discovering half-burned papers in which Harmon has laid out plans for a wall to be built around the community compound—a task the followers find difficult because all their holdings have been placed in Harmon's name in Swiss bank accounts—the destitute group undergoes a harsh winter. The story ends ominously, with the narrator planning to build the wall, noting that the plans, in spite of Harmon's lack of military experience, provide the community with a clear and unimpeded field of fire.

"Child, Dead in the Rose Garden" follows the conventions of a political mystery. Told by Special Agent B. W. Molloy, the story recounts the implications of the discovery of a dead five-year-old boy on White House grounds. Only five months from retirement, Molloy, a twenty-four-year veteran of the Federal Bureau of Investigation

(FBI), gets the case. Suspecting a symbolic act by terrorists, the administration wants the case to be kept secret. Molloy runs into obstructions from the head of the White House Office of Domestic Policy, who insists that a body was never found.

Molloy, however, perseveres and flies to the boy's home in Houston, only to find that the child's immigrant parents, the Guzmans, are being detained by the Immigration and Naturalization Service (INS). Further developments reveal that the boy's father was a gardener for a wealthy Texan, a strong supporter of the president. The source of the mystery turns out to be the Texan's daughter, Chrissie Stevens, who engineered the placement of the boy (who died of natural causes) to shock those who run things into some sense of responsibility. After warning the Office of Domestic Policy at the White House that if the boy's parents are not released by the INS, he will give the story to major newspapers, Molloy resigns from the FBI and writes a letter to the Guzmans, telling them that their son will lie in an unmarked grave in Arlington National Cemetery among others who died for their country.

These are entertaining and diverting stories, relayed by a master storyteller. However, in their simplistic, self-indulgent shots at innocence, ignorance, and naïveté, they fail to provide any important insights into either the nature of human hopes or the national mythos about the American Dream.

*Charles E. May*

## Review Sources

*Booklist* 100, no. 12 (February 15, 2004): 1003.
*The Boston Globe*, May 9, 2004, p. D6.
*International Herald Tribune*, May 17, 2004, p. 12.
*Kirkus Reviews* 72, no. 4 (February 15, 2004): 145.
*Library Journal* 129, no. 4 (March 1, 2004): 110.
*Los Angeles Times*, May 16, 2004, p. R7.
*The New York Times Book Review* 153 (June 27, 2004): 8.
*People* 61, no. 21 (May 31, 2004): 53.
*Publishers Weekly* 251, no. 12 (March 22, 2004): 59.

# THE TRAVELS AND ADVENTURES OF SERENDIPITY
## A Study in Sociological Semantics and the Sociology of Science

*Authors:* Robert K. Merton (1910-2003) and Elinor
 Barber (1924-1999)
*First published: Viaggi e avventure della Serendipity*,
 2002, in Italy
Introduction by James L. Shulman
*Publisher:* Princeton University Press (Princeton, N.J.).
 313 pp. $30.00
*Type of work:* History of science, language, and soci-
 ology

*This study of the creation and diffusion of the word
"serendipity" investigates its move from obscurity into
scholarly use and eventually into the linguistic mainstream; written in 1958, the book uncannily foreshadows
controversies during the second half of the twentieth century about the role of unexpected discovery in science and
the research and funding battles that ensued*

   In *The Travels and Adventures of Serendipity*, Robert Merton and Elinor Barber
draw a map of their intellectual journey that entices readers to follow. They unfold the
story of the word "serendipity," coined by Horace Walpole, English aristocrat and an-
tiquarian, and first used by him in a letter (January 28, 1754) to British diplomat Sir
Horace Mann. Walpole wrote that he had come upon a crucial discovery in an old
book that was of the kind he called "Serendipity." He explained to Mann that the word
derived from "a silly fairy tale" he had read in which "the three Princes of Serendip"
were "always making discoveries, by accidents and sagacity, of things which they
were not in quest of." For the next seventy-nine years, there was no record of "serendipity" appearing in written form.
   Then in 1833, Walpole's letters to Mann were published. Walpole was well
known, and thus his new term theoretically became available for use. However, the
early Victorians did not adopt it, probably because it (and its creator) ran counter to
the tenor of the times, which honored seriousness and competence. Thomas Macau-
lay, distinguished reviewer of Walpole's letters, assessed Walpole as a trifler and a
man of affectation whose word coinages were symptomatic of an "unhealthy and disorganized mind." As the nineteenth century unfolded, however, literary critics began
to afford Walpole more respect, and as his currency rose, so did serendipity's.
   Merton and Barber explain that "serendipity" was eventually noticed by a few collectors and bibliophiles and, forty-two years after Walpole's letters were published,
another writer first used "serendipity" in print. The word stayed within literary circles
until the turn of the twentieth century, when it tiptoed further, particularly through the
attention of Wilfred Meynall. Meynall, magazine editor and literary country squire,

listed serendipity as his re-creation in successive editions of his *Who's Who* entry, and he seemed to be the first to use the word as part of a "moral and intellectual outlook" rather than "incidental whimsy."

So the word began its journey, gathering connotations and variations of meaning, assuming emphases that were most compatible with the given context and the user's purpose. Merton and Barber investigate meaning changes in detail, noting that even the first few users gave "serendipity" their own interpretations. This tendency reflects what the authors call a "single fundamental tension in the concept of accidental discovery: a tension between the attribution of credit for an unexpected discovery to the discoverer on the one hand, and to auspicious external circumstances on the other." In the 1930's, "serendipity" entered the vocabulary of science, where its greatest changes in meaning were to occur. Walter B. Cannon, professor of physiology at Harvard Medical School, was instrumental, using "serendipity" to mean not just accidental discoveries in science but also to express a philosophical approach to scientific research.

*Robert K. Merton was a professor at Columbia University for almost forty years. He is considered one of the most influential sociologists of the twentieth century and credited with coining terms such as "self-fulfilling prophecy" and "role model" and the concept of the focus group. His works include* Social Theory and Social Structure *(1957) and* On the Shoulders of Giants *(1965).*

*Elinor Barber was Research Associate at Columbia University at the time of her death. Her publications include* Bridges to Knowledge *(coauthor, 1985) and* Increasing Faculty Diversity *(coauthor, 2003).*

Serendipity became increasingly of interest within the scientific community, and the term began to be noticed by journalists writing about science for the popular press. Merton and Barber follow the hibernations, meanderings, and permutations of "serendipity" to foreshadow the important and controversial role that the concept of accidental discovery came to play in the scientific framework of the twentieth century. Although the book has chapters on the social history and the moral implications of serendipity and deals with serendipity in the humanities, the primary focus is on its significance in science.

The manuscript that became *The Travels and Adventures of Serendipity* was completed in 1958. Reminiscent, perhaps, of serendipity's own periods of hibernation, Merton and Barber agreed to set their manuscript aside "for a while," where it remained until the 1990's. Then, editors at the Italian press *Il Mulino* approached the authors to publish the work, and permission was granted. Barber died shortly afterward. The book appeared in Italian in 2002, followed two years later by the English edition. The added preface and afterword are authored by Merton alone. He explains that the text was not tampered with because it had become an unintentional time capsule, revealing how the word and its history appeared to him and his coauthor in the 1950's. The only changes were some redivision of chapters and the wording of the subtitle.

In the autobiographical, seventy-page afterword, written shortly before Merton's death in 2003, he pronounces his investigation of serendipity "virtually inevitable," details his encounters with serendipity since the manuscript was written, and investigates how the word and concept have been further adopted—and adapted—in various arenas since 1958. He also amplifies material from the text. One charming example is Merton's account of his 1933 purchase of the unabridged *Oxford English Dictionary* (OED). He was an undergraduate at Harvard when then-President Franklin D. Roosevelt closed all banks for an unspecified period of time in an effort to turn around the influence of the Great Depression. People lost access to their money, but merchants in Cambridge—including a bookseller—devised a method through which certified Harvard students could make purchases on credit. Hoping to convert at least part of his unreachable cash into books, Merton unexpectedly came upon the ten-volume OED, a very expensive reference work. He ended up "spending" almost a third of the cash that was to take him through the school year for the OED, and later remarked: "Still, I now have only to glance at those heavily worn volumes on a nearby bookshelf to reflect on the pleasurable use to which they have been put these last seventy years and to realize yet again the impulsive wisdom of that scholarly investment." Merton says he first saw the word "serendipity" while searching for something else in volume 9 of his OED, and instantly it became a part of his "working vocabulary." In 1945, Merton first used "serendipity" in a published paper.

In addition to humanizing the rather elaborate text, Merton's afterword affords readers new material. For example, it includes different meanings of "serendipity" found in English dictionaries from 1909 to 2000 and discusses how "serendipity" has migrated into other languages, offering translations and transliterations from bilingual dictionaries. Merton explains how his thinking evolved after 1958, for example, how the essential distinction between the psychological and sociological aspects of serendipity came to him in the 1970's, when he was reflecting upon "special sociocultural environments that evidently fostered scientific discoveries." Merton also speculates about the book's belated publication, admitting that had it appeared earlier, "much of the recent research on the role of serendipity in scientific discovery might have begun decades earlier" and "presumably we would now have a more advanced understanding of the process of serendipitous discovery in the evolution of science," which he calls an "intriguing, and rather distressing, counterfactual thought."

Indeed, the prophetic and retrospective perspectives of this text are some of its most compelling aspects. Readers see the routes taken by accomplished intellects from the vantage point of many decades afterward as the authors investigate—through one word—how language changes, knowledge unfolds, and research environments are structured as well as how these aspects are intertwined. Although the book is coauthored, Merton is clearly primary. His longstanding interests as well as terminology he has coined are reflected throughout, most forcefully in the second half of the book. Although Merton makes no mention of the particular role that Barber played, her involvement seems most evident in the early historical chapters.

The introduction by James L. Shulman, executive director of ARTstor, also provides a context within which better to understand *The Travels and Adventures of Serendipity* and its primary author. Shulman suggests that this book can be read as the narrative of "serendipity," but it can also be read as a study of the process of discovery and as a historical document that "foresaw the now-past future." As such, he positions the book within the context of subsequent debates that raged about the role of accidental discovery in science and research structures that relied on carefully planned inquiry. Shulman explains Merton's pivotal role in introducing "serendipity" to the social sciences in the mid-1940's. Shulman also investigates the book as a detective might, examining the evidence to try to figure out why the manuscript was put aside for so long, speculating that this occurred when Merton became fully engaged in work that was to result in his well-known *On the Shoulders of Giants* (1965).

*The Travels and Adventures of Serendipity* unfolds a personal encounter with serendipity, the cornerstone of Merton's research work. The book also investigates the diffusion of the word and its shades of meaning through the social and intellectual sectors in which it has become established. This may seem like a lot of attention for one word, but "serendipity" has a rich history. From its coinage out of thin air, "serendipity" has created space for itself in a wide range of subjects and in everyday parlance. It is the kind of word that many people report a bond with, a delight in, a sense that "serendipity" belongs to them. In the afterword, Merton cites a poll on favorite words in the English language, taken in the year 2000, in which "serendipity" ranked first. In the same year, he says, the Boat Owners Association of the United States listed Serendipity as the tenth most popular boat name. Merton also offers results of his considerable online database searches, which indicate rapid diffusion of "serendipity" into the vernacular as well as its growing imprecision of meaning.

Critics have noted that although the organization of the book is intentionally nonlinear, it seems unfinished in places. There is also rather considerable repetition of cited and quoted material. Overall, *The Travels and Adventures of Serendipity* vibrates in the delight that its authors take in the story of "serendipity." This scholarly, extensively footnoted work will appeal (as the subtitle implies) to those with a background in semantics and the sociology of science. Though it may be slow going at times, the book is also likely to be appreciated by people from other walks of life who have encountered "serendipity" and made it their own. Merton concludes the afterword by stating that although "it is not what I would write now," he is publishing the book—as is—"in the hope that it will be of interest to some who had heard whispers of its existence." This book is likely to be of interest to a wider audience. Filled with an amazing array of intellectual treats as it investigates the propagation and variations of "serendipity," the text creates an environment within which readers are likely to find their own unexpected discoveries.

*Jean C. Fulton*

　　　　　　　　　　　　　　　*Magill's Literary Annual 2005*

## Review Sources

*American Scientist* 92, no. 4 (July/August, 2004): 374.
*Bookforum*, Summer, 2004, p. 16.
*The Boston Globe*, February 1, 2004, p. H5.
*London Review of Books* 26, no. 18 (September 23, 2004): 29.
*New Scientist* 181 (January 31, 2004): 48.
*The New York Times*, January 31, 2004, p. B9.
*Science* 304 (April 9, 2004): 213.
*The Times Literary Supplement*, June 18, 2004, p. 4.
*U.S. News & World Report* 136 (February 2, 2004): 51.
*The Washington Post*, February 8, 2004, p. BW15.

# THE TREE BRIDE

*Author:* Bharati Mukherjee (1940-    )
*Publisher:* Hyperion/Theia (New York). 293 pp. $24.00
*Type of work:* Novel
*Time:* 1820-2001
*Locale:* San Francisco and Sausalito, California;
   Mishtigunj, East Bengal, Bangladesh; Calcutta, Bom-
   bay, and Rishikesh, India; London; Brynnsmere, East
   Anglia, England

*A Calcutta-born woman researching her family history
discovers that even when one ventures into a new life in the
New World, the past inexorably follows*

*Principal characters:*
   TARA BHATTACHARJEE, the protagonist and narrator, a thirty-six-year-
      old divorcé
   BISHWAPRIYA ("BISH") CHATTERJEE, her former husband, a Silicon
      Valley businessman, now disabled
   RABINDRANATH ( "RABI") CHATTERJEE, their fifteen-year-old son
   VICTORIA TREADWELL KHANNA, Tara's gynecologist-obstetrician and
      her friend
   YASH KHANNA, Victoria's husband, formerly Bish's professor at Stan-
      ford
   VIRGIL "VERTIE" TREADWELL, Victoria's grandfather, a British colonial
      officer in India
   TARA LATA GANGOOLY, a martyred Bengal activist, Tara's great-great-
      aunt
   JOHN MIST (JACK SNOW), an orphan, the founder of Mishtigunj
   ABBAS SATTAR HAI, the bomber, a descendant of East Bengal
      Muslims

   Bharati Mukherjee's fiction reflects her preoccupation with cultural conflicts, with
the results of change, and with the influence of the past on the present. Typically her
protagonists are Indian women raised in a society where life is governed by tradition,
as interpreted and enforced by the older members of large extended families. When
such women find themselves in the very different environment of the New World, the
result can be disastrous; in Mukherjee's novel *Wife* (1975), an immigrant brought to
the United States after an arranged marriage feels so lost that she descends into madness and finally murders her husband. For others of Mukherjee's women protagonists, moving to a new country is liberating. In *Jasmine* (1989), a young Hindu widow
who had intended to submit herself to a ritual immolation ends up on the road to California, optimistic about a future that will not be dictated either by custom or by her
relatives.

*Bharati Mukherjee has won awards
for both her essays and her fiction.
In 1981, her essay "An Invisible
Woman" placed second in the
National Magazine Awards
competition, and in 1988, her
collection* The Middleman, and
Other Stories *won a National Book
Critics Circle Award for Best
Fiction. In 1999, she was honored
with a Pushcart Prize. In 1987, she
became a professor of English at the
University of California at Berkeley.*

Although in writing these novels Mukherjee drew on her own experiences as an immigrant, *Desirable Daughters* (2002) was the first of her works that approached autobiography. The title characters of that novel are three sisters born into a family of Bengali Hindu Brahmins living in Calcutta. Like Mukherjee's sisters, one of the young women in the novel becomes a traditional Indian wife, while another moves to the United States and assumes the life of a thoroughly Westernized professional woman. The third sister, Tara Bhattacharjee, who alone of the three has the habit of reflective thought, becomes a writer. More than either of her sisters, Tara is torn between her place in the present and her ties to the past.

Ironically, it is Tara, the real intellectual, whose marriage is arranged by her parents in keeping with ancient tradition. Tara is impressed by the brilliant Bishwapriya ("Bish") Chatterjee, a Silicon Valley multimillionaire. She realizes that she could hardly do better. In upper-class American society, however, Tara discovers that the behavior of a wife and mother is governed by conventions just as rigid as those she left behind. Eventually she obtains a divorce from Bish, taking their son, Rabindranath, or "Rabi," with her. Living in the Haight section of San Francisco with a Zen Buddhist carpenter, she thinks that at last she has attained her freedom, though in fact her new life is also something of a stereotype.

In any case, the idyll does not last long. Tara's lover moves on, and Bish comes back into her life. On one of his frequent visits, Tara's house is fire-bombed. In saving Tara, Bish is badly burned. The arsonist escapes, but the police do discover his identity: His name is Abbas Sattar Hai. The obvious assumption is that Bish's status in the international community somehow made him the target of a criminal conspiracy.

*Desirable Daughters* was written as the first volume in a projected trilogy and, as one might expect, *The Tree Bride* begins where the first book ended. However, while *Desirable Daughters* focused on the options young women are offered and the choices they make, *The Tree Bride* deals more broadly with two Hindu concepts: karma, or fate, over which human beings have no control, and dharma, or right conduct, the only area in which they have a real choice. Significantly, the epigraph to *The Tree Bride* is a passage from the *Mahabharata* beginning, "All kings must see hell at least once." This emphasis on the inevitability of suffering, which dominates the book, is emphasized in the brief prologue with which the novel begins. In it, Tara relives the fire-bombing that took place several months before and comes to terms with the fact that, for the first time in her life, she feels vulnerable. Bish cannot protect her; he is incapacitated, and she is responsible for his care. Nor can she protect Rabi. Moreover, she is pregnant with Bish's child, conceived on the very day of the bombing.

Tara's first-person narrative now proceeds to her first encounter with her new obstetrician, "V. Khanna," who, to her surprise, turns out to be not the Indian doctor she had expected but a Canadian woman whose maiden name was Victoria Treadwell. The doctor's husband, Yash Khanna, is Indian. In fact, he was one of Bish's favorite professors at Stanford University, and, Victoria comments, Bish was her husband's most impressive student. The two couples soon begin to socialize, often at the Khannas' weekend home in Sausalito, which is called *Easy Come* because it was bought with the money Yash realized from his investments in Bish's endeavors.

There is still another connection between Victoria and Tara. Victoria's grandfather was a British civil servant named Virgil Treadwell, or "Vertie," whose final posting was at Mishtigunj, in East Bengal, then the home of the Gangooly family. Because he did not leave Mishtigunj until 1947, Tara believes that he must have known her great-great-aunt, Tara Lata Gangooly.

At the beginning of *Desirable Daughters*, Mukherjee related a story of this family heroine, a story that Tara and her sisters had often heard during their childhoods. When Tara Lata was five, her father, Jai Krishna Gangooly, arranged a marriage for her. However, on his way to the wedding, the boy Tara Lata was to marry was bitten by a snake and died. To save his daughter from a life of disgrace as a woman accursed, and at the same time avoid paying the promised dowry to the boy's father, Jai Krishna decided to marry off Tara Lata immediately. The most convenient bridegroom happened to be a tree. Thus Tara Lata became the "Tree Bride," and her father's scheme succeeded.

Jai Krishna could not foresee, however, that without a human husband, Tara Lata would have the freedom no ordinary wife possessed: She could read, she could learn, she could even develop her own opinions. As a nurse and a healer, Tara Lata gained the respect of her entire community. Eventually she became an activist, fighting for India's independence from Britain, then a martyr and a lasting inspiration to her gender and her nation.

In *Desirable Daughters*, Tara Bhattacharjee had decided to write a book about this remarkable woman. She had even made a couple of trips to Mishtigunj to research her subject. Early in *The Tree Bride*, she recalls her second trip. Six years before the bombing, she traveled to Mishtigunj alone and sought out the house where the Tree Bride once lived. Oddly, an elderly Muslim seemed to be waiting for her. The house was occupied, but he did take Tara on a tour of Mishtigunj, told her about the Tree Bride's donating her dowry to the cause of independence, and gave her a Bengali translation of the life story of John Mist, who had founded the community and whose best friend was her guide's grandfather. The two were hanged at the same time, Tara's informant tells her.

That visit made Tara want to know more, not only about the Tree Bride but about John Mist as well. When Victoria presents her friend with all of Treadwell's papers,

Tara has still another avenue of research to pursue. At the end of part 1 of *The Tree Bride*, Tara promises to tell her readers all that she has learned. She does so in part 2, which is the story of Mist's life, and in part 3, in which an aging Treadwell recalls his years in India.

In the first section of *The Tree Bride*, there are two chapters largely devoted to what Tara, the narrator, describes as a personal rant. Her subject is the evils of British colonialism in India. Although at first these chapters seem to be unnecessary digressions, they pave the way for the second and third parts of the novel, which present two possible ways of living within an alien culture.

Ironically, both Mist and Treadwell are British, and both have the capacity to kill, but otherwise they could not be more different. Mist, born Jack Snow, was a foundling. Reared in an orphanage, he decided to go to sea. On its way to India, his ship was taken by pirates who killed the officers and seized the one woman aboard, the intended bride of a British trader in Calcutta. After her ordeal she was physically and mentally ruined, and the trader wanted nothing to do with her. Because Jack was the only person who could identify her, he knew that the trader would have him killed as soon as he could arrange it.

In desperation, Snow murdered the trader, disappeared, and took the name of John Mist. Years later he surfaced in an area in East Bengal controlled by a native ruler, where Mist founded the settlement of Mishtigunj, built a good school, organized trade, and invited settlers in, as long as they were not Christians. Hindus and Muslims had no trouble getting along with each other. Before long, however, the British found a way to take over the village. Their first act was to hang Mist for a crime that took place five decades earlier and with him, his good friend, the Muslim leader.

Mist had become so much a part of Indian culture that he lost his ability to speak English. By contrast, Vertie Treadwell despised the people he was sent to govern. Part 3 of *The Tree Bride* is set in East Anglia in 1948, a year after the British left India. It is essentially a record of Vertie's thoughts and his conversations with others. After suffering a stroke, Vertie has a long, imaginary dialogue with Prime Minister Winston Churchill. At that point in Vertie's racist diatribe, he pauses to recall his meeting with Tara Lata Gangooly, and it becomes clear that, though he could never admit it, she was the only woman Vertie ever loved.

If Mist's life demonstrates how different cultures can coexist in harmony, Vertie's does just the opposite. His comments reflect not just his unwillingness to learn about unfamiliar customs but also his belief that anyone unlike him is hardly human. If, as Mukherjee suggests, this was a typical attitude among the British civil servants in India, it is no wonder that the Indians rose up against their colonial overlords and ousted them from the country. In these two accounts, the author has contrasted a man who acted unjustly with one who, though not a Hindu, had a commitment to dharma, to doing the right thing.

However, as Mukherjee's epigraph suggested, even the most noble people will, at times, find themselves condemned to suffer. In the final section of *The Tree Bride*, Tara is again reminded that there is no defense against karma, or fate. There is another bombing, this time of the Khannas' retreat in Sausalito, and Victoria is killed.

It does not help that Tara has discovered the chain of events that have made her, not Bish, the target of Abbas Sattar Hai's hostility. The book ends, however, with an expression of dharma. Tara and Bish, who have remarried, take Rabi and their infant daughter, Victoria, to India so that the Tree Bride can at last be honored with a ceremonial funeral.

*Rosemary M. Canfield Reisman*

### Review Sources

*Booklist* 100, nos. 19/20 (June 1-15, 2004): 1671.
*Kirkus Reviews* 72, no. 12 (June 15, 2004): 554.
*Library Journal* 129, no. 13 (August 15, 2004): 69.
*The New York Times*, August 19, 2004, p. E8.
*Publishers Weekly* 251, no. 33 (August 16, 2004): 41.

# TRUE NORTH

*Author:* Jim Harrison (1937- )
*Publisher:* Grove Press (New York). 388 pp. $24.00
*Type of work:* Novel
*Time:* From the 1960's to the 1980's
*Locale:* The Upper Peninsula of Michigan

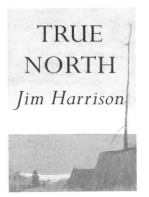

*The disturbed scion of a powerful logging family in Michigan seeks to escape the dark influence of his alcoholic father and discover his own path in life*

Principal characters:

DAVID BURKETT, the narrator, the fourth to bear the name "David Burkett," an heir to a powerful Michigan timber family
CYNTHIA BURKETT, his younger sister
DAVID BURKETT III, his father
FRED, the narrator's uncle, an alcoholic and defrocked Episcopal priest
JESSE, a Mexican immigrant, his father's assistant and aid
CLARENCE, part Finn and part American Indian, his father's handyman
LAURIE, David's first love
RIVA, Fred's girlfriend, who leaves him when he cannot quit drinking
VERNICE, a poet, one of David's lovers

In his memoir *Off to the Side* (2002), Jim Harrison leaps from anecdote to anecdote in his description of his personal history, touching briefly upon the various obsessions that informed his sensibilities and upon the episodes that defined his artistic identity and helped him develop as an artist and a man. Although his book *True North* is a novel and not a memoir, a work of fiction as opposed to autobiography, it nevertheless follows the form of biography in many ways. Typically, novels told in the first-person voice are tightly focused, taking place over a relatively brief period and concentrating on one event or series of events that affect a character's life. Like *Off to the Side*, however, *Truth North* skips from milestone to milestone in a tale of obsession and penitence that spans more than three decades as it recounts David Burkett's quest to eradicate and atone for the evil done by his family to the wilderness and to the poor logging families of the Upper Peninsula in Michigan. Heir to a wealthy timber family that has made its fortune by destroying families' livelihoods and despoiling the land, David is obsessed with exposing his family's sins to the world and, by doing so, perhaps being exonerated of his forefathers' crimes.

The novel begins with a brief, italicized prologue set in the present day. An injured David is rowing his horrifically wounded father (both his father's hands have been severed) off the coast of Veracruz, Mexico. David senses that his father wishes to die, and he pushes him overboard, essentially drowning him. In a way, the entire novel is about the same thing: David seeks to drown out his father's presence and works to remove all influences of his alcoholic and rapacious father from his life. Every choice he makes, as one lover tells him, seems not to be a choice of his own but rather a reaction against the influence of his father.

At first glimpse, *True North* is a familiar American tale, telling the story of the rebellious youth who is fighting back against his unfair and possibly unwholesome wealthy family. However, the sins of the forefathers seem particularly concentrated in David's father, who is more than just a character in the novel—he is a symbol of all that the Burkett men have represented for four generations. In addition to being an alcoholic with little feeling for his children, he is also a "nympholectic"—which is to say that he enjoys having sex with pubescent girls. David's mother deals with his father through alcohol and pills until she is finally able to divorce him and lead a more or less normal life.

The title of *True North* is particularly apt in the case of this novel. David is a young man without purchase, without cause, who is seeking a direction in life. As a teenager, and then after graduating from college, he becomes interested in religion and even considers becoming a minister. After college, rather than choosing either to live a life of indolence on the money left him in

*A native of Michigan's Upper Peninsula, Jim Harrison was raised as an avid outdoorsman. He attended Michigan State University and published his first book of poetry,* Plain Song *(1965), while still a student. His first book of fiction,* Wolf: A False Memoir, *was published in 1971. While considering himself more a poet and publishing more than seven volumes of poetry, Harrison has received greater accolades for his prose in such works as* A Good Day to Die *(1973),* Legends of the Fall *(1979), and* Sundog *(1984).*

trust funds by his father's family or to work for a living, he instead lives modestly on the small allowance provided him by a maternal trust fund and dedicates his life to searching out the history of the Burkett family's crimes against the Upper Peninsula. His quest to prove the corruption of his family's past is, perhaps, a desire to repudiate the innate evil that exists within him as a Burkett.

Two character types work as motifs that anchor the narrative throughout its course. First is the series of surrogate fathers who enter David's life. There is Clarence, the half-Finn, half-Chippewa Indian who works as a handyman for David's father; Jesse, a Mexican man befriended by David's father in World War II, who works as his father's aid and assistant and who knows all of the elder Burkett's dealings; and Fred, David's uncle, his mother's brother, a former Episcopal priest given to drinking too much and chasing his own phantoms. Although each of these surrogate fathers is kind and more interested in David than his own father seems to be, they also seem weak and too accepting of his father's sins. Clarence allows David's father to curse his son and to fire him (although he is soon rehired) because of his son's involvement with Cynthia, David's sister. Jesse continues working for David's father even after the man rapes Jesse's twelve-year-old daughter. Fred is overwhelmed by his own alcoholism and transitory nature.

Mirroring the weak men in David's life are the strong women who, again and again, provide him with either initiative or insight. First there is Cynthia, David's rebellious and courageous younger sister, who as a teenager repudiates their father by leaving the house and getting married to Clarence's son Donald. She proves to David that their father's influence can be resisted. There is Laurie, David's first love, whom he impregnates and who has an abortion; the abortion, as well as her family's silence, is paid for by David's father—indicating to David that he is, indeed, his father's son, and that the family evil that has concentrated itself in his father does indeed live in him.

The reader is also introduced to Vera, Jesse's daughter, who visits the Burketts and who has a schoolgirl crush on David but who is raped by the elder Burkett. Vera, in her beauty and despoiled innocence, becomes a symbol for David's quest. There is Polly, whom David loves and to whom he is briefly married, not so much for herself but because she is a symbol of the people wronged by his family. Riva, Fred's girlfriend (and David's lover for one brief period), as well as Vernice, David's poet lover, both represent voices of reality that let him know his obsession is eminently futile unless he can manage to look beyond himself and live beyond his father.

With the exceptions of Cynthia and Vera, all of these women are David's lovers. It becomes tempting to read this novel, written as a kind of fictional memoir, as a recounting of erotic escapades. David does seem to have more than his share of romantic liaisons, and they all seem preserved in his story in a way that other important events—say, the birth of his sister's children—are not. At the same time, however, his quest for erotic love and romantic fulfillment reflect his other quest, and each obsession stems from the same source: his need to prove himself worthy, whether through expiating his family's deeds or in the arms of a lover.

It is through his various abortive love affairs that David slowly comes to understand who he is and how his need to expose his family history has robbed him of a normal life. Years after his brief relationship with Vernice, he travels to Paris to seek her out. After she rejects him a second time, David spends a few hours taking in the fresh air in the Luxembourg Gardens, where he has an epiphany: "In the midst of my obsessiveness I had rejected many of the forms beauty can take. My depression over my father's wrongdoings and consequently those of my ancestors had prevented me from living a life of wholeness as surely as greed had blinded them."

The inward spiral brought about by David's fixation with his family's history is represented physically by the ankle he breaks a number of times in the novel. He is unable to move on with his life as surely as he is incapable of running or walking for long periods. Despite the time spent away from home in cabins or his trip to Mexico to seek out an adult Vera for forgiveness, as long as he spends his life entirely concentrated on his father and his father's family, he will never truly be able to mature and develop into his own person.

Finally, in the third decade of his quest, while in his late thirties, David comes to realize how his life has been wasted in its childish attempts publicly to deny his patrimony. He seeks out his father in an attempt not for reconciliation but, rather, to forgive him. His father, however, is so inwardly focused and blithe about his actions that he does not acknowledge that he has ever committed any wrongdoing. When David tells him that he wanted to kill him for raping Vera, his father replies, "There's nothing new in that. I wanted to kill my father. He was a mean-minded, self-righteous asshole. The ultimate bully to Richard and me. After being raised by him World War II was a relief." David is forced to realize that his father is the product of his raising in much the way that David is a product—albeit a divergent one—of his own.

The ending pages progress toward the climax that opens the novel. David and his father travel to Mexico to meet with Jesse, where David's father is presented with a chance to apologize and atone for his sins. It almost goes without saying that his father falls bitterly short, failing even to recognize his moment. By the end, however, the mystery of the novel is no longer about the father's actions or the family history but rather the nature of the heart that exists within David. Does he act out of hatred or love when he releases his father over the side of their boat? Will his action finally free him of his patriarchal legacy of obsession and self-loathing, or will it imprison him forever?

*Scott Yarbrough*

## Review Sources

*Booklist* 100, no. 13 (March 1, 2004): 1101.
*Kirkus Reviews* 72, no. 5 (March 1, 2004): 195.
*Library Journal* 129, no. 6 (April 1, 2004): 122.
*The New York Times Book Review* 153 (May 23, 2004): 18.
*Publishers Weekly* 251, no. 14 (April 5, 2004): 38.
*San Francisco Chronicle*, May 30, 2004, p. M3.

# THE TYRANT'S NOVEL

*Author:* Thomas Keneally (1935-    )
*First published:* 2003, in Australia
*Publisher:* Nan A. Talese (New York). 235 pp. $25.00
*Type of work:* Novel
*Time:* 2003
*Locale:* Two detention camps, in an undisclosed Western
country and an unnamed Middle Eastern country

*Alan Sheriff reveals his story of personal and profes-*
*sional devastation under a military dictatorship on a par*
*with that of Saddam Hussein*

*Principal characters:*

ALAN SHERIFF, the protagonist
THE NARRATOR, who visits Sheriff in the detainment camp and learns his
    story
ALICE, a journalist who introduces the narrator to Sheriff
TYRANT/GREAT UNCLE, the feared dictator of the country
SARAH MANNERS SHERIFF, Sheriff's actress wife
ANDREW KENNEDY, the head of the National Broadcasting Network
GRACE KENNEDY, his wife
MATT MCBRIEN, the commissioner of culture and, later, Sheriff's
    guardian
SONIA MCBRIEN, his wife
MRS. CARTER, a widow, the mother of Hugo Carter
PRIVATE HUGO CARTER, a soldier who served with Sheriff and died
    during the Summer Island Battles
PETER COLLINS, a writer who flees to Germany
LOUISE JAMES, Sheriff's former girlfriend, who returns from the United
    States to rescue Sheriff
CAPTAIN MCCAULEY, an oil barge captain and smuggler

Thomas Keneally's *The Tyrant's Novel* is openly based on an article written by
Mark Bowden that appeared in *The Atlantic Monthly* in 2002. Bowden, the author of
*Black Hawk Down* (1999), in this article offered readers an in-depth and somewhat
personal look into Iraqi dictator Saddam Hussein, life under his regime, and his employment of ghostwriters. It was the exploration of the latter that inspired *The Ty-*
*rant's Novel*, which, in Keneally's fashion, explores political, historical, and moral issues affecting its characters and readers alike.

Set in an undisclosed detention camp, undocumented refugee Alan Sheriff finds
that his new host country will not grant him political asylum, nor will they return him
to his homeland for fear that his life would be in danger. As a result, the antihero Sheriff is detained for an indefinite period of time in a double-walled relocation camp with
other refugees who find themselves in similar limbos. During his first three years in

detention, he develops a relationship with a journalist, Alice, and an unnamed writer, the narrator. Sheriff shares his autobiography with the
narrator, which Sheriff admits to be "the saddest
and silliest story you have ever heard."

Sheriff's tale begins in an unnamed country
that bares a striking resemblance to Iraq. A one-
time Middle Eastern ally turned enemy of the
United States, Sheriff's country suffers heavily
under U.S. sanctions and a corrupt dictatorship.
Keneally is able to illustrate the terror and injustice Sheriff's fellow citizens continuously endure living under their tyrant, who has many titles including Great Uncle. Great Uncle lives in
multiple palaces, while his starving citizens, as a
result of untreated water and despicable living conditions, die in the streets from chol-
era and other diseases. Keneally also lets the reader know that there is no saying no to
Great Uncle; if the tyrant wants something, he gets it. In *The Tyrant's Novel*, it is the
writing talent of Sheriff that Great Uncle is after and acquires.

*Thomas Keneally has written more than two dozen books, including the Booker Prize-winning novel* Schindler's Ark *(1982) and the acclaimed* Office of Innocence *(2003). Keneally has also won the Miles Franklin Award, twice, for* Bring Larks and Heroes *(1967) and* Three Cheers for the Paraclete *(1968). In 1983, he was awarded the Order of Australia for his services and contributions to Australian literature.*

Sheriff's life comes crashing down around him when his young, lovely, and talented wife, Sarah Manners, dies suddenly from a cerebral aneurysm. Prior to her
death, Sheriff and Sarah had lived a somewhat privileged life. Sheriff had been a
prominent international writer who received critical acclaim for a collection of short
stories based on his tour of duty in the wars of Summer Island, where his country
fought against an enemy only known as The Others. Nationally loved, Sarah was once
a famous television and stage actress. Her career ended when she refused to act any
longer as a mouthpiece for the state in her daily soap opera. Although she stated a sudden affliction of migraine headaches as her official reason for leaving the small
screen, in truth it was a silent protest against Great Uncle.

At the time of Sarah's death, Sheriff's recently finished first novel was to be published in the United States. The novel told a fictional account of the wars his country
had been through, and the unbearable suffering under which his country continues to
live as a result of the sanctions imposed by the United States. In an act of despair and
mourning, he buried the newly completed manuscript and computer disks with Sarah,
as a tribute to her, and threw his laptop into the river. By doing this, the novel belonged to Sarah, and Sarah alone.

Now alone and on the brink of suicide, Sheriff begins to translate and subtitle
Western films for the National Broadcasting Network, which his close friend, and Sarah's former producer, Andrew Kennedy has been appointed to run by Great Uncle. It
is through his literary work and film translation that Sheriff catches the attention of
Great Uncle. While at work one day, Kennedy and Sheriff's friend Matt McBrien (recently appointed commissioner of culture), escort Sheriff to a waiting car, where he is
blindfolded and taken to one of the tyrant's many palaces. After a thorough decon-
tamination and examination process, Sheriff is taken to meet Great Uncle himself.

It is during this meeting that Sheriff learns of his fate. He is told he must put his talents to use for the good of the nation by capturing and exposing his country's plight and the inhumanity it suffers under the U.S. sanctions. Sheriff also learns that such a novel must be completed before a scheduled international meeting, where it is hoped that the country's devastation will illicit international outrage and will ultimately force the United States to lift its sanctions, allowing the country to prosper once again by controlling its oil sales. Unable to refuse, Sheriff is given one month to write eighty thousand words.

To ensure the deadline is met, Great Uncle provides Sheriff with armed guards stationed outside his home twenty-four hours a day. The guards are to take care of his every whim, as well as track who comes and goes and ultimately keep him under what amounts to a house arrest. His failed author friend-turned-commissioner of culture, McBrien, is appointed to provide Sheriff with literary feedback and support, and—unofficially—vodka. McBrien is optimistic that Sheriff will finish the novel and meet the deadline because he has heard that Sheriff recently completed a novel that already exposes the hardships their country faces under the U.S. sanctions. McBrien assures Sheriff that, with a little polishing and editing here and there, the novel will serve as the voice of their country and will free them of their misery. With the sense that his life is already over, Sheriff tells McBrien that he has buried the novel and all references to it with Sarah; the novel belongs to Sarah and is no longer his to give to Great Uncle.

Suicidal already, Sheriff resolves not to write a word but to wait for Great Uncle's guard to carry out his anxiously awaited death. However, a letter that he receives from a friend, Peter Collins, who fled the country and claimed asylum in Germany, explains that Sheriff's life is not the only life at stake. Collins writes that before he fled, he, too, was given an impossible task to complete by Great Uncle. He was also assigned a supervisor whose role was similar to that of McBrien. After establishing residency in Germany, the friend opened a package he received one morning to find his supervisor's head wrapped in plastic. Sheriff realizes that many lives are now in jeopardy. The thought of being responsible for Matt, his wife, and their unborn child is too great and forces Sheriff to seek desperate measures.

McBrien and Sheriff contact Andrew Kennedy and explain that the finished novel that could save all of their lives is buried six feet below ground with Sarah. Kennedy assures them that he has a friend who is a doctor and is currently studying a newly discovered phenomenon plaguing their country, called sudden adult death syndrome. Kennedy contacts the doctor on Sheriff's behalf, explains the gravity of the situation, and convinces him that Sarah's death would be an optimal case for his studies. It is under this cover that Sheriff agrees to have Sarah's body exhumed and the manuscript to be reclaimed by the living.

Revisiting the novel causes Sheriff to relive the battles of Summer Island. In particular, he remembers one gruesome attack from The Others that resulted in his country's unspoken use of chemical weaponry. With a shift in the wind, the chemicals not only killed The Others but also killed all the soldiers in Sheriff's unit not wearing gas masks and protective gear. One of these soldiers was Sheriff's friend Private Hugo

Carter, whose grieving mother has been under the false hope (provided by the government) that Carter is a prisoner of war. In an attempt to clear his conscience of stealing Sarah's novel from the grave, and promoting the state's cover-up lie that Carter had been captured, Sheriff tells Mrs. Carter the circumstances that led to Hugo's death. The confession is met with rage and disbelief as Mrs. Carter curses Sheriff, ultimately ending in an act of violence.

Away from Mrs. Carter and alone with the manuscript, Sheriff takes only four days to alter the plot to meet the needs of Great Uncle. Great Uncle is overjoyed by the results of Sheriff's labor and impressed that Sheriff finished before his deadline. As a reward for a job well done, Great Uncle bestows the honor of National Storyteller on Sheriff and tells him he will not only be responsible for writing all of the nation's stories and struggles but also will live in a mansion that is currently under construction, be appointed a car and driver, and have guards assigned for his protection and to be at his service.

As the realization of his future role as the tyrant's caged canary sets in, coupled with desecrating Sarah's grave and final tribute, Sheriff finds himself desperate for escape and overwhelmed by the feeling that he no longer has anything to lose. In an act that is half desperation and half self-preservation, Sheriff contacts an oil barge captain, McCauley, after whom he had modeled a sanction-breaking oil smuggler in his tyrant's novel. Sheriff pleads with, and finally convinces, McCauley to smuggle him out of the country in an oil drum. It is after his life-threatening overseas journey that Sheriff eventually ends up imprisoned once again, this time in a refugee detention camp surrounded by others with equally harrowing tales.

After hearing Sheriff's tale, the narrator glances around the detention camp's courtyard and asks of Sheriff, "I wonder if all these people have saddest and silliest stories to rival yours?" To which Sheriff grins and answers, "Oh no, . . . Some of them have been involved in genuine tragedy." *The Tyrant's Novel* is a mixture of personal survival and the desperation of having nothing left to lose.

*Sara Vidar*

## Review Sources

*Booklist* 100, no. 18 (May 15, 2004): 1579.
*Entertainment Weekly*, June 4, 2004, p. 87.
*Kirkus Reviews* 72, no. 8 (April 15, 2004): 350.
*Library Journal* 129, no. 13 (August 15, 2004): 68.
*Los Angeles Times*, June 13, 2004, p. R5.
*The New Leader* 87, no. 4 (July/August, 2004): 31.
*New Statesman* 133 (March 1, 2004): 54.
*The New York Times*, June 17, 2004, p. 1.
*The New York Times Book Review* 153 (July 18, 2004): 11.
*Publishers Weekly* 251, no. 21 (May 25, 2004): 42.
*Time* 163, no. 24 (June 14, 2004): 83.

# UNDERSTANDING ME
## Lectures and Interviews

*Author:* Marshall McLuhan (1911-1980)
Edited by Stephanie McLuhan and David Staines
Foreword by Tom Wolfe
*First published:* 2003, in Canada
*Publisher:* MIT Press (Cambridge, Mass.). 317 pp.
  $22.00
*Type of work:* Media
*Time:* 1959-1979
*Locale:* Toronto

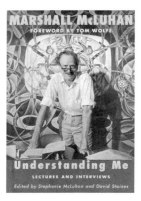

*During his last twenty years, McLuhan made frequent appearances on television, often to discuss the effects of that still-new communications medium; his pronouncements seem prescient to the editors of this volume, who have transcribed and annotated twenty speeches and discussions*

*Principal personages:*
  MARSHALL MCLUHAN, Canadian communication theorist
  TOM BROKAW, news anchorman and correspondent for NBC
  TOM SNYDER, television host for NBC
  GILBERT SELDES, American journalist and cultural critic
  FRANK KERMODE, British literary critic and broadcaster
  TOM WOLFE, inventor and practitioner of the New Journalism

A former librarian of Congress, the historian Daniel Boorstin described the printed book as the most efficient system ever devised for the storage and retrieval of information. Those who share his bias may find it ironic that many hours of Marshall McLuhan's pronouncements on the new electronic media, preserved in long obsolete videotape formats, are now readily accessible in book form. Yet McLuhan was a professor of literature and liked to remind television interviewers such as Tom Brokaw, "I teach books from morning till night."

McLuhan's only quarrel with the print universe was that it promotes linear, sequential thinking that ill prepares people for the electronic universe, where information travels at the speed of light. As he watched his children grow up with television, he realized that the younger generation perceived the world differently than their parents did, that the "generation gap" bewailed in the popular press was really a technology gap. Like Henry David Thoreau in the nineteenth century, McLuhan realized that tools use people as much as people use tools; while Thoreau concentrated on tools of industrial production, however, McLuhan focused on tools of communication. All tools, he said, are extensions of the individual human being.

McLuhan took to the new media more readily than most of his contemporaries, for he was a self-proclaimed "right-brain" man, temperamentally inclined to the creative and simultaneous rather than the rational and sequential. He thought in aphorisms and, while other aphoristic thinkers, such as his colleague Northrop Frye, worked hard to organize their insights into reasoned essays, he did not worry about consistency or coherence but preferred to let readers make their own connections. As a professor of literature and a close student of modernism, he built on the discontinuities of imagism in poetry and cubism in painting. He also anticipated the discontinuities of music videos, news crawlers, and push messages over the Internet.

∽
*Marshall McLuhan wrote and collaborated on many influential studies of media, including* The Gutenberg Galaxy: The Making of Typographic Man *(1962),* Understanding Media: The Extensions of Man *(1964), and The* Medium Is the Message: An Inventory of Effects *(1967).*
∽

Frye acknowledged that McLuhan taught him the importance of discontinuity in the modern world. Other professors were less kind and said McLuhan's books simply did not hold together. Indeed, once he became established as a media commentator, McLuhan tended to collaborate, bringing ideas to a book rather than architectonics.

*Understanding Me* is a posthumous collaboration between McLuhan and his daughter Stephanie, who became a television producer. The collaboration extends to his former student Staines, now a professor of literature himself, and to Tom Wolfe, the American journalist whose 1965 essay on McLuhan asked the inescapable question, "What if He's Right?" Much of the material that Stephanie McLuhan brought to David Staines for editing was already available in *The Video McLuhan* (1996), a set of six videotapes hosted by Wolfe and sold to libraries for $595. Very little is lost in the transposition to print, only McLuhan's cameo appearance in *Annie Hall* (1977) and reminders of how much people smoked in the 1960's and how oddly they dressed in the 1970's. Much is gained, meanwhile, from the addition of short introductions, unobtrusive notes, and a helpful index.

There are, in all, eighteen introductions to thirteen lectures and seven interviews, arranged in chronological sequence. (Some items are paired.) The range of tone is considerably greater than the subtitle's dichotomy suggests. The lectures vary from prepared presentations at academic conferences to after-dinner speeches for businessmen and talks to graduate and undergraduate students on various campuses. The interviews range from a panel discussion to serious conversations with fellow writers and light banter with television hosts. The panel features the venerable American journalist Gilbert Seldes, who covered radio, film, and early television in essays that culminated in *The American Audience* (1950). The conversations include both a studio exchange with the literary critic Frank Kermode and a backyard chat with Wolfe, who clearly "clicks" with McLuhan. The banter touches on topics such as the presidential debates between Gerald Ford and Jimmy Carter in 1976. (One regrets that McLuhan did not live to comment on Ronald Reagan's campaign speeches in 1980.)

McLuhan left most interviewers gasping. "You know," said Tom Snyder, "you're saying things that seem almost to be the opposite of old established truths." That is exactly the point. McLuhan wanted people to confront their preconceptions. In the first published lecture, he warns American educators not to confuse information with the medium used to communicate it and introduces his most famous aphorism, "The medium is the message." In later talks, he nudges the aphorism to maximum advantage; he suggests that a "cool" medium such as television soothes, delivering not only a message but also a massage. A true teacher by temperament, McLuhan never tired of explaining his distinctions, be they hot and cool media, the medium and the message, the figure and the ground, or some other set of terms. Those explanations make this book a highly accessible, if totally unsystematic, account of his thoughts. As Snyder said at the end of their interview, "It was easier listening to you than it is reading you."

As an introduction to McLuhan, this book has the virtue of presenting his thoughts in the decades of his greatest influence, the 1960's and the 1970's, and letting readers see them evolve. His remarks about the "global village" become increasingly pessimistic and, in a late interview, he observes that proximity can breed strife as easily as it can build community. A twenty-first century reader will be able to supply many examples of ethnic struggles reigniting as old political structures collapse and may see parallels between McLuhan's remarks on Vietnam and early twenty-first century commentary on Iraq. McLuhan's suggestion that war is a misguided form of cultural education may raise anew his hope that the American contempt for education will lead politicians to lose interest in war.

The ideas do not change so much as they expand. That is why Tom Wolfe can talk about McLuhan in Silicon Valley, even though McLuhan never saw a personal computer, and why the editors can characterize his comments about the information services as "predicting communication via the Internet." McLuhan would become the "patron saint" of *Wired* magazine, which reported on Internet postings of his pronouncements. In an earlier age, such messages from the dead were said to have come through the "ether," but these traveled by ethernet. Casual references to McLuhan in the popular press confirm that his ideas are as compelling in the age of high-definition television as they were when he called television a medium of "low definition," meaning that viewers had to fill out the shadowy images and thus to become personally involved. Wolfe is surely right to conclude his lively introduction by saying that new communications theorists "will have to contend with McLuhan."

A Canadian reviewer of this book, Bruce Powe, agrees with Wolfe and points to the great paradox of McLuhan: One must be literate, and must read books such as McLuhan's, in order to understand the new media. An American reviewer, Marshall Fishwick, remarks on how McLuhan's great strength was his ability to reconceive history as a story about the media that have recorded it. The history of communication turns out to be the secret of history and the key to understanding modern lives. It follows that one must think about one's life in terms of the communication devices that one has used. Both reviewers know McLuhan's work at first hand and have written about it at length. Both are well worth reading.

Transferring the spoken word to paper is no easy task, especially with a thinker as mercurial as McLuhan, and the editors deserve praise for judiciously punctuating the remarks to make them readable without the verbal inflections and body English on the videotapes. When he is elusive, they let him loose, resisting the temptation to gloss his bon mots and identify all the people he mentions in passing. Anyone unfamiliar with politician Edmund Burke or comedian Carol Burnett can visit an Internet search engine. The important terms become clear from repetition. Readers who have not heard of a "put on" (a deception, as in the question, "Are you putting me on?") will soon realize that McLuhan thinks that an electronic medium, especially television, encourages subjects to "put on" masks, as improvements on their actual humdrum selves, and thus to "put on" the audience. (They will also discover his penchant for puns.) Staines contributes a personal tribute in the book's final pages. He recalls McLuhan's teaching style and, like Wolfe, emphasizes the importance of Catholicism in McLuhan's life and thought.

McLuhan's impromptu reflections, which he liked to call "probes," are ideally suited to a collection. There have been other posthumous gatherings, and one can expect to see more. Eric McLuhan has edited a volume of his father's occasional writings on religion, published as *The Medium and the Light* (2002); he has also collected a boxed set of eighteen publishers' offprints, offered in facsimile as *Marshall McLuhan Unbound* (2004). McLuhan's work has had special appeal in Canada, where he is now recognized as one of the country's seminal thinkers, but the United States is never far from his attention. In a lecture from 1967, the year of Canada's centennial, McLuhan suggested that Americans were no more aware of their environment than fish are of the sea. "As the U.S.A. becomes a world environment through its resources, technology, and enterprises," he said, "Canada takes on the function of making that world environment perceptible to those who occupy it."

In addition to snapshots of McLuhan talking to Wolfe and Staines, there is a striking cover portrait of him, credited to Harry Benson of *Time/Life* but otherwise unidentified. Former students will recognize that it shows McLuhan leaning over his desk in the seminar room of the University of Toronto's Centre for the Study of Culture and Technology, circa 1970. In the background is a swirling mural by a friend, the Toronto architect René Cera. It might be called a modernist mandala on the theme of television, with a large screen in the center and eyes flowering all around. The artist's title, *Pied Pipers All*, is a fair summary of McLuhan's take on the new media. There is no piper, but there are many who watch and listen and who, by watching and listening, call the tune and become part of the show.

*Thomas Willard*

## Review Sources

*Architectural Record* 192, no. 10 (October, 2004): 90.
*Journal of American Culture* 27, no. 2 (June, 2004): 244-245.

# THE UNDRESSED ART
## Why We Draw

*Author:* Peter Steinhart (1943-        )
*Publisher:* Alfred A. Knopf (New York). 259 pp. $23.00
*Type of work:* Fine arts
*Time:* The twenty-first century

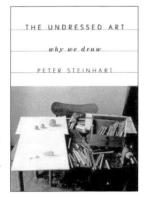

*An illuminating exploration into both what inspires people to draw and the artistic process involved*

*The Undressed Art: Why We Draw* may give the attentive reader the courage to take up a pencil or some pastels and work on the drawing that never seemed just right. Peter Steinhart is a naturalist by training, and he is the author of such wonderful books as *Tracks in the Sky* (1987), *California's Wild Heritage* (1990), *Two Eagles/Dos Aguilas: The Natural World of the U.S. Mexico Borderlands* (1994), and *The Company of Wolves* (1995). His passion for nature comes from having grown up in the Santa Clara Valley of California. In each of his books, Steinhart has told a story of the natural world under siege from the insatiable appetites of humans. *Two Eagles/Dos Aguilas* received the 1995 Silver Medal from the Commonwealth Club.

With the technological advancements of photography and the recognition given to experimental art forms among serious collectors of art, it would seem that the simple act of drawing could be relegated to the mere scribblings of children. In *The Undressed Art*, Steinhart emphatically states that drawing is not becoming an obscure art but is thriving across the United States in the many drawing classes and workshops being offered. His study covers the personal and the universal, from hands-on sketching to the place drawing has held in art history.

Steinhart has divided his book into fourteen chapters, each focusing on a specific element of drawing and especially on the urge to draw, to create. The opening chapter, "Allure," introduces the reader to a session of a weekly drawing group in San Francisco meeting in the home of art teacher Eleanor Dickinson. She has taught drawing for more than three decades. The model for the day is a man named Yoshio Wada. Steinhart provides some details about this elderly man, who, although nude, is "not seductive, not in any way Rabelaisian." Wada's body "tells a story." It reveals a "seriousness, a dignity, a flawed but compelling humanity." These details become obvious to the person who draws and thereby observes. Wada had spent time during World War II in internment camps. This detail is only one of many that make Wada's body what it is at age seventy-eight.

In this opening chapter, Steinhart writes about how the act of drawing has been denigrated in the established art world since abstraction became all the rage in the middle of the twentieth century. With the introduction of the computer, commercial art is almost exclusively created through the use of various software programs. Video art and installation art are what fill contemporary museums. With all this in mind, Steinhart speaks up for the value of drawing, for the process of the special bond between what the human eye observes and what the human hand draws.

While drawing live nudes "used to be something one had to enroll in an art school to do," now amateurs are flocking to their local community art centers and a variety of other venues to experience the act of drawing a live human nude. The phenomenon has taken hold in almost all cities and suburban areas. Steinhart points out that there probably are more than eighty "different drawing groups meeting weekly in the San Francisco Bay Area." As this surge in drawing classes has not been sparked by the art world hierarchy, the author can only assume that the motivating push comes from the artists themselves, from "something innate and human, by a constellation of long-standing behaviors and impulses shaped as much by human nature as by culture."

*Peter Steinhart is the author of four highly regarded books on the natural world. For several years, he served as an editor and columnist at* Audubon *magazine. He was awarded the 1995 Silver Medal from the Commonwealth Club for his extraordinary book* Two Eagles/Dos Aguilas: The Natural World of the U.S. Mexico Borderlands *(1994).*

Steinhart seeks to comprehend why he has become one of these amateur artists who is driven to draw. As a naturalist, he knows how necessary it is for both the nature lover and the artist to be keen observers. Leonardo da Vinci stated that art is "the true born child of nature." Though the author questions what brought him to join a drawing class, it becomes obvious as the book goes on that drawing is a natural extension of who he is as a person. Drawing, as art, is not some foreign code from which only the schooled artist can derive understanding and ultimately pleasure.

Significantly, Steinhart opens *The Undressed Art* with a chapter that wrestles with the issue of drawing's allure, of what moves someone to draw, because it is the central thesis of the entire book. It permeates every chapter. The book moves forward with such chapters as "Ritual," "Learning to Draw," "Connecting," "Waiting for a Muse," "Desire," and "Ambition." For a book like *The Undressed Art*, each of the chapters fits perfectly into the whole that Steinhart so engagingly has constructed. The reader is drawn in by the entertaining and informative anecdotes of the author and those around him.

Steinhart includes enough art history to give authenticity to his central point but not so much as to weigh the work down with dusty academic diatribes. The "drawing groups" are the heart and soul of *The Undressed Art*. In them, each model is sketched with loving technique. The artistic journey that each of these enthusiastic amateurs takes becomes a transforming experience. The process fills their lives with a richness with which few other daily routines can compete.

Steinhart ventures into the world of children and the almost instinctual role drawing plays for them. There is also a brief discussion of how photography has evolved and a scientific explanation of how facial features are recognized. At the end of *The Undressed Art*, the author includes a notes section, in which the reader can find other books that will take up each of the more academic topics. One of the most extraordinary and controversial titles mentioned is *Drawing on the Right Side of the Brain* (1979) by Betty Edwards.

At the heart of *The Undressed Art* is how the very act of drawing connects individuals to the world around them. Steinhart introduces the reader to the artist Jenny Wardrip Keller in his chapter "Connecting." The author includes this portrait of Keller in order to show how a successful artist carries out the process of connecting. Keller lovingly draws peregrine falcons. Her attention to detail in her drawings is a reflection of her feelings of compassion for the falcons.

As an artist and someone who is driven to connect with the natural world around her, Keller has also trained herself to focus on what she is attempting to draw. In another chapter, "Learning to Draw," Steinhart takes up the issue of how the brain learns to lock in on a specific item or focal point. While children in all cultures love to draw at an early age, what they draw is, in actuality, merely a representation of what they see. They do not have the necessary skills to draw a realistic or photographic picture. The trained artist has not only learned hand-eye coordination but also how to focus. The concept of focusing is crucial to all artists. Focusing involves deciding what to leave in and what to leave out.

The ability to remain still is also a crucial factor. Steinhart emphasizes the importance of stillness throughout the discussion on the process of drawing. The artist must have the ability to tune out all that is extraneous, all that is superfluous to making a connection with what he or she is drawing.

Love, or commitment, is yet another aspect of the art. The nineteenth century French artist Edgar Degas remained committed to drawing even after he went blind. Steinhart includes a description of how Degas, after learning that a dear friend had died, felt the need to "trace the contours of the dead man's face with his fingertips." Upon Degas's death, the only words that were to be spoken at his service were: "He greatly loved drawing."

With such chapters as "Why the Figure," "Faces," "What Happened to the Models?," and "Working Naked," Steinhart is at his most immediate. His visits to life-drawing studios take the reader into what can only be described as enchanted settings. The special relationship that is established between artist and model makes for fascinating reading. The author revels in the diversity that he finds in these studios. He states that "Looking at other people may be as essential to growth and maturity as eating and sleeping." The ability to read another person can prove essential to survival.

Each century seems to alter, as Steinhart says, "our sense of what the body means." By the twentieth century, photography had become the preeminent means of visual representation. As Steinhart states, "Photography hijacked so much of the artist's vocation that it is worth asking why people keep on drawing." With this concept as a discussion point, the author delves into why it is still necessary for people to draw. Drawing, after all, is a very personal process. It definitely involves becoming connected to a subject. A photograph can produce a perfect representation of almost anything in an instant, but it does not allow for the same brain stimulation that the methodical process of drawing encourages. As Steinhart so poignantly reflects on after relishing in his encounter with the Bay Area Models' Guild drawing marathon, the eighty artists really are "earnestly seeking to know for themselves what it means to be human."

With *The Undressed Art*, the author has found the appropriate tone for his subject. He is never heavy-handed and does not spend an undo amount of time denigrating other approaches to art in order to bolster his case for the value of drawing. Drawing is the "undressed art" because it is, when done as a true "spontaneous expression of what we see," without affectation. As a naturalist, Steinhart is very good at interjecting scientific theory when necessary. He has found a wonderful balance of personal story and theoretical meditation. Always informative and entertaining, *The Undressed Art* is a compelling read for anyone who has looked at a drawing and been moved.

*Jeffry Jensen*

### Review Sources

*American Artist* 68 (October, 2004): 77.
*Booklist* 100, nos. 19/20 (June 1-15, 2004): 1685.
*Kirkus Reviews* 72, no. 8 (April 15, 2004): 385.
*Library Journal* 129, no. 13 (August 15, 2004): 75.
*Los Angeles Times*, June 21, 2004, p. E11.
*The New York Times Book Review* 153 (September 12, 2004): 7.
*Psychology Today* 37, no. 3 (May/June, 2004): 82.
*Publishers Weekly* 251, no. 16 (April 19, 2004): 50.
*The Washington Post Book World*, June 13, 2004, p. 8.

# AN UNFINISHED SEASON

*Author:* Ward Just (1935-    )
*Publisher:* Houghton Mifflin (Boston). 251 pp. $24.00
*Type of work:* Novel
*Time:* The mid-1950's
*Locale:* Chicago suburbs and downtown

*A sensitive coming-of-age story of a young man during the summer after he graduates from high school and the discoveries he makes about adult relationships*

> Principal characters:
> WILS RAVAN, young man just completing high school
> TEDDY RAVAN, his domineering father, a successful business owner
> JO RAVAN, Wils's mother, who comes from a prestigious Connecticut family
> AURORA BRULE, young woman who becomes Wils's first serious romance
> JACK BRULE, Aurora's divorced father, a psychiatrist and war veteran
> CONSUELA, Brule's companion
> OZIAS TILLEMAN, city editor of a Chicago newspaper where Wils has a summer job

Wils Ravan, age nineteen, lives with his parents in a suburb of Chicago, in a house on the edge of a golf course. His father owns a successful printing business. Wils has been admitted to the University of Chicago as a freshman; he will begin in the fall. For the summer he has a temporary job, obtained through the influence of his father, as a copy boy in the newsroom of a downtown paper. Coming out of his sheltered background, Wils begins to discover a wider world, where it is not at all easy to find one's niche. Ward Just's *An Unfinished Season* contains a series of formative experiences for Wils that will likely remind adult readers of difficulties they had to face in the process of growing up.

The time is the 1950's. Dwight Eisenhower is president, and the Korean conflict has become a stalemate. Wils's father, Teddy Ravan, lectures him about the international Communist menace and un-American influences in the media. Employees at Teddy's print shop have recently formed a labor union, which is threatening to go on strike for higher wages—a development that Teddy attributes to Communist agitators. Wils's mother, Jo, is frightened and wants Teddy to settle with the union.

When no compromise is reached, the workers go on strike, and Teddy hires a crew of rough characters as strikebreakers. A crisis occurs when a brick is thrown through the window of the Ravans' home. The shattered window shows Wils, for the first time, that his father is not always in control. The emotional impact of this event on the young man is condensed into one powerful sentence:

I realized how far from normal our family had become, my mother frightened by cars in the road and threatening telephone calls, my father carrying a gun and worried about the Communists and the future of his business, and I—I, so far on the margins of the family, a spectator only, trying to read between the lines and discovering that the spaces were infinite but that one thing was certainly true, my father and mother loved each other and cared about each other, and then from the moment the brick crashed through the window I knew that was an illusion and the space between them was infinite, too.

Soon after the brick incident, Wils's elderly grandfather in Connecticut has a stroke, so his mother goes East to be with her parents. Teddy and Wils are left on their own, playing golf and pinochle and having extended conversations. Wils's grandfather was part of the moneyed Eastern establishment and held a poor opinion of Chicago. He had expected his daughter to marry and stay in the East and had offered a job to his prospective son-in-law—but Teddy had curtly turned him down. Teddy had never gotten along with Jo's father. When the old man dies, Jo is distraught and goes so far as to blame Teddy for causing her father's death by his antagonistic attitude. Harsh words are spoken, and Wils discovers another gap in his naïve understanding of his parents.

At work at the newspaper, Wils sees that daily stories of shootings, suicides, rapes, and other tragedies are headlined to sell papers. The stories are written to be as sensational as possible. Stories featuring prominent people in the midst of scandal are particularly good sellers. A reporter may pass himself off as a police investigator in order to gain admittance to a crime scene, to take photos or interview a distraught victim. There appear to be no ethical standards that stand in the way of getting information. For Wils, being in such an environment of cutthroat competition is a brand-new experience.

In the evenings, Wils is part of a completely different world. With his upper-middle-class family background, he is invited to numerous debutante parties given by the parents of young women in his peer group. These parties are generally formal; the women wear gowns, and the men wear dinner jackets and dancing shoes. The main activities are dancing, drinking, and polite conversation. Wils tells sensational stories from his newspaper job to provide entertainment for party guests. The young people form an eager audience, as the anecdotes are somewhat risqué. Some of the parents object to his telling such stories because they want to shield their sons and daughters from the roughness of the lower-class world. At one party, Wils becomes acquainted with a girl named Aurora, who is planning to attend an eastern college in the fall. He takes her home after the dance and then begins dating her. She lives in an apartment with her divorced father, who is a psychiatrist.

Meeting Aurora's father, Jack Brule, is an eye-opening experience for Wils. First of all, Jack is divorced, which is uncommon among suburban social circles in the 1950's. Furthermore, Jack is a veteran of World War II, having served in the South Pacific, with traumatic memories of the Bataan Death March, in which many American soldiers died. Winning the war was not a glorious victory for those who came home physically or psychologically wounded. Like many veterans, Jack has been unable to talk openly about his experience in Bataan, referring to it with the euphemism

*Ward Just was a reporter for various*
*newspapers and magazines, including*
The Washington Post *and* Newsweek.
*He is the author of fourteen novels*
*and other works. His awards include*
*the James Fenimore Cooper Prize*
*from the Society of American*
*Historians and the O. Henry Award*
*for short stories.*

"The Hike." He suffers from frequent headaches. On one occasion he tries to explain to Wils the burden that he carries from being unable to overcome his hatred for his Japanese captors. Then Consuela arrives, a woman of Greek heritage whom Wils assumes is Jack's dinner companion for that evening. While Jack is dressing, Consuela talks about herself and Jack with a frankness that makes Wils think to himself, "No one in my straight-laced family would ever tell such stories to a stranger." Later that evening, Wils asks Aurora where Consuela lives. "Aurora looked closely at me and gave a long exasperated sigh, rolling her eyes. She lives here, dummy." Once again, Wils is taken aback when encountering a lifestyle that is outside all of his previous experience.

Wils and Aurora take long walks together and go for drives along Lake Michigan. They talk about their parents, about future goals, about their favorite jazz musicians, about whatever comes to mind. Wils envisions his fondness for Aurora growing into romantic love. On one occasion he tells Aurora that he wants them to have no secrets between them, but she informs him that is impossible. As the daughter of divorced parents, Aurora has developed a maturity and self-awareness that Wils lacks. When he is with her, he realizes how much he still has to learn about life and himself: "I had yet to find a narrative to my life, certainly no narrative that advanced in any coherent order or in which I played anything but a winning cameo role, kid brother or raconteur. It did not seem to me that you could fashion a life until you could make decisions that governed it. Until that time you lived quietly in your father's house."

Just describes the growing affection of Wils for Aurora through their conversations. Wils finds joy in being with Aurora but also finds it difficult to accept when they have disagreements. He learns that some topics are better left alone, that their relationship can progress better when he keeps some of his thoughts to himself. Like with any young couple, Wils blunders into awkward moments. He listens to Aurora's expression of a delicate feeling and treats it as a joke, only to regret his callousness shortly thereafter. Just is a masterful writer in showing how two people have to work to find a bridge between their separate personalities.

Aurora is taking a class at the Chicago Art Institute, and Wils goes to meet her there one day after work. She has missed her class, however, and a phone call to her apartment is unanswered. While Wils is waiting for her, he looks at some paintings and begins to speculate about what story the artist wanted to put on canvas. He tries to imagine what might happen next to the people portrayed in a painting, going beyond color and form to search for a meaningful message. Eventually, Aurora does arrive, but he hardly recognizes her as she stumbles along with an averted face. She has just come from her apartment and tells Wils that her father is dead.

Wils gets a taxi to take Aurora back to her apartment and tries his best to comfort her. The apartment is crowded with Jack's relatives, medical colleagues, and patients who have come to express their condolences. While Aurora retreats to another room, Wils hears from Consuela that Jack actually died by suicide. He shot himself during the night, after he and Consuela had an argument. Suddenly, a sensational story, something one would read about in the newspapers, has entered Wils's personal experience. After the guests leave, Aurora and Consuela have an angry confrontation, witnessed by Wils. He tries to take the role of a referee between the two women. Aurora's fury now turns against Wils. She orders him to get out.

Just's description of Jack's funeral has an unexpected emotional scene. The two women, the daughter and the mistress, walk together to the front of the church holding hands. Their grief has brought them together for this occasion. Wils realizes that he is an outsider to their shared grief and that his relationship with Aurora, which had been so full of promise, is finished. The title of the novel, *An Unfinished Season*, suggests a parallel to a recent big-league baseball season that ended in the middle of the summer because of a dispute between the players and the owners. All hopes for team championships or batting titles came to a sudden halt.

The last chapter of this novel is an epilogue, set on the Mediterranean island of Cyprus. It is several decades later. Wils has become a lawyer and is working for the United Nations (U.N.). He had been sent to Cyprus by the U.N. secretary general to act as a mediator between Greek and Turkish groups on the divided island. He has had some small success at the local level in halting attacks by neighboring villagers, but the basic conflict over who owns the island remains unresolved. Consuela has moved back to Cyprus, where she had grown up. Wils goes to visit her, after being out of touch for many years. Consuela tells him that she is married to a man who does not like coming to this island but that they get together periodically in Athens. Wils also is married, with a wife and two children living in New York. They talk briefly about Aurora, that she has published several novels which Wils had read, but neither one has had any direct communication with her since her father's funeral. Aurora was part of their common history during one summer, but that chapter is closed, and their lives have moved on.

*Hans G. Graetzer*

## Review Sources

*Booklist* 100, no. 18 (May 15, 2004): 1612.
*The Economist* 372 (July 17, 2004): 82.
*Entertainment Weekly*, July 16, 2004, p. 82.
*Kirkus Reviews* 72, no. 9 (May 1, 2004): 415.
*The New York Times Book Review* 153 (July 25, 2004): 7.
*Publishers Weekly* 251, no. 20 (May 17, 2004): 31.

# VANISHING POINT

*Author:* David Markson (1928-    )
*Publisher:* Shoemaker & Hoard (Washington, D.C.).
   191 pp. $15.00
*Type of work:* Novel

   *An unconventional collage of brief anecdotes, facts, and quotations assembled by a character called Author, who is preoccupied with aging, death, and art*

> *Principal character:*
> AUTHOR, a self-effacing collector of notes about artists

   In both *Reader's Block* (1996) and *This Is Not a Novel* (2001), David Markson constructs what seemed to be not novels but instead collections of brief anecdotes, quotations, and factoids. Neither volume is narrated, and neither offers the conventional gratification of observing human lives enmeshed in a plot that proceeds through tension toward resolution. In each case, the reader is invited to impute novelistic design to disparate statements—usually about eight to ten to a page. If "found poetry" is verse whose virtue lies in selection and arrangement, not invention, Markson has demonstrated his mastery of found fiction. He writes nonfiction novels that, unlike the famous cases of Truman Capote's *In Cold Blood* (1966) and Norman Mailer's *The Executioner's Song* (1979), do not attempt to adapt contemporary events to the conventions of nineteenth century narrative. Formally more daring, his books instead offer the raw materials for story in an assemblage of ostensibly random information.
   *Vanishing Point* constitutes the third volume in a cycle begun with *Reader's Block* and *This Is Not a Novel*. In its aspiration toward death and silence, the series might resemble Samuel Beckett's *The Trilogy*, comprising *Molloy* (1951; English translation, 1955), *Malone meurt* (1951; *Malone Dies*, 1956), and *L'Innommable* (1953; *The Unnamable*, 1958). *Vanishing Point*, in fact, quotes the opening line of *Malone Dies:* "I shall soon be quite dead at last in spite of all." Yet Markson is more radical in his challenge to novelistic tradition. His book constitutes a brilliant disappearing act, by a shadowy figure called Author, who, from the beginning, strives to erase his traces. "What Balzac would make of a novel of Author's" is one of the text's fragmentary statements. Through his prodigious creation of the vast, multivolume *La Comédie humaine* (1829-1848; *The Human Comedy*, 1895-1896), Honoré de Balzac became the prototype of the novelist as garrulous storyteller, and it is likely that he would have no idea what to make of Markson's odd, terse effort. It is up to the reader to make a novel out of *Vanishing Point*.
   "T. S. Eliot was afraid of cows." "There are 16,696 lines in the *Iliad*." "Seventy thousand people died in London in the Great Plague of 1665." Instead of satisfying one's curiosity, such curious snippets of information dispersed throughout the book provoke a reader to wonder just what they are doing there and what connection, if

any, they have to one another. Unlike *Reader's Block*, *Vanishing Point* has no character named Reader, but it demands a reader willing to take an active role in discovering patterns where others, like Charles Matthews, writing in the *Chicago Tribune*, might dismiss the disparate entries as so much "intellectual popcorn." One is told that Richard Wagner wore pink underwear but not why that detail is important or relevant. Turning the pages rapidly, compulsively, more than one critic has voraciously devoured such tidbits while questioning whether the entire experience provided any literary substance.

*Born in Albany, New York, David Markson has lived in New York City for most of his life. He received a B.A. from Union College and an M.A. from Columbia University. His books include an early study of the work of his mentor and friend Malcolm Lowry called* Volcano: Myth, Symbol, and Meaning *(1978), his own* Collected Poems *(1993), and the novels* Wittgenstein's Mistress *(1988),* Reader's Block *(1996), and* This Is Not a Novel *(2001).*

Scattered among more than fifteen hundred entries are some that appear to be reflexive, to offer clues to the nature of *Vanishing Point* itself. The terms "Nonlinear. Discontinuous. Collage-like. An assemblage" clearly apply to Markson's own book, as does the paradoxical description "A novel of intellectual reference and allusion, so to speak minus much of the novel." "A seminonfictional semifiction" is another way of characterizing *Vanishing Point*, as is "Obstinately cross-referential and of cryptic interconnective syntax." To discover the cross-references and make the arcane connections, a careful reader must do more than merely quote the book back at itself.

An integral part of experiencing *Vanishing Point* is making the effort to discover patterns and preoccupations in Markson's mélange. To begin with, most of the entries offer information about or statements by writers and other artists. Most emphasize the brevity and the misery of their lives. The poverty suffered by Pierre Corneille, Thomas Chatterton, Edmund Spenser, and others is a recurrent motif, as is the illiteracy of the mothers and wives of writers, including François Villon, Walt Whitman, and Giambattista Vico. Markson names the authors, including Leo Tolstoy, William Wordsworth, and Karl Marx, who begot and neglected illegitimate children, and he mentions the suicides of Virginia Woolf, Vladimir Mayakovsky, and Vincent van Gogh.

Much of *Vanishing Point* is preoccupied with cataloging where, when, and how artists died. One is told that the final mortal moments of Dante were spent in Ravenna, of Paracelsus in Salzburg, of Friedrich Nietzsche in Weimar, and of Richard Tucker in Kalamazoo, Michigan. For two uncharacteristically consistent pages, the book lists a series of times, places, and dates, without any names. Faced with a line that states merely "Haworth Parsonage, Yorkshire. 2 P.M. December 19, 1848," an educated reader might correctly guess Emily Brontë—or else set about tracking down the answer to that literary riddle.

   In addition, it demands both erudition and resourcefulness to identify the source of unattributed quotations scattered throughout the text. Many educated readers can identify William Shakespeare's *King Lear* (1605) as the origin of the question "Who is it that can tell me who I am?" Far fewer can, without investigation, cite the source of "The barometer of his emotional nature was set for a spell of riot." It is from the story "Counterparts," in James Joyce's *Dubliners* (1914), but Markson does not say so. Nor does he explain the origins or significance of "Seventy-two white raisins?" A reader might have to do some research to learn that, though the phrase comes from the Qurʾān, where it refers to the reward awaiting Muslim martyrs in heaven, it was widely mistranslated as seventy-two white virgins. Yet that still does not explain what the line is doing in this book.

   To begin to make sense, or at least a story, out of the enigmatic, independent entries in *Vanishing Point*, a reader has to collate scattered references to the elusive figure called Author. Just about halfway through, the text describes itself as "Author's experiment to see how little of his own presence he can get away with throughout." Consistent with the modernist ideal of self-effacing artist from whose autonomous creation all traces of the creator have vanished, the Flaubertian God who is everywhere present but nowhere visible, he in fact divulges little about himself directly. He seems to delight in the fact that, since almost nothing is known of the life of Livy, Rome's greatest historian has no history of his own. Yet if authors create books, authors qua authors live in their books. The most vital identity of William Shakespeare is the personality embodied in his plays and poems. While David Markson may have disappeared from *Vanishing Point*, its Author lives on, in the sum total of inferences one can draw about his predilections, antipathies, and style.

   He may or may not share biographical characteristics with David Markson, but it is possible to construct a rudimentary identity and plot for Author from clues throughout the book. Author is described as aging and enervated, someone who has begun to lose his balance, bumping into walls and tripping on a curb and on the steps of the apartment building in which he lives. He wears Adidas shoes and continues to use a forty-year-old manual typewriter, for which he is having a hard time finding ribbons and erasers. Author still listens to 33 1/3 rpm vinyl records and is particularly fond of opera, and particularly of performances by Maria Callas. Repeated references to cities and years in which the figure of the Wandering Jew, a figment of the anti-Semitic imagination, was said to have been sighted suggest that Author might himself be Jewish and mindful of the violent history of bigotry toward Jews. Several entries concern the Nazi death camps, while others recall the anti-Semitism of Frédéric Chopin, Fyodor Dostoevsky, and Richard Wagner.

   To judge by the number of entries on the subject, Author seems fascinated by the efficiency of other artists, such as composers, noting that George Frideric Handel completed *The Messiah* (1742) in only twenty-two days, that Johann Wolfgang von Goethe finished *Die Leiden des jungen Werthers* (1774; *The Sorrows of Young Werther*, 1779) in four weeks, and that Friedrich Schiller completed *Wilhelm Tell* (1804; *William Tell*, 1841) in six weeks. Yet, admitting a tendency to procrastinate, he presents this book as a pile of scribbled notes that he has for several weeks postponed typing. He provides them in the form of three-by-five-inch index cards that almost fill two shoebox tops taped together end to end.

Author, who longs for death, has thus effectively vanished from *Vanishing Point*, leaving it up to the reader to deal with the notes left behind. Yet there is an important sense in which Author comes alive only through absence, when the reader assumes the responsibility for deciphering and connecting his notes. According to a familiar literary trope, art is the only stay against ineluctable mortality; poets live on through their poetry. If so, that is also true of poets who, like John Keats and Beckett, express a wish to dissolve. They are most alive when welcoming death, as though artistic distinction enables them to transcend biological extinction.

By providing almost nothing but facts and quotations, *Vanishing Point* is an experiment in erasing its author, and its Author. In the book's final pages, the rhythm becomes more rapid, as the entries, sometimes repeating themselves, become shorter and shorter until halting with the final, single-word entry, "*Selah*"—the Hebrew word that signals the end to a psalm. Author is acutely aware of how capricious and unjust is the mechanism for artistic survival. One entry notes that Sir Walter Scott called Joanna Baillie, who was forgotten even before her death, the best playwright since Shakespeare, and another pronounces *Citizen Kane* (1941), the most admired of all American films, "overrated." In his choice of entries, Author seems to delight in recalling instances in which, oblivious to the judgment of posterity, minor authors heap abuse on major ones. Thus, Walter Savage Landor is quoted as declaring, "Most of Homer is trash." He recalls how Cormac McCarthy dismissed both Henry James and Marcel Proust: "To me that's not literature."

*Vanishing Point* is a short book with long ambitions—to wrest for its mortal Author a permanent place in literature. A compilation of information and quotations available elsewhere, it is a profoundly unoriginal work whose originality lies precisely in its arrangement of existing materials to emphasize the inability to be genuinely original. Even there, Author comes late to his awareness, observing that, in *Anatomy of Melancholy* (1652), Robert Burton had already noted, "We can say nothing but what has been said; the composition and method is ours only." In its idiosyncratic composition and method, *Vanishing Point* is David Markson's alone. If it cannot promise immortality for an anxious, fading author, it at least makes its points in a lively way.

*Steven G. Kellman*

## Review Sources

*Booklist* 100, nos. 9/10 (January 1-15, 2004): 824.
*Chicago Tribune*, March 8, 2004, p. 2.
*Kirkus Reviews* 72, no. 24 (December 15, 2004): 4.
*Library Journal* 129, no. 1 (January 15, 2004): 158.
*The New York Times Book Review* 153 (February 22, 2004): 16.
*Publishers Weekly* 251, no. 4 (January 26, 2004): 231.
*Review of Contemporary Fiction* 24, no. 2 (Summer, 2004): 131.
*The Washington Post Book World*, March 21, 2004, p. T06.

# THE VIENNA PARADOX
## A Memoir

*Author:* Marjorie Perloff (1931-    )
*Publisher:* New Directions (New York). 283 pp. $16.00
*Type of work:* Memoir
*Time:* The twentieth century
*Locale:* Vienna, New York, Washington, D.C., and Los
  Angeles

*An accomplished American literary critic reviews her
Austrian cultural and family heritage*

  *Principal personages:*
    MARJORIE PERLOFF, a teacher and critic
    MAXIMILIAN and ILSE MINTZ, her parents
    RICHARD SCHULLER, her grandfather, a
      prominent Austrian diplomat
    J. CRAIG LADRIERE, her teacher at Catholic University

When Marjorie Perloff announced that she was engaged in a memoir dealing with her Austrian past, it seemed to represent a departure from her usual writing, which consists largely of theoretical and revisionist interpretations of modern poetry ranging from the works of William Butler Yeats to Frank O'Hara. Perhaps Perloff's crowning achievement as a literary critic and historian is *Wittgenstein's Ladder: Poetic Language and the Strangeness of the Ordinary* (1996), in which she makes a strong case for a connection between the questions Ludwig Wittgenstein posed concerning language and the poetic experiments of the avant-garde, beginning with Ezra Pound and T. S. Eliot and continuing through postmodernism.

Wittgenstein's *Tractatus Logico-Philosophicus* (1922) argues a "picture" theory of meaning combined with the idea that logical truths are tautologies. The history of modern poetry from Pound's imagism to the impact of deconstructionist indeterminacy; from obscurantism to the literature of the absurd—all of these trends support Perloff's contention that Ludwig Wittgenstein and literary modernism have a great deal to say to each other. Wittgenstein (1889-1951) was an Austrian, and like Perloff, an Austrian of Jewish background. Although baptized a Catholic, Wittgenstein, the son of a fabulously wealthy industrialist, was representative of a large number of Austrian Jewish intellectuals who did not identify with their Jewishness but who nevertheless were perceived as a group apart. In reviewing her own Austrian past, Perloff is connecting not only with a cluster of ideas that support her critical and intellectual history but is also opening a Pandora's box of cultural and religious identities that haunt her own life.

Despite her gift for penetrating and close analysis of poetic language, Perloff has always contextualized her discoveries in biography or history. In a 1999 review of *Wittgenstein's Ladder* appearing in *Modern Philology*, Robert Gilbert applauds

Perloff for suggesting in commentary on Samuel
Beckett's *Watt* (1953) that the "existential quandaries of Beckett's character may, in fact, reflect
the specific dilemma of Resistance workers (Beckett served in the French Resistance during World
War II) charged with conveying a coded message
they themselves do not understand." In her memoir, *The Vienna Paradox*, Perloff is involved, again
and again, in trying to convey a "coded message"
about her own cultural and religious identity which
she may not, finally, completely understand.

    Perloff's name at birth was Gabriele Mintz.
She begins her memoir with a chapter appropriately titled "Seductive Vienna" in which she discusses the intense devotion of Vienna's Jews to
the city's cultural ideals of "*Bildung, Wissen-*

*Marjorie Perloff is the author of
innumerable books on modernist,
avant-garde, and contemporary
poets, poetics, and art. Much of
her work has focused on the major
currents of modernist and
postmodernist activity in the arts,
including cultural theory and the
visual arts. Perloff has taught at
the University of Maryland, the
University of Southern California,
and Stanford University, where she
is now professor emeritus.*

*schaft*, taste and connoisseurship in the arts." Her namesake was Gabriele von Bulow,
the daughter of the philosopher William Humboldt and the niece of the naturalist Alexander Humboldt. The Humboldt legacy epitomizes all four of the above cultural
ideals that both Prussia and Vienna brought to classical definition.

    Gabriele Mintz eventually swapped her name for Marjorie in 1944, when she be-
came a U.S. citizen. She wanted to be like all the other eighth graders in Riverdale,
New York, where she and her parents found asylum after the Nazi Anschluss of Austria in March, 1938, brought an abrupt end to the happy marriage between Austrian
Jews and German culture. Though the union was no longer a happy one, it still lin-
gered in a kind of intermittent separation; there was never a formal divorce. Perloff
describes at some length the continuing hold of the Viennese past on the descendants
of the Viennese refugees in the United States today. The Neue Galerie in New York,
not far from the Guggenheim Museum, is a lavishly restored beaux arts mansion that
displays Viennese arts and crafts from the early twentieth century and a gathering
place for lovers of Viennese pastries in its Cafe Sabarasky. Perloff dismisses this
scene as nostalgia fodder, but part of her cannot let go of the "energy of modernist Vienna" which she feels was "richly textured" by "the Jewish presence" that was
downplayed by both Gentiles and Jews at the time. Perloff finds this ironic, but it is
closer to the truth to call it tragic. In many ways, what one now calls German and Austrian *Bildung*, that is "cultivation and learning," would probably never have flowered
as it did without the innately Jewish hunger and veneration for learning. *Bildung* also
involves assimilation, as Perloff describes it, and that assimilation went in both directions. Jews introduced a hunger for perfection that went beyond German and Austrian
self-demand.

    Although Perloff conveys with compassion and insight the struggles of her family
to overcome the dislocation and trauma of their forced exodus from Europe, she often
seems to be at the edge, rather than the center, of the very persecution she records.
Much of this can be explained by the distance that she and her family kept from their

own Jewish heritage. When her mother announced that they had to flee in 1938, she put it in these words: "Now we are no longer Austrians. Hitler has taken Austria." Writes Perloff, "There is no mention of our having to leave as Jews, no doubt because despite our nominal Jewishness, we had been brought up as Austrians."

At the end of the memoir Perloff reflects on the fact that even those "only nominally Jewish" are once again targets for assassins in the wake of the September 11, 2001, terrorist attacks in the United States. A "nominal" identity is less than skin deep; it is not felt as a defining force. Indeed it may simply be part of the "noise" of the world—something similar to what characterizes the postmodern world of media and contemporary poetry that Perloff has made her métier as a critic and scholar. She does not deny her Jewishness but does little to affirm it. Since her immediate family was not "openly Jewish," she could not imagine living in New Orleans, the "provincial" hometown of her husband, Joe Perloff, where his "loving but overpowering Jewish family" held court. That phrase—"overpowering Jewish family"—could have come from the mouths of her parents, her uncles and aunts, and many of the other high bourgeois assimilated Viennese refugees one meets in these pages—or from the anti-Semitic world of Perloff's heritage. She constantly assures the reader that the rejection of Jewishness was a condition of time and class among upper class Austrian Jews, but later in her memoir she describes the casually Jewish New York community clustered around the Fieldston School after World War II in similar terms: "No one seemed to be ashamed of being Jewish, no one tried to pass, but being Jewish was a sociocultural premise (or precondition) rather than a religion or even a fixed ethnicity." Most New York Jews, from any class or background, would have difficulty recognizing themselves in such a deracinated and abstract definition.

The most interesting person in this memoir is Perloff's grandfather, Richard Schuller. Born in 1870, the son of a wool manufacturer in what is now the Czech Republic, Schuller went to Vienna to study law and economics. To support his studies he tutored the children of the rich. Although he longed for an academic career, he could not refuse the invitation in 1898 to enter the government. He served in the department of commerce and, after World War I, in the foreign office. As the only Jew in the division, he was subjected to repeated requests to submit to baptism. Perloff writes that "he refused, not because he had any allegiance to the Jewish religion or even to Jewish culture, but because he disliked the idea of what was known as career baptism." Ever since the great poet Heinrich Heine had subjected himself to a "career baptism" in the early nineteenth century and regretted it all of his life, Jews, no matter how distanced they were from their religious and cultural heritage, tended to think dishonorable a religious conversion that had no basis in religious commitment. Christianity meant no more to them than their Judaism.

In his own memoir, *Negotiator of Trust* (1990), Schuller recounts his service to the newly elected social democratic government of Austria in the months of crisis after the end of World War I, when the Habsburg Empire had been dismembered and the people of Vienna were looting shops and stealing wood for fuel. He could not get the Allied powers to extend the necessary loans, so he turned to Italy, a victor in World War I.

The new Italian premier, Benito Mussolini, "seems to have placed great trust in Grandfather's judgment on issues of trade," writes Perloff, "and their fruitful association" helped to curb the inflation at Austria's throat. Later Schuller faithfully served the conservative Austrian government. Once the Austrian Nazis took over after the Anschluss in 1938, Schuller's status became that of just another Austrian Jew who was denied his pension and, like the rest of Perloff's family, forced to flee the country. After a dramatic crossing of the Alps into Italy, where a telegram from his old friend Mussolini prevented the border guards from turning him back, Schuller was united with his family, which had already found temporary asylum in Vallambrosa. Seven-year-old Gabriele Mintz was there to embrace her grandfather.

A less flamboyant figure than Perloff's grandfather, her father, Maximilian Mintz, was nevertheless an impressive example of the ways in which the pursuit of *Bildung* could define a life. Born in 1899, his was perhaps the last generation to savor to its fullest the classical humanistic education of the German and Austrian secondary school (or Gymnasium) which included eight years of Latin and German literature, five of Greek, and three or four of French and English. In 1926 he married Gabriele's mother, Ilse, who was completing her doctorate in economics and was in private law practice with his father. This did not put an end to Maximilian's humanistic endeavors. Since 1921 he had pursued his interests in poetry and the other arts by joining a circle known as the Geistkreis. This group included prominent economists, legal scholars, art historians, political philosophers, historians, mathematicians, and two pheomenologists. Most of these men were Jewish but not all. They were professionals by day; they devoted their evenings to concerts, theater, opera, and meetings of the Geistkreis. They presented papers; Maximilian gave one on Marcel Proust. With such parents, it is easy to see how Perloff became a professor of poetry.

Settled in Washington, D.C., in the mid-1950's with her young doctor husband, Perloff searched for a Ph.D. program in the humanities. Her favorite English professor at Oberlin had two good friends who taught in the one Ph.D. program in the Washington area specializing in literature: Catholic University. The two professors, J. Craig LaDriere and Giovanni Giovannini, proved to be excellent mentors. LaDriere taught a two-semester course, "Introduction to Literary Theory," which was far ahead of its time. Giovannini taught the Russian Formalists, Roman Jakobson, Kenneth Burke, and Charles Morris. Perloff was exposed to a range of theoretical writings in linguistics, rhetoric, and semiotics that set her to thinking about poetry in ways that would not become standard for almost another twenty-five years. She is quite self-effacing here about a lucky break in her education which undoubtedly had a great deal to do with her ensuing sensitivity to the first rumblings of postmodernist indeterminacy in poets like John Ashbery and Frank O'Hara. LaDriere proved to be a difficult taskmaster when it came to writing her dissertation, but she persevered and ultimately accepted a teaching job at Catholic University.

In the 1950's the New Criticism was regnant. LaDriere and Giovannini "scorned Yale's Cleanth Brooks and Robert Penn Warren as mere explicators." W. K. Wimsatt, the prominent Yale critic and aesthetician, was singled out as the worst of the lot. He should have known better, for he was a Catholic and classically trained critic. Perloff confesses to amusement at the notion that the New Critics were champions of "close reading" or "formalism." On the contrary, they "were taught that . . . Wimsatt and Brooks could not get beyond thematics, . . . whereas, we studied problems of form, structure, and language—the very ontology of poetry."

LaDriere and Giovannini were close friends of Ezra Pound, whose reputation as one of the founders of modern poetry suffers from his having been convicted as a traitor for his pro-fascist radio programs during World War II. Perloff goes to considerable lengths to separate them from the racial supremacists and other reactionaries who hovered around Pound while he was incarcerated at St. Elizabeth's. LaDriere and Giovannini never made an anti-Semitic remark, and they never raised any political issues in class. This, of course, does not tell what their political beliefs were. When Pound was discharged in 1958, he stayed for a few weeks at LaDriere's apartment. Although Perloff thinks Pound a great poet, she does not belittle his fascism and anti-Semitism, nor does she excuse the Bollingen jury for giving him his big prize in 1949. "It was much too soon after the war to foreground the work of a poet who had Pound's views." She takes great solace in the fact that in the United States of that time, despite the Cold War, there was a true openness in regard to the Pound controversy. All opinions, for and against giving Pound the prize, were freely aired.

Nevertheless, there is more than a little irony in the fact that Perloff should find herself in a culturally compromised situation in the course of her own professional life that recalls, even if only fleetingly, what happened to her grandfather. He also served masters who disdained his background; he flirted with reactionary leaders, Mussolini and the Austrian chancellor, Engelbert Dollfuss, to help his beloved Austria. Perloff finally left Catholic University. Professor Giovannini claimed that she had been insubordinate regarding the curriculum. Perloff wanted more freedom to serve her idea of what modernism was all about. She maintains that she emerged with a sharper sense of her Jewishness, but she remains uncomfortable with any overtly Jewish ritual or manner. Perhaps, like her grandfather, she had learned that her dignity has something to do with not converting.

Near the end of this memoir Perloff explores the connection between the Austrian Jewish composer Arnold Schoenberg (1874-1951) and his American student John Cage, who himself became an important figure in the history of modern music. The juxtaposition of these two is very suggestive but enigmatic and finally does not seem to do what Perloff hoped it might, namely capture the essence of what the Austrian-American connection is all about. The problem may stem from the fact that Perloff ignores or downplays the most important thing about Schoenberg's American experience, his reconversion to Judaism. America enabled him to rediscover his Judaism—as faith and inspiration for musical composition and not just as a socioeconomic precondition. The pluralism of American life freed him from the notion that he had to suppress his Judaism to be an American. Exactly the opposite proved to be true.

In a moving epilogue to her memoir, Perloff depicts her grandfather in 1970, now one hundred years old, being honored by the Austrian government in her parents' apartment in Washington. Two years after this event, her grandfather was gone—and Kurt Waldheim, the premier of Austria, was exposed as a former SS officer. Perloff soberly concludes that the ironies persist and that although she is free of all the illusions of yesterday, the tug of Vienna will not let her go. In all this, there is both loss and gain. Therein lies the heart of Marjorie-Gabriele's "Vienna paradox."

*Peter Brier*


## Review Sources

*The Times Literary Supplement*, December 17, 2004, p. 24.
*World Literature Today* 79 (January-April, 2005): 111.

# VILLAGES

*Author:* John Updike (1932-      )
*Publisher:* Alfred A. Knopf (New York). 321 pp. $25.00
*Type of work:* Novel
*Time:* From the 1930's to 2002
*Locale:* A series of small towns in Pennsylvania, Connecticut, and Massachusetts

*Updike fashions a relentlessly sexual biography of a fictional computer programmer, Owen Mackenzie, tracing him from his humble birth in the village of Willow, Pennsylvania, through a succession of sexual experimentations and liaisons, to his final home in a posh retirement village in Massachusetts*

*Principal characters:*
> OWEN MACKENZIE, a former computer programmer and sexual athlete
> PHYLLIS MACKENZIE, his beautiful and brainy first wife and mother of his four children
> JULIA MACKENZIE, formerly the wife of a clergyman and now married to Owen
> ED MERVINE, Owen's obese and brilliant partner in a fledgling computer software business
> FAYE,
> VANESSA,
> KAREN, and
> ALLISA, among the sequential cast of "other" women who enjoy "village sex" with Owen through the years

Those familiar with the John Updike corpus will find this latest novel typical of his work: biting humor, description of the ordinary with extraordinary clarity and carefully chosen language, fleshed-out pictures of his flawed but compelling characters. Perhaps predictably, Updike's fleshing out includes pervasively bawdy, sexually explicit scenes which, in spite of their prolonged detail, come off remarkably less sordid than similar descriptions one might find in romance novels. The passages, always well written and stubbornly candid, float above the tawdry and the titillating. They evoke some of Updike's earlier work in *Couples* (1968) and *S.* (1988).

*Villages* introduces to the world a new Updike character, this time a sexually spent seventy-something, Owen Mackenzie. His intensely active professional life is behind him, likewise his sexual glory years. Owen exhausts his well-financed retirement days painting and his dream-filled nights avoiding sexual encounter with his energetic and younger second wife. In many ways Owen possesses the unlikable characteristics that one is accustomed to finding in previous Updike protagonists. The shadow of Rabbit past looms over the figure of Owen present. As a young man, Owen is talented and single-mindedly driven to succeed in the budding software industry.

As he grows older and increasingly successful in business, it is clear that personally he remains shallow, self-absorbed, and only slightly aware of anyone else—unless that someone is sexually attractive to him. Such distractions seem to come generously and often, much like the incessant targets on a carnival shooting gallery stage which keep replicating themselves until all the ammunition has been exhausted. In his dotage there is little that seems to redeem poor Owen. Nevertheless, the reader reads on, perhaps hoping for a deathbed metanoia.

The first chapter finds Owen, retired, in the present. He is determined to avoid the early morning invitation of his wife, Julia, to engage in sex play. He successfully rebuffs her advances, rolls over, and falls back asleep into a bizarre and frightening dream, in which he encounters his wife dead and disrobed in what appears to be a hospital room. The scene is loaded with sexual imagery and unresolved questions. In the dream Owen feels responsible for the wife's death— a suicide—but wakes confused. His wife, very much alive, prepares coffee and listens to early morning radio in quotidian regularity.

*A native Pennsylvanian, John Updike graduated from Harvard University and the Ruskin School of Drawing and Fine Art in Oxford, England. He was on the staff of* The New Yorker *from 1955 to 1957. Among his fifty books are novels, short stories, poems, and criticism. He is the winner of the Pulitzer Prize, the National Book Award, the Rosenthal Award, and the Howells Medal.*

As the succeeding chapters reveal Owen's history, he is portrayed as a normal prepubescent boy, full of the awakenings of sexual desire that one would expect in young males. He observes, tests, and, in some cases, tentatively acts out his fantasies. As he grows to adulthood, sex for Owen becomes more central, almost obsessive in his life. He grows older but apparently does not mature. He marries beautiful Phyllis, who is his intellectual equal but who does not possess the same intensity of sexual drive as her up-and-coming husband. He seeks satisfaction in extensive and varietal sexual activity with a parade of women in lustful fantasies, prolonged and often contrived affairs, and sometimes in one-night stands. Some encounters are sexually restrained, while others are flagrantly frivolous—a kind of potpourri of sexual tastings.

The middle chapters of the book are, appropriately, titled "Village Sex I" through "Village Sex VI." Perhaps the author is trying to underline the ordinariness, as he sees it, of the sexual encounter in the sexually awakened times of the late twentieth century. It is in the unremarkable "village" of ordinary time that an obsessive and insistent pattern drums away and ultimately blocks out the sounds of sane and normal living. Yet rampant sexual encounters are not accepted as orthodox in the small towns of middle America. They are the object of disapproval, sometimes shock, and eventually heartache for the participants as well as for their families. The name of the village where Owen spends a good deal of his life—Middle Falls—may say it all.

Updike's prose is always an amazing cobble of carefully chosen words sparsely crafted into a taut and satisfying picture. Here the reader pages through an album of snapshots from Owen's life from its inception in a small village in Pennsylvania to what the front fly summary calls "the rather geriatric community" of Haskells Crossing, Massachusetts. Owen's origins are modest, his retirement well-heeled. His external life is arguably a metaphor for his sex life. His genitals share with his genesis a gradual "upgrade in sophistication and in experience." From his boyhood Owen is driven both by the urge to put behind him his humble roots and an overly active preoccupation with activities sexual. In his dotage he lives off the profit from the sale of his software company and on the banked memories of his years of rich sexual encounters.

One of the most nicely turned passages—and one which almost avoids the pervasive preoccupation with things sexual that characterize the book—is Updike's detailed description of a wealthy, three-generational family attending Easter church services in staid Haskells Crossing, clearly an upscale village accustomed to enduring money. Commodiously spilling from the two front pews of St. Barnabas Episcopal Church is the elderly family matriarch, blocking the center aisle with her wheelchair and causing those going to Communion to detour around her. There are the youngest generation, granddaughters dressed up and grandsons spit-polished in preppy uniform blazers, red ties, and requisite button-down dress shirts. As they pass by, the boys peck the expected obsequious kiss on the cheek of grandma. These boys "sport the honey tans of winter vacations spent in the Bahamas and weekends spent skiing, and the girls, even those at the awkward age, with braces and acne, display costly dresses and animating hopes of good schools and a fair value on the marriage market. Wealth is health." The middle generation is knitted comfortably into the fabric of church attendance and involvement. This is classic Updike.

Updike describes the male members of this cohort of wealthy society, who "grow more and more polite as the object of their courtesy becomes more and more annoying." Owen (the reader hears more than a hint of a judgmental Updike in the voice of his character) chuckles with restraint as this group goes to severe and sometimes painful extremes to maintain a veneer of civility in the face of situations that would provoke clear discomfort and disapproval in the lives of ordinary, less advantaged mortals. They wear sockless shoes (to show off their "thoroughbred ankles," Owen concludes) and swallow too-hot hors d'oeuvres to avoid the uncouth alternative of spitting them from their burn-assaulted mouths. The reader smiles along with Updike, recognizing and, with him, disapproving the class snobbery he mocks.

In the end the reader grieves for Owen, who never learned that sex is holiday—his phrase—and life is lived in ordinary time. Perhaps the lamentation is also for Updike, whose years and venue are remarkably similar to Owen's. Like all Updike protagonists, Owen is flawed. The reader is prone not only to dislike him but also to feel sorry for him. One feels that his choices could have been better, making life near its term a bit less regrettable. His memories, which formerly detailed the places of his sequential female encounters in Middle Falls and gave Owen a "location," a "somewhere" in life, are now replaced with a series of anonymous "anywheres" in the town of his retirement, the gateway—Haskells Crossing—to his death. An "enlarging hollow in his life" points him toward death. In his sexual activity, he has become "a puppet whose strings old age has snapped."

For those who love Updike, this new offering from the writer of more than fifty books is a treat. It is arguably better than some of his other contemporary writings, exemplified by the reluctantly written autobiographical work *Self-Consciousness* (1989), which contained a whole chapter on psoriasis, or *In the Beauty of the Lilies* (1996), which also examines some of the issues of aging. *Villages* approaches the delight of the funny and bawdy romp of *S*. One could contend that *Villages* is more clearly autobiographical, at least in its retrospective, reflective tone, than his reluctant and explicitly autobiographical memoir.

If one were searching out flaws, one could argue that Updike writes in each new book the same old story of small-town Pennsylvania folk grown sophisticated and perhaps briefly wise. Maybe Owen and his succession of "villages" is merely a newly crafted piecework of parts from the writer's other settings and characters—a kind of safe and benevolent Frankenstein, the alter ego of the author. This new "monster" is entertaining in a bittersweet way, especially for those who share an enduring respect and fondness for the work of this literary giant.

Perhaps this volume is a nostalgic and somewhat ironic swan song for Updike, a slightly sad reflection on his own process of aging and the inevitable wait for the embrace of death. In that, it is both poignant and pertinent. As a memoir of an era where love moved from the confines of committed sheets to comfy sofas installed behind locked office doors or to furtive forests, it is a success. Updike is able still to conjure and craft content to the enjoyment of readers. The best of the book is likely to be found in its beginning and its ending. Sandwiched between, the rich and perhaps not so nourishing accounts of Owen's sexual exploits and his occasional reflective or regretful pauses offer a spicy entertainment with a subtle pinch of retrospective enlightenment. Perhaps the literary and cultural hegemony of explicit, prolonged, sexual accounts is over, and it is time to set a more sober house in order. What better location to do this than in *Villages*?

*Dolores L. Christie*

## Review Sources

*Booklist* 101, no. 1 (September 1, 2004): 7.
*Kirkus Reviews* 72, no. 17 (September 1, 2004): 836.
*Library Journal* 129, no. 16 (October 1, 2004): 74.
*The New York Review of Books* 51, no. 20 (December 16, 2004): 55.
*The New York Times*, October 22, 2004, p. E33.
*The New York Times Book Review* 154 (October 31, 2004): 13.
*People* 62, no. 18 (November 1, 2004): 45.
*Publishers Weekly* 251, no. 36 (September 6, 2004): 44.

# W. B. YEATS: A LIFE
## Volume II: The Arch-Poet, 1915-1939

*Author:* R. F. Foster (1949-    )
*Publisher:* Oxford University Press (New York). Illus-
trated. 798 pp. $45.00
*Type of work:* Literary biography
*Time:* 1915-1939
*Locale:* Ireland, England, France, and Italy

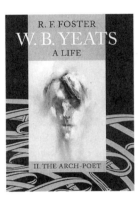

*In this second volume of an authorized biography, his-
torian Foster considers the last quarter century of the life
of Yeats, the major English-language poet of the twentieth
century*

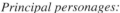

Principal personages:
WILLIAM BUTLER YEATS, Irish poet, play-
wright, and political activist
GEORGE HYDE LEES YEATS, his wife
LADY AUGUSTA GREGORY, his friend and literary and theatrical collabo-
rator
DOROTHY WELLESLEY, the English poet whose home replaced Lady
Gregory's as his retreat

The first volume of R. F. Foster's authorized life of William Butler Yeats, published in 1997 and subtitled *The Apprentice Mage, 1865-1914*, is an exemplary biography by an eminent historian. The present volume, devoted to Yeats's life from age
fifty to his death in 1939 at seventy-four, and a worthy continuation of the first, is enriched by Foster's frequent forays into literary analysis, at which he excels. He also
skillfully copes with other challenges that the latter part of Yeats's life presents, such
as the mysticism that becomes a frequent presence, the so-called automatic writing
that flowed from spiritual sessions in which Yeats and his wife engaged, and the
poet's increasing "intellectual omnivorousness" as he aged.

Further, when Yeats became a public figure (as senator in the Irish Free State parliament and Nobel laureate), his work "repeatedly struck public poses and was put to
public purposes." As Yeats himself sought to determine a pattern to his life (by the
start of his fiftieth year, he already has completed a memoir of his childhood), so must
Foster strive for thematic unity amid a life with major personal, professional, and political conflicts. His subject, after all, was an anomaly. A Protestant in a Catholic
country, he rejected Christianity for mysticism. Devoted to Ireland and a celebrant of
its past, he nevertheless spent much time abroad. Although a nationalist, he was skeptical about the fervency of his fellow Irish and never embraced their anti-British cru-
sades.

This volume begins as Yeats, on the threshold of his sixth decade, starts writing
more introspective poetry, whose elegiac and disillusioned mood reflects his state

of mind, for though he continued his summer retreats at Lady Augusta Gregory's Coole Park estate, he still worried about Abbey Theatre problems, other Dublin cultural matters, and the precarious Irish political situation. In addition, financial problems continued, even after he married George (Georgie Hyde Lees), who had a substantial annual income, partly because he supported his improvident father in New York. To cope, Yeats arranged with John Quinn, a lawyer in that city, to assist John Butler Yeats in exchange for manuscripts.

*R. F. Foster, Carroll Professor of Irish History at Oxford University and fellow of Hertford College, was born and educated in Ireland. Recipient of several honorary degrees, he has written biographies of Lord Randolph Churchill and Charles Stewart Parnell plus books about Irish history, including* Modern Ireland, 1600-1972 *(1988).*

Turning his papers into hard currency and giving public lectures also enabled Yeats to fulfill a dream: to purchase a medieval tower or castle keep, Ballylee, near Coole, which he restored, made into a second home, and used as a symbol for much of his later work. Also becoming increasingly important were psychic investigations, an interest, according to Foster, that stemmed partly from Yeats's "need for verification of life beyond the grave." The plethora of occult activities, abetted by his wife, George, and the discovery of Japanese Noh drama, through his friendship with Ezra Pound, enriched Yeats's work and attracted new patrons and audiences.

When the Easter 1916 Rising occurred in Dublin, Yeats was in London. Surprised by it, he was unsympathetic, having previously disassociated himself from the Gaelic League, Sinn Féin, and revolutionary ideologues. Indicative of his position in the Anglo-Irish conflict is the fact that he was approached about a knighthood, which he rejected, partly because of concern about the reaction of Irish nationalists. Notwithstanding his ambivalence to the rebellion, it inspired some of his most popular poetry, including "Easter 1916" and the play *The Dreaming of the Bones.*

In the midst of European war and Irish rebellion, Yeats in 1917 married George, who had worked with him for several years in occult researches. According to Foster, "joint supernatural investigations marked their relationship from its origin, and would decisively influence their marriage." Half Yeats's age, "she was an autodidact, and read omnivorously in obscure texts, particularly the Neoplatonists. Unlike him, she was both musical and a gifted linguist." The London marriage formalized a close intellectual and spiritual collaboration, and "she would henceforward order, preserve, and arrange drafts of her husband's writing." Marriage also brought tranquillity to his life, heralded in "A Prayer for My Daughter" (Anne, born in 1919), which also "reflects his apprehension at a world descending into formless anarchy." The 1921 publication of *Michael Robartes and the Dancer*, his second collection in two years, suggests the positive effect that marriage had on his output.

With ratification of the Anglo-Irish treaty and establishment of the Free State in 1922, which he supported, Yeats decided to return permanently to Ireland. As Foster says, he came "to a country about to descend into the abyss of civil war, and the outcome would make him question how far the traditions he most valued were really safeguarded by the new state." During this period of personal transition and national turmoil, he wrote the poetic sequence "Meditations in Time of Civil War," as well as lengthy letters of advice to young poets, and was named to the Irish senate. His support of the Free State government wavered as it became more authoritarian, so the appointment to the upper chamber was fortunate, for "he now occupied the kind of platform that suited him best, political but detached from parties."

After winning the 1923 Nobel Prize in Literature, Yeats had another platform, which he unhesitatingly used: as an inveterate lobbyist for government recognition of the Abbey as a national theater and against government censorship and attempts to make Gaelic Ireland's official language. He also challenged the establishment position in parliamentary debates of the divorce issue, which Foster calls "one of WBY's supreme public moments," Yeats's liberalism in the censorship, language, and divorce conflicts "aggressively set himself against his colleagues in the Senate, as well as the presumed opinion of the wider Irish world," so he became politically and intellectually isolated. Indeed, the only official role he had was as head of a commission on Irish coinage.

During this decade of political and social transition for Ireland, Yeats's health necessitated sabbaticals abroad from public life. By the mid-1920's he had completed *A Vision*, his spiritual autobiography, and also a number of poems, including "Leda and the Swan," whose political theme is cloaked in a narrative of overt sexuality, and "Among School Children," ostensibly about the education of youth but actually about his "thoughts on education, art, and life, strangely but potently mixed with memories of his youth . . . through the prism of Neoplatonic philosophy."

The 1927 assassination of Kevin O'Higgins, a friend who had mediated quietly with the British, inspired "Blood and the Moon"; "In Memory of Eva Gore-Booth and Con Markiewicz," another poem of the period, also evokes the tensions spurred by the killing. These deaths and Yeats's uncertain health made him "impatient with any impediments, obstructions, evasions which might come between his work and what he wanted it to say; and he would pursue that lost vigour with a single-minded commitment, determined to demonstrate that he could recapture the force of youth in his life as well as in his work." Notably, he began *The Tower* (1928), a new collection, whose centerpiece was "Sailing to Byzantium," about "the onset of old age and the overwhelming impulse to create an art that would defy mortality." He also wrote poems featuring an alter ego called "Crazy Jane," a deranged woman who safely could make irreverent and scurrilous comments about all subjects and people.

The 1930's began with the possibility of Yeats being named British Poet Laureate, which he considered accepting despite certain negative reaction, because "he owed his creative soul to the great tradition of English literature." In the event, John Masefield got the nod. Soon after, Yeats began a long-standing relationship with the British Broadcasting Corporation (BBC) and then took up residence at Coole Park with Lady Gregory, who was dying of cancer. Not even a frantic letter from his wife about the Abbey's precarious state (as a result of a new government taking power) brought him home. Instead, he went again to London to see Shri Purohit Swami, an Indian monk with whom he was infatuated and whose spiritual autobiography Yeats pronounced a masterpiece; to participate in a celebration of the founding of the Irish Literary Society, to broadcast for the BBC; to find a publisher for Lady Gregory's works; and to negotiate secretly with the British on political matters.

Only then did Yeats come home, but he went again to Coole when Lady Gregory died on May 23, 1932. "I have lost the friend who was my sole adviser for the greater part of my life . . . the one person who knew all that I thought and did," he wrote. Her death, says Foster, "marked a caesura across WBY's life, the cleft driven so deep that he feared the bereavement might even mean the failure of creativity." Problems with her estate and a long American lecture tour drained him, and he was disappointed with the accession of Eamon de Valera, more conservative and anti-British than William T. Cosgrave.

So Yeats largely removed himself from the Irish political scene, except for a flirtation with a nascent Irish fascist movement, which Foster says "should be seen in the light of his own creative stasis," his propensity "to search out themes in unlikely places, and work up his own poetic energies through a willing suspension of incredulity." Concludes Foster, "To an extent unrecognized, WBY's affinity with Fascism (not National Socialism) was a matter of rhetorical style, and the achievement of style, as he himself had decreed long before, was closely connected to shock tactics."

In 1934, Yeats began writing *Dramatis Personae*, a memoir of Lady Gregory, intending that it "would fix both their images in Irish history" and "establish WBY himself at the centre of Irish experience." Concern with legacy also is signaled by the 1933 appearance of his *Collected Poems*; the publication in 1934 of his youthful journalism, *Letters to a New Island*; the preparation of his *Collected Plays* (1934) and an American edition of his works; and the editing of the *Oxford Book of Modern Verse*.

Having undergone a sexual rejuvenation procedure that he believed increased not only his potency but also his creativity, Yeats was actively writing. The most immediate result was *The King of the Great Clock Tower* (1934), an insignificant salmagundi typical of his later work. He also traveled, visiting Italy and pausing for extended stays in England, which continued to be the locus of his artistic activities and where at different times he pursued three women, chief of whom was Dorothy Wellesley, an erstwhile poet whose home became his new Coole Park.

Yeats's seventieth birthday in 1935 occasioned celebrations and commemorations, and though his heart was weakening, he continued to work: writing new poems, including ballads; doing BBC broadcasts; and preparing a new edition of *A Vision*. By 1938, when most Irish and other Europeans were increasingly apprehensive about the prospect of war, "nothing in WBY's correspondence suggests any preoccupation with Hitler." Rather, he seemed detached from international events, focusing instead on an Abbey production of a pair of his plays; dealing with the financial problems of a family publishing operation; and reading widely in eugenics, a new interest. He died January 28, 1939, in France; but largely because of the war, his remains were not returned to Ireland until 1948, by which time, says Foster, "WBY's reputation belonged neither to government nor family, but to the country whose consciousness he had done so much to shape."

Yeats towers above all the heroes of the Irish revolution and struggle for independence, which culminated in the 1948 declaration of a republic, although he avoided most of the conflicts, eschewed militancy, and had close social and professional relationships in England. Long before his death he was internationally regarded as the preeminent Irishman, a reputation that still stands. So a magisterial study such as Foster's is warranted, and because of Yeats's belief that knowledge and biography are inseparable, attention to the minutiae of his life and milieu is appropriate. The result is both a biography of Yeats and an intellectual and social history of his milieu. In addition, Foster offers lucid readings of many poems. That Yeats emerges from Foster's two volumes with his position as poet and icon enhanced is testimony to the excellence of Foster's definitive life.

*Gerald H. Strauss*


## Review Sources

*Commentary* 117, no. 2 (February, 2004): 64.
*Harper's Magazine* 307, no. 1843 (December, 2003): 95.
*Kirkus Reviews* 71, no. 16 (August 15, 2003): 1077.
*New Criterion* 22, no. 9 (May, 2004): 70.
*The New Leader* 86, no. 5 (September/October, 2003): 36.
*The New York Review of Books* 51, no. 3 (February 26, 2004): 12.
*The New York Times*, December 4, 2003, p. E8.
*Publishers Weekly* 250, no. 37 (September 15, 2003): 52.

# WAR TRASH

*Author:* Ha Jin (1956-     )
*Publisher:* Pantheon Books (New York). 352 pp. $25.00
*Type of work:* Novel
*Time:* 1951-1953
*Locale:* The Korean Peninsula and China

*A seventy-four-year-old Chinese man who had served in the army of the People's Republic of China during the Korean War narrates his experience of captivity in U.S. and U.N. prisoner of war camps*

*Principal characters:*
YU YUAN, a Chinese army officer, not a
    Communist Party member
TAO JULAN, Yu's fiancé in Chengdu, mainland China
COMMISSAR PEI, a political officer of Yu's army unit, the leader of the
    Chinese Communist POWs
WANG YONG, the leader of the Chinese Nationalist (Kuomintang) POWs
MR. PARK, the leader of North Korean POWs
DR. GREENE, a U.S. Army medical officer
GENERAL BELL, the U.S. Army commandant of the POW camp

When one considers the émigré writers who have adopted English as the instrument of their craft, one commonly thinks of such luminaries as Joseph Conrad and Vladimir Nabokov. One may soon be adding Ha Jin to that constellation. Although Jin does not indulge in the verbal pyrotechnics of Nabokov or the narratives-within-narratives of Conrad, his unblinkingly lucid prose searches with a steady brilliance and profound compassion into the dark corners of the human psyche and the societal polity.

Having emigrated to the United States in 1985, Jin has since published more than a half dozen highly acclaimed works of fiction, including *Waiting* (1999), which won the National Book Award. *War Trash* is indeed a worthy addition to his impressive repertoire. Like Jin's other fictions, *War Trash* centers on a protagonist from mainland China, although it departs from its predecessors by placing its action in Korea. The time of the novel is the 1950's, and the Korean War is raging. The novel's protagonist is a Chinese soldier captured and held in U.S. and U.N. prisoner of war (POW) camps. The narrator-protagonist provides a forthright, unadorned account of his experience, so seemingly factual that the reader has the illusion of confronting a nonfiction work. The effect is akin to reading Daniel Defoe's *Robinson Crusoe* (1719) or Aleksandr Solzhenitsyn's *Odin den' Ivana Denisovicha* (1962; *One Day in the Life of Ivan Denisovich*, 1963). Jin's novel is realism at its very best.

In the novel's prologue, Jin piques his reader's curiosity by raising two questions

*Ha Jin (also known as Xuefei Jin) has garnered several prestigious awards for his fiction: the National Book Award for* Waiting *(1999), the PEN/Hemingway Award for* Ocean of Words *(1996), the Flannery O'Connor short fiction award for* Under the Red Flag *(1997), and the Asian American Literary Award for the short-story collection* The Bridegroom *(2001). He has also published three volumes of poetry.*

about his narrator. This seventy-three-year-old man from Communist China is writing his memoir while visiting his Chinese American son's family in Atlanta, and he is worried about the anti-American tattoo on his belly. He is worried that at a moment of heightened security concerns, he might be strip-searched at the airport and denied future access to his American family. The reader naturally wonders about the tattoo's provenance.

The other curiosity is this man's deep respect for doctors and his desire that his grandchild should become a doctor—not for the usual financial and social reasons but because he feels that "medicine is a noble, humane profession. . . . Doctors . . . follow a different set of ethics which enables them to transcend political nonsense and man-made enmity and to act with compassion and human decency." Germane to both questions is the problem of "political nonsense and man-made enmity," of the absurd and of hate, a problem that finds its most lethal manifestation in war.

The warrior of Jin's novel is its narrator-protagonist, Yu Yuan, and the body of the book, a memoir of the wartime of his youth, explicates this problem. Yu's memoir begins in 1949. The forces of Communist Party chairman Mao Zedong have wrested control of mainland China away from the Nationalist (Kuomintang) General Chiang Kai-shek, who has retreated to the island of Taiwan. Yu is a cadet at Huangpu (Whampoa) Academy, China's equivalent of West Point, whose commandant had been General Chiang himself. When the Nationalists retreat, Yu remains in mainland China and is absorbed into the Chinese People's Liberation Army as a young officer. Very much a proper Chinese man, Yu puts his family first, and he plans to care for his aging mother and marry his choreographer fiancé.

In 1951, however, the Korean War breaks out, and Yu, like the rest of the Chinese army, is "volunteered" to fight in it. These Chinese People's Volunteers (so-called because China is not officially at war) are ill-equipped, poorly supplied, devoid of air cover, and fragmented in their communication. After crossing the Yalu River into Korea, they suffer horrendous casualties. The men are considered expendable; they are war trash, useful for some political design which they do not comprehend. Yu's unit is soon decimated, and Yu fractures a thigh and is captured by the Americans. He and the handful of wounded survivors are taken to a military hospital at Pusan, South Korea. There his leg is saved from amputation by an American Army major, Dr. Greene.

This doctor astonishes Yu and shatters several stereotypes he holds. This skillful, dedicated doctor who commands many men is a mere woman. This doctor wearing his enemy's uniform exhausts herself to save his leg. This supposedly ignorant American speaks fluent Chinese. (Her parents had been missionaries in China.) Yu realizes that in Dr. Greene's eyes, suffering wears no uniforms, and through her eyes, Yu begins to glimpse a commonality of unaccommodated humanity that transcends race, gender, nationality, political ideology. This encounter with Dr. Greene is at the root of Yu's desire, fifty years later, that one of his flesh and blood should follow this ennobling profession.

Yu's encounter with Dr. Greene is the high point of his Korean War experience. Everything else he experiences afterward is a fall from this peak of noble humanity. When Yu is somewhat recovered from his surgery, he is prematurely moved to a POW camp whose squalid conditions and the ingenious (sometimes ruthless) survival techniques of the inmates are described in meticulous detail. It quickly becomes clear that the camp is a mirror of recent Chinese history. A deep political divide splits the prisoners. On one side are the Nationalists (followers of General Chiang Kai-shek's Kuomintang Party, now ensconced in Taiwan); in the camp they are led by the crude and ill-educated Wang Yong. On the other side are the Communists, led by the astute Commissar Pei, a finely drawn portrait of a complicated man who is a politically correct, intelligent zealot, a dedicated Communist Party leader whose tragedy ultimately is his betrayal by the party which he served with such dedication.

The Nationalists and the Communists are most radically divided on the matter of repatriation, for which the Geneva Convention provides once a truce is reached. Although the United States was not then a signatory to the Geneva Convention, it had stated its intention to abide by it. Since there were two Chinas, the Communist mainland and the Nationalist Taiwan, the repatriation of Chinese POWs had become problematic. The United States was unwilling to force unwilling Nationalist sympathizers to return to Communist China, so it created a system in which Chinese POWs could choose their country of repatriation.

In the realities of the POW camps, this ostensible freedom of choice is perverted into a machinery of coercion created by the prisoners themselves. Yu Yuan, for instance, has mentally chosen to be repatriated to mainland China, not because he is Communist but because he has, in a sense, left hostages there—his mother and his fiancé. Because Yu is a Huangpu-trained officer (and thus valuable to General Chiang) as well as a good English translator, the pro-Nationalists consider him a trophy candidate for repatriation to Taiwan. Their leader, Wang Yong, invites Yu to dinner to persuade him. When talk fails, an accomplice knocks Yu out and brands him by tattooing "Fuck Communism" on his belly. When he regains consciousness, Yu is dismayed, realizing that his tattoo will be a political liability (or worse) in mainland China. The novel is making the ironic point that Yu is being forced in a most unfree manner to "choose" to live in the so-called free world. This incident also provides a partial explanation (or complication) to the initial query raised in the reader's mind about Yu's tattoo.

Despite his brand, Yu still wishes to return to his family. This he declares during a nail-biting scene at the protected U.N. screening process. Henceforth the two factions of Chinese POWs are held in separate compounds to await repatriation. Here Jin excels in conveying the day-to-day events of the prison camp. The Communist prisoners, under Pei's command, organize themselves into a microcosmic socialist state, complete with a written constitution. Deemphasizing the individual, they divide their labor into specialties. (Yu becomes a prime translator.) They put on propaganda plays: Their production of "The Dream of Wall Street," obviously a critique of the American Dream, had an audience of six thousand prisoners and even impressed the American guards. Commissar Pei and the North Korean leader, Mr. Park, a former provincial governor, feel that they must also foment difficulties for their American captors. They come up with a startling plan.

The communist leaders' audacious plan is to kidnap the camp commander, General Bell, and hold him hostage until he approves improvements to conditions in the camp. Pei and Park are really motivated by political propaganda. They wish to create an international media circus to embarrass the United States and the United Nations. The Communist plan succeeds brilliantly. After the abducted general signs off on the prisoners' demands, he is released. The U.S. Army then punishes the prisoners by unleashing tanks and flamethrowers upon them. Hundreds of unarmed prisoners behind barbed wire are killed—a clear violation of the Geneva Convention. The world press is agog. Pei and Park have brought off a signal propaganda coup indeed. Yu, on the other hand, has reservations—he cannot help remembering his comrades who were so readily sacrificed for the sake of propaganda.

One may think at this point that Jin's sense of verisimilitude has gone astray, that he has permitted too much license to his imagination, that this abduction of an American general by his prisoners is beyond belief. If one thinks this, one would be wrong. Such an incident did actually take place at the U.S.-run POW camp on Koje Island off the coast of South Korea. There on May 7, 1952, U.S. Army General Dodd was kidnapped by his Communist prisoners, and events transpired much as Jin relates them (with the officers' names changed).

After this abduction, Pei is placed in isolation, although his ingenuity finds ways of getting his orders out. Camp conditions become harsher. Yu again vacillates between choosing Taiwan and the mainland as he ponders further examples of the dehumanizing tactics of the Communist leadership. Eventually, the prisoners are brought to the Demilitarized Zone (DMZ), and there Yu chooses to return to his family on the mainland. Once in Communist territory, he confesses to his compromising tattoo, and an obliging doctor deletes the necessary letters to transform "Fuck Communism" to "Fuck . . . U.S." Thus is political correctness achieved, and the reader is given the provenance of Yu's tattoo.

Repatriation turns out to be a painful irony for Yu. His mother has died. His former fiancé wants nothing to do with him. Astonishingly, Pei is in disgrace with the party, whose official line is to tout "Martyrs of the Revolution." To be politically correct, Pei and the others should not have allowed themselves to be taken prisoner; they should have just died. Not having been a party member, Yu is allowed to languish in obscurity as a schoolteacher, and he does eventually raise a family. As the novel closes, he sits in Atlanta with his American grandchildren watching his favorite television program, *The Simpsons*.

Through the harrowing details and bitter ironies of *War Trash*, Jin has created a mordantly realistic critique of the absurd in political ideology and the vicious in human hate. Individuals like Jin's protagonist who value reasonableness and love of family are entangled in intrigues, scarred, and re-scarred on the skin and in the heart. It is a marvel of luck that a few such individuals do survive. Jin has fashioned a marvel of a novel that brings such a timely survivor's tale to his lucky readers during a season of war and rumors of war.

*C. L. Chua*

## Review Sources

*Booklist* 100, no. 22 (August 1, 2004): 1872.
*Kirkus Reviews* 72, no. 16 (August 15, 2004): 763.
*Library Journal* 129, no. 13 (August 15, 2004): 67.
*Mother Jones* 29, no. 6 (November/December, 2004): 94.
*The New York Times Book Review* 154 (October 10, 2004): 1, 8-9.
*Publishers Weekly* 251, no. 31 (August 2, 2004): 49.
*San Francisco Chronicle*, October 10, 2004, p. M2.

# WASHINGTON'S CROSSING

*Author:* David Hackett Fischer (1935-    )
*Publisher:* Oxford University Press (New York). 564 pp.
    $35.00
*Type of work:* History
*Time:* 1776-1777

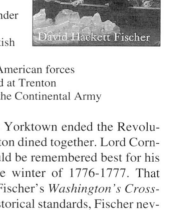

The history and significance of George Washington's famous crossing of the Delaware River and the battles of Trenton and Princeton

Principal personages:
> CHARLES CORNWALLIS, British commander
>     in New Jersey
> RICHARD HOWE, commander of the British
>     in America
> CHARLES LEE, second-in-command of American forces
> JOHANN RALL, Hessian colonel defeated at Trenton
> GEORGE WASHINGTON, commander of the Continental Army

In 1781, after the surrender of the British forces at Yorktown ended the Revolutionary War, Charles Cornwallis and George Washington dined together. Lord Cornwallis proposed a toast asserting that Washington would be remembered best for his brilliant maneuvers along the Delaware River in the winter of 1776-1777. That twelve-week campaign is the focus of David Hackett Fischer's *Washington's Crossing.* If the number of soldiers involved was small by historical standards, Fischer nevertheless believes that the battles of Trenton and Princeton and the famous Christmas night crossing of the Delaware River were significant because they reversed the momentum of the Revolutionary War and demonstrated to the world that a democratic society devoted to freedom could accomplish a great deed through its own conviction, self-discipline, and self-sacrifice.

Professor Fischer has an impressive command not only of the minutiae of these battles but also of their significance. He sees the campaign as a clash not only of three different armies with their own ways of training and sets of tactics but also a conflict of principles. On one hand were the British and Hessians embodying discipline and order. On the other were the Americans, who were struggling to form an army of liberty. To Fischer, the opposing sides were vying for no less than the respect of the free world.

No one felt the difficulties of forging an army of liberty more than Washington. Having served with the British in the French and Indian War, he knew that his opponents were strengthened by the principles of hierarchy, service, loyalty, and discipline. He found that his own soldiers, who were accustomed to unlimited freedom, were difficult to train, and as a consequence, were not reliable under fire. He complained bitterly of the licentious behavior of his men. He also learned to adapt and

compromise, and his leadership of the Continental Army would serve as a prototype for the republican model of government crafted after the
war. When enlistments expired at crucial points—
indeed, in the middle of the Delaware River campaign—he persuaded, rather than commanded,
men to stay. He treated even the lowliest private
as a gentleman; to Washington, the term "gentleman" described not a social position but a moral

~

*David Hackett Fischer, University
Professor of History at Brandeis
University, is author of* Albion's
Seed *(1989),* The Great Wave
*(1996), and* Paul Revere's Ride
*(1994).*

~

condition. Fischer notes that no other army in history had operated on such a principle, certainly not the British or Hessians. Decision making under Washington was not
top-down but an open, democratic process of sharing ideas, a process that Fischer believes led him to some winning strategies in the battles of Trenton and Princeton.

In the first chapter of *Washington's Crossing*, Fischer establishes a context for the
Delaware River battles by backing up a year, to March, 1776, and focusing on Washington in New England and, later, New York City. The New Englanders, having successfully resisted the British, wished Washington a pleasant retirement. Washington,
Fischer notes, knew better. He expected the enemy to return, this time to New York,
nearly indefensible against the greatest naval power in the world. Indeed, he proved
correct. Beginning June 29, 1776, the British launched what Fischer estimates was the
greatest projection of naval power ever ventured by a European country until that
time. Over a six-week period, five hundred transports brought twenty-three thousand
British troops and ten thousand Germans. Some seventy warships prowled in American waters. All told, Fischer estimates that two-thirds of the army and one-half of the
navy of Great Britain were committed to America to put down the rebellion.

This juggernaut rolled over New York. Its officers and men had an overwhelming
advantage in experience, training, and tradition. The fifteen British generals averaged
thirty years experience to the Americans' two. Whereas the typical Continental soldier had only a few months experience, British soldiers were seasoned by the Seven
Years War in Europe, the American French and Indian War, not to mention conflicts
in India, the West Indies, Cuba, the Mediterranean, the Philippines, and Africa. The
British had won every one of these engagements. Moreover, they had recruited a second army to fight with them: the German Hessians were the best-paid military in the
world.

Fischer is the first to acknowledge the excellent work done by researchers of the
Revolution, including studies of not only the British and American participants but of
the Hessians as well. One little-known fact is that the opponents were not so different
philosophically as one might assume. Whereas England's George III was pilloried
as a tyrant, the men he chose to lead his military in America, the Howe brothers—
William, commander in chief of the army, and Richard, of the navy—were both
Whigs and sympathetic to the Americans' desire for their rights. Although longtime
friends of George III, they differed with him on this issue and only agreed to the assignment if they could negotiate to resolve the matter peacefully. Likewise, the philosophical interests of Hessian and colonial American leaders were not so far removed

from each other. Friedrich Wilhelm II, landgraf of Hesse-Cassel, was as interested in the Enlightenment as Benjamin Franklin or Thomas Jefferson. He thought of himself as humane, enlightened, and a social reformer.

The Howes' soft touch may have cost the British a quick victory. Rather than pursuing Washington's fleeing army after New York, William Howe was content to quarter his army for the winter in New Jersey, where there was good foraging. General Henry Clinton may have had a better idea: He urged his superior to march on Philadelphia, arrest the Continental Congress, and cut off Washington's army and destroy it. Fischer speculates that Howe rejected his subordinate's idea because he felt the war was all but won. His purpose in New Jersey was to preserve order and allow the loyalists to take back the state rather than to oppress, and thus alienate, the populace. To be in charge of New Jersey, he selected the like-minded Cornwallis, also a Whig who opposed oppressive measures.

While the British were content to wait out the winter, the fall of New York left the colonists in a crisis. Prominent American Whigs turned Tory. Washington's leadership was challenged by his subordinates, Charles Lee and Horatio Gates. The Continental Army was not only defeated, but, with commissions expiring, half of its men returned home. The remaining fighting force was a disorganized mix of Continentals and state militias, with Washington's portion the smallest at 3,765 men. Lee, his second-in-command and rival, commanded 7,540. Like the country at large, the army was a loose collection of fiercely independent parts.

The Americans rallied. Just a couple of weeks before Washington's crossing in December of 1776, Thomas Paine wrote and distributed his two-cent pamphlet titled *The Crisis*, in which he scorned the summer soldier and sunshine patriot and called for a rebuilt army to oppose the British oppressor. The Continental Congress reorganized the army, giving Washington full command. More attractive incentives made it possible to recruit soldiers for longer commissions. Improved supplying of the army also helped. Even the seeming disaster of General Lee's capture by the British at a tavern where he had unwisely dallied actually strengthened Washington's hand by suddenly bringing Lee's forces under his own direct command. According to Dr. Benjamin Rush, the American response to the crisis typified that of a free republic: It did not rally until almost too late, but when it did, adversity brought out its best.

If Cornwallis was correct, as Fischer implies, then Washington's crossing of the Delaware was the apex of his generalship. Following soon after the rally of the American people, it brought the fame and credibility to the Continental Army that were sorely lacking after the New York fiasco.

The battles of Trenton and Princeton were parts of a web of mischances and opportunities. Washington was adept at adjusting to both. Although he did not direct them, American militia harassed the Hessian and Scottish troops stationed along the New Jersey side of the Delaware River, keeping them in a high state of alert for a week. Washington's plan was to cross the Delaware Christmas night and attack the exhausted and unsuspecting Hessians just before dawn on December 26, 1776. Among the many mischances he encountered were a partially frozen river, a driving snowstorm, eighteen artillery pieces to transport across the icy water, and a stray American regiment commanded by Adam Stephen, whose unauthorized mission of vengeance against the Hessians nearly compromised the surprise attack. Washington, however, benefited from good fortune. The driving snow storm made the ill-clad soldiers miserable but proved essential to retaining the element of surprise. Visibility was so bad that it did not matter that the attack occurred forty minutes after dawn. The artillery, although delaying the implementation of his plans by some four hours, proved to be a decisive factor in the victory. Some nine hundred Hessians were captured, and their commander, Colonel Johann Rall, was killed.

After the victory, more mischances and opportunities presented themselves. As Washington and his generals debated their next move, his men located forty hogsheads of rum, and much having been consumed, no further advance was possible. An annoyed Washington led his men back across the river to Pennsylvania. Along with the missed opportunity, however, came a new one. Colonel John Cadwalader, in charge of two units that were unable to cross the Delaware with Washington Christmas night, notified the commander that he and his men had eventually made it over and were now waiting on the New Jersey side for orders. Although Washington's men were tired and his officers reluctant to re-cross the Delaware, he was convinced that further offensive moves were necessary to deter the British from attacking Philadelphia. Therefore, on the night of December 29, he led his men once again across the river, now completely frozen over.

The plan was to lure eight thousand British troops under Cornwallis into a second battle at Trenton, this time with the Americans firmly established on the heights across Assunpink Creek on the southeast side of town. This second engagement, which occurred January 2, 1777, was less a full-fledged battle than the repulsion of British probes along the creek, including the successful defense of Assunpink Bridge. Fischer estimates 365 British killed or captured. Most important was the morale boost of having held a strong defensive position against the mightiest military power in the world.

The British assumed that the real battle would be fought the following day, but Washington knew that he would eventually be defeated if he stayed in place. He and his officers devised a bold plan to withdraw their troops that night and attack weakly defended Princeton, with a view to moving on to the major garrison at Brunswick and capturing it as well. The maneuver was not an easy one. Some of the continentals were making their third night march in as many nights and actually slept while they walked. Many were barefoot. The Quaker Bridge south of Princeton was not sturdy enough for artillery, so a new bridge had to be constructed during the night. Once again, these delays foiled Washington's plan of attacking before dawn. Ultimately, though, Princeton fell to the Americans, with some 450 British captured, killed, or missing.

Although the exhausted Americans could not finally follow the British to Brunswick and capture that important garrison (Washington felt five hundred fresh soldiers could have done it), the battles of Trenton and Princeton proved to be a turning point in the war. In disarray, the British retreated to Brunswick, not only abandoning Princeton but other outposts as well. They became defensive-minded, the reputation of the Continental Army rapidly rose throughout the colonies and breathed new life into the cause of freedom, and victory in these battles convinced many that the British were not invincible after all.

All through the rest of the winter of 1777, the New Jersey militia, energized by Washington's victories, harassed British foraging parties causing frequent, if not heavy, losses and lowering morale. Although continually annoyed with the militia because they came and went as they pleased, Washington, true to form, made the best of it. In one respect, he had no choice because his own Continentals were reduced to only twenty-five hundred men by March 15, while the militia consisted of some twelve thousand. In another, he must have realized what British colonel William Harcourt pessimistically wrote in a letter: that the colonists would never be defeated because the state militias effectively meant that every man in America was armed and resistant. Victory was not a matter of simply defeating an army, but a whole people.

*Washington's Crossing* is thoroughly documented. Besides its 379 pages of text are 185 pages of back matter including a thorough index, twenty-four appendices, twenty-seven pages of bibliography, and fifty-five pages of notes. Of particular interest is a thirty-two page historiography section that traces the many different interpretations of Washington's crossing, primarily historical but also fictional and artistic, from the nationalistic to the iconoclastic, from romantic to Marxist. One of the strengths of Fischer as a historian is that he has conscientiously considered these many approaches as well as the considerable body of documentary evidence available.

That he has not ignored folk history of the crossing is evidenced by the preface to this book (and its dust cover), which consider the famous painting of Emmanual Leutze and its effect on ordinary Americans' imaginations. The work pictures a resplendent George Washington standing in a boat in the middle of the icy Delaware River. Also in the boat are a diversity of figures including farmers, a wounded soldier, a merchant, a western rifleman, an African American seaman, a Scottish immigrant, and even what Fischer terms an androgynous figure that might, he suggests, be a woman in male clothing. This collection of figures celebrates the United States' democratic values. It is a theme that Fischer follows throughout the book. Primarily through the leadership of George Washington, the Americans were forged by crisis into committed, albeit irregular, fighting units that were able to defeat the mightiest powers of Europe.

*William L. Howard*

## Review Sources

*Booklist* 100, no. 11 (February 1, 2004): 946.
*Library Journal* 129, no. 2 (February 1, 2004): 106.
*National Review* 56, no. 6 (April 5, 2004): 45.
*New Criterion* 22, no. 9 (May, 2004): 66.
*The New York Review of Books* 51, no. 9 (May 27, 2004): 29.
*The New York Times Book Review* 153 (February 15, 2004): 13.
*Publishers Weekly* 251, no. 2 (January 12, 2004): 49.
*School Library Journal* 50, no. 5 (May, 2004): 176.

# WATERBORNE

*Author:* Bruce Murkoff (1953-    )
*Publisher:* Alfred A. Knopf (New York). 397 pp. $25.00
*Type of work:* Novel
*Time:* Primarily the 1930's, with flashbacks to the 1910's and 1920's
*Locale:* The Nevada desert, Wisconsin, Los Angeles, and Oklahoma

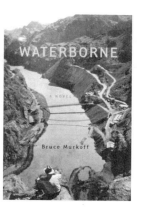

*The construction of the Boulder Dam brings together an unlikely assortment of emotionally wounded characters*

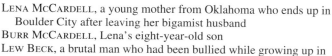

*Principal characters:*

FILIUS POE, a young engineer who leaves Wisconsin after the tragic death of his wife and son

LENA McCARDELL, a young mother from Oklahoma who ends up in Boulder City after leaving her bigamist husband

BURR McCARDELL, Lena's eight-year-old son

LEW BECK, a brutal man who had been bullied while growing up in Los Angeles

In 1922, a report issued to the United States Congress recommended the construction of a dam on the Colorado River in the vicinity of Boulder Canyon, Nevada. It would not be until 1931 that the Bureau of Reclamation would award the bid for the construction of the Boulder Dam to the construction and engineering firm known as the Six Companies. The first concrete at the dam site finally was poured in June, 1933.

During the 1930's, the United States was suffering through the Great Depression. Millions of people had difficulty making ends meet, and there was very little in which Americans, collectively, could take pride. The construction of the dam was a bold stroke taken by a government that needed to make such a gesture, resulting in the largest public works project that the United States had undertaken to date. The dam officially was completed on March 11, 1936. Boulder Dam was the world's highest and largest of its day.

The reservoir, Lake Mead, that was formed by the dam has a capacity of more than thirty-one million acre-feet of water. Lake Mead would remain the largest reservoir in the world until 1959. Through an act of Congress, the name of the dam officially was changed to Hoover Dam in 1947. Within this historical backdrop, Bruce Murkoff has created in his first novel a gripping story of three people who get caught up in the transformation of the Nevada desert.

The narrative spends a great deal of time leading up to the construction of Boulder Dam. The first half of *Waterborne* alternates among the lives of the three lead characters before they converge on the construction area in 1932. Filius Poe grew up in Wis-

*Born in 1953, Bruce Murkoff lived*
*for several years in California,*
*where he worked as a scriptwriter.*
*He now resides in Stone Ridge, New*
*York.* Waterborne *is his first novel.*

consin, where he learned to appreciate what the wilderness had to offer. Water as a life force plays a very prominent role in his story and throughout the novel. At a young age, Poe became enamored with figuring out how things worked. He set his sights on bringing order to the world wherever possible. As a child, he received parental love and encouragement. With this solid foundation, Poe made his way into the world with a confidence that served him well. For example, at seventeen, he took it upon himself to build a boat. He became obsessed with every detail and even created a scale model before building the full-sized *Alpha Dory*.

World War I was coming to an end when Poe reached his eighteenth birthday. By the time he was nineteen, he was a "third-year engineering student, already published in technical journals, courted by prestigious firms in Chicago and New York and by the Bureau of Reclamation in Washington, D.C." A young coed, Addie McCabe, interviewed him for the *Badger Herald*. She was a journalism major, and it was her assignment to get the scoop on this up-and-coming engineering star. Her interview with Poe led to a first date, which led to a relationship and eventually to marriage and a honeymoon in Paris. This storybook love affair is handled in a flashback with care and good humor by Murkoff. He avoids sentimentality at all cost. Poe is truly the emotional center of the novel, so Markoff does well here by not overplaying his hand.

After the honeymoon, Poe went to work for the Chicago Tunnel Company as a superintendent. Part of his job was to inspect railroad tunnels that ran forty feet below the streets of Chicago. Even with his tiring work, Poe found it difficult to sleep. Restless, he could not resist the challenges presented him whenever an interesting new engineering project emerged. By 1931, Poe and Addie had an eight-year-old son, Ray, whom they adored. During the summer of that year, the Poe family was on Lake Michigan in a thirty-foot sailboat. A storm raged on the lake, and tragically, young Ray was lost to one of the surging waves that enveloped the sailboat. The perfect family had been shattered in an instant. Poe's grief at the death of his son was exacerbated when his wife came down with a fever and died after a few weeks in the hospital.

Poe's rock-solid life is now only a distant memory. The once-important career as an engineer comes to a halt. The novel opens with Poe leaving Chicago in 1932. A former colleague has asked him to join the Boulder Dam project, and Poe decides that this project may somehow provide a diversion from his sorrows, a way to come to terms with his loss and the guilt that inhabits his heart. Murkoff's precise writing adds weight to the situation. As the first half of the novel continues to unfold, the reader becomes acquainted with what has brought the other two main characters to the Nevada desert.

While Poe is the wounded hero of *Waterborne*, Lew Beck is most certainly the damaged villain of the saga. He was born Louis Beckman and grew up in the Boyle

Heights section of Los Angeles. He is the first member of his Jewish family to be born in the United States. His father runs Beckman's Kosher Meats, and young Beck is the victim of virulent anti-Semitism. He is repeatedly harassed and beaten up for being Jewish. Always small, young Lew learns to survive by being more brutal than those who attack him. He even takes his anger out on his father by breaking some of his father's fingers. Beck refuses to take any punishment lying down, even from his own father.

While Murkoff has, in his character Poe, created an almost too-noble character, in Beck the author has fashioned a complicated villain who is close to unforgettable. Throughout the history of literature, it has been almost commonplace for the villain to get all the best lines. Murkoff has taken extra care to flesh out Beck with more intriguing and disturbing facets than any other character. This is not to say that the reader will come away condoning Beck's actions. His fits of rage are hard to stomach, but as a life force he is a perfect counterweight to the heroic Poe. Poe is the strong, silent type who may win in the end, but Beck is someone who refuses to hold back or to play the victim.

The third major character, who comes between these two men, is Lena McCardell. She had been happily married to a Bible salesperson living in Oklahoma with her young son, Burr, when she discovered that her husband was a bigamist. An attractive, considerate woman, McCardell never expected to be wronged in such a way. Faced with the reality of her situation, she decided to head West, to stay with a friend in Nevada. Once there, she finds it necessary on several occasions to fight off the advances of men who try to take advantage of her.

At the halfway point of the novel, each of these three characters has arrived at the center of the massive public works project. The patient reader will be rewarded with all of the elements of an epic tale finally coming together. There are flashes of the works of John Steinbeck, E. L. Doctorow, and Don DeLillo in the texture of the tale. Murkoff is especially adept at describing the natural world and the vastness of the Western landscape.

Las Vegas and Boulder City grow dramatically during the construction of Boulder Dam. Although the laborers are forced to live in squalid conditions at the start of the project, by 1932 living conditions have greatly improved with the building of Boulder City. Something of a reservation or fortified camp for individuals who are desperate for work and shelter, Boulder City becomes an oasis. Unfortunately, minority dam workers are forced to live outside of this newly created oasis. In the novel, even the loathsome Beck supports an African American man who is refused the use of a toilet.

Meanwhile, the spirit of new growth is contagious; a grateful nation seems to feel that it is getting a second chance to rise to the top through the efforts of this public works project. Nature can seemingly be controlled by technology and the hard work of many. Poe comes to terms with his past by finding love again. He and McCardell help each other to heal the personal wounds that would have destroyed each of them if allowed to fester. In a dramatic—if somewhat overwrought—conclusion, Poe is given a chance to save McCardell's son from drowning.

For the most part, Murkoff has struck a good balance between character development and historical detail. *Waterborne* is much more than an ambitious first novel; it is a bold, brawling, and thoroughly American novel that can stand alongside many of those written by American literature's most honored icons.

*Jeffry Jensen*

## Review Sources

*Booklist* 100, no. 11 (February 1, 2004): 951.
*The Christian Science Monitor*, February 24, 2004, p. 15.
*Library Journal* 128 (November 15, 2003): 98.
*The Nation* 278, no. 14 (April 12, 2004): 26.
*The New York Times Book Review* 153 (May 2, 2004): 18.
*Publishers Weekly* 251, no. 4 (January 26, 2004): 228.
*The Washington Post Book World*, March 7, 2004, p. 7.

# WHERE SHALL WISDOM BE FOUND?

*Author:* Harold Bloom (1930-    )
*Publisher:* Riverhead Books (New York). 284 pp. $25.00
*Type of work:* Philosophy and literary criticism
*Time:* About 750 B.C.E.-2004
*Locale:* Europe, the Middle East, and the United States

*Bloom seeks to discover the nature and sources of wisdom by exploring some of the major texts and authors of Western civilization*

*Principal personages:*
JOB, biblical character
YAHWEH, the god of the Old Testament
THE PREACHER from the biblical book Ecclesiastes
PLATO, ancient Greek philosopher
HOMER, ancient Greek poet
MIGUEL DE CERVANTES, Spanish novelist
WILLIAM SHAKESPEARE, English playwright
MICHEL DE MONTAIGNE, French essayist
FRANCIS BACON, English essayist
SAMUEL JOHNSON, English writer
JOHANN VON GOETHE, German writer
RALPH WALDO EMERSON, American writer
FRIEDRICH NIETZSCHE, German philosopher
SIGMUND FREUD, inventor of psychoanalysis
MARCEL PROUST, French novelist
SAINT AUGUSTINE, early Christian church father

In an early chapter in this exploration of wisdom, Harold Bloom makes a passing reference to life-threatening "medical ordeals" he has recently survived. Elsewhere he mentions having been at "the gates of death." Although *Where Shall Wisdom Be Found?* is not at all an autobiography, it does seem to spring from a very personal source, out of "personal need," as Bloom himself puts it on the opening page, "reflecting a quest for sagacity that might solace and clarify the traumas of aging, . . . illness, and . . . loss."

The notion of loss seems especially relevant to Bloom; several of the wisdom writers whom he examines in this book, including Samuel Johnson, Marcel Proust, and the author of the biblical book of Ecclesiastes, focus on it and teach acceptance in the face of it.

Acceptance of loss is only one piece of wisdom to be found in this book. In nine chapters focusing on sixteen writers or their works, Bloom identifies several different pieces of wisdom, some of them contradicting each other, some of which he likes better than others. By the end, therefore, the reader is a bit uncertain about what exactly wisdom is for Bloom, and perhaps that is part of Bloom's point: that wisdom is as various and contradictory as life itself.

~

*The Sterling Professor of Humanities at Yale University, Harold Bloom has written more than twenty-five books of literary criticism and theory and has edited numerous anthologies of literary criticism. His best-known book is* The Anxiety of Influence *(1973), a study of the way in which later writers relate to earlier ones.*

~

Bloom begins by examining the biblical Book of Job and finds a harsh, even wicked wisdom in its depiction of the suffering the pious Job is forced to endure so that God can prove a point to Satan. For Bloom, the wisdom that emerges from the Book of Job is that God has the power to inflict suffering and does not care if a good man suffers as a result. The lesson of the book thus seems to be that one should fear God, a lesson Bloom finds difficult to accept.

Bloom much prefers the wisdom of Ecclesiastes, even though it is gloomy in its own way. The Preacher's wisdom in Ecclesiastes is that all is vanity: Everything passes away, dust returns to dust, and the spirit returns to God. This is "the wisdom of annihilation," Bloom says, and he is drawn to it even though, especially now that he has entered his seventies, he says he cannot read it without feeling a chill.

Moving on from the Bible, Bloom then produces a long, odd chapter devoted to arguing with Plato, the ancient Greek philosopher who wanted to ban poets from the Utopia he described in *Politeia* (c. 388-368 B.C.E.; *Republic*, 1701). Plato's desire to ban the poets troubles Bloom because Bloom sees much wisdom in Plato (though he never exactly explains what that wisdom might be) and yet he is very much devoted to poetry of the sort with which Plato wants to do away.

For Bloom, there is more wisdom in poets such as Homer and William Shakespeare than in philosophers such as Plato, and he blames Plato for recent developments in the universities, where he sees Plato's heirs, the postmodernist theorists whom he calls the "commissars of Resentment," attempting to undermine the Western literary tradition.

Bloom is very much devoted to the Western literary tradition and more generally to Western civilization as revealed in its best-known books, from the Bible through the works of Shakespeare, Proust, and Sigmund Freud. It is noteworthy that in this study of wisdom Bloom looks only to books, and only books in the Western tradition. He does not seek wisdom in Nature or in Heaven or in the streets. He also does not seek it from non-Western sources or from the writings of women. Every piece of wisdom writing he examines comes from a male, Western writer.

It is almost as if Bloom is deliberately thumbing his nose at the latest academic fashions, such as feminism, neohistoricism, and cultural and postcolonial studies, casting himself as an old curmudgeon defending old-fashioned views against those who would undermine the Western tradition. He seems committed to ignoring attempts to move beyond the Western tradition. Thus, though he explores the renunciation of desire in the works of Johann von Goethe, he says nothing of the similar sort of renunciation found in Buddhism, nor does he explore any wisdom that might be found in Islam or Hinduism.

For that matter, he devotes very little attention to Christianity. Feeling this lack, he adds a final chapter on Saint Augustine, but it is a very short chapter, and the only wisdom he can find in Augustine is the view that reading is important to spiritual development. This is hardly what one might think of as an essential aspect of Christianity—but it is very much in line with Bloom's devotion to books.

The one other quasi-Christian work Bloom looks at is the apocryphal Gospel of Thomas, which he sees as an expression less of traditional Christianity than of gnosticism, the ancient mystical philosophy devoted to secret knowledge and transcending everyday life.

The mysterious wisdom Bloom sees in the Gospel of Thomas seems strangely at odds with the wisdom he points to elsewhere in his book, notably in his chapter on Michel de Montaigne, the French essayist whom Bloom calls one of the wisest of writers. For Bloom, Montaigne's message is to turn away from transcendental notions (like those in the Gospel of Thomas) and to focus not on divine matters but on living well in the actual conditions and limitations of one's life.

For Montaigne, according to Bloom, it is important to know oneself, to understand one's role, and to perform it as well as possible. "Our great and glorious masterpiece," says Montaigne in a passage quoted by Bloom, "is to live appropriately." According to Montaigne, it is a very human thing to want to be more than human, to seek divine status in some way, but paradoxically those who seek to rise in this manner actually lower themselves. To be truly divine, for Montaigne, is to enjoy one's proper condition and not to despise one's own being.

There is something similar in this wisdom to the wisdom Bloom sees in Miguel de Cervantes' *Don Quixote de la Mancha* (1605, 1615). For Bloom, one of the greatest aspects of Cervantes' novel is the self-knowledge developed by Don Quixote and Sancho Panza in the course of their conversations with each other. Oddly, this wisdom, which amounts to saying "Know thyself," is usually associated with ancient Greek writers such as Plato, the philosopher who troubles Bloom so much.

Another important aspect of *Don Quixote de la Mancha* for Bloom is the suffering the characters in it are forced to endure. This leads Bloom to talk of "the human need to withstand suffering," a subject he returns to in his chapter on Samuel Johnson, quoting Johnson's remark that for human beings "much is to be endured, and little to be enjoyed."

Suffering, loss, and pain are subjects Bloom is drawn to in this book, as if a large part of wisdom consists in realizing that there is much that is negative in human life. Surprisingly, it is this sort of negative wisdom that Bloom emphasizes in the works of Shakespeare. Bloom clearly loves Shakespeare and celebrates his vitality, and yet what he finds in his plays is a dark nihilism. He focuses mostly on Shakespeare's great tragic heroes (Hamlet, Lear, Macbeth) and sees recklessness, excess, and thus defeat in them all.

Perhaps Bloom's experiences of growing old and ill have made him focus on the darker side of Shakespeare's achievement. It is interesting that he has nothing to say about Shakespeare's comedies, though he does discuss the comic character Falstaff, and indeed argues that it is better to be a Falstaff than a Hamlet, just as it is better to be a peasant like Sancho Panza than the overly bookish Don Quixote. "Being mat-

ters more than knowing," he says, as if it is better not to think too much, a somewhat odd position to come to for someone who has devoted his life to thinking about
books.

In the coda at the end of his book, Bloom returns to Hamlet and the issue of thinking, and follows the philosopher William James in saying that wisdom consists in
"learning what to overlook." Hamlet's problem, according to Bloom, is that he over-
looks nothing; he thinks too much; he goes to extremes. Bloom in this passage thus
seems to be recommending restraint, moderation, a recognition of one's limitations,
the sort of approach he found so full of wisdom in the essays of Montaigne.

However, this sort of restraint is not what Bloom seems to be recommending in his
discussion of the only American figure in his book, Ralph Waldo Emerson. Bloom,
who calls himself an Emersonian, approvingly quotes Emerson's comments in favor
of force, the "strong transgressor," and those who act out of a "bold and manly" anger.
Bloom seems to enjoy this "exuberant amoralism," even though he recognizes that it
has "Hamlet-like" destructive aspects.

It is hard to see how this Emersonian philosophy of force and transgression fits in
with the quiet restraint of Montaigne, except perhaps for the emphasis on self found in
both of them. Montaigne emphasizes knowing oneself; Emerson promotes the idea of
self-reliance, something that Bloom sees as central to the American experience. Self-
reliance may also appeal personally to Bloom because of how he sees himself in this
book: as a defender of old-fashioned ways fighting a lonely battle against his own colleagues' transformation of institutions of higher learning into "mediaversities of
multiculturalism."

In the end, readers seeking wisdom may feel baffled, for Bloom does not even attempt to reconcile the varieties of wisdom he has presented. There are some common
themes, it is true, such as the inevitability of loss and suffering. For Bloom, the universe seems a dark place, but it is not entirely clear how he thinks one should deal with
this dark universe. Through acceptance and through knowing one's limitations in the
manner of Montaigne? By fighting against it in an Emersonian manner? Or perhaps
he thinks the best approach is to seek out the sort of hidden wisdom hinted at in the
Gospel of Thomas. He gives no single answer.

On the other hand, Bloom does provide a single clear answer to the literal question
posed by his title. If one is looking for wisdom, the place to find it, according to
Bloom, is among the poets, playwrights, and novelists. At least, that is what Bloom
repeatedly says, especially in his chapter arguing against Plato.

It is interesting, though, that despite saying that the greatest wisdom is to be found
among the poets rather than among the philosophers, the bulk of Bloom's book deals
with philosophers and quasi-philosophical essayists, from Plato through Montaigne
and Francis Bacon to Johnson, Friedrich Nietzsche, and Freud.

Indeed, the longest discussion in the book is the one on Plato. It is true that this discussion consists primarily of a rejection of Plato's antipoetic notions and his defense
of order and reason, but at some level Bloom must think there is something important
in Plato. In fact, he says himself that Plato's *Symposion* (388-368 B.C.E.; *Symposium*,
1701) is nearly as essential as Homer's *Iliad* (c. 725 B.C.E.) and Shakespeare's trage-

dies. There must be some wisdom in Plato, then, though Bloom never really explains what it is.

What the reader is left with, then, are some baffling contradictions. These contradictions, coupled with Bloom's sometimes obscure and idiosyncratic way of writing, produce a sometimes difficult and mysterious work, but perhaps that is exactly what a book about wisdom has to be.

*Sheldon Goldfarb*

## Review Sources

*Booklist* 101, no. 3 (October 1, 2004): 294.
*Kirkus Reviews* 72, no. 17 (September 1, 2004): 845.
*Library Journal* 129, no. 16 (October 1, 2004): 80.
*The New York Times Book Review* 154 (October 10, 2004): 16.
*Publishers Weekly* 251, no. 35 (August 30, 2004): 40.

# WHO ARE WE?
## The Challenges to America's National Identity

*Author:* Samuel P. Huntington (1927-    )
*Publisher:* Simon & Schuster (New York). 428 pp.
  $27.00
*Type of work:* Current affairs

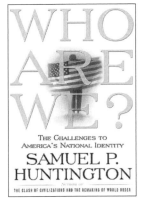

*A distinguished American political scientist examines the character of Americans' perception of their identity, the historical basis of traditional American identity, social and economic forces that may be disintegrating that identity, and the choices that confront Americans for the future of their society and polity*

The United States is now in the throes of a "crisis of identity" that bids fair to undermine the idea of a sovereign American nation governed by the U.S. Constitution. So argues Professor Samuel P. Huntington, for decades professor of government, now University Professor, at Harvard University. Huntington is best known to the reading public for *The Clash of Civilizations and the Remaking of World Order* (1996), an often misunderstood work that has generated considerable attention and controversy. Now Huntington has turned his prodigious talents as social scientist to one of his central concerns as an American citizen. *Who Are We? The Challenges to America's National Identity* examines the roots and substance of traditional American identity, the dynamic social forces altering it, and prospects for the revival and extension of what he calls "the cultural core," which he identifies as "Anglo-Protestant" culture.

This work is no exercise in "value free" social science. On the contrary, Huntington makes it clear that he writes not just as a political scientist but also as a citizen and patriot. He has chosen the present moment for this closely argued but full-throated jeremiad because of his belief that a crisis of identity is upon the United States.

While American identity once included marked elements of race and ethnicity, this is no longer true, as Huntington is at pains to point out. Upon what, then, is American identity now based? Students of American society often take what Swedish sociologist Gunnar Myrdal famously described in 1944 as the "American Creed" to be the common factor that unites Americans in a single identity.

Briefly put, the "creed" includes commitment to political and personal liberty, political equality, equality of opportunity, constitutional democracy founded on popular sovereignty, individual dignity and individualism, and economic freedom. Huntington argues, however, that by itself, adherence to the creed is insufficient to sustain a distinct American identity. Indeed, the "principal theme" of *Who Are We?*, he writes, is "the continuing centrality of the Anglo-Protestant culture to American national identity."

Huntington argues that the ideological element of that identity (the "creed"), while essential, is insufficient to describe, still less to sustain, American identity. If millions—or billions—of people believe or come to believe in the creed, would that make them Americans? If American identity in its entirety consists in the creed, then they are all Americans, just as all those who accept the Roman Catholic faith are all Catholics, and identity must have further substance. That substance, in Huntington's view, is America's founding Anglo-Protestant culture.

*Samuel P. Huntington is Albert J. Weatherhead III University Professor at Harvard University and chairman of the Harvard Academy for International and Area Studies. His many books include* The Third Wave: Democratization in the Late Twentieth Century *(1991) and* The Clash of Civilizations and the Remaking of World Order *(1996).*

American identity is thus built upon a "core" Anglo-Protestant culture consisting of traditions and values "that have been embraced by Americans of all races, ethnicities, and religions and that have been the source of their liberty, unity, power, prosperity, and moral leadership as a force for good in the world."

From this core culture were distilled values of the creed already mentioned, as well as the value of hard work, the centrality of religion in its dissident Protestant form, "ostensibly secular" political principles, and use of the English language.

Religions other than Protestant Christianity, including Catholicism and Judaism, have adapted themselves to this core culture, assimilating its key features. Non-Christian religions, however, are marginal to American identity. Additional features of the "core culture" include a moralist and reform ethic and its reach into foreign policy, illustrated by the figure of John Foster Dulles, son of protestant missionaries, who as secretary of state under Dwight Eisenhower declared the "neutralist" movement of nations to be immoral for their failure to join the West in its struggle with Soviet Communism.

Huntington's talk of the centrality of "Anglo-Protestant" culture has elicited charges of "nativism" from hostile critics. Such claims are not based on a careful and accurate reading of the book, however; and some undoubtedly arise from partisan animus or ill will. Indeed, the author explicitly contradicts nativism in his foreword:

> This is, let me make clear, an argument for the importance of Anglo-Protestant culture, not for the importance of Anglo-Protestant people. I believe one of the greatest achievements, perhaps the greatest achievement, of America is the extent to which it has eliminated the racial and ethnic components that historically were central to its identity and has become a multiethnic, multiracial society in which individuals are to be judged on their merits . . . If [the] commitment [to Anglo-Protestant culture] is sustained, America will still be America long after the WASPish descendants of its founders have become a small and uninfluential minority. That is the America I know and love. It is also, as the evidence in these pages demonstrates, the America that most Americans love and want.

The drama of *Who Are We?* lies in the fact that America's core culture is now under sustained attack from a variety of sources. Much of the book is taken up by analysis of these sources, which include political, economic, and, especially, intellectual elites. These elites hold views about the nature and destiny of American democracy diametrically opposed to those of its citizens.

Manifestations of discontinuity between the American people and influential elites are many and diverse. In the post-Vietnam War era, for example, patriotism was abandoned by the teaching profession and ceased to be part of civic education in American schools, if civic education was addressed at all. Many educators still find the idea of patriotism suspect, if not outright offensive, and are unable to distinguish between national self-affirmation and fascism. Instead, celebration of diversity at the expense of common identity holds sway, as a so-called multiculturalism has swept the nation's schools. Increasingly, adherence to world or "global" citizenship is advocated.

In the past, in the wake of the mass immigration halted in the 1920's, Americans embarked on an intensive "Americanization" campaign. Despite the attempt of the Jordan Commission to resurrect this idea in the 1990's, elites are loathe to give credence to "Americanization," and efforts at assimilation are often ignored in favor of the preservation of difference.

Large numbers of American elites have undergone what Huntington calls "denationalization," abandoning identification with the United States in favor of some notion of transnational democracy and globalism. Thus business elites rejected adherence to American interests and patriotism, illustrated in 1996 when public interest advocate Ralph Nader wrote to the chief executives of one hundred of the nation's largest corporations, suggesting that they open stockholders meetings with the Pledge of Allegiance. Only one agreed, half never responded, and the remainder "brusquely" rejected it.

Intellectual and professional elites exhibit similar attitudes and behavior. Anything approaching patriotism among university faculty in many institutions, especially elite ones, is taboo; instead, forms of transnationalism are de rigueur. In the field of law, advocates proclaim the superiority of "international law" to law under the U.S. Constitution and demand that a nebulous body of "customary international law," to which no nation has consented, should be empowered to trump the U.S. Constitution.

Huntington devotes considerable attention to the single most powerful force in the deconstruction of the American nation into an elementally divided or cleft society, the challenge of Mexican immigration and Hispanization. Political, economic, and intellectual elites have attempted to further the division of America into Spanish- and English-speaking sectors through bilingual education, while most citizens, when asked at elections, reject it. Similarly, the vast majority of citizens want the nation's southern border protected from the millions of illegal aliens, most of them Mexicans, who pour across it annually.

Elites on both the political Left and Right, however, object to closing off this source of eventual electoral support or cheap labor (respectively) and with only modest difficulty consign the majority will to ineffectuality. Presidents, aware of powerful forces favoring porous borders, knowingly allow the flow of illegal immigrants to continue. Those who publicly object are labeled "nativist" or "racist," and proposals to place the Army or National Guard on the border—which would cut off most of the illicit traffic—are said to require the border's "militarization," a term employed to frighten off opposition to the status quo.

By September, 2001, national identification and national self-affirmation seemed to have faded badly. They suddenly reaffirmed themselves in a great burst of patriotism after the terrorist attacks on September 11. Nevertheless, by the time Huntington put pen to paper, this eruption of nationalism seemed likewise to be fading. To retain America as a national idea, albeit with universalist features, Huntington calls for national recommitment to its core Anglo-Protestant culture, upon which the American Creed is based.

This brief recitation of some of the high points of Huntington's argument does scant justice to the richness and complexity of this magisterial work. Each page bristles with the social science learning and acuity for which Huntington's many works are noted.

In the end, Huntington poses three future options for the nation. American identity could be dissolved by re-creating the world in America's image (the "imperial" option); or it could be dissolved in a different way, through large-scale immigration without assimilation of newcomers into core American culture. In the former case, "the world becomes America" through the success of an imperial state; in the latter case, "America becomes the world"—an amorphous cosmopolitan collection of nationalities living under one roof; in essence, Canada.

Both of these potential futures would please various elites; but these options constitute polar antitheses of what most Americans at the opening of the twenty-first century are known to desire—preservation of a distinctive American identity, the third option in Huntington's galaxy. Although Huntington himself clearly prefers it, this option is the least likely outcome of the present struggle to define what is to come for the American polity.

A compelling analysis of American democracy published in 1960 by political scientist E. E. Schattschneider was titled *The Semi-Sovereign People*. The full force and latter-day consequences of the truth supposed by the title of that work is only now coming to light. The supposedly "sovereign" people of democratic myth ("popular sovereignty" being a fundamental principle of any form of democracy) is being systematically thwarted in its desire to preserve and strengthen "the American identity" that, in Huntington's words, "has existed for centuries."

The elites in universities and in the print and electronic media who attack Huntington's work by falsely characterizing it as "nativist" work their arts to ensure that the will of a democratic people, of which they do not approve, is thwarted. In working to dissolve American identity into either of the popularly unauthorized future states that Huntington describes, elites are in the process of systematically undermining American liberal constitutional democracy, transforming it into a postdemocratic transnational regime or some other version of international utopia.

When the work of these elites has reached fruition, as in all probability it will in the twenty-first century, the America born in the seventeenth century, transformed into an independent state through a colonial rebellion in the next century, reborn following a different rebellion in the nineteenth century, and preserved from the menace of fascism and communism in the twentieth century, will be no more. By then, few will bear the profound sense of loss that a society that had not gradually lost its collective memory would have felt. By then, too, American democracy, splintered into Hispanic and other diasporas along with the rump, possibly racist, remnants of Anglo-Protestantism, will be but a shadow of its former self. At that point, the American democracy of today will be revealed to have been a colossal failure, a circumstance assuaged by the likelihood that few will take notice.

*Charles F. Bahmueller*

## Review Sources

*Booklist* 100, no. 17 (May 1, 2004): 1529.
*The Economist* 371, no. 8379 (June 12, 2004): 82.
*Foreign Affairs* 83, no. 3 (May/June, 2004): 120.
*The Nation* 278, no. 23 (June 14, 2004): 18.
*The New Republic* 230, no. 23 (June 21, 2004): 25.
*The New York Times*, May 28, 2004, p. E29.
*The New Yorker* 80, no. 12 (May 17, 2004): 92.

# WHY I WAKE EARLY

*Author:* Mary Oliver (1935-    )
*Publisher:* Beacon Press (Boston). 80 pp. $22.00
*Type of work:* Poetry

*Oliver's nature poetry about birds, animals, and the land concerns the cyclical nature of things, reflects the influence of George Herbert and William Blake, and is devoutly religious*

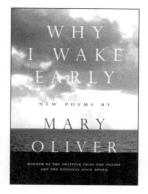

By beginning her book with a quotation from George Herbert, a seventeenth century metaphysical poet, Mary Oliver establishes the religious tone and content of her work. Herbert writes, "Lord! Who hath praise enough?" Oliver's poems offer direct and indirect praise of the creator. Herbert, whose chief work was *The Temple* (1633), found God in nature, just as Oliver does, but her poems lack his liturgical themes, and the structure of *The Temple* is more pronounced. The fourth poem of Oliver's *Why I Wake Early* is titled "Where Does the Temple Begin, Where Does It End?" Unlike Herbert's "temple," with its structure and sense of completion, Oliver's "temple" seems to exist without temporal or topographical boundaries.

Her first poem, "Why I Wake Early," begins with a "hello" addressed to the "best preacher," the maker of the morning, the creator of the world. That world may have its "miserable and crotchety" people, but the "preacher," who speaks through nature, is the source of light and direction, and "ease[s] us with warm touching." The speaker's "Watch now, how I start the day/ in happiness, in kindness" seems addressed not only to the "preacher" but to her readers, who will discover the happiness and kindness in the rest of the poems.

"Bone" is really about the nature of the soul and one's power to fathom it. Comparing it to the ear bone of a pilot whale, the speaker speculates that both are "so hard, so necessary—yet almost nothing." The sea, with its "time-ridiculing roar," seems to mock attempts to define, to reduce "into fractions, and facts" that which cannot be seen but which is nevertheless there. The speaker ends with the realization that "our part is not knowing,/ but looking, and touching, and loving" even without "certainties."

"Looking" is a pervasive theme in the book, and in her poem about the "temple" the speaker returns to the idea that some things, like the soul, cannot be reached, but they can be reached out to. Readers are enjoined to look, which she defines as not just standing around but as standing around "as though with your arms open." Essentially, she regards "looking" as seeing, with the latter word's emphasis on being receptive. Looking will result in things coming closer and coming "cordially," not only warmly, but in its older sense of heart-reviving; even the "blue air" of God seems "close." In the later "Look and See" the speaker concludes, "Oh, Lord, how

*Born in Cleveland, Mary Oliver
attended and taught at schools in
the East. She has written five books
of prose and several volumes of
poetry. Her collection* American
Primitive *(1983) won the Pulitzer
Prize, and her* New and Selected
Poems *(1992) won the National
Book Award.*

shining and festive is your gift to us, if we only
look, and see."

As in her earlier works, Oliver incorporates an
American Indian perspective in some of the poems in *Why I Wake Early*, particularly "Beans"
and "The Arrowhead." In the former, beans appear to give themselves up to the fire or the pot,
just as animals give themselves up to hunters.
Though the speaker acknowledges that these
beans are "only vegetables" and hence not like
intelligent human beings, she is also aware that
all things are creatures. When the speaker finds
an arrowhead, she declares, "Now, it's mine," demonstrating a European American
attitude toward ownership. She vows to show the "imposing trinket" to her friends
and display it on her desk, but, like the quilt in Alice Walker's short story "Everyday
Use," the arrowhead is not a "trinket" to be displayed. As she walks home, the "old
ghost" corrects her assumptions: "I would rather eat mud and die/ than steal as you
still steal,/ than lie as you still lie." The words apply not only to the speaker's taking of
the arrowhead but also ("still") to white Americans' treatment of American Indians.

"What Was Once the Largest Shopping Center in Northern Ohio Was Built Where
There Had Been a Pond I Used to Visit Every Summer Afternoon" contains a related
ecological theme. The speaker, "seeing what has been done to [the earth]," grows cold
as she ponders the fate of the displaced flowers, here personified (a bit more senti-
mentally than usual) with "faces" and "lives." She knows she has more material
things than she needs and wishes she could live a less materialistic life, substituting
"vines for walls," and grass for a carpet, but she also knows that only when she dies
will she be separated from the "buying and selling." When she is "old and cold," she
will have "only the beautiful earth in my heart."

The conflict between what one wants and what one knows will happen is also the
theme of "Something," a poem about the speaker's discovery of "the egg case of an
ocean shell,/ the whelk." Although she admires the beauty of the object, she is not
content until she can identify it with a name. Glib and intelligent, she desires "syntax,
connections, lists" to go with all that she sees in nature so that her world is "named
and orderly." There are two responses to the beauty of the world: one, the spontaneous delight of a "madcap," who sings and applauds with delight; the other, the devout
penitent in thankful prayer to the creator.

"Logos" also illustrates two ways of responding and knowing. "Logos" means reason, but it also has a religious meaning as in the Word or ultimate reality, the creative
spirit of God as it is manifested in Jesus Christ. The speaker speaks of "reality,/ or
what is plain, or what mysterious." The "him" she refers to is Christ, who was "there"
at the creation or reality, and to be there is one way of knowing, but one need not be
"there" to know it; one only needs to "imagine" it and to accept the "miracle" and the
love, the grace, that accompanies it.

Part 1 of the book ends with "'Just a minute,' said a voice," a poem in which a "quaint" unidentified voice requests that the speaker stand still and then after a moment or two thanks her for complying. Aware that she is intruding upon nature with her "great feet" and threatening any "small or unusual thing," she speculates about the source of the voice. Among her speculations is the mention of the "wondrous meeting" of poet William Blake, a religious Romantic poet who found God in nature. As in the poetry of Herbert and Henry Vaughan, the voice is never identified and does not need to be, and the poem concludes with a line about keeping one "wondering." The poem thus serves as a convenient break, "just a minute," between the two parts of the book.

In part 2 the speaker seeks a closer connection with the world of nature. In "This Morning I Watched the Deer" the speaker feels miserable, despite being able to see the deer because she is aware that the world she is in is really their world. She wishes to communicate with them ("sing some sparkling poem into/ the folds of their ears") and go with them "over the hills" and into the "impossible trees," impossible only because she realizes the worlds are different. Similarly, in "The Best I Could Do" her encounter with a pond owl prompts her to desire "some connection," some notion of the way he thinks of her intrusion into "*his* world." The poem ends with an ambiguous vision of his carrying her away while she pleads for her life at the same time that she shouts "*praise, praise, praise.*" As the book begins with a quotation about praise, this is consistent with the theme, but it is also disquieting, unless there is the simultaneous desire to live and to be carried away by something symbolically religious.

The theme of "looking" also pervades part 2. In "Mindful" the speaker states that she was born "to look, to listen,/ to lose myself/ inside this soft world" and to "instruct myself" in not just the extraordinary things in life, those things the world considers worthy of attention, but also the "ordinary" things that become prayers and the praise due the creator. In "The Pinewoods" the speaker uses her "imagination" to reconstruct the visit three deer pay to the pond. She sees beyond "the edge/ of what my eyes actually see" and is not limited by the real. In the quest to know all the answers, too often people forget to be like the mockingbird, who "knows enough already or knows enough to be/ perfectly content not knowing." Again, the speaker in "Daisies" counsels the acceptance of "what is given," a "heavenly" giving up of the quest that may be futile.

*Why I Wake Early* also concerns redemption and resurrection. In "The Wren from Carolina," the wren "delivers such a cantering praise" ("canter" suggests pace, but "canter" also derives from the pace of the "Canterbury pilgrims" and is a possible pun on "cantor," a religious singer). An invention of holiness, he drinks from his small cup of life, "knowing it will refill." The speaker states, "I'm on that list too," and she has her own cup of gladness (like the biblical "cup of trembling" in James Baldwin's short story "Sonny's Blues"). In "One" the speaker states that everything is "redeemable," even the eyes, the imagination, and "you." (It is implied that if the "looking" is not receptive, the insight will be imperfect.) Resurrection is the theme of "The Soul at Last," a poem about the soul's departure from the "closed coffin." The soul is depicted as leaping and dancing in joy and is the perfect manifestation of the "Lord's terrifying kindness."

The last poem in Oliver's book is "Lingering in Happiness," which describes the overall tone of the volume and also symbolically depicts the process by which happiness is dispersed throughout God's world. The rain, after a drought, cleanses but disappears to people's eyes when it enters the ground. What is not seen by people's limited vision is the way that the water, always religiously symbolic, permeates the ground, touching everything, including "small stones, buried for a thousand years." The poem is a fitting conclusion to the book, for happiness and joy pervade Oliver's work, and the "lingering" reference suggests the ongoing acceptance of things as they are.

The speaker is Oliver, a woman writing nature poetry in a field usually dominated by men, who have traditionally approached nature from a masculine point of view. Oliver's speaker brings questions to her quest in nature and seeks instruction, which she often receives, although that "instruction" may be limited, even to a receptive student. Though there is some violence and death in the poems, they seem to be part of a cyclical pattern that the speaker embraces and in which she finds solace. The poems are unabashedly religious, but unlike Herbert, whose poems often involve religious doubt and inner conflict, Oliver writes of serenity and joy as she seeks to provide the "praise" Herbert commented on in his introductory quotation.

*Thomas L. Erskine*

### Review Sources

*The Boston Globe*, April 25, 2004, p. D6.
*The New York Times Book Review* 153 (May 2, 2004): 24.

# WILL IN THE WORLD
## How Shakespeare Became Shakespeare

*Author:* Stephen Greenblatt (1943-     )
*Publisher:* W. W. Norton (New York). Illustrated. 430 pp. $26.95
*Type of work:* Literary biography
*Time:* 1564-1616
*Locale:* Stratford, Lancashire, and London, England

> *Greenblatt explores how William Shakespeare's life and world informed his plays and helped shape Shakespeare into the greatest dramatist in the English language*

*Principal personages:*

WILLIAM SHAKESPEARE, a famous playwright and poet
ANNE HATHAWAY, his wife
JOHN SHAKESPEARE, his father
MARY ARDEN SHAKESPEARE, his mother
HAMNET SHAKESPEARE, his son
JUDITH SHAKESPEARE, his younger daughter, Hamnet's twin sister
SUSANNA SHAKESPEARE, his older and favorite daughter
RICHARD BURBAGE, an actor
ROBERT GREENE, an author
CHRISTOPHER MARLOWE, a dramatist
THOMAS NASHE, a playwright and satirist
HENRY WRIOTHESLEY, third Earl of Southampton, a literary patron and
     the leading contender for the fair youth of Shakespeare's sonnets
ELIZABETH I, queen of England from 1558 to 1603
JAMES I, king of England from 1603 to 1625

In *Will in the World* the eminent Shakespeare scholar Stephen Jay Greenblatt, Cogan University Professor of the Humanities at Harvard, seeks to explain how a young man from the provincial market town of Stratford-upon-Avon became the greatest playwright not only of his own age but of all time. The question has exercised people's imaginations since at least the eighteenth century, when bardolatry began. To some, including Mark Twain, the feat was impossible: Surely the author of such moving sonnets, captivating narrative poems, profound tragedies, and lyrical comedies must have attended university and must have grown up in courtly, or at least aristocratic, circles. Twain agreed with Delia Bacon that her namesake, Francis Bacon, (though no relation) had written the plays, and dozens of other candidates have been proposed over the years as the real playwright and poet.

Scholars have uniformly rejected these anti-Stratfordian arguments and have shown how Shakespeare drew from the world he knew and from books available to him all that his imagination needed. Greenblatt presents no new facts in this biography aimed at the general reader. Rather, he considers how what is known of Shakespeare's life and world affected him in such a way as to prompt him to produce his great works.

*Cogan University Professor of the Humanities at Harvard, Stephen Greenblatt is the founder of new historicism, an approach to literature that situates texts within their historical context. He is the author of eight previous books, including a study of Sir Walter Ralegh and* Hamlet in Purgatory *(2001).*

At the time of Shakespeare's birth, his father was enjoying a period of great prosperity and prestige. John Shakespeare was buying property and holding a series of increasingly responsible posts in local government, culminating in his selection as bailiff, the equivalent of the town's mayor, of Stratford-upon-Avon in 1568. In 1576 John Shakespeare applied for a coat of arms that would, for a fee, transform him and his heirs into gentlemen, an important distinction in the hierarchical Elizabethan world.

In 1577, when William was thirteen, John began to suffer financial reverses. The probable cause was Parliament's enforcement of the laws against illegal trading in wool, England's chief export. John owned two adjacent houses in Henley Street, Stratford. (The houses were subsequently joined.) One is known as the Birthplace, where William was born. The other is the Woolshop, under the floor of which fragments of fleece have been found. In *The Winter's Tale* (1610-1611) Shakespeare reveals an intimate knowledge not only of sheep-shearing festivals but also of the wool business. The young clown in that play, trying to calculate how much money his flock will yield, comments, "Every 'leven wether tods, every tod yields pound and odd shilling." A tod is twenty-eight pounds of wool, which in the 1570's sold for twenty-one shillings, or precisely "pound and odd shilling."

John began mortgaging and selling off properties. His bid for a coat of arms languished because he could not afford the fees. According to Nicholas Rowe, who included a biography in his 1709 edition of Shakespeare's works, William was forced to withdraw from school to help his father in the glove trade John was licensed to practice.

For Greenblatt, this loss of status helped impel Shakespeare to the theatrical world, which allowed commoners to become kings, if only for a brief moment. Actors wore clothes otherwise allowed by the sumptuary laws of the time only to the gentry, and actors acquired skills, such as fencing, that marked their betters. The magic of theatrical illusion transforms Christopher Sly from a drunken commoner into a gentleman in Shakespeare's early *The Taming of the Shrew* (1593-1594). Sonnet 87, in which Shakespeare laments the loss of the fair youth's love, concludes, "Thus have I had thee as a dream doth flatter:/ In sleep a king, but waking no such matter." Bottom the weaver could be transformed into Pyramus in the play-within-a-play in *A Midsummer Night's Dream* (1595-1596). Legally, actors were at best servants of the aristocrats who acted as their patrons, at worst lumped with rogues and vagabonds when they lacked such aristocratic protection. Yet they could not only pretend to gentility but also, if successful as Shakespeare was, actually gentle their condition, as Shakespeare did in 1596 when he bought that coat of arms his father had sought twenty years earlier.

Greenblatt speculates that John Shakespeare's fate affected his famous son in another way as well. Greenblatt suggests that either as cause or effect of John's decline, the playwright's father turned to drink. Greenblatt notes further that in Shakespeare's plays excessive drinking is condemned, perhaps as a reaction to what William saw at home. Hamlet objects to Claudius's draining "his draughts of Rhenish down." Cassio's drinking in *Othello* (1604) not only loses him his lieutenancy but also sets in motion events that allow Iago to pursue his plot more easily. Falstaff embodies all the deadly sins, but his drinking figures prominently among his vices.

Falstaff is clearly a father figure to Prince Hal, whom Greenblatt links to Shakespeare. One of Greenblatt's original observations in this book is that one of Shakespeare's models for Falstaff was the playwright, novelist, and pamphleteer Robert Greene. Greene was one of the university wits who dominated the London literary scene when Shakespeare first arrived in the metropolis in the late 1580's. Greenblatt quotes Gabriel Harvey's description of Greene: "Lo, a wild head, full of mad brain and a thousand crotchets: A Scholar, a Discourser, a Courtier, a Ruffian, a Gamester, a Lover, a Soldier, a Traveler, a Merchant, a Broker, an Artificer, a Botcher, a Pettifogger, a Player, a Cozener, a Railer, a Beggar, . . . an Image of Idleness; an Epitome of Fantasticality; a Mirror of Vanity."

Falstaff embodies many of these qualities. Moreover, Greene was married to a woman named Doll, whom he abandoned for a mistress. Shakespeare's Doll Tearsheet, Falstaff's mistress (and others'), may take her name from Greene's wife. All but one of the university wits died young. Shakespeare knew these men, probably drank with them, yet, like Prince Hal, remained somewhat aloof. Perhaps because of his father's reverses, Shakespeare was cautious financially, politically, and religiously.

His was an age in which caution was wise. Shakespeare's chief rival, Christopher Marlowe, was involved in espionage and was killed in what may well have been a staged brawl in Deptford. Catholics were subject to fines and sometimes worse penalties. Decades after Shakespeare's death, Richard Davies, a chaplain at Corpus Christi College, Oxford, wrote that Shakespeare "died a papist." Greenblatt presents the argument, first offered by Ernest Honigmann in *Shakespeare: The Lost Years* (1985), that in the early 1580's the future dramatist went to Lancashire, a Catholic stronghold, to escape persecution in the Midlands led by Sir Thomas Lucy (whom some see as the model for Justice Shallow in the 1597 play *The Merry Wives of Windsor*), who lived about four miles from Stratford. A William Shakeshafte is mentioned as a player in a will dated August 3, 1581. The testator, Alexander Hoghton, lived near Fernando, Lord Strange, whose acting company included many of Shakespeare's later associates. Greenblatt goes so far as to speculate that in Lancashire Shakespeare could have met Edmund Campion, leader of a Catholic mission to England in 1580. If Shakespeare was involved with these Catholic intrigues and households, he hid his connections well.

His daring appeared rather in his drama. Another of Greenblatt's fascinating insights concerns Shakespeare's discovery, as he was writing *Hamlet* (1600-1601), that literary works are more interesting when clear motivation is removed. In Shakespeare's sources for *Hamlet*, the prince at the time of his father's death is too young to revenge the murder. To stay alive until he grows up, he feigns madness. Shakespeare's Hamlet is at least twenty, if not thirty, years old; and his madness, far from deflecting suspicion, arouses it. Why, then, does he "put an antic disposition on"? Similarly, in *Othello*, Shakespeare muddies Iago's motive for his malevolence. Again, the source is clear: Iago wants Desdemona. Shakespeare offers Iago so many motives—anger at being passed over for a promotion; the thought that Othello has cuckolded him; Cassio's goodness; perhaps even lust for Desdemona—that one can never be certain what drives him. The result is a more complex character than existed in earlier accounts.

Greenblatt suggests that the dissatisfaction with easy explanations resulted from the death of Hamnet Shakespeare in 1596, an event that defied reason and bred increased skepticism in the playwright. In his chapter on *Hamlet*, "Speaking with the Dead," Greenblatt links Hamnet's death to another feature of the play: the ghost (played by Shakespeare and regarded as his finest role). Here Greenblatt presents in condensed form the argument he set forth in *Hamlet in Purgatory* (2001). Protestantism rejected the belief in ghosts as well as in Purgatory and thereby sundered the link between living and dead that is a feature of Catholicism. Whatever Shakespeare's own religious beliefs, his psychological need to remain connected with his dead son surfaces in the play named for the boy: Hamnet and Hamlet were used interchangeably in Stratford documents. That same desire for reunion seems to underlie the late romances, with their recovery of lost children. This restoration may be most poignant in *The Winter's Tale*. Leontes' son, Mamilius, dies in act 3 at about the same age as Hamnet. In act 4 the boy who plays this role returns as Perdita, Leontes' lost daughter with whom he eventually is reunited. Greenblatt does not mention this bit of staging, but it is of a piece with his argument.

At least as daring is Shakespeare's sympathy with the outsider. In "Laughter at the Scaffold," Greenblatt contrasts Marlowe's treatment of the Jew Barabus in *The Jew of Malta* (1589) with Shylock in Shakespeare's *The Merchant of Venice* (1596-1597). Barabas is energetic and clever, but he is a villain drawn from anti-Semitic stereotypes. Shylock is not. Greenblatt, like many other critics, links Shakespeare's Jewish play with the 1594 execution of Dr. Ruy Lopez, physician to Queen Elizabeth. Lopez was born Jewish but had converted to Protestantism. He was caught up in the political battles between the earl of Essex and the Cecils and was condemned for allegedly plotting to assassinate his royal patient. Moved by Lopez's plight and capitalizing on an interest in Jews (none of whom legally resided in England, though in fact about two hundred were living in London, some of them near Shakespeare), Shakespeare created an alternative to Barabas, a Jew more sympathetic than his Christian antagonists. Similarly, nearly a decade later Shakespeare would champion an African Moor against the Europeans, and in one of his last plays, *The Tempest* (1611), would raise questions about colonialism in showing how Prospero enslaves the native population of an island much like Bermuda (though located in the Mediterranean Sea).

What is the source of this sympathy with the outsider, and how did Shakespeare transmute these feelings into poetry that is daily recited on stages and in classrooms around the world? Greenblatt's book finally does not answer these questions because no one can explain genius. *Will in the World* does shed much light on the playwright and his world, though, and for that it deserves to be savored.

*Joseph Rosenblum*

## Review Sources

*Booklist* 101, no. 1 (September 1, 2004): 39.
*Harper's Magazine* 309 (September, 2004): 85.
*Kirkus Reviews* 72, no. 13 (July 1, 2004): 616.
*The New York Review of Books* 51, no. 20 (December 16, 2004): 34.
*The New York Times Book Review* 154 (October 3, 2004): 22.
*The New Yorker* 80, no. 26 (September 13, 2004): 90-95.
*Publishers Weekly* 251, no. 29 (July 19, 2004): 152.
*The Wall Street Journal* 244, no. 60 (September 24, 2004): W7.

# WITH

*Author:* Donald Harington (1935-     )
*First published:* 2003, in Great Britain
*Publisher:* Toby Press (New Milford, Conn.). 492 pp.
   $20.00
*Type of work:* Novel
*Time:* 2003
*Locale:* The towns of Harrison and Stay More and Madewell
   Mountain, in Arkansas

Donald Harington

*Robin Kerr escapes the sexual designs of her kidnapper,
pedophile Sog Alan, because of his deteriorating health.
When he dies, she is left to grow up alone on a remote Arkansas mountaintop homestead with no modern amenities and
only assorted animals and the spirit of a twelve-year-old boy
for company*

   *Principal characters:*
      ROBIN KERR, an eight-year-old girl who is kidnapped
      SUGRUE (SOG) ALAN, the man who kidnaps Robin to be his child bride
      ADAM MADEWELL, the spirit of Adam when he was twelve and also the
         living, now-middle-aged man
      HREAPHA, a mongrel dog who manages the menagerie of animals at the
         homestead

   The latest of Donald Harington's Stay More novels, *With*, attempts to create a
mythical world in which a young girl of eight can grow up safely without any other
people in the innocence of the natural world that surrounds her. The eighteen-year-
old nature goddess who emerges from these years is then ripe and ready for the
middle-aged man who returns to his family's abandoned homestead to find in her true
love.
   No matter how clever this novel becomes (and it is shameless in the chances it
takes), it is telling the same old sad story that Hollywood has been filming for decades: The young, beautiful girl and the older, experienced man find in each other a
match made in heaven—or, perhaps, the typical fantasy of middle-aged men, dressed
up in fancy to make it palatable.
   The first chapter of *With* starts out trying to hoodwink the reader. Knowing, as the
author must, that almost every reader will have seen at least the cover blurb and have
an idea of the book's plot, he opens with a third-person narrative of a female who has
been beaten and abused by a man who took her away from her mother. For several
pages, the author lures the reader into believing that this is Robin Kerr's experience,
until mounting details reveal that the female is a dog. Hreapha, as she calls herself, is
the dog of Robin's kidnapper, who thinks and "speaks" in a fairly sophisticated

voice—not a human voice, but every "hreapha!" she utters is freighted with meaning, which she conveys to the reader. She also "speaks" to other dogs, some of which "speak" back in uneducated, country diction.

Hreapha's tale begins in the midst of Sugrue (Sog) Alan's preparations to steal a young girl and retreat into a hermitlike existence with her. Sog has come into the possession of nearly a half million dollars in drug money cash while making a traffic stop on a lonely highway, and this becomes his stake to realize his ultimate fantasy. No longer will he have to depend on leafing through his worn copy of *Nudist Moppets*, although he takes it along anyway. He stocks a long-deserted homestead on top of Madewell Mountain with all manner of supplies, trusting to the abilities of himself and his purloined "bride" to make a living from the land once they run out.

> *Donald Harington has written eleven other novels—including* The Cockroaches of Stay More *(1989),* Ekaterina *(1993), and* Thirteen Albatrosses *(2002)—with most of them set in his fictional world of Stay More. He has taught art history at a variety of colleges and written books about artists. In 2003, he won the Robert Penn Warren Award.*

Ensuing chapters alternate between various characters' points of view. Most of the time, these are presented as third-person narratives, with occasional chapters told in first-person voice. Often the tales overlap, presenting the story from two or more sides. Each character speaks in a unique voice, and Harington does a good job both of finding a character's voice and determining who will provide the best focus for each particular point in the story.

Robin becomes Sog's victim by chance. He sees her in the parking lot, waiting by her mother's car. He cannot abduct her then, but he reacts physically to her blond beauty and decides that she is the girl he will take away with him. After being thwarted once by Robin's stepgrandfather, Sog manages to steal Robin away from a birthday party at a roller-skating rink.

The abduction itself is where Harington begins to have trouble with his plot. So that Sog can snatch Robin without being seen, Harington invents a ludicrous, open balcony that extends from the skating rink floor out above the alleyway, with the floor at eye level and convenient for Sog to grab the girl, who comes out alone to cool off. The obvious access such a structure would give to people trying to sneak into the skating rink is ignored; no guard has been posted to prevent this. By this time, alert readers realize that Harington does not hesitate to manipulate facts and events to make his story work in the way that he wants.

This young girl has been abducted by a pedophile and taken away where no one will find her. Because the author plans for Robin to remain virginal until she is grown, he must introduce reasons for Sog not to fall upon and ravish the girl as soon as he has her alone. At first, Sog is tired from the long, harrowing hike from his truck to the homestead. He wants to give Robin a chance to calm down and accept her situation. Such a reprobate, however, could not control himself for long, and so Harington has Sog's health deteriorate, with impotency as the first symptom. It appears that his only purpose was to get Robin up to the mountain and to start her in her new life. Sog remains alive long enough to teach Robin many of the "old-time" ways of living, but his health has declined too much to teach her all she needs to know. He even loses the power of coherent speech.

Conveniently, another character appears who can give Robin advice based on experience. Harington has created a new kind of ghost: the spirit of someone still living. He calls this an "in-habit" because the spirit inhabits the place where the person who left it was most happy. The in-habit residing at Madewell Mountain is that of Adam Madewell, who was forced to leave the homestead when he was twelve years old. Harington takes the most liberties with his unique creation, not choosing to adhere to the rules he himself makes up for its existence. At first, Adam's in-habit cannot be seen and cannot be touched. He can mentally communicate to the dog, Hreapha, and she can communicate to him in return. Gradually he comes to speak out loud with Robin. He provides the guidance she needs to survive in the homestead, which has no running water, no electricity or gas, and a dwindling food supply.

The problem with Adam's in-habit is that, even though he feels frustrated that he cannot physically help Robin, this does not stop the author from allowing Adam to engage in sexual intercourse with Robin when she becomes a teenager and invites him to do so. The author tries to get away with this by having Robin declare more than once that she knows she is really only imagining their escapades, and this both preserves her virginity and gives her a preview of Adam as her lover.

For any reader who might be disappointed by the lack of sexual activity between humans, there are occasions of animal mating taking place at the homestead and in the surrounding mountains. When Hreapha decides she must journey down to the nearly abandoned town of Stay More to mate with her old friend, Yowrfrowr, their experience is detailed in a tender, romantic interlude. This is followed, however, by an absurd scene in which Hreapha is raped by a gang of male coyotes on her way back to the homestead.

There are five parts to *With*. Part 1, "Parted with," concerns Robin's abduction, being parted from her loved ones and the life she knew. Part 2, "Sleeping with," which might slyly seem to indicate sexual experience, is about merely sleeping—only briefly with an impotent, exhausted Sog but mostly with Hreapha and the bobcat kitten, Robert, that Hreapha brings home for Robin's ninth birthday present. In this second section, Robin uses an Ouija board that Sog gives her to communicate with both Hreapha, who puts her paw on the planchette and moves it to Yes or No, and the in-habit, who does not yet reveal his identity.

The third part, "Without," contains the death of Sog, who wants Robin to shoot him to end his misery. When she refuses, he attempts to molest her. This angers Robin enough to prompt her to shoot him after all. He is sitting in the two-seat outhouse with the door open when she levels the shotgun at him, and there he stays, in full view of the house, rotting until his bones are picked clean by crows and buzzards. Harington apparently does not think such a constant sight should affect Robin. At one point she props a bottle of Jack Daniels whiskey in the skeleton's hand and leaves it there. At the end of the story, the skeleton remains in its outhouse in the yard.

# WITHOUT BLOOD

*Author:* Alessandro Baricco (1958-    )
*First published: Senza sangue*, 2002, in Italy
Translated from the Italian by Ann Goldstein
*Publisher:* Alfred A. Knopf (New York). 97 pp. $18.00
*Type of work:* Novella
*Time:* 2004
*Locale:* A small town

*Three partisans visit a farmhouse and kill a father and son; a daughter survives to confront one of the killers and resolve the assassinations in a highly personal fashion*

Principal characters:
　　MANUEL ROCA, a former hospital director
　　　　accused of war crimes
　　NINA ROCA, his four-year-old daughter, who survives her father's assassination
　　TITO (also known as PEDRO CANTOS), a twenty-year-old partisan who invades Roca's farmhouse and spares Nina
　　SALINAS, a leader of partisans
　　EL GURRE, a machine gunner accompanying Salinas

*Without Blood* begins ominously, with a lonely farmhouse silhouetted against a dark sky as a Mercedes flies by on a dusty country road. Manuel Roca, resident of the house, hides his daughter, Nina, in a cellar, and with his teenage son awaits intruders. When he refuses to leave the house, they spray machine gun fire and quickly gain entrance.

Roca is accused of war crimes against patients at a hospital, which he denies, and Salinas, head of the intruders, whose brother was brutalized at that hospital, shoots Roca in the knee. Roca's son comes to his father's defense and is machine-gunned, and when the father begins screaming, he too is killed. As the three assassins search the house, the youngest, Tito, finds Roca's daughter, Nina, hidden below the floor and cannot bring himself to reveal her to the others, who then torch the house.

Fifty years later, a gray-haired woman stops at a lottery kiosk and asks the attendant to accompany her for a drink. During their conversation, the man, an aging Tito, now calling himself Pedro Cantos, admits he recognized the woman immediately as the girl he saw in the cellar. As they trade stories, the reader learns that the other two partisans have met untimely deaths—one by poisoning and one by a bullet in the back—and that Cantos has been waiting for his demise.

Each understands the past differently, presenting radically different explanations for Nina's survival. She has been told that her adoptive father wagered her in a card game and lost to a wealthy count, while Cantos heard that the same count, who had been a double agent during the war, was charged with eliminating the young woman.

~

*Alessandro Baricco has earned a reputation as a musicologist and television personality in his native Italy for shows on opera and literature. He has written two plays, one of which,* Novecento *(1994), was made into the film* The Legend of 1900 *(1998). His novel* Silk *(1997) brought him international acclaim and inspired an opera by Andre Previn. Baricco founded a school of writing in Turin called Holden, in honor of the protagonist in J. D. Salinger's* The Catcher in the Rye *(1951).*

~

Both stories agree that she and the count married and that she had three sons and lived quietly thereafter. When discussing the war, she insists that Cantos explain his motives and what exactly he hoped to accomplish with all the fighting and reprisals.

Eventually she asks if he would like to make love to her, and they retire to a hotel. The novel ends with each character contemplating the past, and Nina huddling close to a sleeping Cantos, wrapped in the same posture that she assumed when hiding under the floorboards.

Although described as a novel, *Without Blood* is barely a novella, a slim narrative characterized by sparseness and simplicity. There is nothing of narratorial baroqueness, and it is devoid of the self-consciousness of minimalists and maximalists alike. The sparseness of Baricco's prose is matched by sparse plot. Divided into two sections, the novel concerns two principal events: the assault at the farmhouse and a middle-aged couple having a discussion in a bar. It is, however, the various interpretations of events offstage, which are open to considerable debate and are never resolved by the narrator, that hypnotize the reader.

One wonders whether Roca was a Hispanic Mengele, as Salinas insists, or an innocent pawn, as the doctor contends? Was Nina adopted and then given away in a card game, or, as Cantos claims, was she married off to a man commissioned to kill her? Cantos further announces that Salinas was later believed to have been poisoned by Nina's pharmacist stepfather and El Gurre discovered with a bullet in his back and Nina's name in his pocket. For her part, Nina offers neither refutation nor elaboration of these events, thus they hang suspended in the narrative air, awaiting clarification.

What the novel suggests most powerfully is that everyone has a story, and each person is more committed to his or her version than anything else. Thus issues such as truth, accountability, and the cold, hard facts are ultimately elusive and indeterminate. Consequently, in spite of his radically trimmed style, Alessandro Baricco has much in common with more obviously flashy postmodern writers.

Repeatedly critics have described Baricco's fiction as fables or morality tales, and, indeed, with the exception of *City* (1999), his novels are abbreviated affairs that cut to the quick of detailed exposition and narrative evaluation. Fables and morality tales are always characterized by a distinct ethical code or point of view; their dominant function is didactic. Good and evil, in such tales, are presented as palpable presences in the narrative world and are typically easy to identify. The so-called "moral" of these stories is usually unequivocal, as for instance in Aesop's stories of the turtle and hare or the cricket and grasshopper.

However, *Without Blood* is more elusive. Evil is not easy to discern, existing either nowhere entirely or everywhere. His characters, while they do unspeakable things to one another, are all victims, and all, in spite of their ethical limitations, are pathetic creatures who suffer horribly. Salinas, Roca's avenging angel, is so overcome by his victim's pain that he covers his ears, pleading with his accomplices to silence the victim. The result is that the reader cannot escape the heart-scalding pain that visits each life and can find no convenient scapegoat for all the grief.

If, indeed, fable is an apt description for this work, then the subject for moral consideration is warfare itself. It appears that the war to which all the characters refer is a civil one in some unnamed country (possibly Spain or South America, though Baricco offers in a disclaimer that the choice of Hispanic names "is due purely to their music and is not intended to suggest a historic or geographical location") where each side has clearly been brutalized. While having drinks, Nina asks Cantos to explain how such a cataclysm could take place. His answer is simple—to create a better world—"And we fought for that, to be able to do what was right." From Nina's point of view, though, the motive was revenge.

Such certitude and dedication come with a steep price—lives that are forever eclipsed by the shadow of warfare. Americans seem addicted to the nonsensical, feel-good phrase of "moving on" when tragedy occurs; there is no moving on in Baricco's world. Cantos admits, "You can't turn back, when people begin to murder each other you can't go back." Nina admits that feelings of terror have never left her, and she warns that in order to survive the war, Cantos and others like him "burned your entire life, and you no longer even know." In the end they are forced to live truncated lives: "She was a phantom and he a man whose real life ended a long time ago."

The novel also explores the less obvious effects of war, the psychic pain and dislocation that attend any severely traumatic experience and, like memories of the war itself, these effects never "move on" or disappear. Given the opening scene where Roca's knee explodes, his son is turned into a rag doll, and the father's head is then blown off, one might expect that the story will be a graphic horror show. However, the concern is less with physical violence than with psychic dislocation.

Both the victims and victimizers are devastated and find themselves living in a tortured intimacy with one another, as the relationship between Nina and Cantos indicates. They appear like creatures on a northern tundra, frozen in a moment that occurred fifty years earlier. Cantos frequently drifts off during their discussions, disbelieving circumstances and questioning where he is and, as he says, "life is never complete—there is always a piece missing." Although he has yearned to unburden himself of these memories, "it all seemed absurd." Their conversation is full of gaps and dramatic ellipses. Nina admits that for most of her life she has been mute, and Cantos has "felt how difficult it was to give a name to what had happened to him in the war, as if there were a spell under which those who had lived couldn't tell a story, and those who knew how to tell the story had not been fated to live."

So much pain produces awesome guilt and a desire to achieve some kind of reckoning. Cantos admits to himself that he no longer fears his own execution and will not resist it. Nina has her own sense of reckoning but a far more humane one—she has sex with one of her family's brutalizers. While she hides in the cellar, she becomes conscious of her cramped quarters and takes comfort in the security of her fetal position:

*"she liked this—she was shell and animal, her own shelter, she was everything for herself, nothing could hurt her as long as she remained in that position."* Immediately after having sex, she assumes the same position, cradling herself against Cantos's back. "She smiled. Animal and shell."

It is this curious position that initially overwhelmed the young Tito and encouraged him to spare her, *"It was all so orderly. It was all so complete."* Fifty years later, sitting in a bar, he realizes what that vision meant to him: "He knew that the word 'peace' was not enough to describe what he had felt, and yet nothing else occurred to him, except perhaps the idea that it had been like seeing something that was infinitely complete." Indeed, at the novel's close, with love replacing vengeance, a sense of completeness is achieved, if only symbolically.

*Without Blood* is a deceptive novella, a seemingly slight effort that probes deeply into timeless themes of war, childhood, and suffering. Baricco's control of the material is firm and the style mesmerizing, as if one had fallen into ravishing trance. He has produced a work that is not easily forgotten and that deserves a wide audience.

*David W. Madden*

## Review Sources

*Booklist* 100, no. 15 (April 1, 2004): 1345.
*The Daily Telegraph*, May 8, 2004, p. 8.
*Kirkus Reviews* 72, no. 6 (March 15, 2004): 235
*Library Journal* 129, no. 7 (April 15, 2004): 122.
*Los Angeles Times*, June 20, 2004, p. R4.
*Review of Contemporary Fiction* 24, no. 2 (Summer, 2004): 147.
*San Francisco Chronicle*, June 20, 2004, p. M3.
*The Times Literary Supplement*, May 7, 2004, p. 22.

# WODEHOUSE
## A Life

*Author:* Robert McCrum (1953-    )
*Publisher:* W. W. Norton (New York). 530 pp. $28.00
*Type of work:* Literary biography
*Time:* 1881-1975
*Locale:* England, France, Belgium, Germany, New York
City, Long Island, and Los Angeles

*One of the most popular comic writers of the twentieth
century is revealed to have been obsessed with his work at
the expense of other aspects of his life*

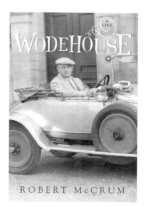

Principal personages:
> SIR PELHAM GRENVILLE WODEHOUSE, nov-
> elist, playwright, and lyricist
> ETHEL WODEHOUSE, his wife
> LEONORA WODEHOUSE CAZALET, his stepdaughter

Robert McCrum's examination of the life of Pelham Grenville Wodehouse (1881-1975) is the seventh major Wodehouse biography. McCrum tries to distinguish his study from earlier ones by emphasizing the significance of Wodehouse's considerable theatrical work, by making suppositions about his relations with his wife, Ethel, a free spirit, and by drawing a more complete portrait of the darkest period of Wodehouse's life, his questionable behavior during his internment by the Germans during World War II. Often seen as a jovial man without a care in the world, Wodehouse was much more complex. McCrum weaves acute literary criticism into his narrative, making a strong case for the greatness of the creator of Jeeves, Bertie Wooster, Psmith, Ukridge, and Mr. Mulliner.

Wodehouse came from a family of colonial administrators whose values were encompassed "by near-feudal attitudes." Young Pelham, called Plum, and his two older brothers were never close to their parents, especially their mother. When the boys were two, four, and six, Eleanor and Ernest Wodehouse deposited them with a nanny and spent three years in Hong Kong. Between the ages of three and fifteen, Wodehouse spent about six months with his parents. As an old man, he wrote that he and his brothers considered their mother a stranger. McCrum, who based some of his conclusions upon an interview with a child psychologist, sees this separation as central to the writer's solitary, self-sufficient nature and his ability to insulate himself from emotional distress. His unstable childhood led Wodehouse, never close to his brothers, to crave the certainty of daily routines and contributed to his unusual devotion to his craft.

McCrum traces the cold, remote parents in Wodehouse's fiction to this upbringing, unfortunately typical of the Victorian colonial class. Rudyard Kipling, George Orwell, and Somerset Maugham had similar childhoods. The time the boy Plum spent

*A native of Cambridge, England, Robert McCrum has degrees from Cambridge University and the University of Pennsylvania. After many years as an editor at Faber & Faber, he became literary editor of* The Observer *in 1996. The author of several novels and children's books, McCrum is the coauthor, with Robert MacNeil, of* The Story of English *(1986) and has also written the memoir* My Year Off *(1998), detailing his recovery from a stroke.*

with a variety of aunts and uncles is also reflected in his fiction, especially with the contrast between Bertie Wooster's sympathetic Aunt Dahlia and the fearsome Aunt Agatha.

Wodehouse began writing stories and poems when he was five and read all the Victorian children's classics during his formative years. His literary interests were encouraged at Dulwich, the boarding school he attended in suburban London. This time at Dulwich was the high point of Wodehouse's life, providing a security missing elsewhere. In many senses, Wodehouse remained frozen in time as a Dulwich boy, with the emotional age of his male protagonists arrested at fifteen. Wodehouse later observed, "Mentally, I seem not to have progressed a step since I was eighteen."

Though Wodehouse's feelings toward his father were benign, Ernest Wodehouse's inexplicable behavior led to the major disappointment of his son's life in deciding that Plum, unlike his elder brothers, would not attend Oxford because the family could not afford to send three sons there. If he had gone, however, he might have followed his father's path into the Foreign Office of the civil service and not become a writer.

As it was, young Wodehouse began an immensely boring job with a branch of the Hongkong and Shanghai Bank, work that nevertheless inspired some of his early fiction about bumbling young men slaving away in offices. He was soon neglecting the bank for his freelance journalism, turning out eighty stories and articles while in its employ. Through a former Dulwich schoolmaster, Wodehouse was soon working for the daily newspaper the *Globe* and was making enough money to quit the bank. In 1903 alone, he published forty-seven items in his favorite publication, *Punch*.

Wodehouse created a distinctive, unsentimental London "where aristocrats chased actresses, where American money pursued British class, where bookmakers and barmaids mixed on equal terms with Cabinet ministers and newspaper editors, and where everyone read the *Sporting Times*." The attitudes Wodehouse developed during this period, a contrast between fascination with the hurly-burly of the city and the peaceful calm of rural climes, solidified and rarely varied for the remainder of his more than sixty years as a writer.

Wodehouse liberated himself from his family in 1904 by moving to the United States for the first time. In New York, he wrote lyrics for several musicals. By connecting the words to the actions in the plays, he helped create, says McCrum, the modern musical comedy. Because he had so loved the theater as a schoolboy, he always considered his stage work much more glamorous and satisfying than his fiction. He contributed to fourteen productions from 1916 to 1919, including collaborations with Jerome Kern.

McCrum is especially good at showing that while Wodehouse discovered his subject early on—lovestruck young men getting into all sorts of scraps—he took his time discovering his true voice. Wodehouse begins to do so with the invention of Psmith and becomes a true comic artist in the 1920's with the creation of the unflappable Jeeves, straight man to the chaos that is Bertie Wooster. While McCrum acknowledges the almost mathematical precision of Wodehouse's complicated plots, he never quite grasps that what is so wonderful about the Jeeves stories and novels is Bertie's boundless optimism. If one scheme fails, another will certainly pave the path to true happiness.

Bertie finds women so bewildering because his creator did, too. In New York, writes McCrum, "Wodehouse seems to have been the kind of young man who, like Bingo Little, falls in love easily, but lightly, not letting real emotions interfere." McCrum is intrigued by the apparent absence of a Wodehouse libido, speculating that a 1901 bout with mumps may have decreased or even eliminated his sex drive. If such a drive ever existed, McCrum guesses that Wodehouse sublimated it first in sports such as boxing and rugby and later by engrossing himself in his work.

Nevertheless, in 1914, he met and fell in love with the twice-widowed Ethel Newton Rowley Wayman and married her two months later. In strong contrast to Plum, Ethel was social, noisy, and extravagant. More significant, she was also highly sexed, leading to a series of extramarital relationships. Whether they were innocent flirtations or full-blown affairs, McCrum does not say. What is important is Wodehouse's complete devotion to and tolerance of his wife.

Ethel brought with her a ten-year-old daughter, Leonora. Wodehouse loved the girl as if she were his own, and as she grew older, Leonora became his confidant and adviser, gradually taking charge of the running of his and Ethel's lives. She tried to sort out the long-standing tax problems about which McCrum perhaps goes on too much.

The Wodehouses returned to London in 1919 as Plum began the most productive decade of his career: twenty books, four plays, and lyrics for twelve musicals. He also achieved his greatest successes, with *The Inimitable Jeeves* selling three million copies between 1923 and 1939. Always eager to try new ventures, Wodehouse began the first of two sojourns in Hollywood in 1930 and spent the following decade bouncing between California, New York, and England before settling in Le Touquet, France, in the late 1930's.

After World War II began in 1939, the Wodehouses remained in France despite the pleadings of Leonora, now married and living in England, and other friends and relatives. Plum and Ethel were devoted to their pets and did not want to be separated from their beloved Pekinese during a mandatory British quarantine. When the Germans finally invaded, Wodehouse was taken into custody and, after stops in France and Belgium, sent to an internment camp in Germany. He amused his fellow prisoners with comic accounts of their confinement. After nearly a year, he was transferred in July, 1941, to much more comfortable quarters in a Berlin hotel and was soon joined by Ethel.

Then the only controversial phase of Wodehouse's life began, when he was asked to give some talks on German radio. Wodehouse always said he agreed because of a need to assure his fans, especially those in the United States, that he was all right. The comments with which he had regaled his fellow prisoners did not, however, come across the same in this context, and he was soon accused of collaborating with the Nazis in exchange for greater freedom. Even though Leonora pleaded in letters for him to stop, he continued the broadcasts and was soon denounced in the British press and in Parliament.

Wodehouse's behavior has been defended by many, most notably by Orwell, and the talks seem mostly innocuous. Delivering them at the behest of the enemy, however, is another matter. McCrum devotes by far the largest portion of the biography to this episode, looking at it from all possible angles in an attempt to understand why Wodehouse did it and why he was unable, after the war, truly to fathom what all the uproar was about.

During this period, the Wodehouses were devastated when Leonora died during routine surgery. At the end of the war, they cut all ties to their native country, moving to Manhattan and later to Long Island, never to return to Europe. The final years of Wodehouse's life were fairly uneventful, as he surrounded himself with an ever-increasing family of dogs and cats, went for long walks, and watched soap operas and baseball games on television. Despite health problems, he remained as productive as ever, though with gradually declining quality, and was working on a manuscript when he died in 1975.

In addition to his rather unusual relationship with his wife, Wodehouse had few close friends and went long periods without seeing them. He not only lived for his work; he saw it as a refuge. "Better to be alone than take the risk of company," writes McCrum. "Better to enjoy the fiendish complexity of plot than the troubling complexity of everyday life. Better to exert control over an imaginary world and keep the demons at bay than suffer the manipulations of fate and allow the intrusion of melancholy." McCrum presents Wodehouse as a man of many contradictions: outgoing and friendly yet cold and withdrawn, timid yet bold about some matters, single-minded yet uncertain, loving yet indifferent, innocent yet sophisticated. All that matters, finally, was the work; the rest of life was an afterthought.

While McCrum's biography has been called definitive by some reviewers, a few have criticized it for being too defensive of its subject, and others have complained that McCrum never clearly explains Wodehouse's psychological makeup. Joseph Connolly, whose revised edition of *P. G. Wodehouse: An Illustrated Biography*, first published in 1979, appeared within days of McCrum's book, not only objected to the refusal of the Wodehouse estate to allow him to use quotations from the writer's works, in deference to McCrum, but also claimed that McCrum offered no new information.

While that objection may have some validity, McCrum strives to dig deeper into interpreting Wodehouse's life, to draw larger conclusions than his predecessors. He also devotes considerable attention to the process of Wodehouse's writing, showing how the seemingly effortless was the result of painstaking planning and multiple revisions. He also perfectly captures the essence of Wodehouse when describing Wodehouse's greatness as coming from his providing "a release from everyday cares into a paradise of innocent comic mayhem, narrated in a prose so light and airy, and so perfectly pitched, that the perusal of a few pages rarely fails to banish the demons of darkness, sickness and despair."

*Michael Adams*

## Review Sources

*The Atlantic Monthly* 294 (November, 2004): 136.
*Booklist* 101, no. 2 (September 15, 2004): 194.
*The Economist* 373 (November 20, 2004): 86.
*Kirkus Reviews* 72, no. 18 (September 15, 2004): 904.
*National Review* 56, no. 23 (December 13, 2004): 53.
*New Statesman* 133 (September 20, 2004): 49.
*The New York Times Book Review* 154 (December 5, 2004): 48.
*Publishers Weekly* 251, no. 35 (August 30, 2004): 39.
*The Times Literary Supplement*, October 8, 2004, p. 12.
*The Wall Street Journal* 244, no. 100 (November 19, 2004): W16.

# WONDROUS STRANGE
## The Life and Art of Glenn Gould

*Author:* Kevin Bazzana (1963-    )
*Publisher:* Oxford University Press (New York). 528 pp.
    $35.00
*Type of work:* Biography and music
*Time:* 1932-1982
*Locale:* Toronto, New York, and Europe

*This account of the life of the pianist takes an unconventional form and focuses on Gould's Canadian background while providing detailed musicological analyses of his works*

Principal personages:
    GLENN GOULD, a Canadian pianist
    FLORENCE GOULD, his mother
    BERT GOULD, his father
    ALBERTO GUERRERO, his piano teacher

After retiring from the concert stage in 1964, the pianist Glenn Gould embarked on a variety of new careers, including one as a radio documentary maker. One of the earliest and best of his documentaries was a study of the Canadian Arctic called *The Idea of the North*. Characteristically, it did not focus on facts or figures or topical issues but instead presented a collage of interviews to create a sense of the North and its isolated nature.

In *Wondrous Strange: The Life and Art of Glenn Gould*, Kevin Bazzana has done something similar. Instead of presenting a conventional, linear account, tracing Gould's life in strict chronological order, he has created a swirling, time-shifting study which seeks to give a sense of the famous Canadian pianist and his isolated nature.

Gould was born in Toronto in 1932 and lived his whole life there, leaving only for concert tours, New York recording sessions, and holidays in northern Ontario. Another of Bazzana's departures from convention is to emphasize this Canadian background in an attempt to show that Gould did not spring out of nowhere. One result of this is his solid portrayal of the proper middle-class Toronto neighborhood where Gould grew up.

Bazzana shows that Gould's Toronto was very British and Protestant, conservative and puritanical, and suggests that Gould's own puritanism stemmed from this background. Perhaps it did, but at times Bazzana seems to push too hard for his theory of the importance of Canadian influence on Gould. A comparison of Gould's austere piano style with the barren Canadian Arctic seems unconvincing, as does the suggestion that Gould's interest in communications theory was particularly Canadian.

At the end of the book, one might expect Bazzana to explore this question further, but he does not. He recounts Gould's sudden death and simply says that within a year of it, his recordings were being rereleased, his writings were being collected, and plans were being made for various commemorations. "The extraordinary posthumous life of Glenn Gould had begun," he comments, and the book ends there. It might have been useful to explore that posthumous life further and to try, after writing a whole book on the man, to explain what about him turned him into a cult figure.

Perhaps Bazzana comes closest to an explanation when he compares Gould to the American popular culture figures Elvis Presley and James Dean. Bazzana does not say so, but perhaps part of the source of the cult appeal in all these cases is the sense that despite the great achievement, there could have been greater achievement still. Perhaps one of the reasons for Gould's continuing appeal is that he left people wanting more.

On the other hand, perhaps Bazzana leaves this question unanswered because it has no good answer. What he does succeed in doing is to give a sense of who Glenn Gould was: a brilliant pianist full of quirky mannerisms that irritated his early critics; an unconventional interpreter of the piano repertoire who outraged some commentators but who won praise from some of the leading figures in the music world, while at the same time appealing to ordinary listeners from New York to Moscow.

Above all, Bazzana sketches the central paradox of an artist who wanted to communicate and who theorized about the best way to communicate in his art but who, in his personal life, hardly ever went out, except to his recording studio. Bazzana records the amusing fact that when Gould agreed to host a documentary about Toronto, he ended up on film wandering around a city with which he was obviously not very familiar, even though he had lived there his whole life. In fact, at times he shook his head in disbelief at what he was seeing, as if he had never even seen it before.

Bazzana has some other amusing anecdotes, mostly to do with Gould's legendary hypochondria. One time Gould protested that it was not true that he went around with a suitcase full of pills. It was only a briefcase, he said. Another time he worried in his diary about some strange spots he had noticed on his stomach, agonizing over what they might be. At the end of the diary entry, though, there is a postscript stating that he had taken a bath and the spots had vanished.

Oddly, Bazzana relegates some of these sorts of anecdotes to his footnotes. In any case, if it is anecdotes one is after, Friedrich has more of them. Bazzana is less interested in stories than in analysis—and, oddly, lists. For some reason, from time to time, he inserts lists of concerts or lists of recordings or lists of topics about which Gould wrote. Not what one would expect in a conventional biography, but this is not a conventional biography. It is more of a Glenn Gouldian collage.

*Sheldon Goldfarb*

## Review Sources

*Booklist* 100, no. 16 (April 15, 2004): 1415.
*Library Journal* 129, no. 10 (June 1, 2004): 136.
*The Nation* 278, no. 23 (June 14, 2004): 15.
*New Statesman* 133 (October 11, 2004): 53.
*The New York Review of Books* 51, no. 15 (October 7, 2004): 10.
*Publishers Weekly* 251, no. 16 (April 19, 2004): 53.
*The Times Literary Supplement*, August 20, 2004, p. 16.
*The Washington Post*, March 28, 2004, p. BW15.

# THE WORKING POOR
## Invisible in America

*Author:* David K. Shipler (1942-    )
*Publisher:* Alfred A. Knopf (New York). 319 pp. $25.00
*Type of work:* Sociology and current affairs
*Time:* 2004
*Locale:* The United States

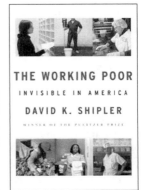

*This study of working people is based on interviews with Americans whose income places them above the official poverty line but for whom mishaps, such as car trouble, child care interruptions, or illness, represent crises which could result in sudden joblessness and extreme poverty*

Throughout his book, David K. Shipler depicts real people to show that the "invisible poor" are found throughout the United States. He demonstrates how the lives of the rich and the middle class are touched by those of the working poor almost every day. The latter are thought to be invisible because of the nature of the work that they do. For example, most consumers do not associate the produce that they buy at the supermarket with the workers who harvest the crops. Most white-collar employees have gone home for the day before the cleaning crew arrives to vacuum their offices. Even consumers who scrupulously avoid buying clothing made in countries where sweatshop labor is a known problem may unwittingly purchase made-in-the-U.S.A. garments from a factory whose workers are denied their legal wages and rights.

In *The Working Poor*, Shipler examines the minimum wage, the poverty line, federal welfare reform, and the gap between rich and poor, though these issues are not the focus of his study. He prefers to concentrate on laborers in various sectors of the economy, including farmworkers, retail employees, parking attendants, restaurant employees, and garment workers. Shipler also visits public schools to glimpse how children of the poor and the working class spend their days, what resources are available to them through education, and what factors in their home lives set them up for success or failure. Shipler draws conclusions throughout the book and, in the final chapter, offers some astute prescriptions for these problems.

In evaluating the scope of Shipler's work, one might note that his total sample is not large. Nowhere does he state his methodology—how he selected his interview subjects or how he gained these people's confidence and made them willing to share their life stories with him. Likewise, Shipler does not attempt a standardized survey, which would have enabled the collection of at least some data from a larger group of people. He does occasionally use figures from previous sociological studies, among other sources, to support his findings.

The book's strength, then, is the interviews with working people, which the author

*Former professor and journalist David K. Shipler is the author of several books, including* A Country of Strangers: Blacks and Whites in America *(1997) and the Pulitzer Prize-winning* Arab and Jew: Wounded Spirits in a Promised Land *(1986).*

says he began in 1997. They create a series of unique portraits from which some common themes emerge. Subjects include former welfare recipients, former convicts, and legal and illegal immigrants. Shipler speaks with social case workers and job skills trainers. In some of the most revealing conversations, he talks to employers such as farmers and Wal-Mart managers. The author's portraits of the bosses are largely sympathetic, although in generalized terms he blasts greedy corporate executives and he makes no secret of where his political sympathies lie. Although agile, the prose does not have the zing of a firsthand account of life among the working poor, such as Barbara Ehrenreich's *Nickel and Dimed* (2001). A notable feature of Shipler's work, however, is that it is well organized into eleven distinct chapters.

The introduction, "At the Edge of Poverty," describes the broad range of problems encountered by those stuck for whatever reason in low-wage jobs. Pluses and minuses of the 1996 welfare reform act are given a paragraph, and Shipler then makes a point to which he will return:

> Breaking away and moving a comfortable distance from poverty seems to require a perfect lineup of favorable conditions. A set of skills, a good starting wage, and a job with the likelihood of promotion are prerequisites. But so are clarity of purpose, courageous self-esteem, a lack of substantial debt, the freedom from illness or addiction, a functional family, a network of upstanding friends, and the right help from private or governmental agencies.

Shipler reminds the reader of the fabular American belief that any individual can, through hard work and mindful living, attain prosperity. The author notes that this "American Myth" is also a convenient way to lay blame on those who do not rise to a position of material comfort and stay there.

With the problem thus stated, chapter 1 describes facets of being poor that may not be familiar to readers. For example, those who qualify can receive payment of the federal earned income credit (EIC). This payment is available only to people who have earned some income the previous year. In order to get the money, one has to apply for it, and in order to apply for it, one has to know about it. The author describes con artists as well as institutions that take advantage of the poor, such as a well-known tax preparation service that is reported to charge up to 410 percent interest on its "rapid refund" loan service—which it does not refer to as a "loan." Shipler also shows how the poor pay more than other people do to maintain bank accounts and for credit in the forms of car loans, cellular phone contracts, "payday loans," and late fees and fines. Personal examples pepper this chapter, wherein one subject simply says, "Being poor is very expensive."

Set within the context of a society that greatly needs the labor performed for cheap by low-skilled workers, the chapter titled "Work Doesn't Work" conveys the life circumstances of three single mothers. These women, two in Ohio and one in New Hampshire, are able-minded but not highly educated, able-bodied but not skilled, and they have experienced various setbacks which are detailed here. Particularly striking is the story of Caroline, who will not be promoted to a checker's position at her company, Wal-Mart, anytime soon because of an "unwritten part of the job description" that she is missing: some of her teeth. Again Shipler emphasizes how poverty engenders circumstances that promote continued poverty.

A reader may be wondering at this point in the book if the rest of the narrative will consist of case studies. It is somewhat of a relief that the next chapter offers a general discussion of the garment manufacturing industry in Los Angeles. Here is an eye-opening account of how clothing is constructed, who does the work (almost always immigrants) and for whom (well-known designer companies and retailers). Laws regarding working conditions and pay are circumvented in ways that a worker concerned about his or her immigration status in the United States might be loathe to question. For example, a rise in the state's minimum hourly pay usually precedes a rise in the number of pieces employees are required to produce per hour. The text recounts infamous cases (including one of slavery), saying that those who "want to protest sweatshops [do not] have to look for exploitation in poor nations; they can find more immediate targets . . . in L.A., where the bad publicity would surely provoke speedier results."

In a chapter-long discussion of immigrant farmworkers, the author tells of his visits to some of their living quarters and sees their isolation on farms as well as their dependence on their supervisors for life's every need. The homesickness expressed by these men is heartbreaking. Most native-born Americans are not aware of the extreme need for opportunities of any kind that drives foreigners to cross into the United States illegally, in spite of the inherent dangers. As elsewhere in the book, views of employers are presented. In this chapter, North Carolina grower Jimmy Burch details some problems that farmers face, such as the floods that wiped out three entire crops one year. Federal subsidies were inadequate to cover the damage, and seed, fertilizer, and pesticide had all doubled in cost during a decade.

Reliant as most Americans are on underpriced labor, Burch expresses a deep need for laborers who would work reliably and then return the following season. Toward this end, he installed workers in homes on his own property and cosigned loans for some of them. Only a minority of growers, however, are so willing to help. Shipler points out the costs of being undocumented, including a reluctance to complain about wages or working conditions. He also reiterates that there are less obvious costs of being poor. For example, the process of transferring money home to Mexico invokes extra bank fees for workers who do not have bank accounts. "In other words, American government and business gain financially from your inability to legalize your presence in this country," Shipler comments.

A section titled "The Daunting Workplace" focuses on the need for job preparation and job readiness skills among those seeking work. What may seem like a big hurdle for a former welfare recipient to overcome—getting hired—can be just the beginning of a job's challenges. Often, employers cannot understand why workers arrive late, why they fail to show up but do not call, and why some do not even comb their hair before coming to work. These basics have to be taught to workers in many cases. Bosses would often prefer for their employees to be versed in the "soft skills" of diligence, punctuality, and positive attitude over, for example, math skills that are not essential to every job. Among the supervisors with whom Shipler spoke, many were surprised to learn of the deep-seated feelings of inadequacy among employees that would lead workers to believe that there is no point in calling work when they are sick because, they reason, their presence at the workplace makes no difference. Such people perceive themselves to be invisible, and frequently they are treated by their employers as being so.

The author reveals that the causes of such feelings of worthlessness are many. "Even though I never posed the question," he writes, "sooner or later most of the impoverished women I interviewed mentioned that they had been sexually abused as children." Shipler's discussion of child abuse and other problems related to youth returns his attention to individual histories. This is some of the toughest reading in the book; among the other issues affecting children covered here are malnutrition and underfunded public schools.

In his penultimate chapter, "Work Works," Shipler begins with an inside view of job training programs (the sponsors of these programs are not revealed) and moves on to the narratives of first Ricky and then Leary, both former drug addicts who found and kept gainful employment. Both have problems relating to family members—a situation that cuts across all class lines and one which reinforces Shipler's assertion that many factors contribute to one's success as a wage earner, let alone as a happy and fulfilled individual.

The book's concluding chapter is an impressive summation of issues that need to be addressed by a society attempting to overcome the scourge of poverty. The author again describes the elements that contribute to individuals' ability to support themselves and their children. "Holistic remedies," he says, "are vital . . . and [gateways] are best established at intersections through which working poor families are likely to travel." His prescription calls for such intersections—hospitals, welfare offices, schools, police departments, and so on—to receive the financing and the creative management that would allow them to "reach beyond their mandates, create connections of services, and become portals through which the distressed could pass into a web of assistance."

Current political trends that Shipler cites seem to be moving things in the opposite direction. One way to provide adequate resources to those institutions would be to gain greater advocacy for the poor among legislators. The lower one's income, however, the less likely one is to vote. Shipler believes that the problems of the working class would become a lot more interesting to politicians if the poor and nearly poor were to cast ballots in larger numbers and according to their own needs. However, when one is caught in an exhausting struggle to make ends meet, it is hard to imagine finding the energy to become a follower of, much less a participant in, the political process. The author offers additional, and specific, policy suggestions for both gov-

ernment and business. He also entreats politicians to work across party lines and reminds the reader that workers at the edge of poverty are essential to the economic
health of the United States.

*Elizabeth Ferry Slocum*

## Sources for Further Study

*America* 191, no. 6 (September 13, 2004): 24.
*Kirkus Reviews* 71, no. 24 (December 15, 2003): 1442.
*Library Journal* 129, no. 2 (February 1, 2004): 114.
*The Nation* 278, no. 10 (March 15, 2004): 25.
*The New York Times*, February 18, 2004, p. E8.
*The New York Times Book Review* 153 (February 15, 2004): 7.
*Publishers Weekly* 251, no. 1 (January 5, 2004): 51.
*Time* 163, no. 7 (February 16, 2004): 76.

# A YEAR AT THE RACES
## Reflections on Horses, Humans, Love, Money, and Luck

*Author:* Jane Smiley (1950-    )
*Publisher:* Alfred A. Knopf (New York). 287 pp. $22.00
*Type of work:* Essays and memoir
*Time:* 1993-2003
*Locale:* California

*Organized loosely around a year the author spent preparing her most promising horse to race, these essays on the care and training of thoroughbreds bring insights of modern psychology to the mysterious and ancient bond between horse and human*

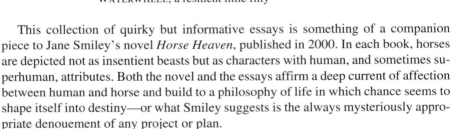

*Principal personages:*
> JANE SMILEY, a novelist and the owner of a stable of thoroughbred horses
> ALEXIS, her trainer
> HALI, a so-called animal psychic
> HORNBLOWER, an ambitious gray stallion, renamed WOWIE
> PERSEY, a fearful, emotionally fragile filly
> MR. T, Smiley's unusually prescient first horse
> WATERWHEEL, a resilient little filly

This collection of quirky but informative essays is something of a companion piece to Jane Smiley's novel *Horse Heaven*, published in 2000. In each book, horses are depicted not as insentient beasts but as characters with human, and sometimes superhuman, attributes. Both the novel and the essays affirm a deep current of affection between human and horse and build to a philosophy of life in which chance seems to shape itself into destiny—or what Smiley suggests is the always mysteriously appropriate denouement of any project or plan.

Only incidentally about horse racing, *A Year at the Races* is an informal series of essays which discuss the psychology of horses as well as the psychology of the humans who love them. As in *Horse Heaven*, Smiley does not concentrate on one unified narrative thread but moves along in an open and unpredictable way, using the various ups and downs of life with her horses to draw larger philosophical lessons. Peppered with fifteen photographs of Smiley's horses, her trainer, or herself, the narrative is personal as well, its first-person voice establishing a conversational relationship with the reader.

For Smiley, every horse story is a love story, and each chapter concerns not simply the ins and outs of raising thoroughbreds but also the more intimate story of the mysterious and often intense bonds between herself and her horses. While Smiley quotes liberally from various expert texts on horses, and includes a scholarly bibliography at the end of her book, *A Year at the Races* is nevertheless an informal, anecdotal narrative which develops portraits of her own horses as individuals. Of equal importance is Smiley's own psychological journey, which began when, after winning the Pulitzer Prize for fiction in 1992, she treated herself to the purchase of her first horse, a thoroughbred gelding named Mr. T. Although appearing to be a scruffy and unprepossessing creature, Mr. T surprises Smiley with his uncanny intelligence, very similar to that of a horse of the same name who appears in Smiley's novel *Horse Heaven*. It is the redoubtable Mr. T who launches a career for Smiley as an owner and trainer of horses.

Although this new occupation threatens to displace her identity as a novelist, Smiley celebrates the new endeavor as a life-changing one that has allowed her to realize her true destiny. In one of the book's most significant passages, Smiley confesses that it was Mr. T who forced her to address her fears, as if together they were conducting a secret course of therapy for her.

*Jane Smiley is the author of numerous novels as well as a biography of Charles Dickens. She is the recipient of a Pulitzer Prize and was inducted into the American Academy of Arts and Letters in 2001. She is the owner of several horses and lives in California.*

She goes on to suggest that all the anxieties and problems she has experienced in the course of raising her thoroughbreds has, ironically, resulted in making her more serene, accepting, and philosophically optimistic than she was before she entered the world of horses.

In addition to exploring the healing nature of her relationships with the horses in her stable, Smiley uses her novelist's feeling for character to develop a series of convincing portraits of horses that have fairly complicated personalities, with specific emotional issues, opinions, and life stories. Mr. T's unusual intelligence and love of ritual is one example of Smiley's central thesis: that horses, like people, have unique personalities and histories. Her horse Persey, for instance, is a skittish filly whose fragile personality seems to have been a result of mother-daughter problems often disclosed on the human psychotherapist's couch. As Smiley diagnoses Persey's feelings of maternal abandonment, the reader witnesses modern psychology being brought to bear on equine inner lives. Alternating theoretical passages with case histories of her horses, Smiley uses chapters with titles such as "Neurosis," "Ambition," and "IQ" to persuade the reader that horses are animals with aspirations, intellectual and social skills, and even psychic abilities, that can love and be loved just as human beings can.

Smiley allows herself to digress while describing the world of turf and paddock, touching at times on arcane lore and other times on widely held theories of horse behavior, occasionally citing her life as a mother and a writer, at other times allowing the reader into her moments of introspection and self-analysis. There is, nevertheless, a basic narrative arc to this book, namely the careers of her two most promising thoroughbreds, Wowie and Waterwheel, through a season at the track—the year at the races of the title. As Smiley grooms Wowie as a potential winner, she speculates on the mystery of why one horse wins and another fails, suggesting that what the horse is thinking and how it is feeling may play an important role in its ability to perform at the track. Smiley's fascination with the inner lives of her horses leads her to consult Hali, a beautiful, blond "horse communicator" to help her with her difficulties in training her potential winner, whom she had named Hornblower. Hali suggests the horse would prefer the name Wowie and goes on to make many other suggestions and predictions, not only about Wowie but about other horses in Smiley's stable as well. Not unlike the character of Elizabeth Zada, the animal psychic in *Horse Heaven*, Hali is an important figure in this work because she helps develop Smiley's central point, which is that, if one has ears to hear, horses will tell all about themselves, and what they have to say will be quite illuminating.

Like human beings, the horses in these essays have inner lives and feelings and also seem preternaturally attuned to the human beings around them—in fact, the horses suggest a supernatural dimension to the lives of people. That mystical dimension, also present in *Horse Heaven*, can be seen in Smiley's readiness to interpret her entire involvement in the world of thoroughbreds as less about winning and losing than about life lessons. As a result, this book can be seen as not simply a how-to book on raising horses but as a contribution to the category of writing known as wisdom literature. Although Smiley does prepare Wowie for racing, the fact that he never comes close to winning is not a source of major disappointment for her. When, at the end of the year, Hali informs Smiley that Wowie feels that the dilemma of his life has been solved, this reward is enough for the romantic, empathic, and newly philosophical Smiley, whose own dilemma seems to have been solved as well.

Another major theme in this book is that of women and horses. Using herself as a prime example, Smiley suggests that women have always had a special feel for horses and a special talent for relating to them. She points out that the racing community has failed to capitalize on a natural audience—namely, girls and women—instead creating a male-oriented workplace and sporting arena. The two other major figures in this book, Alexis and Hali, are also women who have a remarkable way with horses. It is the portrait Smiley presents of herself, however—sometimes comical but always intellectually curious and highly empathic and maternal—who dominates this book. This is not so much a departure from her previous identities as a novelist and mother as an extension and development of them—she employs both her novelist's interest in character and motive and a mother's capacity for care in this latest and most highly evolved version of herself.

Perhaps the most important aspect of this book is its argument for compassionate and ethical treatment of animal companions. Smiley here is treating the ownership of animals not simply in terms of utility but with the assumption that developing an understanding of the character of horses and other animals is important, as is the meaning of their roles in one's life. Although Smiley makes a case for the superior physical powers of the horse, it is the animals' inner lives, their intuitive capabilities, and their ideas and affections that she feels requires emphasis. Horses, Smiley suggests, can make intelligent decisions and know far more than one thinks they can. They will thrive and develop under the guidance of humans who realize this. In this regard, this book is of a piece with the larger movement for the ethical treatment of animals, so that while Smiley's ideas are not really new and radical, her essays are part of a growing literature questioning modern mechanistic interpretations of the animal mind and moving into an acceptance of alternative spiritual interpretations of both the self and its animal companions. In this group of essays, she is calling attention to the animal world, affirming the integrity and dignity of animals in a culture she finds too insensitive and exploitive. In addition, the metaphysical aspect of her essays adds a magical element to her work. As in fairy tales or wonder stories, the horses in Smiley's book have an otherworldly aspect and indicate a real connection with a supernatural plain of existence. Her work celebrates the mystery of animals and the way in which they are inherently marvelous.

With her regular consultation of a horse astrology Web site and her interest in the psychic and the telepathic, Smiley's *A Year at the Races* contains elements that some readers may find overly invested in what is known as New Age thought. Additionally, Smiley's attempts to weave together factual information, personal anecdotes, and metaphysics does not always appear to be a seamless process. One problem is that, although the book is very detailed and comprehensive, it often fails to build the kind of narrative momentum one has come to associate with a writer of Smiley's talent. There is some repetition of her earlier novel *Horse Heaven* here as well, not only in theme but also in terms of returning characters. This return to the subject of horses in nonfiction may have been inspired, or at least encouraged, by the popularity of nonfiction books about thoroughbreds, notably Laura Hillenbrand's *Seabiscuit* (2001). Smiley's love of horses and good-natured enthusiasm about the subject is genuine, however, and is something she communicates to her readers in a way that invites them to catch the spirit. As a result, this collection of essays should please casually curious readers, inveterate horse lovers, and those interested in an inspiring story of how one woman's midlife venture led to a series of personal and philosophical affirmations.

*Margaret Boe Birns*

## Review Sources

*Booklist* 100, no. 14 (March 15, 2004): 1242.
*Entertainment Weekly*, April 23, 2004, p. 85.
*Library Journal* 129, no. 7 (April 15, 2004): 93.
*The New York Times Book Review* 153 (June 27, 2004): 22.
*Publishers Weekly* 251, no. 13 (March 29, 2004): 51.
*USA Today*, April 20, 2004, p. D04.
*The Wall Street Journal* 243, no. 75 (April 16, 2004): W8.
*The Washington Post*, May 2, 2004, p. WBK09.

# THE YOM KIPPUR WAR
## The Epic Encounter That Transformed the Middle East

*Author:* Abraham Rabinovich (1933-    )
*Publisher:* Schocken Books (New York). Illustrated.
  543 pp. $27.50
*Type of work:* History
*Time:* 1973
*Locale:* The Middle East

*Rabinovich presents a carefully researched and brilliantly written account of the October, 1973, Egyptian and Syrian attack on Israel, which saw some of the most intense armored combat since World War II and which ultimately made possible the Egyptian-Israeli Peace Accord of 1978*

Principal personages:
  ANWAR SADAT, president of Egypt
  GOLDA MEIR, prime minister of Israel
  MOSHE DAYAN, defense minister of Israel
  DAVID ELAZAR, Israeli military chief of staff
  ARIEL SHARON, Israeli general
  HENRY KISSINGER, United States secretary of state

Abraham Rabinovich's *The Yom Kippur War: The Epic Encounter That Transformed the Middle East* is a fast-moving and authoritative account of the war Egypt and Syria launched against Israel in October, 1973. Caught by surprise, the Israelis nearly suffered a disastrous defeat before regaining the initiative. This war saw the greatest tank battles since World War II. At the end of nineteen days of intense fighting, the Israeli Defense Forces were threatening both enemy capitals. The cost was high. The Israelis killed in the war numbered 2,656. Proportionally, in less than three weeks Israel lost three times as many fighters per capita than the United States lost in a decade of combat in Vietnam. Arab losses were much higher. Despite this, the biggest victor in the war was Egyptian president Anwar Sadat, because the honorable showing of his military in the conflict would make possible his later diplomatic visit to Jerusalem and an Egyptian-Israeli peace accord later in the decade. Thus, for all its bloody ferocity, the Yom Kippur War did ultimately bring one corner of peace to the tumultuous Middle East.

Rabinovich is a distinguished journalist whose work has appeared in a number of American and Israeli papers. He covered the Yom Kippur War for the *Jerusalem Post*. In this book, Rabinovich has supplemented personal experience with extensive research. Despite his efforts, his account is largely one-sided. Many Arab sources of information are still closed to outsiders, especially in Syria. Any definitive record of the Egyptian and Syrian war efforts in 1973 will have to wait until those are more open societies. Fortunately, thanks to some published memoirs and interviews,

Rabinovich is able to present a fair picture of
Egyptian and Syrian intentions and actions.

Rabinovich is able to do much better with the
United States and the Soviet Union. For both
these Cold War superpowers, the Yom Kippur
War took on the character of a proxy war by allied states. The conduct and outcome of the conflict quickly became a matter of prestige and
threatened to upset the policy of détente being
pursued by U.S. president Richard Nixon and
Soviet premier Leonid Brezhnev. The United States and the Soviet Union rushed
arms to their allies and played major roles in brokering the cease-fire that would bring
the fighting to a halt. Rabinovich's greatest contribution is the exhaustive pains that
he has taken going through Israeli sources on the war. He has digested a small library
of published works and studied many recently declassified government documents.
Rabinovich has also interviewed dozens of veterans and officials. As a result, he has
produced the most comprehensive account yet of the Yom Kippur War.

*Abraham Rabinovich graduated
from Brooklyn College and served
in the United States Army. He
worked for* Newsday *before joining
the* Jerusalem Post. *He is the author
of several books and lives in
Jerusalem.*

Rabinovich's history is more than a work of impeccable scholarship. It is also an
engaging and exciting read. Rabinovich writes with the assured eye for detail of an
experienced journalist. His narrative ranges freely from the front lines, through the Israeli and Arab high commands, to councils of state in Washington and Moscow. He is
able vividly to evoke the experience of those caught up in the organized chaos of battle. Yet he does not refrain from magisterial judgments of the success or failure of the
combatants' strategy and tactics. *The Yom Kippur War* is military history at its best.

The tale that Rabinovich tells is replete with ironies and surprises. Among the most
telling: Sadat would launch the war to make peace, and the vaunted Israeli military
would come within a hair of defeat because of its own hubris. Both the ironies and the
surprises would be shaped by the aftermath of the 1967 Six-Day War. In that earlier
conflict, the Israelis attacked Egyptian and Syrian forces gathering against them and
inflicted a devastating defeat on the Arabs. They captured the Sinai Peninsula from
the Egyptians and the strategic Golan Heights from the Syrians. When the Jordanians
intervened in the war, the Israelis conquered the West Bank of the Jordan River.

The Israelis were elated by their dramatic success in the war. Their victory fed a
sense of military superiority over their Arab opponents that reflected a reality but also
bred a dangerous overconfidence. The Israelis hoped that with territories that they
could use as bargaining chips, a comprehensive peace could be negotiated with their
hostile neighbors. The very magnitude of the Israeli victory, however, robbed it of any
diplomatic value. The Israelis' Arab opponents were humiliated by the thoroughness
of their defeat in the Six-Day War. Their forces were routed. Images of fleeing troops
harried by the seemingly invincible Israeli army and air force haunted them. The
Arabs had not only been defeated; they had been dishonored. Thus they refused to deal
with the Israelis. Instead they fell back upon the barren strategy of reiterating their determination to eradicate the Jewish state that they denounced as the "Zionist Entity."

Egypt was regarded as the leader of the Arab world. Its president Gamal Abdel

Nasser had precipitated the Six-Day War and symbolically embodied the anti-Israeli cause. Along the Suez Canal, across which Egyptian and Israeli forces now faced each other, fighting flared up again in March, 1969. In what came to be known as the War of Attrition, the Egyptians struck at the Israelis with intense artillery bombardments. Hundreds of Israeli soldiers were killed. The Israelis retaliated with air strikes and commando raids. In August, 1970, the Egyptians accepted a cease-fire. The satisfactions of the War of Attrition for the Egyptians were meager indeed. They had dealt blows to the hated enemy, but their attacks had been repaid with interest by the Israelis. The twilight zone between peace and war in which Egyptians lived was demoralizing. The Egyptian economy was staggering under the burden, and the Israelis still were entrenched along the Suez Canal.

Nasser died at the end of September, 1970. He was succeeded by Sadat. Unlike his predecessor, Sadat was a realist who recognized that Egypt could no longer afford its official hostility to Israel. He was determined to make peace with Israel. In order to do this, he had to restore Egyptian self-respect. He had to be able to treat the Israelis as equals. Hence, while Sadat stirred diplomatic waters with talk about readiness to make peace if the Israelis withdrew from all occupied Arab lands, he built up his army and trumpeted his willingness to fight. The Israelis noted both Sadat's talk of peace and military buildup. Given what they believed was a position of strength, they were not prepared to make concessions without expressions of good faith that the Egyptian leader was not in a political position to give. This left Sadat in a box. He realized that the only way out was to fight a war to restore Egyptian honor.

Sadat made careful preparations for his war. Egypt had been a client of the Soviet Union since Nasser's time. The Soviets had armed and trained the Egyptian army. However, they discouraged talk of war because they did not believe that the Egyptians could win. The Soviet presence was thus an embarrassing complication for Sadat. He also realized that if he was to make peace with Israel, he would have to make use of the good offices of the United States.

Thus in May, 1972, Sadat took advantage of the growing détente between the United States and the Soviet Union to expel his Soviet advisers. This helped pave the way for war and provided an opening to the Americans. Early in 1973, Sadat's national security adviser met with Henry Kissinger in Washington. The two discussed diplomatic initiatives. Kissinger expressed sympathy for Egyptian concerns but urged his counterpart to be realistic given Israeli military superiority. When Sadat learned of this, he accelerated his war planning. The Syrians readily agreed to join in a strike against Israel. They dreamed of recapturing the Golan Heights. Troops began flowing to the front lines.

While the Arabs readied themselves, the Israelis discounted talk of war. The Israeli prime minister, Golda Meir, was a highly capable politician and diplomat, but as a grandmother in her seventies, she made no pretense of having military expertise. For that, she relied on her defense minister, the legendary soldier Moshe Dayan, and the Israel Defense Forces chief of staff David Elazar, a hero of the Six-Day War. These men, in turn, depended on Israeli military intelligence which, because of past successes, enjoyed a redoubtable reputation.

This time, however, the military intelligence office would prove to be disastrously wrong. Despite mounting evidence to the contrary, the chiefs of military intelligence refused to believe that a war was coming. They, like all the Israeli leadership, were still infected by the euphoria of the Six-Day War. They recklessly underestimated their Arab opponents. This proved nearly fatal. The Israeli battle plan depended upon timely notice of the imminence of war. The Israelis, in part because of their contempt for their enemy, guarded their frontiers with very light forces. Most of their armed might would have to be called up from reserve, optimally with a week's warning and in an emergency, two days'. Ultimately, the Israeli intelligence services would give the military only a few hours' advance notice.

The Arabs attacked on October 6, 1973, the Jewish holiday of Yom Kippur, when they knew most Israeli soldiers would be at home with their families. They came in overwhelming force. The Israeli fortifications on the Suez Canal were held by 450 men. In a carefully planned and expertly executed assault, the Egyptians put thirty-two thousand soldiers across the canal within three-and-a-half hours. On the Golan Heights, 177 Israeli tanks found themselves facing 1,460 Syrian tanks. The Israelis received more unpleasant surprises. They had grown used to their tanks and air force routing superior numbers of the enemy, but the Egyptians and Syrians had equipped their infantry with Soviet-made rocket propelled grenades and Sagger missiles. They protected their airspace with the surface-to-air missile defense system. Israeli tanks and warplanes charging into battle were knocked out in great numbers.

For a time, the Israeli high command reeled in confusion and dismay. Only the skill and tenacity of ordinary Israeli soldiers hanging on in the Sinai and the Golan Heights gave their leaders the time to rally and organize effective counterattacks. The Syrians were thrust back and Damascus threatened. In the Sinai, Sadat's goal had been to take the area around the Suez Canal and then hunker down behind a shield of missiles. In a hard-fought battle, Israeli troops led by Ariel Sharon fought their way across the canal, resulting in the eventual isolation of an Egyptian army. At this point the superpowers, after flexing their military muscles at each other, negotiated a cease-fire.

Though the Israelis were on the offensive when the war ended, the conflict was inconclusive enough to make possible a flurry of diplomatic activity. Kissinger came into his own as he shuttled from one Middle Eastern capital to another. Sadat's strategy was vindicated as an Egyptian-Israeli peace was negotiated at Camp David in 1978.

*The Yom Kippur War* teaches timeless but necessary lessons. Rabinovich's well-told story of this important conflict reminds one that the world can be a hard place where war can be seen as a necessary and creative act, that intelligence services will often fail their political masters, and that often only the bloody sacrifices of ordinary people can redeem the mistakes of their leaders. This makes the lessons of this book not only timeless but timely.

*Daniel P. Murphy*

## Review Sources

*Booklist* 100, no. 8 (December 15, 2003): 724.
*Foreign Affairs* 83, no. 3 (May/June, 2004): 154.
*Kirkus Reviews* 71, no. 22 (November 15, 2003): 1355.
*The Nation* 278, no. 21 (May 31, 2004): 23.
*The New York Times Book Review* 153 (February 15, 2004): 29.
*Publishers Weekly* 250, no. 45 (November 10, 2003): 51.

MAGILL'S
LITERARY ANNUAL
2005

# BIOGRAPHICAL WORKS BY SUBJECT

## 2005

AUDUBON, JOHN JAMES
John James Audubon (Rhodes), 414

BORGES, JORGE LUIS
Borges (Williamson), 89
BREWSTER, KINGMAN
Guardians, The (Kabaservice), 306
BRONTË, ANNE
Brontë Myth, The (Miller), 94
BRONTË, CHARLOTTE
Brontë Myth, The (Miller), 94
BRONTË, EMILY
Brontë Myth, The (Miller), 94

CAMUS, ALBERT
Camus and Sartre (Aronson), 104
CLINTON, WILLIAM JEFFERSON "BILL"
My Life (Clinton), 533

DYLAN, BOB
Chronicles (Dylan), 128

FOWLES, JOHN
John Fowles (Warburton), 404

GARDNER, JOHN
John Gardner (Silesky), 409
GODARD, JEAN-LUC
Godard (MacCabe), 294
GOLDBERG, NATALIE
Great Failure, The (Goldberg), 298
GOULD, GLENN
Wondrous Strange (Bazzana), 874
GREENE, GRAHAM
Life of Graham Greene, The, 1955-1991 (Sherry), 450
GUTHRIE, WOODY
Ramblin' Man (Cray), 649

HAMILTON, ALEXANDER
Alexander Hamilton (Chernow), 24
HOWLIN' WOLF
Moanin' at Midnight (Segrest and Hoffman), 511
HUTCHINSON, ANNE
American Jezebel (LaPlante), 47

ISHERWOOD, CHRISTOPHER
Isherwood (Parker), 387

KEILLOR, GARRISON
Homegrown Democrat (Keillor), 334

LUTHER, MARTIN
Martin Luther (Marty), 498

McLUHAN, MARSHALL
Understanding Me (McLuhan), 796
MARY, QUEEN OF SCOTS
Queen of Scots (Guy), 640
MAUGHAM, W. SOMERSET
Somerset Maugham (Meyers), 729

NERUDA, PABLO
Pablo Neruda (Feinstein), 605
NIGHTINGALE, FLORENCE
Nightingales (Gill), 552

PATRICK, SAINT
St. Patrick of Ireland (Freeman), 695
PERLOFF, MARJORIE
Vienna Paradox, The (Perloff), 812
POWELL, ANTHONY
Anthony Powell (Barber), 66

ROBBINS, JEROME
Jerome Robbins (Jowitt), 400

SARTRE, JEAN-PAUL
Camus and Sartre (Aronson), 104

# CATEGORY INDEX

## 2005

ANTHROPOLOGY. *See* SOCIOLOGY,
ARCHAEOLOGY, and
ANTHROPOLOGY

ARCHAEOLOGY. *See* SOCIOLOGY,
ARCHAEOLOGY, and
ANTHROPOLOGY

AUTOBIOGRAPHY, MEMOIRS,
DIARIES, and LETTERS
Blood Horses (Sullivan), 80
Book Nobody Read, The (Gingerich),
84
Brontë Myth, The (Miller), 94
Chronicles (Dylan), 128
Dress Your Family in Corduroy and
Denim (Sedaris), 231
Great Failure, The (Goldberg), 298
Homegrown Democrat (Keillor), 334
My Life (Clinton), 533
Politics of Truth, The (Wilson), 626
Sonata for Jukebox (O'Brien), 738
Vienna Paradox, The (Perloff), 812
Year at the Races, A (Smiley), 884

BIOGRAPHY. *See also* LITERARY
BIOGRAPHY
Alexander Hamilton (Chernow), 24
American Jezebel (LaPlante), 47
Chance Meeting, A (Cohen), 119
Godard (MacCabe), 294
Guardians, The (Kabaservice), 306
Harriet Tubman (Clinton), 310
Jerome Robbins (Jowitt), 400
John James Audubon (Rhodes), 414
Judging Thomas (Foskett), 422
Martin Luther (Marty), 498
Moanin' at Midnight (Segrest and
Hoffman), 511
Natalie Wood (Lambert), 537
Nightingales (Gill), 552
Queen of Scots (Guy), 640
Ramblin' Man (Cray), 649
St. Patrick of Ireland (Freeman), 695
Stalin (Montefiore), 755
Wondrous Strange (Bazzana), 874

CURRENT AFFAIRS and SOCIAL
ISSUES
Against All Enemies (Clarke), 14
Allies (Shawcross), 33

# CATEGORY INDEX

# TITLE INDEX

## 2005

# AUTHOR INDEX

## 2005

ALLISON, GRAHAM
Nuclear Terrorism, 566
ANONYMOUS
Imperial Hubris, 360
ARONSON, RONALD
Camus and Sartre, 104

BAKER, NICHOLSON
Checkpoint, 123
BANKS, RUSSELL
Darling, The, 179
BARBER, ELINOR, and ROBERT K.
MERTON
Travels and Adventures of
Serendipity, The, 778
BARBER, MICHAEL
Anthony Powell, 66
BARICCO, ALESSANDRO
Without Blood, 865
BARNES, JULIAN
Lemon Table, The, 441
BARRY, JOHN M.
Great Influenza, The, 302
BAZZANA, KEVIN
Wondrous Strange, 874
BEZMOZGIS, DAVID
Natasha, and Other Stories, 541
BLOOM, HAROLD
Where Shall Wisdom Be Found?,
841
BOATWRIGHT, MARY T., DANIEL J.
GARGOLA, and RICHARD J. A.
TALBERT
Romans, The, 677
BOYLE, T. CORAGHESSAN
Inner Circle, The, 373
BROOKNER, ANITA
Rules of Engagement, The, 686

BURUMA, IAN, and AVISHAI
MARGALIT
Occidentalism, 575
BYATT, A. S.
Little Black Book of Stories, 464

CALDWELL, IAN, and DUSTIN
THOMASON
Rule of Four, The, 682
CHERNOW, RON
Alexander Hamilton, 24
CHEVALIER, TRACY
Lady and the Unicorn, The, 432
CHRISTIAN, DAVID
Maps of Time, 493
CHRISTOPHER, NICHOLAS
Crossing the Equator, 167
CLARKE, RICHARD A.
Against All Enemies, 14
CLARKE, SUSANNA
Jonathan Strange and Mr. Norrell, 418
CLINTON, CATHERINE
Harriet Tubman, 310
CLINTON, WILLIAM JEFFERSON
"BILL"
My Life, 533
COHEN, RACHEL
Chance Meeting, A, 119
CRAY, ED
Ramblin' Man, 649

DALTON, JOHN
Heaven Lake, 320
DANTICAT, EDWIDGE
Dew Breaker, The, 213
DEVINE, T. M.
Scotland's Empire and the Shaping of
the Americas, 1600-1815, 699